COMMAND-MENTS and PROMISES OF GOD

COMMAND-MENTS and PROMISES OF GOD

BERNARD P. BROCKBANK

Deseret Book Company
Salt Lake City, Utah

First printing January 1983
Second printing March 1984

Library of Congress Cataloging in Publication Data
Main entry under title:

Commandments and promises of God.

   Includes index.
   1. Bible—Indexes, Topical. 2. Mormon Church—
Sacred books—Indexes. I. Brockbank, Bernard P.,
1909-   II. Brigham, Janet.
BS432.C63   1983   241'.04933   82-23629
ISBN 0-87747-889-9

Contents

Preface

One day, a lawyer tempted the Savior with the question: "Master, which is the great commandment in the law?" The Savior's answer illuminates the heart of the commandments. He said, "Thou shalt love the Lord thy God with all thy heart, and with all thy soul, and with all thy mind. This is the first and great commandment. And the second is like unto it, Thou shalt love thy neighbour as thyself. On these two commandments hang all the laws and the prophets." (Matt. 22:37-40.) The Savior also explained very simply how we can demonstrate that love: "If ye love me, keep my commandments." (John 14:15.)

The plea that God's sons and daughters love him for the sake of their own happiness is recorded throughout the scriptures. Similarly, the charge that all the Lord's commandments be obeyed is recorded as early as Genesis and as late as the Doctrine and Covenants.

Buy why obey commandments? The Lord states through Joseph Smith that "there is a law, irrevocably decreed in heaven before the foundations of this world, upon which all blessings are predicated—and when we obtain any blessing from God, it is by obedience to that law upon which it is predicated." (D&C 130:20-21.) He further explains, "All who will have a blessing at my hands shall abide the law which was appointed for that blessing, and the conditions thereof, as were instituted from before the foundation of the world." (D&C 132:5.)

Focusing on the commandments themselves, as the Lord and his servants spoke them, is critical. The Savior's closing counsel to his apostles before he ascended to heaven was this: "Go ye therefore, and teach all nations, baptizing them in the name of the Father, and of the Son, and of the Holy Ghost: teaching them to observe all things whatsoever I have commanded you: and, lo, I am with you alway, even unto the end of the world." (Matt. 28:19-20.) True followers of Christ are thus commanded to teach whatsoever he has commanded.

Furthermore, awareness of the promises—the blessings and cursings—that accompany God's commandments is vital. God does not capriciously hand out blessings to favored children; we ourselves determine by our behavior and our hearts how blessed we are. In other words, we can choose some blessing or achievement and set about to receive it at the Lord's hand, though God determines the nature and extent of our blessings. Often, in fact, promises are the natural result of obeying or not obeying a specific commandment.

These, then, are the reasons why this book has been compiled. For ease in use, the listing of commandments and promises in this book has been set in a certain format. First, a brief topical introduction at the beginning of each section serves to synthesize and focus the entries. Second, all entries are differentiated by type. Promises are printed in italic, all else is in roman. Third, scriptural references are in parentheses immediately after each entry. Abbreviations used are those found in the front of the 1981 edition of the Book of Mormon, Doctrine and Covenants, and Pearl of Great Price (triple combination). The texts of Joseph Smith Translation (JST) references all are contained in the explanatory notes of the 1979 Latter-day Saint edition of the King James Version of the Bible. The notation "similar scripture" indicates a scripture that is identical or nearly identical with the quoted passage.

Though the number of commandments and promises may appear overwhelming, we are not expected to absorb them all at once. The Lord has given us "line upon line, precept upon precept." (Isa. 28:10; 2 Ne. 28:30; D&C 98:12.) He tells us, "See that all these things are done in wisdom and order; for it is not requisite that a man should run faster than he has strength. And again, it is expedient that he should be diligent, that thereby he might win the prize." (Mosiah 4:27.) By careful and diligent application of the commandments in our lives, we can obtain, among the many promises of God, his greatest gift: "If you keep my commandments and endure to the end you shall have eternal life, which gift is the greatest of all the gifts of God." (D&C 14:7.)

Acknowledgments

Many thanks and deep appreciation are extended to Janet Brigham, whose work in the preparation of this book has covered several years. The assistance of the following persons is also gratefully acknowledged: Larry Morris, Sharon Ray, and Richard Tice.

Subject Guide to Commandments and Promises

Note: Words in italic refer to sections of the book.

Kindness
Kingdom of heaven, entering. See *Baptism and Spiritual Rebirth;*
    Coming to God; Purity
Knowing God and His Ways
Knowledge

Language. See *Blasphemy and Evil Communication*
Learning. See *Knowledge*
Levity. See *Foolishness*
Liberty. See *Agency, Use of*
Life, eternal. See *Authority and Stewardship; Good Works; Hope;*
    Looking to God; Obedience; Patience; Receiving God, His Teachings
    and His Servants; Sacrifice; Steadfastness/Enduring to the End
Life, sanctity of. See *Murder and Violence*
Lightmindedness. See *Foolishness*
Listening to God and His Servants
Looking to God
Loving God
Loving Others
Loyalty. See *Faithfulness*
Lying. See *False Witness, Bearing; Honesty*
Lust. See *Purity of Heart; Sexual Morality*

Malice. See *Loving Others*
Manifestations. See *Signs and Miracles, Seeking*
Marriage
Meditation and Purity of Thought
Meekness
Meetings
Mercy
Miracles. See *Believing in God; Faith*
Missionary work. See *Example, Being an; Teaching the Gospel*
Mocking. See *Foolishness*
Moderation. See *Health*
Morality. See *Honesty; Sexual Morality*
Motherhood. See *Family Responsibilities*
Motivation. See *Initiative; Zeal*
Mourning
Murder and Violence
Murmuring and Complaining

COMMAND-MENTS and PROMISES OF GOD

Abiding in God/Becoming God's People

We must know and comprehend who we are. God created man in his own image; and while each individual has an eternal identity, all must commune with God and keep his commandments to become known as his people.

"I am the vine, ye are the branches: He that abideth in me, and I in him, the same bringeth forth much fruit: for without me ye can do nothing." (John 15:5.) We are God's most important creation. By recognizing and partaking of the portion of God's kingdom given to men, we become fruitful branches of the plant from whose roots we grew. We receive renewed life from God as we abide in him. Through righteousness, we live in communion with his Spirit.

As we sense a need for God's companionship, we recognize our longing to return to his presence. As we yield to his will and direction, we begin on the path that leads to his presence. As we, his spirit offspring and his mortal creations, choose to abide in him, we indeed become his.

Commandments and Promises

Those that be planted in the house of the Lord *shall flourish in the courts of our God. They shall still bring forth fruit in old age; they shall be fat and flourishing.* (Ps. 92:13-14.)

As a shepherd seeketh out his flock in the day that he is among his sheep that are scattered; so will I seek out my sheep, and will deliver them out of all places where they have been scattered in the cloudy and dark day. And I will bring them out from the people, and gather them from the countries, and will bring them to their own land, and feed them upon the mountains of Israel by the rivers, and in all the inhabited places of the country. I will feed them in a good pasture, and upon the high mountains of Israel shall their fold be: there shall they lie in a good fold, and in a fat pasture shall they feed upon the mountains of

1

Israel. I will feed my flock, and I will cause them to lie down, saith the Lord God. (Ezek. 34:12-15.)

The kingdom and dominion, and the greatness of the kingdom under the whole heaven, shall be given to the people of the saints of the most High, whose kingdom is an everlasting kingdom, and all dominions shall serve and obey him. (Dan. 7:27.)

The sheep hear his voice: *and he calleth his own sheep by name, and leadeth them out. And when he putteth forth his own sheep, he goeth before them, and the sheep follow him:* for they know his voice. (John 10:3-4.)

My sheep hear my voice, and I know them, and they follow me: *and I give unto them eternal life; and they shall never perish, neither shall any man pluck them out of my hand. My Father, which gave them me, is greater than all; and no man is able to pluck them out of my Father's hand.* (John 10:27-29.)

Abide in me, *and I in you. As the branch cannot bear fruit of itself, except it abide in the vine; no more can ye, except ye abide in me. I am the vine, ye are the branches:* He that abideth in me, *and I in him,* the same bringeth forth much fruit: *for without me ye can do nothing. If a man abide not in me, he is cast forth as a branch, and is withered; and men gather them, and cast them into the fire, and they are burned.* If ye abide in me, and my words abide in you, *ye shall ask what ye will, and it shall be done unto you.* (John 15:4-7.)

Let every man, wherein he is called, therein abide with God. (1 Cor. 7:24.)

If ye be Christ's, *then are ye Abraham's seed, and heirs according to the promise.* (Gal. 3:29.)

And now, little children, abide in him; *that, when he shall appear, we may have confidence, and not be ashamed before him at his coming.* (1 Jn. 2:28.)

Whosoever abideth in him sinneth not: whosoever sinneth hath not seen him, neither known him. (1 Jn. 3:6; see also JST 1 Jn. 3:6.)

He gathereth his children from the four quarters of the earth; and he numbereth his sheep, and they know him; and there shall be one fold and one shepherd; and he shall feed his sheep, and in him they shall find pasture. (1 Ne. 22:25.)

I will be merciful unto my people, but the wicked shall perish. (2 Ne. 23:22.)

He that will hear my voice *shall be my sheep; and him shall ye receive into the church, and him will I also receive.* (Mosiah 26:21.)

The good shepherd doth call you; yea, and in his own name he doth call you, which is the name of Christ; and if ye will not hearken unto the voice of the good shepherd, to the name by which ye are called, behold, *ye are not the sheep of the good shepherd.* And now if ye are not the sheep of the good shepherd, *of what fold are ye? Behold, I say unto you, that the devil is your shepherd, and ye are of his fold.* (Alma 5:38-39.)

I know my sheep, and they are numbered. (3 Ne. 18:31.)

I will gather my people together as a man gathereth his sheaves into the floor. For I will make my people with whom the Father hath covenanted, yea, I will make thy horn iron, and I will make thy hoofs brass. And thou shalt beat in pieces many people; and I will consecrate their gain unto the Lord, and their substance unto the Lord of the whole earth. (3 Ne. 20:18-19.)

Whosoever belongeth to my church *need not fear, for such shall inherit the kingdom of heaven.* (D&C 10:55.)

Whosoever is of my church, and endureth of my church to the end, *him will I establish upon my rock, and the gates of hell shall not prevail against them.* (D&C 10:69.)

Adversity, Reacting to

(See also Coming to God; Patience; Trusting in God.)

Few, if any, of us are immune to adversity. Often we seem to have little control over what another person—or what life itself—does to us. Whether in waves or trickles, adversity saturates us all with conflicts and concerns that can be our blessing or our downfall.

What determines whether we overcome adversity or it overcomes us? Since often we cannot control the difficulties we encounter, the only variable is our control over our reactions. When we face adversity maturely and wisely, following God's counsel, we have his repeated promise that all things will work together for our good.

While Joseph Smith was incarcerated at Liberty, Missouri, the Lord said, "Thine adversity and thine afflictions shall be but a small moment; and then, if thou endure it well, God shall exalt thee on high; thou shalt triumph over all thy foes." (D&C 121:7-8.) Also, "All these things shall give thee experience, and shall be for thy good." (D&C 122:7.)

How do we endure so that adversity works to our benefit?

If we turn to the Lord, patient endurance is simpler; the experiences can strengthen our faith. The refiner's fire can purge our souls and lead us to humility. We have Christ's assurance that if we ask, he will help us endure.

The story of the captivity of Alma's people, told in Mosiah 24, is witness to these assurances. Alma and his people were in servitude to Amulon, a wicked Lamanite ruler. "So great were their afflictions that they began to cry mightily to God," which prompted Amulon to condemn to death all who were caught praying.

The Nephites then prayed in their hearts to God, who responded with a spoken promise that he would deliver them from bondage. In the meantime, he said, "I will also ease the burdens which are put upon your shoulders, that even you cannot feel them upon your backs, even while you are in bondage." He explained: "This will I do that ye may stand as witnesses for me hereafter, and that ye may know of a surety that I, the Lord God, do visit my people in their afflictions."

The promise was fulfilled; the Lord made the burdens light and made the people of Alma strong so that "they could bear up their burdens with ease." Waiting for deliverance, the people submitted "cheerfully and with patience to all the will of the Lord." The day of deliverance came when the Lord miraculously freed Alma's people and led them to the land of Zarahemla, where king Mosiah "did also receive them with joy." (Mosiah 24: 9-25.)

The Lord can similarly bless us when adversities weigh on our minds and hearts. And if we develop patience and faith, all things can work for our benefit, for our growth and eventual joy.

Commandments and Promises

Cast thy burden upon the Lord, *and he shall sustain thee: he shall never suffer the righteous to be moved.* (Ps. 55:22.)

Blessed are they which are persecuted for righteousness' sake: *for theirs is the kingdom of heaven. Blessed* are ye, when men shall revile you, and persecute you, and shall say all manner of evil against you falsely, for my sake. Rejoice, and be exceeding glad: *for great is your reward in heaven: for so persecuted they the prophets which were before you.* (Matt. 5:10-12.)

Ye shall be hated of all men for my name's sake: but he that endureth to the end *shall be saved.* (Matt. 10:22; similar scripture, Mark 13:13.)

Come unto me, all ye that labour and are heavy laden, *and I will give you rest.* Take my yoke upon you, and learn of me; for I am meek and lowly in heart: *and ye shall find rest unto your souls. For my yoke is easy, and my burden is light.* (Matt. 11:28-30.)

We glory in tribulations also: knowing that tribulation *worketh patience; and patience, experience; and experience, hope: and hope maketh not ashamed; because the love of God is shed abroad in our hearts by the Holy Ghost which is given unto us.* (Rom. 5:3-5.)

If so be that we suffer with [Christ], . . . *we may be also glorified together*. (Rom. 8:17.)

As ye are partakers of the sufferings, *so shall ye be also of the consolation*. (2 Cor. 1:7.)

So that we ourselves glory in you in the churches of God for your patience and faith in all your persecutions and tribulations that ye endure: which is a manifest token of the righteous judgment of God, *that ye may be counted worthy of the kingdom of God*, for which ye also suffer. (2 Thes. 1:4-5.)

Be not thou therefore ashamed of the testimony of our Lord, nor of me his prisoner: but be thou partaker of the afflictions of the gospel according to the power of God. (2 Tim. 1:8.)

Thou therefore endure hardness, as a good soldier of Jesus Christ. (2 Tim. 2:3.)

All that will live godly in Christ Jesus shall suffer persecution. But evil men and seducers shall wax worse and worse, deceiving, and being deceived. But continue thou in the things which thou hast learned and hast been assured of, knowing of whom thou hast learned them. (2 Tim. 3:12-14.)

Watch thou in all things, endure afflictions. (2 Tim. 4:5.)

My brethren, count it all joy when ye fall into divers temptations; knowing this, *that the trying of your faith worketh patience*. But let patience have her perfect work, *that ye may be perfect and entire, wanting nothing*. (James 1:2-4; see also JST James 1:2.)

Blessed is the man that endureth temptation: for when he is tried, *he shall receive the crown of life, which the Lord hath promised to them that love him*. (James 1:12; see also JST James 1:12.)

Take, my brethren, the prophets, who have spoken in the name of the Lord, for an example of suffering affliction, and of patience. (James 5:10.)

Is any among you afflicted? let him pray. Is any merry? let him sing psalms. (James 5:13.)

For this is thankworthy, if a man for conscience toward God endure grief, suffering wrongfully. *For what glory is it,* if, when ye be buffeted for your faults, ye shall take it patiently? but if, when ye do well, and suffer for it, ye take it patiently, *this is acceptable with God.* For even hereunto were ye called: because Christ also suffered for us, leaving us an example, that ye should follow his steps. (1 Pet. 2:19-21.)

If ye suffer for righteousness' sake, *happy are ye:* and be not afraid of their terror, neither be troubled. (1 Pet. 3:14.)

Forasmuch then as Christ hath suffered for us in the flesh, arm yourselves likewise with the same mind: for he that hath suffered in the flesh hath ceased from sin. (1 Pet. 4:1; see also JST 1 Pet. 4:2.)

Think it not strange concerning the fiery trial which is to try you, as though some strange thing happened unto you: but rejoice, inasmuch as ye are partakers of Christ's sufferings; *that, when his glory shall be revealed, ye may be glad also with exceeding joy.* If ye be reproached for the name of Christ, *happy are ye; for the spirit of glory and of God resteth upon you:* on their part he is evil spoken of, but on your part he is glorified. . . . If any man suffer as a Christian, let him not be ashamed; but let him glorify God on this behalf. (1 Pet. 4:12-14, 16.)

Let them that suffer according to the will of God commit the keeping of their souls to him in well doing, as unto a faithful Creator. (1 Pet. 4:19.)

Marvel not, my brethren, if the world hate you. (1 Jn. 3:13.)

Because thou sayest, I am rich, and increased with goods, and have need of nothing; and knowest not that thou art wretched, and miserable, and poor, and blind, and naked: I counsel thee to buy of me gold tried in the fire, *that thou mayest be rich.* (Rev. 3:17-18.)

[to Jacob] In thy childhood thou hast suffered afflictions and much sorrow, because of the rudeness of thy brethren. Nevertheless, Jacob, my firstborn in the wilderness, thou knowest the greatness of God; *and he shall consecrate thine afflictions for thy gain. Wherefore, thy soul shall be blessed, and thou shalt dwell safely with thy brother, Nephi; and thy days shall be spent in the service of thy God. Wherefore, I know that thou art redeemed, because of the righteousness of thy Redeemer.* (2 Ne. 2:1-3.)

The righteous, the saints of the Holy One of Israel, they who have believed in the Holy One of Israel, they who have endured the crosses of the world, and despised the shame of it, *they shall inherit the kingdom of God, which was prepared for them from the foundation of the world, and their joy shall be full forever.* (2 Ne. 9:18.)

I, Jacob, would speak unto you that are pure in heart. Look unto God with firmness of mind, and pray unto him with exceeding faith, *and he will console you in your afflictions, and he will plead your cause, and send down justice upon those who seek your destruction.* (Jacob 3:1.)

The voice of the Lord came to them in their afflictions, saying: Lift up your heads and be of good comfort, for I know of the covenant which ye have made unto me; *and I will covenant with my people and deliver them out of bondage. And I will also ease the burdens which are put upon your shoulders, that even you cannot feel them upon your backs, even while you are in bondage; and this will I do that ye may stand as witnesses for me hereafter, and that ye may know of a surety that I, the Lord God, do visit my people in their afflictions.* (Mosiah 24:13-14.)

I would exhort you to have patience, and that ye bear with all manner of afflictions; that ye do not revile against those who do cast you out because of your exceeding poverty, lest ye become sinners like unto them; but that ye have patience, and bear with those afflictions, with a firm hope that ye shall one day rest from all your afflictions. (Alma 34:40-41.)

Blessed are all they who are persecuted for my name's sake, *for theirs is the kingdom of heaven. And blessed are ye* when men shall revile you and persecute, and shall say all manner of evil against you falsely, for my sake; *for ye shall have great joy and be exceedingly glad, for great shall be your reward in heaven; for so persecuted they the prophets who were before you.* (3 Ne. 12:10-12.)

Fear not, little flock; do good; let earth and hell combine against you, for if ye are built upon my rock, *they cannot prevail.* (D&C 6:34.)

Be patient in afflictions, for thou shalt have many; but endure them, *for, lo, I am with thee, even unto the end of thy days.* (D&C 24:8.)

[to Peter Whitmer, Jr.] Be you afflicted in all his [Oliver Cowdery's] afflictions, ever lifting up your heart unto me in prayer and faith, for his and your deliverance. (D&C 30:6.)

Be patient in afflictions, revile not against those that revile. (D&C 31:9.)

After much tribulation *come the blessings. Wherefore the day cometh that ye shall be be crowned with much glory; the hour is not yet, but is nigh at hand.* (D&C 58:4.)

Verily I say unto you my friends, fear not, let your hearts be comforted; yea, rejoice evermore, and in everything give thanks; waiting patiently on the Lord, for your prayers have entered into the ears of the Lord of Sabaoth, and are recorded with this seal and testament— the Lord hath sworn and decreed that they shall be granted. Therefore, he giveth this promise unto you, with an immutable covenant that they shall be fulfilled; *and all things wherewith you have been afflicted shall work together for your good, and to my name's glory, saith the Lord.* (D&C 98:1-3.)

If men will smite you, or your families, once, and ye bear it patiently and revile not against them, neither seek revenge, *ye shall be rewarded;* but if ye bear it not patiently, *it shall be accounted unto you as being meted out as a just measure against you.* And again, if your enemy shall smite you the second time, and you revile not against your enemy, and bear it patiently, *your reward shall be an hundred-fold.* And again, if he shall smite you the third time, and ye bear it patiently, *your reward shall be doubled unto you four-fold; and these three testimonies shall stand against your enemy if he repent not, and shall not be blotted out.* (D&C 98:23-27.)

Verily I say unto you, concerning your brethren who have been afflicted, and persecuted, and cast out from the land of their inheritance—I, the Lord, have suffered the affliction to come upon them, wherewith they have been afflicted, in consequence of their transgressions; *yet I will own them, and they shall be mine in that day when I shall come to make up my jewels.* Therefore, they must needs be chastened and tried, even as Abraham, who was commanded to offer up his only son. For all those who will not endure chastening, but deny me, *cannot be sanctified.* (D&C 101:1-5.)

All they who suffer persecution for my name, and endure in faith, though they are called to lay down their lives for my sake *yet shall they partake of all this glory.* Wherefore, fear not even unto death; *for in this world your joy is not full, but in me your joy is full.* (D&C 101:35-36.)

After much tribulation, as I have said unto you in a former commandment, *cometh the blessing.* (D&C 103:12.)

My people must needs be chastened until they learn obedience, if it must needs be, by the things which they suffer. (D&C 105:6.)

Inasmuch as there are those who have hearkened unto my words, I have prepared a blessing and an endowment for them, if they continue faithful. *I have heard their prayers, and will accept their offering;* and it is expedient in me that they should be brought thus far for a trial of their faith. (D&C 105:18-19.)

My son, peace be unto thy soul; thine adversity and thine afflictions shall be but a small moment; and then, if thou endure it well, *God shall exalt thee on high; thou shalt triumph over all thy foes.* (D&C 121:7-8.)

I am the Lord your God, and will save all those of your brethren who have been pure in heart, and have been slain in the land of Missouri, saith the Lord. (D&C 124:54.)

If they persecute you, so persecuted they the prophets and righteous men that were before you. *For all this there is a reward in heaven.* (D&C 127:4.)

Agency, Use of

Agency is an eternal right, a right that is so important that God is willing to risk our using it wrongly and not being exalted. The Lord allows us to use our agency, but he also holds us accountable for our choices. Each of us can choose to use agency in a variety of ways. We can yield it to God, abdicate it, abuse it, or destroy it through our choices.

We are commanded to use our agency to do good, to keep us from the entanglements of sin. Every decision can bring us closer to perfection. The Lord wants us to develop our decision-making abilities and to exercise initiative: "For behold, it is not meet that I should command in all things." (D&C 58:26.)

However, we must remember that we can lose our freedom as we make an incorrect choice. As the Lord told Adam of his choice in the Garden of Eden, "Thou mayest choose for thyself, for it is given unto thee; but, remember that I forbid it, for in the day thou eatest thereof thou shalt surely die." (Moses 3:17.) Our agency may end when we make a choice, for we don't have the agency to choose the consequences.

Our lives and our choices are not predestined. "For the power is in them, wherein they are agents unto themselves," the Lord declared. (D&C 58:28.) That power is twofold: first, we have power to make choices; and second, by making correct choices, we enhance and increase that power.

Commandments and Promises

I call heaven and earth to record this day against you, that I have set before you life and death, blessing and cursing: therefore choose life, *that both thou and thy seed may live.* (Deut. 30:19.)

Choose you this day whom ye will serve. (Josh. 24:15.)

Let not sin therefore reign in your mortal body, that ye should obey it in the lusts thereof. Neither yield ye your members as instruments of unrighteousness unto sin: but yield yourselves unto God, as those that are alive from the dead, and your members as instruments of righteousness unto God. (Rom. 6:12-13.)

Let every soul be subject unto the higher powers. For there is no power but of God: the powers that be are ordained of God. Whosoever therefore resisteth the power, resisteth the ordinance of God: and they that resist *shall receive to themselves damnation.* (Rom. 13:1-2; see also JST Rom. 13:1.)

Stand fast therefore in the liberty wherewith Christ hath made us free, and be not entangled again with the yoke of bondage. (Gal. 5:1.)

Ye have been called unto liberty; only use not liberty for an occasion to the flesh, but by love serve one another. (Gal. 5:13.)

Submit yourselves therefore to God. Resist the devil, *and he will flee from you.* (James 4:7.)

Behold, here is wisdom, and let every man choose for himself until I come. (D&C 37:4.)

It is not meet that I should command in all things; for he that is compelled in all things, the same is a slothful and not a wise servant; *wherefore he receiveth no reward.* Verily I say, men should be anxiously engaged in a good cause, and do many things of their own free will, and bring to pass much righteousness; for the power is in them, wherein they are agents unto themselves. And inasmuch as men do good, *they shall in nowise lose their reward.* But he that doeth not anything until he is commanded, and receiveth a commandment with doubtful heart, and keepeth it with slothfulness, *the same is damned.* (D&C 58:26-29.)

I, the Lord God, commanded the man, saying: Of every tree of the garden thou mayest freely eat, but of the tree of the knowledge of good and evil, thou shalt not eat of it, nevertheless, thou mayest choose for thyself, for it is given unto thee; but, remember that I forbid it, *for in the day thou eatest thereof thou shalt surely die.* (Moses 3:16-17; similar scripture, Gen. 2:16-17.)

Anger

(See also Adversity; Patience.)

Being angry may sometimes seem natural and justified. But allowing anger to overtake us is an incorrect way to react to aggravation. Expression of anger doesn't just happen to us; we choose it, dangerous and inefficient as it is.

Showing anger is not just a venting of frustrations. When we harbor and nourish angry feelings, we damage ourselves and risk hurting others. Perhaps anger is one of the faults implied in the epistle to the Hebrews, where members are told to look "diligently . . . lest any root of bitterness springing up trouble you, and thereby many be defiled." (Heb. 12:15.)

The condition of never being angry may seem distant to a struggling, frustrated mortal. But difficult as it is, people have achieved it through understanding others, forgiveness, spirituality, discipline, and self-control. If we feel angered, we should control our expression of it; we should not use anger as an excuse to hurt others. If we don't overcome our anger, we are dangerous to ourselves and are of no use to God: "For the wrath of man worketh not the righteousness of God." (James 1:20.)

If we are quick to anger and slow to overcome it, we do not learn patience. We deny ourselves the blessings of a disciplined body and spirit.

Commandments and Promises

Wrath *killeth the foolish man.* (Job 5:2.)

Cease from anger, and forsake wrath: fret not thyself in any wise to do evil. (Ps. 37:8.)

He that is soon angry dealeth foolishly. (Prov. 14:17.)

Be not hasty in thy spirit to be angry: *for anger resteth in the bosom of fools.* (Eccl. 7:9.)

14

Unto them that are contentious, and do not obey the truth, but obey unrighteousness, *indignation and wrath, tribulation and anguish, upon every soul of man* that doeth evil, *of the Jew first, and also of the Gentile.* (Rom. 2:8-9.)

Now the works of the flesh are manifest, which are these; [adultery, idolatry, hatred, wrath, strife, murders, drunkenness], and such like: *of the which I tell you before, as I have also told you in time past, that they which do such things shall not inherit the kingdom of God.* (Gal. 5:19-21.)

If ye be angry, . . . sin not: let not the sun go down upon your wrath. (Eph. 4:26; see also JST Eph. 4:26.)

Let all bitterness, and wrath, and anger, and clamour, and evil speaking, be put away from you, with all malice: and be ye kind one to another, tenderhearted, forgiving one another, even as God for Christ's sake hath forgiven you. (Eph. 4:31-32.)

Now ye also put off all these; anger, wrath, malice, blasphemy, filthy communication out of your mouth. (Col. 3:8.)

Men shall be . . . fierce: . . . *from such turn away. . . . They shall proceed no further: for their folly shall be manifest unto all men.* (2 Tim. 3:2-5, 9.)

Let every man be swift to hear, slow to speak, slow to wrath: for the wrath of man *worketh not the righteousness of God.* (James 1:19-20.)

Wo unto all those who tremble, and are angry because of the truth of God! (2 Ne. 28:28.)

Ye have heard that it hath been said by them of old time, and it is also written before you, that you shalt not kill, and whosoever shall kill *shall be in danger of the judgment of God;* but I say unto you, that whosoever is angry with his brother *shall be in danger of his judgment.* And whosoever shall say to his brother, Raca, *shall be in danger of the council;* and whosoever shall say, Thou fool, *shall be in danger of hell fire.* (3 Ne. 12:21-22; similar scripture, Matt. 5:21-22.)

Authority and Stewardship

(See also Glorifying God.)

In a world prone to engender power-mad despots, the Savior's teaching must seem revolutionary: "He that is greatest among you shall be your servant." (Matt. 23:11.)

This truth is reinforced in latter-day scripture: "He that is ordained of God and sent forth, the same is appointed to be the greatest, notwithstanding he is the least and the servant of all." (D&C 50:26.)

Just as Jesus Christ served others through his leadership, so we are to fulfill our stewardships. We should fulfill them as Christ would, in dedication and humility. As he washed the apostles' feet, the Savior admonished, "If I then, your Lord and Master, have washed your feet; ye also ought to wash one another's feet. For I have given you an example, that ye should do as I have done to you." (John 13:14-15.)

With every action, Christ showed that being King meant being Servant.

Commandments and Promises

Let them [rulers] judge the people at all seasons: and it shall be, that every great matter they shall bring unto thee [Moses], but every small matter they shall judge: *so shall it be easier for thyself, and they shall bear the burden with thee.* (Ex. 18:22.)

Cursed be he that doeth the work of the Lord deceitfully. (Jer. 48:10.)

Son of man, prophesy against the shepherds of Israel, prophesy, and say unto them, Thus saith the Lord God unto the shepherds; *Woe* be to the shepherds of Israel that do feed themselves! should not the shepherds feed the flocks? Ye eat the fat, and ye clothe you with the wool, ye kill them that are fed: but ye feed not the flock. The diseased have ye not strengthened, neither have ye healed that which was sick, neither have ye bound up that which was broken, neither have ye brought again that which was driven away, neither have ye sought that which was lost; but with force and with cruelty have ye ruled them. And they were scattered, because there is no shepherd: and they became meat to all the beasts of the field, when they were scattered. My sheep wandered through all the mountains, and upon every high hill: yea, my flock was scattered upon all the face of the earth, and none did search or seek after them. Therefore, ye shepherds, hear the word of the Lord; As I live, saith the Lord God, surely because my flock became a prey, and my flock became meat to every beast of the field, because there was no shepherd, neither did my shepherds search for my flock, but the shepherds fed themselves, and fed not my flock; therefore, O ye shepherds, hear the word of the Lord; Thus saith the Lord God; *Behold, I am against the shepherds; and I will require my flock at their hand, and cause them to cease from feeding the flock; neither shall the shepherds feed themselves any more; for I will deliver my flock from their mouth, that they may not be meat for them.* (Ezek. 34:2-10.)

Woe to the idol shepherd that leaveth the flock! *the sword shall be upon his arm, and upon his right eye: his arm shall be clean dried up, and his right eye shall be utterly darkened.* (Zech. 11:17.)

Be not ye called Rabbi: for one is your Master, even Christ; and all ye are brethren. And call no man your father upon the earth: for one is your Father, which is in heaven. Neither be ye called masters: for one is your Master, even Christ. But he that is greatest among you shall be your servant. And whosoever shall exalt himself *shall be abased;* and he that shall humble himself *shall be exalted.* (Matt. 23:8-12; see also JST Matt. 23:6-7.)

[the Savior relates the parable of the talents] Well done, thou good and faithful servant: thou hast been faithful over a few things, *I will make thee ruler over many things: enter thou into the joy of thy lord.* (Matt. 25:21.)

And the Lord said, Who then is that faithful and wise steward, *whom his lord shall make ruler over his household, to give them their portion of meat in due season? Blessed* is that servant, whom his lord when he cometh shall find so doing. (Luke 12:42-43; similar scripture, Matt. 24:45-46.)

Well, thou good servant: because thou hast been faithful in a very little, *have thou authority over ten cities.* (Luke 19:17.)

Feed my sheep. (John 21:17.)

Take heed therefore unto yourselves, and to all the flock, over the which the Holy Ghost hath made you overseers, to feed the church of God, which he hath purchased with his own blood. (Acts 20:28.)

Having then gifts differing according to the grace that is given to us, whether prophecy, let us prophesy according to the proportion of faith; or ministry, let us wait on our ministering: or he that teacheth, on teaching; or he that exhorteth, on exhortation: he that giveth, let him do it with simplicity; he that ruleth, with diligence; he that sheweth mercy, with cheerfulness. (Rom. 12:6-8.)

Let a man so account of us, as of the ministers of Christ, and stewards of the mysteries of God. Moreover it is required in stewards, that a man be found faithful. (1 Cor. 4:1-2.)

Let every man abide in the same calling wherein he was called. Art thou called being a servant? care not for it: but if thou mayest be made free, use it rather. For he that is called in the Lord, being a servant, is the Lord's freeman: likewise also he that is called, being free, is Christ's servant. Ye are bought with a price; be not ye the servants of men. Brethren, let every man, wherein he is called, therein abide with God. (1 Cor. 7:20-24.)

I therefore, the prisoner of the Lord, beseech you that ye walk worthy of the vocation wherewith ye are called, with all lowliness and meekness, with longsuffering, forbearing one another in love; endeavouring to keep the unity of the Spirit in the bond of peace. (Eph. 4:1-3.)

Lift up the hands which hang down, and the feeble knees; and make straight paths for your feet, lest that which is lame be turned out of the way; but let it rather be healed. Follow peace with all men, and holiness, *without which no man shall see the Lord:* looking diligently lest any man fail of the grace of God; lest any root of bitterness springing up trouble you, and thereby many be defiled. (Heb. 12: 12-15.)

Obey them that have rule over you, and submit yourselves: for they watch for your souls, as they that must give account, that they may do it with joy, and not with grief: *for that is unprofitable for you.* (Heb. 13:17; see also Heb. 13:7.)

As every man hath received the gift, even so minister the same one to another, as good stewards of the manifold grace of God. If any man speak, let him speak as the oracles of God; if any man minister, let him do it as of the ability which God giveth: that God in all things may be glorified through Jesus Christ, to whom be praise and dominion for ever and ever. (1 Pet. 4:10-11.)

The elders which are among you I exhort, who am also an elder, and a witness of the sufferings of Christ, *and also a partaker of the glory that shall be revealed:* Feed the flock of God which is among you, taking the oversight thereof, not by constraint, but willingly; not for filthy lucre, but of a ready mind; neither as being lords over God's heritage, but being ensamples to the flock. *And when the chief Shepherd shall appear, ye shall receive a crown of glory that fadeth not away.* Likewise, ye younger, submit yourselves unto the elder. Yea, all of you be subject one to another, and be clothed with humility: *for God resisteth the proud, and giveth grace to the humble.* (1 Pet. 5:1-5.)

Stand fast in the work wherewith I have called you, *and a hair of your head shall not be lost, and you shall be lifted up at the last day.* (D&C 9:14.)

Magnify thine office. (D&C 24:3.)

Attend to thy calling *and thou shalt have wherewith to magnify thine office, and to expound all scriptures, and continue in laying on of the hands and confirming the churches.* (D&C 24:9.)

The elders, priests and teachers of this church shall teach the principles of my gospel, which are in the Bible and the Book of Mormon, in the which is the fulness of the gospel. And they shall observe the covenants and church articles to do them, and these shall be their teachings, as they shall be directed by the Spirit. *And the Spirit shall be given unto you* by the prayer of faith; and if ye receive not the Spirit ye shall not teach. And all this ye shall observe to do as I have commanded concerning your teaching, until the fulness of my scriptures is given. (D&C 42:12-15.)

Every man shall be made accountable unto me, a steward over his own property, or that which he has received by consecration, as much as is sufficient for himself and family. (D&C 42:32.)

Thou shalt stand in the place of thy stewardship. (D&C 42:53.)

He that receiveth of God, let him account it of God; and let him rejoice that he is accounted of God worthy to receive. (D&C 50:34.)

Whoso is found a faithful, a just, and a wise steward *shall enter into the joy of his Lord, and shall inherit eternal life.* (D&C 51:19.)

You shall stand fast in the office whereunto I have appointed you. (D&C 54:2.)

Behold, they have been sent to preach my gospel among the congregations of the wicked; wherefore, I give unto them a commandment, thus: Thou shalt not idle away thy time, neither shalt thou bury thy talent that it may not be known. (D&C 60:13.)

Even the bishop, who is a judge, and his counselors, if they are not faithful in their stewardships *shall be condemned, and others shall be planted in their stead.* (D&C 64:40.)

Lay your hands upon the sick, *and they shall recover.* (D&C 66:9.)

Keep these sayings, for they are true and faithful; *and thou shalt magnify thine office, and push many people to Zion with songs of everlasting joy upon their heads.* Continue in these things [missionary work and righteousness] even unto the end, *and you shall have a crown of eternal life at the right hand of my Father.* (D&C 66:11-12.)

A promise I give unto you that have been ordained unto this ministry, that inasmuch as you strip yourselves from jealousies and fears, and humble yourselves before me, for ye are not sufficiently humble, *the veil shall be rent and you shall see me and know that I am—not with the carnal neither natural mind, but with the spiritual.* (D&C 67:10.)

This is an ensample unto all those who were ordained unto this priesthood, whose mission is appointed unto them to go forth—and this is the ensample unto them, that they shall speak as they are moved upon by the Holy Ghost, *and whatsoever they shall speak when moved upon by the Holy Ghost shall be scripture, shall be the will of the Lord, shall be the mind of the Lord, shall be the word of the Lord, shall be the voice of the Lord, and the power of God unto salvation.* (D&C 68:2-4.)

Go ye into all the world, preach the gospel to every creature, acting in the authority which I have given you, baptizing in the name of the Father, and of the Son, and of the Holy Ghost. (D&C 68:8.)

My servants who are abroad in the earth should send forth the accounts of their stewardships to the land of Zion. (D&C 69:5.)

It is required of the Lord, at the hand of every steward, to render an account of his stewardship, both in time and in eternity. (D&C 72:3.)

Every elder in this part of the vineyard must give an account of his stewardship unto the bishop in this part of the vineyard. (D&C 72:16.)

He that is a faithful and wise steward *shall inherit all things.* (D&C 78:22.)

Be faithful; stand in the office which I have appointed unto you; succor the weak, lift up the hands which hang down, and strengthen the feeble knees. (D&C 81:5.)

The sons of Moses and also the sons of Aaron shall offer an acceptable offering and sacrifice in the house of the Lord, which house shall be built unto the Lord in this generation, upon the consecrated spot as I have appointed—*and the sons of Moses and of Aaron shall be filled with the glory of the Lord, upon Mount Zion in the Lord's house, whose sons are ye; and also many whom I have called and sent forth to build up my church.* For whoso is faithful unto the obtaining these two priesthoods of which I have spoken, and the magnifying their calling, *are sanctified by the Spirit unto the renewing of their bodies. They become the sons of Moses and of Aaron and the seed of Abraham, and the church and kingdom, and the elect of God.* And also all they who receive this priesthood *receive me, saith the Lord; for he that receiveth my servants receiveth me; and he that receiveth me receiveth my Father; and he that receiveth my Father receiveth my Father's kingdom; therefore all that my Father hath shall be given unto him. And this is according to the oath and covenant which belongeth to the priesthood.* Therefore, all those who receive the priesthood, *receive this oath and covenant of my Father, which he cannot break, neither can it be moved.* But whoso breaketh this covenant after he hath received it, and altogether turneth therefrom, *shall not have forgiveness of sins in this world nor in the world to come.* And *wo* unto all those who come not unto this priesthood which ye have received. (D&C 84:31-42.)

Therefore, let every man stand in his own office, and labor in his own calling; and let not the head say unto the feet it hath no need of the feet; for without the feet how shall the body be able to stand? (D&C 84:109.)

[regarding government leaders] *In his hot displeasure, and in his fierce anger, in his time, [the Lord] will cut off* those wicked, unfaithful, and unjust stewards, *and appoint them their portion among hypocrites, and unbelievers; even in outer darkness, where there is weeping, and wailing, and gnashing of teeth.* (D&C 101:90-91.)

It is wisdom in me; therefore, a commandment I give unto you, that ye shall organize yourselves and appoint every man his stewardship; that every man may give an account unto me of the stewardship which is appointed unto him. (D&C 104:11-12.)

Now let every man learn his duty, and to act in the office in which he is appointed, in all diligence. He that is slothful *shall not be counted worthy to stand,* and he that learns not his duty and shows himself not approved *shall not be counted worthy to stand.* (D&C 107: 99-100.)

The rights of the priesthood are inseparably connected with the powers of heaven, and . . . the powers of heaven cannot be controlled nor handled only upon the principles of righteousness. That they may be conferred upon us, it is true; but when we undertake to cover our sins, or to gratify our pride, our vain ambition, or to exercise control or dominion or compulsion upon the souls of the children of men, in any degree of unrighteousness, behold, *the heavens withdraw themselves; the Spirit of the Lord is grieved; and when it is withdrawn, Amen to the priesthood or the authority of that man. Behold, ere he is aware, he is left unto himself, to kick against the pricks, to persecute the saints, and to fight against God.* We have learned by sad experience that it is the nature and disposition of almost all men, as soon as they get a little authority, as they suppose, they will immediately begin to exercise unrighteous dominion. *Hence many are called, but few are chosen.* (D&C 121:36-40.)

No power or influence can or ought to be maintained by virtue of the priesthood, only by persuasion, by long-suffering, by gentleness and meekness, and by love unfeigned; by kindness, and pure knowledge, *which shall greatly enlarge the soul without hypocrisy, and without guile*—reproving betimes with sharpness, when moved upon by the Holy Ghost; and then showing forth afterwards an increase of love toward him whom thou has reproved, *lest he esteem thee to be his enemy; that he may know that thy faithfulness is stronger than the cords of death.* Let thy bowels also be full of charity towards all men, and to the household of faith, and let virtue garnish thy thoughts unceasingly; *then shall thy confidence wax strong in the presence of God; and the doctrine of the priesthood shall distil upon thy soul as the dews from heaven. The Holy Ghost shall be thy constant companion, and thy scepter an unchanging scepter of righteousness and truth; and thy dominion shall be an everlasting dominion, and without compulsory means it shall flow unto thee forever and ever.* (D&C 121:41-46.)

Let him [Robert B. Thompson] remember that his stewardship will I require at his hands. (D&C 124:14.)

Thou shalt be diligent in preserving what thou hast, that thou mayest be a wise steward. (D&C 136:27.)

Who, then, is a faithful and wise servant, *whom his lord hath made ruler over his household, to give them meat in due season? Blessed* is that servant whom his lord, when he cometh, shall find so doing; *and verily I say unto you, he shall make him ruler over all his goods.* (JS–M 1:49-50.)

Baptism and Spiritual Rebirth

(See also Covenants; Receiving and Following the Holy Ghost; Sacrament.)

Baptism is a perfect combination of symbol and covenant. The best of symbols do more than merely represent an idea or principle; they embody it in tone, conveying the message on rational, emotional, and sensory levels.

Baptism represents not only the beginning but also the ending, not only birth but also death and resurrection. It cleanses the baptized person from sin and opens a new earthly life and an eternal life to him. Keeping the baptismal covenant qualifies him for the companionship of the Holy Ghost, for baptism of the Spirit as well as of the body.

Baptism is a serious commitment, a sacred covenant. Alma, baptizing his people at the waters of Mormon, gave them this charge as they were baptized:

"Now, as ye are desirous to come into the fold of God, and to be called his people, and are willing to bear one another's burdens, that they may be light; yea, and are willing to mourn with those that mourn; yea, and comfort those that stand in need of comfort and to stand as witnesses of God at all times and in all things, and in all places that ye may be in, even until death, . . . what have you against being baptized in the name of the Lord, as a witness before him that ye have entered into a covenant with him, that ye will serve him and keep his commandments . . . ?"

The people clapped their hands for joy, exclaiming, "This is the desire of our hearts." (Mosiah 18:8-11.)

Just as Alma's believers were baptized in the waters of Mormon, so we assume those same covenants, obligations, and potential blessings through baptism. By making the covenants of baptism and receiving the Holy Ghost, we become eligible for a spiritual rebirth, the godly transformation that means we are born not only of water but also of Spirit.

We are commanded to seek these blessings through baptism. It is the only "strait gate" that leads to eternal life.

Commandments and Promises

Then cometh Jesus from Galilee to Jordan unto John, to be baptized of him. But John forbad him, saying, I have need to be baptized of thee, and comest thou to me? And Jesus answering said unto him, Suffer it to be so now: for thus it becometh us to fulfil all righteousness. (Matt. 3:13-15.)

Enter ye in at the strait gate: for wide is the gate, and broad is the way, *that leadeth to destruction*, and many there be which go in thereat: because strait is the gate, and narrow is the way, *which leadeth unto life*, and few there be that find it. (Matt. 7:13-14.)

He that believeth and is baptized *shall be saved*; but he that believeth not *shall be damned*. (Mark 16:16.)

Except a man be born again, *he cannot see the kingdom of God*. (John 3:3.)

Peter said unto them, Repent, and be baptized every one of you in the name of Jesus Christ for the remission of sins, *and ye shall receive the gift of the Holy Ghost. For the promise is unto you, and to your children, and to all that are afar off, even as many as the Lord our God shall call.* (Acts 2:38-39.)

[Peter] commanded them to be baptized in the name of the Lord. (Acts 10:48.)

[to Saul] Arise, and be baptized, *and wash away thy sins*, calling on the name of the Lord. (Acts 22:16.)

Know ye not, that so many of us as were baptized into Jesus Christ were baptized into his death? Therefore we are buried with him by baptism unto death: *that like as Christ was raised up from the dead by the glory of the Father, even so we also should walk in newness of life.* For if we have been planted together in the likeness of his death, *we shall be also in the likeness of his resurrection: knowing this, that our old man is crucified with him, that the body of sin might be destroyed, that henceforth we should not serve sin.* (Rom. 6:3-6.)

Be not conformed to this world: but be ye transformed by the renewing of your mind, that ye may prove what is that good, and acceptable, and perfect, will of God. (Rom. 12:2.)

Put off concerning the former conversation the old man, which is corrupt according to the deceitful lusts; and be renewed in the spirit of your mind; and that ye put on the new man, which after God is created in righteousness and true holiness. (Eph. 4:22-24.)

Seeing ye have purified your souls in obeying the truth through the Spirit unto unfeigned love of the brethren, see that ye love one another with a pure heart fervently: being born again, not of corruptible seed, but of incorruptible, by the word of God, which liveth and abideth for ever. (1 Pet. 1:22-23.)

Whosoever is born of God *doth not commit sin; for his seed remaineth in him: and he cannot sin,* because he is born of God. (1 Jn. 3:9; see also JST 1 Jn. 3:9.)

He commandeth all men that they must repent, and be baptized in his name, having perfect faith in the Holy One of Israel, *or they cannot be saved in the kingdom of God.* And if they will not repent and believe in his name, and be baptized in his name, and endure to the end, *they must be damned; for the Lord God, the Holy One of Israel, has spoken it.* (2 Ne. 9:23-24.)

The Father said: Repent ye, repent ye, and be baptized in the name of my Beloved Son. And also, the voice of the Son came unto me, saying: He that is baptized in my name, *to him will the Father give the Holy Ghost, like unto me;* wherefore, follow me, and do the things which ye have seen me do. Wherefore, my beloved brethren, I know that if ye shall follow the Son, with full purpose of heart, acting no hypocrisy and no deception before God, but with real intent, repenting of your sins, witnessing unto the Father that ye are willing to take upon you the name of Christ, by baptism—yea, following your Lord and your Savior down into the water, according to his word, *behold, then shall ye receive the Holy Ghost; yea, then cometh the baptism of fire and of the Holy Ghost; and then can ye speak with the tongue of angels, and shout praises unto the Holy One of Israel.* (2 Ne. 31: 11-13.)

The gate by which ye should enter is repentance and baptism by water; *and then cometh a remission of your sins by fire and by the Holy Ghost.* (2 Ne. 31:17.)

If ye will enter in by the way, and receive the Holy Ghost, *it will show unto you all things what ye should do.* (2 Ne. 32:5.)

Repent ye, and enter in at the strait gate, and continue in the way which is narrow, *until ye shall obtain eternal life.* (Jacob 6:11.)

As ye are desirous to come into the fold of God, and to be called his people, and are willing to bear one another's burdens, *that they may be light;* yea, and are willing to mourn with those that mourn; yea, and comfort those that stand in need of comfort, and to stand as witnesses of God at all times and in all things, and in all places that ye may be in, even until death, *that ye may be redeemed of God, and be numbered with those of the first resurrection, that ye may have eternal life*—Now I say unto you, if this be the desire of your hearts, what have you against being baptized in the name of the Lord, as a witness before him that ye have entered into a covenant with him, that ye will serve him and keep his commandments, *that he may pour out his Spirit more abundantly upon you?* (Mosiah 18:8-10.)

He commanded them that there should be no contention one with another, but that they should look forward with one eye, having one faith and one baptism, having their hearts knit together in unity and in love one towards another. And thus he commanded them to preach. *And thus they became the children of God.* (Mosiah 18:21-22.)

The Lord said unto me: Marvel not that all mankind, yea, men and women, all nations, kindreds, tongues and people, must be born again; yea, born of God, changed from their carnal and fallen state, to a state of righteousness, *being redeemed of God, becoming his sons and daughters; and thus they become new creatures;* and unless they do this, *they can in nowise inherit the kingdom of God.* (Mosiah 27: 25-26.)

I [Alma] speak by way of command unto you that belong to the church; and unto those who do not belong to the church I speak by way of invitation, saying: Come and be baptized unto repentance, *that ye also may be partakers of the fruit of the tree of life.* (Alma 5:62.)

Now I say unto you that ye must repent, and be born again; for the spirit saith if ye are not born again *ye cannot inherit the kingdom of heaven;* therefore come and be baptized unto repentance, *that ye may be washed from your sins, that ye may have faith on the Lamb of God, who taketh away the sins of the world, who is mighty to save and to cleanse from all unrighteousness.* Yea, I say unto you come and fear not, and lay aside every sin, which easily doth beset you, which doth bind you down to destruction, yea, come and go forth, and show unto your God that ye are willing to repent of your sins and enter into a covenant with him to keep his commandments, and witness it unto him this day by going into the waters of baptism. And whosoever doeth this, and keepeth the commandments of God from thenceforth, *the same will remember that I say unto him, yea, he will remember that I have said unto him, he shall have eternal life, according to the testimony of the Holy Spirit, which testifieth in me.* (Alma 7:14-16.)

Blessed are they who humble themselves without being compelled to be humble; or rather, in other words, *blessed* is he that believeth in the word of God, and is baptized without stubbornness of heart, yea, without being brought to know the word, or even compelled to know, before they will believe. (Alma 32:16.)

If I had not been born of God, *I should not have known these things; but God has, by the mouth of his holy angel, made these things known unto me,* not of any worthiness of myself. (Alma 36:5.)

Many have been born of God, *and have tasted as I have tasted, and have seen eye to eye as I have seen; therefore they do know of these things of which I have spoken, as I do know; and the knowledge which I have is of God.* (Alma 36:26.)

I would not that ye should think that I know these things of myself, but it is the Spirit of God which is in me which maketh these things known unto me; for if I had not been born of God *I should not have known these things.* (Alma 38:6.)

Whoso believeth in me, and is baptized, *the same shall be saved; and they are they who shall inherit the kingdom of God.* (3 Ne. 11:33-34.)

Ye must repent, and become as a little child, and be baptized in my name, *or ye can in nowise receive these things [record borne of the Savior, through fire and the Holy Ghost].* And again I say unto you, ye must repent, and be baptized in my name, and become as a little child, *or ye can in nowise inherit the kingdom of God.* (3 Ne. 11: 37-38.)

After that ye are baptized with water, *behold, I will baptize you with fire and with the Holy Ghost; therefore blessed are ye* if ye shall believe in me and be baptized, after that ye have seen me and know that I am. *And again, more blessed* are they who shall believe in your words because that ye shall testify that ye have seen me, and that ye know that I am. Yea, *blessed* are they who shall believe in your words, and come down into the depths of humility and be baptized, *for they shall be visited with fire and with the Holy Ghost, and shall receive a remission of their sins.* (3 Ne. 12:1-2.)

Whosoever will hearken unto my words and repenteth and is baptized, *the same shall be saved.* (3 Ne. 23:5.)

Whoso repenteth and is baptized in my name *shall be filled;* and if he endureth to the end, *behold, him will I hold guiltless before my Father at that day when I shall stand to judge the world.* (3 Ne. 27:16.)

Now this is the commandment: Repent, all ye ends of the earth, and come unto me and be baptized in my name, *that ye may be sanctified by the reception of the Holy Ghost, that ye may stand spotless before me at the last day.* (3 Ne. 27:20.)

Enter ye in at the strait gate; for strait is the gate, and narrow is the way *that leads to life, and few there be that find it;* but wide is the gate, and broad the way *which leads to death, and many there be that travel therein, until the night cometh, wherein no man can work.* (3 Ne. 27:33.)

Come unto me, and be baptized in my name, *that ye may receive a remission of your sins, and be filled with the Holy Ghost, that ye may be numbered with my people who are of the house of Israel.* (3 Ne. 30:2.)

Repent ye, and come unto me, and be ye baptized, and build up again my church, *and ye shall be spared.* (Morm. 3:2.)

Therefore repent, and be baptized in the name of Jesus, and lay hold upon the gospel of Christ. (Morm. 7:8.)

If it so be that ye believe in Christ, and are baptized, first with water, then with fire and with the Holy Ghost, following the example of our Savior, according to that which he hath commanded us, *it shall be well with you in the day of judgment.* (Morm. 7:10.)

He that believeth and is baptized *shall be saved,* but he that believeth not *shall be damned.* (Morm. 9:23.)

See that ye are not baptized unworthily. (Morm. 9:29.)

Repent all ye ends of the earth, and come unto me, and believe in my gospel, and be baptized in my name; for he that believeth and is baptized *shall be saved.* (Ether 4:18.)

Repent all ye ends of the earth, and come unto me, and be baptized in my name, and have faith in me, *that ye may be saved.* (Moro. 7:34.)

As many as repent and are baptized in my name, which is Jesus Christ, and endure to the end, *the same shall be saved.* (D&C 18:22.)

All men must repent and be baptized, and not only men, but women, and children who have arrived at the years of accountability. (D&C 18:42.)

And again, by way of commandment to the church concerning the manner of baptism—All those who humble themselves before God, and desire to be baptized, and come forth with broken hearts and contrite spirits, and witness before the church that they have truly repented of all their sins, and are willing to take upon them the name of Jesus Christ, having a determination to serve him to the end, and truly manifest by their works that they have received the Spirit of Christ unto the remission of their sins, shall be received by baptism into his church. (D&C 20:37.)

Baptism is to be administered in the following manner unto all those who repent—the person who is called of God and has authority from Jesus Christ to baptize, shall go down into the water with the person who has presented himself or herself for baptism, and shall say, calling him or her by name: Having been commissioned of Jesus Christ, I baptize you in the name of the Father, and of the Son, and of the Holy Ghost. Amen. Then shall he immerse him or her in the water, and come forth again out of the water. (D&C 20:72-74; similar scripture, 3 Ne. 11:22-26.)

Enter ye in at the gate, as I have commanded, and seek not to counsel your God. (D&C 22:4.)

Repent and be baptized, every one of you, *for a remission of your sins;* yea, be baptized even by water, *and then cometh the baptism of fire and of the Holy Ghost.* (D&C 33:11.)

I give unto thee a commandment, that thou shalt baptize by water, *and they shall receive the Holy Ghost by the laying on of the hands, even as the apostles of old.* (D&C 35:6.)

[to James Covill] *Behold, the days of thy deliverance are come,* if thou wilt hearken to my voice, which saith unto thee: Arise and be baptized, and wash away your sins, calling on my name, *and you shall receive my Spirit, and a blessing so great as you have never known.* And if thou do this, *I have prepared thee for a greater work.* (D&C 39:10-11.)

[Believe on Jesus Christ and] repent and be baptized in the name of Jesus Christ, according to the holy commandment, *for the remission of sins; and whoso doeth this shall receive the gift of the Holy Ghost, by the laying on of the hands of the elders of the church.* (D&C 49:12-14.)

[to W.W. Phelps] After thou hast been baptized by water, which if you do with an eye single to my glory, *you shall have a remission of your sins and a reception of the Holy Spirit by the laying on of hands.* (D&C 55:1.)

Their children shall be baptized *for the remission of their sins when eight years old, and receive the laying on of the hands.* (D&C 68:27.)

By reason of transgression cometh the fall, which fall bringeth death, and inasmuch as ye were born into the world by water, and blood, and the spirit, which I have made, and so became of dust a living soul, even so ye must be born again into the kingdom of heaven, of water, and of the Spirit, and be cleansed by blood, even the blood of mine Only Begotten; *that ye might be sanctified for all sin, and enjoy the words of eternal life in this world, and eternal life in the world to come, even immortal glory; for by the water ye keep the command-ment; by the Spirit ye are justified, and by the blood ye are sanctified; therefore it is given to abide in you; the record of heaven; the Com-forter; the peaceable things of immortal glory; the truth of all things; that which quickeneth all things, which maketh alive all things; that which knoweth all things, and hath all power according to wisdom, mercy, truth, justice, and judgment.* (Moses 6:59-61.)

[Noah preaching] Believe and repent of your sins and be baptized in the name of Jesus Christ, the Son of God, even as our fathers, *and ye shall receive the Holy Ghost, that ye may have all things made man-ifest; and if ye do not this, the floods will come in upon you.* (Moses 8:24.)

Believing in God

(See also Faith.)

"Believe in God," King Benjamin taught his people. He listed what they should believe about God and compared man's abilities to His: "Believe that he is, and that he created all things, both in heaven and in earth; believe that he has all wisdom and power, both in heaven and in earth; believe that man doth not comprehend all the things which the Lord can comprehend."

King Benjamin then taught what men must believe about their actions: "Believe that ye must repent of your sins and forsake them, and humble yourselves before God; and ask in sincerity of heart that he would forgive you."

As did other prophets and teachers and the Savior, King Benjamin detailed many things we should believe. Belief is a critical basis for our relationship with Deity. It is a prerequisite for baptism, a necessity for keeping the commandments. But King Benjamin, like others, did not stop with belief: "And now, if you believe all these things see that ye do them." (Mosiah 4:9-10.)

Commandments and Promises

Believe in the Lord your God, *so shall ye be established*; believe his prophets, *so shall ye prosper*. (2 Chr. 20:20.)

Then was the king exceeding glad for him [Daniel], and commanded them they should take Daniel up out of the den. So Daniel was taken up out of the den, *and no manner of hurt was found upon him*, because he believed in his God. (Dan. 6:23.)

Jesus said unto the centurion, Go thy way; and as thou hast believed, *so be it done unto thee*. (Matt. 8:13.)

Jesus said unto them, A prophet is not without honour, save in his own country, and in his own house. *And he did not many mighty works there* because of their unbelief. (Matt. 13:57-58.)

All things, whatsoever ye shall ask in prayer, believing, *ye shall receive.* (Matt. 21:22.)

The time is fulfilled, and the kingdom of God is at hand: repent ye, and believe the gospel. (Mark 1:15.)

Be not afraid, only believe. (Mark 5:36.)

Jesus said unto him, If thou canst believe, *all things are possible to him that believeth.* And straightway the father of the child cried out, and said with tears, Lord, I believe; help thou mine unbelief. (Mark 9:23-24.)

For verily I say unto you, That whosoever shall say unto this mountain, Be thou removed, and be thou cast into the sea; and shall not doubt in his heart, but shall believe that those things which he saith shall come to pass; *he shall have whatsoever he saith.* Therefore I say unto you, What things soever ye desire, when ye pray, believe that ye receive them, *and ye shall have them.* (Mark 11:23-24.)

He that believeth and is baptized *shall be saved;* but he that believeth not *shall be damned. And these signs shall follow them that believe; In my name they shall cast out devils; they shall speak with new tongues; they shall take up serpents; and if they drink any deadly thing, it shall not hurt them: they shall lay hands on the sick, and they shall recover.* (Mark 16:16-18.)

Blessed is she [Mary] that believed: *for there shall be a performance of those things which are told her from the Lord.* (Luke 1:45.)

Now the parable is this: The seed is the word of God. Those by the way side are they that hear ; then cometh the devil, and taketh away the word out of their hearts, lest they should believe *and be saved.* They on the rock are they, which, when they hear, receive the word with joy; and these have no root, which for a while believe, *and in time of temptation fall away.* (Luke 8:11-13.)

But when Jesus heard it, he answered him, saying, Fear not: believe only, *and she [Jairus's daughter] shall be made whole.* (Luke 8:50.)

As many as received him, *to them gave he power to become the sons of God*, even to them that believe on his name: which were born, not of blood, nor of the will of the flesh, nor of the will of man, but of God. (John 1:12-13.)

He that believeth on him *is not condemned:* but he that believeth not *is condemned already*, because he hath not believed in the name of the only begotten Son of God. (John 3:18; see also JST John 3:18.)

He that believeth on the Son *hath everlasting life:* and he that believeth not the Son *shall not see life; but the wrath of God abideth on him.* (John 3:36; see also JST John 3:36.)

He that heareth my word, and believeth on him that sent me, *hath everlasting life, and shall not come into condemnation; but is passed from death unto life.* (John 5:24.)

This is the will of him that sent me, that everyone which seeth the Son, and believeth on him, *may have everlasting life: and I will raise him up at the last day.* (John 6:40; see also JST John 6:40.)

He that believeth on me *hath everlasting life.* (John 6:47.)

He that believeth on me, as the scripture hath said, *out of his belly shall flow rivers of living water.* (John 7:38.)

I said therefore unto you, *that ye shall die in your sins:* for if ye believe not that I am he, *ye shall die in your sins.* (John 8:24.)

If I do not the works of my Father, believe me not. But if I do, though ye believe not me, believe the works: *that ye may know, and believe, that the Father is in me, and I in him.* (John 10:37-38.)

I am the resurrection, and the life: he that believeth in me, though he were dead, *yet shall he live:* and whosoever liveth and believeth in me *shall never die.* (John 11:25-26.)

Jesus saith unto her, Said I not unto thee, that, if thou wouldest believe, *thou shouldest see the glory of God?* (John 11:40.)

While ye have light, believe in the light, *that ye may be the children of light.* (John 12:36.)

I am come a light into the world, that whosoever believeth on me *should not abide in darkness.* (John 12:46.)

Let not your heart be troubled: ye believe in God, believe also in me. (John 14:1.)

Believe me that I am in the Father, and the Father in me: or else believe me for the very works' sake. (John 14:11.)

Neither pray I for these [the apostles] alone, but for them also which shall believe on me through their word; *that they all may be one; as thou, Father, art in me, and I in thee, that they also may be one in us:* that the world may believe that thou hast sent me. (John 17:20-21.)

Then saith he to Thomas, Reach hither thy finger, and behold my hands; and reach hither thy hand, and thrust it into my side: and be not faithless, but believing. And Thomas answered and said unto him, My Lord and my God. Jesus saith unto him, Thomas, because thou hast seen me, thou hast believed: *blessed* are they that have not seen, and yet have believed. (John 20:27-29.)

These are written, that ye might believe that Jesus is the Christ, the Son of God; and that believing *ye might have life through his name.* (John 20:31.)

To him give all the prophets witness, that through his name whosoever believeth in him *shall receive remission of sins.* (Acts 10:43.)

By him all that believe *are justified from all things, from which ye could not be justified by the law of Moses.* (Acts 13:39.)

Believe on the Lord Jesus Christ, *and thou shalt be saved, and thy house.* (Acts 16:31.)

I am not ashamed of the gospel of Christ: *for it is the power of God unto salvation* to every one that believeth; to the Jew first, and also to the Greek. (Rom. 1:16.)

Whosoever believeth on him *shall not be ashamed.* (Rom. 9:33.)

Christ is the end of the law for righteousness to every one that believeth. (Rom. 10:4.)

If thou shalt confess with thy mouth the Lord Jesus, and shalt believe in thine heart that God hath raised him from the dead, *thou shalt be saved. For with the heart man believeth unto righteousness; and with the mouth confession is made unto salvation.* For the scripture saith, Whosoever believeth on him *shall not be ashamed.* (Rom. 10:9-11.)

The scripture hath concluded all under sin, *that the promise by faith of Jesus Christ might be given* to them that believe. (Gal. 3:22.)

With all deceivableness of unrighteousness in them that perish; because they received not the love of the truth, *that they might be saved.* And for this cause God shall send them strong delusion, that they should believe a lie: *that they all might be damned* who believed not the truth, but had pleasure in unrighteousness. (2 Thes. 2:10-12.)

We both labour and suffer reproach, because we trust in the living God, *who is the Saviour of all men*, specially of those that believe. (1 Tim. 4:10.)

Be thou an example of the believers, in word, in conversation, in charity, in spirit, in faith, in purity. (1 Tim. 4:12.)

Unto the pure *all things are pure:* but unto them that are defiled and unbelieving *is nothing pure; but even their mind and conscience is defiled.* (Titus 1:15; see also JST Titus 1:15.)

Take heed, brethren, lest there be in any of you an evil heart of unbelief, in departing from the living God. (Heb. 3:12.)

To whom *sware he that they should not enter into his rest*, but to them that believed not? So we see that *they could not enter in* because of unbelief. (Heb. 3:18-19.)

We which have believed *do enter into rest, as he said.* (Heb. 4:3; see also JST Heb. 4:3.)

Without faith it is impossible to please him: for he that cometh to God must believe that he is, and that he is a rewarder of them that diligently seek him. (Heb. 11:6.)

Unto you therefore which believe *he is precious.* (1 Pet. 2:7.)

This is his commandment, That we should believe on the name of his Son Jesus Christ, and love one another, as he gave us commandment. And he that keepeth his commandments *dwelleth in him, and he in him. And hereby we know that he abideth in us, by the Spirit which he hath given us.* (1 Jn. 3:23-24.)

Believe not every spirit, but try the spirits whether they are of God: because many false prophets are gone out into the world. (1 Jn. 4:1.)

Whosoever believeth that Jesus is the Christ *is born of God.* (1 Jn. 5:1.)

The fearful, and unbelieving . . . *shall have their part in the lake which burneth with fire and brimstone: which is the second death.* (Rev. 21:8.)

Blessed art thou, Nephi, because thou believest in the Son of the most high God; *wherefore, thou shalt behold the things which thou hast desired.* (1 Ne. 11:6.)

When the time cometh that they shall dwindle in unbelief, after they have received so great blessings from the hand of the Lord—having a knowledge of the creation of the earth, and all men, knowing the great and marvelous works of the Lord from the creation of the world; having power given them to do all things by faith; having all the commandments from the beginning, and having been brought by his infinite goodness into this precious land of promise—behold, I say, if the day shall come that they will reject the Holy One of Israel, the true Messiah, their Redeemer and their God, behold, *the judgments of him that is just shall rest upon them.* (2 Ne. 1:10.)

He is the firstfruits unto God, inasmuch as he shall make intercession for all the children of men; and they that believe in him *shall be saved*. (2 Ne. 2:9.)

According to the words of the prophet, the Messiah will set himself again the second time to recover them; wherefore, *he will manifest himself unto them in power and great glory, unto the destruction of their enemies*, when that day cometh when they shall believe in him; *and none will he destroy* that believe in him. And they that believe not in him *shall be destroyed, both by fire, and by tempest, and by earthquakes, and by bloodsheds, and by pestilence, and by famine. And they shall know that the Lord is God, the Holy One of Israel*. (2 Ne. 6:14-15.)

The righteous, the saints of the Holy One of Israel, they who have believed in the Holy One of Israel, they who have endured the crosses of the world, and despised the shame of it, *they shall inherit the kingdom of God, which was prepared for them from the foundation of the world, and their joy shall be full forever*. (2 Ne. 9:18.)

If they will not repent and believe in his name, and be baptized in his name, and endure to the end, *they must be damned*; for the Lord God, the Holy One of Israel, has spoken it. (2 Ne. 9:24.)

The right way is to believe in Christ, and deny him not; and Christ is the Holy One of Israel, wherefore ye must bow down before him, and worship him with all your might, mind, and strength, and your whole soul; and if ye do this *ye shall in nowise be cast out*. (2 Ne. 25:29.)

It shall come to pass that the Jews which are scattered also shall begin to believe in Christ; and they shall begin to gather in upon the face of the land; and as many as shall believe in Christ *shall also become a delightsome people*. (2 Ne. 30:7.)

Hearken unto these words and believe in Christ; and if ye believe not in these words believe in Christ. And if ye shall believe in Christ *ye will believe in these words*, for they are the words of Christ, and he hath given them unto me; and they teach all men that they should do good. (2 Ne. 33:10.)

We would to God that we could persuade all men not to rebel against God, to provoke him to anger, but that all men would believe in Christ, and view his death, and suffer his cross and bear the shame of the world. (Jacob 1:8.)

[Enos] cried unto [God] continually, for he had said unto me: Whatsoever thing ye shall ask in faith, believing that ye shall receive in the name of Christ, *ye shall receive it.* (Enos 1:15.)

Come unto God, the Holy One of Israel, and believe in prophesying, and in revelations, and in the ministering of angels, and in the gift of speaking with tongues, and in the gift of interpreting languages, and in all things which are good; for there is nothing which is good save it comes from the Lord; and that which is evil cometh from the devil. (Omni 1:25.)

Men drink damnation to their own souls except they humble themselves and become as little children, and believe that salvation was, and is, and is to come, in and through the atoning blood of Christ, the Lord Omnipotent. (Mosiah 3:18.)

Believe in God; believe that he is, and that he created all things, both in heaven and in earth; believe that he has all wisdom, and all power, both in heaven and in earth; believe that man doth not comprehend all the things which the Lord can comprehend. And again, believe that ye must repent of your sins and forsake them, and humble yourselves before God; and ask in sincerity of heart that he would forgive you; and now, if you believe all these things see that ye do them. (Mosiah 4:9-10.)

All those who have hearkened unto [the prophets'] words, and believed that the Lord would redeem his people, and have looked forward to that day for a remission of their sins, I say unto you, that *these are his seed, or they are the heirs of the kingdom of God.* (Mosiah 15:11.)

He has all power to save every man that believeth on his name and bringeth forth fruit meet for repentance. (Alma 12:15.)

His arm is extended to all people who will repent and believe on his name. (Alma 19:36.)

If thou wilt bow down before God, yea, if thou wilt repent of all thy sins, and will bow down before God, and call on his name in faith, believing that ye shall receive, *then shalt thou receive the hope which thou desirest.* (Alma 22:16.)

He is a merciful Being, even unto salvation, to those who will repent and believe on his name. (Alma 26:35.)

Blessed are they who humble themselves without being compelled to be humble; or rather, in other words, *blessed* is he that believeth in the word of God, and is baptized without stubbornness of heart, yea, without being brought to know the word, or even compelled to know, before they will believe. (Alma 32:16.)

I would that ye should remember, that *God is merciful* unto all who believe on his name; therefore he desireth, in the first place, that ye should believe, yea, even on his word. (Alma 32:22.)

Cast about your eyes and begin to believe in the Son of God, that he will come to redeem his people, and that he shall suffer and die to atone for their sins; and that he shall rise again from the dead, which shall bring to pass the resurrection, that all men shall stand before him, to be judged at the last and judgment day, according to their works. (Alma 33:22.)

He shall bring salvation to all those who shall believe on his name; this being the intent of this last sacrifice, to bring about the bowels of mercy, which overpowereth justice, and bringeth about means unto men that they may have faith unto repentance. (Alma 34:15.)

Thus we see that *the gate of heaven is open* unto all, even to those who will believe on the name of Jesus Christ, who is the Son of God. (Hel. 3:28.)

The Lord began to pour out his Spirit upon the Lamanites, because of their easiness and willingness to believe in his words. (Hel. 6:36.)

Whosoever shall believe on the Son of God, *the same shall have everlasting life.* (Hel. 14:8.)

As many as have received me, *to them have I given to become the sons of God; and even so will I* to as many as shall believe on my name, for behold, by me redemption cometh, and in me is the law of Moses fulfilled. (3 Ne. 9:17.)

The Father commandeth all men, everywhere, to repent and believe in me. Whoso believeth in me, and is baptized, *the same shall be saved; and they are they who shall inherit the kingdom of God.* And whoso believeth not in me, and is not baptized, *shall be damned.* (3 Ne. 11:32-34.)

Blessed are ye if ye shall believe in me and be baptized, after that ye have seen me and know that I am. *And again, more blessed are they* who shall believe in your words because that ye shall testify that ye have seen me, and that ye know that I am. *Yea, blessed are they* who shall believe in your words, and come down into the depths of humility and be baptized, *for they shall be visited with fire and with the Holy Ghost, and shall receive a remission of their sins.* (3 Ne. 12:1-2.)

I have given you the law and the commandments of my Father, that ye shall believe in me, and that ye shall repent of your sins, and come unto me with a broken heart and a contrite spirit. Behold, ye have the commandments before you, and the law is fulfilled. Therefore come unto me *and be ye saved.* (3 Ne. 12:19-20.)

Because of stiffneckedness and unbelief *they [the other sheep] understood not my word; therefore I was commanded to say no more of the Father concerning this thing unto them.* (3 Ne. 15:18.)

Blessed are the Gentiles, because of their belief in me, in and of the Holy Ghost, which witnesses unto them of me and of the Father. (3 Ne. 16:6.)

So great faith have I never seen among all the Jews; *wherefore I could not show unto them so great miracles,* because of their unbelief. (3 Ne. 19:35.)

When they shall have received this, which is expedient that they should have first, to try their faith, and if it shall so be that they shall believe these things *then shall the greater things be made manifest unto them.* And if it so be that they will not believe these things, *then shall the greater things be withheld from them, unto their condemnation.* (3 Ne. 26:9-10.)

There were no gifts from the Lord, and the Holy Ghost did not come upon any, because of their wickedness and unbelief. (Morm. 1:14.)

This people shall be scattered, and shall become a dark, a filthy, and a loathsome people, beyond the description of that which ever hath been amongst us, yea, even that which hath been among the Lamanites, and this because of their unbelief and idolatry. (Morm. 5:15.)

Know ye that ye must come to the knowledge of your fathers, and repent of all your sins and iniquities, and believe in Jesus Christ, that he is the Son of God, and that he was slain by the Jews, and by the power of the Father he hath risen again, whereby he hath gained the victory over the grave; and also in him is the sting of death swallowed up. (Morm. 7:5.)

The reason why he ceaseth to do miracles among the children of men is because that they dwindle in unbelief, and depart from the right way, and know not the God in whom they should trust. Behold, I say unto you, that whoso believeth in Christ, doubting nothing, *whatsoever he shall ask the Father in the name of Christ it shall be granted him; and this promise is unto all, even unto the ends of the earth.* (Morm. 9:20-21.)

Doubt not, but be believing, and begin as in times of old, and come unto the Lord with all your heart. (Morm. 9:27.)

The Lord . . . showed unto the brother of Jared all the inhabitants of the earth which had been, and also all that would be; and he withheld them not from his sight, even unto the ends of the earth. For he had said unto him in times before, that if he would believe in him *that he could show unto him all things—it should be shown unto him; therefore the Lord could not withhold anything from him,* for he knew that the Lord could show him all things. (Ether 3:25-26.)

He that believeth these things which I have spoken, *him will I visit with the manifestations of my Spirit, and he shall know and bear record. For because of my Spirit he shall know that these things are true; for it persuadeth men to do good.* (Ether 4:11.)

Come unto me, O ye Gentiles, and *I will show unto you the greater things, the knowledge which is hid up* because of unbelief. Come unto me, O ye house of Israel, and *it shall be made manifest unto you how great things the Father hath laid up for you, from the foundation of the world; and it hath not come unto you,* because of unbelief. Behold, when ye shall rend that veil of unbelief *which doth cause you to remain in your awful state of wickedness, and hardness of heart, and blindness of mind, then shall the great and marvelous things which have been hid up from the foundation of the world from you*—yea, when ye shall call upon the Father in my name, with a broken heart and a contrite spirit, *then shall ye know that the Father hath remembered the covenant which he made unto your fathers, O house of Israel.* (Ether 4:13-15.)

Repent all ye ends of the earth, and come unto me, and believe in my gospel, and be baptized in my name; for he that believeth and is baptized *shall be saved;* but he that believeth not *shall be damned; and signs shall follow them* that believe in my name. (Ether 14:28.)

[Ether] did cry from the morning, even until the going down of the sun, exhorting the people to believe in God unto repentance *lest they should be destroyed,* saying . . . whoso believeth in God *might with surety hope for a better world, yea, even a place at the right hand of God, which hope* cometh of faith, *maketh an anchor to the souls of men, which would make them sure and steadfast, always abounding in good works, being led to glorify God.* (Ether 12:4.)

It is by faith *that miracles are wrought;* and it is by faith *that angels appear and minister unto men; wherefore, if these things have ceased wo be unto the children of men,* for it is because of unbelief, *and all is vain.* (Moro. 7:37.)

All these gifts of which I have spoken, which are spiritual, never will be done away, even as long as the world shall stand, only according to the unbelief of the children of men. (Moro. 10:19.)

If the day cometh that the power and gifts of God shall be done away among you, it shall be because of unbelief. (Moro. 10:24.)

Whosoever believeth on my words, *them will I visit with the manifestation of my Spirit; and they shall be born of me, even of water and of the Spirit.* (D&C 5:16.)

Oliver Cowdery, verily, verily, I say unto you *that assuredly as the Lord liveth, who is your God and your Redeemer, even so surely shall you receive a knowledge of whatsoever things* you shall ask in faith, with an honest heart, believing that you shall receive a knowledge. . . . *Yea, behold, I will tell you in your mind and in your heart, by the Holy Ghost, which shall come upon you and which shall dwell in your heart. Now, behold, this is the spirit of revelation.* (D&C 8:1-3.)

[to Hyrum Smith] *Behold, thou hast a gift, or thou shalt have a gift* if thou wilt desire of me in faith, with an honest heart, believing in the power of Jesus Christ, or in my power which speaketh unto thee. (D&C 11:10.)

[to Hyrum Smith] *I will impart unto you of my Spirit, which shall enlighten your mind, which shall fill your soul with joy; and then shall ye know, or by this shall ye know, all things whatsoever ye desire of me, which are pertaining unto things of righteousness,* in faith believing in me that you shall receive. (D&C 11:13-14.)

It shall come to pass, that if you shall ask the Father in my name, in faith believing, *you shall receive the Holy Ghost, which giveth utterance, that you may stand as a witness of the things of which you shall both hear and see, and also that you may declare repentance unto this generation.* (D&C 14:8.)

Ask the Father in my name, in faith believing that you shall receive, *and you shall have the Holy Ghost, which manifesteth all things which are expedient unto the children of men.* (D&C 18:18.)

Those who harden their hearts in unbelief, and reject it, *it shall turn to their own condemnation.* (D&C 20:15.)

As many as would believe and be baptized in his holy name, and endure in faith to the end, *should be saved.* (D&C 20:25.)

We know that all men must repent and believe on the name of Jesus Christ, and worship the Father in his name, and endure in faith on his name to the end, *or they cannot be saved in the kingdom of God.* (D&C 20:29.)

Thus did I, the Lord God, appoint unto man the days of his probation—*that by his natural death he might be raised in immortality unto eternal life,* even as many as would believe; and they that believe not *unto eternal damnation; for they cannot be redeemed from their spiritual fall,* because they repent not; for they love darkness rather than light, and their deeds are evil, and they receive their wages of whom they list to obey. (D&C 29:43-45.)

[Jesus Christ] so loved the world that he gave his own life, that as many as would believe *might become the sons of God. Wherefore you* [Orson Pratt] *are my son; and blessed are you* because you have believed. (D&C 34:3-4.)

I am God, and mine arm is not shortened; *and I will show miracles, signs, and wonders,* unto all those who believe on my name. (D&C 35:8.)

They who have not faith to do these things [to be healed], but believe in me, *have power to become my sons;* and inasmuch as they break not my laws *thou shalt bear their infirmities.* (D&C 42:52.)

Unto them that believed on my name *gave I power to obtain eternal life.* (D&C 45:8.)

Believe on the name of the Lord Jesus, who was on the earth, and is to come, the beginning and the end; repent and be baptized in the name of Jesus Christ, according to the holy commandment, for the remission of sins; and whoso doeth this *shall receive the gift of the Holy Ghost, by the laying on of the hands of the elders of the church.* (D&C 49:12-14.)

If [Edward Partridge] repent not of his sins, which are unbelief and blindness of heart, let him take heed *lest he fall.* (D&C 58:15.)

The sound must go forth from this place into all the world, and unto the uttermost parts of the earth—the gospel must be preached unto every creature, *with signs following* them that believe. (D&C 58:64.)

Let the unbelieving hold their lips, *for the day of wrath shall come upon them as a whirlwind, and all flesh shall know that I am God.* (D&C 63:6.)

The fearful, and the unbelieving . . . *shall have their part in that lake which burneth with fire and brimstone, which is the second death.* (D&C 63:17.)

He that believeth and is baptized *shall be saved,* and he that believeth not *shall be damned.* And he that believeth *shall be blest with signs following, even as it is written.* (D&C 68:9-10.)

Every soul who believeth on your words, and is baptized by water for the remission of sins, *shall receive the Holy Ghost. And these signs shall follow them that believe—In my name they shall do many wonderful works; in my name they shall cast out devils; in my name they shall heal the sick; in my name they shall open the eyes of the blind, and unstop the ears of the deaf; and the tongue of the dumb shall speak; and if any man shall administer poison unto them it shall not hurt them; and the poison of a serpent shall not have power to harm them.* But a commandment I give unto them, that they shall not boast themselves of these things, neither speak them before the world; *for these things are given unto you for your profit and for salvation....* They who believe not on your words, and are not baptized in water in my name, for the remission of their sins, that they may receive the Holy Ghost, *shall be damned, and shall not come into my Father's kingdom where my Father and I am.* (D&C 84:64-74.)

Search diligently, pray always, and be believing, *and all things shall work together for your good,* if ye walk uprightly and remember the covenant wherewith ye have covenanted one with another. (D&C 90:24.)

He that believeth and is baptized *shall be saved*, and he that believeth not, and is not baptized, *shall be damned*. (D&C 112:29.)

As many as believed in the Son, and repented of their sins, *should be saved*; and as many as believed not and repented not, *should be damned*; and the words went forth out of the mouth of God in a firm decree; *wherefore they must be fulfilled*. (Moses 5:15.)

Enoch continued his speech, saying: Behold, our father Adam taught these things, and many have believed *and become the sons of God*, and many have believed not, *and have perished in their sins, and are looking forth with fear, in torment, for the fiery indignation of the wrath of God to be poured out upon them*. (Moses 7:1.)

Believe and repent of your sins and be baptized in the name of Jesus Christ, the Son of God, even as our fathers, *and ye shall receive the Holy Ghost, that ye may have all things made manifest*; and if ye do not this, *the floods will come in upon you*. (Moses 8:24.)

Blasphemy and Evil Communication

(See also Edifying and Strengthening Others; Name of Jesus Christ, Bearing the; Sacredness.)

Words are, of themselves, neither good nor bad. The way men choose and use them is what determines their desirability and effect. Words used in corrupt ways, or for incorrect and evil purposes, are condemned by the Lord.

The sin of blasphemy—irreverence toward that which is sacred—is so serious that it was punishable by death under Mosaic law. Blasphemy may involve more than a misuse of words, however. The most serious and least repentable sin is blasphemy against the Holy Ghost. That sin is defined in scripture, and its consequences are repeated several times. These are the scriptural definitions:

"The blasphemy against the Holy Ghost, which shall not be forgiven in the world nor out of the world, is in that ye commit murder wherein ye shed innocent blood, and assent unto my death, after ye have received my new and everlasting covenant, saith the Lord God; and he that abideth not this law can in nowise enter into my glory, but shall be damned, saith the Lord." (D&C 132:27.)

"They are vessels of wrath, doomed to suffer the wrath of God, with the devil and his angels in eternity; concerning whom I have said there is no forgiveness in this world nor in the world to come—having denied the Holy Spirit after having received it, and having denied the Only Begotten Son of the Father, having crucified him unto themselves and put him to an open shame." (D&C 76:33-35.)

"All manner of sin and blasphemy shall be forgiven unto men: but the blasphemy against the Holy Ghost shall not be forgiven unto men. And whosoever speaketh a word against the Son of man, it shall be forgiven him: but whosoever speaketh against the Holy Ghost, it shall not be forgiven him, neither in this world, neither in the world to come." (Matt. 12:31-32.)

50

Not all blasphemies and ill-used words are as dramatically defined, and not all carry such serious consequences. Misuses of the gift of communication include backbiting and talebearing. Profanely and idly using the name of Deity is condemned. Speaking evilly and critically of others is forbidden, as is "filthy" or "corrupt" communication.

How then should we speak? "Let your speech be alway with grace, seasoned with salt," Paul wrote to the Colossians, "that ye may know how ye ought to answer every man." (Col. 4:6.) With the blessing of such perfected communication, we are likely to have no desire or need to express ourselves through less acceptable means.

Commandments and Promises

Thou shalt not take the name of the Lord thy God in vain; *for the Lord will not hold him guiltless that taketh his name in vain.* (Ex. 20:7; similar scriptures, Deut. 5:11; Mosiah 13:15.)

Neither shalt thou profane the name of thy God: I am the Lord. (Lev. 18:21.)

Ye shall not swear by my name falsely, neither shalt thou profane the name of thy God: I am the Lord. (Lev. 19:12.)

I will set my face against that man [whosoever gives any of his seed to Molech], *and will cut him off from among his people*; because he hath given of his seed to Molech, to defile my sanctuary, and to profane my holy name. (Lev. 20:3.)

They shall be holy unto their God, and not profane the name of their God: for the offerings of the Lord made by fire, and the bread of their God, they do offer: therefore they shall be holy. (Lev. 21:6.)

Neither shall ye profane my holy name; but I will be hallowed among the children of Israel: I am the Lord which hallow you, that brought you out of the land of Egypt, to be your God: I am the Lord. (Lev. 22:32-33.)

Lord, who shall abide in thy tabernacle? who shall dwell in thy holy hill? . . . He that backbiteth not with his tongue, nor doeth evil to his neighbour, nor taketh up a reproach against his neighbour. (Ps. 15: 1-3; see also JST Ps. 15:1.)

Keep thy tongue from evil, and thy lips from speaking guile. (Ps. 34:13.)

Surely thou wilt slay the wicked, O God: depart from me therefore, ye bloody men. For they speak against thee wickedly, and thine enemies take thy name in vain. (Ps. 139:19-20.)

Death and life are in the power of the tongue: and they that love it *shall eat the fruit thereof.* (Prov. 18:21.)

Be not rash with thy mouth, and let not thine heart be hasty to utter any thing before God: for God is in heaven, and thou upon earth: therefore let thy words be few. (Eccl. 5:2.)

Suffer not thy mouth to cause thy flesh to sin. (Eccl. 5:6.)

Every one that sweareth *shall be cut off as on that side according to it.* (Zech. 5:3.)

Swear not at all; neither by heaven; for it is God's throne: nor by the earth; for it is his footstool: neither by Jerusalem; for it is the city of the great King. Neither shalt thou swear by thy head, because thou canst not make one hair white or black. But let your communication be, Yea, yea; Nay, nay; for whatsoever is more than these cometh of evil. (Matt. 5:34-37; similar scripture, 3 Ne. 12:34-37.)

Let no corrupt communication proceed out of your mouth, but that which is good to the use of edifying, *that it may minister grace unto the hearers.* (Eph. 4:29.)

Let all . . . evil speaking . . . be put away from you. (Eph. 4:31.)

Put off all these; anger, wrath, malice, blasphemy, filthy communication out of your mouth. (Col. 3:8.)

Let the word of God dwell in you richly in all wisdom; teaching and admonishing one another in psalms and hymns and spiritual songs, singing with grace in your hearts to the Lord. (Col. 3:16.)

Let your speech be alway with grace, seasoned with salt, *that ye may know how ye ought to answer every man.* (Col. 4:6.)

Likewise must the deacons be grave, not doubletongued. . . . Even so must their wives be grave, not slanderers. (1 Tim. 3:8, 11.)

Refuse profane and old wives' fables, and exercise thyself rather unto godliness. (1 Tim. 4:7.)

Be thou an example of the believers, in word, in conversation, in charity, in spirit, in faith, in purity. (1 Tim. 4:12.)

Keep that which is committed to thy trust, avoiding profane and vain babblings, and oppositions of science falsely so called. (1 Tim. 6:20.)

Shun profane and vain babblings: *for they will increase unto more ungodliness.* (2 Tim. 2:16.)

In all things shewing thyself a pattern of good works: in doctrine shewing uncorruptness, gravity, sincerity, sound speech that cannot be condemned; *that he that is of the contrary part may be ashamed, having no evil thing to say of you.* (Titus 2:7-8.)

Put them in mind to . . . speak evil of no man. (Titus 3:1-2.)

If any man among you seem to be religious, and bridleth not his tongue, but deceiveth his own heart, *this man's religion is vain.* (James 1:26.)

Out of the same mouth proceedeth blessing and cursing. My brethren, these things ought not so to be. (James 3:10.)

Who is a wise man and endued with knowledge among you? let him shew out of a good conversation his works with meekness of wisdom. (James 3:13.)

Speak not evil one of another, brethren. He that speaketh evil of his brother, and judgeth his brother, speaketh evil of the law, and judgeth the law. (James 4:11.)

Above all things, my brethren, swear not, neither by heaven, neither by earth, neither by any other oath: but let your yea be yea; and your nay, nay; *lest ye fall into condemnation.* (James 5:12.)

[Lay] aside all malice, and all guile, and hypocrisies, and envies, and all evil speakings. (1 Pet. 2:1.)

He that will love life, and see good days, let him refrain his tongue from evil, and his lips that they speak no guile. (1 Pet. 3:10.)

Let none of you suffer as . . . a busybody in other men's matters. (1 Pet. 4:15.)

The Lord knoweth how to deliver the godly out of temptations, and to reserve the unjust unto the day of judgment to be punished: but chiefly them that walk after the flesh in the lust of uncleanness, and despise government. Presumptuous are they, selfwilled, they are not afraid to speak evil of dignities. . . . These, as natural brute beasts, made to be taken and destroyed, speak evil of the things that they understand not; *and shall utterly perish in their own corruption; and shall receive the reward of unrighteousness, as they that count it pleasure to riot in the day time. Spots they are and blemishes, sporting themselves with their own deceivings while they feast with you.* (2 Pet. 2:9-10.)

The Lord God hath commanded that men should not . . . take the name of the Lord their God in vain; . . . that they should not contend one with another; . . . *for whoso doeth them shall perish.* (2 Ne. 26:32.)

If ye do not watch yourselves, and your thoughts, and your words, and your deeds, and observe the commandments of God, and continue in the faith of what ye have heard concerning the coming of the Lord, even unto the end of your lives, *ye must perish.* And now, O man, remember, *and perish not.* (Mosiah 4:30.)

Fools mock, *but they shall mourn.* (Ether 12:26.)

[to teachers in the priesthood] See that there is no iniquity in the church, neither hardness with each other, neither lying, backbiting, nor evil speaking. (D&C 20:54.)

Thou shalt not speak evil of thy neighbor, nor do him any harm. (D&C 42:27.)

He that speaketh, whose spirit is contrite, whose language is meek and edifieth, *the same is of God* if he obey mine ordinances. (D&C 52:16.)

Let all men beware how they take my name in their lips—for behold, verily I say, that many there be who are under this condemnation, who use the name of the Lord, and use it in vain, having not authority. (D&C 63:61-62.)

Inasmuch as there are those among you who deny my name, *others shall be planted in their stead and receive their bishopric.* (D&C 114:2.)

The blasphemy against the Holy Ghost, *which shall not be forgiven in the world nor out of the world,* is in that ye commit murder wherein ye shed innocent blood, and assent unto my death, after ye have received my new and everlasting covenant, saith the Lord God; and he that abideth not this law *can in nowise enter into my glory, but shall be damned, saith the Lord.* (D&C 132:27.)

Keep yourselves from evil to take the name of the Lord in vain, for I am the Lord your God, even the God of your fathers, the God of Abraham and of Isaac and of Jacob. (D&C 136:21.)

Cease to speak evil one of another. . . . Let your words tend to edifying one another. (D&C 136:23-24.)

Building the Kingdom of God

The work of building up God's kingdom on earth is done by mortals. God has commanded his followers: "Enlarge the place of thy tent, and let them stretch forth the curtains of thine habitations: spare not, lengthen thy cords, and strengthen thy stakes." (Isa. 54:2.)

Building the kingdom involves more than just teaching the gospel throughout all the world to all who will hear. It involves establishing Christ's church wherever men will repent, building up Zion "in beauty, and in holiness." (D&C 82:14.)

The Lord gave specific instructions to those building a temple in Ohio, telling them measurement by measurement how his house should be constructed. (See D&C 94.) Less than a month later, when the temple remained unplanned, the Lord chastized the people and again specified the dimensions. "Let the house be built, not after the manner of the world, . . . let it be built after the manner which I shall show unto . . . you." (D&C 95:13-14.)

He is equally specific regarding the building of his kingdom—a lesson some members of the restored church learned as they moved to Missouri in 1843. The Lord gave them this revelation: "Talk not of judgments, neither boast of faith nor of mighty works, but carefully gather together, as much in one region as can be, consistently with the feelings of the people." (D&C 105:24.) In the case of these Saints, who violated this advice, the Lord made it clear that just building up the Church was not enough. It had to be built the right way.

Commandments and Promises

Awake, awake; put on thy strength, O Zion; put on thy beautiful garments, O Jerusalem, the holy city: for henceforth there shall no more come into thee the uncircumcised and the unclean. (Isa. 52:1.)

Enlarge the place of thy tent, and let them stretch forth the curtains of thine habitations: spare not, lengthen thy cords, and strengthen thy stakes; *for thou shalt break forth on the right hand and on the left; and thy seed shall inherit the Gentiles, and make the desolate cities to be inhabited.* (Isa. 54:2-3.)

Blessed are they who shall seek to bring forth my Zion at that day, *for they shall have the gift and the power of the Holy Ghost;* and if they endure unto the end *they shall be lifted up at the last day, and shall be saved in the everlasting kingdom of the Lamb;* and whoso shall publish peace, yea, tidings of great joy, *how beautiful upon the mountains shall they be.* (1 Ne. 13:37.)

The laborer in Zion shall labor for Zion; for if they labor for money *they shall perish.* (2 Ne. 26:31.)

Go to, and call servants, that we may labor diligently with our might in the vineyard, that we may prepare the way, *that I may bring forth again the natural fruit, which natural fruit is good and the most precious above all other fruit.* (Jacob 5:61.)

Because ye have been diligent in laboring with me in my vineyard, and have kept my commandments, and have brought unto me again the natural fruit, *that my vineyard is no more corrupted, and the bad is cast away, behold, ye shall have joy with me because of the fruit of my vineyard.* (Jacob 5:75.)

Blessed art thou because thou hast established a church among this people; *and they shall be established, and they shall be my people.* (Mosiah 26:17.)

The Lord did say unto me [Mormon]: Cry unto this people—Repent ye, and come unto me, and be ye baptized, and build up again my church, *and ye shall be spared.* (Morm. 3:2.)

Seek to bring forth and establish the cause of Zion. (D&C 6:6; similar scriptures, D&C 11:6, 12:6, 14:6.)

Keep my commandments and assist to bring forth my work, according to my commandments, *and you shall be blessed.* (D&C 6:9; similar scripture, D&C 11:9.)

Build upon my rock, which is my gospel. (D&C 11:24.)

If you shall build up my church, upon the foundation of my gospel and my rock, *the gates of hell shall not prevail against you.* (D&C 18:5.)

[to Joseph Smith and Oliver Cowdery] Thou shalt devote all thy service in Zion; *and in this thou shalt have strength.* (D&C 24:7.)

Inasmuch as ye shall find them that will receive you ye shall build up my church in every region. (D&C 42:8.)

Go ye forth into the western countries, call upon the inhabitants to repent, and inasmuch as they do repent, build up churches unto me. (D&C 45:64.)

Let them build up churches, inasmuch as the inhabitants of the earth will repent. (D&C 58:48.)

If ye believe me, ye will labor while it is called today. (D&C 64:25.)

Zion must increase in beauty, and in holiness; her borders must be enlarged; her stakes must be strengthened; yea, verily I say unto you, Zion must arise and put on her beautiful garments. (D&C 82:14.)

Zion cannot be built up unless it is by the principles of the law of the celestial kingdom; *otherwise I cannot receive her unto myself.* (D&C 105:5.)

[to the Saints who were gathering in Missouri] Talk not of judgments, neither boast of faith nor of mighty works, but carefully gather together, as much in one region as can be, consistently with the feelings of the people; *and behold, I will give unto you favor and grace in their eyes, that you may rest in peace and safety, while you are saying unto the people: Execute judgment and justice for us according to law, and redress us of our wrongs.* (D&C 105:24-25.)

I command you again to build a house to my name, even in this place, that you may prove yourselves unto me that ye are faithful in all things whatsoever I command you, *that I may bless you, and crown you with honor, immortality, and eternal life.* (D&C 124:55.)

Cheerfulness

(See also Adversity, Reacting to; Courage; Mourning; Rejoicing.)

The Savior has always encouraged his followers through his prophets to be of good cheer. "Let your heart be glad," the Lord said through Joseph Smith. (D&C 79:4.) "Cheer up your heart," Nephi told his brethren.

Cheerfulness is an attitude we can choose. While it may come easier for some than for others, it can help all of us. An optimistic, cheerful perspective will help us to "remember that [we] are free to act for [ourselves]—to choose the way of everlasting death or the way of eternal life." (2 Ne. 10:23.) By choosing cheerfulness as a means to achieve that end, we bless others as well as ourselves.

Commandments and Promises

Fret not thyself because of evil men, neither be thou envious at the wicked. (Prov. 24:19.)

Remove sorrow from thy heart, and put away evil from thy flesh. (Eccl. 11:10.)

Jesus seeing their faith said unto the sick of the palsy; Son, be of good cheer; thy sins be forgiven thee. (Matt. 9:2.)

When the disciples saw him walking on the sea, they were troubled, saying, It is a spirit; and they cried out for fear. But straightway Jesus spake unto them, saying, Be of good cheer; it is I; be not afraid. (Matt. 14:26-27; similar scripture, Mark 6:49-50.)

These things I have spoken unto you, that in me ye might have peace. In the world ye shall have tribulation: but be of good cheer; I have overcome the world. (John 16:33.)

He that sheweth mercy, [let him do it] with cheerfulness. (Rom. 12:8.)

Cheer up your hearts, and remember that ye are free to act for yourselves—to choose the way of everlasting death or the way of eternal life. (2 Ne. 10:23.)

The voice of the Lord came to them [Alma and his people] in their afflictions, saying: Lift up your heads and be of good comfort, for I know of the covenant which ye have made unto me; *and I will covenant with my people and deliver them out of bondage.* (Mosiah 24:13.)

[to Nephi] Lift up your head and be of good cheer; for behold, the time is at hand, and on this night shall the sign be given, and on the morrow come I into the world. (3 Ne. 1:13.)

Be of good cheer, little children; for I am in your midst, and I have not forsaken you. (D&C 61:36.)

Be of good cheer, and do not fear, for I the Lord am with you, and will stand by you. (D&C 68:6.)

Ye cannot bear all things now; nevertheless, be of good cheer, for I will lead you along. The kingdom is yours and the blessings thereof are yours, and the riches of eternity are yours. (D&C 78:18.)

Let your heart be glad, my servant Jared Carter, and fear not, saith your Lord. (D&C 79:4.)

[to Thomas B. Marsh] Let thy heart be of good cheer before my face. (D&C 112:4.)

Let us cheerfully do all things that lie in our power; *and then may we stand still, with the utmost assurance, to see the salvation of God, and for his arm to be revealed.* (D&C 123:17.)

Church Organization and Government

(See also Authority and Stewardship.)

The Lord has established patterns of Church organization and government for the church that bears his name. "It must needs be that they be organized according to my laws; if otherwise, they will be cut off." (D&C 51:2.)

Jesus Christ's church is led by leaders he chooses, who must be attuned to the continuing revelation Christ gives. Through a system of stewardship and accountability, the work of the kingdom proceeds. All in the Church are commanded to follow basic principles of Church government: "Obey them that have rule over you." (Heb. 13:17.) "Thou shalt not command him who is at thy head, and at the head of the church." (D&C 28:6.) "All things shall be done by common consent in the church." (D&C 26:2.) "It shall not be given to any one to go forth to preach my gospel, or to build up my church, except he be ordained by some one who has authority." (D&C 42:11.) "Thou shalt take the things which thou hast received, which have been given unto thee in my scriptures for a law, to be my law to govern my church." (D&C 42:59.)

When the members follow those guidelines and others and live as they should, the Church functions as it should. The Lord said several times that all things must be done by prayer and faith: "By the prayer of your faith ye shall receive my law," he said, "that ye may know how to govern my church and have all things right before me." (D&C 41:3.)

Commandments and Promises

Obey them that have the rule over you, and submit yourselves: for they watch for your souls, as they that must give account, *that they may do it with joy, and not with grief: for that is unprofitable for you.* (Heb. 13:17.)

He also commanded them that the priests whom he had ordained should labor with their own hands for their support. . . . The priests were not to depend upon the people for their support; but for their labor *they were to receive the grace of God, that they might wax strong in the Spirit, having the knowledge of God, that they might teach with power and authority from God.* (Mosiah 18:24, 26.)

If it so be that the church is built upon my gospel *then will the Father show forth his own works in it.* But if it be not built upon my gospel, and is built upon the works of men, or upon the works of the devil, *verily I say unto you they have joy in their works for a season, and by and by the end cometh, and they are hewn down and cast into the fire, from whence there is no return. For their works do follow them, for it is because of their works that they are hewn down.* (3 Ne. 27:10-12.)

All things shall be done by common consent in the church, by much prayer and faith, for all things you shall receive by faith. (D&C 26:2.)

Thou shalt not command him who is at thy head, and at the head of the church. (D&C 28:6.)

All things must be done in order, and by common consent in the church, by the prayer of faith. (D&C 28:13.)

I give unto the church in these parts a commandment, that certain men among them shall be appointed, and they shall be appointed by the voice of the church; and they shall look to the poor and the needy, and administer to their relief *that they shall not suffer;* and send them forth to the place which I have commanded them. (D&C 38: 34-35.)

By the prayer of your faith ye shall receive my law, *that ye may know how to govern my church and have all things right before me.* (D&C 41:3.)

It shall not be given to any one to go forth to preach my gospel, or to build up my church, except he be ordained by some one who has authority, and has been regularly ordained by the heads of the church. (D&C 42:11.)

Thou shalt take the things which thou hast received, which have been given unto thee in my scriptures for a law, to be my law to govern my church. (D&C 42:59.)

I give unto you a commandment, that when ye are assembled together ye shall instruct and edify each other, *that ye may know how to act and direct my church, how to act upon the points of my law and commandments, which I have given. And thus ye shall become instructed in the law of my church, and be sanctified by that which ye have received,* and ye shall bind yourselves to act in all holiness before me—that inasmuch as ye do this, *glory shall be added to the kingdom which ye have received.* Inasmuch as ye do it not, *it shall be taken, even that which ye have received.* (D&C 43:8-10.)

It must needs be that they be organized according to my laws; if otherwise, *they will be cut off.* (D&C 51:2.)

Let the residue of the elders watch over the churches, and declare the word in the regions round about them; and let them labor with their own hands *that there be no idolatry nor wickedness practised.* (D&C 52:39.)

Behold, the laws which ye have received from my hand are the laws of the church, and in this light ye shall hold them forth. (D&C 58:23.)

It must needs be that there be an organization of my people, in regulating and establishing the affairs of the storehouse for the poor of my people, both in this place and in the land of Zion. (D&C 78:3.)

It is wisdom in me; therefore, a commandment I give unto you, that ye shall organize yourselves and appoint every man his stewardship; that every man may give an account unto me of the stewardship which is appointed unto him. For it is expedient that I, the Lord, should make every man accountable, as a steward over earthly blessings, which I have made and prepared for my creatures. (D&C 104:11-13.)

Citizenship

The Lord's people are to be obedient both to the laws of God and to the laws of man. Christ taught such obedience, as have prophets since his day.

Not only have we been taught to obey the laws, we have also been taught to bear with patience imperfect laws and rulers. Regarding this the Lord said, "Be subject to the powers that be, until he reigns whose right it is to reign." (D&C 58:22.)

In particular, members who live in the United States are told to uphold the Constitution of the United States. Since it was established by the Lord for the abolition of slavery (see D&C 101:79), the Constitution "should be maintained for the rights and protection of all flesh." (D&C 101:77.) In the land protected by the Constitution, the Lord was able to bring forth his restored gospel. He was able to raise up a people freed by law to practice their chosen religion.

Although we are to obey and sustain the law, the Lord does not ask us to be passive. "Honest and wise men should be sought for diligently," we learn. (D&C 98:10.) When the Missouri members of the Church were suffering persecution, they were instructed to "continue to importune for redress, and redemption, by the hands of those who are placed as rulers and are in authority." (D&C 101:76.)

Obeying and upholding the laws, however, is not enough. When redress is sought, a governor or president who does not heed the complaints of the Lord's people will be "cut off" and cast out. The nation will be vexed. "Pray ye, therefore, that their ears may be opened unto your cries," the Lord told the members, "that I may be merciful unto them." (D&C 101:92.)

Commandments and Promises

Then saith [Jesus] unto them, Render therefore unto Caesar the things which are Caesar's; and unto God the things that are God's. (Matt. 22:21; similar scripture, Mark 12:17.)

Render therefore to all their dues: tribute to whom tribute is due; custom to whom custom; fear to whom fear; honour to whom honour. (Rom. 13:7.)

I exhort therefore, that, first of all, supplications, prayers, intercessions, and giving of thanks, be made for all men; for kings, and for all that are in authority; *that we may lead a quiet and peaceable life in all godliness and honesty. For this is good and acceptable in the sight of God our Saviour.* (1 Tim. 2:1-3.)

Put them in mind to be subject to principalities and powers, to obey magistrates, to be ready to every good work. (Titus 3:1.)

Submit yourselves to every ordinance of man for the Lord's sake: whether it be to the king, as supreme; or unto governors, as unto them that are sent by him for the punishment of evildoers, and for the praise of them that do well. (1 Pet. 2:13-14.)

Honour the king. (1 Pet. 2:17.)

[Alma to his people] I desire that ye should stand fast in this liberty wherewith ye have been made free, and that ye trust no man to be a king over you. And also trust no one to be your teacher nor your minister, except he be a man of God, walking in his ways and keeping his commandments. (Mosiah 23:13-14.)

Verily I say unto you, my law shall be kept on this land. Let no man think he is ruler; but let God rule him that judgeth, according to the counsel of his own will, or, in other words, him that counseleth or sitteth upon the judgment seat. Let no man break the laws of the land, for he that keepeth the laws of God hath no need to break the laws of the land. Wherefore, be subject to the powers that be, until he reigns whose right it is to reign, and subdues all enemies under his feet. (D&C 58:19-22.)

Concerning the laws of the land, it is my will that my people should observe to do all things whatsoever I command them. And that law of the land which is constitutional, supporting that principle of freedom in maintaining rights and privileges, belongs to all mankind, and is justifiable before me. (D&C 98:4-5.)

Honest men and wise men should be sought for diligently, and good men and wise men ye should observe to uphold. (D&C 98:10.)

Those who have been scattered by their enemies, it is my will that they should continue to importune for redress, and redemption, by the hands of those who are placed as rulers and are in authority over you—according to the laws and constitution of the people, which I have suffered to be established, and should be maintained for the rights and protection of all flesh, according to just and holy principles; *that every man may act in doctrine and principle pertaining to futurity, according to the moral agency which I have given unto him, that every man may be accountable for his own sins in the day of judgment.* (D&C 101:76-78.)

Pray ye, therefore, that their [governor's and president's] ears may be opened unto your cries, *that I may be merciful unto them, that these things [vexing the nation] may not come upon them.* (D&C 101:92.)

Cleaving to God

(See also Abiding in God; Following God and His Servants.)

To cleave unto the Lord means to obey him and be faithful. But the meaning of *cleave* is stronger still: it means to adhere to something firmly, closely, and unwaveringly. These attributes are crucial in our service to the Lord.

The commandment to cleave to God is often mentioned in the same sentence with phrases such as "all your soul," "all your heart," and "full purpose of heart." Cleaving is not lukewarm dedication; it is total devotion.

On introspection, many of us find that we do not cleave to God as closely as we cleave to material things or false values. But as we make renewed efforts in that direction, we can be assured of receiving the same blessing given to Hezekiah: "For he clave to the Lord, and . . . kept his commandments, . . . and the Lord was with him; and he prospered whithersoever he went forth." (2 Kgs. 18:6-7.)

Commandments and Promises

Thou shalt fear the Lord thy God; him shalt thou serve, and to him shalt thou cleave, and swear by his name. (Deut. 10:20.)

[Moses to Israel] If ye shall diligently keep all these commandments which I command you, to do them, to love the Lord your God, to walk in all his ways, and to cleave unto him, *then will the Lord drive out all these nations from before you, and ye shall possess greater nations and mightier than yourselves. Every place whereon the soles of your feet shall tread shall be yours; from the wilderness and Lebanon, from the river, the river Euphrates, even unto the uttermost sea shall your coast be. There shall no man be able to stand before you: for the Lord your God shall lay the fear of you and the dread of you upon all the land that ye shall tread upon, as he hath said unto you.* (Deut. 11:22-25.)

Ye shall walk after the Lord your God, and fear him, and keep his commandments, and obey his voice, and ye shall serve him, and cleave unto him. (Deut. 13:4.)

Take diligent heed to do the commandment and the law, which Moses the servant of the Lord charged you, to love the Lord your God, and to walk in all his ways, and to keep his commandments, and to cleave unto him, and to serve him with all your heart and with all your soul. (Josh. 22:5.)

Cleave unto the Lord your God, as ye have done unto this day. (Josh. 23:8.)

[Barnabas] when he came, and had seen the grace of God, was glad, and exhorted them all, that with purpose of heart they would cleave unto the Lord. (Acts 11:23.)

I beseech of you in words of soberness that ye would repent, and come with full purpose of heart, and cleave unto God as he cleaveth unto you. And while his arm of mercy is extended towards you in the light of day, harden not your hearts. (Jacob 6:5.)

[to Hyrum Smith] Cleave unto me with all your heart, *that you may assist in bringing to light those things of which has been spoken—yea, the translation of my work.* (D&C 11:19.)

I give unto you a commandment, that ye shall forsake all evil and cleave unto all good, that ye shall live by every word which proceedeth forth out of the mouth of God. (D&C 98:11.)

Coming to God

(See also Abiding in God; Following God and His Servants; Receiving and Following the Holy Ghost.)

Spiritually, we have the mobility to move closer to or further from God. We are commanded to use our freedom to approach the God who gave us that freedom. The commandment is simple: "Come unto me."

We can approach him through prayer, worship, following him, and becoming like him. All these actions require that we approach him as surely as if we were actually walking toward him. By coming to him, we have his help and can benefit from a proximity to his glory.

Commandments and Promises

O house of Jacob, come ye, and let us walk in the light of the Lord. (Isa. 2:5; similar scripture, 2 Ne. 12:5.)

Assemble yourselves and come; draw near together, ye that are escaped of the nations: they have no knowledge that set up the wood of their graven image, and pray unto a god that cannot save. Tell ye, and bring them near; yea, let them take counsel together: who hath declared this from ancient time? who hath told it from that time? have not I the Lord? and there is no God else beside me; a just God and a Saviour; there is none beside me. (Isa. 45:20-21.)

Come ye near unto me. (Isa. 48:16; similar scripture, 1 Ne. 20:16.)

Every one that thirsteth, come ye to the waters, and he that hath no money; come ye, buy, and eat; yea, come, buy wine and milk without money and without price. (Isa. 55:1; similar scripture, 2 Ne. 26:25.)

Incline your ear, and come unto me: hear, *and your soul shall live; and I will make an everlasting covenant with you, even the sure mercies of David.* (Isa. 55:3.)

Turn you to the strong hold, ye prisoners of hope: *even to day do I declare that I will render double unto thee.* (Zech. 9:12.)

Come unto me, all ye that labour and are heavy laden, *and I will give you rest.* Take my yoke upon you, and learn of me; for I am meek and lowly in heart: *and ye shall find rest unto your souls.* For my yoke is easy, and my burden is light. (Matt. 11:28-30.)

Jesus said unto them, I am the bread of life: he that cometh to me *shall never hunger.* (John 6:35.)

All that the Father giveth me shall come to me; and him that cometh to me *I will in no wise cast out.* (John 6:37.)

Jesus stood and cried, saying, If any man thirst, let him come unto me, *and drink.* (John 7:37.)

Let us therefore come boldly unto the throne of grace, *that we may obtain mercy, and find grace to help in time of need.* (Heb. 4:16.)

He is able also to save them to the uttermost that come unto God by him, *seeing he ever liveth to make intercession for them.* (Heb. 7:25.)

Let us draw near with a true heart in full assurance of faith, having our hearts sprinkled from an evil conscience, and our bodies washed with pure water. (Heb. 10:22.)

He that cometh to God must believe that he is, and that *he is a rewarder of them* that diligently seek him. (Heb. 11:6.)

Draw nigh to God, *and he will draw nigh to you.* (James 4:8; see also D&C 88:63.)

All men must come unto him, *or they cannot be saved.* (1 Ne. 13:40.)

Come unto Christ, who is the Holy One of Israel, and partake of his salvation, and the power of his redemption. Yea, come unto him, and offer your whole souls as an offering unto him, and continue in fasting and praying, and endure to the end; *and as the Lord liveth ye will be saved.* (Omni 1:26.)

Come unto me *and ye shall partake of the fruit of the tree of life; yea, ye shall eat and drink of the bread and the waters of life freely;* yea, come unto me and bring forth works of righteousness, *and ye shall not be hewn down and cast into the fire.* (Alma 5:34-35.)

Whosoever will come *may come and partake of the waters of life freely;* and whosoever will not come *the same is not compelled to come; but in the last day it shall be restored unto him according to his deeds.* (Alma 42:27.)

O repent ye, repent ye! Why will ye die? Turn ye, turn ye unto the Lord your God. (Hel. 7:17.)

If ye will come unto me *ye shall have eternal life. Behold, mine arm of mercy is extended towards you,* and whosoever will come, *him will I receive; and blessed* are those who come unto me. (3 Ne. 9:14.)

Whoso repenteth and cometh unto me as a little child, *him will I receive, for of such is the kingdom of God. Behold, for such I have laid down my life, and have taken it up again;* therefore repent, and come unto me ye ends of the earth, and be saved. (3 Ne. 9:22.)

Blessed are the poor in spirit who come unto me, *for theirs is the kingdom of heaven.* (3 Ne. 12:3.)

I have given you the law and the commandments of my Father, that ye shall believe in me, and that ye shall repent of your sins, and come unto me with a broken heart and a contrite spirit. Behold, ye have the commandments before you, and the law is fulfilled. Therefore come unto me *and be ye saved;* for verily I say unto you, that except ye shall keep my commandments, which I have commanded you at this time, *ye shall in no case enter into the kingdom of heaven.* (3 Ne. 12:19-20.)

Ye see that I have commanded that none of you should go away, but rather have commanded that ye should come unto me, *that ye might feel and see;* even so shall ye do unto the world; and whosoever breaketh this commandment *suffereth himself to be led into temptation.* (3 Ne. 18:25.)

At that day whosoever will not repent and come unto my Beloved Son, *them will I cut off from among my people, O house of Israel; and I will execute vengeance and fury upon them, even as upon the heathen, such as they have not heard.* (3 Ne. 21:20-21.)

Now this is the commandment: Repent, all ye ends of the earth, and come unto me and be baptized in my name, *that ye may be sanctified by the reception of the Holy Ghost, that ye may stand spotless before me at the last day.* (3 Ne. 27:20.)

Repent ye, and come unto me, and be ye baptized, and build up again my church, *and ye shall be spared.* (Morm. 3:2.)

Doubt not, but be believing, and begin as in times of old, and come unto the Lord with all your heart, and work out your own salvation with fear and trembling before him. (Morm. 9:27.)

Come unto me, O ye Gentiles, *and I will show unto you the greater things, the knowledge which is hid up because of unbelief.* Come unto me, O ye house of Israel, *and it shall be made manifest unto you how great things the Father hath laid up for you, from the foundation of the world; and it hath not come unto you,* because of unbelief. (Ether 4:13-14.)

Repent all ye ends of the earth, and come unto me, and believe in my gospel, and be baptized in my name. (Ether 4:18.)

If it so be that they repent and come unto the Father in the name of Jesus, *they shall be received into the kingdom of God.* (Ether 5:5.)

Repent all ye ends of the earth, and come unto me, and be baptized in my name, and have faith in me, *that ye may be saved.* (Moro. 7:34.)

Come unto Christ, and lay hold upon every good gift, and touch not the evil gift, nor the unclean thing. (Moro. 10:30.)

Come unto Christ, and be perfected in him, and deny yourselves of all ungodliness. (Moro. 10:32.)

Canst thou be humble and meek, and conduct thyself wisely before me? Yea, come unto me thy Savior. (D&C 19:41.)

Even so I have sent mine everlasting covenant into the world, to be a light to the world, and to be a standard for my people, and for the Gentiles to seek to it, and to be a messenger before my face to prepare the way before me. Wherefore, come ye unto it, and with him that cometh *I will reason as with men in days of old, and I will show unto you my strong reasoning.* (D&C 45:9-10.)

Whoso cometh not unto me *is under the bondage of sin.* (D&C 84:51.)

Draw near unto me *and I will draw near unto you.* (D&C 88:63; see also James 4:8.)

Verily, thus saith the Lord: It shall come to pass that every soul who forsaketh his sins and cometh unto me, and calleth on my name, and obeyeth my voice, and keepeth my commandments, *shall see my face and know that I am.* (D&C 93:1.)

I give unto you these sayings that you may understand and know how to worship, and know what you worship, that you may come unto the Father in my name, *and in due time receive of his fulness.* (D&C 93:19.)

The scattered remnants are exhorted to return to the Lord from whence they have fallen; which if they do, *the promise of the Lord is that he will speak to them, or give them revelation.* (D&C 113:10.)

I am the Lord thy God; and I give unto you this commandment—that no man shall come unto the Father but by me or by my word, which is my law, saith the Lord. (D&C 132:12.)

Companions and Friends, Choosing

The commandment to choose companions carefully may seem to present a paradox. On one hand, we are commanded to spread the gospel to those who do not have it, while, on the other hand, we are commanded to avoid associating with transgressors. How can we do both?

Paul uses a helpful metaphor when he speaks of marriage: "Be ye not unequally yoked together with unbelievers." (2 Cor. 6:14.) Associating with and fellowshipping unbelievers is not the same as being "yoked" with them, where unbelievers would be expected to pull weight alongside believers.

Paul also says, "Have no fellowship with the unfruitful works of darkness, but rather reprove them." (Eph. 5:11.) Here, fellowship implies more than mere association.

Again, Paul admonishes us to "have no company" with those who choose not to obey Paul's epistle, "Yet count him not as an enemy, but admonish him as a brother." (2 Thes. 3:14-15.) Those we do not choose as companions need not become our enemies.

Being friends is different than being fellow partakers of the same sins. The Lord himself associated with numerous sinners, demonstrating his love through teaching and healing. His servants and his Spirit visit unrepentant souls whom the Lord loves but who do not yet love him; however, the continual companionship of the Spirit is reserved for those worthy of it, those who do not "grieve" him. We should follow that example in choosing companions, those who walk with us daily, those we emulate, those with whom we join in pulling burdens. Many can be our friends, and many should receive our love. Only those worthy should be chosen for our companions.

Commandments and Promises

Thou shalt make no covenant with them [Canaanites, Hittites, etc.], nor with their gods. They shall not dwell in thy land, *lest they make thee sin against me: for if thou serve their gods, it will surely be a snare unto thee.* (Ex. 23:32-33.)

Blessed is the man that walketh not in the counsel of the ungodly, nor standeth in the way of sinners, nor sitteth in the seat of the scornful. But his delight is in the law of the Lord; and in his law doth he meditate day and night. *And he shall be like a tree planted by the rivers of water, that bringeth forth his fruit in his season; his leaf also shall not wither; and whatsoever he doeth shall prosper.* (Ps. 1:1-3.)

Walk not thou in the way with [sinners]; refrain thy foot from their path. (Prov. 1:15.)

He that walketh with wise men *shall be wise:* but a companion of fools *shall be destroyed.* (Prov. 13:20.)

Go from the presence of a foolish man, when thou perceivest not in him the lips of knowledge. (Prov. 14:7.)

Make no friendship with an angry man; and with a furious man thou shalt not go: *lest thou learn his ways, and get a snare to thy soul.* (Prov. 22:24-25.)

Eat thou not the bread of him that hath an evil eye, neither desire thou his dainty meats: for as he thinketh in his heart, so is he: Eat and drink, saith he to thee; but his heart is not with thee. (Prov. 23:6-7.)

Be not thou envious against evil men, neither desire to be with them. For their heart studieth destruction, and their lips talk of mischief. (Prov. 24:1-2.)

Now I beseech you, brethren, mark them which cause divisions and offences contrary to the doctrine which ye have learned; and avoid them. For they that are such serve not our Lord Jesus Christ, but their own belly; and by good words and fair speeches *deceive the hearts of the simple.* (Rom. 16:17-18.)

Now I have written unto you not to keep company, if any man that is called a brother be a fornicator, or covetous, or an idolater, or a railer, or a drunkard, or an extortioner; with such an one no not to eat. (1 Cor. 5:11-12.)

Be ye not unequally yoked together with unbelievers: for what fellowship hath righteousness with unrighteousness? and what communion hath light with darkness? (2 Cor. 6:14.)

Come out from among them, and be ye separate, saith the Lord, and touch not the unclean thing; *and I will receive you. And will be a Father unto you, and ye shall be my sons and daughters, saith the Lord Almighty.* (2 Cor. 6:17-18.)

Have no fellowship with the unfruitful works of darkness, but rather reprove them. (Eph. 5:11.)

Withdraw yourselves from every brother that walketh disorderly, and not after the tradition which he received of us. (2 Thes. 3:6.)

If any man obey not our word by this epistle, note that man, and have no company with him, *that he may be ashamed.* Yet count him not as an enemy, but admonish him as a brother. (2 Thes. 3:14-15.)

Lay hands suddenly on no man, neither be partaker of other men's sins: keep thyself pure. (1 Tim. 5:22.)

Flee also youthful lusts: but follow righteousness, faith, charity, peace, with them that call on the Lord out of a pure heart. (2 Tim. 2:22.)

A man that is an heretick after the first and second admonition reject; knowing that he that is such is subverted, and sinneth, being condemned of himself. (Titus 3:10-11.)

Go ye out from among the wicked. Save yourselves. Be ye clean that bear the vessels of the Lord. (D&C 38:42.)

Contention

(See also Anger; Murder and Violence.)

Contention was one of the many sins of the Nephites who were driven back by the Lamanites. Helaman recorded that "in the fifty and fourth year there were many dissensions in the church, and there was also a contention among the people, insomuch that there was much bloodshed." The rebels driven from the land stirred the Lamanites to war against the Nephites. In the ensuing years of battle, the Nephites lost severely. The loss would not have occurred, we are told, "had it not been for their wickedness and their abomination which was among them; yea, and it was among those also who professed to belong to the church of God." (Hel. 4:1-11.) Contention is clearly stated as part of that wickedness.

The Lord does not strengthen those who are contentious. Instead, he shows favor to those who avoid contention. "Do all things without murmurings and disputings," Paul wrote the Philippians, "that ye may be blameless and harmless, the sons of God, without rebuke, in the midst of a crooked and perverse nation, among whom ye shine as lights in the world." (Philip. 2:14-15.)

Commandments and Promises

Thou shalt not go up and down as a talebearer among thy people: neither shalt thou stand against the blood of thy neighbour: I am the Lord. (Lev. 19:16.)

Devise not evil against thy neighbour, seeing he dwelleth securely by thee. Strive not with a man without cause, if he have done thee no harm. (Prov. 3:29-30.)

These ... things doth the Lord hate: ... he that soweth discord among brethren. (Prov. 6:16-19.)

All that watch for iniquity *are cut off:* that make a man an offender for a word, and lay a snare for him that reproveth in the gate, and turn aside the just for a thing of naught. (Isa. 29:20-21; similar scripture, 2 Ne. 27:31-32.)

Agree with thine adversary quickly, whiles thou art in the way with him; *lest at any time the adversary deliver thee to the judge, and the judge deliver thee to the officer, and thou be cast into prison. Verily I say unto thee, Thou shalt by no means come out thence, till thou hast paid the uttermost farthing.* (Matt. 5:25-26; similar scripture, 3 Ne. 12:25-26.)

[God] will render to every man according to his deeds: to them who by patient continuance in well doing seek for glory and honour and immortality, *eternal life:* but unto them that are contentious, and do not obey the truth, but obey unrighteousness, *indignation and wrath, tribulation and anguish,* upon every soul of man that doeth evil. (Rom. 2:6-9.)

The night is far spent, the day is at hand: let us therefore cast off the works of darkness, and let us put on the armour of light. Let us walk honestly, as in the day; not in rioting and drunkenness, not in chambering and wantonness, not in strife and envying. (Rom. 13:12-13.)

Him that is weak in the faith receive ye, but not to doubtful disputations. (Rom. 14:1.)

Now I beseech you, brethren, mark them which cause divisions and offences contrary to the doctrine which ye have learned; and avoid them. (Rom. 16:17.)

If ye bite and devour one another, take heed that ye be not consumed one of another. (Gal. 5:15.)

The works of the flesh are . . . hatred, variance, emulations, wrath, strife, seditions, of the which I tell you before, as I have also told you in time past, that they which do such things *shall not inherit the kingdom of God.* (Gal. 5:19-21.)

Let us not be desirous of vain glory, provoking one another, envying one another. (Gal. 5:26.)

Let all bitterness, and wrath, and anger, and clamour, and evil speaking, be put away from you, with all malice: and be ye kind one to another, tenderhearted, forgiving one another, even as God for Christ's sake hath forgiven you. (Eph. 4:31-32.)

Let nothing be done through strife or vainglory; but in lowliness of mind let each esteem other better than themselves. (Phil. 2:3.)

Do all things without murmurings and disputings: *that ye may be blameless and harmless, the sons of God, without rebuke, in the midst of a crooked and perverse nation, among whom ye shine as lights in the world.* (Phil. 2:14-15.)

They that have believing masters, let them not despise them, because they are brethren; but rather do them service, because they are faithful and beloved, partakers of the benefit. These things teach and exhort. If any man teach otherwise, and consent not to wholesome words, even the words of our Lord Jesus Christ, and to the doctrine which is according to godliness; he is proud, knowing nothing, but doting about questions and strifes of words, *whereof cometh envy, strife, railings, evil surmisings, perverse disputings of men of corrupt minds, and destitute of the truth, supposing that gain is godliness:* from such withdraw thyself. (1 Tim. 6:2-5.)

Foolish and unlearned questions avoid, knowing that they *do gender strifes.* (2 Tim. 2:23.)

Put them in mind . . . to speak evil of no man, to be no brawlers, but gentle, shewing all meekness unto all men. (Titus 3:1-2.)

Avoid foolish questions, and genealogies, and contentions, and strivings about the law; *for they are unprofitable and vain.* (Titus 3:9.)

Grudge not one against another, brethren, *lest ye be condemned: behold, the judge standeth before the door.* (James 5:9.)

The Lord hath commanded that men . . . should not contend one with another; . . . for whoso doeth them [envy, malice, contentions, etc.] *shall perish.* (2 Ne. 26:32.)

Beware lest there shall arise contentions among you, and ye list to obey the evil spirit, which was spoken of by my father Mosiah. (Mosiah 2:32.)

Ye will not suffer your children that they . . . fight and quarrel one with another. (Mosiah 4:14.)

He commanded them that there should be no contention one with another, but that they should look forward with one eye, having one faith and one baptism, having their hearts knit together in unity and in love one towards another. And thus he commanded them to preach. *And thus they became the children of God.* (Mosiah 18:21-22.)

Thus did Alma teach his people, that every man should love his neighbor as himself, that there should be no contention among them. (Mosiah 23:15.)

Those priests who did go forth among the people did preach against all . . . envyings, and strifes, and malice, and revilings, . . . crying that these things ought not so to be. (Alma 16:18.)

Your hearts are not drawn out unto the Lord, but they do swell with great pride, unto boasting, and unto great swelling, envyings, strifes, malice, persecutions, and murders, and all manner of iniquities. *For this cause hath the Lord God caused that a curse should come upon the land, and also upon your riches, and this* because of your iniquities. (Hel. 13:22-23.)

There shall be no disputations among you. (3 Ne. 11:22.)

There shall be no disputations among you, as there have hitherto been; neither shall there be disputations among you concerning the points of my doctrine, as there have hitherto been. For verily, verily I say unto you, he that hath the spirit of contention is not of me, but is of the devil, who is the father of contention, and he stirreth up the hearts of men to contend with anger, one with another. Behold, this is not my doctrine, to stir up the hearts of men with anger, one against another; but this is my doctrine, that such things should be done away. (3 Ne. 11:28-30.)

It is also written before you, that thou shalt not kill, and whosoever shall kill shall be in danger of the judgment of God; but I say unto you, that whosoever is angry with his brother shall be in danger of his judgment. And whosoever shall say to his brother, Raca, shall be in danger of the council; and whosoever shall say, Thou fool, shall be in danger of hellfire. (3 Ne. 12:21-22; similar scripture, Matt. 5:21-22.)

Behold what the scripture says—man shall not smite, neither shall he judge; for judgment is mine, saith the Lord, and vengeance is mine also, and I will repay. (Morm. 8:20.)

Contend against no church, save it be the church of the devil. (D&C 18:20.)

Revile not against those that revile. (D&C 31:9.)

[Proclaim] my word against the congregations of the wicked, not in haste, neither in wrath nor with strife. (D&C 60:14.)

Contrite Heart and Spirit

(See also Sacrifice.)

The Holy Ghost can speak only to a softened heart, to a willing spirit. In the Savior's gospel of love, a contrite heart is the mark of a believer. In fact, the Lord commanded the Jews to "circumcise therefore the foreskin of [their] heart" (Deut. 10:16), a commandment parallel to the covenant sign of Abraham's people.

The Lord had for centuries commanded his people to sacrifice specific offerings to him. That type of sacrifice, stated in the Law of Moses, was replaced by the commandments the Savior gave during and after his mortal ministry. He told the Nephites that for a sacrifice each was to offer "a broken heart and a contrite spirit," and he promised, "him will I baptize with fire and with the Holy Ghost." (3 Ne. 9:19-20.)

Commandments and Promises

Circumcise therefore the foreskin of your heart, and be no more stiff-necked. (Deut. 10:16.)

If there be among you a poor man of one of thy brethren within any of thy gates in the land which the Lord thy God giveth thee, thou shalt not harden thine heart, nor shut thine hand from thy poor brother. (Deut. 15:7.)

[to Saul] Rebellion is as the sin of witchcraft, and stubbornness is as iniquity and idolatry. Because thou hast rejected the word of the Lord, *he hath also rejected thee from being king.* (1 Sam. 15:23.)

The Lord is nigh unto them that are of a broken heart; *and saveth* such as be of a contrite spirit. (Ps. 34:18.)

The sacrifices of God are a broken spirit: a broken and a contrite heart, O God, *thou wilt not despise.* (Ps. 51:17.)

Forasmuch as this people draw near me with their mouth, and with their lips do honour me, but have removed their heart far from me, and their fear toward me is taught by the precept of men: *therefore, behold, I will proceed to do a marvellous work among this people, even a marvellous work and a wonder: for the wisdom of their wise men shall perish, and the understanding of their prudent men shall be hid.* (Isa. 29:13-14.)

To this man will I look, even to him that is poor and of a contrite spirit, and trembleth at my word. (Isa. 66:2.)

Break up your fallow ground, and sow not among thorns. Circumcise yourselves to the Lord, and take away the foreskins of your heart, ye men of Judah and inhabitants of Jerusalem: *lest my fury come forth like fire, and burn that none can quench it, because of the evil of your doings.* (Jer. 4:3-4.)

As the Holy Ghost saith, To day if ye will hear his voice, harden not your hearts, as in the provocation, in the day of temptation in the wilderness: when your fathers tempted me, proved me, and saw my works forty years. Wherefore I was grieved with that generation, and said, They do alway err in their heart; and they have not known my ways. *So I sware in my wrath, They shall not enter into my rest.* (Heb. 3:7-11; similar scripture, Ps. 95:7-11.)

I beseech of you in words of soberness that ye would repent, and come with full purpose of heart, and cleave unto God as he cleaveth unto you. And while his arm of mercy is extended towards you in the light of the day, harden not your hearts. Yea, today, *if ye will hear his voice,* harden not your hearts: *for why will ye die?* (Jacob 6:5-6; similar scripture, Heb. 4:7.)

[regarding Abinadi's preaching] They have hardened their hearts against my words; they have repented not of their evil doings; *therefore, I will visit them in my anger, yea, in my fierce anger will I visit them in their iniquities and abominations.* (Mosiah 12:1.)

Therefore, he that will harden his heart, *the same receiveth the lesser portion of the word;* and he that will not harden his heart, *to him is given the greater portion of the word, until it is given unto him to know the mysteries of God until he know them in full.* They that will harden their hearts, *to them is given the lesser portion of the word until they know nothing concerning his mysteries; and then they are taken captive by the devil, and led by his will down to destruction. Now this is what is meant by the chains of hell.* (Alma 12:10-11.)

If our hearts have been hardened, yea, if we have hardened our hearts against the word, insomuch that it has not been found in us, *then will our state be awful, for then we shall be condemned. For our words will condemn us, yea, all our works will condemn us; we shall not be found spotless; and our thoughts will also condemn us; and in this awful state we shall not dare to look up to our God; and we would fain be glad if we could command the rocks and the mountains to fall upon us to hide us from his presence.* (Alma 12:13-14.)

If ye will repent, and harden not your hearts, *then will I have mercy upon you, through mine Only Begotten Son;* therefore, whosoever repenteth, and hardeneth not his heart, *he shall have claim on mercy through mine Only Begotten Son, unto a remission of his sins; and these shall enter into my rest.* And whosoever will harden his heart and will do iniquity, *behold, I swear in my wrath that he shall not enter into my rest.* And now, my brethren, behold I say unto you, that if ye will harden your hearts *ye shall not enter into the rest of the Lord; therefore your iniquity provoketh him that sendeth down his wrath upon you as in the first provocation, yea, according to his word in the last provocation as well as the first, to the everlasting destruction of your souls; therefore, according to his word, unto the last death, as well as the first.* And now, my brethren, seeing we know these things, and they are true, let us repent, and harden not our hearts, *that we provoke not the Lord our God to pull down his wrath upon us in these his second commandments which he has given unto us;* but let us enter into the rest of God, which is prepared according to his word. (Alma 12:33-37.)

I would that ye would come forth and harden not your hearts any longer; for behold, now is the time and the day of your salvation; and therefore, if ye will repent and harden not your hearts, *immediately shall the great plan of redemption be brought about unto you.* (Alma 34:31.)

The Spirit of the Lord began to withdraw from the Nephites, because of the wickedness and the hardness of their hearts. And thus we see that *the Lord began to pour out his Spirit upon the Lamanites,* because of their easiness and willingness to believe in his words. (Hel. 6:35-36.)

O repent ye, repent ye! *Why will ye die?* Turn ye, turn ye unto the Lord your God. *Why has he forsaken you?* It is because you have hardened your hearts; yea, ye will not hearken unto the voice of the good shepherd; yea, ye have provoked him to anger against you. And behold, *instead of gathering you, except ye will repent, behold, he shall scatter you forth that ye shall become meat for dogs and wild beasts.* (Hel. 7:17-19.)

Because of the hardness of the hearts of the people of the Nephites, except they repent *I will take away my word from them, and I will withdraw my Spirit from them, and I will suffer them no longer, and I will turn the hearts of their brethren against them.* (Hel. 13:8.)

And ye shall offer for a sacrifice unto me a broken heart and a contrite spirit. And whoso cometh unto me with a broken heart and a contrite spirit, *him will I baptize with fire and with the Holy Ghost, even as the Lamanites, because of their faith in me at the time of their conversion, were baptized with fire and with the Holy Ghost, and knew it not.* (3 Ne. 9:20.)

I have given you the law and the commandments of my Father, that ye shall believe in me, and that ye shall repent of your sins, and come unto me with a broken heart and a contrite spirit. (3 Ne. 12:19.)

If they will repent and hearken unto my words, and harden not their hearts, *I will establish my church among them, and they shall come in unto the covenant and be numbered among this the remnant of Jacob, unto whom I have given this land for their inheritance.* (3 Ne. 21:22.)

Neither did they receive any unto baptism save they came forth with a broken heart and a contrite spirit, and witnessed unto the church that they truly repented of all their sins. (Moro. 6:2.)

Their testimony shall also go forth unto the condemnation of this generation if they harden their hearts against them; *for a desolating scourge shall go forth among the inhabitants of the earth, and shall continue to be poured out from time to time, if they repent not, until the earth is empty, and the inhabitants thereof are consumed away and utterly destroyed by the brightness of my coming.* (D&C 5:18-19.)

If this generation harden not their hearts, *I will establish my church among them.* (D&C 10:53.)

I will gather them as a hen gathereth her chickens under her wings, if they will not harden their hearts. (D&C 10:65.)

Those who harden their hearts in unbelief, and reject [this work], *it shall turn to their own condemnation.* (D&C 20:15.)

Mine elect hear my voice and harden not their hearts. (D&C 29:7.)

Even so will I cause the wicked to be kept, that will not hear my voice but harden their hearts, *and wo, wo, wo, is their doom.* (D&C 38:6.)

Hearken, O ye people of my church, and ye elders listen together, and hear my voice while it is called today, and harden not your hearts. (D&C 45:6.)

He that prayeth, whose spirit is contrite, *the same is accepted of me* if he obey mine ordinances. He that speaketh, whose spirit is contrite, whose language is meek and edifieth, *the same is of God if he obey mine ordinances.* (D&C 52:15-16.)

[to Newel Knight] *If your brethren desire to escape their enemies,* let them repent of all their sins, and become truly humble before me and contrite. (D&C 54:3.)

Wo unto you poor men, whose hearts are not broken, whose spirits are not contrite, and whose bellies are not satisfied, and whose hands are not stayed from laying hold upon other men's goods, whose eyes are full of greediness, and who will not labor with your own hands. *But blessed* are the poor who are pure in heart, whose hearts are broken, and whose spirits are contrite, *for they shall see the kingdom of God coming in power and great glory unto their deliverance; for the fatness of the earth shall be theirs.* (D&C 56:17-18.)

Courage

The commandment to have courage differs from other commandments in one respect: explanations of why we should be courageous frequently accompany the commandment. Because of this, the explanations in this section as well as the promises are italicized. In fact, the reasons for not being fearful are much like promises, except they aren't contingent on obedience to the commandment.

Fear, we learn, does not come from God. "For God hath not given us the spirit of fear; but of power, and of love, and of a sound mind." (2 Tim. 1:7.) When the Lord promises blessings for being fearless, those promises are significant, and the condemnations for the reverse are stern. We are told that the fearful will "have part in . . . the second death" and that the reason "ye did not receive" was because of the "fears in your hearts." (D&C 63:17 and 67:3.) On the other hand, those who strip themselves of fears "shall see me and know that I am." (D&C 67:10.)

Commandments and Promises (reasons for having courage also in italics)

Be strong and of a good courage, fear not, nor be afraid of them: *for the Lord thy God, he it is that doth go with thee; he will not fail thee, nor forsake thee.* (Deut. 31:6.)

Have I not commanded thee? Be strong and of good courage; be not afraid, neither be thou dismayed: *for the Lord thy God is with thee whithersoever thou goest.* (Josh. 1:9.)

Samuel said unto the people, Fear not: ye have done all this wickedness: yet turn not aside from following the Lord, but serve the Lord with all your heart; and turn ye not aside: *for then should ye go after vain things, which cannot profit nor deliver;* for they are vain. *For the Lord will not forsake his people for his great name's sake: because it hath pleased the Lord to make you his people.* (1 Sam. 12:20-22.)

Be of good courage, and let us behave ourselves valiantly for our people, and for the cities of our God: and let the Lord do that which is good in his sight. (1 Chr. 19:13.)

Wait on the Lord: be of good courage, *and he shall strengthen thine heart:* wait, I say, on the Lord. (Ps. 27:14.)

When thou liest down, thou shalt not be afraid: yea, thou shalt lie down, and thy sleep shall be sweet. Be not afraid of sudden fear, neither of the desolation of the wicked, when it cometh. *For the Lord shall be thy confidence, and shall keep thy foot from being taken.* (Prov. 3:24-26.)

Say to them that are of a fearful heart, Be strong, fear not: *behold, your God will come with vengeance, even God with a recompence; he will come and save you.* (Isa. 35:4.)

Fear thou not; *for I am with thee:* be not dismayed; *for I am thy God: I will strengthen thee; yea, I will help thee; yea, I will uphold thee with the right hand of my righteousness.* (Isa. 41:10.)

Fear not, thou worm Jacob, and ye men of Israel; *I will help thee,* saith the Lord, and thy redeemer, the Holy One of Israel. (Isa. 41:14.)

Fear not: *for I am with thee.* (Isa. 43:5.)

Fear not, O Jacob, my servant; and thou, Jesurun, whom I have chosen. (Isa. 44:2.)

Fear ye not, neither be afraid: have not I told thee from that time, and have declared it? (Isa. 44:8.)

Thus saith the Lord, Learn not the way of the heathen, and be not dismayed at the signs of heaven; for the heathen are dismayed at them. (Jer. 10:2.)

Fear thou not, O my servant Jacob, saith the Lord; neither be dismayed, O Israel: *for, lo, I will save thee from afar, and thy seed from the land of their captivity; and Jacob shall return, and shall be in rest, and be quiet, and none shall make him afraid.* (Jer. 30:10.)

Fear not thou, O my servant Jacob, and be not dismayed, O Israel: *for, behold, I will save thee from afar off, and thy seed from the land of their captivity; and Jacob shall return, and be in rest and at ease, and none shall make him afraid.* Fear not thou, Jacob, my servant, saith the Lord: *For I am with thee; for I will make a full end of all the nations whither I have driven thee: but I will not make a full end of thee, but correct thee in measure; yet will I not leave thee wholly unpunished.* (Jer. 46:27-28.)

According to the word that I covenanted with you when ye came out of Egypt, so my Spirit remaineth among you: fear ye not. (Hag. 2:5.)

Fear [your persecutors] not therefore: *for there is nothing covered, that shall not be revealed; and hid, that shall not be known.* (Matt. 10:26.)

Fear not them which kill the body, but are not able to kill the soul: but rather fear him which is able to destroy both soul and body in hell. (Matt. 10:28; see also Luke 12:4-5.)

When the disciples saw him walking on the sea, they were troubled, saying, It is a spirit; and they cried out for fear. But straightway Jesus spake unto them, saying, Be of good cheer; it is I; be not afraid. (Matt. 14:26-27; see also Mark 6:49-50.)

While [Peter] yet spake, behold, a bright cloud overshadowed them: and behold a voice out of the cloud, which said, This is my beloved Son, in whom I am well pleased; hear ye him. And when the disciples heard it, they fell on their face, and were sore afraid. And Jesus came and touched them, and said, Arise, and be not afraid. (Matt. 17:5-7.)

When they saw him walking upon the sea, they supposed it had been a spirit, and cried out: For they all saw him, and were troubled. And immediately he talked with them, and saith unto them, Be of good cheer: it is I; be not afraid. (Mark 6:4-50; see also Matt. 14:26-27.)

When ye shall hear of wars and rumours of wars, be ye not troubled: *for such things must needs be; but the end shall not be yet. For nation shall rise against nation, and kingdom against kingdom: and there shall be earthquakes in divers places, and there shall be famines and troubles: these are the beginnings of sorrows.* (Mark 13:7-8.)

Jesus said unto Simon, Fear not; from henceforth thou shalt catch men. (Luke 5:10.)

When Jesus heard [that Jairus's daughter was dead], he answered him, saying, Fear not: believe only, and she shall be made whole. (Luke 8:50.)

I say unto you my friends, Be not afraid of them that kill the body, and after that have no more that they can do. But I will forewarn you whom ye shall fear: Fear him, which after he hath killed hath power to cast into hell; yea, I say unto you, fear him. (Luke 12:4-5; see also Matt. 10:28.)

Are not five sparrows sold for two farthings, and not one of them is forgotten before God? But even the very hairs of your head are all numbered. Fear not therefore: *ye are of more value than many sparrows.* (Luke 12:6-7; similar scripture, Matt. 10:29-31.)

Fear not, little flock; *for it is your Father's good pleasure to give you the kingdom.* (Luke 12:32.)

When ye shall hear of wars and commotions, be not terrified: *for these things must first come to pass; but the end is not by and by.* (Luke 21:9.)

Peace I leave with you, my peace I give unto you: not as the world giveth, give I unto you. Let not your heart be troubled, neither let it be afraid. (John 14:27.)

If thou do that which is evil, be afraid. (Rom. 13:4.)

In nothing [be] terrified by your adversaries: which is to them an evident token of perdition, but to you salvation, and that of God. (Philip. 1:28; see also JST Philip. 1:28.)

Be not soon shaken in mind, or be troubled, neither by spirit, nor by word, nor by letter as from us, as that the day of Christ is at hand. (2 Thes. 2:2.)

Cast not away therefore your confidence, *which hath great recompence of reward.* (Heb. 10:35.)

[to Alma and his people] Lift up your heads and be of good comfort, *for I know of the covenant which ye have made unto me; and I will covenant with my people and deliver them out of bondage. And I will also ease the burdens which are put upon your shoulders, that even you cannot feel them upon your backs, even while you are in bondage; and this will I do that ye may stand as witnesses for me hereafter, and that ye may know of a surety that I, the Lord God, do visit my people in their afflictions.* (Mosiah 24:13-14.)

Fear not to do good, my sons, *for whatsoever ye sow, that shall ye also reap; therefore, if ye sow good ye shall also reap good for your reward.* Therefore, fear not, little flock; do good; let earth and hell combine against you, *for if ye are built upon my rock, they cannot prevail.* (D&C 6:33-34.)

Look unto me in every thought; doubt not, fear not. (D&C 6:36.)

[to Peter Whitmer] Fear not, but give heed unto the words of advice of your brother, which he shall give you. (D&C 30:5.)

You shall ever open your mouth in my cause, not fearing what man can do, *for I am with you.* (D&C 30:11.)

Fear not, little flock, *the kingdom is yours until I come.* (D&C 35:27.)

Be ye strong from henceforth; fear not, *for the kingdom is yours.* (D&C 38:15.)

Fear not, little children, for you are mine, and I have overcome the world, and you are of them that my Father hath given me; *and none of them that my Father hath given me shall be lost.* (D&C 50:41-42.)

I, the Lord, have said that the fearful, and the unbelieving, . . . *shall have their part in that lake which burneth with fire and brimstone, which is the second death. Verily I say, that they shall not have part in the first resurrection.* (D&C 63:17-18.)

Ye endeavored to believe that ye should receive the blessing which was offered unto you; but behold, verily I say unto you there were fears in your hearts, *and verily this is the reason that ye did not receive.* (D&C 67:3.)

It is your privilege, and a promise I give unto you that have been ordained unto this ministry, that inasmuch as you strip yourselves from jealousies and fears, and humble yourselves before me, for ye are not sufficiently humble, *the veil shall be rent and you shall see me and know that I am—not with the carnal neither natural mind, but with the spiritual.* (D&C 67:10.)

Be of good cheer, and do not fear, *for I the Lord am with you, and will stand by you.* (D&C 68:6.)

Let your heart be glad, my servant Jared Carter, and fear not, saith your Lord, even Jesus Christ. (D&C 79:4.)

Fear not, let your hearts be comforted; yea, rejoice evermore, and in everything give thanks. (D&C 98:1.)

Be not afraid of your enemies, *for I have decreed in my heart, saith the Lord, that I will prove you in all things, whether you will abide in my covenant, even unto death, that you may be found worthy.* (D&C 98:14.)

Let not your hearts be troubled; *for in my Father's house are many mansions, and I have prepared a place for you; and where my Father and I am, there ye shall be also.* (D&C 98:18.)

Let your hearts be comforted; *for all things shall work together for good to them that walk uprightly, and to the sanctification of the church.* (D&C 100:15.)

Fear not even unto death; for in this world your joy is not full, *but in me your joy is full.* (D&C 101:36.)

As your fathers were led at the first, even so shall the redemption of Zion be. Therefore, let not your hearts faint, *for I say not unto you as I said unto your fathers: Mine angel shall go up before you, but not my presence. But I say unto you: Mine angels shall go up before you, and also my presence, and in time ye shall possess the goodly land.* (D&C 103:18-20.)

Fear not what man can do, *for God shall be with you forever and ever.*
(D&C 122:9.)

Go thy way and do as I have told you, and fear not thine enemies; *for*
they shall not have power to stop my work. (D&C 136:17.)

Fear not thine enemies, *for they are in mine hands and I will do my*
pleasure with them. (D&C 136:30.)

Covenants

(See also Baptism and Spiritual Rebirth; Sacrament.)

Moroni, the chief commander of the Nephite armies, wrote the "title of liberty" on his coat and challenged: "Behold, whosoever will maintain this title upon the land, let them come forth in the strength of the Lord, and enter into a covenant that they will maintain their rights, and their religion, that the Lord God may bless them."

The people made the covenant, "running together with their armor girded about their loins, rending their garments in token, or as a covenant, that they would not forsake the Lord their God." If they fell into transgression, they expected to be "cast . . . at the feet of our enemies, even as we have cast our garments at thy feet to be trodden under foot." (Alma 46:11-22.)

We can learn much about covenants from that example. While we may not find ourselves faced with such a spontaneous covenant, the covenants we enter into or renew at baptism, through the sacrament, in the temple, or at other times can also have serious consequences.

Just as the people of Moroni's army covenanted not to fall into transgression lest they should lose the deliverance of their Lord, our covenants can protect us through the influence of the Holy Ghost. Participating in the sacrament covenant, for example, demonstrates a willingness to take upon us Christ's name, to remember him and to keep his commandments—with the promise that his Spirit will always be with us. (Moro. 4:3; 5:2.)

Is obedience not enough? Why must God's sons and daughters enter into formal covenants with him? That answer is simple: "That the Lord God may bless them." (Alma 46:20.) Without the framework of covenants, we might lack incentive and commitment to do what is expected of us and obtain the resultant blessings.

Commandments and Promises

If ye will obey my voice indeed, and keep my covenant, *then ye shall be a peculiar treasure unto me above all people:* for all the earth is mine: *and ye shall be unto me a kingdom of priests, and an holy nation.* (Ex. 19:5-6.)

He declared unto you [people of Moses at Mt. Horeb] his covenant, which he commanded you to perform, even ten commandments; and he wrote them upon two tables of stone. (Deut. 4:13.)

Keep therefore the words of this covenant, and do them, *that ye may prosper in all that ye do.* . . . Thou shouldest enter into covenant with the Lord thy God, and into his oath, which the Lord thy God maketh with thee this day: *that he may establish thee to day for a people unto himself, and that he may be unto thee a God.* . . . Neither with you [people of Moses] only do I make this covenant and this oath; but with him . . . that is not here with us this day. (Deut. 29:9-15.)

When ye have transgressed the covenant of the Lord your God, which he commanded you, and have gone and served other gods, and bowed yourselves to them; *then shall the anger of the Lord be kindled against you, and ye shall perish quickly from off the good land which he hath given unto you.* (Josh. 23:16.)

All the paths of the Lord are mercy and truth unto such as keep his covenant and his testimonies. (Ps. 25:10.)

When thou vowest a vow unto God, defer not to pay it; for he hath no pleasure in fools: pay that which thou hast vowed. Better is it that thou shouldest not vow, than that thou shouldest vow and not pay. (Eccl. 5:4-5.)

The earth also is defiled under the inhabitants thereof; because they have transgressed the laws, changed the ordinance, broken the everlasting covenant. (Isa. 24:5.)

Thus saith the Lord: *Even the captives of the mighty shall be taken away, and the prey of the terrible shall be delivered; for the Mighty God shall deliver* his covenant people. For thus saith the Lord: *I will contend with them that contendeth with thee—and I will feed them that oppress thee, with their own flesh; and they shall be drunken with their own blood as with sweet wine; and all flesh shall know that I the Lord am thy Savior and thy Redeemer, the Mighty One of Jacob.* (2 Ne. 6:17-18.)

We are willing to enter into a covenant with our God to do his will, and to be obedient to his commandments in all things that he shall command us, all the remainder of our days, *that we may not bring upon ourselves a never-ending torment, as has been spoken by the angel, that we may not drink out of the cup of the wrath of God.* (Mosiah 5:5.)

[Moroni speaking] Whosoever will maintain this title [of liberty] upon the land, let them come forth in the strength of the Lord, and enter into a covenant that they will maintain their rights, and their religion, *that the Lord God may bless them.* (Alma 46:20.)

Cleave unto the covenants which thou hast made. (D&C 25:13.)

Thus ye shall become instructed in the law of my church, and be sanctified by that which ye have received, and ye shall bind yourselves to act in all holiness before me—that inasmuch as ye do this, *glory shall be added to the kingdom which ye have received.* Inasmuch as ye do it not, *it shall be taken, even that which ye have received.* (D&C 43:9-10.)

Come ye unto it [my everlasting covenant], and with him that cometh *I will reason as with men in days of old, and I will show unto you my strong reasoning.* (D&C 45:10.)

Bind yourselves by this covenant [in the administration of stewardship], *and it shall be done according to the laws of the Lord.* (D&C 82:15.)

Whoso is faithful unto the obtaining these two priesthoods of which I have spoken, and the magnifying of their calling, *are sanctified by the Spirit unto the renewing of their bodies. They become the sons of Moses and of Aaron and the seed of Abraham, and the church and kingdom, and the elect of God. And also all they who receive this priesthood re-*

ceive me, saith the Lord; for he that receiveth my servants receiveth me; and he that receiveth me receiveth my Father; and he that re- ceiveth my Father receiveth my Father's kingdom; therefore all that my Father hath shall be given unto him. And this is according to the oath and covenant which belongeth to the priesthood. Therefore, all those who receive the priesthood, receive this oath and covenant of my Father, *which he cannot break, neither can it be moved.* (D&C 84: 33-40.)

Search diligently, pray always, and be believing, *and all things shall work together for your good,* if ye walk uprightly and remember the covenant wherewith ye have covenanted one with another. (D&C 90:24.)

Be not afraid of your enemies, for I have decreed in my heart, saith the Lord, that I will prove you in all things, whether you will abide in my covenant, even unto death, *that you may be found worthy.* (D&C 98:14.)

[to Lyman Sherman] Arise up and be more careful henceforth in ob- serving your vows, which you have made and do make, *and you shall be blessed with exceeding great blessings.* (D&C 108:3.)

As pertaining to the new and everlasting covenant, it was instituted *for the fulness of my glory; and he that receiveth a fulness thereof* must and shall abide the law, *or he shall be damned, saith the Lord God.* (D&C 132:6.)

Go ye, therefore, and do the works of Abraham; enter ye into my law *and ye shall be saved.* (D&C 132:32.)

Covetousness

(See also False Gods; Worldliness.)

The Lord gave Martin Harris a curiously stated commandment in 1830: "Thou shalt not covet thine own property, but impart it freely to the printing of the Book of Mormon." (D&C 19:26.) Prior commandments, notably the tenth of the Ten Commandments, speak of not coveting others' possessions. "Thou shalt not covet thy neighbour's house," Moses recorded. (Ex. 20:17.) "Envy thou not the oppressor," Proverbs says. (Prov. 3:31.) "Let your conversation be without covetousness; and be content with such things as ye have," wrote Paul in Hebrews. (Heb. 13:5.) Actually, the Lord's instructions to Martin Harris not to covet his own property are in harmony with the Lord's teachings in the New Testament: "Take heed, and beware of covetousness: for a man's life consisteth not in the abundance of the things which he possesseth." (Luke 12:15.)

Covetousness is a matter of mixed priorities. Not only should we be content with our own possessions and not desire those of others, but we should not value our possessions too highly, instead keeping foremost the needs of the Lord's kingdom.

Commandments and Promises

Thou shalt not covet thy neighbour's house, thou shalt not covet thy neighbour's wife, nor his manservant, nor his maidservant, nor his ox, nor his ass, nor any thing that is thy neighbour's. (Ex. 20:17; similar scriptures, Deut. 5:21, Mosiah 13:24.)

Envy thou not the oppressor, and choose none of his ways. (Prov. 3:31.)

Let not thine heart envy sinners. (Prov. 23:17.)

Be not thou envious against evil men, neither desire to be with them. (Prov. 24:1.)

Fret not thyself because of evil men, neither be thou envious at the wicked. (Prov. 24:19.)

Take heed, and beware of covetousness: for a man's life consisteth not in the abundance of the things which he possesseth. (Luke 12:15.)

Let us walk honestly, as in the day; not in [envying, etc.]. But put ye on the Lord Jesus Christ, and make not provision for the flesh, to fulfil the lusts thereof. (Rom. 13:13-14.)

Nor thieves, nor covetous. . . *shall inherit the kingdom of God*. (1 Cor. 6:10.)

The works of the flesh are manifest, which are these; [idolatry, envyings, etc.]: of the which I tell you before, as I have also told you in time past, that *they which do such things shall not inherit the kingdom of God*. (Gal. 5:19-21.)

Let us not be desirous of vain glory, provoking one another, envying one another. (Gal. 5:26.)

Fornication, and all uncleanness, or covetousness, let it not be once named among you, as becometh saints; . . . for this ye know, that no . . . covetous man, who is an idolater, *hath any inheritance in the kingdom of Christ and of God*. (Eph. 5:3-5.)

Mortify therefore your members which are upon the earth; [covetousness, which is idolatry, etc.]: *for which things' sake the wrath of God cometh on the children of disobedience*. (Col. 3:5-6.)

A bishop then must be . . . not covetous. . . . Likewise must the deacons be . . . not greedy of filthy lucre. (1 Tim. 3:2-3, 8.)

In the last days perilous times shall come. For men shall be lovers of their own selves, covetous, . . . having a form of godliness; but denying the power thereof: from such turn away. . . . *But they shall proceed no further: for their folly shall be manifest unto all men*. (2 Tim. 3:1-9.)

Let your conversation be without covetousness; and be content with such things as ye have: for he hath said, I will never leave thee, nor forsake thee. (Heb. 13:5.)

Laying aside all [envies, etc.], as newborn babes, desire the sincere milk of the word, *that ye may grow thereby: if so be ye have tasted that the Lord is gracious.* (1 Pet. 2:1-3.)

They should not envy. (2 Ne. 26:32.)

Now, if God, who has created you, on whom you are dependent for your lives and for all that ye have and are, doth grant unto you whatsoever ye ask that is right, in faith, believing that ye shall receive, O then, how ye ought to impart of the substance that ye have one to another. And if ye judge the man who putteth up his petition to you for your substance that he perish not, and condemn him, how much more just will be your condemnation for withholding your substance, which doth not belong to you but to God, to whom also your life belongeth; and yet ye put up no petition, nor repent of the thing which thou hast done. I say unto you, *wo be unto that man, for his substance shall perish with him*; and now, I say these things unto those who are rich as pertaining to the things of this world. And again, I say unto the poor, ye who have not and yet have sufficient, that ye remain from day to day; I mean all you who deny the beggar, because ye have not; I would that ye say in your hearts that: I give not because I have not; but if I had I would give. And now, if ye say this in your hearts *ye remain guiltless, otherwise ye are condemned; and your condemnation is just* for ye covet that which ye have not received. (Mosiah 4:21-25.)

Is there one among you who is not stripped of envy? I say unto you that such an one is not prepared; and I would that he should prepare quickly, for the hour is close at hand, and he knoweth not when the time shall come; *for such an one is not found guiltless.* (Alma 5:29.)

Now those priests who did go forth among the people did preach against all . . . envyings, stealing, robbing, plundering, . . . crying that these things ought not so to be. (Alma 16:18.)

Ye do not remember the Lord your God in the things with which he hath blessed you, but ye do always remember your riches, not to thank the Lord your God for them; yea, your hearts are not drawn out unto the Lord, but they do swell with great pride, unto boasting, and unto great swelling, envyings, strifes, malice, persecutions and murders, and all manner of iniquities. *For this cause hath the Lord God caused that a curse should come upon the land, and also upon your riches,* and this because of your iniquities. (Hel. 13:22-23.)

[to Martin Harris] I command thee that thou shalt not covet thy neighbor's wife; nor seek thy neighbor's life. And again, I command thee that thou shalt not covet thine own property, but impart it freely to the printing of the Book of Mormon. (D&C 19:25-26.)

Wo unto you poor men, whose hearts are not broken, whose spirits are not contrite, and whose bellies are not satisfied, and whose hands are not stayed from laying hold upon other men's goods, whose eyes are full of greediness, and who will not labor with your own hands! (D&C 56:17.)

[to those ordained to the ministry] Inasmuch as you strip yourselves from jealousies and fears, and humble yourselves before me, for ye are not sufficiently humble, *the veil shall be rent and you shall see me and know that I am—not with the carnal neither natural mind, but with the spiritual.* (D&C 67:10.)

Cease to be covetous. (D&C 88:123.)

Inasmuch as some of my servants have not kept the commandment, but have broken the covenant through covetousness, and with feigned words, *I have cursed them with a very sore and grievous curse.* (D&C 104:4.)

Covet not that which is thy brother's. (D&C 136:20.)

Diligence
(See also Zeal.)

In this commandment the Lord tells us how to do all that we do: "I would that ye would be diligent and temperate in all things." (Alma 38:10.) With such a blend, we will not "run faster or labor more than [we] have strength and means." (D&C 10:4.) However, we ought to do all we can, as well as we can, as quickly as we should.

Commandments and Promises

He becometh poor that dealeth with a slack hand: but the hand of the diligent *maketh rich.* (Prov. 10:4.)

The soul of the sluggard desireth, *and hath nothing:* but the soul of the diligent *shall be made fat.* (Prov. 13:4.)

He that ruleth, [let him do it] with diligence. (Rom. 12:8.)

[Be] not slothful in business; [be] fervent in spirit; serving the Lord. (Rom. 12:11.)

We desire that every one of you do shew the same diligence to the full assurance of hope unto the end. (Heb. 6:11.)

Giving all diligence, add to your faith virtue; and to virtue knowledge; and to knowledge temperance; and to temperance patience; and to patience godliness; and to godliness brotherly kindness; and to brotherly kindness charity. For if these things be in you, and abound, *they make you that ye shall neither be barren nor unfruitful in the knowledge of our Lord Jesus Christ.* But he that lacketh these things *is blind, and cannot see afar off, and hath forgotten that he was purged from his old sins.* (2 Pet. 1:5-9.)

Give diligence *to make your calling and election sure: for if ye do these things, ye shall never fall: for so an entrance shall be ministered unto you abundantly into the everlasting kingdom of our Lord and Saviour Jesus Christ.* (2 Pet. 1:10-11.)

Seeing that ye look for such things [new heavens and a new earth], be diligent *that ye may be found of him in peace, without spot, and blameless.* (2 Pet. 3:14.)

How blessed are they who have labored diligently in his vineyard. (Jacob 6:3.)

It is expedient that he should be diligent, *that thereby he might win the prize.* (Mosiah 4:27.)

Now I would that ye should be humble . . . ; being temperate in all things; being diligent in keeping the commandments of God at all times. (Alma 7:23.)

If ye will nourish the word, yea, nourish the tree as it beginneth to grow, by your faith with great diligence, and with patience, looking forward to the fruit thereof, *it shall take root; and behold it shall be a tree springing up unto everlasting life.* And because of your diligence and your faith and your patience with the word in nourishing it, *that it may take root in you, behold, by and by ye shall pluck the fruit thereof, which is most precious, which is sweet above all that is sweet, and which is white above all that is white, yea, and pure above all that is pure; and ye shall feast upon this fruit even until ye are filled, that ye hunger not, neither shall ye thirst.* (Alma 32:41-42.)

They were slothful, and forgot to exercise their faith and diligence *and then those marvelous works [of the Liahona] ceased, and they did not progress in their journey.* (Alma 37:41.)

As ye have begun to teach the word even so I would that ye should continue to teach; and I would that ye would be diligent and temperate in all things. (Alma 38:10.)

Remember faith, . . . temperance, . . . diligence. (D&C 4:6.)

Be diligent. (D&C 6:18.)

Be faithful and diligent in keeping the commandments of God, *and I will encircle thee in the arms of my love.* (D&C 6:20.)

[to Joseph Smith] Do not run faster or labor more than you have strength and means provided to enable you to translate; but be diligent unto the end. (D&C 10:4.)

If [Joseph] shall be diligent in keeping my commandments *he shall be blessed unto eternal life.* (D&C 18:8.)

He that doeth not anything until he is commanded, and receiveth a commandment with doubtful heart, and keepeth it with slothfulness, *the same is damned.* (D&C 58:29.)

They shall also be crowned with blessings from above, yea, and with commandments not a few, and with revelations in their time—they that are faithful and diligent before me. (D&C 59:4.)

Let every man be diligent in all things. And the idler *shall not have place in the church,* except he repent and mend his ways. (D&C 75:29.)

All victory and glory is brought to pass unto you through your diligence, faithfulness, and prayers of faith. (D&C 103:36.)

It is my will that you shall humble yourselves before me, and *obtain this blessing [stewardship]* by your diligence and humility and the prayer of faith. (D&C 104:79.)

[to Joseph Smith] Inasmuch as you are diligent and humble, and exercise the prayer of faith, behold, *I will soften the hearts of those to whom you are in debt, until I shall send means unto you for your deliverance.* (D&C 104:80.)

Let every man learn his duty, and to act in the office in which he is appointed, in all diligence. He that is slothful *shall not be counted worthy to stand,* and he that learns not his duty and shows himself not approved *shall not be counted worthy to stand.* (D&C 107: 99-100.)

When I give a commandment to any of the sons of men to do a work unto my name, and those sons of men go with all their might and with all they have to perform that work, and cease not their diligence, and their enemies come upon them and hinder them from performing that work, behold, *it behooveth me to require that work no more at the hands of those sons of men, but to accept of their offerings.* (D&C 124:49.)

Let the work of my temple, and all the works which I have appointed unto you, be continued on and not cease; and let your diligence, and your perseverance, and patience, and your works be redoubled, *and you shall in nowise lose your reward, saith the Lord of Hosts.* (D&C 127:4.)

Doubt

(See also Believing in God; Faith.)

Doubt is a companion to fear and is the opposite of faith. While some people may see doubt as a healthy protection against letdowns, the Lord does not concur—at least where He and his word are concerned.

To doubt is to infer that God is a liar, to deny the reality of his promises, to insist on proof before we exercise faith. Like Thomas, the apostle who refused to believe in Christ's appearance after his death until he had seen the Savior himself, we suspend our belief before the intangible. Christ told Thomas, "Because thou hast seen me, thou hast believed; blessed are they that have not seen, and yet have believed." (John 20:29.)

Many blessings depend on our overcoming doubt. God's response to our petitions depends on our not doubting. "But let him ask in faith, nothing wavering. For he that wavereth is like a wave of the sea driven with the wind and tossed." (James 1:5-6.) Furthermore, the skeptic who "receiveth a commandment with doubtful heart and keepeth it with slothfulness" is, succinctly, "damned."(D&C 58:29.)

The rewards for not doubting are remarkable. God will deliver, will preserve, and will grant whatever is asked. And to him who does not doubt, "will I confirm all my words." (Morm. 9:25.)

Commandments and Promises

Whosoever shall say unto this mountain, Be thou removed, and be thou cast into the sea; and shall not doubt in his heart, but shall believe that those things which he saith shall come to pass; *he shall have whatsoever he saith.* Therefore I say unto you, What things soever ye desire, when ye pray, believe that ye receive them, *and ye shall have them.* (Mark 11:23-24.)

Seek not ye what ye shall eat, or what ye shall drink, neither be ye of doubtful mind. For all these things do the nations of the world seek after: and your Father knoweth that ye have need of these things. (Luke 12:29-30.)

Now the just shall live by faith: but if any man draw back, *my soul shall have no pleasure in him.* (Heb. 10:38.)

If any of you lack wisdom, let him ask of God, that giveth to all men liberally, and upbraideth not; *and it shall be given him.* But let him ask in faith, nothing wavering. For he that wavereth *is like a wave of the sea driven with the wind and tossed. Let not that man think that he shall receive any thing of the Lord.* (James 1:5-7.)

[The stripling sons] had been taught by their mothers, that if they did not doubt, *God would deliver them.* (Alma 56:47.)

We do justly ascribe *[the stripling sons' preservation]* to the miraculous power of God, because of their exceeding faith in that which they had been taught to believe—that there was a just God, and whosoever did not doubt, *that they should be preserved by his marvelous power.* (Alma 57:26.)

Whoso believeth in Christ, doubting nothing, *whatsoever he shall ask the Father in the name of Christ it shall be granted him; and this promise is unto all, even unto the ends of the earth.* (Morm. 9:21.)

Whosoever shall believe in my name, doubting nothing, *unto him will I confirm all my words, even unto the ends of the earth.* (Morm. 9:25.)

O then despise not, and wonder not, but hearken unto the words of the Lord, and ask the Father in the name of Jesus for what things soever ye shall stand in need. Doubt not, but be believing. (Morm. 9:27.)

Doubt not, fear not. (D&C 6:36.)

[to Oliver Cowdery] Doubt not, for [the gift of Aaron] is the gift of God. (D&C 8:8.)

He that doeth not anything until he is commanded, and receiveth a commandment with doubtful heart, and keepeth it with slothfulness, *the same is damned.* (D&C 58:29.)

Edifying and Strengthening Others

All of us have different strengths and different degrees of strengths. So that we can benefit from each other's strengths, Christ has commanded us to strengthen one another.

Sharing strength is a mutual venture. A leader is strengthened by the love, prayers, and support of those he or she serves. Those served are in turn strengthened by the leader's strength. In this way none of us carries a burden alone, and none of us—not even a prophet—carries all burdens.

Between 1829 and 1831, the Lord commanded various men and groups to support Joseph Smith, not only temporally but spiritually. Oliver Cowdery was commanded to "stand by my servant Joseph, faithfully, in whatsoever difficult circumstances he may be for the word's sake." (D&C 6:18.) Sidney Rigdon was commanded to "watch over him that his faith fail not." (D&C 35:19.) The elders of the Church were commanded to "uphold him . . . by the prayer of faith" and to "provide for him food and raiment, and whatsoever thing he needeth to accomplish the work." (D&C 43:12-14.) This commandment is similar to the many pleas the Apostle Paul made to the Saints to pray for him. All of us, even those seemingly strong ones who through their callings bear many burdens, need each other's help and strength.

As Alma baptized his people at the waters of Mormon, he gave the stipulation that those entering the fold of God be "willing to bear one another's burdens, that they may be light" and be "willing to mourn with those that mourn; yea, and comfort those that stand in need of comfort." (Mosiah 18:8-9.) Just as the Lord has at various times lightened his people's burdens, so can we similarly lighten the burdens of others.

Commandments and Promises

Strengthen ye the weak hands, and confirm the feeble knees. Say to them that are of a fearful heart, Be strong, fear not: behold, your God will come with vengeance, even God with a recompence; he will come and save you. (Isa. 35:3-4.)

Woe be to the shepherds of Israel that do feed themselves! should not the shepherds feed the flocks? Ye eat the fat, and ye clothe you with the wool, ye kill them that are fed: but ye feed not the flock. The diseased have ye not strengthened, neither have ye healed that which was sick, neither have ye bound up that which was broken, neither have ye brought again that which was driven away, neither have ye sought that which was lost; but with force and with cruelty have ye ruled them. . . . As I live, saith the Lord God, surely because my flock became a prey, and my flock became meat to every beast of the field, because there was no shepherd, neither did my shepherds search for my flock, but the shepherds fed themselves, and fed not my flock; *behold, I am against the shepherds; and I will require my flock at their hand, and cause them to cease from feeding the flock; neither shall the shepherds feed themselves any more; for I will deliver my flock from their mouth, that they may not be meat for them.* (Ezek. 34:2-10.)

When thou art converted, strengthen thy brethren. (Luke 22:32.)

I have shewed you all things, how that so labouring ye ought to support the weak, and to remember the words of the Lord Jesus, how he said, It is more blessed to give than to receive. (Acts 20:35.)

Him that is weak in the faith receive ye, but not to doubtful disputations. (Rom. 14:1.)

Let us therefore follow after the things which make for peace, and things wherewith one may edify another. (Rom. 14:19.)

We then that are strong ought to bear the infirmities of the weak, and not to please ourselves. Let every one of us please his neighbour for his good to edification. (Rom. 15:1-2.)

If a man be overtaken in a fault, ye which are spiritual, restore such an one in the spirit of meekness; considering thyself, lest thou also be tempted. Bear ye one another's burdens, and so fulfill the law of Christ. (Gal. 6:1-2.)

Let no corrupt communication proceed out of your mouth, but that which is good to the use of edifying, *that it may minister grace unto the hearers.* (Eph. 4:29.)

Comfort yourselves together, and edify one another, even as also ye do. (1 Thes. 5:11.)

Warn them that are unruly, comfort the feebleminded, support the weak, be patient toward all men. (1 Thes. 5:14.)

Rebuke not an elder, but intreat him as a father; and the younger men as brethren; the elder women as mothers; the younger as sisters, with all purity. Honour widows that are widows indeed. (1 Tim. 5:1-3.)

Exhort one another daily, while it is called To day; *lest any of you be hardened through the deceitfulness of sin.* (Heb. 3:13.)

Lift up the hands which hang down, and the feeble knees; and make straight paths for your feet, *lest that which is lame be turned out of the way;* but let it rather be healed. Follow peace with all men, and holiness, without which no man shall see the Lord: looking diligently lest any man fail of the grace of God; *lest any root of bitterness springing up trouble you, and thereby many be defiled.* (Heb. 12:12-15.)

Brethren, if any of you do err from the truth, and one convert him; let him know, that he which converteth the sinner from the error of his way *shall save a soul from death, and shall hide a multitude of sins.* (James 5:19-20.)

[to Gaius] Thou doest faithfully whatsoever thou doest to the brethren, and to strangers; which have borne witness of thy charity before the church: whom if thou bring forward on their journey after a godly sort, *thou shalt do well:* because that for his name's sake they went forth, taking nothing of the Gentiles. We therefore ought to receive such, that we might be fellowhelpers to the truth. (3 Jn. 1:5-8.)

Of some have compassion, making a difference: and others save with fear, pulling them out of the fire; hating even the garment spotted by the flesh. (Jude 1:22-23.)

Be watchful, and strengthen the things which remain, that are ready to die. (Rev. 3:2; see also JST Rev. 3:2.)

[to Oliver Cowdery] Be diligent; stand by my servant Joseph, faithfully, in whatsoever difficult circumstances he may be for the word's sake. (D&C 6:18.)

[to Sidney Rigdon]Watch over him [Joseph Smith] that his faith fail not, *and it shall be given by the Comforter, the Holy Ghost, that knoweth all things.* (D&C 35:19.)

Let every man esteem his brother as himself, and practise virtue and holiness before me. And again I say unto you, let every man esteem his brother as himself. (D&C 38:24-25.)

If ye desire the glories of the kingdom, appoint ye my servant Joseph Smith, Jun., and uphold him before me by the prayer of faith. And again, I say unto you, *that if ye desire the mysteries of the kingdom,* provide for him food and raiment, and whatsoever thing he needeth to accomplish the work wherewith I have commanded him; and if ye do it not *he shall remain unto them that have received him, that I may reserve unto myself a pure people before me.* (D&C 43:12-14.)

Succor the weak, lift up the hands which hang down, and strengthen the feeble knees. (D&C 81:5.)

If any man among you be strong in the Spirit, let him take with him him that is weak, *that he may be edified in all meekness, that he may become strong also.* (D&C 84:106.)

The duty of a president over the office of a deacon is to preside over twelve deacons, to sit in council with them, and to teach them their duty, edifying one another, as it is given according to the covenants. (D&C 107:85.)

Strengthen your brethren in all your conversation, in all your prayers, in all your exhortations, and in all your doings. *And behold, and lo, I am with you to bless you and deliver you forever.* (D&C 108:7-8.)

Let your words tend to edifying one another. (D&C 136:24.)

Example, Being an

The sons of Mosiah approached their missionary travels with one goal: "that they might be an instrument in the hands of God." As they sought to convert the Lamanites to a knowledge of the truth, they fasted and prayed. Responding to their desires through the voice of his Spirit, the Lord said, "Go forth among the Lamanites, thy brethren, and establish my word; yet ye shall be patient in long-suffering and afflictions, that ye may show forth good examples unto them in me." The Spirit promised that they would thus be instruments in God's hands "unto the salvation of many souls." (Alma 17:9-11.)

We have been commanded to do as the sons of Mosiah, who were admonished to exhibit Godlike traits to "show forth good examples unto them in me." But how should we be examples? Should we consciously decide to make our good deeds known? How do we balance this commandment with the one which says, "When thou doest alms, let not thy left hand know what thy right hand doeth: that thine alms may be in secret." How do we make our good deeds known without sounding a trumpet, figuratively, as did the hypocrites in the synagogues? (Matt. 6:2-4.)

We must realize that however small our sphere of influence, others see our actions and justify their actions by ours. A sad instance of this is recorded in Alma's reproof of Corianton, his wayward son: "How great iniquity ye brought upon the Zoramites; for when they saw your conduct they would not believe in my words." (Alma 39:11.) Similarly, believers are admonished in the book of Hebrews: "Let us labour therefore to enter into that rest, lest any man fall after the same example of unbelief." (Heb. 4:11.) In other words, one reason for our righteousness is so that we will not lead others into unrighteousness, which is itself a sin.

The commandment to "let your light so shine before men" is not a justification for boasting. The rest of that statement of the Savior, from the Sermon on the Mount, explains the reason: "that they may see your good works, and glorify your Father which is in heaven."

(Matt. 5:16.) The goal is not to earn the praise of men but to inspire men to recognize and praise God.

When we act as God himself would act, as much as is possible, we make the ideal real for others and motivate them to do good works with the same divine incentive that motivates us. As we perform God's work with his goals in mind, we become literal tools in his hands.

Commandments and Promises

Arise, shine; for thy light is come, and the glory of the Lord is risen upon thee. (Isa. 60:1.)

Let your light so shine before men, *that they may see your good works, and glorify your Father which is in heaven.* (Matt. 5:16; similar scripture, 3 Ne. 12:16.)

Take heed lest by any means this liberty of yours *become a stumbling-block to them that are weak.* (1 Cor. 8:9.)

Abstain from all appearance of evil. (1 Thes. 5:22.)

Be thou an example of the believers, in word, in conversation, in charity, in spirit, in faith, in purity. (1 Tim. 4:12.)

Meditate upon these things [of the gospel]; give thyself wholly to them; *that thy profiting may appear to all.* Take heed unto thyself, and unto the doctrine; continue in them: for in doing this *thou shalt both save thyself, and them that hear thee.* (1 Tim. 4:15-16.)

In all things [shew] thyself a pattern of good works: in doctrine shewing uncorruptness, gravity, sincerity, sound speech, that cannot be condemned; *that he that is of the contrary part may be ashamed, having no evil thing to say of you.* (Titus 2:7-8.)

Let us labour therefore to enter into that rest, *lest any man fall after the same example of unbelief.* (Heb. 4:11.)

Lift up the hands which hang down, and the feeble knees; and make straight paths for your feet, *lest that which is lame be turned out of the way;* but let it rather be healed. (Heb. 12:12-13.)

[to the elders] Feed the flock of God which is among you, taking the oversight thereof, not by constraint, but willingly; not for filthy lucre, but of a ready mind. neither as being lords over God's heritage, but being ensamples unto the flock. *And when the chief Shepherd shall appear, ye shall receive a crown of glory that fadeth not away.* (1 Pet. 5:2-4.)

[to the sons of Mosiah] Go forth among the Lamanites, thy brethren, and establish my word; yet ye shall be patient in long-suffering and afflictions, *that ye may show forth good examples unto them in me, and I will make an instrument of thee in my hands unto the salvation of many souls.* (Alma 17:11.)

[to Corianton] How great iniquity ye brought upon the Zoramites; for when they saw your conduct *they would not believe in my words.* And now the Spirit of the Lord doth say unto me: Command thy children to do good, *lest they lead away the hearts of many people to destruction;* therefore I command you, my son, in the fear of God, that ye refrain from your iniquities. (Alma 39:11-12.)

I give unto you to be the light of this people. (3 Ne. 12:14.)

Hold up your light that it may shine unto the world. Behold I am the light which ye shall hold up—that which ye have seen me do. (3 Ne. 18:24.)

Blessed are ye if ye continue in my goodness, a light unto the Gentiles, and through this priesthood, a savior unto my people Israel. (D&C 86:11.)

Arise and shine forth, *that thy light may be a standard for the nations.* (D&C 115:5.)

Faith

(See also Faithfulness; Hope.)

Some people seem to have inborn faith: it comes naturally and easily for them. Timothy was one of these. The apostle Paul wrote to Timothy: "I call to remembrance the unfeigned faith that is in thee, which dwelt first in thy grandmother Lois, and thy mother Eunice; and I am persuaded that in thee also." (2 Tim. 1:5.) For others, however, acquiring faith may take a lifetime of adversity and prayer. In either case and all others, God commands us to have faith. We are told to "have faith" and "follow faith," and reference is made to "taking the shield of faith" and "holding faith." The scriptures are clear on how we should and shouldn't seek faith.

"Faith cometh not by signs, but . . . signs come by faith," the Lord says. (D&C 63:9-10.) We cannot expect faith to come simply by our observing God's works. Building faith takes more effort and, as Alma explains, involves exercising "a particle of faith" and letting "this desire work in you." (Alma 32:27.) Seedling faith must be nourished until it grows.

Moroni taught what this faith is, and how we obtain it: "Faith is things which are hoped for and not seen; wherefore, dispute not because ye see not, for ye receive no witness until after the trial of your faith." (Ether 12:6.) He explains that only after men exercise whatever extent of faith they have can God perform miracles. (See Ether 12.) Later, he explains one manifestation of faith: "They who have faith in him will cleave unto every good thing." (Moro. 7:28.)

Faith, therefore, cannot be passive. It must be active—particularly since "faith, if it hath not works, is dead, being alone" (James 2:17)—but just what that activity involves depends on an individual's situation and capabilities. The exercise of faith varies, since each person's faith meets with different trials and duties.

For all who build and maintain faith, the blessings are many. Those who have faith in Christ "shall have power to do whatsoever thing is expedient in me." (Moro. 7:33.) One blessing coming through faith is to have hope. (See Ether 12:4.) Hope and faith are mutually supportive: "How is it that ye can attain unto faith, save ye shall have hope?" Moroni asks. "And what is it that ye shall hope for? Behold I say unto you that ye shall have hope through the atonement of Christ and the power of his resurrection, to be raised into life eternal, and this because of your faith in him according to the promise." (Moro. 7:40-41.)

Faith, then, is not based on wild expectations or unmade promises. We cannot decide what God will do for us and then, through "faith," bind him to our wills; such faith is vain. Rather, faith comes from God through the exercise of hope in the promise of life eternal.

Commandments and Promises

If ye have faith as a grain of mustard seed, ye shall say unto this mountain, Remove hence to yonder place; *and it shall remove; and nothing shall be impossible unto you.* (Matt. 17:20.)

If ye have faith, and doubt not, *ye shall not only do this which is done to the fig tree,* but also if ye shall say unto this mountain, Be thou removed, and be thou cast into the sea; *it shall be done. And all things, whatsoever ye shall ask in prayer, believing, ye shall receive.* (Matt. 21:21-22.)

Woe unto you, scribes and Pharisees, hypocrites! for ye pay tithe of mint and anise and cummin, and have omitted the weightier matters of the law, judgment, mercy, and faith: these ought ye to have done, and not to leave the other undone. (Matt. 23:23.)

Have faith in God, for verily I say unto you, That whosoever shall say unto this mountain, Be thou removed, and be thou cast into the sea; and shall not doubt in his heart, but shall believe that those things which he saith shall come to pass; *he shall have whatsoever he saith.* (Mark 11:22-23.)

Therefore *being justified* by faith, we have peace with God through our Lord Jesus Christ: *by whom also we have access* by faith *into this grace wherein we stand, and rejoice in hope of the glory of God.* (Rom. 5:1-2.)

Having then gifts differing according to the grace that is given to us, whether prophecy, let us prophesy according to the proportion of faith. (Rom. 12:6.)

Whatsoever is not of faith *is sin.* (Rom. 14:23.)

By faith *ye stand.* (2 Cor. 1:24.)

They which are of faith, *the same are the children of Abraham.* (Gal. 3:7.)

The just shall live by faith. (Gal. 3:11.)

For by grace are ye saved through faith; *and that not of yourselves: it is the gift of God: not of works, lest any man should boast.* (Eph. 2:8-9.)

Above all, [take] the shield of faith, *wherewith ye shall be able to quench all the fiery darts of the wicked.* (Eph. 6:16; similar scripture, D&C 27:17.)

I [Paul] count all things but loss for the excellency of the knowledge of Christ Jesus my Lord: for whom I have suffered the loss of all things, and do count them but dung, that I may win Christ, and be found in him, not having mine own righteousness, which is of the law, but that which is through the faith of Christ, *the righteousness which is of God* by faith: *that I may know him, and the power of his resurrection, and the fellowship of his sufferings, being made conformable unto his death.* (Philip. 3:8-10.)

Let us, who are of the day, be sober, putting on the breastplate of faith and love; and for an helmet, the hope of salvation. (1 Thes. 5:8.)

Now the end of the commandment is charity out of a pure heart, and of a good conscience, and of faith unfeigned. (1 Tim. 1:5.)

This charge I commit unto thee, son Timothy, according to the prophecies which went before on thee, that thou by them mightest war a good warfare; holding faith, and a good conscience; which some having put away concerning faith *have made shipwreck.* (1 Tim. 1:18-19.)

Be thou an example of the believers, in word, in conservation, in charity, in spirit, in faith, in purity. (1 Tim. 4:12.)

Thou, O man of God, . . . follow after righteousness, godliness, faith, love, patience, meekness. Fight the good fight of faith. (1 Tim. 6: 11-12.)

Flee also youthful lusts: but follow righteousness, faith, charity, peace, with them that call on the Lord out of a pure heart. (2 Tim. 2:22.)

Speak thou the things which become sound doctrine: That the aged men be sober, grave, temperate, sound in faith, in charity, in patience. (Titus 2:1-2.)

Cast not away therefore your confidence, *which hath great recompence of reward.* (Heb. 10:35.)

Now faith is the substance of things hoped for, the evidence of things not seen. For by it *the elders obtained a good report.* Through faith *we understand that the worlds were framed by the word of God, so that things which are seen were not made of things which do appear.* (Heb. 11:1-3; see also JST Heb. 11:1.)

By faith Abel offered unto God a more excellent sacrifice than Cain, *by which he obtained witness that he was righteous, God testifying of his gifts: and by it he being dead yet speaketh.* (Heb. 11:4.)

By faith *Enoch was translated that he should not see death; and was not found, because God had translated him: for before his translation he had this testimony, that he pleased God.* But without faith *it is impossible to please him:* for he that cometh to God must believe that he is, and that he is a rewarder of them that diligently seek him. (Heb. 11:5-6.)

By faith Noah, being warned of God of things not seen as yet, moved with fear, prepared an ark *to the saving of his house;* by the which he condemned the world, and *became heir of righteousness* which is by faith. (Heb. 11:7.)

By faith Abraham, when he was called to go out into a place which he should after receive for an inheritance, obeyed; and he went out, not knowing whither he went. By faith *he sojourned in the land of promise, as in a strange country, dwelling in tabernacles with Isaac and Jacob, the heirs with him of the same promise:* for he looked for a city which hath foundations, whose builder and maker is God. Through faith also *Sara herself received strength to conceive seed, and was delivered of a child when she was past age,* because she judged him faithful who had promised. *Therefore sprang there even of one, and him as good as dead, so many as the stars of the sky in multitude, and as the sand which is by the sea shore innumerable.* (Heb. 11:8-11.)

These all died in faith, not having received the promises, but having seen them afar off, and were persuaded of them, and embraced them, and confessed that they were strangers and pilgrims on the earth. For they that say such things declare plainly that they seek a country. And truly, if they had been mindful of that country from whence they came out, they might have had opportunity to have returned. But now they desire a better country, that is, an heavenly: *wherefore God is not ashamed to be called their God: for he hath prepared for them a city.* (Heb. 11:13-16.)

By faith Isaac *blessed Jacob and Esau concerning things to come.* By faith Jacob, when he was a dying, *blessed both the sons of Joseph.* (Heb. 11:20-21.)

Through faith [Moses] kept the passover, and the sprinkling of blood, *lest he that destroyed the firstborn should touch [the children of Israel].* By faith *they passed through the Red sea as by dry land: which the Egyptians assaying to do were drowned.* (Heb. 11:28-29.)

By faith *the walls of Jericho fell down, after they were compassed about seven days.* By faith *the harlot Rahab perished not with them that believed not, when she had received the spies with peace.* (Heb. 11:30-31.)

And what shall I more say? for the time would fail me to tell of Gedeon, and of Barak, and of Samson, and of Jephthae; of David also, and Samuel, and of the prophets: who through faith *subdued kingdoms, wrought righteousness, obtained promises, stopped the mouths of lions, quenched the violence of fire, escaped the edge of the sword, out of weakness were made strong, waxed valiant in fight, turned to flight the armies of the aliens. Women received their dead raised to life again:* and others were tortured, not accepting deliverance; *that they might obtain a better resurrection.* (Heb. 11:32-35; see also JST Heb. 11:35.)

And these all *[obtained] a good report* through faith. (Heb. 11:39.)

If any of you lack wisdom, let him ask of God, that giveth to all men liberally, and upbraideth not; *and it shall be given him.* But let him ask in faith, nothing wavering. For he that wavereth *is like a wave of the sea driven with the wind and tossed. For let not that man think that he shall receive any thing of the Lord.* (James 1:5-7.)

The prayer of faith *shall save the sick, and the Lord shall raise him up; and if he have committed sins, they shall be forgiven him.* (James 5:15.)

I, Nephi, will show unto you that *the tender mercies of the Lord are over all those whom he hath chosen,* because of their faith, *to make them mighty even unto the power of deliverance.* (1 Ne. 1:20.)

How is it that ye have forgotten that *the Lord is able to do all things according to his will, for the children of men,* if it so be that they exercise faith in him? Wherefore, let us be faithful to him. (1 Ne. 7:12.)

The angel said unto me: Look! and I looked, and beheld three generations pass away in righteousness; and their garments were white even like unto the Lamb of God. And the angel said unto me: *These are made white in the blood of the Lamb,* because of their faith in him. (1 Ne. 12:11.)

He commandeth all men that they must repent, and be baptized in his name, having perfect faith in the Holy One of Israel, *or they cannot be saved in the kingdom of God.* (2 Ne. 9:23.)

We are made alive in Christ because of our faith. (2 Ne. 25:25.)

He manifesteth himself unto all those who believe in him, by the power of the Holy Ghost; yea, unto every nation, kindred, tongue, and people, *working mighty miracles, signs, and wonders, among the children of men* according to their faith. (2 Ne. 26:13.)

Because of faith and great anxiety, *it truly had been made manifest unto us concerning our people, what things should happen unto them.* (Jacob 1:5.)

Look unto God with firmness of mind, and pray unto him with exceeding faith, *and he will console you in your afflictions, and he will plead your cause, and send down justice upon those who seek your destruction.* (Jacob 3:1.)

Be reconciled unto him through the atonement of Christ, his Only Begotten Son, *and ye may obtain a resurrection, according to the power of the resurrection which is in Christ, and be presented as the first-fruits of Christ unto God,* having faith, *and obtained a good hope of glory in him before he manifesteth himself in the flesh.* (Jacob 4:11.)

There came a voice unto me, saying: Enos, *thy sins are forgiven thee, and thou shalt be blessed.* And I, Enos, knew that God could not lie; *wherefore, my guilt was swept away.* And I said: Lord, how is it done? And he said unto me: Because of thy faith in Christ, whom thou hast never before heard nor seen. And many years pass away before he shall manifest himself in the flesh; wherefore, go to, thy faith *hath made thee whole.* (Enos 1:5-8.)

Whatsoever thing ye shall ask in faith, believing that ye shall receive in the name of Christ, *ye shall receive it.* (Enos 1:15.)

He cometh unto his own, that *salvation might come unto the children of men* even through faith on his name. (Mosiah 3:9.)

Wo, wo unto him who knoweth that he rebelleth against God! For *salvation cometh to none such* except it be through repentance and faith on the Lord Jesus Christ. (Mosiah 3:12.)

The time shall come when the knowledge of the Savior shall spread throughout every nation, kindred, tongue, and people. And behold, when that time cometh, *none shall be found blameless before God, except it be little children*, only through repentance and faith on the name of the Lord God Omnipotent. (Mosiah 3:20-21.)

I would that ye should remember, and always retain in remembrance, the greatness of God, and your own nothingness, and his goodness and long-suffering towards you, unworthy creatures, and humble yourselves even in the depths of humility, calling on the name of the Lord daily, and standing steadfastly in the faith of that which is to come, which was spoken by the mouth of the angel. And behold, I say unto you that if ye do this *ye shall always rejoice, and be filled with the love of God, and always retain a remission of your sins; and ye shall grow in the knowledge of the glory of him that created you, or in the knowledge of that which is just and true.* (Mosiah 4:11-12.)

If ye do not watch yourselves, and your thoughts, and your words, and your deeds, and observe the commandments of God, and continue in the faith of what ye have heard concerning the coming of our Lord, even unto the end of your lives, *ye must perish.* And now, O man, remember, *and perish not.* (Mosiah 4:30.)

God has provided a means that man, through faith, *might work mighty miracles; therefore he becometh a great benefit to his fellow beings.* (Mosiah 8:18.)

He commanded them that there should be no contention one with another, but that they should look forward with one eye, having one faith and one baptism, having their hearts knit together in unity and in love one towards another. And thus he commanded them to preach. *And thus they became the children of God.* (Mosiah 18:21-22.)

Thou [Alma] art blessed because of thy exceeding faith in the words alone of my servant Abinadi. (Mosiah 26:15.)

According to his faith *there was a mighty change wrought in his heart.* (Alma 5:12.)

See that ye have faith, hope, and charity, *and then ye will always abound in good works.* (Alma 7:24.)

May the peace of God rest upon you, and upon your houses and lands, and upon your flocks and herds, and all that you possess, your women and your children, according to your faith and good works, from this time forth and forever. (Alma 7:27.)

There were many who were ordained and became high priests of God; and it was on account of their exceeding faith and repentance, and their righteousness before God, they choosing to repent and work righteousness rather than to perish; *therefore they were called after this holy order, and were sanctified, and their garments were washed white through the blood of the Lamb. Now they, after being sanctified by the Holy Ghost, having their garments made white, being pure and spotless before God, could not look upon sin save it were with abhorrence; and there were many, exceedingly great many, who were made pure and entered into the rest of the Lord their God.* (Alma 13:10-12.)

I wish from the inmost part of my heart, yea, with great anxiety even unto pain, that ye would hearken unto my words, and cast off your sins, and not procrastinate the day of your repentance; but that ye would humble yourselves before the Lord, and call on his holy name, and watch and pray continually, that ye may not be tempted above that which ye can bear, and thus be led by the Holy Spirit, becoming humble, meek, submissive, patient, full of love and all long-suffering; having faith on the Lord; having a hope that ye shall receive eternal life; having the love of God always in your hearts, *that ye may be lifted up at the last day and enter into his rest.* (Alma 13: 27-29.)

A portion of that Spirit dwelleth in me, which giveth me knowledge, and also power according to my faith and desires which are in God. (Alma 18:35.)

The Lord provided for them that they should hunger not, neither should they thirst; yea, and he also gave them strength, that they should suffer no manner of afflictions, save it were swallowed up in the joy of Christ. Now this was according to the prayer of Alma; and this because he prayed in faith. (Alma 31:38.)

If ye will awake and arouse your faculties, even to an experiment upon my words, and exercise a particle of faith, yea, even if ye can no more than desire to believe, let this desire work in you, *even until ye believe in a manner that ye can give place for a portion of my words.* Now, we will compare the word unto a seed. Now, if ye give place, that a seed may be planted in your heart, behold, if it be a true seed, or a good seed, if ye do not cast it out by your unbelief, that ye will resist the Spirit of the Lord, behold, *it will begin to swell within your breasts;* and when you feel these swelling motions, ye will begin to say within yourselves—It must needs be that this is a good seed, or that the word is good, *for it beginneth to enlarge my soul; yea, it beginneth to enlighten my understanding, yea, it beginneth to be delicious to me.* (Alma 32:27-28.)

Neither must ye lay aside your faith, for ye have only exercised your faith to plant the seed that ye might try the experiment to know if the seed was good. And behold, as the tree beginneth to grow, ye will say: Let us nourish it with great care, that it may get root, that it may grow up, and bring forth fruit unto us. And now behold, if ye nourish it with much care *it will get root, and grow up, and bring forth fruit.* But if ye neglect the tree, and take no thought for its nourishment, *behold it will not get any root;* and when the heat of the sun cometh and scorcheth it, because it hath no root *it withers away, and ye pluck it up and cast it out.* Now, this is not because the seed was not good, neither is it because the fruit thereof would not be desirable; but it is because your ground is barren, and ye will not nourish the tree, *therefore ye cannot have the fruit thereof.* And thus, if ye will not nourish the word, looking forward with an eye of faith to the fruit thereof, *therefore ye cannot have the fruit thereof.* And thus, if ye will not nourish the word, looking forward with an eye of faith to the fruit thereof, *ye can never pluck of the fruit of the tree of life.* (Alma 32: 36-39.)

But if ye will nourish the word, yea, nourish the tree as it beginneth to grow, by your faith and great diligence, and with patience, looking forward to the fruit thereof, *it shall take root; and behold it shall be a tree springing up unto everlasting life.* And because of your diligence and your faith and your patience with the word in nourishing it, that it may take root in you, behold, *by and by ye shall pluck the fruit thereof, which is most precious, which is sweet above all that is sweet, and which is white above all that is white, yea, and pure above all that is pure; and ye shall feast upon this fruit even until ye are filled, that ye hunger not, neither shall ye thirst.* Then, my brethren, ye shall reap the rewards of your faith, and your diligence, and patience, and long-suffering, waiting for the tree to bring forth fruit unto you. (Alma 32:40-43.)

I desire that ye shall plant this word in your hearts, and as it beginneth to swell even so nourish it by your faith. *And behold, it will become a tree, springing up in you unto everlasting life. And then may God grant unto you that your burdens may be light,* through the joy of his Son. *And even all this can ye do* if ye will. (Alma 33:23.)

[The Liahona] did work for them according to their faith in God; therefore, if they had faith to believe that God could cause that those spindles should point the way they should go, *behold, it was done; therefore they had this miracle, and also many other miracles wrought by the power of God, day by day. Nevertheless, because those miracles were worked by small means it did show unto them marvelous works.* They were slothful, and forgot to exercise their faith and diligence and *then those marvelous works ceased, and they did not progress in their journey.* (Alma 37:40-41.)

[The stripling Ammonite warriors] did obey and observe to perform every word of command with exactness; yea, and even according to their faith *it was done unto them.* (Alma 57:21.)

[The stripling warriors'] preservation was astonishing to our whole army, yea, that they should be spared while there was a thousand of our brethren who were slain. And we do justly ascribe it to the miraculous power of God, because of their exceeding faith in that which they had been taught to believe—that there was a just God, and whosoever did not doubt, *that they should be preserved by his marvelous power.* (Alma 57:26.)

Peace, peace be unto you, because of your faith in my Well Beloved, who was from the foundation of the world. (Hel. 5:47.)

Heavy destruction awaiteth [the Nephites], and it surely cometh unto this people, and *nothing can save this people save it* be repentance and faith on the Lord Jesus Christ. (Hel. 13:6.)

Blessed are ye because of your faith. (3 Ne. 17:20.)

[Jesus Christ praying] Father, I thank thee that *thou hast purified those whom I have chosen*, because of their faith, and I pray for them and also for them who shall believe on their words, that *they may be purified in me*, through faith on their words, *even as they are purified in me*. (3 Ne. 19:28.)

Nothing entereth into his rest save it be those who have washed their garments in my blood, because of their faith, and the repentance of all their sins, and their faithfulness unto the end. (3 Ne. 27:19.)

In that day that they shall exercise faith in me, saith the Lord, even as the brother of Jared did, *that they may become sanctified in me, then will I manifest unto them the things which the brother of Jared saw, even to the unfolding unto them all my revelations*, saith Jesus Christ, the Son of God, the Father of the heavens and of the earth, *and all things that in them are*. (Ether 4:7.)

By faith *all things are fulfilled*—wherefore, whoso believeth in God *might with surety hope for a better world, yea, even a place at the right hand of God, which hope* cometh of faith, *maketh an anchor to the souls of men, which would make them sure and steadfast, always abounding in good works, being led to glorify God*. (Ether 12:3-4.)

Repent all ye ends of the earth, and come unto me, and be baptized in my name, and have faith in me, *that ye may be saved*. (Moro. 7:34.)

No man can be saved, according to the words of Christ, save they shall have faith in his name; wherefore, if these things [miracles] have ceased, then has faith ceased also; and *awful is the state of man, for they are as though there had been no redemption made*. (Moro. 7:38.)

If ye have not faith in him *then ye are not fit to be numbered among the people of his church.* (Moro. 7:39.)

Ye shall have hope through the atonement of Christ and the power of his resurrection, to be raised unto life eternal, and this because of your faith in him according to the promise. Wherefore, if a man have faith *he must needs have hope;* for without faith *there cannot be any hope.* And again, behold, I say unto you that he cannot have faith and hope, save he shall be meek, and lowly of heart. If so, his faith and hope *is vain, for none is acceptable before God,* save the meek and lowly in heart; and if a man be meek and lowly in heart, and confess by the power of the Holy Ghost that Jesus is the Christ, he must needs have charity; for if he have not charity *he is nothing;* wherefore he must needs have charity. (Moro. 7:41-44.)

There must be faith; and if there must be faith there must also be hope; and if there must be hope there must also be charity. (Moro. 10:20.)

Christ truly said unto our fathers: If ye have faith *ye can do all things which are expedient unto me.* (Moro. 10:23.)

Faith, hope, charity and love, with an eye single to the glory of God, *qualify him for the work.* Remember faith, . . . knowledge, . . . charity. (D&C 4:5-6.)

Have patience, faith, hope and charity. (D&C 6:19.)

[to Oliver Cowdery] Remember that without faith *you can do nothing;* therefore ask in faith. Trifle not with these things; do not ask for that which you ought not. Ask that you may know the mysteries of God, and that you may translate and receive knowledge from all those ancient records which have been hid up, that are sacred; and according to your faith *shall it be done unto you.* (D&C 8:10-11.)

[to Hyrum Smith] *Thou hast a gift, or thou shalt have a gift* if thou wilt desire of me in faith, with an honest heart, believing in the power of Jesus Christ, or in my power which speaketh unto thee. (D&C 11:10.)

I will impart unto you of my Spirit, *which shall enlighten your mind, which shall fill your soul with joy; and then shall ye know, or by this shall you know, all things whatsoever you desire of me, which are pertaining unto things of righteousness*, in faith believing in me that you shall receive. (D&C 11:13-14.)

No one can assist in this work except he shall be humble and full of love, having faith, hope, and charity, being temperate in all things, whatsoever shall be entrusted to his care. (D&C 12:8.)

If you shall ask the Father in my name, in faith believing, *you shall receive the Holy Ghost, which giveth utterance, that you may stand as a witness of the things of which you shall both hear and see, and also that you may declare repentance unto this generation.* (D&C 14:8.)

Ask the Father in my name, in faith believing that you shall receive, *and you shall have the Holy Ghost, which manifesteth all things which are expedient unto the children of men.* (D&C 18:18.)

All men must repent and believe on the name of Jesus Christ, and worship the Father in his name, and endure in faith on his name to the end, *or they cannot be saved in the kingdom of God.* (D&C 20:29.)

Wherefore, meaning the church, thou shalt give heed unto all [Joseph Smith's] words and commandments which he shall give unto you as he receiveth them, walking in all holiness before me; for his word ye shall receive, as if from mine own mouth, in all patience and faith. *For by doing these things the gates of hell shall not prevail against you; yea, and the Lord God will disperse the powers of darkness from before you, and cause the heavens to shake for your good, and his name's glory.* (D&C 21:4-6.)

Whatsoever ye shall ask in faith, being united in prayer according to my command, *ye shall receive.* (D&C 29:6.)

They shall have faith in me *or they can in nowise be saved.* (D&C 33:12.)

Whoso shall ask it in my name in faith, *they shall cast out devils; they shall heal the sick; they shall cause the blind to receive their sight, and the deaf to hear, and the dumb to speak, and the lame to walk.* (D&C 35:9.)

By the prayer of your faith *ye shall receive my law, that ye may know how to govern my church and have all things right before me.* (D&C 41:3.)

The Spirit shall be given unto you by the prayer of faith; and if ye receive not the Spirit ye shall not teach. (D&C 42:14.)

He that hath faith in me to be healed, and is not appointed unto death, *shall be healed.* He who hath faith to see *shall see.* He who hath faith to hear *shall hear.* The lame who hath faith to leap *shall leap.* (D&C 42:48-51.)

Inasmuch as they are faithful, and exercise faith in me, *I will pour out my Spirit upon them in the day that they assemble themselves together.* (D&C 44:2.)

According to men's faith *it shall be done unto them.* (D&C 52:20.)

Through faith [Sidney Gilbert and W. W. Phelps] *shall overcome.* And inasmuch as they are faithful *they shall be preserved, and I, the Lord, will be with them.* (D&C 61:9-10.)

Signs come by faith, not by the will of men, nor as they please, but by the will of God. Yea, *signs come* by faith, *unto mighty works,* for without faith *no man pleaseth God; and with whom God is angry he is not well pleased; wherefore, unto such he showeth no signs, only in wrath unto their condemnation. Wherefore, I, the Lord, am not pleased with those among you* who have sought after signs and wonders for faith, and not for the good of men unto my glory. (D&C 63:10-12.)

He that endureth in faith and doeth my will, *the same shall overcome, and shall receive an inheritance upon the earth when the day of transfiguration shall come.* (D&C 63:20.)

Establish a house, even a house of prayer, a house of fasting, a house of faith, a house of learning, a house of glory, a house of order, a house of God. (D&C 88:119; similar scripture, D&C 109:8.)

All they who suffer persecution for my name, and endure in faith, though they are called to lay down their lives for my sake *yet shall they partake of all this glory.* (D&C 101:35.)

All victory and glory is brought to pass unto you through your diligence, faithfulness, and prayers of faith. (D&C 103:36.)

[to Joseph Smith] Inasmuch as you are diligent and humble, and exercise the prayer of faith, behold, *I will soften the hearts of those to whom you are in debt, until I shall send means unto you for your deliverance.* (D&C 104:80.)

The decisions of these quorums, or either of them, are to be made in all righteousness, in holiness, and lowliness of heart, meekness and long suffering, and in faith, and virtue, and knowledge, temperance, patience, godliness, brotherly kindness and charity; *because the promise is,* if these things abound in them *they shall not be unfruitful in the knowledge of the Lord.* (D&C 107:30-31.)

Faithfulness

(See also Covenants; Enduring to the End; Faith; Obedience.)

Faithfulness involves loyalty, conscientiousness, and constancy. We can trust those who are faithful; we expect them to be faithful in keeping their promises.

The Lord expects the same of us, and the significance of being faithful to him is illustrated in a parable he related which tells of a man who delivers his goods to his servants before he travels to a far country. He gives five talents to one servant, two to another, and one to another. "After a long time the lord of those servants cometh, and reckoneth with them." The first servant now has ten talents, the second four. To both of them the master says, "Well done, thou good and faithful servant: thou hast been faithful over a few things, I will make thee ruler over many things: enter thou into the joy of thy lord." The third servant, however, failed to increase his talents; he is condemned to outer darkness, to "weeping and gnashing of teeth." (Matt. 25:14-30.)

Each of us has been given "talents," and the Lord commands us to be faithful, to increase them. In the parable the Lord says exactly the same thing to each of the first two servants, even though one had ten talents and the other four. Though we have different abilities and opportunities the Lord will judge us accordingly. Our responsibility is to be faithful in our own station in life. Each individual who lives true to his potential will someday hear from the Lord of Lords, "Well done, thou good and faithful servant."

Commandments and Promises

A faithful man *shall abound with blessings.* (Prov. 28:20.)

He that hath my word, let him speak my word faithfully. (Jer. 23:28.)

[to a faithful servant] Well done, thou good and faithful servant: thou has been faithful over a few things, *I will make thee ruler over many things: enter thou into the joy of thy lord.* (Matt. 25:21.)

Even so must [bishops' and deacons'] wives be grave, not slanderers, sober, faithful in all things. (1 Tim. 3:11.)

Fear none of those things which thou shalt suffer: behold, the devil shall cast some of you into prison, that ye may be tried; and ye shall have tribulation ten days: be thou faithful unto death, *and I will give thee a crown of life.* (Rev. 2:10.)

If it so be that we are faithful to him, *we shall obtain the land of promise; and ye shall know at some future period that the word of the Lord shall be fulfilled concerning the destruction of Jerusalem.* (1 Ne. 7:13.)

Be faithful unto his words, and choose eternal life, according to the will of his Holy Spirit. (2 Ne. 2:28.)

Now ye see that this is the true faith of God; yea, ye see that *God will support, and keep, and preserve us,* so long as we are faithful unto him, and unto our faith, and our religion; *and never will the Lord suffer that we shall be destroyed* except we should fall into transgression and deny our faith. (Alma 44:4.)

No unclean thing *can enter into his kingdom; therefore nothing entereth into his rest* save it be those who have washed their garments in my blood, because of their faith, and the repentance of all their sins, and their faithfulness unto the end. (3 Ne. 27:19.)

Blessed is he that is found faithful unto my name at the last day, *for he shall be lifted up to dwell in the kingdom prepared for him from the foundation of the world.* (Ether 4:19.)

[to Martin Harris] You should not have feared man more than God. Although men set at naught the counsels of God, and despise his words—yet you should have been faithful; *and he would have extended his arm and supported you against all the fiery darts of the adversary; and he would have been with you in every time of trouble.* (D&C 3:7-8.)

If thou art faithful in keeping my commandments, *thou shalt be lifted up at the last day.* (D&C 5:35.)

If thou wilt do good, yea, and hold out faithful to the end, *thou shalt be saved in the kingdom of God, which is the greatest of all the gifts of God; for there is no gift greater than the gift of salvation.* (D&C 6:13.)

Be faithful and diligent in keeping the commandments of God, *and I will encircle thee in the arms of my love.* (D&C 6:20.)

Be faithful, keep my commandments, *and ye shall inherit the kingdom of heaven.* (D&C 6:37.)

[to Oliver Cowdery] Do this thing which I have commanded you, *and you shall prosper.* Be faithful, and yield to no temptation. (D&C 9:13.)

[to Joseph Smith] See that you are faithful and continue on unto the finishing of the remainder of the work of translation as you have begun. (D&C 10:3.)

If thou art faithful and walk in the paths of virtue before me, *I will preserve thy life, and thou shalt receive an inheritance in Zion.* (D&C 25:2.)

Lift up your hearts and rejoice, and gird up your loins, and take upon you my whole armor, *that ye may be able to withstand the evil day,* having done all, *that ye may be able to stand.* Stand, therefore, having your loins girt about with truth, having on the breastplate of righteousness, and your feet shod with the preparation of the gospel of peace, which I have sent mine angels to commit unto you; taking the shield of faith *wherewith ye shall be able to quench all the fiery darts of the wicked;* and take the helmet of salvation, and the sword of my Spirit, which I will pour out upon you, and my word which I reveal unto you, and be agreed as touching all things whatsoever ye ask of me, and be faithful until I come, *and ye shall be caught up, that where I am ye shall be also.* (D&C 27:15-18.)

Be faithful unto the end, *and lo, I am with you.* (D&C 31:13; similar scripture, D&C 105:41.)

Be faithful, praying always, having your lamps trimmed and burning, and oil with you, *that you may be ready at the coming of the Bridegroom.* (D&C 33:17.)

If you are faithful, *behold, I am with you until I come—and verily, verily, I say unto you, I come quickly. I am your Lord and your Redeemer.* (D&C 34:11-12.)

Inasmuch as they are faithful, and exercise faith in me, *I will pour out my Spirit upon them in the day that they assemble themselves together.* (D&C 44:2.)

[regarding John Whitmer] *It shall be given him,* inasmuch as he is faithful, *by the Comforter, to write these things.* (D&C 47:4.)

Blessed are they who are faithful and endure, whether in life or in death, *for they shall inherit eternal life.* (D&C 50:5.)

Whoso is found a faithful, a just, and a wise steward *shall enter into the joy of his Lord, and shall inherit eternal life.* (D&C 51:19.)

[to Sidney Rigdon and Joseph Smith] *It shall also,* inasmuch as they are faithful, *be made known unto them the land of your inheritance. And inasmuch as they are not faithful, they shall be cut off, even as I will, as seemeth me good.* (D&C 52:5-6.)

He that is faithful *shall be made ruler over many things.* (D&C 52:13.)

He that is faithful, *the reward of the same shall be kept and blessed with much fruit.* (D&C 52:34.)

Blessed is he that keepeth my commandments, whether in life or in death; and he that is faithful in tribulation, *the reward of the same is greater in the kingdom of heaven.* (D&C 58:2.)

They shall also be crowned with blessings from above, yea, and with commandments not a few, and with revelations in their time—they that are faithful and diligent before me. (D&C 59:4.)

If they are not more faithful unto me, *it shall be taken away, even that which they have.* (D&C 60:3.)

He that is faithful among you [Joseph Smith and ten elders on the Missouri River] shall not perish by the waters. (D&C 61:6.)

Inasmuch as [Sidney Gilbert and William W. Phelps] are faithful *they shall be preserved, and I, the Lord, will be with them.* (D&C 61:10.)

I will that my saints should be assembled upon the land of Zion; and that every man should take righteousness in his hands and faithfulness upon his loins, and lift a warning voice unto the inhabitants of the earth; and declare both by word and by flight that desolation shall come upon the wicked. (D&C 63:36-37.)

He that is faithful and endureth *shall overcome the world.* (D&C 63:47.)

He that is faithful *shall be made strong in every place; and I, the Lord, will go with you.* (D&C 66:8.)

[to Joseph Smith and Sidney Rigdon] Confound your enemies; call upon them to meet you both in public and private; and inasmuch as ye are faithful *their shame shall be made manifest.* (D&C 71:7.)

He who is faithful and wise in time *is accounted worthy to inherit the mansions prepared for him of my Father.* (D&C 72:4.)

If ye are faithful *ye shall be laden with many sheaves, and crowned with honor, and glory, and immortality, and eternal life.* (D&C 75:5.)

Gird up your loins and be faithful, *and ye shall overcome all things, and be lifted up at the last day.* (D&C 75:22; similar scripture, D&C 75:16.)

He that is a faithful and wise steward *shall inherit all things.* (D&C 78:22.)

Be faithful; stand in the office which I have appointed unto you; succor the weak, lift up the hands which hang down, and strengthen the feeble knees. And if thou art faithful unto the end *thou shalt have a crown of immortality, and eternal life in the mansions which I have prepared in the house of my Father.* (D&C 81:5-6.)

Any man that shall go and preach this gospel of the kingdom, and fail not to continue faithful in all things, *shall not be weary in mind, neither darkened, neither in body, limb, nor joint; and a hair of his head shall not fall to the ground unnoticed. And they shall not go hungry, neither athirst.* (D&C 84:80.)

If you are faithful *you shall receive the fulness of the record of John.* (D&C 93:18.)

He will give unto the faithful *line upon line, precept upon precept.* (D&C 98:12.)

All victory and glory is brought to pass unto you through your diligence, faithfulness, and prayers of faith. (D&C 103:36.)

With promise immutable and unchangeable, that inasmuch as those whom I commanded were faithful *they should be blessed with a multiplicity of blessings;* but inasmuch as they were not faithful *they were nigh unto cursing.* (D&C 104:2-3.)

Inasmuch as they are faithful, *behold I will bless, and multiply blessings upon them....* And, inasmuch as they are faithful, *I will multiply blessings upon them and their seed after them, even a multiplicity of blessings.* (D&C 104:31, 33; similar scriptures, D&C 104:38, 42, 46.)

Inasmuch as ye are humble and faithful and call upon my name, *behold, I will give you the victory.* (D&C 104:82.)

I have prepared a great endowment and blessing to be poured out upon them, inasmuch as they are faithful and continue in humility before me. (D&C 105:12.)

Let all my people who dwell in the regions round about be very faithful. (D&C 105:23.)

Be ye faithful before me unto my name. (D&C 112:12.)

Be faithful until I come, for I come quickly; *and my reward is with me to recompense every man according as his work shall be.* (D&C 112:34.)

Let him be faithful and true in all things from henceforth, *and he shall be great in mine eyes.* (D&C 124:13.)

[to the Saints at Winter Quarters] Let every man use all his influence and property to remove this people to the place where the Lord shall locate a stake of Zion. And if ye do this with a pure heart, in all faithfulness, *ye shall be blessed; you shall be blessed in your flocks, and in your herds, and in your fields, and in your houses, and in your families.* (D&C 136:10-11.)

Ye can not yet bear my glory; but *ye shall behold it* if ye are faithful in keeping all my words that I have given you, from the days of Adam to Abraham, from Abraham to Moses, from Moses to Jesus and his apostles, and from Jesus and his apostles to Joseph Smith, whom I did call upon by mine angels, my ministering servants, and by mine own voice out of the heavens, to bring forth my work; which foundation he did lay, and was faithful; *and I took him to myself.* (D&C 136:37-38.)

False Gods

(See also Knowing God; Worship.)

We tend to become like those we worship. Perhaps that is one reason God commands us to worship him, the actual God of power, and abandon all false gods.

Man-made gods and idol worship have been a problem in all eras, preventing men from finding the true God and becoming like him. The children of Israel, surrounded by those who worshiped idols, were warned repeatedly, "Take heed to yourselves, that your heart be not deceived, and ye turn aside, and serve other gods, and worship them." (Deut. 11:16.)

The Apostle Paul spoke to the Athenians at Mars Hill: "Ye men of Athens, I perceive that in all things ye are too superstitious. For as I passed by, and beheld your devotions, I found an altar with this inscription, TO THE UNKNOWN GOD. Whom therefore ye ignorantly worship, him declare I unto you." (Acts 17:22-23.) Paul then gave a startling declaration to the Athenians steeped in their Hellenistic traditions.

Paul taught them that God made the world. God was not a statue dwelling in temples and was not to be worshiped as the Athenians worshiped their gods. Paul declared that men are God's offspring, and therefore they should not think that the Godhead is "like unto gold, or silver, or stone, graven by art and man's device." While God once "winked" at this ignorance, the time had now come for all men to repent. (Acts 17:24-30.)

The Athenians mocked Paul's teaching of the resurrection. The false gods, having no power, had not blinded the Athenians; the people had blinded themselves by yielding allegiance to traditions of foolishness. By worshiping false gods, they denied the godly potential in themselves.

Our idols today may not be as easily defined as those of the Athenians. The people we emulate, the endeavors or goods which command our dedication and resources may have become our gods. By devoting our lives to such false ends, we deny ourselves the blessings of wholeheartedly worshiping the true and living God.

Commandments and Promises

Thou shalt have no other gods before me. Thou shalt not make unto thee any graven image, or any likeness of any thing that is in heaven above, or that is in the earth beneath, or that is in the water under the earth: thou shalt not bow down thyself to them, nor serve them: for I the Lord thy God am a jealous God, *visiting the iniquity of the fathers upon the children unto the third and fourth generation of them* that hate me; *and shewing mercy unto thousands of them* that love me, and keep my commandments. (Ex. 20:3-6; similar scriptures, Deut. 5:7-10, Mosiah 12:35-36, 13:12-14.)

In all things that I have said unto you be circumspect: and make no mention of the name of other gods, neither let it be heard out of thy mouth. (Ex. 23:13.)

Thou shalt not bow down to their gods, nor serve them, nor do after their works: but thou shalt utterly overthrow them, and quite break down their images. (Ex. 23:24.)

Thou shalt worship no other god: for the Lord, whose name is Jealous, is a jealous God. *Lest thou make a covenant with the inhabitants of the land, and they go a whoring after their gods, and do sacrifice unto their gods, and one call thee, and thou eat of his sacrifice; and thou take of their daughters unto thy sons, and their daughters go a whoring after their gods, and make thy sons go a whoring after their gods.* Thou shalt make thee no molten gods. (Ex. 34:14-17.)

Turn ye not unto idols, nor make to yourselves molten gods: I am the Lord your God. (Lev. 19:4.)

Ye shall not go after other gods, of the gods of the people which are round about you; (for the Lord thy God is a jealous God among you) *lest the anger of the Lord thy God be kindled against thee, and destroy thee from off the face of the earth.* (Deut. 6:14-15.)

[regarding the Canaanites] The graven images of their gods shall ye burn with fire: thou shalt not desire the silver or gold that is on them, nor take it unto thee, *lest thou be snared therein: for it is an abomination to the Lord thy God.* (Deut. 7:25.)

Take heed to yourselves, that your heart be not deceived, and ye turn aside, and serve other gods, and worship them; *and then the Lord's wrath be kindled against you, and he shut up the heaven, that there be no rain, and that the land yield not her fruit; and lest ye perish quickly from off the good land which the Lord giveth you.* (Deut. 11:16-17.)

Neither shalt thou set thee up any image; which the Lord thy God hateth. (Deut. 16:22.)

Cursed be the man that maketh any graven or molten image, an abomination unto the Lord, the work of the craftsman, and putteth it in a secret place. (Deut. 27:15.)

When ye have transgressed the covenant of the Lord your God, which he commanded you, and have gone and served other gods, and bowed yourselves to them; *then shall the anger of the Lord be kindled against you, and ye shall perish quickly from off the good land which he hath given unto you.* (Josh. 23:16.)

Fear the Lord, and serve him in sincerity and in truth: and put away the gods which your fathers served on the other side of the flood, and in Egypt; and serve ye the Lord. (Josh. 24:14.)

Because they have forsaken me, and have burned incense unto other gods, *that they might provoke me to anger with all the works of their hands; therefore my wrath shall be kindled against this place, and shall not be quenched.* (2 Kgs. 22:17.)

Great is the Lord, and greatly to be praised: he also is to be feared above all gods. (1 Chr. 16:25.)

They that are far from thee *shall perish: thou hast destroyed all them* that go a whoring from thee. (Ps. 73:27.)

There shall no strange god be in thee; neither shalt thou worship any strange god. (Ps. 81:9.)

Confounded be all they that serve graven images, that boast themselves of idols: worship him, all ye gods. (Ps. 97:7.)

They shall be turned back, they shall be greatly be ashamed, that trust in graven images, that say to the molten images, Ye are our gods. (Isa. 42:17.)

I will bring evil upon this place [Tophet], the which whosoever heareth, his ears shall tingle. Because they have forsaken me, and have estranged this place, and have burned incense in it unto other gods, whom neither they nor their fathers have known, nor the kings of Judah, and have filled this place with the blood of innocents; they have built also the high places of Baal, to burn their sons with fire for burnt offerings unto Baal, which I commanded not, nor spake it, neither came it into my mind. . . . *And I will make void the counsel of Judah and Jerusalem in this place; and I will cause them to fall by the sword before their enemies, and by the hands of them that seek their lives: and their carcases will I give to be meat for the fowls of the heaven, and for the beasts of the earth. And I will make meat for the fowls of the heaven, and for the beasts of the earth. And I will make this city [Jerusalem] desolate, and an hissing; every one that passeth thereby shall be astonished and hiss because of all the plagues thereof. And I will cause them to eat the flesh of their sons and the flesh of their daughters, and they shall eat every one the flesh of his friend in the siege and straitness, wherewith their enemies, and they that seek their lives, shall straiten them.* (Jer. 19:3-9.)

The houses of Jerusalem, and the houses of the kings of Judah, shall be defiled as the place of Tophet, because of all the houses upon whose roofs they have burned incense unto all the host of heaven, and have poured out drink offerings unto other gods. (Jer. 19:13.)

If a man be just, and do that which is lawful and right, . . . neither hath lifted up his eyes to the idols of the house of Israel, . . . *he shall surely live, saith the Lord God.* (Ezek. 18:5-9.)

Cast ye away every man the abominations of his eyes, and defile not yourselves with the idols of Egypt: I am the Lord your God. (Ezek. 20:7.)

Walk ye not in the statutes of your fathers, neither observe their judgments, nor defile yourselves with their idols: I am the Lord your God; walk in my statutes, and keep my judgments, and do them; and hallow my sabbaths; *and they shall be a sign between me and you, that ye may know that I am the Lord your God.* (Ezek. 20:18-20.)

I am the Lord thy God from the land of Egypt, and thou shalt know no god but me: for there is no saviour beside me. (Hosea 13:4.)

The wrath of God is revealed from heaven against all ungodliness and unrighteousness of men, who hold the truth in unrighteousness; because that which may be known of God is manifest in them; for God hath shewed it unto them. For the invisible things of him from the creation of the world are clearly seen, being understood by the things that are made, even his eternal power and Godhead; *so that they are without excuse:* because that, when they knew God, they glorified him not as God, neither were thankful; but became vain in their imaginations, and their foolish heart was darkened. Professing themselves to be wise, they became fools, and changed the glory of the uncorruptible God into an image made like to corruptible man, and to birds, and four-footed beasts, and creeping things. (Rom. 1:18-23; see also JST Rom. 1:18.)

Neither be ye idolators. (1 Cor. 10:7.)

Flee from idolatry. (1 Cor. 10:14.)

No whoremonger, nor unclean person, nor covetous man, who is an idolater, *hath any inheritance in the kingdom of Christ and of God.* (Eph. 5:5.)

Keep yourselves from idols. (1 Jn. 5:21.)

Idolaters . . . *shall have their part in the lake which burneth with fire and brimstone: which is the second death.* (Rev. 21:8.)

Wo unto those that worship idols, *for the devil of all devils delighteth in them.* (2 Ne. 9:37.)

This people shall be scattered, and shall become a dark, a filthy, and a loathsome people, beyond the description of that which ever hath

been amongst us, yea, even that which hath been among the Lamanites, and this because of their unbelief and idolatry. (Morm. 5:15.)

*The anger of the Lord is kindled, and his sword is bathed in heaven,
and it shall fall upon the inhabitants of the earth. And the arm of the
Lord shall be revealed; and the day cometh* that they who will not
hear the voice of the Lord, neither the voice of his servants, neither
give heed to the words of the prophets and apostles, *shall be cut off
from among the people;* for they have strayed from mine ordinances,
and have broken mine everlasting covenant; they seek not the Lord to
establish his righteousness, but every man walketh in his own way,
and after his image of his own god, whose image is in the likeness of
the world, and whose substance is that of an idol, which waxeth old
and shall perish in Babylon. (D&C 1:13-16.)

The Son of Man cometh not in the form of a woman, neither of a man
traveling on the earth. Wherefore, be not deceived, but continue in
steadfastness, looking forth for the heavens to be shaken, and the
earth to tremble and to reel to and fro as a drunken man, and for the
valleys to be exalted, and for the mountains to be made low, and for
the rough places to become smooth—and all this when the angel
shall sound his trumpet. (D&C 49:22-23.)

Let [the elders] labor with their own hands that there be no idolatry
nor wickedness practised. (D&C 52:39.)

False Teachers and Teachings

(See also False Gods; Worldliness; Knowing God and His Ways.)

Without a sound knowledge of God and his ways, lacking the enlightenment of the Spirit or refusing the Spirit and hearkening to Satan, many pervert God's messages and lead men into warped perspective and sin. God's people thus are cautioned against being deceived by evil teachings. One such warning is given to the Church in latter-day revelation: "That which the Spirit testifies unto you even so I would that ye should do in all holiness of heart, walking uprightly before me, considering the end of your salvation, doing all things with prayer and thanksgiving, that ye may not be seduced by evil spirits, or doctrines of devils, or the commandments of men; for some are of men, and others of devils. Wherefore, beware lest ye are deceived; and that ye may not be deceived seek ye earnestly the best gifts, always remembering for what they are given." (D&C 46:7-8.)

Man has a godly ability to discern. However, mere reasoning or rationality is not enough to keep his mind free from false ideas. Righteousness and the Spirit are his only protection against becoming a false teacher and his only defense against being deceived by one.

Commandments and Promises

Therefore shall ye keep mine ordinance, that ye commit not any one of these abominable customs, which were committed before you, and that ye defile not yourselves therein: I am the Lord your God. (Lev. 18:30.)

Regard not them that have familiar spirits, neither seek after wizards, to be defiled by them: I am the Lord your God. (Lev. 19:31.)

The soul that turneth after such as have familiar spirits, and after wizards, to go a whoring after them, *I will even set my face against that soul, and will cut him off from among his people.* (Lev. 20:6.)

If there arise among you a prophet, or a dreamer of dreams, and giveth thee a sign or a wonder, and the sign or the wonder come to pass, whereof he spake unto thee, saying, Let us go after other gods, which thou hast not known, and let us serve them; thou shalt not hearken unto the words of that prophet, or that dreamer of dreams: for the Lord your God proveth you, to know whether ye love the Lord your God with all your heart and with all your soul. Ye shall walk after the Lord your God, and fear him, and keep his commandments, and obey his voice, and ye shall serve him, and cleave unto him. (Deut. 13:1-4.)

There shall not be found among you any one that maketh his son or daughter to pass through fire, or that useth divination, or an observer of times, or an enchanter, or a witch, or a charmer, or a consulter with familiar spirits, or a wizard, or a necromancer. For all that do these things *are an abomination unto the Lord: and because of these abominations the Lord thy God doth drive them out from before thee.* (Deut. 18:10-12.)

The prophet, which shall presume to speak a word in my name, which I have not commanded him to speak, or that shall speak in the name of other gods, *even that prophet shall die.* And if thou say in thine heart, How shall we know the word which the Lord hath not spoken? When a prophet speaketh in the name of the Lord, if the thing follow not, nor come to pass, *that is the thing which the Lord hath not spoken, but the prophet hath spoken it presumptuously:* thou shalt not be afraid of him. (Deut. 18:20-22.)

Cease, my son, to hear the instruction that causeth to err from the words of knowledge. (Prov. 19:27.)

Bring no more vain oblations; incense is an abomination unto me; the new moons and sabbaths, the calling of assemblies, I cannot away with; it is iniquity, even the solemn meeting. Your new moons and your appointed feasts my soul hateth: they are a trouble unto me; I am weary to bear them. (Isa. 1:13-14.)

Learn not the way of the heathen, and be not dismayed at the signs of heaven; for the heathen are dismayed at them. (Jer. 10:2.)

Woe be unto the pastors that destroy and scatter the sheep of my pasture! saith the Lord. Therefore thus saith the Lord God of Israel against the pastors that feed my people; Ye have scattered my flock, and driven them away, and have not visited them: *behold, I will visit upon you the evil of your doings, saith the Lord.* (Jer. 23:1-2.)

I have seen also in the prophets of Jerusalem an horrible thing: they commit adultery, and walk in lies: they strengthen also the hands of evildoers, that none doth return from his wickedness: they are all of them unto me as Sodom, and the inhabitants thereof as Gomorrah. Therefore thus saith the Lord of hosts concerning the prophets; Behold, *I will feed them with wormwood, and make them drink the water of gall:* for from the prophets of Jerusalem is profaneness gone forth into all the land. Thus saith the Lord of hosts, Hearken not unto the words of the prophets that prophesy unto you: *they make you vain:* they speak a vision of their own heart, and not out of the mouth of the Lord. (Jer. 23:14-16.)

Woe unto the foolish prophets, that follow their own spirit, and have seen nothing! (Ezek. 13:3.)

Thus saith the Lord concerning the prophets that make my people err, that bite with their teeth, and cry, Peace; and he that putteth not into their mouths, they even prepare war against him. *Therefore night shall be unto you, that ye shall not have a vision; and it shall be dark unto you, that ye shall not divine; and the sun shall go down over the prophets, and the day shall be dark over them. Then shall the seers be ashamed, and the diviners confounded: yea, they shall all cover their lips; for there is no answer of God.* (Micah 3:5-7.)

Beware of false prophets, which come to you in sheep's clothing, but inwardly they are ravening wolves. *Ye shall know them by their fruits. Do men gather grapes of thorns, or figs of thistles?* (Matt. 7:15-16; similar scripture, 3 Ne. 14:15-16.)

The scribes and the Pharisees sit in Moses' seat: all therefore whatsoever they bid you observe, that observe and do; but do not ye after their works: for they say, and do not. (Matt. 23:2-3.)

Woe unto you, ye blind guides, which say, Whosoever shall swear by the temple, it is nothing; but whosoever shall swear by the gold of the temple, he is a debtor! (Matt. 23:16.)

Jesus answered and said unto them, Take heed that no man deceive you. For many shall come in my name, saying, I am Christ; and shall deceive many. (Matt. 24:4-5; similar scriptures, Mark 13:5-6, JS-M 1:5-6.)

Then if any man shall say unto you, Lo, here is Christ, or there; believe it not. For there shall arise false Christs, and false prophets, and shall shew great signs and wonders; insomuch that, if it were possible, they shall deceive the very elect. (Matt. 24:23-24; similar scriptures, Mark 13:21-22, JS-M 1:21-22.)

If they shall say unto you, Behold, he is in the desert; go not forth: behold, he is in the secret chambers; believe it not. (Matt. 24:26; similar scripture, JS-M 1:25.)

Beware of the scribes, which love to go in long clothing, and love salutations in the marketplaces, and the chief seats in the synagogues, and the uppermost rooms at feasts: which devour widows' houses, and for a pretence make long prayers: *these shall receive greater damnation.* (Mark 12:38-40; similar scripture, Luke 20:46-47.)

Woe unto you, lawyers! for ye have taken away the key of knowledge: ye entered not in yourselves, and them that were entering in ye hindered. (Luke 11:52; see also JST Luke 11:53.)

Take heed that ye be not deceived: for many shall come in my name, saying, I am Christ; and the time draweth near: go ye not therefore after them. (Luke 21:8.)

Let us not therefore judge one another any more: but judge this rather, that no man put a stumblingblock or an occasion to fall in his brother's way. (Rom. 14:13.)

Mark them which cause divisions and offences contrary to the doctrine which ye have learned; and avoid them. (Rom. 16:17.)

If any man preach any other gospel unto you than that ye have received, *let him be accursed.* (Gal. 1:9.)

Let no man deceive you with vain words: for because of these things *cometh the wrath of God upon the children of disobedience.* Be not ye therefore partakers with them. (Eph. 5:6-7.)

Beware of evil workers, beware of the concision. (Philip. 3:2.)

Beware lest any man spoil you through philosophy and vain deceit, after the tradition of men, after the rudiments of the world, and not after Christ. (Col. 2:8.)

Let no man beguile you of your reward in a voluntary humility and worshipping of angels, intruding into those things which he hath not seen, vainly puffed up by his fleshly mind. (Col. 2:18.)

Let no man decieve you by any means. (2 Thes. 2:3.)

[Paul to Timothy] I besought thee to abide still at Ephesus, when I went into Macedonia, that thou mightest charge some that they teach no other doctrine, neither give heed to fables and endless genealogies, which minister questions, rather than godly edifying which is in faith: so do. (1 Tim. 1:3-4.)

Now the Spirit speaketh expressly, that in the latter times some shall depart from the faith, giving heed to seducing spirits, and doctrines of devils; speaking lies in hypocrisy; having their conscience seared with a hot iron; forbidding to marry, and commanding to abstain from meats. . . . If thou put the brethren in remembrance of these things, *thou shalt be a good minister of Jesus Christ, nourished up in the words of faith and of good doctrine, whereunto thou hast attained.* But refuse profane and old wives' fables, and exercise thyself rather unto godliness. (1 Tim. 4:1-7.)

All that will live godly in Christ Jesus shall suffer persecution. But evil men and seducers shall wax worse and worse, deceiving, and being deceived. But continue thou in the things which thou hast learned and hast been assured of, knowing of whom thou hast learned them; and that from a child thou hast known the holy scriptures, *which are able to make thee wise unto salvation* through faith which is in Christ Jesus. (2 Tim. 3:12-15.)

Be not carried about with divers and strange doctrines. For it is a good thing that the heart be established with grace; not with meats, which have not profited them that have been occupied therein. (Heb. 13:9.)

Be sober, be vigilant; because your adversary the devil, as a roaring lion, walketh about, seeking whom he may devour: whom resist stedfast in the faith, knowing that the same afflictions are accomplished in your brethren that are in the world. (1 Pet. 5:8-9.)

There were false prophets also among the people, even as there shall be false teachers among you, who privily shall bring in damnable heresies, even denying the Lord that brought them, *and bring upon themselves swift destruction.* And many shall follow their pernicious ways; by reason of whom the way of truth shall be evil spoken of. And through covetousness shall they with feigned words make merchandise of you: *whose judgment now of a long time lingereth not, and their damnation slumbereth not.* (2 Pet. 2:1-3.)

The Lord knoweth how to deliver the godly out of temptations, and to reserve the unjust unto the day of judgment to be punished: but chiefly them that walk after the flesh in the lust of uncleanness, and despise government. Presumptuous are they, selfwilled, they are not afraid to speak evil of dignities. . . . But these, as natural brute beasts, *made to be taken and destroyed,* speak evil of the things that they understand not; *and shall utterly perish in their own corruption; and shall receive the reward of unrighteousness,* as they that count it pleasure to riot in the day time. Spots they are and blemishes, sporting themselves with their own deceivings while they feast with you; having eyes full of adultery, and that cannot cease from sin; beguiling unstable souls: an heart they have exercised with covetous practices; cursed children: which have forsaken the right way, and are gone astray. . . . These are wells without water, clouds that are carried with a tempest; *to whom the mist of darkness is reserved for ever.* (2 Pet. 2:9-17.)

For when they speak great swelling words of vanity, they allure through the lusts of the flesh, through much wantonness, those that were clean escaped from them who live in error. While they promise them liberty, *they themselves are the servants of corruption: for of whom a man is overcome, of the same is he brought in bondage.* (2 Pet. 2:18-19.)

As also in all his [Paul's] epistles, speaking in them of these things; in which are some things hard to be understood, which they that are unlearned and unstable wrest, as they do also the other scriptures, *unto their own destruction.* Ye therefore, beloved, seeing ye know these things before, beware lest ye also, being led away with the error of the wicked, *fall from your own stedfastness.* (2 Pet. 3:16-17; see also JST 2 Pet. 3:17.)

Believe not every spirit, but try the spirits whether they are of God: because many false prophets are gone out into the world. (1 Jn. 4:1.)

Many deceivers are entered into the world, who confess not that Jesus Christ is come in the flesh. This is a deceiver and an antichrist. Look to yourselves, *that we lose not those things which we have wrought, but that we receive a full reward.* Whosoever transgresseth, and abideth not in the doctrine of Christ, *hath not God.* He that abideth in the doctrine of Christ, *he hath both the Father and the Son.* If there come any unto you, and bring not this doctrine, receive him not into your house, neither bid him God speed: for he that biddeth him God speed is partaker of his evil deeds. (2 Jn. 1:7-11.)

The fearful, and unbelieving, and the abominable, and murderers, and whoremongers, and sorcerers, and idolaters, and all liars, *shall have their part in the lake which burneth with fire and brimstone: which is the second death.* (Rev. 21:8; see also D&C 63:17.)

The time speedily shall come that all churches which are built up to get gain, and all those who are built up to get power over the flesh, and those who are built up to become popular in the eyes of the world, and those who seek the lusts of the flesh and the things of the world, and to do all manner of iniquity; yea, in fine, all those who belong to the kingdom of the devil *are they who need fear, and tremble, and quake; they are those who must be brought low in the dust; they are those who must be consumed as stubble; and this is according to the words of the prophet.* (1 Ne. 22:23.)

When they are learned they think they are wise, and they hearken not unto the counsel of God, for they set it aside, supposing they know of themselves, *wherefore, their wisdom is foolishness and it profiteth them not. And they shall perish.* (2 Ne. 9:28-29.)

Wo unto them that call evil good, and good evil, that put darkness for light, and light for darkness, that put bitter for sweet, and sweet for bitter! *Wo* unto the wise in their own eyes and prudent in their own sight! (2 Ne. 15:20-21.)

He commandeth that there shall be no priestcrafts; for, behold, priestcrafts are that men preach and set themselves up for a light unto the world, that they may get gain and praise of the world; but they seek not the welfare of Zion. (2 Ne. 26:29.)

O the wise, and the learned, and the rich, that are puffed up in the pride of their hearts, and all those who preach false doctrines, and all those who commit whoredoms, and pervert the right way of the Lord, *wo, wo, wo be unto them, saith the Lord God Almighty, for they shall be thrust down to hell!* (2 Ne. 28:15.)

Wo be unto him that crieth: All is well! Yea, *wo* be unto him that hearkeneth unto the precepts of men, and denieth the power of God, and the gift of the Holy Ghost! Yea, *wo* be unto him that saith: We have received, and we need no more! And in fine, *wo* unto all those who tremble, and are angry because of the truth of God! For behold, he that is built upon the rock *receiveth it with gladness;* and he that is built upon a sandy foundation *trembleth lest he shall fall. Wo* be unto him that shall say: We have received the word of God, and we need no more of the word of God, for we have enough! (2 Ne. 28:25-29.)

I say unto you, *wo* be unto you for perverting the ways of the Lord! For if ye understand these things ye have not taught them; therefore, ye have perverted the ways of the Lord. (Mosiah 12:26.)

Trust no one to be your teacher nor your minister, except he be a man of God, walking in his ways and keeping his commandments. (Mosiah 23:14.)

The good shepherd doth call after you; and if you will hearken unto his voice *he will bring you into his fold, and ye are his sheep*; and he commandeth you that ye suffer no ravenous wolf to enter among you, *that ye may not be destroyed.* (Alma 5:60.)

O ye wicked and ye perverse generation; ye hardened and ye stiffnecked people, how long will ye suppose that the Lord will suffer you? Yea, how long will ye suffer yourselves to be led by foolish and blind guides? Yea, how long will ye choose darkness rather than light? *Yea, behold, the anger of the Lord is already kindled against you; behold, he hath cursed the land because of your iniquity. And behold, the time cometh that he curseth your riches, that they become slippery, that ye cannot hold them; and in the days of your poverty ye cannot retain them. And in the days of your poverty ye shall cry unto the Lord; and in vain shall ye cry, for your desolation is already come upon you, and your destruction is made sure; and then shall ye weep and howl in that day, saith the Lord of Hosts. And then shall ye lament, and say: O that I had repented, and had not killed the prophets, and stoned them, and cast them out. Yea, in that day ye shall say: O that we had remembered the Lord our God in the day that he gave us our riches, and then they would not have become slippery that we should lose them; for behold, our riches are gone from us. Behold, we lay a tool here and on the morrow it is gone; and behold, our swords are taken from us in the day we have sought them for battle. Yea, we have hidden up our treasures and they have slipped away from us, because of the curse of the land.* (Hel. 13:29-35.)

At that day when the Gentiles shall sin against my gospel, and shall reject the fulness of my gospel, and shall be lifted up in the pride of their hearts above all nations, and above all the people of the whole earth, and shall be filled with all manner of lyings, and of deceits, and of mischiefs, and all manner of hypocrisy, and murders, and priestcrafts, and whoredoms, and of secret abominations; and if they shall do all those things, and shall reject the fulness of my gospel, *behold, saith the Father, I will bring the fulness of my gospel from among them.* (3 Ne. 16:10.)

Whatsoever nation shall uphold such secret combinations, to get power and gain, until they shall spread over the nation, behold, *they shall be destroyed; for the Lord will not suffer that the blood of the saints, which shall be shed by them, shall always cry unto him from the ground for vengeance upon them and yet avenge them not.* (Ether 8:22.)

He that supposeth that little children need baptism *is in the gall of bitterness and in the bonds of iniquity, for he hath neither faith, hope, nor charity; wherefore, should he be cut off while in the thought, he must go down to hell.* (Moro. 8:14.)

He that saith that little children need baptism denieth the mercies of Christ, and setteth at naught the atonement of him and the power of his redemption. *Wo unto such, for they are in danger of death, hell, and endless torment.* I speak it boldly; God hath commanded me. Listen unto them and give heed, *or they stand against you at the judgment-seat of Christ.* (Moro. 8:20-21.)

It is they who do not fear me, neither keep my commandments but build up churches unto themselves to get gain, yea, and all those that do wickedly and build up the kingdom of the devil—yea, verily, verily, I say unto you, that *it is they that I will disturb, and cause to tremble and shake to the center.* (D&C 10:56.)

This is my doctrine—whosoever repenteth and cometh unto me, *the same is* my church. Whosoever declareth more or less than this, the same is not of me, but is against me; *therefore he is not of my church.* (D&C 10:67-68.)

This shall be a law unto you, that ye receive not the teachings of any that shall come before you as revelations or commandments; and this I give unto you *that you may not be deceived, that you may know they are not of me.* (D&C 43:5-6.)

That which the Spirit testifies unto you even so I would that ye should do in all holiness of heart, walking uprightly before me, considering the end of your salvation, doing all things with prayer and thanksgiving, *that ye may not be seduced by evil spirits, or doctrines of devils, or the commandments of men; for some are of men, and others of devils. Wherefore, beware lest ye are deceived; and that ye may not be deceived* seek ye earnestly the best gifts, always remembering for what they are given. (D&C 46:7-8.)

Whoso forbiddeth to marry *is not ordained of God*, for marriage is ordained of God unto man. (D&C 49:15.)

Whoso forbiddeth to abstain from meats, that man should not eat the same, *is not ordained of God*. (D&C 49:18.)

Wo unto them that are deceivers and hypocrites, *for, thus saith the Lord, I will bring them to judgment*. (D&C 50:6.)

I, the Lord, have said that the fearful, and the unbelieving, and all liars, and whosoever loveth and maketh a lie, and the whoremonger, and the sorcerer, *shall have their part in that lake which burneth with fire and brimstone, which is the second death*. (D&C 63:17; see also Rev. 21:8.)

False Witness, Bearing

(See also Honesty.)

The Lord's warning not to bear false witness is important enough to be included in the Ten Commandments. But what does it mean to bear false witness? It means to lie, but much more is implied than just speaking falsehoods. A witness is one called on to testify truthfully before others. A false witness betrays that truth: he knowingly deceives. He bears testimony against the truth, to the detriment of others.

The scriptures make it clear that we can bear false witness in many ways: by allowing others to be deceived without actually speaking untrue words, by being hypocrites, by failing to testify of the truth because of fear or embarrassment, by plotting revenge, or by accusing others falsely.

The Lord is a God of truth; the devil is the father of lies, a liar from the beginning. The more strictly we obey the commandment to not bear false witness, the closer we move toward godhood.

Commandments and Promises

Thou shalt not bear false witness against thy neighbour. (Ex. 20:16; similar scriptures, Deut. 5:20, Matt. 19:18, Mosiah 13:23.)

These six things doth the Lord hate: yea, seven are an abomination unto him: a lying tongue, . . . an heart that deviseth wicked imaginations, . . . a false witness that speaketh lies. (Prov. 6:16-19.)

Be not a witness against thy neighbour without cause; and deceive not with thy lips. Say not, I will do so to him as he hath done to me: I will render to the man according to his work. (Prov. 24:28-29.)

Let none of you imagine evil in your hearts against his neighbour; and love no false oath: for all these are things *that I hate*, saith the Lord. (Zech. 8:17.)

I will come near to you in judgment; and I will be a swift witness against . . . false swearers. (Mal. 3:5; similar scripture, 3 Ne. 24:5.)

The soldiers likewise demanded of him, saying, And what shall we do? And he said unto them, Do violence to no man, neither accuse any falsely. (Luke 3:14.)

Men shall be . . . boasters, . . . trucebreakers, false accusers, . . . traitors. . . . *But they shall proceed no further: for their folly shall be manifest unto all men.* (2 Tim. 3:2-9.)

Speak thou the things which become sound doctrine: . . . the aged women likewise, that they be in behaviour as becometh holiness, not false accusers. (Titus 2:1-3.)

Those who swear falsely against my servants, that they might bring them into bondage and death—*wo unto them; because they have of-fended my little ones they shall be severed from the ordinances of mine house. Their basket shall not be full, their houses and their barns shall perish, and they themselves shall be despised by those that flattered them. They shall not have right to the priesthood, nor their posterity after them from generation to generation. It had been better for them that a millstone had been hanged about their necks, and they drowned in the depth of the sea.* (D&C 121:18-23.)

Family Responsibilities

Most of us spend most of our lives as part of a living family. Our duties may shift from being a son to being a father, or from being a great-grandchild of an ancestor whose temple work needs doing to being a grandmother, but family responsibilities always remain in the eternal family.

Children have certain responsibilities to their parents, and parents have responsibilities in return. These duties are clear in scripture. Children are to honor their parents and to obey them in righteousness. Parents are to discipline their children lovingly into correct behavior and an understanding of God. Families are responsible for those among them who are without other support.

God could have created us so that our offspring could raise themselves without parents, or so that our offspring would require only minimal training. For instance, butterflies aren't trained by their parents, and fish eggs simply hatch into fish, without parental coddling. But we were created so that much of our adult life is spent in parenthood.

Why would God make us spend decades raising offspring? One answer might be that man's growth involves learning to be part of a family—particularly learning to be a parent. God is not only raising children, he is raising parents—parents who can someday fulfill eternal parental roles as God fulfills His.

Commandments and Promises

Honour thy father and thy mother: *that thy days may be long upon the land which the Lord thy God giveth thee.* (Ex. 20:12; similar scriptures, Matt. 19:19, 1 Ne. 17:55, Mosiah 13:20; see also Deut. 5:16.)

Ye shall fear every man his mother, and his father. (Lev. 19:3.)

Only take heed to thyself, and keep thy soul diligently, lest thou forget the thing which thine eyes have seen, and lest they depart from thy heart all the days of thy life: but teach them thy sons, and thy sons' sons. (Deut. 4:9.)

Honour thy father and thy mother, as the Lord thy God hath commanded thee; *that thy days may be prolonged, and that it may go well with thee, in the land which the Lord thy God giveth thee.* (Deut. 5:16; see also Ex. 20:12.)

Ye shall teach [the Lord's words to] your children, speaking of them when thou sittest in thine house, and when thou walkest by the way, when thou liest down, and when thou risest up. And thou shalt write them upon the door posts of thine house, and upon thy gates: *that your days may be multiplied, and the days of your children, in the land which the Lord sware unto your fathers to give them, as the days of heaven upon the earth.* (Deut. 11:19-21.)

Cursed be he that setteth light by his father or his mother. (Deut. 27:16.)

My son, hear the instruction of thy father, and forsake not the law of thy mother. (Prov. 1:8.)

Hear, ye children, the instruction of a father, and attend to know understanding. For I give you good doctrine, forsake ye not my law. (Prov. 4:1-2.)

He that troubleth his own house *shall inherit the wind.* (Prov. 11:29.)

Chasten thy son while there is hope, and let not thy soul spare for his crying. (Prov. 19:18.)

The just man walketh in his integrity: *his children are blessed after him.* (Prov. 20:7.)

Withhold not correction from the child. (Prov. 23:13.)

Hearken unto thy father that begat thee, and despise not thy mother when she is old. (Prov. 23:22.)

The rod and reproof *give wisdom:* but a child left to himself *bringeth his mother to shame.* (Prov. 29:15.)

Correct thy son, *and he shall give thee rest; yea, he shall give delight unto thy soul.* (Prov. 29:17.)

All thy children shall be taught of the Lord; *and great shall be the peace of thy children.* (Isa. 54:13.)

Children, obey your parents in the Lord: for this is right. Honour thy father and mother; (which is the first commandment with promise;) *that it may be well with thee, and thou mayest live long on the earth.* And ye fathers, provoke not your children to wrath: but bring them up in the nurture and admonition of the Lord. (Eph. 6:1-4.)

Wives, submit yourselves unto your own husbands, as it is fit in the Lord. Husbands, love your wives, and be not bitter against them. Children, obey your parents in all things: *for this is well pleasing unto the Lord.* Fathers, provoke not your children to anger, *lest they be discouraged.* (Col. 3:18-21.)

[Jacob to the Nephites] Ye shall remember your children, how that ye have grieved their hearts because of the example that ye have set before them; and also remember that ye may, because of your filthiness, *bring your children unto destruction, and their sins shall be heaped upon your heads at the last day.* (Jac. 3:10.)

Ye will not suffer your children that they go hungry, or naked; neither will ye suffer that they transgress the laws of God, and fight and quarrel one with another, and serve the devil, who is the master of sin, or who is the evil spirit which hath been spoken of by our fathers, he being an enemy to all righteousness. But ye will teach them to walk in the ways of truth and soberness; ye will teach them to love one another, and to serve one another. (Mosiah 4:14-15.)

The Spirit of the Lord doth say unto me [Alma]: Command thy children to do good, *lest they lead away the hearts of many people to destruction;* therefore I command you, my son, in the fear of God, that ye refrain from your iniquities. (Alma 39:12.)

The Lord has said that: Ye shall defend your families even unto bloodshed. (Alma 43:47.)

Every member of the church of Christ having children is to bring them unto the elders before the church, who are to lay their hands upon them in the name of Jesus Christ, and bless them in his name. (D&C 20:70.)

[to Thomas B. Marsh] Govern your house in meekness. (D&C 31:9.)

Inasmuch as parents have children in Zion, or in any of her stakes which are organized, that teach them not to understand the doctrine of repentance, faith in Christ the Son of the living God, and of baptism and the gift of the Holy Ghost by the laying on of the hands, when eight years old, *the sin be upon the heads of the parents.* For this shall be a law unto the inhabitants of Zion, or in any of her stakes which are organized. And their children shall be baptized for the remission of their sins when eight years old, and receive the laying on of the hands. And they shall also teach their children to pray, and to walk uprightly before the Lord. (D&C 68:25-28.)

Every man who is obliged to provide for his own family, let him provide, *and he shall in nowise lose his crown.* (D&C 75:28.)

Women have claim on their husbands for their maintenance, until their husbands are taken. (D&C 83:2.)

All children have claim upon their parents for their maintenance until they are of age. (D&C 83:4.)

I have commanded you to bring up your children in light and truth. (D&C 93:40.)

A commandment I give unto you [Frederick G. Williams]—*if you will be delivered* you shall set in order your own house, for there are many things that are not right in your house. (D&C 93:43.)

My servant Newel K. Whitney also, a bishop of my church, hath need to be chastened, and set in order his family, and see that they are more diligent and concerned at home, and pray always, *or they shall be removed out of their place.* (D&C 93:50.)

Seek diligently to turn the hearts of the children to their fathers, and the hearts of the fathers to the children; and again, the hearts of the Jews unto the prophets, and the prophets unto the Jews; *lest I come and smite the whole earth with a curse, and all flesh be consumed before me.* (D&C 98:16-17.)

Let us present in his holy temple, when it is finished, a book containing the records of our dead, which shall be worthy of all acceptation. (D&C 128:24.)

I give unto you a commandment, to teach these things freely unto your children, saying: That by reason of transgression cometh the fall, which fall bringeth death, and inasmuch as ye were born into the world by water, and blood, and the spirit, which I have made, and so became of dust a living soul, even so ye must be born again into the kingdom of heaven, of water, and of the Spirit, and be cleansed by blood, even the blood of mine Only Begotten; *that ye might be sanctified from all sin, and enjoy the words of eternal life in this world, and eternal life in the world to come, even immortal glory.* (Moses 6:58-59.)

Fasting

(See also Prayer; Sabbath Observance.)

Fasting, like prayer, must be done correctly to be effective. Correct fasting sharpens our spiritual perception, demonstrates our faith, empowers our prayers, and ennobles our motives. The Lord tells us how to fast so that we can be worthy of the vast blessings available through fasting.

Fasting cannot stand alone. Without prayer, our fast is not consecrated to the Lord. If we do not direct our thoughts and desires heavenward and direct our goodness toward our fellowmen, we are not fed spiritually by our Father.

Commandments and Promises

Ye fast for strife and debate, and to smite with the fist of wickedness: ye shall not fast as ye do this day, to make your voice to be heard on high. Is it such a fast that I have chosen? a day for a man to afflict his soul? is it to bow down his head as a bulrush, and to spread sackcloth and ashes under him? wilt thou call this a fast, and an acceptable day to the Lord? Is not this the fast that I have chosen? to loose the bands of wickedness, to undo the heavy burdens, and to let the oppressed go free, and that ye break every yoke? Is it not to deal thy bread to the hungry, and that thou bring the poor that are cast out to thy house? when thou seest the naked, that thou cover him; and that thou hide not thyself from thine own flesh? *Then shall thy light break forth as the morning, and thine health shall spring forth speedily: and thy righteousness shall go before thee; the glory of the Lord shall be thy rereward. Then shall thou call, and the Lord shall answer; thou shalt cry, and he shall say, Here I am.* If thou take away from the midst of thee the yoke, the putting forth of the finger, and speaking vanity; and if thou draw out thy soul to the hungry, and satisfy the afflicted soul; *then shall thy light rise in obscurity, and thy darkness be as the noonday: and the Lord shall guide thee continually, and satisfy thy soul in drought, and make fat thy bones: and thou shalt be like a watered garden, and like a spring of water, whose waters fail not.* (Isa. 58:4-11.)

164

Turn ye even to me with all your heart, and with fasting, and with weeping, and with mourning: and rend your heart, and not your garments, and turn unto the Lord your God. (Joel 2:12-13.)

Moreover when ye fast, be not, as the hypocrites, of a sad countenance: for they disfigure their faces, that they may appear unto men to fast. Verily I say unto you, *They have their reward.* But thou, when thou fastest, anoint thine head, and wash thy face; that thou appear not unto men to fast, but unto thy Father which is in secret: *and thy Father, which seeth in secret, shall reward thee openly.* (Matt. 6:16-18; similar scripture, 3 Ne. 13:16-18.)

Continue in fasting and praying, and endure to the end; *and as the Lord liveth ye will be saved.* (Omni 1:26.)

The children of God were commanded that they should gather themselves together oft, and join in fasting and mighty prayer in behalf of the welfare of the souls of those who knew not God. (Alma 6:6.)

[The sons of Mosiah] had given themselves to much prayer, and fasting; *therefore they had the spirit of prophecy, and the spirit of revelation, and when they taught, they taught with power and authority of God.* (Alma 17:3.)

On [the Lord's holy] day thou shalt do none other thing, only let thy food be prepared with singleness of heart *that thy fasting may be perfect, or, in other words, that thy joy may be full.* Verily, this is fasting and prayer, or in other words, rejoicing and prayer. Inasmuch as ye do these things with thanksgiving, with cheerful hearts and countenances, not with much laughter, for this is sin, but with a glad heart and a cheerful countenance—verily I say, that inasmuch as ye do this, *the fulness of the earth is yours, the beasts of the field and the fowls of the air, and that which climbeth upon the trees and walketh upon the earth.* (D&C 59:13-16.)

Continue in prayer and fasting from this time forth. (D&C 88:76.)

Establish a house, even a house of prayer, a house of fasting. (D&C 88:119; similar scripture, D&C 109:8.)

Fearing God

(See also Knowing God and His Ways; Worship.)

God wants us to love him, but he also wants us to be aware of his power. This awareness, combined with respect and awe, is the "fear" of God. We must realize that God is not a whimsical being far removed from our lives. He is a God of power: omnipotent and omniscient.

Deuteronomy records that the "Lord commanded us to do all these statutes, to fear the Lord our God, *for our good always.*" (Deut. 6:24, italics added.) God does not command us to fear him simply to build his ego; rather, he commands us for our own benefit.

Such awareness, or fear, does more than keep us righteous for fear of recrimination. It helps us increase the godliness in ourselves through awareness of the vast duties and powers God has that we might obtain. We are thus taught to reverence what we can become.

Commandments and Promises

Thou shalt fear the Lord thy God, and serve him, and shalt swear by his name. (Deut. 6:13.)

The Lord commanded us to do all these statutes, to fear the Lord our God, *for our own good always, that he might preserve us alive, as it is at this day.* (Deut. 6:24.)

Thou shalt keep the commandments of the Lord thy God, to walk in his ways, and to fear him. (Deut. 8:6.)

Israel, what doth the Lord thy God require of thee, but to fear the Lord thy God, to walk in all his ways, and to love him, and to serve the Lord thy God with all thy heart and with all thy soul, to keep the commandments of the Lord, and his statutes, which I command thee this day *for thy good?* (Deut. 10:12-13.)

Thou shalt fear the Lord thy God; him shalt thou serve, and to him shalt thou cleave, and swear by his name. (Deut. 10:20.)

Ye shall walk after the Lord your God, and fear him, and keep his commandments, and obey his voice, and ye shall serve him, and cleave unto him. (Deut. 13:4.)

Fear the Lord, and serve him in sincerity and in truth: and put away the gods which your fathers served on the other side of the flood, and in Egypt; and serve ye the Lord. (Josh. 24:14.)

If ye will fear the Lord, and serve him, and obey his voice, and not rebel against the commandment of the Lord, *then shall both ye and also the king that reigneth over you continue following the Lord your God;* but if ye will not obey the voice of the Lord, but rebel against the commandment of the Lord, *then shall the hand of the Lord be against you, as it was against your fathers.* (1 Sam. 12:14-15.)

Ye that fear the Lord, praise him; all ye the seed of Jacob, glorify him; and fear him, all ye the seed of Israel. (Ps. 22:23.)

Oh how great is thy goodness, which thou hast laid up for them that fear thee; *which thou hast wrought* for them that trust in thee before the sons of men! *Thou shalt hide them in the secret of thy presence from the pride of man: thou shalt keep them secretly in a pavilion from the strife of tongues.* (Ps. 31:19-20.)

The eye of the Lord is upon them that fear him, upon them that hope in his mercy; *to deliver their soul from death, and to keep them alive in famine.* (Ps. 33:18-19.)

The angel of the Lord encampeth round about them that fear him, *and delivereth them.* (Ps. 34:7.)

O fear the Lord, ye his saints: *for there is no want* to them that fear him. (Ps. 34:9.)

O worship the Lord in the beauty of holiness: fear before him, all the earth. (Ps. 96:9.)

The fear of the Lord *is the beginning of wisdom.* (Ps. 111:10; see also Prov. 9:10.)

Praise ye the Lord. *Blessed* is the man that feareth the Lord, that delighteth greatly in his commandments. *His seed shall be mighty upon the earth: the generation of the upright shall be blessed. Wealth and riches shall be in his house: and his righteousness endureth for ever.* (Ps. 112:1-3.)

He will bless them that fear the Lord, both small and great. (Ps. 115:13.)

Blessed is every one that feareth the Lord; that walketh in his ways. *For thou shalt eat the labour of thine hands: happy shalt thou be, and it shall be well with thee. Thy wife shall be as a fruitful vine by the sides of thine house: thy children like olive plants round about thy table. Behold, that thus shall the man be blessed* that feareth the Lord. *The Lord shall bless thee out of Zion: and thou shalt see the good of Jerusalem all the days of thy life. Yea, thou shalt see thy children's children, and peace upon Israel.* (Ps. 128:1-6.)

He will fulfil the desire of them that fear him: *he also will hear their cry, and will save them.* (Ps. 145:19.)

The Lord taketh pleasure in them that fear him, in those that hope in his mercy. (Ps. 147:11.)

The fear of the Lord is to hate evil: pride, and arrogancy, and the evil way, and the froward mouth, *do I hate.* (Prov. 8:13.)

The fear of the Lord *is the beginning of wisdom:* and the knowledge of the holy *is understanding.* (Prov. 9:10; see also Ps. 111:10.)

The fear of the Lord *prolongeth days: but the years* of the wicked *shall be shortened.* (Prov. 10:27.)

In the fear of the Lord *is strong confidence: and his children shall have a place of refuge.* (Prov. 14:26.)

Let not thine heart envy sinners: but be thou in the fear of the Lord all the day long. (Prov. 23:17.)

Happy is the man that feareth alway: but he that hardeneth his heart *shall fall into mischief.* (Prov. 28:14.)

Favour *is deceitful*, and beauty *is vain:* but a woman that feareth the Lord, *she shall be praised.* (Prov. 31:30.)

In the multitude of dreams and many words *there are also divers vanities:* but fear thou God. (Eccl. 5:7.)

Fear God, and keep his commandments: for this is the whole duty of man. For God shall bring every work into judgment, with every secret thing, whether it be good, or whether it be evil. (Eccl. 12:13-14.)

Sanctify the Lord of hosts himself; and let him be your fear, and let him be your dread. (Isa. 8:13; similar scripture, 2 Ne. 18:13.)

Then they that feared the Lord spake often one to another: *and the Lord hearkened, and heard it, and a book of remembrance was written before him* for them that feared the Lord, and that thought upon his name. (Mal. 3:16; similar scripture, 3 Ne. 24:16.)

Unto you that fear my name *shall the Sun of righteousness arise with healing in his wings; and ye shall go forth, and grow up as calves of the stall. And ye shall tread down the wicked; for they shall be ashes under the soles of your feet in the day that I shall do this, saith the Lord of hosts.* (Mal. 4:2-3; similar scripture, 3 Ne. 25:2-3.)

His mercy is on them that fear him from generation to generation. (Luke 1:50.)

Be not high-minded, but fear. (Rom. 11:20.)

Let us cleanse ourselves from all filthiness of the flesh and spirit, perfecting holiness in the fear of God. (2 Cor. 7:1.)

[Submit] yourselves one to another in the fear of God. (Eph. 5:21.)

Wherefore we receiving a kingdom which cannot be moved, let us have grace, *whereby we may serve God acceptably with reverence and godly fear.* (Heb. 12:28.)

If ye call on the Father, who without respect of persons judgeth according to every man's work, pass the time of your sojourning here in fear. (1 Pet. 1:17.)

Fear God. (1 Pet. 2:17.)

Sanctify the Lord God in your hearts: and be ready always to give an answer to every man that asketh you a reason of the hope that is in you with meekness and fear: having a good conscience; that, whereas they speak evil of you, as of evildoers, *they may be ashamed that falsely accuse your good conversation in Christ.* (1 Pet. 3:15-16.)

Come unto the Lord with all your heart, and work out your own salvation with fear and trembling before him. (Morm. 9:27.)

He that trembleth under my power *shall be made strong, and shall bring forth fruits of praise and wisdom, according to the revelations and truths which I have given you.* (D&C 52:17.)

I, the Lord, am merciful and gracious unto those who fear me, *and delight to honor those* who serve me in righteousness and in truth unto the end. *Great shall be their reward and eternal shall be their glory. And to them will I reveal all mysteries, yea, all the hidden mysteries of my kingdom from days of old, and for ages to come, will I make known unto them the good pleasure of my will concerning all things pertaining to my kingdom. Yea, even the wonders of eternity shall they know, and things to come will I show them, even the things of many generations. And their wisdom shall be great, and their understanding reach to heaven; and before them the wisdom of the wise shall perish, and the understanding of the prudent shall come to naught. For by my Spirit will I enlighten them, and by my power will I make known unto them the secrets of my will—yea, even those things which eye has not seen, nor ear heard, nor yet entered into the heart of men.* (D&C 76:5-10.)

Fleeing Evil

(See also Companions and Friends, Choosing; Repentance; Righteousness.)

Though we should avoid sin as much as is possible, we should not entirely avoid sinners, especially if we wish to share God's love and truth with them and to help them to repentance. Christ himself associated and showed us how to associate with sinful people, making clear that none of us are without sin. But when sin surrounds and threatens to overpower us, we are commanded to do as Joseph did when Potiphar's wife sought to seduce him: "he left his garment in her hand, and fled, and got him out." (Gen. 39:12.)

Commandments and Promises

Keep thy tongue from evil, and thy lips from speaking guile. Depart from evil, and do good; seek peace, and pursue it. (Ps. 34:14.)

Depart from evil, and do good; *and dwell evermore.* (Ps. 37:27.)

If sinners entice thee, consent thou not. (Prov. 1:10.)

Be not wise in thine own eyes: fear the Lord, and depart from evil. (Prov. 3:7.)

Enter not into the path of the wicked, and go not in the way of evil men. Avoid it, pass not by it, turn from it, and pass away. (Prov. 4: 14-15.)

Go ye forth of Babylon, flee ye from the Chaldeans, with a voice of singing declare ye, tell this, utter it even to the end of the earth; say ye, The Lord hath redeemed his servant Jacob. (Isa. 48:20; similar scripture, 1 Ne. 20:20.)

With many other words did he testify and exhort, saying, Save yourselves from this untoward generation. (Acts 2:40.)

Abhor that which is evil; cleave to that which is good. (Rom. 12:9.)

Put away from among yourselves that wicked person. (1 Cor. 5:13.)

Flee from idolatry. (1 Cor. 10:14.)

Come out from among them [idols], and be ye separate, saith the Lord, and touch not the unclean thing; *and I will receive you, and will be a Father unto you, and ye shall be my sons and daughters, saith the Lord Almighty.* (2 Cor. 6:17-18.)

Beware of dogs, beware of evil workers, beware of the concision. (Philip. 3:2.)

Abstain from all appearance of evil. (1 Thes. 5:22.)

If any man . . . consent not to wholesome words, even the words of our Lord Jesus Christ, and to the doctrine which is according to godliness; *he is proud, knowing nothing, but doting about questions and strifes of words, whereof cometh envy, strife, railings, evil surmisings, perverse disputings of men of corrupt minds, and destitute of the truth, supposing that gain is godliness:* from such withdraw thyself. (1 Tim. 6:1-5.)

The love of money is the root of all evil: which while some coveted after, they have erred from the faith, and pierced themselves through with many sorrows. But thou, O man of God, flee these things; and follow after righteousness, godliness, faith, love, patience, meekness. (1 Tim. 6:10-11.)

Flee also youthful lusts: but follow righteousness, faith, charity, peace, with them that call on the Lord out of a pure heart. (2 Tim 2:22.)

This know also, that in the last days perilous times shall come. For men shall be lovers of their own selves, covetous, boasters, proud, blasphemers, disobedient to parents, unthankful, unholy, without natural affection, trucebreakers, false accusers, incontinent, fierce, despisers of those that are good, traitors, heady, highminded, lovers of pleasures more than lovers of God; having a form of godliness, but denying the power thereof: from such turn away. (2 Tim. 3:1-5.)

He that will love life, and see good days, let him refrain his tongue from evil, and his lips that they speak no guile: let him eschew evil, and do good; let him seek peace, and ensue it. (1 Pet. 3:10-11.)

All you that are desirous to follow the voice of the good shepherd, come ye out from the wicked, and be ye separate, and touch not their unclean things; and behold, *their names shall be blotted out, that the names of the wicked shall not be numbered among the names of the righteous, that the word of God may be fulfilled, which saith: The names of the wicked shall not be mingled with the names of my people.* (Alma 5:57.)

Go ye out from among the wicked. Save yourselves. Be ye clean that bear the vessels of the Lord. (D&C 38:42.)

Go ye out from Babylon. Be ye clean that bear the vessels of the Lord. (D&C 133:5.)

Go ye out of Babylon; gather ye out from among the nations, from the four winds, from one end of heaven to the other. (D&C 133:7.)

Go ye out from among the nations, even from Babylon, from the midst of wickedness, which is spiritual Babylon. (D&C 133:14.)

Following God and His Servants

(See also Obedience.)

Scripture frequently uses the image of a path or way that leads to celestial glory. An example of this is the vision of Lehi and Nephi, in which "a strait and narrow path" leads to the tree of life. In Lehi's dream, many who try to follow the path "lose their way" in the mist of darkness. (1 Ne. 8:20, 23.)

Considering that image, we can understand why the Lord commands us repeatedly to follow him and his appointed servants along a path of righteousness. None of us is the first to walk that path. By following the counsel and example of the Lord and his servants, we can reach the destination of God's kingdom.

Commandments of Promises

The Lord appeared to Abram, and said unto him, I am the Almighty God; walk before me, and be thou perfect. *And I will make my covenant between me and thee, and will multiply thee exceedingly.* (Gen. 17:1-2.)

I am the Lord your God: ye shall therefore sanctify yourselves, and ye shall be holy; for I am holy. (Lev. 11:44.)

The Lord spake unto Moses, saying, Speak unto all the congregation of the children of Israel, and say unto them, Ye shall be holy: for I the Lord your God am holy. (Lev. 19:1-2.)

The Lord's anger was kindled the same time, and he sware, saying, Surely none of the men that came up out of Egypt, from twenty years old and upward, shall see the land which I sware unto Abraham, unto Isaac, and unto Jacob; because they have not wholly followed me: save Caleb the son of Jephunneh the Kenezite, and Joshua the son of Nun: for they have wholly followed the Lord. *And the Lord's anger was kindled against Israel, and he made them wander in the wilderness forty years, until all the generation, that had done evil in the sight of the Lord, was consumed.* (Num. 32:10-13.)

Ye shall walk after the Lord your God, and fear him, and keep his commandments, and obey his voice, and ye shall serve him, and cleave unto him. (Deut. 13:4.)

The Lord thy God will raise up unto thee a Prophet from the midst of thee, of thy brethren, like unto me; unto him ye shall hearken. (Deut. 18:15.)

Samuel said unto the people, Fear not: ye have done all this wicked-ness: yet turn not aside from following the Lord, but serve the Lord with all your heart; and turn ye not aside: *for then should ye go after vain things, which cannot profit nor deliver, for they are vain.* (1 Sam. 12:20-21.)

Blessed is the man that walketh not in the counsel of the ungodly, nor standeth in the way of sinners, nor sitteth in the seat of the scornful. But his delight is in the law of the Lord; and in his law doth he medi-tate day and night. *And he shall be like a tree planted by the rivers of water, that bringeth forth his fruit in his season; his leaf also shall not wither; and whatsoever he doeth shall prosper.* (Ps. 1:1-3.)

My son, give me thine heart, and let thine eyes observe my ways. (Prov. 23:26.)

Turn ye unto him from whom the children of Israel have deeply re-volted. (Isa. 31:6.)

Behold my servant, whom I uphold; mine elect, in whom my soul de-lighteth; I have put my spirit upon him: he shall bring forth judg-ment to the Gentiles. (Isa. 42:1.)

Thus saith the Lord, Stand ye in the ways, and see, and ask for the old paths, where is the good way, and walk therein, *and ye shall find rest for your souls.* (Jer. 6:16.)

If ye will not hearken to me, to walk in my law, which I have set be-fore you, to hearken to the words of my servants the prophets, whom I sent unto you, both rising up early, and sending them, but ye have not hearkened; *then will I make this house like Shiloh, and will make this city a curse to all the nations of the earth.* (Jer. 26:4-6; see also JST Jer. 26:6.)

It is written, Man shall not live by bread alone, but by every word that proceedeth out of the mouth of God. (Matt. 4:4.)

Jesus, walking by the sea of Galilee, saw two brethren, Simon called Peter, and Andrew his brother, casting a net into the sea: for they were fishers. And he saith unto them, Follow me, *and I will make you fishers of men.* (Matt. 4:18-19; similar scripture, Mark 1:17; see also JST Matt. 4:18.)

Be ye therefore perfect, even as your Father which is in heaven is perfect. (Matt. 5:48.)

He that taketh not his cross, and followeth after me, *is not worthy of me.* (Matt. 10:38.)

Jesus said unto him, *If thou wilt be perfect,* go and sell that thou hast, and give to the poor, *and thou shalt have treasure in heaven:* and come and follow me. (Matt. 19:21; see also Mark 10:21.)

Ye which have followed me, in the regeneration when the Son of man shall sit in the throne of his glory, *ye also shall sit upon twelve thrones, judging the twelve tribes of Israel.* And every one that hath forsaken houses, or brethren, or sisters, or father, or mother, or wife, or children, or lands, for my name's sake, *shall receive an hundredfold, and shall inherit everlasting life.* (Matt. 19: 28-29; see also JST Matt. 19:28.)

Whosoever will come after me, let him deny himself, and take up his cross, and follow me. (Mark 8:34; similar scripture, Luke 9:23.)

Jesus beholding him loved him, and said unto him, One thing thou lackest: go thy way, sell whatsoever thou hast, and give to the poor, *and thou shalt have treasure in heaven:* and come, take up the cross, and follow me. (Mark 10:21; see also Matt. 19:21.)

He said unto another, Follow me. But he said, Lord, suffer me first to go and bury my father. Jesus said unto him, let the dead bury their dead: but go thou and preach the kingdom of God. (Luke 9:59-60; similar scripture, Matt. 8:22.)

Go, and do thou likewise [as the good Samaritan did]. (Luke 10:37.)

He that is not with me is against me: and he that gathereth not with me scattereth. (Luke 11:23.)

Whosoever doth not bear his cross, and come after me, *cannot be my disciple*. (Luke 14:27; see also JST Luke 14:27-28.)

I am the light of the world: he that followeth me *shall not walk in darkness, but shall have the light of life*. (John 8:12.)

If any man serve me, let him follow me; *and where I am, there shall also my servant be:* if any man serve me, *him will my Father honour*. (John 12:26.)

I have given you an example, tnat ye should do as I have done to you. (John 13:15.)

[Christ to Peter] Follow thou me. (John 21:22.)

Wherefore I beseech you, be ye followers of me [Paul]. (1 Cor. 4:16.)

Be ye followers of me [Paul], even as I also am of Christ. (1 Cor. 11:1.)

Be ye therefore followers of God, as dear children; and walk in love, as Christ also hath loved us, and hath given himself for us an offering and a sacrifice to God for a sweetsmelling savour. (Eph. 5:1-2.)

Let this mind be in you, which was also in Christ Jesus. (Philip. 2:5.)

Be followers together of me [Paul], and mark them which walk so as ye have us for an ensample. (Philip. 3:17.)

Whatsoever things are true, whatsoever things are honest, whatsoever things are just, whatsoever things are pure, whatsoever things are lovely, whatsoever things are of good report; if there be any virtue, and if there be any praise, think on these things. Those things, which ye have both learned, and received, and heard, and see in me, do: *and the God of peace shall be with you*. (Philip. 4:8-9.)

As ye have therefore received Christ Jesus the Lord, so walk ye in him: rooted and built up in him, and stablished in the faith, as ye have been taught, *abounding therein with thanksgiving*. (Col. 2:6-7.)

See that none render evil for evil unto any man; but ever follow that which is good, both among yourselves, and to all men. (1 Thes. 5:15.)

Hold fast the form of sound words, which thou hast heard of me, in faith and love which is in Christ Jesus. (2 Tim. 1:13.)

We ought to give the more earnest heed to the things which we have heard, *lest at any time we should let them slip.* (Heb. 2:1.)

Take heed, brethren, *lest there be in any of you an evil heart of unbelief,* in departing from the living God. (Heb. 3:12.)

We desire that every one of you do shew the same diligence to the full assurance of hope unto the end: that ye be not slothful, but followers of them who through faith and patience *inherit the promises.* (Heb. 6:11-12.)

Remember them which have the rule over you, who have spoken unto you the word of God: whose faith follow, considering the end of their conversation. (Heb. 13:7.)

Obey them that have rule over you, and submit yourselves: for they watch for your souls, as they that must give account, that they may do it with joy, and not with grief: for that is unprofitable for you. (Heb. 13:17.)

So speak ye, and so do, as they that shall be judged by the law of liberty. (James 2:12.)

Draw nigh to God, *and he will draw nigh to you.* (James 4:8.)

Take, my brethren, the prophets, who have spoken in the name of the Lord, for an example of suffering affliction, and of patience. (James 5:10.)

If we say that we have fellowship with him, and walk in darkness, *we lie, and do not the truth:* but if we walk in the light, as he is in the light, *we have fellowship one with another, and the blood of Jesus Christ his Son cleanseth us from all sin.* (1 Jn. 1:6-7.)

Hear ye the words of the prophet, which were written unto all the house of Israel, and liken them unto yourselves, *that ye may have*

hope as well as your brethren from whom ye have been broken off.
(1 Ne. 19:24.)

He said unto the children of men: Follow thou me. Wherefore, my beloved brethren, can we follow Jesus save we shall be willing to keep the commandments of the Father? (2 Ne. 31:10.)

He that is baptized in my name, *to him will the Father give the Holy Ghost, like unto me;* wherefore, follow me, and do the things which ye have seen me do. Wherefore, my beloved brethren, I know that if ye shall follow the Son, with full purpose of heart, acting no hypocrisy and no deception before God, but with real intent, repenting of your sins, witnessing unto the Father that ye are willing to take upon you the name of Christ, by baptism—yea, by following your Lord and your Savior down into the water, according to his word, behold, *then shall ye receive the Holy Ghost; yea, then cometh the baptism of fire and of the Holy Ghost; and then can ye speak with the tongue of angels, and shout praises unto the Holy One of Israel.* (2 Ne. 31: 12-13.)

Unless a man shall endure to the end, in following the example of the Son of the living God, *he cannot be saved.* (2 Ne. 31:16.)

Is there not a type in this thing? For just as surely as this director did bring our fathers, by following its course, to the promised land, *shall the words of Christ,* if we follow their course, *carry us beyond this vale of sorrow into a far better land of promise.* (Alma 37:45.)

[Jesus Christ to the Nephites] *Blessed* are ye if ye shall give heed unto the words of these twelve whom I have chosen from among you to minister unto you, and to be your servants; and unto them I have given power that they may baptize you with water; and after that ye are baptized with water, behold, *I will baptize you with fire and with the Holy Ghost; therefore blessed are ye* if ye shall believe in me and be baptized, after that ye have seen me and know that I am. (3 Ne. 12:1.)

The works which ye have seen me do that shall ye also do; for that which ye have seen me do even that shall ye do; therefore, if ye do these things *blessed are ye, for ye shall be lifted up at the last day.* (3 Ne. 27:21-22.)

What manner of men ought ye to be? Verily I say unto you, even as I am. (3 Ne. 27:27.)

The day cometh that they who will not hear the voice of the Lord, neither the voice of his servants, neither give heed to the words of the prophets and apostles, *shall be cut off from among the people.* (D&C 1:14.)

[to Martin Harris] *Misery thou shalt receive* if thou wilt slight these counsels, yea, *even the destruction of thyself and property.* (D&C 19:33.)

Thou shalt not command him who is at thy head, and at the head of the church. (D&C 28:6.)

They shall give heed to that which is written, and pretend to no other revelation. (D&C 32:4.)

Hear my voice and follow me, *and you shall be a free people, and ye shall have no laws but my laws when I come, for I am your lawgiver, and what can stay my hand?* (D&C 38:22.)

Hearken, O ye inhabitants of Zion, and all ye people of my church who are afar off, and hear the word of the Lord which I give unto my servant Joseph Smith, Jun., and also unto my servant Martin Harris, and also unto my servant Oliver Cowdery, and also unto my servant John Whitmer, and also unto my servant Sidney Rigdon, and also unto my servant William W. Phelps, by the way of commandment unto them. (D&C 70:1.)

Follow me, and listen to the counsel which I shall give unto you. (D&C 100:2.)

Inasmuch as they [the Saints in Missouri] follow the counsel which they receive, *they shall have power after many days to accomplish all things pertaining to Zion.* (D&C 105:37.)

Foolishness
(See also Soberness.)

Scripture condemns those who engage in either lighthearted or serious foolishness and implies that foolishness is more serious than some might believe. Foolish talking and jesting are listed with such sins as fornication, uncleanness, covetousness, and filthiness, and foolishness with evil thoughts, adulteries, murders, thefts, wickedness, deceit, lasciviousness, an evil eye, blasphemy, and pride. (See Eph. 5:3-5 and Mark 7:21-23.)

This does not mean that we should always be without humor or that we should deny ourselves joy. Instead, our expressions should be appropriate: we must not give light treatment or consideration to serious matters. Nephi writes: "For the reward of their pride and their foolishness they shall reap destruction; for because they yield unto the devil and choose works of darkness rather than light, therefore they must go down to hell." (2 Ne. 26:10)

Commandments of Promises

The foolish *shall not stand in thy sight: thou hatest all workers of iniquity.* (Ps. 5:5.)

Forsake the foolish, *and live;* and go in the way of understanding. (Prov. 9:6.)

Fools *die for want of wisdom.* (Prov. 10:21.)

Judgments are prepared for scorners, *and stripes* for the back of fools. (Prov. 19:29.)

The thought of foolishness *is sin:* and the scorner *is an abomination to men.* (Prov. 24:9.)

Be not over much wicked, neither be thou foolish: *why shouldest thou die before thy time?* (Eccl. 7:17.)

Fornication, and all uncleanness, or covetousness, let it not be once named among you, as becometh saints; neither filthiness, nor foolish talking, nor jesting, which are not convenient: but rather giving of thanks. (Eph. 5:3-5.)

See then that we walk circumspectly, not as fools, but as wise. (Eph. 5:15.)

Foolish and unlearned questions avoid, knowing that they do gender strifes. (2 Tim. 2:23.)

Avoid foolish questions, and genealogies, and contentions, and strivings about the law; for they are unprofitable and vain. (Titus 3:9-11.)

When these things have passed away a speedy destruction cometh unto my people; for, notwithstanding the pains of my soul, I have seen it; wherefore, I know that it shall come to pass; and they sell themselves for naught; for, for the reward of their pride and their foolishness *they shall reap destruction;* for because they yield unto the devil and choose works of darkness rather than light, *therefore they must go down to hell.* (2 Ne. 26:10.)

Forgiving Others
(See also Retribution.)

We must do three things to be granted forgiveness: we must be worthy of forgiveness, ask for forgiveness, and forgive others. But how can we turn our grudges into goodness, our resentment into righteous desire? How do we truly forgive?

In the Sermon on the Mount, Christ explains: "Love your enemies, bless them that curse you, do good to them that hate you, and pray for them which despitefully use you, and persecute you." (Matt. 5:44.) We can develop forgiveness for others by praying for them, asking God to bless them, and doing good to them. Furthermore, we must be willing to do these things each time we are wronged, for we are commanded to forgive others "until seventy times seven." (Matt. 18: 21-22.)

With eloquence, Paul instructs the Corinthian saints to forgive everyone who has "caused grief" and to "comfort him," lest he be "swallowed up with overmuch sorrow." "Confirm your love toward him," Paul teaches. (2 Cor. 2:5-8.) Such love must conquer resentment and hatred. Forgiveness must be total and sincere to benefit the forgiving as well as the forgiven.

Commandments and Promises

Thou shalt not avenge, nor bear any grudge against the children of thy people, but thou shalt love thy neighbour as thyself: I am the Lord. (Lev. 19:18.)

Leave there thy gift before the altar, and go thy way; first be reconciled to thy brother, and then come and offer thy gift. (Matt. 5:24.)

Ye have heard that it hath been said, An eye for an eye, and a tooth for a tooth: but I say unto you, That ye resist not evil: but whosoever shall smite thee on thy right cheek, turn to him the other also. And if any man will sue thee at the law, and take away thy coat, let him have thy cloke also. (Matt. 5:38-40; similar scripture, 3 Ne. 12:38-40.)

Ye have heard that it hath been said, Thou shalt love thy neighbour, and hate thine enemy. But I say unto you, Love your enemies, bless them that curse you, do good to them that hate you, and pray for them which despitefully use you, and persecute you; *that ye may be the children of your Father which is in heaven:* for he maketh his sun to rise on the evil and on the good, and sendeth rain on the just and the unjust. (Matt. 5:43-45; similar scripture, 3 Ne. 12:43-45.)

For if ye forgive men their trespasses, *your heavenly Father will also forgive you:* but if ye forgive not men their trespasses, *neither will your Father forgive your trespasses.* (Matt. 6:14-15; similar scripture, 3 Ne. 13:14-15.)

Then came Peter to him, and said, Lord, how oft shall my brother sin against me, and I forgive him? till seven times? Jesus saith unto him, I say not unto thee, Until seven times: but, Until seventy times seven. (Matt. 18:21-22.)

When ye stand praying, forgive, if ye have ought against any: *that your Father also which is in heaven may forgive you your trespasses.* But if ye do not forgive, *neither will your Father which is in heaven forgive your trespasses.* (Mark 11:25-26.)

Take heed to yourselves: If thy brother trespass against thee, rebuke him; and if he repent, forgive him. And if he trespass against thee seven times in a day, and seven times in a day turn again to thee, saying, I repent; thou shalt forgive him. (Luke 17:3-4.)

If any have caused grief, he hath not grieved me, but in part: *that I may not overcharge you all. Sufficient to such a man is this punishment, which was inflicted of many.* So that contrariwise ye ought rather to forgive him, and comfort him, *lest perhaps such a one should be swallowed up with overmuch sorrow.* Wherefore I beseech you that ye would confirm your love toward him. (2 Cor. 2:5-8.)

Let all bitterness, and wrath, and anger, and clamour, and evil speaking, be put away from you, with all malice: and be ye kind one to another, tenderhearted, forgiving one another, even as God for Christ's sake hath forgiven you. (Eph. 4:31-32.)

Put on therefore, as the elect of God, holy and beloved, bowels of mercies, kindness, humbleness of mind, meekness, longsuffering; forbearing one another, and forgiving one another, if any man have a quarrel against any: even as Christ forgave you, so also do ye. (Col. 3:12-13.)

Grudge not one against another, brethren, *lest ye be condemned: behold, the judge standeth before the door.* (James 5:9.)

Whosoever transgresseth against me, him shall ye judge according to the sins which he has committed; and if he confess his sins before thee and me, and repenteth in the sincerity of his heart, him shall ye forgive, *and I will forgive him also.* (Mosiah 26:29.)

Ye shall also forgive one another your trespasses; for verily I say unto you, he that forgiveth not his neighbor's trespasses when he says that he repents, *the same hath brought himself under condemnation.* (Mosiah 26:31.)

If ye shall come unto me, or shall desire to come unto me, and rememberest that thy brother hath aught against thee—go thy way unto thy brother, and first be reconciled to thy brother, and then come unto me with full purpose of heart, *and I will receive you.* (3 Ne. 12:23-24.)

Ye ought to forgive one another; for he that forgiveth not his brother his trespasses *standeth condemned before the Lord; for there remaineth in him the greater sin.* I, the Lord, will forgive whom I will forgive, but of you it is required to forgive all men. (D&C 64:9-10.)

If after thine enemy has come upon thee the first time, he repent and come unto thee praying thy forgiveness, thou shalt forgive him, and shalt hold it no more as a testimony against thine enemy—and so on unto the second and third time; and as oft as thine enemy repenteth of the trespass wherewith he has trespassed against thee, thou shalt forgive him, until seventy times seven. And if he trespass against thee and repent not the first time, nevertheless thou shalt forgive him. And if he trespass against thee the second time, and repent not, nevertheless thou shalt forgive him. And if he trespass against thee the third time, and repent not, thou shalt also forgive him. But if he trespass against thee the fourth time thou shalt not forgive him, but shalt bring these testimonies before the Lord; and they shall not be blotted out until he repent and reward thee four-fold in all things wherewith he has trespassed against thee. And if he do this, thou shalt forgive him with all thine heart; and if he do not this, *I the Lord, will avenge thee of thine enemy an hundred-fold; and upon his children, and upon his children's children of all them that hate me, unto the third and fourth generation.* (D&C 98:39-46.)

Let mine handmaid [Emma Smith] forgive my servant Joseph his trespasses; *and then shall she be forgiven her trespasses, wherein she has trespassed against me; and I, the Lord thy God, will bless her, and multiply her, and make her heart to rejoice.* (D&C 132:56.)

Generosity

(See also Covetousness; Kindness; Mercy; Tithes and Offerings.)

With the commandment to give freely, we are promised that we will receive. "For with the same measure that ye mete withal it shall be measured to you again," Luke explains. (Luke 6:38.)

But is is not enough just to give. We must do it correctly—"with simplicity" (Rom. 12:8) and "not grudgingly, or of necessity" (2 Cor. 9:7). Our hearts, as well as our gifts, must be right.

Commandments and Promises

When ye reap the harvest of your land, thou shalt not wholly reap the corners of thy field, neither shalt thou gather the gleanings of thy harvest. And thou shalt not glean thy vineyard, neither shalt thou gather every grape of thy vineyard; thou shalt leave them for the poor and stranger. (Lev. 19:9-10.)

Thou shalt not harden thine heart, nor shut thine hand from thy poor brother: but thou shalt open thine hand wide unto him, and shalt surely lend him sufficient for his need, in that which he wanteth. Beware that there be not a thought in thy wicked heart, saying, The seventh year, the year of release, is at hand; and thine eye be evil against thy poor brother, and thou givest him nought; and he cry unto the Lord against thee, *and it be sin unto thee.* Thou shalt surely give him, and thine heart shall not be grieved when thou givest unto him: because that for this thing *the Lord thy God shall bless thee in all thy works, and in all that thou puttest thine hand unto.* For the poor shall never cease out of the land: therefore I command thee, saying, Thou shalt open thine hand wide unto thy brother, to thy poor, and to thy needy, in thy land. (Deut. 15:7-11.)

The righteous sheweth mercy, and giveth. (Ps. 37:21.)

Blessed is he that considereth the poor: *the Lord will deliver him in time of trouble. The Lord will preserve him, and keep him alive; and he shall be blessed upon the earth.* (Ps. 41:1-2.)

The liberal soul *shall be made fat:* and he that watereth *shall be watered also himself.* He that withholdeth corn, *the people shall curse him: but blessing shall be upon the head* of him that selleth it. (Prov. 11:25-26.)

He that hath pity upon the poor *lendeth unto the Lord; and that which he hath given will he pay him again.* (Prov. 19:17.)

He that giveth unto the poor *shall not lack:* but he that hideth his eyes *shall have many a curse.* (Prov. 28:27.)

Cast thy bread upon the waters: *for thou shalt find it after many days.* Give a portion to seven, and also to eight. (Eccl. 11:1-2.)

If any man will sue thee at the law, and take away thy coat, let him have thy cloke also. And whosoever shall compel thee to go a mile, go with him twain. Give to him that asketh thee, and from him that would borrow of thee turn not thou away. (Matt. 5:40-42.)

Heal the sick, cleanse the lepers, raise the dead, cast out devils: freely ye have received, freely give. (Matt. 10:8.)

If thou [the rich young man] wilt be perfect, go and sell that thou hast, and give to the poor, *and thou shalt have treasure in heaven.* (Matt. 19:21; similar scriptures, Mark 10:21, Luke 18:22.)

He that hath two coats, let him impart to him that hath none; and he that hath meat, let him do likewise. (Luke 3:11.)

Give to every man that asketh of thee; and of him that taketh away thy goods ask them not again. (Luke 6:30.)

Give, *and it shall be given unto you; good measure, pressed down, and shaken together, and running over, shall men give into your bosom.* For with the same measure that ye mete withal *it shall be measured to you again.* (Luke 6:38.)

When thou makest a dinner or a supper, call not thy friends, nor thy brethren, neither thy kinsmen, nor thy rich neighbours; *lest they also bid thee again, and a recompence be made thee.* But when thou makest a feast, call the poor, the maimed, the lame, the blind: *and thou shalt be blessed;* for they cannot recompense thee: *for thou shalt be recompensed at the resurrection of the just.* (Luke 14:12-14.)

He that giveth, let him do it with simplicity. (Rom. 12:8.)

We then that are strong ought to bear the infirmities of the weak, and not to please ourselves. (Rom. 15:1.)

Let no man seek his own, but every man another's wealth. (1 Cor. 10:24; see also JST 1 Cor. 10:24.)

Every man according as he purposeth in his heart, so let him give; not grudgingly, or of necessity: *for God loveth a cheerful giver.* (2 Cor. 9:7.)

This I say therefore, and testify in the Lord, that ye henceforth walk not as other Gentiles walk, in the vanity of their mind, having the understanding darkened, being alienated from the life of God through the ignorance that is in them, because of the blindness of their heart: who being past feeling have given themselves over unto lasciviousness, to work all uncleanness with greediness. (Eph. 4:17-19.)

Look not every man on his own things, but every man also on the things of others. (Philip. 2:4.)

Charge them that are rich in this world, that they be not highminded, nor trust in uncertain riches, but in the living God, who giveth us richly all things to enjoy; that they do good, that they be rich in good works, ready to distribute, willing to communicate; laying up in store for themselves a good foundation against the time to come, *that they may lay hold on eternal life.* (1 Tim. 6:17-19.)

Think of your brethren like unto yourselves, and be familiar with all and free with your substance, *that they may be rich like unto you.* (Jacob 2:17.)

Ye will administer of your substance unto him that standeth in need; and ye will not suffer that the beggar putteth up his petition to you in vain, and turn him out to perish. Perhaps thou shalt say: The man has brought upon himself his misery; therefore I will stay my hand,

and will not give unto him of my food, nor impart unto him of my substance that he may not suffer, for his punishments are just—but I say unto you, O man, whosoever doeth this the same *hath great cause to repent*; and except he repenteth of that which he hath done *he perisheth forever, and hath no interest in the kingdom of God.* (Mosiah 4:16-18.)

Alma commanded that the people of the church should impart of their substance, every one according to that which he had; if he have more abundantly he should impart more abundantly; and of him that had but little, but little should be required; and to him that had not should be given. And thus they should impart of their substance of their own free will and good desires towards God, and to those priests that stood in need, yea, and to every needy, naked soul. (Mosiah 18:27-28.)

If ye turn away the needy, and the naked, and visit not the sick and af-flicted, and impart of your substance, if ye have, to those who stand in need—I say unto you, if ye do not any of these things, behold, *your prayer is vain, and availeth you nothing, and ye are as hypocrites who do deny the faith.* Therefore, if ye do not remember to be charitable, *ye are as dross, which the refiners do cast out (it being of no worth) and is trodden under foot of men.* (Alma 34:28-29.)

I would that ye should do alms unto the poor; but take heed that ye do not your alms before men to be seen of them; *otherwise ye have no reward of your Father who is in heaven.* (3 Ne. 13:1.)

Remember in all things the poor and the needy, the sick and the af-flicted, for he that doeth not these things, *the same is not my disciple.* (D&C 52:40.)

My servant Ezra Thayre must repent of his pride, and of his selfish-ness. (D&C 56:8.)

Wo unto you rich men, that will not give your substance to the poor, *for your riches will canker your souls; and this shall be your lamenta-tion in the day of visitation, and of judgment, and of indignation: The harvest is past, the summer is ended, and my soul is not saved! Wo* unto you poor men, whose hearts are not broken, whose spirits are not contrite, and whose bellies are not satisfied, and whose hands are not stayed from laying hold upon other men's goods, whose eyes are full of greediness, and who will not labor with your own hands! (D&C 56:16-17.)

I, the Lord, am not well pleased with the inhabitants of Zion, for there are idlers among them; and their children are also growing up in wickedness; they also seek not earnestly the riches of eternity, but their eyes are full of greediness. (D&C 68:31.)

See that ye love one another; cease to be covetous; learn to impart one to another as the gospel requires. (D&C 88:123.)

If any man shall take of the abundance which I have made, and impart not his portion, according to the law of my gospel, unto the poor and the needy, *he shall, with the wicked, lift up his eyes in hell, being in torment.* (D&C 104:18.)

Gentleness

Gentleness is an attribute, a gift, and a requirement of God. Paul, writing to the Corinthians, refers to "the meekness and gentleness of Christ." (2 Cor. 10:1.) Writing to the Galatian church, he includes gentleness as "the fruit of the Spirit." (Gal. 5:22-23.) Gentleness, especially with similar qualities such as meekness and humility, is characteristic of the relationships of the Lord's servant with others.

Commandments and Promises

The servant of the Lord must not strive; but be gentle unto all men, apt to teach, patient, in meekness instructing those that oppose themselves; if God peradventure will give them repentance to the acknowledging of the truth; *and that they may recover themselves out of the snare of the devil, who are taken captive by him at his will.* (2 Tim. 2:24-26.)

Put them in mind . . . to speak evil of no man, to be no brawlers, but gentle, shewing all meekness unto all men. (Titus 3:1-2.)

I would that ye should be humble, and be submissive and gentle; easy to be entreated; full of patience and long-suffering. (Alma 7:23.)

No power or influence can or ought to be maintained by virtue of the priesthood, only by persuasion, by long-suffering, by gentleness and meekness, and by love unfeigned; by kindness, and pure knowledge, *which shall greatly enlarge the soul without hypocrisy, and without guile.* (D&C 121:41-42.)

Glorifying God

In the Doctrine and Covenants, the Savior, referring to the Atonement, says that "[my] suffering caused myself, even God, the greatest of all, to tremble because of pain, and to bleed at every pore. . . . Nevertheless, glory be to the Father, and I partook of the bitter cup and finished my preparations unto the children of men." (D&C 19:18-19.)

In this scripture we see an important part of Christ's purposes. Christ said, "Glory be to the Father," and remained true to what he had said in the premortal existence: "Father, thy will be done, and the glory be thine forever." (Moses 4:2.) True to this always, Christ suffered but took no glory for himself.

Glorifying God is closely related to loving him. The closer we draw to God and the more we feel his love and realize what he has done for us, the more we want to honor and praise him. Just as children honor or glorify their parents when they accomplish good, we glorify God when we are faithful.

Glorifying God is not a denial of self; rather, it affirms who we really are: spirit children of God. As we work toward genuine spiritual goals, we take pride in striving for quality, and we assert ourselves to bring honor to God. By striving to live good lives and by not setting our hearts on worldly things, we let our lights so shine that others see our actions and our joy and are led to glorify God.

Commandments and Promises

It is not good to eat much honey: so for men to search their own glory is not glory. (Prov. 25:27.)

Hear the word of the Lord, ye that tremble at his word; Your brethren that hated you, that cast you out for my name's sake, said, Let the Lord be glorified: *but he shall appear to your joy, and they shall be ashamed.* (Isa. 66:5.)

Let your light so shine before men, *that they may see your good works, and glorify your Father which is in heaven.* (Matt. 5:16.)

There arose a reasoning among them, which of them should be greatest. And Jesus, perceiving the thought of their heart, took a child, and set him by him. And said unto them, Whosoever shall receive this child in my name *receiveth me:* and whosoever shall receive me *receiveth him that sent me:* for he that is least among you all, *the same shall be great.* (Luke 9:46-48.)

He that speaketh of himself seeketh his own glory: but he that seeketh his glory that sent him, *the same is true, and no unrighteousness is in him.* (John 7:18.)

Jesus answered, If I honour myself, *my honour is nothing:* it is my Father that honoureth me; of whom ye say, that he is your God. (John 8:54.)

Whatsoever ye shall ask in my name, that will I do, *that the Father may be glorified in the Son.* (John 14:13.)

Herein is my Father glorified, that ye bear much fruit; so shall ye be my disciples. (John 15:8.)

Now the God of patience and consolation grant you to be likeminded one toward another according to Christ Jesus: *that ye may with one mind and one mouth glorify God, even the Father of our Lord Jesus Christ.* (Rom. 15:5-6.)

Abstain from fleshly lusts, which war against the soul; having your conversation honest among the Gentiles: *that,* whereas they speak against you as evildoers, *they may by your good works, which they shall behold, glorify God in the day of visitation.* (1 Pet. 2:11-12.)

If any man speak, let him speak as the oracles of God; if any man minister, let him do it as of the ability which God giveth: *that God in all things may be glorified through Jesus Christ,* to whom be praise and dominion for ever and ever. (1 Pet. 4:11.)

Let no man glory in man, but rather let him glory in God, who shall subdue all enemies under his feet. (D&C 76:61.)

Thus saith the Lord, it is expedient that all things be done unto my glory, by you who are joined together in this order [storehouse for the poor]. (D&C 78:8.)

If your eye be single to my glory, *your whole bodies shall be filled with light, and there shall be no darkness in you; and that body which is filled with light comprehendeth all things.* (D&C 88:67.)

There are many called, but few are chosen. And why are they not chosen? Because their hearts are set so much upon the things of this world, and aspire to the honors of men, *that they do not learn this one lesson—that the rights of the priesthood are inseparably connected with the powers of heaven, and that the powers of heaven cannot be controlled nor handled only upon the principles of righteousness.* (D&C 121:34-36.)

[Joseph Smith recalling Moroni's words] I must have no other object in view in getting the plates but to glorify God, and must not be influenced by any other motive than that of building his kingdom; *otherwise I could not get them.* (JS–H 1:46.)

Good Works

We reap what we sow. If our lives are sown with good works, we reap goodness, and that goodness nourishes others.

Good intentions, however, are not enough; we must do good works. James counsels: "Be ye doers of the word, and not hearers only, deceiving your own selves." (James 1:22.) As we do good, we become worthy of having good rewarded to us. "For that which ye do send out shall return unto you again, and be restored," Alma writes. "Therefore, the word restoration more fully condemneth the sinner, and justifieth him not at all." (Alma 41:15.)

The Lord gives us hope for even the least significant of our good works, beyond the reward we receive for doing them. "Be not weary in well-doing," he counsels, "for ye are laying the foundation of a great work. And out of small things proceedeth that which is great." (D&C 64:33.)

Commandments and Promises

If thou [Cain] doest well, *shalt thou not be accepted?* and if thou doest not well, *sin lieth at the door.* (Gen. 4:7; similar scripture, Moses 5:23.)

Thou [children of Israel] shalt do that which is right and good in the sight of the Lord: *that it may be well with thee, and that thou mayest go in and possess the good land which the Lord sware unto thy fathers, to cast out all thine enemies from before thee.* (Deut. 6:18-19.)

Thou shalt surely give him [thy poor brother], and thine heart shall not be grieved when thou givest unto him: *because that for this thing the Lord thy God shall bless thee in all thy works, and in all that thou puttest thine hand unto.* For the poor shall never cease out of the land: therefore I command thee, saying, Thou shalt open thine hand wide unto thy brother, to thy poor, and to thy needy, in thy land. (Deut. 15:10-11.)

Be ye strong therefore, and let not your hands be weak: *for your work shall be rewarded.* (2 Chr. 15:7.)

Lord, who shall abide in thy tabernacle? who shall dwell in thy holy hill? He that walketh uprightly, and worketh righteousness, and speaketh the truth in his heart. (Ps. 15:1-2; see also JST Ps. 15:1.)

Depart from evil, and do good. (Ps. 34:14.)

Trust in the Lord, and do good; so shalt thou dwell in the land, *and verily thou shalt be fed.* (Ps. 37:3.)

Whoso rewardeth evil for good, *evil shall not depart from his house.* (Prov. 17:13.)

Wash you, make you clean; put away the evil of your doings from before mine eyes; cease to do evil; learn to do well; seek judgment, relieve the oppressed, judge the fatherless, plead for the widow. (Isa. 1:16-17.)

I the Lord search the heart, I try the reins, *even to give every man* according to his ways, and according to the fruit of his doings. (Jer. 17:10.)

I will punish you according to the fruit of your doings, saith the Lord. (Jer. 21:14.)

Let your light so shine before men, *that they may see your good works, and glorify your Father which is in heaven.* (Matt. 5:16.)

Ye have heard that it hath been said, Thou shalt love thy neighbour, and hate thine enemy. But I say unto you, Love your enemies, bless them that curse you, do good to them that hate you, and pray for them which despitefully use you, and persecute you; *that ye may be the children of your Father which is in heaven:* for he maketh his sun to rise on the evil and on the good, and sendeth rain on the just and on the unjust. (Matt. 5:43-45.)

Take heed that ye do not your alms before men, to be seen of them: *otherwise ye have no reward of your Father which is in heaven.* Therefore when thou doest thine alms, do not sound a trumpet before thee, as the hypocrites do in the synagogues and in the streets, *that they may have glory of men. Verily I say unto you, They have their reward.*

But when thou doest alms, let not thy left hand know what thy right hand doeth: that thine alms may be in secret: *and thy Father which seeth in secret himself shall reward thee openly.* (Matt. 6:1-4.)

For the Son of man shall come in the glory of his Father with his angels; and *then he shall reward every man* according to his works. (Matt. 16:27.)

Love your enemies, do good to them which hate you. (Luke 6:27.)

[God] will render to every man according to his deeds: to them who by patient continuance in well doing seek for glory and honour and immortality, *eternal life.* (Rom. 2:6-7.)

Glory, honour, and peace, to every man that worketh good, to the Jew first, and also to the Gentile: for there is no respect of persons with God. (Rom. 2:10-11.)

For not the hearers of the law are just before God, but the doers of the law *shall be justified.* (Rom. 2:13.)

Do that which is good, *and thou shalt have praise of the same.* (Rom. 13:3.)

Every man shall receive his own reward according to his own labour. (1 Cor. 3:8.)

Every man's work *shall be made manifest: for the day shall declare it, because it shall be revealed by fire; and the fire shall try every man's work of what sort it is.* (1 Cor. 3:13.)

He which soweth sparingly *shall reap also sparingly;* and he which soweth bountifully *shall reap also bountifully.* (2 Cor. 9:6.)

Whatsoever a man soweth, *that shall he also reap.* For he that soweth to his flesh *shall of the flesh reap corruption;* but he that soweth to the Spirit *shall of the Spirit reap life everlasting.* And let us not be weary in well doing: *for in due season we shall reap, if we faint not.* As we have therefore opportunity, let us do good unto all men, especially unto them who are of the household of faith. (Gal. 6:7-10.)

Whatsoever things are true, whatsoever things are honest, what-soever things are just, whatsoever things are pure, whatsoever things are lovely, whatsoever things are of good report; if there be any vir-tue, and if there be any praise, think on these things. Those things, which ye have both learned, and received, and heard, and seen in me, do: *and the God of peace shall be with you.* (Philip. 4:8-9.)

Whatsoever ye do in word or deed, do all in the name of the Lord Jesus, giving thanks to God and the Father by him. (Col. 3:17.)

Whatsoever ye do, do it heartily, as to the Lord, and not unto men; knowing that *of the Lord ye shall receive the reward of the inheritance:* for ye serve the Lord Christ. But he that doeth wrong *shall receive for the wrong which he hath done: and there is no respect of persons.* (Col. 3:23-25.)

Be not weary in well doing. (2 Thes. 3:13.)

I will therefore that men pray every where, lifting up holy hands, without wrath and doubting. In like manner also, that women adorn themselves in modest apparel, with shamefacedness and sobriety; not with broided hair, or gold, or pearls, or costly array; but (which becometh women professing godliness) with good works. (1 Tim. 2:8-10.)

Charge them that are rich in this world, that they be not high-minded, nor trust in uncertain riches, but in the living God, who giveth us richly all things to enjoy; that they do good, that they be rich in good works, ready to distribute, willing to communicate; laying up in store for themselves a good foundation against the time to come, *that they may lay hold on eternal life.* (2 Tim. 6:17-19.)

In all things [shew] thyself a pattern of good works: in doctrine shewing uncorruptness, gravity, sincerity, sound speech, that cannot be condemned; *that he that is of the contrary part may be ashamed, having no evil thing to say of you.* (Titus 2:7-8.)

Put them in mind to be subject to principalities and powers, to obey magistrates, to be ready to every good work. (Titus 3:1.)

Let us consider one another to provoke unto love and to good works. (Heb. 10:24.)

To do good and to communicate forget not: for with such sacrifices *God is well pleased.* (Heb. 13:16.)

Make you perfect in every good work to do his will, working in you *that which is wellpleasing in his sight,* through Jesus Christ. (Heb. 13:21.)

Be ye doers of the word, and not hearers only, deceiving your own selves. For if any be a hearer of the word, and not a doer, he is like unto a man beholding his natural face in a glass: for he beholdeth himself, and goeth his way, and straightway forgetteth what manner of man he was. But whoso looketh into the perfect law of liberty, and continueth therein, he being not a forgetful hearer, but a doer of the work, *this man shall be blessed in his deed.* (James 1:22-25.)

By works *a man is justified,* and not by faith only. (James 2:24.)

Who is a wise man and endued with knowledge among you? let him shew out of a good conversation his works with meekness of wisdom. (James 3:13.)

Abstain from fleshly lusts, which war against the soul; having your conversation honest among the Gentiles: *that,* whereas they speak against you as evildoers, *they may by your good works, which they shall behold, glorify God in the day of visitation.* (1 Pet. 2:11-12.)

So is the will of God, that with well doing *ye may put to silence the ignorance of foolish men.* (1 Pet. 2:15.)

He that will love life, and see good days, let him refrain his tongue from evil, and his lips that they speak no guile: let him eschew evil, and do good; let him seek peace, and ensue it. (1 Pet. 3:10-11.)

I will give unto every one of you according to your works. (Rev. 2:23.)

He that leadeth into captivity *shall go into captivity:* he that killeth with the sword *must be killed with the sword.* Here is the patience and the faith of the saints. (Rev. 13:10.)

That great pit which hath been digged for the destruction of men shall be filled by those who digged it, unto their utter destruction, saith the Lamb of God. (1 Ne. 14:3.)

They shall be judged, every man according to his works, whether they be good, or whether they be evil. (Mosiah 3:24.)

Believe that ye must repent of your sins and forsake them, and humble yourselves before God; and ask in sincerity of heart that he would forgive you; and now, if ye believe all these things see that ye do them. (Mosiah 4:10.)

I would that ye should be steadfast and immovable, always abounding in good works, *that Christ, the Lord God Omnipotent, may seal you his, that you may be brought to heaven, that ye may have everlasting salvation and eternal life, through the wisdom, and power, and justice, and mercy of him who created all things, in heaven and in earth, who is God above all.* (Mosiah 5:15.)

Even this mortal shall put on immortality, and this corruption shall put on incorruption, and shall be brought to stand before the bar of God, to be judged of him according to their works whether they be good or whether they be evil—if they be good, *to the resurrection of endless life and happiness;* and if they be evil, *to the resurrection of endless damnation, being delivered up to the devil, who hath subjected them, which is damnation.* (Mosiah 16:10-11.)

Come unto me and bring forth works of righteousness, *and ye shall not be hewn down and cast into the fire—for behold, the time is at hand that* whosoever bringeth forth not good fruit, or whosoever doeth not the works of righteousness, *the same have cause to wail and mourn.* (Alma 5:35-36.)

The ax is laid at the root of the tree; therefore every tree that bringeth not forth good fruit *shall be hewn down and cast into the fire, yea, a fire which cannot be consumed, even an unquenchable fire.* (Alma 5:52.)

May the peace of God rest upon you, and upon your houses and lands, and upon your flocks and herds, and all that you possess, your women and your children, according to your faith and good works, *for this time forth and forever.* (Alma 7:27.)

After ye have done all these things, if ye turn away the needy, and the naked, and visit not the sick and the afflicted, and impart of your substance, if ye have, to those who stand in need—I say unto you if ye do not any of these things, *behold, your prayer is vain, and availeth you nothing, and ye are as hypocrites who do deny the faith.* (Alma 34:28.)

It is requisite with the justice of God that men should be judged according to their works; and if their works were good in this life, and the desires of their hearts were good, *that they should also, at the last day, be restored unto that which is good.* And if their works are evil *they shall be restored unto them for evil. Therefore, all things shall be restored to their proper order, every thing to its natural frame.* (Alma 41:3-4.)

My son, see that you are merciful unto your brethren; deal justly, judge righteously, and do good continully; and if ye do all these things *then shall ye receive your reward; yea, ye shall have mercy restored unto you again; ye shall have justice restored unto you again; ye shall have a righteous judgment restored unto you again; and ye shall have good rewarded unto you again. For that which ye do send out shall return unto you again, and be restored; therefore, the word restoration more fully condemneth the sinner, and justifieth him not at all.* (Alma 41:14-15.)

[Moroni's] heart did glory . . . not in the shedding of blood but in doing good, in preserving his people, yea, in keeping the commandments of God, yea, and resisting iniquity. Yea, verily, verily I say unto you, if all men had been, and were, and ever would be, like unto Moroni, behold, *the very powers of hell would have been shaken forever; yea, the devil would never have power over the hearts of the children of men.* (Alma 48:16-17.)

They that have done good *shall have everlasting life;* and they that have done evil *shall have everlasting damnation. And thus it is.* (Hel. 12:26.)

Ye know the things that ye must do in my church; for the works which ye have seen me do that shall ye also do; for that which ye have seen me do even that shall ye do; therefore, if ye do these things *blessed are ye, for ye shall be lifted up at the last day.* (3 Ne. 27:21-22.)

According to his works *shall his wages be.* (Morm. 8:19.)

If thou wilt do good, yea, and hold out faithful to the end, *thou shalt be saved in the kingdom of God, which is the greatest of all the gifts of God; for there is no gift greater than the gift of salvation.* (D&C 6:13.)

Fear not to do good, my sons, for whatsoever ye sow, *that shall ye also reap*; therefore, if ye sow good *ye shall also reap good for your reward.* Therefore, fear not, little flock; do good. (D&C 6:33-34.)

By way of commandment to the church concerning the manner of baptism—All those who humble themselves before God, and desire to be baptized, and come forth with broken hearts and contrite spirits, and witness before the church that they have truly repented of all their sins, and are willing to take upon them the name of Jesus Christ, having a determination to serve him to the end, and truly manifest by their works that they have received of the Spirit of Christ unto the remission of their sins, *shall be received by baptism into his church.* (D&C 20:37.)

The members shall manifest before the church, and also before the elders, by a godly walk and conversation, that they are worthy of it, that there may be works and faith agreeable to the holy scriptures— walking in holiness before the Lord. (D&C 20:69.)

According to that which they do *they shall receive, even in lands for their inheritance.* (D&C 56:13.)

Men should be anxiously engaged in a good cause, and do many things of their own free will, and bring to pass much righteousness; for the power is in them, wherein they are agents unto themselves. And inasmuch as men do good *they shall in nowise lose their reward.* (D&C 58:27-28.)

Those [faithful of Zion] that live *shall inherit the earth*, and those that die *shall rest from all their labors*, and their works *shall follow them; and they shall receive a crown in the mansions of my Father, which I have prepared for them.* (D&C 59:2.)

He who doeth the works of righteousness *shall receive his reward, even peace in this world, and eternal life in the world to come.* (D&C 59:23.)

Be not weary in well-doing, for ye are laying the foundation of a great work. And out of small things *proceedeth that which is great.* (D&C 64:33.)

They shall be judged according to their works, *and every man shall receive according to his own works, his own dominion, in the mansions which are prepared.* (D&C 76:111.)

The indignation of the Lord is kindled against their abominations and all their wicked works. (D&C 97:24.)

I must gather together my people, according to the parable of the wheat and the tares, that the wheat *may be secured in the garners to possess eternal life, and be crowned with celestial glory, when I shall come in the kingdom of my Father to reward every man* according as his work shall be; while the tares *shall be bound in bundles, and their bands made strong, that they may be burned with unquenchable fire.* (D&C 101:65-66.)

Let us cheerfully do all things that lie in our power; *and then may we stand still, with the utmost assurance, to see the salvation of God, and for his arm to be revealed.* (D&C 123:17.)

Instead of blessings, ye, by your own works, *bring cursings, wrath, indignation, and judgments upon your own heads,* by your follies, and by all your abominations, which you practise before me, saith the Lord. (D&C 124:48.)

Let the work of my temple, and all the works which I have appointed unto you, be continued on and not cease; and let your diligence, and your perseverance, and patience, and your works be redoubled, *and you shall in nowise lose your reward,* saith the Lord of Hosts. (D&C 127:4.)

Health

Since the time the children of Israel left Egypt, health laws have had an important place in God's commandments. Although different commandments have been emphasized at different times, instructions regarding health have always helped keep bodies strong and healthy, provided an opportunity to demonstrate obedience, and identified God's people. Being healthy means being free of disease, but to an individual trying to be Christlike the word *health* also connotes soundness of body and spirit, strength and vigor, and a flourishing condition.

Sometimes the wisdom of following health commandments becomes evident later. The Saints in Joseph Smith's time may not have understood why tobacco and strong drink were forbidden by the Lord, but today—a century and a half later—the harmful effects of both are well known.

The principal health commandment now is the Word of Wisdom—the revelation found in Doctrine and Covenants 89. This section was not originally given as a commandment, but prophets of God have since been inspired to establish it as one. The *letter* of the Word of Wisdom states that we are not to partake of coffee, tea, alcohol, or tobacco, or to misuse drugs. The *spirit* of the law tells us to use wisdom to avoid all harmful food and drink and to follow other basic rules of good health. Both are essential to the keeping of the law.

Commandments and Promises

He that loveth wine and oil *shall not be rich.* (Prov. 21:17.)

Be not among winebibbers; among riotous eaters of flesh: for the drunkard and the glutton *shall come to poverty: and drowsiness shall clothe a man with rags.* (Prov. 23:20-21.)

Woe unto them that rise in the morning, that they may follow strong drink; that continue until night, till wine inflame them! (Isa. 5:11; similar scripture, 2 Ne. 15:11.)

205

Woe unto them that are mighty to drink wine, and men of strength to mingle strong drink: *which justify the wicked for reward, and take away the righteousness of the righteous from him!* (Isa. 5:22-23; similar scripture, 2 Ne. 15:22-23.)

Be not deceived: neither fornicators, . . . nor drunkards, . . . *shall inherit the kingdom of God.* (1 Cor. 6:9-10.)

Now the works of the flesh are manifest, which are these; . . . drunkenness, revellings, and such like: of the which I tell you before, as I have also told you in time past, that they which do such things *shall not inherit the kingdom of God.* (Gal. 5:19-21.)

Be not drunk with wine, wherein is excess; but be filled with the Spirit. (Eph. 5:18.)

A bishop then must be . . . sober, . . . not given to wine. (1 Tim. 3:2-3; similar scripture, Titus 1:7.)

Likewise must the deacons be . . . not given to much wine. (1 Tim. 3:8.)

Whoso forbiddeth to abstain from meats, that man should not eat the same, *is not ordained of God.* (D&C 49:18.)

All things which come of the earth, in the season thereof, are made for the benefit and the use of man, both to please the eye and to gladden the heart; yea, for food and for raiment, for taste and for smell, to strengthen the body and to enliven the soul. And it pleaseth God that he hath given all these things unto men; for unto this end were they made to be used, with judgment, not to excess, neither by extortion. (D&C 59:18-20.)

Lay your hands upon the sick, *and they shall recover.* (D&C 66:9.)

Cease to be idle; cease to be unclean; cease to find fault one with another; cease to sleep longer than is needful; retire to thy bed early, *that ye may not be weary;* arise early, *that your bodies and your minds may be invigorated.* (D&C 88:124.)

Strong drinks are not for the belly, but for the washing of your bodies. And again, tobacco is not for the body, neither for the belly, and is not good for man, but is an herb for bruises and all sick cattle, to be used with judgment and skill. And again, hot drinks are not for the body or belly. (D&C 89:7-9; see promise in D&C 89:18-21.)

All wholesome herbs God hath ordained for the constitution, nature, and use of man—every herb in the season thereof, and every fruit in the season thereof; all these to be used with prudence and thanksgiving. Yea, flesh also of beasts and of the fowls of the air, I, the Lord, have ordained for the use of man with thanksgiving; nevertheless they are to be used sparingly; and it is pleasing unto me that they should not be used, only in times of winter, or of cold, or famine. All grain is ordained for the use of man and of beasts, to be the staff of life, not only for man but for the beasts of the field, and the fowls of heaven, and all wild animals that run or creep on the earth; and these hath God made for the use of man only in times of famine and excess of hunger. All grain is good for the food of man; as also the fruit of the vine; that which yieldeth fruit, whether in the ground or above the ground—nevertheless, wheat for man, and corn for the ox, and oats for the horse, and rye for the fowls and for swine, and for all beasts of the field, and barley for all useful animals, and for mild drinks, as also other grain. (D&C 89:10-17; see promise in D&C 89:18-21.)

All saints who remember to keep and do these sayings, walking in obedience to the commandments, *shall receive health in their navel and marrow to their bones; and shall find wisdom and great treasures of knowledge, even hidden treasures; and shall run and not be weary, and shall walk and not faint. And I, the Lord, give unto them a promise, that the destroying angel shall pass by them, as the children of Israel, and not slay them.* (D&C 89:18-21.)

Holiness

(See also Purity; Sacredness; Sanctification; Worldliness; Worship.)

As the Lord commands us throughout ancient and modern scripture to become holy, he is commanding us to set ourselves apart for a divine purpose. The world may not recognize holiness, nor even acknowledge a need for it, yet despite the irreverence of the world for holy things we must respect teachings, objects, and people which have been designated for sacred purposes.

Our lives can demonstrate respect for God's purposes if we dedicate and consecrate ourselves to be instruments of his will. Such dedication is not dependent on high Church callings or great natural ability. Each believing individual can present himself to God as "a living sacrifice, holy, acceptable unto God." (Rom. 12:1.)

Commandments and Promises

I am the Lord your God: ye shall therefore sanctify yourselves, and ye shall be holy; for I am holy. (Lev. 11:44; similar scripture, Lev. 20:7.)

The Lord spake unto Moses, saying, Speak unto all the congregation of the children of Israel, and say unto them, Ye shall be holy: for I the Lord your God am holy. (Lev. 19:1-2.)

Worship the Lord in the beauty of holiness. (1 Chr. 16:29; similar scriptures, Ps. 29:2, 96:9.)

I speak after the manner of men because of the infirmity of your flesh: for as ye have yielded your members servants to uncleanness and to iniquity unto iniquity; even so now yield your members servants to righteousness unto holiness. (Rom. 6:19.)

Present your bodies a living sacrifice, holy, acceptable unto God, which is your reasonable service. (Rom. 12:1.)

Having therefore these promises [that God will be our Father and we his children], dearly beloved, let us cleanse ourselves from all filthiness of the flesh and spirit, perfecting holiness in the fear of God. (2 Cor. 7:1.)

God hath not called us unto uncleanness, but unto holiness. (1 Thes. 4:7.)

Refuse profane and old wives' fables, and exercise thyself rather unto godliness. For bodily exercise profiteth little: but godliness *is profitable unto all things, having promise of the life that now is, and of that which is to come.* (1 Tim. 4:7-8.)

For men shall be . . . unholy, . . . having a form of godliness; but denying the power thereof: from such turn away. . . . *But they shall proceed no further: for their folly shall be manifest unto all men.* (2 Tim. 3:2-9.)

A bishop must be . . . holy. (Titus 1:7-8.)

Speak thou [Titus] the things which become sound doctrine: that . . . the aged women . . . be in behaviour as becometh holiness. (Titus 2:1-3.)

Follow peace with all men, and holiness, *without which no man shall see the Lord.* (Heb. 12:14.)

As he which hath called you is holy, so be ye holy in all manner of conversation; because it is written, Be ye holy; for I am holy. (1 Pet. 1:15-16.)

Giving all diligence, add to your faith virtue; and to virtue knowledge; and to knowledge temperance; and to temperance patience; and to patience godliness; and to godliness brotherly kindness; and to brotherly kindness charity. For if these things be in you, and abound, *they make you that ye shall neither be barren nor unfruitful in the knowledge of our Lord Jesus Christ.* But he that lacketh these things *is blind, and cannot see afar off, and hath forgotten that he was purged from his old sins.* (2 Pet. 1:5-9.)

The Lord knoweth how to deliver the godly *out of temptations, and to reserve* the unjust *unto the day of judgment to be punished.* (2 Pet. 2:9.)

If ye were holy *I would speak unto you of holiness;* but as ye are not holy, and ye look upon me as a teacher, *it must needs be expedient that I teach you the consequences of sin.* (2 Ne. 9:48.)

[Angels] are subject unto him, *to minister according to the word of his command, showing themselves unto them* of strong faith and a firm mind in every form of godliness. (Moro. 7:30.)

Remember . . . virtue, . . . godliness, charity. (D&C 4:6.)

The members shall manifest before the church, and also before the elders, by a godly walk and conversation, that they are worthy of [baptism], *that there may be works and faith agreeable to the holy scriptures*—walking in holiness before the Lord. (D&C 20:69.)

Wherefore, meaning the church, thou shalt give heed unto all his words and commandments which he shall give unto you as he receiveth them, walking in all holiness before me. (D&C 21:4.)

Ye shall become instructed in the law of my church, and be sanctified by that which ye have received, and ye shall bind yourselves to act in all holiness before me—that inasmuch as ye do this, *glory shall be added to the kingdom which ye have received.* Inasmuch as ye do it not, *it shall be taken, even that which ye have received.* (D&C 43: 9-10.)

That which the Spirit testifies unto you even so I would that ye should do in all holiness of heart, walking uprightly before me, considering the end of your salvation, doing all things with prayer and thanksgiving, *that ye may not be seduced by evil spirits, or doctrines of devils, or the commandments of men; for some are of men, and others of devils.* (D&C 46:7.)

Ye must practise virtue and holiness before me continually. (D&C 46:33.)

In this place let them lift up their voice and declare my word with loud voices, without wrath or doubting, lifting up holy hands upon them. *For I am able to make you holy, and your sins are forgiven you.* (D&C 60:7.)

Stand ye in holy places, and be not moved, until the day of the Lord come; for behold, it cometh quickly, saith the Lord. (D&C 87:8.)

It is my will, that all they who call on my name, and worship me according to mine everlasting gospel, should gather together, and stand in holy places. (D&C 101:22.)

The decisions of these quorums, or either of them, are to be made in all righteousness, in holiness, and lowliness of heart, meekness and long suffering, and in faith, and virtue, and knowledge, temperance, patience, godliness, brotherly kindness and charity; because *the promise is*, if these things abound in them *they shall not be unfruitful in the knowledge of the Lord*. (D&C 107:30-31.)

Honest in Heart

(See also Honesty.)

The heart has long represented the innermost character, feelings, and inclinations of man. Those who are honest in heart are inwardly truthful, honorable, upright, and full of integrity. For God's people, honest hearts are requisite to receiving a knowledge of whatever is asked of God. (See D&C 8:1.) It is a condition preceding acceptance by God. (See D&C 97:8.)

Another reason honesty within self is important is this: if we know something is a sin, then we have to deceive ourselves somehow to commit that sin. Thus the more honest we are with ourselves, the less we sin.

Only through being honest with ourselves can we see and overcome our weaknesses. "And because thou hast seen thy weakness thou shalt be made strong," the Lord tells Moroni, "even unto the sitting down in the place which I have prepared in the mansions of my Father." (Ether 12:37.)

Commandments and Promises

Stand in awe, and sin not: commune with your own heart upon your bed, and be still. (Ps. 4:4.)

Lord, who shall abide in thy tabernacle? who shall dwell in thy holy hill? He that walketh uprightly, and worketh righteousness, and speaketh the truth in his heart. (Ps. 15:1-2; see also JST Ps. 15:1.)

These six things doth the Lord hate: yea, seven are an abomination unto him: a proud look, a lying tongue, and hands that shed innocent blood, an heart that deviseth wicked imaginations, feet that be swift in running to mischief, a false witness that speaketh lies, and he that soweth discord among brethren. (Prov. 6:16-19.)

In them is fulfilled the prophecy of Esaias, which saith, *By hearing ye shall hear, and shall not understand; and seeing ye shall see, and shall not perceive;* for this people's heart is waxed gross, and their ears are dull of hearing, and their eyes they have closed; *lest at any time they should see with their eyes, and hear with their ears, and should understand with their heart, and should be converted, and I should heal them.* (Matt. 13:14-15.)

Thou therefore which teachest another, teachest thou not thyself? thou that preachest a man should not steal, dost thou steal? Thou that sayest a man should not commit adultery, dost thou commit adultery? thou that abhorrest idols, dost thou commit sacrilege? Thou that makest thy boast of the law, through breaking the law dishonourest thou God? (Rom. 2:21-23.)

Let no man deceive himself. If any man among you seemeth to be wise in this world, let him become a fool, *that he may be wise.* (1 Cor. 3:18.)

Let us keep the feast, not with old leaven, neither with the leaven of malice and wickedness; but with the unleavened bread of sincerity and truth. (1 Cor. 5:8.)

If we would judge ourselves, *we should not be judged.* (1 Cor. 11:31.)

Examine yourselves, whether ye be in the faith; prove your own selves. Know ye not your own selves, how that Jesus Christ is in you, except ye be reprobates? (2 Cor. 13:5.)

Now the end of the commandment is charity out of a pure heart, and of a good conscience, and of faith unfeigned. (1 Tim. 1:5.)

[Hold] faith, and a good conscience; which some having put away concerning faith have made shipwreck. (1 Tim. 1:19.)

Now as Jannes and Jambres withstood Moses, so do these also resist the truth: men of corrupt minds, reprobate concerning the faith. *But they shall proceed no further: for their folly shall be manifest unto all men, as theirs also was.* (2 Tim. 3:8-9.)

Unto the pure *all things are pure:* but unto them that are defiled and unbelieving *is nothing pure;* but even their mind and conscience is defiled. They profess that they know God; but in works they deny him, being abominable and disobedient, and unto every good work reprobate. (Titus 1:15-16; see JST Titus 1:15.)

A double minded man *is unstable in all his ways.* (James 1:8.)

Be ye doers of the word, and not hearers only, deceiving your own selves. (James 1:22.)

If any man among you seem to be religious, and bridleth not his tongue, but deceiveth his own heart, *this man's religion is vain.* (James 1:26.)

If ye have bitter envying and strife in your hearts, glory not, and lie not against the truth. (James 3:14.)

Purify your hearts, ye doubleminded. (James 4:8.)

Laying aside all malice, and all guile, and hypocrisies, and envies, and all evil speakings, as newborn babes, desire the sincere milk of the word, *that ye may grow thereby:* if so be ye have tasted that the Lord is gracious. (1 Pet. 2:1-3.)

If we say that we have no sin, we deceive ourselves, *and the truth is not in us.* (1 John 1:8.)

Wo unto them that seek deep to hide their counsel from the Lord! (2 Ne. 27:27.)

If ye shall follow the Son, with full purpose of heart, acting no hypocrisy and no deception before God, but with real intent, repenting of your sins, witnessing unto the Father that ye are willing to take upon you the name of Christ, by baptism—yea, by following your Lord and your Savior down into the water, according to his word, behold, *then shall ye receive the Holy Ghost; yea, then cometh the baptism of fire and of the Holy Ghost; and then can ye speak with the tongue of angels, and shout praises unto the Holy One of Israel.* (2 Ne. 31:13.)

I desire that ye should deny the justice of God no more. Do not endeavor to excuse yourself in the least point because of your sins, by denying the justice of God; but do you let the justice of God, and his mercy, and his long-suffering have full sway in your heart; and let it bring you down to the dust in humility. (Alma 42:30.)

At that day when the Gentiles shall sin against my gospel, and shall reject the fulness of my gospel, and shall be lifted up in the pride of their hearts above all nations, and above all the people of the whole earth, and shall be filled with all manner of lyings, and of deceits, and of mischiefs, and all manner of hypocrisy, and murders, and priestcrafts, and whoredoms, and of secret abominations; and if they shall do all those things, and shall reject the fulness of my gospel, behold, saith the Father, *I will bring the fulness of my gospel from among them.* (3 Ne. 16:10.)

Because thou hast seen thy weakness *thou shalt be made strong, even unto the sitting down in the place which I have prepared in the mansions of my Father.* (Ether 12:37.)

Oliver Cowdery, verily, verily, I say unto you, that assuredly as the Lord liveth, who is your God and your Redeemer, *even so surely shall you receive a knowledge of whatsoever things you shall ask* in faith, with an honest heart, believing that you shall receive a knowledge. . . . *Yea, behold, I will tell you in your mind and in your heart, by the Holy Ghost, which shall come upon you and which shall dwell in your heart. Now, behold, this is the spirit of revelation.* (D&C 8: 1-3.)

The hypocrites *shall be detected and shall be cut off, either in life or in death, even as I will; and wo unto them who are cut off from my church, for the same are overcome of the world.* (D&C 50:8.)

All among them who know their hearts are honest, and are broken, and their spirits contrite, and are willing to observe their covenants by sacrifice—yea, every sacrifice which I, the Lord, shall command— *they are accepted of me.* (D&C 97:8.)

Honesty

(See also False Witness; Honest in Heart; Stealing.)

The Apostle Paul with this reason enjoins Christ's followers to be honest: "for we are members one of another." (Eph. 4:25.) The Lord, in commanding Edward Partridge to handle the temporal arrangements for settling in Ohio, stipulates honesty and equality among his people: "that ye may be one, even as I have commanded you." (D&C 51:9.) Dishonesty evidently does much more than rob a man of his property or reputation. Dishonesty undermines charity, destroys unity, and fosters mistrust.

Commandments and Promises

Ye shall not steal, neither deal falsely, neither lie one to another. (Lev. 19:11.)

The Lord shall cut off all flattering lips, and the tongue that speaketh proud things. (Ps. 12:3.)

Who shall ascend into the hill of the Lord? or who shall stand in his holy place? He that hath clean hands, and a pure heart; who hath not lifted up his soul unto vanity, nor sworn deceitfully. (Ps. 24:3-4.)

Thou lovest all devouring words, O thou deceitful tongue. *God shall likewise destroy thee for ever, he shall take thee away, and pluck thee out of thy dwelling place, and root thee out of the land of the living.* (Ps. 52:4-5.)

These six things doth the Lord hate: yea, seven are an abomination unto him: a proud look, a lying tongue, and hands that shed innocent blood, an heart that deviseth wicked imaginations, feet that be swift in running to mischief, a false witness that speaketh lies, and he that soweth discord among brethren. (Prov. 6:16-19.)

Buy the truth, and sell it not; also wisdom, and instruction, and understanding. (Prov. 23:23.)

If a man be just, and do that which is lawful and right, . . . and hath not oppressed any, but hath restored to the debtor his pledge, . . . he that hath not given forth upon usury, neither hath taken any increase, that hath withdrawn his hand from iniquity, hath executed true judgment between man and man, hath walked in my statutes, and hath kept my commandments, to deal truly; *he is just, he shall surely live,* saith the Lord God. (Ezek. 18:5-9.)

These are the things that ye shall do; Speak ye every man the truth to his neighbour; execute the judgment of truth and peace in your gates: and let none of you imagine evil in your hearts against his neighbour; and love no false oath: for all these are things *that I hate,* saith the Lord. (Zech. 8:16-17.)

Putting away lying, speak every man truth with his neighbour: for we are members one of another. (Eph. 4:25.)

Take unto you the whole armour of God, *that ye may be able to withstand in the evil day, and having done all, to stand.* Stand therefore, having your loins girt about with truth. (Eph. 6:13-14.)

Lie not one to another, seeing that ye have put off the old man with his deeds; and have put on the new man, which is renewed in knowledge after the image of him that created him. (Col. 3:9-10.)

Masters, give unto your servants that which is just and equal; knowing that ye also have a Master in heaven. (Col. 4:1.)

A bishop must be blameless, . . . not given to filthy lucre. (Titus 1:7.)

Go to now, ye rich men, weep and howl for your miseries that shall come upon you. Your riches are corrupted, and your garments are motheaten. Your gold and silver is cankered; and the rust of them shall be a witness against you, and shall eat your flesh as it were fire. Ye have heaped treasure together for the last days. Behold, the hire of the labourers who have reaped down your fields, which is of you kept back by fraud, crieth: and the cries of them which have reaped are entered into the ears of the Lord of sabaoth. (James 5:1-4.)

Having your conversation honest among the Gentiles: that, whereas they speak against you as evildoers, they may by your good works, which they shall behold, *glorify God in the day of visitation.* (1 Pet. 2:12.)

He that saith, I know him, and keepeth not his commandments, is a liar, *and the truth is not in him.* (1 Jn. 2:4.)

The fearful, and unbelieving, and the abominable, and murderers, and whoremongers, and sorcerers, and idolaters, and all liars, *shall have their part in the lake which burneth with fire and brimstone: which is the second death.* (Rev. 21:8; see also D&C 63:17.)

Wo unto the liar, *for he shall be thrust down to hell.* (2 Ne. 9:34.)

Those priests who did go forth among the people did preach against all lyings, and deceivings, and envyings, and strifes, and malice, and revilings,and stealing,robbing, plundering, murdering, committing adultery, and all manner of lasciviousness, crying that these things ought not so to be. (Alma 16:18.)

At that day when the Gentiles shall sin against my gospel, and shall reject the fulness of my gospel, and shall be lifted up in the pride of their hearts above all nations, and above all the people of the whole earth, and shall be filled with all manner of lyings, and of deceits, and of mischiefs, and all manner of hypocrisy, and murders, and priestcrafts, and whoredoms, and of secret abominations; and if they shall do all those things, and shall reject the fulness of my gospel, behold, saith the Father, *I will bring the fulness of my gospel from among them.* (3 Ne. 16:10.)

Wo be unto him that lieth to deceive because he supposeth that another lieth to deceive, *for such are not exempt from the justice of God.* (D&C 10:28.)

Take upon you the name of Christ, and speak the truth in soberness. (D&C 18:21.)

Thou shalt not lie; he that lieth and will not repent *shall be cast out.* (D&C 42:21.)

Let every man deal honestly, and be alike among this people, and receive alike, *that ye may be one, even as I have commanded you.* (D&C 51:9.)

I, the Lord, have said that the fearful, and the unbelieving, and all liars, and whosoever loveth and maketh a lie, and the whoremonger, and the sorcerer, *shall have their part in that lake which burneth with fire and brimstone, which is the second death.* (D&C 63:17; see also Rev. 21:8.)

Inasmuch as some of my servants have not kept the commandment, but have broken the covenant through covetousness, and with feigned words, *I have cursed them with a very sore and grievous curse.* (D&C 104:4.)

When we undertake to cover our sins, or to gratify our pride, our vain ambition, or to exercise control or dominion or compulsion upon the souls of the children of men, in any degree of unrighteousness, behold, *the heavens withdraw themselves; the Spirit of the Lord is grieved; and when it is withdrawn, Amen to the priesthood or the authority of that man. Behold, ere he is aware, he is left unto himself, to kick against the pricks, to persecute the saints, and to fight against God.* (D&C 121:37-38.)

Those who are not pure, and who have said they were pure, *shall be destroyed*, saith the Lord God. (D&C 132:52.)

Keep all your pledges one with another. (D&C 136:20.)

If thou borrowest of thy neighbour, thou shalt restore that which thou hast borrowed; and if thou canst not repay then go straightway and tell thy neighbor, *lest he condemn thee.* If thou shalt find that which thy neighbor has lost, thou shalt make diligent search till thou shalt deliver it to him again. (D&C 136:25-26.)

Hope

(See also Faith; Loving Others.)

Faith, hope, charity, and humility are inextricably intertwined. "Now abideth faith, hope, charity, these three," Paul writes. (1 Cor. 13:13.) And Moroni teaches, "There must be faith; and if there must be faith there must also be hope; and if there must be hope there must also be charity." (Moro. 10:20.) Also, "If a man have faith he must needs have hope; for without faith there cannot be any hope. And . . . he cannot have faith and hope, save he shall be meek, and lowly of heart." (Moro. 7:42-43.)

Without faith, we have no hope; we are in despair. We have little spiritual strength to share with others, and we feel incapable of acknowledging the love of God.

A lack of hope is painful, but what can we do when despair and depression grip us, when hope ebbs?

First, we can realize that hope is an attitude, and that our attitudes affect our actions. "Have patience, and bear with those afflictions, with a firm hope that ye shall one day rest from all your afflictions." (Alma 34:41.) We can *choose* hopefulness rather than pessimism or skepticism.

Additionally, we can act as if we have hope, "always abounding in good works, being led to glorify God."(Ether 12:4.) This is similar to the commandments recorded in scripture that God's people were to have faith in the Resurrection and Atonement even before it happened. If we persist in active righteousness that benefits others, our hope will be strengthened as our feelings of charity strengthen. We will avoid the selfish inwardness that leads to despair. As we approach life with gratitude—glorifying and thanking God instead of blaming him—we can more easily recognize the good that can come through any experience in life. At the same time, we must eliminate the iniquity that, according to Moroni, brings us despair. (See Moro. 10:22.)

As we thus struggle upward, the Lord will lift us through his

Spirit. We can gain hope through the Spirit, since hope is a gift of the Spirit. Paul wrote: "The God of hope fill you with all joy and peace in believing, that ye may abound in hope, through the power of the Holy Ghost." (Rom. 15:13.)

With Godly hope in our lives, our souls are anchored to the Lord and his truths. We can then stand as does an anchored ship—at times tossed and troubled by storms of adversity, but nonetheless "sure and steadfast." (Ether 12:4.)

Commandments and Promises

The eye of the Lord is upon them that fear him, upon them that hope in his mercy; *to deliver their soul from death, and to keep them alive in famine.* (Ps. 33:18-19.)

Let thy mercy, O Lord, be upon us, according as we hope in thee. (Ps. 33:22.)

The Lord taketh pleasure in them that fear him, in those that hope in his mercy. (Ps. 147:11.)

We are saved by hope: but hope that is seen is not hope: for what a man seeth, why doth he yet hope for? But if we hope for that we see not, then do we with patience wait for it. (Rom. 8:24-25.)

[Be] rejoicing in hope; patient in tribulation; continuing instant in prayer. (Rom. 12:12.)

Now the God of hope fill you with all joy and peace in believing, that ye may abound in hope, through the power of the Holy Ghost. (Rom. 15:13.)

For our sakes, no doubt, this is written: that he that ploweth should plow in hope; and that he that thresheth in hope *should be partaker of his hope.* (1 Cor. 9:10.)

If in this life only we have hope in Christ, *we are of all men most miserable.* (1 Cor. 15:19.)

And you, that were sometime alienated and enemies in your mind by wicked works, yet now hath he reconciled in the body of his flesh through death, to present you holy and unblameable and unreproveable in his sight: if ye continue in the faith grounded and settled, and be not moved away from the hope of the gospel, which ye have heard, and which was preached to every creature which is under heaven. (Col. 1:21-23.)

Let us, who are of the day, be sober, putting on the breastplate of faith and love; and for an helmet, the hope of salvation. (1 Thes. 5:8.)

The grace of God that bringeth salvation hath appeared to all men, teaching us that, denying ungodliness and worldly lusts, we should live soberly, righteously, and godly, in this present world; looking for that blessed hope, and the glorious appearing of the great God and our Saviour Jesus Christ; who gave himself for us, that he might redeem us from all iniquity, and purify unto himself a peculiar people, zealous of good works. These things speak, and exhort, and rebuke with all authority. (Titus 2:11-15.)

Christ's house are we, if we hold fast the confidence and the rejoicing of the hope firm unto the end. (Heb. 3:6.)

God, willing more abundantly to shew unto the heirs of promise the immutability of his counsel, *confirmed it by an oath: that* by two immutable things, in which it was impossible for God to lie, *we might have a strong consolation,* who have fled for refuge *to lay hold upon the hope set before us:* which hope *we have as an anchor of the soul, both sure and stedfast, and which entereth into that within the veil.* (Heb. 6:17-19.)

The law made nothing perfect, but the bringing in of a better hope *did; by the which we draw nigh unto God.* (Heb. 7:19; see also JST Heb. 7:19.)

Gird up the loins of your mind, be sober, and hope to the end *for the grace that is to be brought unto you at the revelation of Jesus Christ.* (1 Pet. 1:13.)

Sanctify the Lord God in your hearts: and be ready always to give an answer to every man that asketh you a reason of the hope that is in you with meekness and fear: having a good conscience; *that*, whereas they speak evil of you, as of evildoers, *they may be ashamed that falsely accuse your good conversation in Christ.* (1 Pet. 3:15-16; see also JST 1 Pet. 3:16.)

Now are we the sons of God, and it doth not yet appear what we shall be: but we know that, when he shall appear, we shall be like him; for we shall see him as he is. And every man that hath this hope in him *purifieth himself, even as he is pure.* (1 Jn. 3:2-3.)

Building up yourselves on your most holy faith, praying in the Holy Ghost, keep yourselves in the love of God, looking for the mercy of our Lord Jesus Christ *unto eternal life.* (Jude 1:20-21.)

Ye must press forward with a steadfastness in Christ, having a perfect brightness of hope, and a love of God and of all men. (2 Ne. 31:20.)

Be reconciled unto him through the atonement of Christ, his Only Begotten Son, *and ye may obtain a resurrection, according to the power of the resurrection which is in Christ, and be presented as the first-fruits of Christ unto God,* having faith, and obtained a good hope of glory in him before he manifesteth himself in the flesh. (Jacob 4:11.)

Whosoever has heard the words of the prophets, yea, all the holy prophets who have prophesied concerning the coming of the Lord—I say unto you, that all those who have hearkened unto their words, and believed that the Lord would redeem his people, and have looked forward to that day for a remission of their sins, *I say unto you, that these are his seed, or they are the heirs of the kingdom of God. For these are they whose sins he has borne; these are they for whom he has died, to redeem them from their transgressions. And now, are they not his seed?* (Mosiah 15:11-12.)

Let us be wise and look forward to these things, and do that which will make for the peace of this people. (Mosiah 29:10.)

See that ye have faith, hope, and charity, *and then ye will always abound in good works.* (Alma 7:24.)

I [Alma] wish . . . that ye would hearken unto my words . . . having faith on the Lord; having a hope that ye shall receive eternal life; having the love of God always in your hearts, *that ye may be lifted up at the last day and enter into his rest.* (Alma 13:27-29.)

If ye will nourish the word, yea, nourish the tree as it beginneth to grow, by your faith with great diligence, and with patience, looking forward to the fruit thereof, *it shall take root; and behold it shall be a tree springing up unto everlasting life.* (Alma 32:41.)

Have patience, and bear with those afflictions, with a firm hope that ye shall one day rest from all your afflictions. (Alma 34:41.)

Whoso believeth in God might with surety hope for a better world, yea, even a place at the right hand of God, which hope cometh of faith, *maketh an anchor to the souls of men, which would make them sure and steadfast, always abounding in good works, being led to glorify God.* (Ether 12:4.)

Man must hope, *or he cannot receive an inheritance in the place which thou hast prepared.* (Ether 12:32.)

What is it that ye shall hope for? Behold I say unto you that ye shall have hope through the atonement of Christ and the power of his resurrection, to be raised unto life eternal, and this because of your faith in him according to the promise. (Moro. 7:41.)

There must be faith; and if there must be faith there must also be hope; and if there must be hope there must also be charity. And except ye have charity *ye can in nowise be saved in the kingdom of God; neither can ye be saved in the kingdom of God* if ye have not faith; *neither can ye* if ye have no hope. And if ye have no hope *ye must needs be in despair; and despair cometh because of iniquity.* (Moro. 10: 20-22.)

Faith, hope, charity and love, with an eye single to the glory of God, *qualify him for the work.* (D&C 4:5.)

[to Oliver Cowdery] Have patience, faith, hope and charity. (D&C 6:19.)

No one can assist in this work except he shall be humble and full of love, having faith, hope, and charity, being temperate in all things, whatsoever shall be entrusted to his care. (D&C 12:8.)

If you have not faith, hope, and charity, *you can do nothing.* (D&C 18:19.)

Humility

(See also Honest in Heart; Meekness; Trusting God.)

Humility develops as we learn who we are and come to accept and love ourselves. Humility comes from recognizing our total dependence on Christ, from realizing that he is our true strength and that only through him can we overcome.

This does not preclude self-confidence, however. When our confidence is based on our belief in God, we are able to accomplish more and progress in ways that otherwise would be closed to us. We must not, however, let confidence lead us to the opposites of humility, which are pride and "stiffneckedness." Prideful people have falsely placed their confidence.

We can achieve humility through prayer, through repentance, through trusting in God, through worship, through subjecting our wills to God's will. If we try too hard in the wrong way to be humble, our humility will be artificial or even self-deprecating. Rather than thinking "I will now be humble," we must attempt to live Christlike lives, and genuine humility will follow.

The Lord details numerous rewards for the humble, among them this rich and simply stated promise: "Be thou humble; and the Lord thy God shall lead thee by the hand, and give thee answer to thy prayers." (D&C 112:10.)

Commandments and Promises

Speak not thou in thine heart, after that the Lord thy God hath cast them out from before thee, saying, For my righteousness the Lord hath brought me in to possess this land: but for the wickedness of these nations *the Lord doth drive them out from before thee.* Not for thy righteousness, or for the uprightness of thine heart, *dost thou go to possess their land:* but for the wickedness of these nations the Lord thy God *doth drive them out from before thee, and that he may perform the word which the Lord sware unto thy fathers, Abraham, Isaac, and Jacob.* Understand therefore, that *the Lord thy God giveth thee not this good land to possess it* for thy righteousness; for thou art a stiffnecked people. (Deut. 9:4-6.)

If I shut up heaven that there be no rain, or if I command the locusts to devour the land, or if I send pestilence among my people; if my people, which are called by my name, shall humble themselves, and pray, and seek my face, and turn from their wicked ways; *then will I hear from heaven, and will forgive their sin, and will heal their land.* (2 Chr. 7:13-14.)

When the Lord saw that [the princes of Israel and the king] humbled themselves, the word of the Lord came to Shemaiah, saying, They have humbled themselves; *therefore I will not destroy them, but I will grant them some deliverance; and my wrath shall not be poured out upon Jerusalem by the hand of Shishak.* (2 Chr. 12:7.)

He forgetteth not the cry of the humble. (Ps. 9:12.)

The Lord shall cut off all flattering lips, and the tongue that speaketh proud things: who have said, With our tongue we will prevail; our lips are our own: who is lord over us? (Ps. 12:3-4.)

Thou wilt save the afflicted people; *but wilt bring down* high looks. (Ps. 18:27.)

Who shall ascend into the hill of the Lord? or who shall stand in his holy place? He that hath clean hands, and a pure heart; who hath not lifted up his soul unto vanity, nor sworn deceitfully. (Ps. 24:3-4.)

The humble shall see this, *and be glad: and your heart shall live* that seek God. (Ps. 69:32.)

The Lord preserveth the simple: I was brought low, *and he helped me.* (Ps. 116:6.)

The entrance of thy words giveth light; it giveth understanding unto the simple. (Ps. 119:130.)

Though the Lord be high, yet hath he respect unto the lowly: but the proud *he knoweth afar off.* (Ps. 138:6.)

Be not wise in thine own eyes: fear the Lord, and depart from evil. (Prov. 3:7.)

He giveth grace unto the lowly. (Prov. 3:34.)

These six things doth the Lord hate: yea, seven are an abomination unto him: A proud look, a lying tongue, and hands that shed innocent blood, an heart that deviseth wicked imaginations, feet that be swift in running to mischief, a false witness that speaketh lies, and he that soweth discord among brethren. (Prov. 6:16-19.)

The fear of the Lord is to hate evil: pride, and arrogancy, and the evil way, and the froward mouth, *do I [wisdom] hate.* (Prov. 8:13.)

Only by pride *cometh contention:* but with the well advised *is wisdom.* (Prov. 13:10.)

The Lord will destroy the house of the proud: *but he will establish the border* of the widow. (Prov. 15:25.)

Every one that is proud in heart *is an abomination to the Lord: though hand join in hand, he shall not be unpunished.* (Prov. 16:5.)

Pride *goeth before destruction*, and an haughty spirit *before a fall.* Better it is to be of an humble spirit with the lowly, than to divide the spoil with the proud. (Prov. 16:19.)

Labour not to be rich: cease from thine own wisdom. (Prov. 23:4.)

Boast not thyself of to morrow; for thou knowest not what a day may bring forth. (Prov. 27:1.)

Let another man praise thee, and not thine own mouth; a stranger, and not thine own lips. (Prov. 27:2.)

He that is of a proud heart *stirreth up strife.* (Prov. 28:25.)

A man's pride *shall bring him low:* but honour *shall uphold* the humble in spirit. (Prov. 29:23.)

The lofty looks of man *shall be humbled*, and the haughtiness of men *shall be bowed down, and the Lord alone shall be exalted in that day.*

For the day of the Lord of hosts shall be upon every one that is proud and lofty, *and upon every one* that is lifted up, *and he shall be brought low.* . . . And the loftiness of man *shall be bowed down,* and the haughtiness of men *shall be made low: and the Lord alone shall be exalted in that day.* (Isa. 2:11-17; similar scripture, 2 Ne. 12:11-17.)

Because the daughters of Zion are haughty, and walk with stretched forth necks and wanton eyes, walking and mincing as they go, and making a tinkling with their feet: *therefore the Lord will smite with a scab the crown of the head of the daughters of Zion, and the Lord will discover their secret parts.* (Isa. 3:16-17; similar scripture, 2 Ne. 13:16-17.)

Woe be unto them that are wise in their own eyes, and prudent in their own sight! (Isa. 5:21; similar scripture, 2 Ne. 15:21.)

Hear ye, and give ear; be not proud: for the Lord has spoken. Give glory to the Lord your God, *before he cause darkness, and before your feet stumble upon the dark mountains, and while ye look for light, he turn it into the shadow of death, and make it gross darkness.* But if ye will not hear it, *my soul shall weep in secret places* for your pride; *and mine eye shall weep sore, and run down with tears; because the Lord's flock is carried away captive.* (Jer. 13:15-17.)

Have ye forgotten the wickedness of your fathers, and the wickedness of their wives, and your own wickedness, and the wickedness of your wives, which they have committed in the land of Judah, and in the streets of Jerusalem? They are not humbled even unto this day, neither have they feared, nor walked in my law, nor in my statutes, that I set before you and before your fathers. *Therefore thus saith the Lord of Hosts, the God of Israel; Behold, I will set my face against you for evil, and to cut off all Judah. And I will take the remnant of Judah, that have set their faces to go into the land of Egypt to sojourn there, and they shall all be consumed, and fall in the land of Egypt; they shall even be consumed by the sword of famine: they shall die, from the least even unto the greatest, by the sword and by the famine: and they shall be an execration, and an astonishment, and a curse, and a reproach.* (Jer. 44:9-12.)

What doth the Lord require of thee, but to do justly, and to love mercy, and to walk humbly with thy God? (Micah 6:8.)

The day cometh, that shall burn as an oven; and all the proud, yea, and all that do wickedly, *shall be stubble: and the day that cometh shall burn them up, saith the Lord of hosts, that it shall leave them neither root nor branch.* (Mal. 4:1; similar scripture, 3 Ne. 25:1.)

Think not to say within yourselves, We have Abraham to our father: for I say unto you, that God is able of these stones to raise up children unto Abraham. (Matt. 3:9.)

Blessed are the poor in spirit: *for theirs is the kingdom of heaven.* (Matt. 5:3.)

Except ye be converted, and become as little children, *ye shall not enter into the kingdom of heaven.* Whosoever therefore shall humble himself as this little child, *the same is greatest in the kingdom of heaven.* (Matt. 18:3-4.)

Whosoever shall exalt himself *shall be abased;* and he that shall humble himself *shall be exalted.* (Matt. 23:12.)

From within, out of the heart of men, proceed evil thoughts, adulteries, fornications, murders, thefts, covetousness, wickedness, deceit, lasciviousness, an evil eye, blasphemy, pride, foolishness: all these evil things come from within, and *defile the man.* (Mark 7:21-23.)

Whosoever shall not receive the kingdom of God as a little child, *he shall not enter therein.* (Mark 10:15.)

He hath shewed strength with his arm; he hath scattered the proud in the imagination of their hearts. *He hath put down* the mighty *from their seats, and exalted them* of low degree. (Luke 1:51-52.)

Blessed be ye poor: *for yours is the kingdom of God.* (Luke 6:20.)

Woe unto you, Pharisees! for ye love the uppermost seats in the synagogues, and greetings in the markets. (Luke 11:43.)

Whosoever exalteth himself *shall be abased;* and he that humbleth himself *shall be exalted.* (Luke 14:11.)

Whosoever shall not receive the kingdom of God as a little child *shall in no wise enter therein.* (Luke 18:17.)

He that speaketh of himself seeketh his own glory: but he that seeketh his glory that sent him, *the same is true, and no unrighteousness is in him.* (John 7:18.)

If the firstfruit be holy, the lump is also holy: and if the root be holy, so are the branches. And if some of the branches be broken off, and thou, being a wild olive tree, wert graffed in among them, and with them partakest of the root and fatness of the olive tree; boast not against the branches. But if thou boast, thou bearest not the root, but the root thee. (Rom. 11:16-18.)

Be not highminded, but fear. (Rom. 11:20.)

I say, through the grace given unto me, to every man that is among you, not to think of himself more highly than he ought to think, but to think soberly, according as God hath dealt to every man the measure of faith. (Rom. 12:3.)

Be of the same mind one toward another. Mind not high things, but condescend to men of low estate. Be not wise in your own conceits. (Rom. 12:16.)

Let no man glory in men. (1 Cor. 3:21.)

These things, brethren, I have in a figure transferred to myself and to Apollos for your sakes; that ye might learn in us not to think of men above that which is written, that no one of you be puffed up for one against another. For who maketh thee to differ from another? and what hast thou that thou didst not receive? now if thou didst receive it, why dost thou glory, as if thou hadst not received it? (1 Cor. 4:6-7.)

He that glorieth, let him glory in the Lord. For not *he* that commendeth himself *is approved, but whom the Lord commendeth.* (2 Cor. 10:17-18.)

Let us not be desirous of vain glory, provoking one another, envying one another. (Gal. 5:26.)

Walk worthy of the vocation wherewith ye are called, with all lowliness and meekness. (Eph. 4:1-2.)

Let nothing be done through strife or vainglory; but in lowliness of mind let each esteem other better than themselves. (Philip. 2:3.)

Let no man beguile you of your reward in a voluntary humility and worshiping of angels, intruding into those things which he hath not seen, vainly puffed up by his fleshly mind. (Col. 2:18.)

Put on therefore, as the elect of God, holy and beloved, bowels of mercies, kindness, humbleness of mind, meekness, longsuffering. (Col. 3:12.)

A bishop then must be . . . not a novice, lest being lifted up with pride *he fall into the condemnation of the devil.* (1 Tim. 3:2-6.)

If any man teach otherwise, and consent not to wholesome words, even the words of our Lord Jesus Christ, and to the doctrine which is according to godliness; he is proud, knowing nothing, but doting about questions and strifes of words, *whereof cometh envy, strife, railing, evil surmisings, perverse disputings of men of corrupt minds, and destitute of the truth, supposing that gain is godliness.* (1 Tim. 6:3-5.)

Charge them that are rich in this world, that they be not highminded. (1 Tim. 6:17.)

For men shall be lovers of their own selves, covetous, boasters, proud, . . . heady, highminded . . . : from such turn away. . . . *But they shall proceed no further: for their folly shall be manifest unto all men.* (2 Tim. 3:2-9.)

A bishop must be . . . not self-willed. (Titus 1:7.)

If ye have respect to persons, *ye commit sin, and are convinced of the law as transgressors.* (James 2:9.)

Who is a wise man and endued with knowledge among you? let him shew out of a good conversation his works with meekness of wisdom. (James 3:13.)

God resisteth the proud, *but giveth grace* unto the humble. (James 4:6.)

Humble yourselves in the sight of the Lord, *and he shall lift you up.* (James 4:10.)

All of you be subject one to another, and be clothed with humility: for *God resisteth* the proud, *and giveth grace* to the humble. Humble yourselves therefore under the mighty hand of God, *that he may exalt you in due time:* casting all your care upon him; for he careth for you. (1 Pet. 5:5-7.)

The Lord knoweth how to deliver the godly out of temptations, and to reserve the unjust unto the day of judgment to be punished: but chiefly them that walk after the flesh in the lust of uncleanness, and despise government. Presumptuous are they, selfwilled, they are not afraid to speak evil of dignities. (2 Pet. 2:9-10.)

The Lord spake unto me, saying: *Blessed* art thou, Nephi, because of thy faith, for thou hast sought me diligently, with lowliness of heart. (1 Ne. 2:19.)

The day soon cometh that all the proud and they who do wickedly *shall be as stubble; and the day cometh that they must be burned.* (1 Ne. 22:15.)

They sell themselves *for naught;* for, for the reward of their pride and their foolishness *they shall reap destruction;* for because they yield unto the devil and choose works of darkness rather than light, *therefore they must go down to hell.* (2 Ne. 26:10.)

O the wise, and the learned, and the rich, that are puffed up in the pride of their hearts, and all those who preach false doctrines, and all those who commit whoredoms, and pervert the right way of the Lord, *wo, wo, wo be unto them, saith the Lord God Almighty, for they shall be thrust down to hell!* (2 Ne. 28:15.)

The hand of providence hath smiled upon you most pleasingly, that you have obtained many riches; and because some of you have obtained more abundantly than that of your brethren ye are lifted up in the pride of your hearts, and wear stiff necks and high heads because of the costliness of your apparel, and persecute your brethren because ye suppose that ye are better than they. And now, my brethren, do ye suppose that God justifieth you in this thing? Behold, I say unto you, *Nay. But he condemneth you*, and if ye persist in these things *his judgments must speedily come unto you*. (Jacob 2:13-14.)

O that ye would listen unto the word of his commands, and let not this pride of your hearts *destroy your souls!* (Jacob 2:16.)

Men drink damnation to their own souls except they humble themselves and become as little children, and believe that salvation was, and is, and is to come, in and through the atoning blood of Christ, the Lord Omnipotent. *For the natural man is an enemy to God, and has been from the fall of Adam, and will be, forever and ever,* unless he yields to the enticings of the Holy Spirit, and putteth off the natural man and becometh a saint through the atonement of Christ the Lord, and becometh as a child, submissive, meek, humble, patient, full of love, willing to submit to all things which the Lord seeth fit to inflict upon him, even as a child doth submit to his father. (Mosiah 3: 18-19.)

Believe that ye must repent of your sins and forsake them, and humble yourselves before God; and ask in sincerity of heart that he would forgive you; and now, if you believe all these things see that ye do them. (Mosiah 4:10.)

Remember, and always retain in remembrance, the greatness of God, and your own nothingness, and his goodness and long-suffering towards you, unworthy creatures, and humble yourselves even in the depths of humility, calling on the name of the Lord daily, and standing steadfastly in the faith of that which is to come, which was spoken by the mouth of the angel. (Mosiah 4:11.)

Ye shall not esteem one flesh above another, or one man shall not think himself above another. (Mosiah 23:7.)

He did deliver them because they did humble themselves before him; and because they cried mightily unto him *he did deliver them out of bondage; and thus doth the Lord work by his power in all cases among the children of men, extending the arm of mercy towards them* that put their trust in him. (Mosiah 29:20.)

Are ye stripped of pride? I say unto you, if ye are not *ye are not prepared to meet God.* Behold ye must prepare quickly; for the kingdom of heaven is soon at hand, and such an one *hath not eternal life.* (Alma 5:28.)

I would that ye should be humble. (Alma 7:23.)

I would that ye should humble yourselves before God, and bring forth fruit meet for repentance, *that ye may also enter into that rest.* (Alma 13:13.)

I wish from the inmost part of my heart, yea, with great anxiety even unto pain, that ye would hearken unto my words, and cast off your sins, and not procrastinate the day of your repentance; but that ye would humble yourselves before the Lord, and call on his holy name, and watch and pray continually, *that ye may not be tempted above that which ye can bear, and thus be led by the Holy Spirit, becoming humble, meek, submissive, patient, full of love and all long-suffering; having faith on the Lord; having a hope that ye shall receive eternal life; having the love of God always in your hearts, that ye may be lifted up at the last day and enter into his rest.* (Alma 13:27-29.)

Now, as I said unto you, that because ye were compelled to be humble *ye were blessed,* do ye not suppose that *they were more blessed* who truly humble themselves because of the word? Yea, he that truly humbleth himself, and repenteth of his sins, and endureth to the end, *the same shall be blessed—yea, much more blessed than they who are compelled to be humble because of their exceeding poverty. Therefore, blessed* are they who humble themselves without being compelled to be humble; or rather, in other words, *blessed* is he that believeth in the word of God, and is baptized without stubbornness of heart, yea, without being brought to know the word, or even compelled to know, before they will believe. (Alma 32:14-16.)

Humble yourselves even to the dust. (Alma 34:38.)

See that ye are not lifted up unto pride; yea, see that ye do not boast in your own wisdom, nor of your much strength. (Alma 38:11.)

Do not say: O God, I thank thee that we are better than our brethren; but rather say: O Lord, forgive my unworthiness, and remember my brethren in mercy—yea, acknowledge your unworthiness before God at all times. (Alma 38:14.)

Do not endeavor to excuse yourself in the least point because of your sins, by denying the justice of God; but do you let the justice of God, and his mercy, and his long-suffering have full sway in your heart; and let it bring you down to the dust in humility. (Alma 42:30.)

It was because of the pride of their hearts, because of their exceeding riches, yea, it was because of their oppression to the poor, withholding their food from the hungry, withholding their clothing from the naked, and smiting their humble brethren upon the cheek, making a mock of that which was sacred, denying the spirit of prophecy and of revelation, murdering, plundering, lying, stealing, committing adultery, rising up in great contentions, and deserting away into the land of Nephi, among the Lamanites—and because of this their great wickedness, and their boastings in their own strength, *they were left in their own strength; therefore they did not prosper, but were afflicted and smitten, and driven before the Lamanites, until they had lost possession of almost all their lands.* (Hel. 4:12-13.)

Wo shall come unto you because of that pride which ye have suffered to enter your hearts, which has lifted you up beyond that which is good because of your exceedingly great riches! (Hel. 7:26.)

Your hearts are not drawn out unto the Lord, but they do swell with great pride, unto boasting, and unto great swelling, envyings, strifes, malice, persecutions and murders, and all manner of iniquities. *For this cause hath the Lord God caused that a curse should come upon the land, and also upon your riches, and this* because of your iniquities. (Hel. 13:22-23.)

Ye must repent, and become as a little child, and be baptized in my name, or *ye can in nowise receive these things [witness of the Holy Ghost].* And again I say unto you, ye must repent, and be baptized in my name, and become as a little child, *or ye can in nowise inherit the kingdom of God.* (3 Ne. 11:37-38.)

Blessed are they who shall believe in your words, and come down into the depths of humility and be baptized, *for they shall be visited with fire and with the Holy Ghost, and shall receive a remission of their sins.* Yea, blessed are the poor in spirit who come unto me, *for theirs is the kingdom of heaven.* (3 Ne. 12:2-3.)

Because of stiffneckedness and unbelief *they understood not my word; therefore I was commanded to say no more of the Father concerning this thing unto them.* (3 Ne. 15:18.)

At that day when the Gentiles shall sin against my gospel, and shall reject the fulness of my gospel, and shall be lifted up in the pride of their hearts above all nations, and above all the people of the whole earth, and shall be filled with all manner of lyings, and of deceits, and of mischiefs, and all manner of hypocrisy, and murders, and priestcrafts, and whoredoms, and of secret abominations; and if they shall do all those things, and shall reject the fulness of my gospel, *behold, saith the Father, I will bring the fulness of my gospel from among them.* (3 Ne. 16:10.)

Repent ye, and humble yourselves before him, *lest he shall come out in justice against you—lest a remnant of the seed of Jacob shall go forth among you as a lion, and tear you in pieces, and there is none to deliver.* (Morm. 5:24.)

When they had humbled themselves sufficiently before the Lord *he did send rain upon the face of the earth; and the people began to revive again, and there began to be fruit in the north countries, and in all the countries round about. And the Lord did show forth his power unto them in preserving them from famine.* (Ether 9:35.)

If men come unto me *I will show unto them their weakness.* I give unto men weakness *that they may be humble; and my grace is sufficient* for all men that humble themselves before me; for if they humble themselves before me, and have faith in me, *then will I make weak things become strong unto them.* (Ether 12:27.)

Because thou [Moroni] hast seen thy weakness *thou shalt be made strong, even unto the sitting down in the place which I have prepared in the mansions of my Father.* (Ether 12:37.)

The pride of this nation, or the people of the Nephites, *hath proven their destruction* except they should repent. (Moro. 8:27.)

Inasmuch as they were humble *they might be made strong, and blessed from on high, and receive knowledge from time to time.* (D&C 1:28.)

Although a man may have many revelations, and have power to do many mighty works, yet if he boasts in his own strength, and sets at naught the counsels of God, and follows after the dictates of his own will and carnal desires, *he must fall and incur the vengeance of a just God upon him.* (D&C 3:4.)

Faith, hope, charity and love, with an eye single to the glory of God, qualify him for the work. Remember faith, . . . brotherly kindness, . . . charity, humility. (D&C 4:5-6.)

Put your trust in that Spirit which leadeth to do good—yea, to do justly, and walk humbly, to judge righteously; and this is my Spirit. (D&C 11:12.)

No one can assist in this work except he shall be humble and full of love, having faith, hope, and charity, being temperate in all things, whatsoever shall be entrusted to his care. (D&C 12:8.)

Thou shalt do it [publish glad tidings] with all humility, trusting in me, reviling not against the revilers. (D&C 19:30.)

By way of commandment to the Church concerning the matter of baptism—All those who humble themselves before God, and desire to be baptized, and come forth with broken hearts and contrite spirits, and witness before the church that they have truly repented of all their sins, and are willing to take upon them the name of Jesus Christ, having determination to serve him to the end, and truly manifest by their works that they have received of the Spirit of Christ unto the remission of their sins, *shall be received by baptism into his church.* (D&C 20:37.)

Enter ye in at the gate, as I have commanded, and seek not to counsel your God. (D&C 22:4.)

Beware of pride, *lest thou shouldst enter into temptation.* (D&C 23:1.)

Continue in the spirit of meekness, and beware of pride. (D&C 25:14.)

[Jesus Christ] will gather his people even as a hen gathereth her chickens under her wings, even as many as will hearken to my voice and humble themselves before me, and call upon me in mighty prayer. (D&C 29:2.)

The hour is nigh and the day soon at hand when the earth is ripe; and all the proud and they that do wickedly *shall be as stubble; and I will burn them up, saith the Lord of Hosts, that wickedness shall not be upon the earth.* (D&C 29:9.)

Beware of pride, *lest ye become as the Nephites of old.* (D&C 38:39.)

Thou shalt not be proud in thy heart. (D&C 42:40.)

Ezra Thayre must repent of his pride, and of his selfishness. (D&C 56:8.)

Let [Martin Harris] repent of his sins, for he seeketh the praise of the world. (D&C 58:59.)

Inasmuch as you have humbled yourselves before me, *the blessings of the kingdom are yours.* (D&C 61:37.)

I, the Lord, am not pleased with my servant Sidney Rigdon; he exalted himself in his heart, and received not counsel, but grieved the Spirit. (D&C 63:55.)

Tomorrow all the proud and they that do wickedly *shall be as stubble; and I will burn them up, for I am the Lord of Hosts; and I will not spare any that remain in Babylon.* (D&C 64:24.)

It is your privilege, and a promise I give unto you that have been ordained unto this ministry, that inasmuch as you strip yourselves from jealousies and fears, and humble yourselves before me, for ye are not sufficiently humble, *the veil shall be rent and you shall see me and know that I am—not with the carnal neither natural mind, but with the spiritual.* (D&C 67:10.)

Let no man glory in man, but rather let him glory in God, *who shall subdue all enemies under his feet.* (D&C 76:61.)

A commandment I give unto them, that they shall not boast themselves of these things, neither speak them before the world; for these things are given unto you *for your profit and for salvation.* (D&C 84:73.)

Cease from all your . . . pride. (D&C 88:121.)

Be not ashamed, neither confounded; but be admonished in all your high-mindedness and pride, *for it bringeth a snare upon your souls.* (D&C 90:17.)

He that exalteth himself *shall be abased*, and he that abaseth himself *shall be exalted.* (D&C 101:42.)

[to Joseph Smith] It is my will that you shall humble yourselves before me, and *obtain this blessing* by your diligence and humility and the prayer of faith. And inasmuch as you are diligent and humble, and exercise the prayer of faith, *behold, I will soften the hearts of those to whom you are in debt, until I shall send means unto you for your deliverance.* (D&C 104:79-80.)

Inasmuch as ye are humble and faithful and call upon my name, behold, *I will give you the victory.* (D&C 104:82.)

I have prepared a great endowment and blessing to be poured out upon them, inasmuch as they are faithful and continue in humility before me. (D&C 105:12.)

Let all my people who dwell in the regions round about be very faithful, and prayerful, and humble before me. (D&C 105:23.)

Talk not of judgments, neither boast of faith nor of mighty works, but carefully gather together, as much in one region as can be, consistently with the feelings of the people; *and behold, I will give unto you favor and grace in their eyes, that you may rest in peace and safety, while you are saying unto the people: Execute judgment and justice for us according to law, and redress us of our wrongs.* (D&C 105:24-25.)

Blessed is my servant Warren [Cowdery], for I will have mercy on him; and, notwithstanding the vanity of his heart, *I will lift him up* inasmuch as he will humble himself before me. *And I will give him grace and assurance wherewith he may stand.* (D&C 106:7-8.)

The decisions of these quorums, or either of them, are to be made in all righteousness, in holiness, and lowliness of heart, meekness and long suffering, and in faith, and virtue, and knowledge, temperance, patience, godliness, brotherly kindness and charity; *because the promise is,* if these things abound in them *they shall not be unfruitful in the knowledge of the Lord.* (D&C 107:30-31.)

Inasmuch as thou hast abased thyself *thou shalt be exalted; therefore, all thy sins are forgiven thee.* (D&C 112:3.)

Be thou humble; *and the Lord thy God shall lead thee by the hand, and give thee answer to thy prayers.* (D&C 112:10.)

After their temptations, and much tribulation, behold, *I, the Lord, will feel after them,* and if they harden not their hearts, and stiffen not their necks against me, *they shall be converted, and I will heal them.* (D&C 112:13.)

Exalt not yourselves; rebel not against my servant Joseph. (D&C 112:15.)

Let the residue continue to preach from that hour, and if they will do this in all lowliness of heart, in meekness and humility, and long-suffering, *I, the Lord, give unto them a promise that I will provide for their families; and an effectual door shall be opened for them, from henceforth.* (D&C 118:3.)

Let my servant William Law . . . be humble before me, and be without guile, *and he shall receive of my Spirit even the Comforter, which shall manifest unto him the truth of all things, and shall give him, in the very hour, what he shall say. And these signs shall follow him—he shall heal the sick, he shall cast out devils, and shall be delivered from those who would administer unto him deadly poison; and he shall be led in paths where the poisonous serpent cannot lay hold upon his heel, and he shall mount up in the imagination of his thoughts as upon eagles' wings. (D&C 124:97-99.)*

Initiative

(See also Agency, Use of; Willingness.)

In the Doctrine and Covenants, the Lord tells us: "It is not meet that I should command in all things; for he that is compelled in all things, the same is a slothful and not a wise servant; wherefore he receiveth no reward." (D&C 58:26.) It is not enough merely to do good; we must take the initiative in doing it. We cannot wait to be commanded. We must use our free will to perform righteousness and good works.

The Lord further states: "He that doeth not anything until he is commanded, and receiveth a commandment with doubtful heart, and keepeth it with slothfulness, the same is damned." (D&C 58:29.)

Commandments and Promises

If his offering be a burnt sacrifice of the herd, let him offer a male without blemish: he shall offer it of his own voluntary will at the door of the tabernacle of the congregation before the Lord. (Lev. 1:3.)

For the kingdom of heaven is as a man travelling into a far country, who called his own servants, and delivered unto them his goods. And unto one he gave five talents, to another two, and to another one; to every man according to his several ability; and straightway took his journey. Then he that had received the five talents went and traded with the same, and made them other five talents. And likewise he that had received two, he also gained other two. But he that had received one went and digged in the earth, and hid his lord's money. After a long time the lord of those servants cometh, and reckoneth with them. And so he that had received five talents came and . . . his lord said unto him, *Well done, thou good and faithful servant:* thou hast been faithful over a few things, *I will make thee ruler over many things: enter thou into the joy of thy lord.* He also that had received two talents came and . . . his lord said unto him [likewise]. Then he which had received the one talent came and . . . his lord . . . said unto him, *Thou wicked and slothful servant. . . . Take therefore the talent from him, and give it unto him which hath ten talents. For unto every one that hath shall be given, and he shall have abundance: but from him that hath not shall be taken away even that which he hath. And cast ye the unprofitable servant into outer darkness: there shall be weeping and gnashing of teeth.* (Matt. 25:14-30.)

That servant, which knew his lord's will, and prepared not himself, neither did according to his will, *shall be beaten with many stripes.* But he that knew not, and did commit things worthy of stripes, *shall be beaten with few stripes.* For unto whomsoever much is given, *of him shall much be required:* and to whom men have committed much, *of him they will ask the more.* (Luke 12:47-48.)

They should impart of their substance of their own free will and good desires towards God, and to those priests that stood in need, yea, and to every needy, naked soul. (Mosiah 18:28.)

He that truly humbleth himself, and repenteth of his sins, and endureth to the end, *the same shall be blessed—yea much more blessed* than they who are compelled to be humble because of their exceeding poverty. Therefore, *blessed* are they who humble themselves without being compelled to be humble; or rather, in other words, *blessed* is he that believeth in the word of God, and is baptized without stubbornness of heart, yea, without being brought to know the word, or even compelled to know, before they will believe. (Alma 32:15-16.)

It is not meet that I should command in all things; for he that is compelled in all things, *the same is a slothful and not a wise servant; wherefore he receiveth no reward.* Verily I say, men should be anxiously engaged in a good cause, and do many things of their own free will, and bring to pass much righteousness; for the power is in them, wherein they are agents unto themselves. And inasmuch as men do good *they shall in nowise lose their reward.* But he that doeth not anything until he is commanded, and receiveth a commandment with doubtful heart, and keepeth it with slothfulness, *the same is damned.* (D&C 58:26-29.)

Judging Others

(See also Just, Being.)

The Savior uses the example of the mote and the beam to explain his commandment to "judge not, that ye be not judged." (Matt. 7:1.) He asks, why do you see the mote (splinter) in your brother's eye, and yet not consider the beam (plank) in your own? "First cast out the beam out of thine own eye; and then shalt thou see clearly to cast out the mote out of thy brother's eye." (Matt. 7:3-5.)

We cannot improve others by judging and being critical. We help others work toward perfection by eliminating their stumbling blocks, by being an example, by not speaking evilly of them, and by understanding the root of their weaknesses.

Moroni, addressing those who would someday read his words, tells us to what good end our discernment of others' weaknesses may work: "Condemn me not because of mine imperfection, . . . but rather give thanks unto God that he hath made manifest unto you our imperfections, that ye may learn to be more wise than we have been." (Morm. 9:31.)

Commandments and Promises

Thou shalt not follow a multitude to do evil; neither shalt thou speak in a cause to decline after many to wrest judgment. (Ex. 23:2.)

Thou shalt not wrest the judgment of thy poor in his cause. (Ex. 23:6.)

Ye shall do no unrighteousness in judgment: thou shalt not respect the person of the poor, nor honour the person of the mighty: but in righteousness shalt thou judge thy neighbour. (Lev. 19:15.)

[Moses to judges of Israel] Ye shall not respect persons in judgment; but ye shall hear the small as well as the great; ye shall not be afraid of the face of man; for the judgment is God's: and the cause that is too hard for you, bring it unto me, and I will hear it. (Deut. 1:17.)

Thou shalt not wrest judgment; thou shalt not respect persons, neither take a gift: for a gift doth blind the eyes of the wise, and pervert the words of the righteous. (Deut. 16:19.)

Hate the evil, and love the good, and establish judgment in the gate. (Amos 5:15.)

Shall horses run upon the rock? will one plow there with oxen? for ye have turned judgment *into gall*, and the fruit of righteousness *into hemlock.* (Amos 6:12.)

Execute true judgment, and shew mercy and compassions every man to his brother: and oppress not the widow, nor the fatherless, the stranger, nor the poor; and let none of you imagine evil against his brother in your heart. (Zech. 7:9-10.)

Judge not, *that ye be not judged. For with what judgment ye judge, ye shall be judged: and with what measure ye mete, it shall be measured to you again.* And why beholdest thou the mote that is in thy brother's eye, but considerest not the beam that is in thine own eye? Or how wilt thou say to thy brother, Let me pull out the mote out of thine eye; and, behold, a beam is in thine own eye? Thou hypocrite, first cast out the beam out of thine own eye; *and then shalt thou see clearly to cast out the mote out of thy brother's eye.* (Matt. 7:1-5.; similar scriptures, Luke 6:41-42, 3 Ne. 14:1-5; see also JST Matt. 7:1-8.)

Judge not, *and ye shall not be judged:* condemn not, *and ye shall not be condemned:* forgive, *and ye shall be forgiven.* (Luke 6:37.)

Judge not according to the appearance, but judge righteous judgment. (John 7:24; see also JST John 7:24.)

So when they continued asking him, he lifted up himself, and said unto them, He that is without sin among you, let him first cast a stone at her. (John 8:7.)

Thou art inexcusable, O man, whosoever thou art that judgest: for wherein thou judgest another, *thou condemnest thyself*; for thou that judgest doest the same things. *But we are sure that the judgment of*

God is according to truth against them which commit such things. (Rom. 2:1-2.)

Let us not therefore judge any more: but judge this rather, that no man put a stumblingblock or an occasion to fall in his brother's way. (Rom. 14:13.)

Have not the faith of the Lord Jesus Christ, the Lord of glory, with respect of persons. For if there come unto your assembly a man with a gold ring, in goodly apparel, and there come in also a poor man in vile raiment; and ye have respect to him that weareth the gay clothing, and say unto him, Sit thou here in a good place; and say to the poor, Stand thou there, or sit here under my footstool: are ye not then partial in yourselves, and are become judges of evil thoughts? Hearken my beloved brethren, *Hath not God chosen the poor of this world rich in faith, and heirs of the kingdom which he hath promised to them* that love him? But ye have despised the poor. Do not rich men oppress you, and draw you before the judgment seats? Do not they blaspheme that worthy name by the which ye are called? If ye fulfil the royal law according to the scripture, Thou shalt love thy neighbour as thyself, *ye do well:* but if ye have respect to persons, *ye commit sin, and are convinced of the law as transgressors.* (James 2:1-9; see also JST James 2:1, 4.)

Speak not evil one of another, brethren. He that speaketh evil of his brother, and judgeth his brother, *speaketh evil of the law, and judgeth the law:* but if thou judge the law *thou art not a doer of the law, but a judge.* (James 4:11.)

For assuredly as the Lord liveth they shall see that . . . all that watch for iniquity *are cut off;* and they that make a man an offender for a word, and lay a snare for him that reproveth in the gate, and turn aside the just for a thing of naught. (2 Ne. 27:31-32.)

A commandment I give unto you, which is the word of God, that ye revile no more against them [Lamanites] because of the darkness of their skins; neither shall ye revile against them because of their filthiness; but ye shall remember your own filthiness, and remember that their filthiness came because of their fathers. (Jacob 3:9.)

If ye judge the man who putteth up his petition to you for your substance that he perish not, and condemn him, *how much more just will be your condemnation* for withholding your substance, which doth not belong to you but to God, to whom also your life belongeth; and yet ye put up no petition, nor repent of the thing which thou hast done. I say unto you, *wo be unto that man, for his substance shall perish with him.* (Mosiah 4:22-23.)

He that condemneth, let him be aware *lest he shall be in danger of hell fire.* And he that saith: Show unto me, or ye shall be smitten—let him beware *lest he commandeth that which is forbidden of the Lord.* For behold, the same that judgeth rashly *shall be judged rashly again;* for according to his works *shall his wages be;* therefore, he that smiteth *shall be smitten again, of the Lord.* Behold what the scripture says—man shall not smite, neither shall he judge; for judgment is mine, saith the Lord, and vengeance is mine also, *and I will repay.* (Morm. 8:17-20; see also D&C 82:23.)

Condemn me not because of mine imperfection, neither my father, because of his imperfection, neither them who have written before him; but rather give thanks unto God that he hath made manifest unto you our imperfections, *that ye may learn to be more wise than we have been.* (Morm. 9:31.)

Seeing that ye know the light by which ye may judge, which light is the light of Christ, see that ye do not judge wrongfully; for with that same judgment which ye judge *ye shall also be judged.* (Moro. 7:18.)

Let every man esteem his brother as himself, and practise virtue and holiness before me. And again I say unto you, let every man esteem his brother as himself. (D&C 38:24-25.)

Leave judgment alone with me, for it is mine and I will repay. (D&C 82:23; see also Morm. 8:20.)

Cease to find fault one with another. (D&C 88:124.)

Just, Being
(See also Judging Others.)

All things will be restored: righteousness to the righteous, mercy to the merciful, and justice to the just. To be worthy of that restoration, we must deal justly in all our affairs, not favoring one over another because of money or status, or favoring friends over strangers. Those who combine justice, faithfulness, and wisdom in managing their stewardships have the Lord's promise that they "shall enter into the joy of [their] Lord, and shall inherit eternal life." (D&C 51:19.)

Commandments and Promises

Ye shall do no unrighteousness in judgment: thou shalt not respect the person of the poor, nor honour the person of the mighty: but in righteousness shalt thou judge thy neighbour. (Lev. 19:15.)

Ye shall do no unrighteousness in judgment, in meteyard, in weight, or in measure. Just balances, just weights, a just ephah, and a just hin, shall ye have. (Lev. 19:35-36.)

I [Moses] charged your judges at that time, saying, Hear the causes between your brethren, and judge righteously between every man and his brother, and the stranger that is with him. Ye shall not respect persons in judgment; but ye shall hear the small as well as the great; ye shall not be afraid of the face of man; for the judgment is God's: and the cause that is too hard for you, bring it unto me, and I will hear it. (Deut. 1:16-17.)

That which is altogether just shalt thou follow, *that thou mayest live, and inherit the land which the Lord thy God giveth thee.* (Deut. 16:20.)

He that ruleth over men must be just, ruling in the fear of God. *And he shall be as the light of the morning, when the sun riseth, even a morning without clouds; as the tender grass springing out of the earth by clear shining after rain.* (2 Sam. 23:3-4.)

Lord, who shall abide in thy tabernacle? who shall dwell in thy holy hill? He that walketh uprightly, and worketh righteousness, and speaketh the truth in his heart. He that backbiteth not with his tongue, nor doeth evil to his neighbour, nor taketh up a reproach against his neighbour. In whose eyes a vile person is condemned; but he honoureth them that fear the Lord. He that sweareth to his own hurt, and changeth not. He that putteth not out his money to usury, nor taketh reward against the innocent. *He that doeth these things shall never be moved.* (Ps. 15:1-5; see also JST Ps. 15:1.)

The path of the just *is as the shining light, that shineth more and more unto the perfect day.* (Prov. 4:18.)

Blessings are upon the head of the just: *but violence covereth the mouth* of the wicked. *The memory* of the just *is blessed: but the name* of the wicked *shall rot.* (Prov. 10:6-7.)

Through knowledge shall the just *be delivered.* (Prov. 11:9.)

A good man *leaveth an inheritance to his children's children: and the wealth of the sinner is laid up* for the just. (Prov. 13:22.)

The just man walketh in his integrity: *his children are blessed after him.* (Prov. 20:7.)

The way of the just is uprightness: *thou, most upright, dost weigh the path of the just.* (Isa. 26:7.)

The terrible one *is brought to nought,* and the scorner *is consumed,* and all that watch for iniquity *are cut off:* that make a man an offender for a word, and lay a snare for him that reproveth at the gate, and turn aside the just for a thing of nought. (Isa. 29:20-21; similar scripture, 2 Ne. 27:31-32.)

Keep ye judgment, and do justice: for my salvation is near to come, and my righteousness to be revealed. *Blessed* is the man that doeth this, and the son of man that layeth hold on it. (Isa. 56:1-2.)

Execute ye judgment and righteousness, and deliver the spoiled out of the hand of the oppressor: and do no wrong, do no violence to the stranger, the fatherless, nor the widow, neither shed innocent blood in this place. For if ye do this thing indeed, *then shall there enter in by the gates of this house kings sitting upon the throne of David, riding in chariots and on horses, he, and his servants, and his people.* But if ye will not hear these words, *I swear by myself, saith the Lord, that this house shall become a desolation.* (Jer. 22:3-5.)

If a man be just, and do that which is lawful and right, . . . he is just, *he shall surely live, saith the Lord God.* (Ezek. 18:5-9.)

Hate the evil, and love the good, and establish judgment in the gate: *it may be that the Lord God of hosts will be gracious unto the remnant of Joseph.* (Amos 5:15.)

What doth the Lord require of thee, but to do justly, and to love mercy, and to walk humbly with thy God? (Micah 6:8.)

Execute true judgment, and shew mercy and compassions every man to his brother. (Zech. 7:9.)

These are the things that ye shall do; Speak ye every man the truth to his neighbour; execute the judgment of truth and peace in your gates. (Zech. 8:16.)

So shall it be at the end of the world: *the angels shall come forth, and sever the wicked* from among the just. (Matt. 13:49.)

Woe unto you, scribes and Pharisees, hypocrites! for ye pay tithe of mint and anise and cummin, and have omitted the weightier matters of the law, judgment, mercy, and faith: these ought ye to have done, and not to leave the other undone. (Matt. 23:23.)

Woe unto you, Pharisees! for ye tithe mint and rue and all manner of herbs, and pass over judgment and the love of God: these ought ye to have done, and not to leave the other undone. (Luke 11:42.)

I charge thee before God, and the Lord Jesus Christ, and the elect angels, that thou observe these things without preferring one before another, doing nothing by partiality. (1 Tim. 5:21.)

A bishop must be blameless, . . . sober, just, holy. (Titus 1:7-8.)

See that you are merciful unto your brethren; deal justly, judge righteously, and do good continually; and if ye do all these things *then shall ye receive your reward; yea, ye shall have mercy restored unto you again; ye shall have justice restored unto you again; ye shall have a righteous judgment restored unto you again; and ye shall have good rewarded unto you again. For that which ye do send out shall return unto you again, and be restored.* (Alma 41:14-15.)

Put your trust in that Spirit which leadeth to do good—yea, to do justly, to walk humbly, to judge righteously; and this is my Spirit. (D&C 11:12.)

Whoso is found a faithful, a just, and a wise steward *shall enter into the joy of his Lord, and shall inherit eternal life.* (D&C 51:19.)

Kindness

Kindness is a necessity for those given priesthood authority from God. It is necessary for knowing God, for spiritual perceptiveness, and for approval as "ministers of God." (2 Cor. 6:4.)

The necessity of exercising priesthood authority with kindness is stated in the Doctrine and Covenants: "The decisions of these quorums . . . are to be made in . . . brotherly kindness," and "no power or influence can or ought to be maintained by virtue of the priesthood, only by . . . kindness." (D&C 107:30 and 121:41-42.)

Peter writes of kindness as a trait valued alongside diligence, faith, virtue, knowledge, temperance, patience, godliness, charity. (2 Pet. 1:5-9.) Although kindness is not mentioned in the scriptures with great frequency, when it is mentioned its importance is clear enough.

Commandments and Promises

Be kindly affectioned one to another with brotherly love; in honour preferring one another. (Rom. 12:10.)

In all things approving ourselves as the ministers of God, . . . by longsuffering, by kindness. (2 Cor. 6:4-6.)

Be ye kind one to another, tenderhearted. (Eph. 4:32.)

Put on therefore, as the elect of God, holy and beloved, bowels of mercies, kindness, humbleness of mind, meekness, longsuffering. (Col. 3:12.)

Be ye all of one mind, having compassion one of another, love as brethren, be pitiful, be courteous. (1 Pet. 3:8.)

Giving all diligence, add to your faith virtue; and to virtue knowledge; and to knowledge temperance; and to temperance patience; and to patience godliness; and to godliness brotherly kindness; and to brotherly kindness charity. For if these things be in you, and abound, *they make you that ye shall neither be barren nor unfruitful*

253

in the knowledge of our Lord Jesus Christ. But he that lacketh these things *is blind, and cannot see afar off, and hath forgotten that he was purged from his old sins.* (2 Pet. 1:5-9.)

Decisions of these quorums . . . are to be made in . . . long suffering, and in faith, and virtue, . . . patience, godliness, brotherly kindness and charity; *because the promise is,* if these things abound in them *they shall not be unfruitful in the knowledge of the Lord.* (D&C 107:30-31.)

No power or influence can or ought to be maintained by virtue of the priesthood, only by persuasion, by long-suffering, by gentleness and meekness, and by love unfeigned; by kindness, and pure knowledge, *which shall greatly enlarge the soul without hypocrisy, and without guile*—reproving betimes with sharpness, when moved upon by the Holy Ghost; and then showing forth afterwards an increase of love toward him whom thou hast reproved, *lest he esteem thee to be his enemy; that he may know that thy faithfulness is stronger than the cords of death.* (D&C 121:41-44.)

Knowing God and His Ways

A man who struggled with grief after the death of his wife wrote: "Not that I am (I think) in much danger of ceasing to believe in God. The real danger is of coming to believe such dreadful things about him." (C. S. Lewis, *A Grief Observed* [Bantam Books, New York: 1976], p. 5.) Those who do not know the traits and ways of God may think dreadful things about him as they cope with adversity. Loving or trusting a seemingly capricious or uncaring God would be difficult, but those who know the goodness and purposes of God know the security of his strength and feel the depth of his love. They can worship, love, and trust him more fully and freely.

The Lord commands us to know him: "Be still, and know that I am God." (Ps. 46:10.) Peter writes, "Grow in grace, and in the knowledge of our Lord and Saviour Jesus Christ." (2 Pet. 3:18.) But how can we know beings we have not seen or heard?

If we would know God, we must know his teachings. We must learn of him and his ways. We must study his dealings with his children, recorded in ancient and latter-day scriptures. We can know him by striving to be like him. We can also know him through the godliness in others, through considering the magnitude of our universe and the harmony of its creations, through listening to the whisperings of the Spirit, through humble prayer.

"O taste and see that the Lord is good." (Ps. 34:8.) Those who don't believe with commitment, who haven't tried to keep the commandments, who haven't sought to endure to the end, who haven't prayed with full purpose of heart, who haven't humbled themselves in repentance, are those who may never know the goodness of God. "Hereby we do know that we know him, if we keep his commandments." (1 Jn. 2:3.)

Commandments and Promises

Know therefore this day, and consider it in thine heart, that the Lord he is God in heaven above, and upon the earth beneath: there is none else. (Deut. 4:39.)

Know therefore that the Lord thy God, the faithful God, *which keepeth covenant and mercy with them* that love him and keep his commandments *to a thousand generations; and repayeth them* that hate him *to their face, to destroy them: he will not be slack to him* that hateth him, *he will repay him to his face.* (Deut. 7:9-10.)

O taste and see that the Lord is good. (Ps. 34:8.)

Be still, and know that I am God: I will be exalted among the heathen, I will be exalted in the earth. (Ps. 46:10.)

Come and see the works of God: he is terrible in his doing toward the children of men. (Ps. 66:5.)

Know ye that the Lord he is God: it is he that made us, and not we ourselves; *we are his people, and the sheep of his pasture.* (Ps. 100:3.)

The knowledge of the holy *is understanding* (Prov. 9:10.)

If thou seest the oppression of the poor, and violent perverting of judgment and justice in a province, marvel not at the matter: for he that is higher than the highest regardeth; and there be higher than they. (Eccl. 5:8.)

Consider the work of God: for who can make that straight, which he hath made crooked? (Eccl. 7:13.)

Lift up your eyes on high, and behold who hath created these things, that bringeth out their host by number: he calleth them all by names by the greatness of his might, for that he is strong in power; not one faileth. (Isa. 40:26.)

Lift up your eyes to the heavens, and look upon the earth beneath; *for the heavens shall vanish away like smoke, and the earth shall wax old like a garment, and they that dwell therein shall die in like manner: but my salvation shall be for ever, and my righteousness shall not be abolished.* (Isa. 51:6; similar scripture, 2 Ne. 8:6.)

Such as do wickedly against the covenant *shall he corrupt by flatteries:* but the people that do know their God *shall be strong, and do exploits.* (Dan. 11:32.)

Hear the word of the Lord, ye children of Israel: for *the Lord hath a controversy with the inhabitants of the land,* because there is no truth, nor mercy, nor knowledge of God in the land. (Hosea 4:1.)

They will not frame their doings to turn unto their God: for the spirit of whoredoms is in the midst of them, and they have not known the Lord. And the pride of Israel doth testify to his face: *therefore shall Israel and Ephraim fall in their iniquity; Judah also shall fall with them.* (Hosea 5:4-5.)

Come, and let us return unto the Lord: for he hath torn, and he will heal us; he hath smitten, and he will bind us up. After two days will he revive us: in the third day he will raise us up, *and we shall live in his sight. Then shall we know,* if we follow on to know the Lord: *his going forth is prepared as the morning; and he shall come unto us as the rain, as the latter and former rain unto the earth.* (Hosea 6:1-3.)

Think not that I am come to destroy the law, or the prophets: I am not come to destroy, but to fulfil. (Matt. 5:17; similar scripture, 3 Ne. 12:17.)

And this is life eternal, that they might know thee the only true God, and Jesus Christ, whom thou hast sent. (John 17:3.)

To you who are troubled rest with us, when the Lord Jesus shall be revealed from heaven with his mighty angels, *in flaming fire taking vengeance* on them that know not God, and that obey not the gospel of our Lord Jesus Christ: *who shall be punished with everlasting destruction from the presence of the Lord, and from the glory of his power; when he shall come to be glorified in his saints, and to be admired in all them that believe* (because our testimony among you was believed) *in that day.* (2 Thes. 1:7-10.)

Let no man say when he is tempted, I am tempted of God: for God cannot be tempted with evil, neither tempteth he any man. (James 1:13.)

To him that knoweth to do good, and doeth it not, *to him it is sin.* (James 4:17.)

Grace and peace be multiplied unto you through the knowledge of God, and of Jesus our Lord, *according as his divine power hath given unto us all things that pertain unto life and godliness,* through the knowledge of him that hath called us to glory and virtue. (2 Pet. 1:2-3.)

Be not ignorant of this one thing, that one day is with the Lord as a thousand years, and a thousand years as one day. (2 Pet. 3:8.)

Grow in grace, and in the knowledge of our Lord and Saviour Jesus Christ. (2 Pet. 3:18.)

Hereby *we do know that we know him,* if we keep his commandments. (1 Jn. 2:3.)

We are of God: he that knoweth God *heareth us;* he that is not of God *heareth not us.* Hereby *know we the spirit of truth, and the spirit of error.* (1 Jn. 4:6.)

He that loveth not *knoweth not God;* for God is love. (1 Jn. 4:8.)

[Lehi to his son Jacob] Thou knowest the greatness of God; *and he shall consecrate thine afflictions for thy gain. Wherefore, thy soul shall be blessed, and thou shalt dwell safely with thy brother, Nephi; and thy days shall be spent in the service of thy God.* (2 Ne. 2:2-3.)

If ye have come to a knowledge of the goodness of God, and his matchless power, and his wisdom, and his patience, and his long-suffering towards the children of men; and also, the atonement which has been prepared from the foundation of the world, that thereby salvation might come to him that should put his trust in the Lord, and should be diligent in keeping his commandments, and continue in the faith even unto the end of his life, I mean the life of the mortal body—*I say, that this is the man who receiveth salvation, through the atonement which was prepared from the foundation of the world for all mankind, which ever were since the fall of Adam, or who are, or who ever shall be, even unto the end of the world.* (Mosiah 4:6-7.)

Believe in God; believe that he is, and that he created all things, both in heaven and in earth; believe that he has all wisdom, and all power, both in heaven and in earth; believe that man doth not comprehend all the things which the Lord can comprehend. (Mosiah 4:9.)

As ye have come to the knowledge of the glory of God, or if ye have known of his goodness and have tasted of his love, and have received a remission of your sins, which causeth such exceedingly great joy in your souls, even so I would that ye should remember, and always retain in remembrance, the greatness of God, and your own nothingness, and his goodness and long-suffering towards you, unworthy creatures, and humble yourselves even in the depths of humility, calling on the name of the Lord daily, and standing steadfastly in the faith of that which is to come, which was spoken by the mouth of the angel. And behold, I say unto you that if ye do this *ye shall always rejoice, and be filled with the love of God, and always retain a remission of your sins; and ye shall grow in the knowledge of the glory of him that created you, or in the knowledge of that which is just and true. And ye will not have a mind to injure one another, but to live peaceably, and to render to every man according to that which is his due.* (Mosiah 4:11-13.)

In my name are they called; and if they know me *they shall come forth, and shall have a place eternally at my right hand. And it shall come to pass that when the second trump shall sound then shall they* that never knew me *come forth and shall stand before me. And then shall they know that I am the Lord their God, that I am their Redeemer;* but they would not be redeemed. *And then I will confess unto them that I never knew them; and they shall depart into everlasting fire prepared for the devil and his angels.* (Mosiah 26:24-27.)

Know ye that ye must come to the knowledge of your fathers, and repent of all your sins and iniquities, and believe in Jesus Christ, that he is the Son of God, and that he was slain by the Jews, and by the power of the Father he hath risen again, whereby he hath gained the victory over the grave; and also in him is the sting of death swallowed up. (Morm. 7:5.)

The reason why he ceaseth to do miracles among the children of men is because that they dwindle in unbelief, and depart from the right way, and know not the God in whom they should trust. (Morm. 9:20.)

The Lord said unto him [the brother of Jared]: Believest thou the words which I shall speak? And he answered: Yea, Lord, I know that thou speakest the truth, for thou art a God of truth, and canst not lie.

And when he had said these words, behold, the Lord showed himself unto him, and said: Because thou knowest these things *ye are redeemed from the fall; therefore ye are brought back into my presence; therefore I show myself unto you.* (Ether 3:11-13.)

Because of the knowledge of this man [the brother of Jared] *he could not be kept from beholding within the veil; and he saw the finger of Jesus, which, when he saw, he fell with fear; for he knew that it was the finger of the Lord; and he had faith no longer, for he knew, nothing doubting.* Wherefore, having this perfect knowledge of God, *he could not be kept from within the veil; therefore he saw Jesus; and he did minister unto him.* (Ether 3:19-20.)

Whatsoever thing is good is just and true; wherefore, nothing that is good denieth the Christ, but acknowledgeth that he is. *And ye may know that he is,* by the power of the Holy Ghost; wherefore I would exhort you that ye deny not the power of God; for he worketh by power, according to the faith of the children of men, the same today and tomorrow, and forever. (Moro. 10:6-7.)

Learn of me, and listen to my words; walk in the meekness of my Spirit, *and you shall have peace in me.* (D&C 19:23.)

Let the wicked take heed, and let the rebellious fear and tremble; and let the unbelieving hold their lips, *for the day of wrath shall come upon them as a whirlwind, and all flesh shall know that I am God.* (D&C 63:6.)

Let your hearts be comforted concerning Zion; for all flesh is in mine hands; be still and know that I am God. (D&C 101:16.)

Strait is the gate, and narrow the way that leadeth unto the exaltation and continuation of the lives, and few there be that find it, because ye receive me not in the world neither do ye know me. (D&C 132:22.)

Knowledge

(See also False Teachers and Teachings; Understanding; Wisdom.)

The Lord insists that his people be knowledgeable. Yet while he commands individuals and peoples to grow in knowledge, he stipulates that they also grow in truth.

The Lord commanded the Prophet Joseph Smith "to obtain a knowledge of history, and of countries, and of kingdoms, of laws of God and man." (D&C 93:53.) Yet Paul, writing to the Colossian saints, cautioned, "Beware lest any man spoil you through philosophy and vain deceit, after the tradition of men, after the rudiments of the world, and not after Christ." (Col. 2:8.)

Is that a contradiction? No, not if learning teaches wisdom. Jacob writes: "O the vainness, and the frailties, and the foolishness of men! When they are learned they think they are wise, and they hearken not unto the counsel of God, for they set it aside, supposing they know of themselves, wherefore, their wisdom is foolishness and it profiteth them not. And they shall perish." (2 Ne. 9:28.)

Any learning can be good if man applies wisdom and understanding to harvest truth.

Commandments and Promises

Take fast hold of instruction; let her not go: keep her; for she is thy life. (Prov. 4:13.)

Through knowledge *shall the just be delivered.* (Prov. 11:9.)

Hear counsel, and receive instruction, *that thou mayest be wise in thy latter end.* (Prov. 19:20.)

Apply thine heart unto instruction, and thine ears to the words of knowledge. (Prov. 23:12.)

Buy the truth, and sell it not; also wisdom, and instruction, and understanding. (Prov. 23:23.)

My people are destroyed for lack of knowledge: because thou hast rejected knowledge, *I will also reject thee, that thou shalt be no priest to me:* seeing thou hast forgotten the law of thy God, *I will also forget thy children.* (Hosea 4:6.)

In all things approving ourselves as the ministers of God, . . . by knowledge. (2 Cor. 6:4-6.)

Beware lest any man spoil you through philosophy and vain deceit, after the tradition of men, after the rudiments of the world, and not after Christ. (Col. 2:8.)

Beside this, giving all diligence, add to your faith virtue; and to virtue knowledge; and to knowledge temperance; and to temperance patience; and to patience godliness; and to godliness brotherly kindness; and to brotherly kindness charity. For if these things be in you, and abound, *they make you that ye shall neither be barren nor unfruitful in the knowledge of our Lord Jesus Christ.* But he that lacketh these things *is blind, and cannot see afar off, and hath forgotten that he was purged from his old sins.* (2 Pet. 1:5-9.)

If after they have escaped the pollutions of the world through the knowledge of the Lord and Saviour Jesus Christ, they are again entangled therein, and overcome, *the latter end is worse with them than the beginning. For it had been better for them* not to have known the way of righteousness, than, after they have known it, to turn from the holy commandment delivered unto them. *But it is happened unto them according to the true proverb, The dog is turned to his own vomit again; and the sow that was washed to her wallowing in the mire.* (2 Pet. 2:20-22.)

O that cunning plan of the evil one! O the vainness, and the frailties, and the foolishness of men! When they are learned they think they are wise, and they hearken not unto the counsel of God, for they set it aside, supposing they know of themselves, wherefore, their wisdom is foolishness and *it profiteth them not. And they shall perish.* But to be learned *is good* if they hearken unto the counsels of God. (2 Ne. 9:28-29.)

I am God and have spoken it; these commandments are of me, and were given unto my servants in their weakness, after the manner of their language, *that they might come to understanding.* And inasmuch as they erred *it might be made known;* and inasmuch as they sought wisdom *they might be instructed;* and inasmuch as they sinned *they might be chastened, that they might repent;* and inasmuch as they were humble *they might be made strong, and blessed from on high, and receive knowledge from time to time.* (D&C 1: 24-28.)

Ye shall become instructed in the law of my church, and be sanctified by that which ye have received, and ye shall bind yourselves to act in all holiness before me—that inasmuch as ye do this, *glory shall be added to the kingdom which ye have received.* Inasmuch as ye do it not, *it shall be taken, even that which ye have received.* (D&C 43: 9-10.)

Behold, ye are little children and ye cannot bear all things now; ye must grow in grace and in the knowledge of the truth. (D&C 50:40.)

As all have not faith, seek ye diligently and teach one another words of wisdom; yea, seek ye out of the best books words of wisdom; seek learning, even by study and also by faith. (D&C 88:118; similar scripture, D&C 109:7.)

Establish a house, even . . . a house of faith, a house of learning, . . . a house of God. (D&C 88:119; similar scripture, D&C 109:8.)

Set in order the churches, and study and learn, and become acquainted with all good books, and with languages, tongues, and people. (D&C 90:15.)

[to Joseph Smith]It is my will that you should hasten to translate my scriptures, and to obtain a knowledge of history, and of countries, and of kingdoms, of laws of God and man, and all this *for the salvation of Zion.* (D&C 93:53.)

The decisions of these quorums, or either of them, are to be made in all righteousness, in holiness, and lowliness of heart, meekness and long suffering, and in faith, and virtue, and knowledge, temperance, patience, godliness, brotherly kindness and charity; *because the promise is,* if these things abound in them *they shall not be unfruitful in the knowledge of the Lord.* (D&C 107:30-31.)

No power or influence can or ought to be maintained by virtue of the priesthood, only by persuasion, by long-suffering, by gentleness and meekness, and by love unfeigned; by kindness, and pure knowledge, *which shall greatly enlarge the soul without hypocrisy, and without guile.* (D&C 121:41-42.)

Whatever principle of intelligence we attain unto this life, *it will rise with us in the resurrection.* And if a person gains more knowledge and intelligence in this life through his diligence and obedience than another, *he will have so much the advantage in the world to come.* (D&C 130:18-19.)

Listening to God and His Servants

As if to say "Listen to me!" the Savior frequently begins statements with the word *behold*. In fact, references to that word take up eleven columns of type in one Bible concordance. The word is used repeatedly to call the reader's attention to what is said next. Similarly, the Lord often says, "Hear," or "Come and hear," or "Hearken to me," or just "Listen."

As Christ was transfigured, and as he appeared to Joseph Smith in the Sacred Grove, God the Father spoke these words: "This is my beloved Son, in whom I am well pleased; hear ye him." (Matt. 17:5; also JS–H 1:17.)

The Lord speaks to us through his own voice, through the Holy Ghost, and through his servants—"whether by mine own voice or by the voice of my servants, it is the same." (D&C 1:38.) To further establish this authority, the Lord declares of his servants: "Whatsoever they shall speak when moved upon by the Holy Ghost shall be scripture, shall be the will of the Lord, shall be the mind of the Lord, shall be the word of the Lord, shall be the voice of the Lord, and the power of God unto salvation." (D&C 68:4.)

Listening with an open mind and an open heart is the first step to comprehending and incorporating the gospel. The mightiest manifestations and the subtlest whisperings of the Spirit affect us only if we listen.

Commandments and Promises (see scriptural references for texts of specific messages)

The Lord came down in the pillar of the cloud, and stood in the door of the tabernacle, and called Aaron and Miriam: and they both came forth. And he said, Hear now my words. (Num. 12:5-6.)

I will raise them up a Prophet from among their brethren, like unto thee, and will put my words in his mouth; and he shall speak unto them all that I shall command him. Whosoever will not hearken unto my words which he shall speak in my name, *I will require it of him.* But the prophet, which shall presume to speak a word in my name, which I have not commanded him to speak, or that shall speak in the name of other gods, *even that prophet shall die.* And if thou say in thine heart, How shall we know the word which the Lord hath not spoken? *When a prophet speaketh in the name of the Lord, if the thing follow not, nor come to pass, that is the thing which the Lord hath not spoken, but the prophet hath spoken it presumptuously:* thou shalt not be afraid of him. (Deut. 18:18-22.)

Hear this, all ye people; give ear, all ye inhabitants of the world: both low and high, rich and poor, together. (Ps. 49:1-2.)

Come and hear, all ye that fear God, and I will declare what he hath done for my soul. (Ps. 66:16.)

Hear, O my son, and receive my sayings; *and the years of thy life shall be many.* (Prov. 4:10.)

Hear; for I will speak of excellent things; and the opening of my lips shall be right things. (Prov. 8:6.)

Now therefore hearken unto me, O ye children: for *blessed* are they that keep my ways. Hear instruction, and be wise, and refuse it not. *Blessed* is the man that heareth me, watching daily at my gates, waiting at the posts of my doors. (Prov. 8:32-34.)

Hear counsel, and receive instruction, *that thou mayest be wise in thy latter end.* (Prov. 19:20.)

Hear thou, my son, and be wise, and guide thine heart in the way. (Prov. 23:19.)

All ye inhabitants of the world, and dwellers on the earth, see ye, when he lifteth up an ensign on the mountains; and when he bloweth a trumpet, hear ye. (Isa. 18:3.)

Hear the word of the Lord, ye scornful men, that rule this people which is in Jerusalem. (Isa. 28:14.)

Hear, ye that are far off, what I have done; and, ye that are near, acknowledge my might. (Isa. 33:13.)

Come near, ye nations, to hear; and hearken, ye people: let the earth hear, and all that is therein; the world, and all things that come forth of it. (Isa. 34:1.)

Hear, ye deaf; and look, ye blind, that ye may see. (Isa. 42:18.)

Hearken unto me, ye stouthearted, that are far from righteousness: I bring near my righteousness; it shall not be far off, and my salvation shall not tarry: and I will place salvation in Zion for Israel my glory. (Isa. 46:12-13.)

Hear ye this, O house of Jacob, which are called by the name of Israel. (Isa. 48:1; similar scripture, 1 Ne. 20:1.)

Hearken unto me, O Jacob and Israel, my called; I am he; I am the first, I also am the last. (Isa. 48:12.)

Listen, O isles, unto me; and hearken, ye people, from far. (Isa. 49:1.)

Hearken to me, ye that follow after righteousness, ye that seek the Lord: look unto the rock whence ye are hewn, and to the hole of the pit whence ye are digged. (Isa. 51:1; similar scripture, 2 Ne. 8:1.)

Hear now this, thou afflicted, and drunken, but not with wine: Thus saith thy Lord the Lord, and thy God that pleadeth the cause of his people, Behold, I have taken out of thine hand the cup of trembling, even the dregs of the cup of my fury; *thou shalt no more drink it again.* (Isa. 51:21-22; similar scripture, 2 Ne. 8:21-22.)

Hearken diligently unto me, and eat ye that which is good, and let your soul delight itself in fatness. Incline your ear, and come unto me: hear, *and your soul shall live; and I will make an everlasting covenant with you, even the sure mercies of David.* (Isa. 55:2-3.)

Hear the word of the Lord, ye that tremble at his word. (Isa. 66:5.)

Hear ye the word of the Lord, O house of Jacob, and all the families of the house of Israel. (Jer. 2:4.)

Declare this in the house of Jacob, and publish it in Judah, saying, hear now this, O foolish people, and without understanding; which have eyes, and see not; which have ears, and hear not. (Jer. 5:20-21.)

Hear ye the word which the Lord speaketh unto you, O house of Israel. (Jer. 10:1.)

The word that came to Jeremiah from the Lord, saying, hear ye the words of this covenant, and speak unto the men of Judah, and to the inhabitants of Jerusalem. (Jer. 11:1-2.)

Hear ye, and give ear; be not proud: for the Lord hath spoken. Give glory to the Lord your God, before he cause darkness, and before your feet stumble upon the dark mountains, and, while ye look for light, he turn it into the shadow of death, and make it gross darkness. But if ye will not hear it, *my soul shall weep in secret places for your pride; and mine eye shall weep sore, and run down with tears, because the Lord's flock is carried away captive.* (Jer. 13:15-17.)

Thus saith the Lord of hosts, the God of Israel; Behold, I will bring upon this city and upon all her towns all the evil that I have pronounced against it, because they have hardened their necks, that they might not hear my words. (Jer. 19:15.)

Thus saith the Lord; Execute ye judgment and righteousness, and deliver the spoiled out of the hand of the oppressor: and do no wrong, do no violence to the stranger, the fatherless, nor the widow, neither shed innocent blood in this place. For if ye do this thing indeed, *then shall there enter in by the gates of this house kings sitting upon the throne of David, riding in chariots and on horses, he, and his servants, and his people.* But if ye will not hear these words, *I swear by myself, saith the Lord, that this house shall become a desolation.* (Jer. 22: 3-5.)

O earth, earth, earth, hear the word of the Lord. (Jer. 22:29.)

Jeremiah said unto all the people, and to all the women, Hear the word of the Lord, all Judah that are in the land of Egypt: . . . hear ye the word of the Lord, all Judah that dwell in the land of Egypt. (Jer. 44:24-26.)

Hear the counsel of the Lord, that he hath taken against Edom; and his purposes, that he hath purposed against the inhabitants of Teman. (Jer. 49:20.)

Ye shepherds, hear the word of the Lord. (Ezek. 34:7; similar scripture, Ezek. 34:9.)

Hear this word that the Lord hath spoken against you, O children of Israel, against the whole family which I brought up from the land of Egypt. (Amos 3:1.)

Hear ye now what the Lord saith. (Micah 6:1.)

He that hath ears to hear, let him hear. (Matt. 11:15; similar scriptures, Matt. 13:9, 43; Mark 4:23, 7:16; Rev. 13:9.)

Therefore speak I to them in parables: because they seeing see not; and hearing they hear not, neither do they understand. And in them is fulfilled the prophecy of Esaias, which saith, By hearing ye shall hear, and shall not understand; and seeing ye shall see, and shall not perceive: for this people's heart is waxed gross, and their ears are dull of hearing, and their eyes they have closed; *lest at any time they should see with their eyes, and hear with their ears, and should understand with their heart, and should be converted, and I should heal them. But blessed are your eyes,* for they see: *and your ears,* for they hear. (Matt. 13:13-16.)

He called the multitude, and said unto them, Hear, and understand. (Matt. 15:10.)

While he [Peter] yet spake, behold, a bright cloud overshadowed them: and behold a voice out of the cloud, which said, This is my beloved Son, in whom I am well pleased; hear ye him. (Matt. 17:5; similar scriptures, Mark 9:7, Luke 9:35, 3 Ne. 11:7.)

Take heed therefore how ye hear. (Luke 8:18.)

Let these sayings sink down into your ears. (Luke 9:44.)

Abraham saith unto him, They have Moses and the prophets; let them hear them. . . . And he said unto him, If they hear not Moses and the prophets, *neither will they be persuaded, though one rose from the dead.* (Luke 16:29-31.)

He that heareth my word, and believeth on him that sent me, *hath everlasting life, and shall not come into condemnation; but is passed from death unto life.* (John 5:24.)

Moses truly said unto the fathers, A prophet shall the Lord your God raise up unto you of your brethren, like unto me; him shall ye hear in all things whatsoever he shall say unto you. And it shall come to pass, that every soul, which will not hear that prophet, *shall be destroyed from among the people.* (Acts 3:22-23; similar scripture, 1 Ne. 22:20; see also Deut. 18:18-19, D&C 133:63.)

Faith cometh by hearing, *and hearing* by the word of God. (Rom. 10:17.)

Consider what I say; *and the Lord give thee understanding in all things.* (2 Tim. 2:7.)

We ought to give the more earnest heed to the things which we have heard, *lest at any time we should let them slip.* (Heb. 2:1.)

To day if ye will hear his voice, harden not your hearts, as in the provocation, in the day of temptation in the wilderness. (Heb. 3:7-8.)

I beseech you, brethren, suffer the word of exhortation: for I have written a letter unto you in few words. (Heb. 13:22.)

Let every man be swift to hear, slow to speak, slow to wrath. (James 1:19.)

He that hath an ear, let him hear what the Spirit saith unto the churches. (Rev. 2:7; similar scriptures, Rev. 2:29; 3:6, 13, 22.)

I stand at the door, and knock: if any man hear my voice, and open the door, *I will come in to him, and will sup with him, and he with me.* (Rev. 3:20.)

He [Lehi] did exhort them [Laman and Lemuel] then with all the feeling of a tender parent, that they would hearken to his words, *that perhaps the Lord would be merciful to them, and not cast them off;* yea, my father did preach unto them. (1 Ne. 8:37.)

If the Gentiles shall hearken unto the Lamb of God in that day that he shall manifest himself unto them in word, and also in power, in very deed, unto the taking away of their stumbling blocks—and harden not their hearts against the Lamb of God, *they shall be numbered among the seed of thy father; yea, they shall be numbered among the house of Israel; and they shall be a blessed people upon the promised land forever; they shall be no more brought down into captivity; and the house of Israel shall no more be confounded.* (1 Ne. 14:1-2.)

Whoso would hearken unto the word of God, and would hold fast unto it, *they would never perish; neither could the temptations and the fiery darts of the adversary overpower them unto blindness, to lead them away to destruction.* (1 Ne. 15:24.)

Hear ye the words of the prophet, ye who are a remnant of the house of Israel, a branch who have been broken off; hear ye the words of the prophet, which were written unto all the house of Israel, and liken them unto yourselves, *that ye may have hope as well as your brethren from whom ye have been broken off; for after this manner has the prophet written.* (1 Ne. 19:24.)

All ye, assemble yourselves, and hear. (1 Ne. 20:14.)

Hearken, O ye house of Israel, all ye that are broken off and are driven out because of the wickedness of the pastors of my people; yea, all ye that are broken off, that are scattered abroad, who are of my people, O house of Israel. Listen, O isles, unto me, and hearken ye people from far. (1 Ne. 21:1.)

Awake! and arise from the dust, and hear the words of a trembling parent, whose limbs ye must soon lay down in the cold and silent grave, from whence no traveler can return. (2 Ne. 1:14.)

O that cunning plan of the evil one! O the vainness, and the frailties, and the foolishness of men! When they are learned they think they are wise, and they hearken not unto the counsel of God, for they set it aside, supposing they know of themselves, *wherefore, their wisdom is foolishness and it profiteth them not. And they shall perish. But to be learned is good* if they hearken unto the counsels of God. (2 Ne. 9: 28-29.)

Wo unto the deaf that will not hear; *for they shall perish.* (2 Ne. 9:31.)

Hearken diligently unto me, and remember the words which I have spoken. (2 Ne. 9:51.)

I will be a light unto them forever, that will hear my words. (2 Ne. 10:14.)

I will give unto the children of men line upon line, precept upon precept, here a little and there a little; and *blessed* are those who hearken unto my precepts, and lend an ear unto my counsel, *for they shall learn wisdom;* for unto him that receiveth *I will give more;* and from them that shall say, We have enough, *from them shall be taken away even that which they have. Cursed is he* that putteth his trust in man, or maketh flesh his arm, or shall hearken unto the precepts of men, save their precepts shall be given by the power of the Holy Ghost. (2 Ne. 28:30-31.)

Now, my beloved brethren, and also Jew, and all ye ends of the earth, hearken unto these words and believe in Christ. (2 Ne. 33:10.)

O that ye would listen unto the word of his commands, and let not this pride of your hearts destroy your souls! (Jacob 2:16.)

O my brethren, hearken unto my words. (Jacob 3:11.)

O my people, beware lest there shall arise contentions among you, and ye list to obey the evil spirit, which was spoken of by my father Mosiah. For behold, *there is a wo pronounced upon him* who listeth to obey that spirit; for if he listeth to obey him, and remaineth and dieth in his sins, *the same drinketh damnation to his own soul; for he receiveth for his wages an everlasting punishment,* having transgressed the law of God contrary to his own knowledge. (Mosiah 2: 32-33.)

Whosoever has heard the words of the prophets, yea, all the holy prophets who have prophesied concerning the coming of the Lord—I say unto you, that all those who have hearkened unto their words, and believed that the Lord would redeem his people, and have looked forward to that day for a remission of their sins, *I say unto you, that these are his seed, or they are the heirs of the kingdom of God. For these are they whose sins he has borne; these are they for whom he has died, to redeem them from their transgressions.* (Mosiah 15:11-12.)

The time shall come when all shall see the salvation of the Lord; when every nation, kindred, tongue, and people shall see eye to eye and shall confess before God that his judgments are just. *And then shall the wicked be cast out, and they shall have cause to howl, and weep, and wail, and gnash their teeth;* and this because they would not hearken unto the voice of the Lord; *therefore the Lord redeemeth them not.* (Mosiah 16:1-2.)

He that will hear my voice *shall be my sheep; and him shall ye receive into the church, and him will I also receive.* (Mosiah 26:21.)

I wish from the inmost part of my heart, yea, with great anxiety even unto pain, that ye would hearken unto my words, and cast off your sins, and not procrastinate the day of your repentance. (Alma 13:27.)

Behold ye, the people of this great city [Zarahemla], and hearken unto my words; yea, hearken unto the words which the Lord saith; for behold, *he saith that ye are cursed* because of your riches, *and also are your riches cursed* because ye have set your hearts upon them, and have not hearkened unto the words of him who gave them unto you. (Hel. 13:21.)

If they will not turn unto me, and hearken unto my voice, *I will suffer them, yea, I will suffer my people, O house of Israel, that they shall go through among them, and shall tread them down, and they shall be as salt that hath lost its savor, which is thenceforth good for nothing but to be cast out, and to be trodden under foot of my people, O house of Israel.* (3 Ne. 16:15.)

If they will repent and hearken unto my words, and harden not their hearts, *I will establish my church among them, and they shall come in unto the covenant and be numbered among this the remnant of Jacob, unto whom I have given this land for their inheritance.* (3 Ne. 21:22.)

Whosoever will hearken unto my words and repenteth and is baptized, *the same shall be saved.* (3 Ne. 23:5.)

Hearken unto the words of the Lord. (Morm. 9:27.)

Listen to the words of Christ, your Redeemer, your Lord and your God. (Moro. 8:8.)

Hearken, O ye people of my church, saith the voice of him who dwells on high, and whose eyes are upon all men; yea, verily I say: Hearken ye people from afar; and ye that are upon the islands of the sea, listen together. (D&C 1:1.)

The voice of the Lord is unto the ends of the earth, that all that will hear *may hear.* (D&C 1:11.)

The day cometh that they who will not hear the voice of the Lord, neither the voice of his servants, neither give heed to the words of the prophets and apostles, *shall be cut off from among the people.* (D&C 1:14.)

Woe shall come unto the inhabitants of the earth if they will not hearken unto my words. (D&C 5:5.)

I am God; give heed unto my word, which is quick and powerful, sharper than a two-edged sword, to the dividing asunder of both joints and marrow; therefore give heed unto my words. (D&C 6:2; similar scriptures, D&C 11:2, 12:2, 14:2.)

Hearken, my servant John (Whitmer), and listen to the words of Jesus Christ, your Lord and your Redeemer. (D&C 15:1; similar scripture, D&C 16:1.)

Learn of me, and listen to my words. (D&C 19:23.)

His [the prophet's] word ye shall receive, as if from mine own mouth, in all patience and faith. (D&C 21:5.)

It shall be given thee in the very moment what thou shalt speak and write, and they shall hear it, *or I will send unto them a cursing instead of a blessing.* (D&C 24:6.)

Hearken unto the voice of the Lord your God, while I speak unto you, Emma Smith. (D&C 25:1.)

Listen to the voice of Jesus Christ, your Lord, your God, and your Redeemer, whose word is quick and powerful. (D&C 27:1.)

Listen to the voice of Jesus Christ, your Redeemer, the Great I AM, whose arm of mercy hath atoned for your sins. (D&C 29:1.)

It shall come to pass, because of the wickedness of the world, *that I will take vengeance upon the wicked,* for they will not repent; for the cup of mine indignation is full; for behold, *my blood shall not cleanse them* if they hear me not. (D&C 29:17.)

Give heed unto these things and be diligent in keeping my commandments, *and you shall be blessed unto eternal life.* (D&C 30:8.)

They shall give heed unto these words and trifle not, *and I will bless them.* (D&C 32:5.)

My servants Ezra [Thayre] and Northrop [Sweet], open ye your ears and hearken to the voice of the Lord your God, whose word is quick and powerful, sharper than a two-edged sword, to the dividing asunder of the joints and marrow, soul and spirit; and is a discerner of the thoughts and intents of the heart. (D&C 33:1.)

Listen to the voice of the Lord your God, even Alpha and Omega, the beginning and the end, whose course is one eternal round, the same today as yesterday, and forever. (D&C 35:1.)

Even so will I cause the wicked to be kept, that will not hear my voice but harden their hearts, *and wo, wo, wo, is their doom.* (D&C 38:6.)

Hear my voice and follow me, *and you shall be a free people, and ye shall have no laws but my laws when I come, for I am your lawgiver, and what can stay my hand?* (D&C 38:22.)

Hearken and listen to the voice of him who is from all eternity to all eternity, the Great I AM, even Jesus Christ. (D&C 39:1.)

The days of thy deliverance are come, if thou wilt hearken to my voice, which saith unto thee: Arise and be baptized, and wash away your sins, calling on my name, *and you shall receive my Spirit, and a blessing so great as you never have known.* (D&C 39:10.)

Hearken and hear, O ye my people, saith the Lord and your God, *ye whom I delight to bless with the greatest of all blessings,* ye that hear me; and ye that hear me not *will I curse,* that have professed my name, *with the heaviest of all cursings.* (D&C 41:1.)

Hearken, O ye elders of my church, who have assembled yourselves together in my name. . . . Again I say unto you, hearken and hear and obey the law which I shall give unto you. (D&C 42:1-2.)

O hearken, ye elders of my church, and give ear to the words which I shall speak unto you. (D&C 43:1.)

Hearken ye elders of my church, whom I have appointed: Ye are not sent forth to be taught, but to teach the children of men the things which I have put into your hands by the power of my Spirit. (D&C 43:15.)

Hearken ye, for, behold, the great day of the Lord is nigh at hand. (D&C 43:17.)

Hearken ye to these words. Behold, I am Jesus Christ, the Savior of the world. (D&C 43:34.)

Hearken, O ye people of my church, to whom the kingdom has been given; hearken ye and give ear to him who laid the foundation of the earth, who made the heavens and all the hosts thereof, and by whom all things were made which live, and move, and have a being. And again I say, hearken unto my voice, *lest death shall overtake you; in an hour when ye think not the summer shall be past, and the harvest ended, and your souls not saved.* Listen to him who is the advocate with the Father, who is pleading your cause before him. (D&C 45: 1-3.)

Hearken, O ye my people of my church, and ye elders listen together, and hear my voice while it is called today, and harden not your hearts. (D&C 45:6.)

Hearken ye together and let me show unto you even my wisdom—the wisdom of him whom ye say is the God of Enoch, and his brethren. (D&C 45:11.)

Hearken *and I will reason with you, and I will speak unto you and prophesy, as unto men in days of old. And I will show it plainly as I showed it unto my disciples as I stood before them in the flesh, and spake unto them, saying: As ye have asked of me concerning the signs of my coming, in the day when I shall come in my glory in the clouds of heaven, to fulfil the promises that I have made unto your fathers.* (D&C 45:15-16.)

Hearken, O ye people of my church; for verily I say unto you that these things were spoken unto you *for your profit and learning.* (D&C 46:1.)

Hearken unto my word, my servants Sidney [Rigdon], and Parley [P. Pratt], and Leman [Copley]. (D&C 49:1.)

Hearken, O ye elders of my church, and give ear to the voice of the living God; and attend to the words of wisdom which shall be given unto you, according as ye have asked and are agreed as touching the church. (D&C 50:1.)

Blessed are you who are now hearing these words of mine from the mouth of my servant, *for your sins are forgiven you.* (D&C 50:36.)

Hearken unto me, saith the Lord your God. (D&C 51:1.)

Hearken, O ye elders of my church, saith the Lord your God. (D&C 57:1.)

Hearken, O ye elders of my church, and give ear to my word, and learn of me what I will concerning you, and also concerning this land unto which I have sent you. (D&C 58:1.)

Behold, and hearken unto the voice of him who has all power, who is from everlasting to everlasting, even Alpha and Omega, the beginning and the end. (D&C 61:1.)

Hearken, O ye people, and open your hearts and give ear from afar; and listen, you that call yourselves the people of the Lord, and hear the word of the Lord and his will concerning you. Yea, verily, I say, hear the word of him whose anger is kindled against the wicked and rebellious. (D&C 63:1-2.)

Hearken ye and hear, and receive my will concerning you. (D&C 64:1.)

Hearken, and lo, a voice as of one sent down from on high, who is mighty and powerful, whose going forth is unto the ends of the earth, yea, whose voice is unto men—Prepare ye the way of the Lord, make his paths straight. (D&C 65:1.)

Behold and hearken, O ye elders of my church, who have assembled yourselves together, whose prayers I have heard, and whose hearts I know, and whose desires have come up before me. (D&C 67:1.)

Behold, and hearken, O ye inhabitants of Zion, and all ye people of my church who are afar off, and hear the word of the Lord which I give unto my servant. (D&C 70:1.)

I give unto them [my servants] a commandment; wherefore hearken and hear, for thus saith the Lord unto them—I, the Lord, have appointed them, and ordained them to be stewards over the revelations and commandments which I have given unto them, and which I shall hereafter give unto them; and an account of this stewardship will I require of them in the day of judgment. (D&C 70:2-4.)

Hearken, and listen to the voice of the Lord, O ye who have assembled yourselves together, who are the high priests of my church, to whom the kingdom and power have been given. (D&C 72:1.)

Hearken, O ye who have given your names to go forth to proclaim my gospel, and to prune my vineyard. (D&C 75:2.)

Hear, O ye heavens, and give ear, O earth, and rejoice ye inhabitants thereof, for the Lord is God, and beside him there is no Savior. (D&C 76:1.)

Hearken unto me, saith the Lord your God, who are ordained unto the high priesthood of my church, who have assembled yourselves together; and listen to the counsel of him who has ordained you from on high, who shall speak in your ears the words of wisdom, *that salvation may be unto you in that thing which you have presented before me, saith the Lord God.* (D&C 78:1-2.)

I now give unto you a commandment to beware concerning yourselves, to give diligent heed to the words of eternal life. For you shall live by every word that proceedeth forth from the mouth of God. (D&C 84:43-44.)

Every one that hearkeneth to the voice of the Spirit *cometh unto God, even the Father. And the Father teacheth him of the covenant which he has renewed and confirmed upon you . . . for your sakes, and not for your sakes only, but for the sake of the whole world.* (D&C 84:47-48.)

Follow me, and listen to the counsel which I shall give unto you. (D&C 100:2.)

They were slow to hearken unto the voice of the Lord their God; *therefore, the Lord their God is slow to hearken unto their prayers, to answer them in the day of their trouble.* (D&C 101:7.)

Inasmuch as there are those who have hearkened unto my words, *I have prepared a blessing and an endowment for them,* if they continue faithful. (D&C 105:18.)

Let him [Robert B. Thompson], therefore, hearken to your counsel, and *I will bless him with a multiplicity of blessings.* (D&C 124:13.)

If my people will hearken unto my voice, and unto the voice of my servants whom I have appointed to lead my people, behold, verily I say unto you, *they shall not be moved out of their place.* But if they will not hearken to my voice, nor unto the voice of these men whom I have appointed, *they shall not be blest*, because they pollute mine holy grounds, and mine holy ordinances, and charters, and my holy words which I give unto them. (D&C 124:45-46.)

Hearken, O ye people of my church, saith the Lord your God, and hear the word of the Lord concerning you. (D&C 133:1.)

Hearken and hear, O ye inhabitants of the earth. Listen, ye elders of my church together, and hear the voice of the Lord; for he calleth upon all men, and he commandeth all men everywhere to repent. (D&C 133:16.)

Upon them that hearken not to the voice of the Lord *shall be fulfilled that which was written by the prophet Moses, that they should be cut off from among the people.* (D&C 133:63.)

Hearken, O ye people of my church; and ye elders listen together; you have received my kingdom. (D&C 136:41.)

Noah and his sons hearkened unto the Lord, and gave heed, *and they were called the sons of God.* (Moses 8:13.)

Looking to God

(See also Trusting God; Following God and His Teachings.)

Looking to God implies trusting him, being willing to follow him, and turning to him and his word for guidance and strength. "Look unto me in every thought," the Lord declared to Joseph Smith and Oliver Cowdery. (D&C 6:36.) Not only does this imply looking to Jesus Christ as an example, but also looking to him as a source of strength.

Where we look for entertainment, for companionship, for guidance, for strength determines our directions. A Church leader counsels: "The direction of our look is critical. From the rooftop King David 'saw a woman washing herself; and the woman was very beautiful to look upon' (2 Sam. 11:2). He looked across the way, and his heart was filled with lust. He looked; he fell. . . .

"Our looks must not be allowed to wander across the way or to become fixed upon the perishable things of the world. The eye, 'that light of the body' (Matt. 6:22), must be trained to look upward. We must look to God and live!" (Carlos E. Asay, "Look to God and Live," *Ensign*, Nov. 1978, p. 54.)

Commandments and Promises

Unto thee lift I up mine eyes, O thou that dwellest in the heavens. Behold, as the eyes of servants look unto the hand of their masters, and as the eyes of a maiden unto the hand of her mistress; so our eyes wait upon the Lord our God, *until that he have mercy upon us.* (Ps. 123:1-2.)

Hear, ye deaf; and look ye blind, *that ye may see.* (Isa. 42:18.)

Look unto me, *and be ye saved*, all the ends of the earth: for I am God, and there is none else. (Isa. 45:22.)

[Lehi to sons] I would that ye should look to the great Mediator, and hearken unto his great commandments; and be faithful unto his words, and choose eternal life. (2 Ne. 2:28.)

[Alma to his son Helaman] The way is prepared, and if we will look *we may live forever.* And now, my son, see that ye take care of these sacred things, yea, see that ye look to God *and live.* Go unto this people and declare the word, and be sober. (Alma 37:46-47.)

As many as should look upon the Son of God with faith, having a contrite spirit, *might live, even unto that life which is eternal.* (Hel. 8:15.)

Behold, I am the law, and the light. Look unto me, and endure to the end, *and ye shall live;* for unto him that endureth to the end *will I give eternal life.* (3 Ne. 15:9.)

Look unto me in every thought; doubt not, fear not. (D&C 6:36.)

Loving God

(See also Faith; Hope; Loving Others.)

The Lord commands his followers to love him—to love him with all their heart, soul, and might. (See Deut. 6:5.) But unlike human beings, to whom we can demonstrate love concretely by kind acts, forgiveness, and physical affection, how can we show love for God, who is not physically present, who does not sin and therefore needs no forgiveness, and who cannot receive our physical affection? God also gives us that answer: "If ye love me, keep my commandments." (John 14:15.) And, "inasmuch as ye have done it unto one of the least of these my brethren, ye have done it unto me." (Matt. 25:40.)

Thus we see that we can grow into a total love for our God by giving our heart, soul, and strength to keeping his commandments. We show love for him by perfecting ourselves and loving others.

Moroni confirms this: "Come unto Christ, and be perfected in him, and deny yourselves of all ungodliness . . . and love God with all your might, mind and strength." If we do this, "his grace [is] sufficient for [us], that by his grace [we] may be perfect in Christ." (Moro. 10:32.)

Commandments and Promises

Thou shalt not bow down thyself unto them [graven images], nor serve them: *for I the Lord thy God am a jealous God, visiting the iniquity of the fathers upon the children unto the third and fourth generation* of them that hate me, *and shewing mercy unto thousands of them* that love me and keep my commandments. (Deut. 5:9-10; similar scripture, Mosiah 13:13.)

Thou shalt love the Lord thy God with all thine heart, and with all thy soul, and with all thy might. (Deut. 6:5; see also Matt. 22:37-38, Mark 12:28-30, Luke 10:25-28.)

Know therefore that the Lord thy God, he is God, the faithful God, *which keepeth covenant and mercy* with them that love him and keep his commandments to a thousand generations; *and repayeth* them that hate him *to their face, to destroy them: he will not be slack* to him that hateth him, *he will repay him to his face.* (Deut. 7:9-10.)

Now, Israel, what doth the Lord thy God require of thee, but to fear the Lord thy God, to walk in all his ways, and to love him, and to serve the Lord thy God with all thy heart and with all thy soul, to keep the commandments of the Lord, and his statutes, which I command thee this day for thy good? (Deut. 10:12-13.)

Thou shalt love the Lord thy God, and keep his charge, and his statutes, and his judgments, and his commandments, alway. (Deut. 11:1.)

If ye shall diligently keep all these commandments which I command you, to do them, to love the Lord your God, to walk in all his ways, and to cleave unto him; *then will the Lord drive out all these nations from before you, and ye shall possess greater nations and mightier than yourselves. Every place whereon the soles of your feet shall tread shall be yours: from the wilderness and Lebanon, from the river, the river Euphrates, even unto the uttermost sea shall your coast be. There shall no man be able to stand before you: for the Lord your God shall lay the fear of you and the dread of you upon all the land that ye shall tread upon, as he hath said unto you.* (Deut. 11:22-25.)

The Lord thy God will circumcise thine heart, and the heart of thy seed, to love the Lord thy God with all thine heart, and with all thy soul, *that thou mayest live.* (Deut. 30:6.)

God . . . keepeth covenant and mercy for them that love him and observe his commandments. (Neh. 1:5.)

Let them also that love thy name be joyful in thee. (Ps. 5:11.)

O love the Lord, all ye his saints: *for the Lord preserveth the faithful, and plentifully rewardeth the proud doer.* (Ps. 31:23.)

Ye that love the Lord, hate evil: *he preserveth the souls of his saints; he delivered them out of the hand of the wicked.* (Ps. 97:10.)

The Lord preserveth all them that love him: but all the wicked *will he destroy.* (Ps. 145:20.)

My son, despise not the chastening of the Lord; neither be weary of his correction: for whom the Lord loveth *he correcteth; even as a father the son in whom he delighteth.* (Prov. 3:11-12.)

I love them that love me; and those that seek me early *shall find me.* (Prov. 8:17.)

Cursed be the man that trusteth in man, and maketh flesh his arm, and whose heart departeth from the Lord. *For he shall be like the heath in the desert, and shall not see when good cometh; but shall inhabit the parched places in the wilderness, in a salt land, and not inhabited.* (Jer. 17:5-6.)

[Daniel] prayed unto the Lord . . . , O Lord, the great and dreadful God, *keeping the covenant and mercy* to them that love him, and to them that keep his commandments. (Dan. 9:4.)

Hate the evil, and love the good, and establish judgment in the gate: *it may be that the Lord God of hosts will be gracious unto the remnant of Joseph.* (Amos 5:15.)

Love the truth and peace. (Zech. 8:19.)

He that loveth father or mother more than me *is not worthy of me:* and he that loveth son or daughter more than me *is not worthy of me.* (Matt. 10:37.)

Thou shalt love the Lord thy God with all thy heart, and with all thy soul, and with all thy mind. This is the first and great commandment. (Matt. 22:37-38; see also Deut. 6:5, Mark 12:28-30, Luke 10: 25-28.)

One of the scribes . . . asked him, Which is the first commandment of all? And Jesus answered him, The first of all the commandments is, Hear, O Israel; the Lord our God is one Lord: and thou shalt love the Lord thy God with all thy heart, and with all thy soul, and with all thy mind, and with all thy strength: this is the first commandment. (Mark 12:28-30; see also Deut. 6:5, Matt. 22:37-38, Luke 10:25-28.)

Blessed is he, whosoever shall not be offended in me. (Luke 7:23.)

Whosoever shall be ashamed of me and of my words, *of him shall the Son of man be ashamed, when he shall come in his own glory, and in his Father's and of the holy angels.* (Luke 9:26; see also JST Luke 9:26.)

A certain lawyer stood up, and tempted him, saying, Master, what shall I do to *inherit eternal life?* He said unto him, What is written in the law? how readest thou? And he answering said, Thou shalt love the Lord thy God with all thy heart, and with all thy soul, and with all thy strength, and with all thy mind; and thy neighbour as thyself. And he said unto him, Thou hast answered right: this do, *and thou shalt live.* (Luke 10:25-28; see also Deut. 6:5, Matt. 22:37-38, Mark 12:28-30.)

Woe unto you, Pharisees! for ye tithe mint and rue and all manner of herbs, and pass over judgment and the love of God: these ought ye to have done, and not to leave the other undone. (Luke 11:42.)

If ye love me, keep my commandments. (John 14:15.)

He that hath my commandments, and keepeth them, he it is that loveth me: and he that loveth me *shall be loved of my Father, and I will love him, and will manifest myself to him.* (John 14:21.)

If a man love me, he will keep my words: *and my Father will love him, and we will come unto him, and make our abode with him.* (John 14:23.)

As the Father hath loved me, so have I loved you: continue ye in my love. (John 15:9.)

He that hateth me *hateth my Father also.* (John 15:23.)

We know that *all things work together for good to them* that love God, to them who are called according to his purpose. (Rom. 8:28.)

As it is written, *Eye hath not seen, nor ear heard, neither have entered into the heart of man, the things which God hath prepared* for them that love him. *But God hath revealed them unto us by his Spirit: for the Spirit searcheth all things, yea, the deep things of God.* (1 Cor. 2: 9-10.)

If any man love God, *the same is known of him.* (1 Cor. 8:3.)

Be not thou therefore ashamed of the testimony of our Lord, nor of me his prisoner: but be thou partaker of the afflictions of the gospel according to the power of God. (2 Tim. 1:8.)

Men shall be lovers of their own selves, . . . without natural affection, lovers of pleasures more than lovers of God; . . . from such turn away. . . . *But they shall proceed no further: for their folly shall be manifest unto all men.* (2 Tim. 3:2-9.)

Blessed is the man that endureth temptation: for when he is tried, *he shall receive the crown of life, which the Lord hath promised* to them that love him. (James 1:12; see also JST James 1:12.)

Hath not God chosen the poor of this world rich in faith, and heirs of *the kingdom which he hath promised* to them that love him? (James 2:5.)

Ye must press forward with a steadfastness in Christ, having a perfect brightness of hope, and a love of God and of all men. (2 Ne. 31:20.)

O all ye that are pure in heart, lift up your heads and receive the pleasing word of God, and feast upon his love; *for ye may, if your minds are firm, forever.* (Jacob 3:2.)

[Have] the love of God always in your hearts, *that ye may be lifted up at the last day and enter into his rest.* (Alma 13:29.)

Let all thy thoughts be directed unto the Lord; yea, let the affections of thy heart be placed upon the Lord forever. (Alma 37:36.)

Sanctification cometh because of their yielding their hearts unto God. (Hel. 3:35.)

If ye shall deny yourselves of all ungodliness, and love God with all your might, mind and strength, *then is his grace sufficient for you, that by his grace ye may be perfect in Christ;* and if by the grace of God ye are perfect in Christ, *ye can in nowise deny the power of God.* (Moro. 10:32.)

[God] gave unto them commandments that they should love and serve him, the only living and true God, and that he should be the only being whom they should worship. (D&C 20:19.)

We know also, that *sanctification through the grace of our Lord and Savior Jesus Christ is just and true,* to all those who love and serve God with all their mights, minds, and strength. (D&C 20:31.)

I give unto them a commandment, saying thus: Thou shalt love the Lord thy God with all thy heart, with all thy might, mind, and strength; and in the name of Jesus Christ thou shalt serve him. (D&C 59:5.)

The Lord requireth the heart and a willing mind. (D&C 64:34.)

Great and marvelous are the works of the Lord, and the mysteries of his kingdom which he showed unto us, which surpass all understanding in glory, and in might, and in dominion; which he commanded us we should not write while we were yet in the Spirit, and are not lawful for man to utter; neither is man capable to make them known, for they are only to be seen and understood by the power of the Holy Spirit, which God bestows on those who love him, and purify themselves before him; to whom *he grants this privilege of seeing and knowing for themselves; that through the power and manifestation of the Spirit, while in the flesh, they may be able to bear his presence in the world of glory.* (D&C 76:114-118.)

If ye love me, keep my commandments; *and the sickness of the land shall redound to your glory.* (D&C 124:87.)

Loving Others

(See also Faith; Hope; Loving God.)

We are commanded to love all men, not just those for whom a pure, Christlike love comes naturally. To have this love, we might have to bear great burdens, endure provocation, or be patient in suffering. But it is the nature of love that "charity suffereth long, and is kind; charity envieth not; charity vaunteth not itself, is not puffed up. Doth not behave itself unseemly, seeketh not her own, is not easily provoked, thinketh no evil; rejoiceth not in iniquity, but rejoiceth in the truth; beareth all things, believeth all things, hopeth all things, endureth all things." (1 Cor. 13:4-7.)

We shouldn't allow others' actions or our own faults to interfere with our love for others, for without this love we are nothing. Paul says, "Though I speak with the tongues of men and of angels, and have not charity, I am become as sounding brass, or a tinkling cymbal. And though I have the gift of prophecy, and understand all the mysteries, and all knowledge; and though I have all faith, so that I could remove mountains, and have not charity, I am nothing." (1 Cor. 13:1-2.)

But where does charity come from? How does pure love fill a human heart? Scriptures indicate that charity comes from God: "Pray unto the Father with all the energy of heart, that ye may be filled with this love, which he hath bestowed upon all who are true followers of his Son, Jesus Christ." (Moro. 7:48.) Love can come as a gift of the Spirit to those willing to accept and share it. Love fills and directs the purified heart. "Bridle all your passions, that ye may be filled with love." (Alma 38:12.)

We have not only the eternal promises of eternal life and salvation, but also this earthly promise: "He that dwelleth in love dwelleth in God, and God in him." (1 Jn. 4:16.)

Commandments and Promises

Thou shalt not hate thy brother in thine heart: thou shalt in any wise rebuke thy neighbour, and not suffer sin upon him. Thou shalt not

289

avenge, nor bear any grudge against the children of thy people, but thou shalt love thy neighbour as thyself. (Lev. 19:17-18.)

The stranger that dwelleth with you shall be unto you as one born among you, and thou shalt love him as thyself; for ye were strangers in the land of Egypt. (Lev. 19:34; similar scripture, Deut. 10:19.)

Hatred stirreth up strifes: but love *covereth all sins.* (Prov. 10:12.)

Let none of you imagine evil in your hearts against his neighbour; and love no false oath: *for all these are things that I hate, saith the Lord.* (Zech. 8:17.)

Ye have heard that it hath been said, Thou shalt love thy neighbour, and hate thine enemy. But I say unto you, Love your enemies, bless them that curse you, do good to them that hate you, and pray for them which despitefully use you, and persecute you; *that ye may be the children of your Father which is in heaven:* for he maketh his sun to rise on the evil and on the good, and sendeth rain on the just and on the unjust. (Matt. 5:43-45; similar scriptures, Luke 6:27-28, 3 Ne. 12:44-45; see also Luke 6:31-35.)

Then one of them, which was a lawyer, asked him a question, tempting him, and saying, Master, which is the great commandment in the law? Jesus said unto him, Thou shalt love the Lord thy God with all thy heart, and with all thy soul, and with all thy mind. This is the first and great commandment. And the second is like unto it, Thou shalt love thy neighbour as thyself. On these two commandments hang all the law and the prophets. (Matt. 22:35-40; similar scripture, Mark 12:28-31.)

As ye would that men should do to you, do ye also to them likewise. For if ye love them which love you, *what thank have ye?* for sinners also love those that love them. And if ye do good to them which do good to you, *what thank have ye?* for sinners also do even the same. And if ye lend to them of whom ye hope to receive, *what thank have ye?* for sinners also lend to sinners, to receive as much again. But love ye your enemies, and do good, and lend, hoping for nothing again; *and your reward shall be great, and ye shall be the children of the*

Highest: for he is kind unto the unthankful and to the evil. (Luke 6: 31-35; see also Matt. 5:43-45.)

A new commandment I give unto you, That ye love one another; as I have loved you, that ye also love one another. *By this shall all men know that ye are my disciples*, if ye have love one to another. (John 13:34-35; similar scripture, John 15:12.)

Let love be without dissimulation. Abhor that which is evil; cleave to that which is good. Be kindly affectioned one to another with brotherly love; in honour preferring one another. (Rom. 12:9-10.)

Owe no man any thing, but to love one another: for he that loveth another *hath fulfilled the law.* For this, thou shalt not commit adultery, Thou shalt not kill, Thou shalt not steal, Thou shalt not bear false witness, Thou shalt not covet; and if there be any other commandment, it is briefly comprehended in this saying, namely, Thou shalt love thy neighbour as thyself. Love *worketh no ill to his neighbour: therefore love is the fulfilling of the law.* (Rom. 13:8-10.)

Though I speak with the tongues of men and of angels, and have not charity, *I am become as sounding brass, or a tinkling cymbal.* And though I have the gift of prophecy, and understand all mysteries, and all knowledge; and though I have all faith, so that I could remove mountains, and have not charity, *I am nothing.* And though I bestow all my goods to feed the poor, and though I give my body to be burned, and have not charity, *it profiteth me nothing.* (1 Cor. 13:1-3.)

Charity suffereth long, and is kind; charity envieth not; charity vaunteth not itself, is not puffed up. Doth not behave itself unseemly, seeketh not her own, is not easily provoked, thinketh no evil; rejoiceth not in iniquity, but rejoiceth in the truth; beareth all things, believeth all things, hopeth all things, endureth all things. Charity *never faileth:* but whether there be prophecies, *they shall fail;* whether there be tongues, *they shall cease;* whether there be knowledge, *it shall vanish away.* (1 Cor. 13:4-8; see also Moro. 7:45-46.)

Let all your things be done with charity. (1 Cor. 16:14.)

If any have caused grief, *he hath not grieved me, but in part: that I may not overcharge you all. Sufficient to such a man is this punishment, which was inflicted of many.* So that contrariwise ye ought rather to forgive him, and comfort him, *lest perhaps such a one should be swallowed up with overmuch sorrow.* Wherefore I beseech you that ye would confirm your love toward him. (2 Cor. 2:5-8.)

In all things approving ourselves as the ministers of God, in much patience, . . . by longsuffering, by kindness, . . . by love unfeigned. (2 Cor. 6:4-6.)

Ye have been called unto liberty; only use not liberty for an occasion to the flesh, but by love serve one another. For all the law is fulfilled in one word, even in this; Thou shalt love thy neighbour as thyself. (Gal. 5:13-14.)

Now the works of the flesh are manifest, which are these; Adultery, fornication, . . . hatred, . . . wrath, strife, . . . and such like: *of the which I tell you before, as I have also told you in time past, that* they which do such things *shall not inherit the kingdom of God.* (Gal. 5: 19-21.)

I therefore, the prisoner of the Lord, beseech you that ye walk worthy of the vocation wherewith ye are called, with all lowliness and meekness, with longsuffering, forbearing one another in love. (Eph. 4:1-2.)

Walk in love, as Christ also hath loved us, and hath given himself for us an offering and a sacrifice to God for a sweetsmelling savour. (Eph. 5:2.)

Now ye also put off all these; anger, wrath, malice. (Col. 3:8.)

Put on therefore, as the elect of God, holy and beloved, bowels of mercies, kindness, humbleness of mind, meekness, longsuffering; forbearing one another, and forgiving one another, if any man have a quarrel against any: even as Christ forgave you, so also do ye. And above all these things put on charity, *which is the bond of perfectness.* (Col. 3:12-14.)

He therefore that despiseth, despiseth not man, but God, who hath also given unto us his holy Spirit. But as touching brotherly love ye need not that I write unto you: for ye yourselves are taught of God to love one another. And indeed ye do it toward all the brethren which are in all Macedonia: but we beseech you, brethren, that ye increase more and more. (1 Thes. 4:8-10.)

Let us, who are of the day, be sober, putting on the breastplate of faith and love. (1 Thes. 5:8.)

Be thou an example of the believers, in word, in conversation, in charity, in spirit, in faith, in purity. (1 Tim. 4:12.)

O man of God, . . . follow after righteousness, godliness, faith, love, patience, meekness. (1 Tim. 6:11.)

Flee also youthful lusts: but follow righteousness, faith, charity, peace, with them that call on the Lord out of a pure heart. (2 Tim. 2:22.)

Speak thou the things which become sound doctrine: that the aged men be . . . sound in faith, in charity, in patience. The aged women likewise, that they be in behavior as becometh holiness. (Titus 2:1-3.)

Let us consider one another to provoke unto love and to good works. (Heb. 10:24.)

Let brotherly love continue. (Heb. 13:1.)

If ye fulfil the royal law according to the scripture, Thou shalt love thy neighbour as thyself, *ye do well:* But if ye have respect to persons, *ye commit sin, and are convinced of the law as transgressors.* For whosoever shall keep the whole law, and yet offend in one point, *he is guilty of all.* (James 2:8-10)

Seeing *ye have purified your souls* in obeying the truth through the Spirit unto unfeigned love of the brethren, see that ye love one another with a pure heart fervently: being born again, not of corruptible seed, but of incorruptible, by the word of God, which liveth and abideth for ever. (1 Pet. 1:22-23.)

Laying aside all malice, and all guile, and all hypocrisies, and envies, and all evil speakings, as newborn babes, desire the sincere milk of the word, *that ye may grow thereby:* if so be ye have tasted that the Lord is gracious. (1 Pet. 2:1-3.)

Love as brethren. (1 Pet. 3:8.)

Above all things have fervent charity among yourselves: *for charity shall cover the multitude of sins.* (1 Pet. 4:8; see also JST 1 Pet. 4:8.)

He that hateth his brother *is in darkness, and walketh in darkness, and knoweth not whither he goeth, because that darkness hath blinded his eyes.* (1 Jn. 2:11.)

In this the children of God are manifest, and the children of the devil: whosoever doeth not righteousness *is not of God,* neither he that loveth not his brother. For this is the message that ye heard from the beginning, that we should love one another. (1 Jn. 3:10-11.)

He that loveth not his brother *abideth in death.* Whosoever hateth his brother *is a murderer: and ye know that no murderer hath eternal life abiding in him.* (1 Jn. 3:14-15.)

Let us not love in word, neither in tongue; but in deed and in truth. (1 Jn. 3:18.)

This is his commandment, That we should believe on the name of his Son Jesus Christ, and love one another, as he gave us commandment. And he that keepeth his commandments *dwelleth in him, and he in him. And hereby we know that he abideth in us, by the Spirit which he hath given us.* (1 Jn. 3:23-24.)

Beloved, let us love one another: for love is of God; and every one that loveth *is born of God, and knoweth God.* He that loveth not *knoweth not God;* for God is love. (1 Jn. 4:7-8.)

Beloved, if God so loved us, we ought also to love one another. (1 Jn. 4:11.)

God is love; and he that dwelleth in love *dwelleth in God, and God in him.* (1 Jn. 4:16.)

This commandment have we from him, That he who loveth God love his brother also. (1 Jn. 4:21.)

Now I beseech thee, lady, not as though I wrote a new commandment unto thee, but that which we had from the beginning, that we love one another. And this is love, that we walk after his commandments. (2 Jn. 1:5-6.)

The Lord God hath given a commandment that all men should have charity, which charity is love. And except they should have charity *they were nothing.* Wherefore, if they should have charity *they would not suffer the laborer in Zion to perish.* (2 Ne. 26:30.)

The Lord God hath commanded that men . . . should not have malice; that they should not contend one with another; that they should not commit whoredoms; . . . *for whoso doeth them shall perish.* (2 Ne. 26:32.)

Ye must press forward with a steadfastness in Christ, having a perfect brightness of hope, and a love of God and of all men. (2 Ne. 31:20.)

The natural man is an enemy to God, and has been from the fall of Adam, and will be, forever and ever, unless he yields to the enticings of the Holy Spirit, and putteth off the natural man and becometh a saint through the atonement of Christ the Lord, and becometh as a child, submissive, meek, humble, patient, full of love, willing to submit to all things which the Lord seeth fit to inflict upon him, even as a child doth submit to his father. (Mosiah 3:19.)

He commanded them that there should be no contention one with another, but that they should look forward with one eye, having one faith and one baptism, having their hearts knit together in unity and in love one towards another. And thus he commanded them to preach. *And thus they became the children of God.* (Mosiah 18:21-22.)

Thus did Alma teach his people, that every man should love his neighbor as himself, that there should be no contention among them. (Mosiah 23:15.)

See that ye have faith, hope, and charity, *and then ye will always abound in good works.* (Alma 7:24.)

[Become] humble, meek, submissive, patient, full of love and all long-suffering. (Alma 13:28.)

If ye do not remember to be charitable, *ye are as dross, which the refiners do cast out, (it being of no worth) and is trodden under foot of men.* (Alma 34:29.)

This love which thou hast had for the children of men is charity; wherefore, except men shall have charity *they cannot inherit that place which thou hast prepared in the mansions of thy Father.* Wherefore, I know by this thing which thou hast said, that if the Gentiles have not charity, because of our weakness, *that thou wilt prove them, and take away their talent, yea, even that which they have received, and give unto them who shall have more abundantly.* (Ether 12:34-35.)

If a man be meek and lowly in heart, and confesses by the power of the Holy Ghost that Jesus is the Christ, he must needs have charity; for if he have not charity *he is nothing;* wherefore he must needs have charity. (Moro. 7:44.)

Charity suffereth long, and is kind, and envieth not, and is not puffed up, seeketh not her own, is not easily provoked, thinketh no evil, and rejoiceth not in iniquity but rejoiceth in the truth, beareth all things, believeth all things, hopeth all things, endureth all things. Wherefore, my beloved brethren, if ye have not charity, *ye are nothing,* for charity never faileth. Wherefore, cleave unto charity, which is the greatest of all, for all things must fail—but charity is the pure love of Christ, and it endureth forever; and whoso is found possessed of it at the last day, *it shall be well with him.* Wherefore, my beloved brethren, pray unto the Father with all the energy of heart, *that ye may be filled with this love, which he hath bestowed upon all who are true followers of his Son, Jesus Christ; that ye may become the sons of God; that when he shall appear we shall be like him, for we shall see him as he is; that we may have this hope; that we may be purified even as he is pure.* (Moro. 7:45-48; see also 1 Cor. 13:4-8.)

If there must be hope there must also be charity. And except ye have charity *ye can in nowise be saved in the kingdom of God; neither can ye be saved in the kingdom of God* if ye have not faith; *neither can ye* if ye have no hope. (Moro. 10:20-21.)

Faith, hope, charity and love, with an eye single to the glory of God, *qualify him for the work.* (D&C 4:5.)

No one can assist in this work except he shall be humble and full of love, having faith, hope, and charity, being temperate in all things, whatsoever shall be entrusted to his care. (D&C 12:8.)

Thou shalt live together in love, insomuch that thou shalt weep for the loss of them that die, and more especially for those that have not hope of a glorious resurrection. (D&C 42:45.)

Above all things, clothe yourselves with the bond of charity, as with a mantle, *which is the bond of perfectness and peace.* (D&C 88:125.)

The decisions of these quorums, or either of them, are to be made in all righteousness, in holiness, and lowliness of heart, meekness and long suffering, and in faith, and virtue, and knowledge, temperance, patience, godliness, brotherly kindness and charity; *because the promise is,* if these things abound in them *they shall not be unfruitful in the knowledge of the Lord.* (D&C 107:30-31.)

Be not partial towards them [thy brethren] in love above many others, but let thy love be for them as for thyself; and let thy love abound unto all men, and unto all who love my name. (D&C 112:11.)

No power or influence can or ought to be maintained by virtue of the priesthood, only by persuasion, by long-suffering, by gentleness and meekness, and by love unfeigned; by kindness, and pure knowledge, *which shall greatly enlarge the soul without hypocrisy, and without guile*—reproving betimes with sharpness, when moved upon by the Holy Ghost; and then showing forth afterwards an increase of love toward him whom thou hast reproved, *lest he esteem thee to be his enemy; that he may know that thy faithfulness is stronger than the cords of death.* Let thy bowels also be full of charity towards all men, and to the household of faith, and let virtue garnish thy thoughts unceasingly; *then shall thy confidence wax strong in the presence of God; and the doctrine of the priesthood shall distil upon thy soul as the dews from heaven.* (D&C 121:41-45.)

Unto thy brethren have I said, and also given commandment, that they should love one another, and that they should choose me, their

Father; but behold, they are without affection, and they hate their own blood; *and the fire of mine indignation is kindled against them; and in my hot displeasure will I send in the floods upon them, for my fierce anger is kindled against them.* (Moses 7:33-34.)

Marriage

The commandment to marry is basic both to the needs of individuals and to the perpetuation of mankind. Marriage establishes long-lasting bonds of love and responsibility. It takes us out of ourselves, yet satisfies our need for meaningful companionship and understanding. When children are born, it places the development of human beings in our hands.

Marriage is also a legal promise and covenant between two people before society and God to be responsible for each other and their children. It is a declaration of love, honor, and trust, a commitment to mutual upbuilding. As such, marriage is not an easy path to happiness, but can be the well-spring of eternal joy.

The Lord directs men and women to build marriages on Christlike principles. The Apostle Paul wrote that the husband is to lead his family as Christ leads his church: he is commanded to love his wife "even as Christ also loved the church, and gave himself for it." (Eph. 5:22-28.) Elsewhere in the Bible we learn many other principles upon which godly marriages are based. Latter-day scripture tells us the blessings possible for those who base their marriage on covenants and righteousness.

Marriage, we learn, should be eternal. It is an essential step toward godhood. The participants in this covenant are eligible for the highest degree of the celestial kingdom and for an eternal increase. (See D&C 131:1-4.) An eternal marriage is one sealed by the Holy Spirit of Promise, and though its responsibilities are awesome, its promise is much more so.

Commandments and Promises

So God created man in his own image, in the image of God created he him; male and female created he them. And God blessed them, and God said unto them, Be fruitful, and multiply, and replenish the earth, and subdue it. (Gen. 1:27-28.)

Unto the woman [Eve] he said, *I will greatly multiply thy sorrow and thy conception; in sorrow thou shalt bring forth children; and thy desire shall be to thy husband, and he shall rule over thee.* (Gen. 3:16; similar scripture, Moses 4:22.)

God blessed Noah and his sons, and said unto them, Be fruitful, and multiply, and replenish the earth. (Gen. 9:1.)

Be ye fruitful, and multiply; bring forth abundantly in the earth, and multiply therein. (Gen. 9:7.)

God said unto him [Jacob], I am God Almighty: be fruitful and multiply; *a nation and a company of nations shall be of thee, and kings shall come out of thy loins; and the land which I gave Abraham and Isaac, to thee I will give it, and to thy seed after thee will I give the land.* (Gen. 35:11-12.)

Neither shall he [the king] multiply wives to himself, *that his heart turn not away.* (Deut. 17:17.)

Whoso findeth a wife *findeth a good thing, and obtaineth favour of the Lord.* (Prov. 18:22; see also JST Prov. 18:22.)

Live joyfully with the wife whom thou lovest all the days of the life of thy vanity, which he hath given thee under the sun, all the days of thy vanity: for that is thy portion in this life, and in thy labour which thou takest under the sun. (Eccl. 9:9.)

Take heed to your spirit, and let none deal treacherously against the wife of his youth. (Mal. 2:15.)

[Christ] answered and said unto them, Have ye not read, that he which made them at the beginning made them male and female, and said, For this cause shall a man leave father and mother, and shall cleave to his wife: and they twain shall be one flesh? Wherefore they are no more twain, but one flesh. What therefore God hath joined together, let no man put asunder. (Matt. 19:4-6; similar scriptures, Gen. 2:24, Mark 10:6-9, Eph. 5:31.)

Let the husband render unto the wife due benevolence: and likewise also the wife unto the husband. (1 Cor. 7:3.)

Unto the married I command, yet not I, but the Lord, Let not the wife depart from her husband. (1 Cor. 7:10.)

Neither is the man without the woman, neither the woman without the man, in the Lord. For as the woman is of the man, even so is the man also by the woman; but all things of God. (1 Cor. 11:11.)

Wives, submit yourselves unto your own husbands, as unto the Lord. For the husband is the head of the wife, even as Christ is the head of the church: and he is the saviour of the body. Therefore as the church is subject unto Christ, so let the wives be to their own husbands in every thing. Husbands, love your wives, even as Christ also loved the church, and gave himself for it; *that he might sanctify and cleanse it with the washing of water by the word, that he might present it to himself a glorious church, not having spot, or wrinkle, or any such thing; but that it should be holy and without blemish.* So ought men to love their wives as their own bodies. He that loveth his wife *loveth himself.* (Eph. 5:22-28.)

Nevertheless let every one of you in particular so love his wife even as himself; and the wife see that she reverence her husband. (Eph. 5:33.)

Wives, submit yourselves unto your own husbands, as it is fit in the Lord. Husbands, love your wives, and be not bitter against them. (Col. 3:18-19.)

A bishop then must be . . . the husband of one wife, . . . one that ruleth well his own house, having his children in subjection with all gravity. (1 Tim. 3:2-4.)

Let the deacons be the husbands of one wife, ruling their children and their own houses well. (1 Tim. 3:12.)

I will therefore that the younger women marry, bear children, guide the house, give none occasion to the adversary to speak reproachfully. (1 Tim. 5:14.)

Speak thou the things which become sound doctrine: that . . . the aged women . . . may teach the young women to be sober, to love their husbands, to love their children, to be discreet, chaste, keepers at home, good, obedient to their own husbands, *that the word of God be not blasphemed.* (Titus 2:1-5.)

Marriage *is honourable in all,* and the bed *undefiled.* (Heb. 13:4.)

Likewise, ye wives, be in subjection to your own husbands; *that, if any obey not the word, they also may without the word be won by the conversation of the wives;* while they behold your chaste conversation coupled with fear. (1 Pet. 3:1-2; see also JST 1 Pet. 3:1-2.)

Likewise, ye husbands, dwell with them according to knowledge, giving honour unto the wife, as unto the weaker vessel, and as being heirs together of the grace of life; *that your prayers be not hindered.* (1 Pet. 3:7.)

It was not meet for him, Lehi, that he should take away his family into the wilderness alone; but that his sons should take daughters to wife, that they might raise up seed unto the Lord in the land of promise. (1 Ne. 7:1.)

[The Lamanites] have not forgotten the commandment of the Lord, which was given unto our father—that they should have save it were one wife, and concubines they should have none. (Jacob 3:5; similar scripture, Jacob 2:27.)

[to Emma Smith] The office of thy calling shall be for a comfort unto my servant, Joseph Smith, Jun., thy husband, in his afflictions with consoling words, in the spirit of meekness. (D&C 25:5.)

[to Emma Smith] Continue in the spirit of meekness, and beware of pride. Let thy soul delight in thy husband, and the glory which shall come upon him. (D&C 25:14.)

Thou shalt love thy wife with all thy heart, and shalt cleave unto her and none else. (D&C 42:22.)

Whoso forbiddeth to marry *is not ordained of God,* for marriage is ordained of God unto man. Wherefore, it is lawful that he should have one wife, and they twain shall be one flesh, and all this *that the earth might answer the end of its creation; and that it might be filled with the measure of man, according to his creation before the world was made.* (D&C 49:15-17.)

In the celestial glory there are three heavens or degrees; and in order to obtain the highest, a man must enter into this order of the priesthood [meaning the new and everlasting covenant of marriage]; *and if he does not, he cannot obtain it. He may enter into the other, but that is the end of his kingdom; he cannot have an increase.* (D&C 131:1-4.)

Prepare thy heart to receive and obey the instructions which I am about to give unto you; for all those who have this law revealed unto them must obey the same. For behold, I reveal unto you a new and an everlasting covenant; and if ye abide not that covenant, *then are ye damned;* for no one can reject this covenant *and be permitted to enter into my glory. For all who will have a blessing at my hands* shall abide the law which was appointed *for that blessing,* and the conditions thereof, as were instituted from before the foundation of the world. And as pertaining to the new and everlasting covenant, it was insti-tuted *for the fulness of my glory; and he that receiveth a fulness thereof* must and shall abide the law, *or he shall be damned, saith the Lord God.* (D&C 132:3-6.)

If a man marry a wife by my word, which is my law, and by the new and everlasting covenant, and it is sealed unto them by the Holy Spirit of promise, by him who is anointed, unto whom I have ap-pointed this power and the keys of this priesthood; and it shall be said unto them—*Ye shall come forth in the first resurrection; and if it be after the first resurrection, in the next resurrection; and shall in-herit thrones, kingdoms, principalities, and powers, dominions, all heights and depths—* . . . and if ye abide in my covenant, and com-mit no murder whereby to shed innocent blood, *it shall be done unto them in all things whatsoever my servant hath put upon them, in time, and through all eternity; and shall be of full force when they are out of the world; and they shall pass by the angels, and the gods, which are set there, to their exaltation and glory in all things, as hath been sealed upon their heads, which glory shall be a fulness and a continuation of the seeds forever and ever. Then shall they be gods, because they have no end; therefore shall they be from everlasting to everlasting, because they continue; then shall they be above all, be-*

cause all things are subject to them. Then shall they be gods, because they have all power, and the angels are subject unto them. Verily, verily, I say unto you, except ye abide my law *ye cannot attain to this glory.* (D&C 132:19-21.)

We are not teaching polygamy or plural marriage, nor permitting any person to enter into its practice. . . . And I now publicly declare that my advice to the Latter-day Saints is to refrain from contracting any marriage forbidden by the law of the land. [Signed by Wilford Woodruff.] (D&C Official Declaration–1.)

Meditation and Purity
of Thought
(See also Prayer; Purity; Sexual Morality; Word of God, Studying the.)

The Lord commands us to meditate on his truths. Moroni's promise to those who pray for a knowledge of the truthfulness of the Book of Mormon is prefaced by this: "When ye shall read these things, . . . remember how merciful the Lord hath been unto the children of men, . . . and ponder it in your hearts." (Moro. 10:3.) Similarly, the Savior told the Nephites to "go ye unto your homes, and ponder upon the things which I have said, and ask of the Father, in my name, that ye may understand." (3 Ne. 17:3.)

Understanding cannot come if we pollute our minds with unholy and unworthy thoughts. It comes when our minds are worthy to receive the Holy Ghost. When we are worthy of such companionship, we can have the Lord's help in guiding our lives. The Lord directs us to learn and make choices in this manner: "You must study it out in your mind; then you must ask me if it be right." Then, the Lord says, we will have a confirmation of truth or a forgetfulness of our error. (D&C 9:8-9.) Clearly, purity of thought and meditation of God's truths are indispensible to receiving a witness of his Spirit.

Commandments and Promises

Stand in awe, and sin not: commune with your own heart upon your bed, and be still. (Ps. 4:4.)

Be still, and know that I am God. (Ps. 46:10.)

Ponder the path of thy feet, and let all thy ways be established. (Prov. 4:26.)

Hear, O earth: behold, *I will bring evil upon this people, even the fruit of their thoughts*, because they have not hearkened unto my words, nor to my law, but rejected it. (Jer. 6:19.)

Whosoever looketh on a woman to lust after her *hath committed adultery with her already in his heart.* (Matt. 5:28; similar scripture, 3 Ne. 12:28.)

Whatsoever things are true, whatsoever things are honest, whatsoever things are just, whatsoever things are pure, whatsoever things are lovely, whatsoever things are of good report; if there be any virtue, and if there be any praise, think on these things. (Philip. 4:8.)

Meditate upon these things; give thyself wholly to them; *that thy profiting may appear to all.* (1 Tim. 4:15.)

Consider what I say; *and the Lord give understanding in all things.* (2 Tim. 2:7.)

If ye do not watch yourselves, and your thoughts, and your words, and your deeds, and observe the commandments of God, and continue in the faith of what ye have heard concerning the coming of our Lord, even unto the end of your lives, *ye must perish.* And now, O man, remember, *and perish not.* (Mosiah 4:30.)

[Christ speaking to the Nephites] Go ye unto your homes, and ponder upon the things which I have said, and ask of the Father, in my name, that ye may understand, and prepare your minds for the morrow, and I come unto you again. (3 Ne. 17:3.)

They that feared the Lord spake often one to another, and the Lord hearkened and heard; *and a book of remembrance was written before him* for them that feared the Lord, and that thought upon his name. *And they shall be mine, saith the Lord of Hosts, in that day when I make up my jewels; and I will spare them as a man spareth his own son that serveth him.* (3 Ne. 24:16-17.)

I would exhort you that when ye shall read these things, if it be wisdom in God that ye should read them, that ye would remember how merciful the Lord hath been unto the children of men, from the creation of Adam even down until the time that ye shall receive these things, and ponder it in your hearts. (Moro. 10:3.)

Look unto me in every thought; doubt not, fear not. (D&C 6:36.)

You must study it out in your mind; then you must ask me if it be right, and if it is right *I will cause that your bosom shall burn within you; therefore, you shall feel that it is right.* But if it be not right *you shall have . . . a stupor of thought that shall cause you to forget the thing which is wrong.* (D&C 9:8-9.)

He that looketh upon a woman to lust after her *shall deny the faith, and shall not have the Spirit;* and if he repents not *he shall be cast out.* (D&C 42:23.)

Treasure these things up in your hearts, and let the solemnities of eternity rest upon your minds. (D&C 43:34.)

He that looketh on a woman to lust after her, or if any man shall commit adultery in their hearts, *they shall not have the Spirit, but shall deny the faith and shall fear.* (D&C 63:16.)

Remember the great and last promise which I have made unto you; cast away your idle thoughts and your excess of laughter far from you. (D&C 88:69.)

Let those whom they have warned in their traveling call on the Lord, and ponder the warning in their hearts which they have received, for a little season. (D&C 88:71.)

Then shall the second angel sound his trump, and reveal the secret acts of men, and the thoughts and intents of their hearts, and the mighty works of God in the second thousand years. (D&C 88:109.)

Let thy bowels also be full of charity towards all men, and to the household of faith, and let virtue garnish thy thoughts unceasingly; *then shall thy confidence wax strong in the presence of God; and the doctrine of the priesthood shall distil upon thy soul as the dews from heaven. The Holy Ghost shall be thy constant companion, and thy scepter an unchanging scepter of righteousness and truth; and thy dominion shall be an everlasting dominion, and without compulsory means it shall flow unto thee forever and ever.* (D&C 121:45-46.)

Meekness

(See also Humility; Receiving and Following the Holy Ghost.)

We must be meek: gentle, forgiving, benevolent. (See Matt. 5:5, footnote 5a, 1979 LDS edition, King James Bible.) We are told to reprove (Gal. 6:1), to serve (Eph. 4:1-2), to receive God's word (James 1:21), to govern our homes (D&C 31:9), to teach and warn (D&C 38:41), to exercise authority (D&C 107:30-31), and to maintain power and influence (D&C 121:41-42), all in meekness. Admonitions to and rewards for meekness are numerous.

Like many virtues, meekness comes through the Spirit of God: "Be led by the Holy Spirit, becoming humble, meek." (Alma 13:28.) Likewise, the Lord counsels: "Walk in the meekness of my Spirit, and you shall have peace in me." (D&C 19:23.) Paul writes, "The fruit of the Spirit is . . . meekness." (Gal. 5:22.)

As we follow the Spirit's guidance in meekness, we become eligible for numerous blessings, among which is this promise: "The meek will he guide in judgment: and the meek will he teach his way." (Ps. 25:9.) Thus through meekness can we continually increase in knowledge and wisdom.

Commandments and Promises

The meek *shall eat and be satisfied.* (Ps. 22:26.)

The meek *will he guide in judgment:* and the meek *will he teach his way.* (Ps. 25:9.)

The meek *shall inherit the earth; and shall delight themselves in the abundance of peace.* (Ps. 37:11; see also Matt. 5:5.)

God arose to judgment, to save all the meek of the earth. (Ps. 76:9.)

The Lord lifteth up the meek. (Ps. 147:6.)

The Lord taketh pleasure in his people: he will beautify the meek *with salvation.* (Ps. 149:4.)

The meek *also shall increase their joy in the Lord.* (Isa. 29:19.)

Seek ye the Lord, all ye meek of the earth, which have wrought his judgment; seek righteousness, seek meekness: *it may be ye shall be hid in the day of the Lord's anger.* (Zeph. 2:3.)

Blessed are the meek: *for they shall inherit the earth.* (Matt. 5:5; similar scripture, 3 Ne. 12:5; see also Ps. 37:11.)

Ye have heard that it hath been said, An eye for an eye, and a tooth for a tooth: but I say unto you, That ye resist not evil: but whosoever shall smite thee on thy right cheek, turn to him the other also. (Matt. 5:38-39; similar scripture, 3 Ne. 12:39; see also JST Luke 6:29-30.)

Except ye be converted, and become as little children, *ye shall not enter into the kingdom of heaven.* (Matt. 18:3.)

Whosoever shall not receive the kingdom of God as a little child, *he shall not enter therein.* (Mark 10:15; similar scripture, Luke 18:17.)

Unto him that smiteth thee on the one cheek offer also the other; and him that taketh away thy cloke forbid not to take thy coat also. (Luke 6:29; see also JST Luke 6:29-30.)

The fruit of the Spirit is love, joy, peace, longsuffering, gentleness, goodness, faith, meekness, temperance: against such there is no law. (Gal. 5:22-23.)

If a man be overtaken in a fault, ye which are spiritual, restore such an one in the spirit of meekness; considering thyself, *lest thou also be tempted.* (Gal. 6:1.)

I therefore, the prisoner of the Lord, beseech you that ye walk worthy of the vocation wherewith ye are called, with all lowliness and meekness, with longsuffering, forbearing one another in love; endeavouring to keep the unity of the Spirit in the bond of peace. (Eph. 4:1-3.)

Put on therefore, as the elect of God, holy and beloved, bowels of mercies, kindness, humbleness of mind, meekness, longsuffering. (Col. 3:12.)

Follow after righteousness, godliness, faith, love, patience, meekness. (1 Tim. 6:11.)

Put them in mind to be subject to principalities and powers, to obey magistrates, to be ready to every good work, to speak evil of no man, to be no brawlers, but gentle, shewing all meekness unto all men. (Titus 3:1-2.)

Receive with meekness the engrafted word, *which is able to save your souls.* (James 1:21.)

Let [the adorning of wives] not be that outward adorning of plaiting the hair, and of wearing of gold, or of putting on of apparel; but let it be the hidden man of the heart, in that which is not corruptible, even the ornament of a meek and quiet spirit, *which is in the sight of God of great price.* (1 Pet. 3:3-4.)

The meek *also shall increase, and their joy shall be in the Lord.* (2 Ne. 27:30.)

The natural man is an enemy to God, and has been from the fall of Adam, and will be, forever and ever, unless he yields to the enticings of the Holy Spirit, and putteth off the natural man and becometh a saint through the atonement of Christ the Lord, and becometh as a child, submissive, meek, humble, patient, full of love, willing to submit to all things which the Lord seeth fit to inflict upon him, even as a child doth submit to his father. (Mosiah 3:19.)

Humble yourselves before the Lord, and call on his holy name, and watch and pray continually, *that ye may not be tempted above that which ye can bear, and thus be led by the Holy Spirit, becoming humble, meek, submissive, patient, full of love and all long-suffering.* (Alma 13:28.)

Ye must repent, and become as a little child, and be baptized in my name, *or ye can in nowise receive these things [witness of the Holy Ghost].* And again I say unto you, ye must repent, and be baptized in my name, and become as a little child, *or ye can in nowise inherit the kingdom of God.* (3 Ne. 11:37-38.)

Walk in the meekness of my Spirit, *and you shall have peace in me.* (D&C 19:23.)

Continue in the spirit of meekness, and beware of pride. (D&C 25:14.)

Govern your house in meekness. (D&C 31:9.)

Let your preaching be the warning voice, every man to his neighbor, in mildness and in meekness. (D&C 38:41.)

[W. W. Phelps] hath need to repent, for I, the Lord, am not well pleased with him, for he seeketh to excel, and he is not sufficiently meek before me. (D&C 58:41.)

If any man among you [missionaries] be strong in the Spirit, let him take with him him that is weak, *that he may be edified in all meekness, that he may become strong also.* (D&C 84:106.)

I, the Lord, show mercy unto all the meek, and upon all whomsoever I will, *that I may be justified when I shall bring them unto judgment.* (D&C 97:2.)

Declare whatsoever thing ye declare in my name, in solemnity of heart, in the spirit of meekness, in all things. *And I give unto you this promise, that inasmuch as ye do this the Holy Ghost shall be shed forth in bearing record unto all things whatsoever ye shall say.* (D&C 100:7-8.)

The decisions of these quorums, or either of them, are to be made in all righteousness, in holiness, and lowliness of heart, meekness and long suffering, and in faith, and virtue, and knowledge, temperance, patience, godliness, brotherly kindness and charity; *because the promise is, if these things abound in them they shall not be unfruitful in the knowledge of the Lord.* (D&C 107:30-31.)

Let the residue continue to preach from that hour, and if they will do this in all lowliness of heart, in meekness and humility, and long-suffering, *I, the Lord, give unto them a promise that I will provide for their families; and an effectual door shall be opened for them, from henceforth.* (D&C 118:3.)

No power or influence can or ought to be maintained by virtue of the priesthood, only by persuasion, by long-suffering, by gentleness and meekness, and by love unfeigned; by kindness, and pure knowledge, *which shall greatly enlarge the soul without hypocrisy, and without guile.* (D&C 121:41-42.)

My servant Lyman Wight should continue in preaching for Zion, in the spirit of meekness, confessing me before the world; *and I will bear him up as on eagles' wings; and he shall beget glory and honor to himself and unto my name.* (D&C 124:18.)

Meetings

(See also Sabbath Observance; Worship.)

A meeting on its own merits is not necessarily good; thus the Lord specifies why and how the followers of God should meet. Meetings should be edifying. (1 Cor. 14:26.) They should involve fasting and prayer to benefit those not yet among God's flock. (Alma 6:6.) They should be frequent and open to all. (3 Ne. 18:22-23.) They should manifest unity on God's teachings. (D&C 41:2.) They should be directed by the Spirit of God. (D&C 46:2.) They should provide a place for edification and instruction to "know how to act and direct [Christ's] church, how to act upon the points of [his] law and commandments." (D&C 43:8.) When the Lord's people are so gathered in his name, they have his promise: "There am I." (Matt. 18:20.)

Commandments and Promises

How is it then, brethren? when ye come together, every one of you hath a psalm, hath a doctrine, hath a tongue, hath a revelation, hath an interpretation. Let all things be done *unto edifying.* (1 Cor. 14:26.)

Not forsaking the assembling of ourselves together, as the manner of some is; but exhorting one another: and so much the more, as ye see the day approaching. (Heb. 10:25.)

The children of God were commanded that they should gather themselves together oft, and join in fasting and mighty prayer in behalf of the welfare of the souls of those who knew not God. (Alma 6:6.)

Ye shall meet together oft; and ye shall not forbid any man from coming unto you when ye shall meet together, but suffer them that they may come unto you and forbid them not; but ye shall pray for them, and shall not cast them out; and if it so be that they come unto you oft ye shall pray for them unto the Father, in my name. (3 Ne. 18:22-23.)

Where two or three are gathered together in my name, as touching one thing, *behold, there will I be in the midst of them—even so am I in the midst of you.* (D&C 6:32; similar scripture, Matt. 18:20.)

Hearken, O ye elders of my church whom I have called, behold I give unto you a commandment, that ye shall assemble yourselves together to agree upon my word. (D&C 41:2.)

As ye have assembled yourselves together according to the commandment wherewith I commanded you, and are agreed as touching this one thing, and have asked the Father in my name, *even so ye shall receive.* (D&C 42:3.)

I give unto you a commandment, that when ye are assembled together ye shall instruct and edify each other, *that ye may know how to act and direct my church, how to act upon the points of my law and commandments, which I have given. And thus ye shall become instructed in the law of my church, and be sanctified by that which ye have received,* and ye shall bind yourselves to act in all holiness before me—that inasmuch as ye do this, *glory shall be added to the kingdom which ye have received.* Inasmuch as ye do it not, *it shall be taken, even that which ye have received.* (D&C 43:8-10.)

It has always been given to the elders of my church from the beginning, and ever shall be, to conduct all meetings as they are directed and guided by the Holy Spirit. Nevertheless ye are commanded never to cast any one out from your public meetings, which are held before the world. Ye are also commanded not to cast any one who belongeth to the church out of your sacrament meetings; nevertheless, if any have trespassed, let him not partake until he makes reconciliation. And again I say unto you, ye shall not cast any out of your sacrament meetings who are earnestly seeking the kingdom—I speak this concerning those who are not of the church. And again I say unto you, concerning your confirmation meetings, that if there be any that are not of the church, that are earnestly seeking after the kingdom, ye shall not cast them out. (D&C 46:2-6.)

Assemble yourselves upon the land of Zion; and hold a meeting and rejoice together, and offer a sacrament unto the Most High. (D&C 62:4.)

Thus saith the Lord unto you who have assembled yourselves together to receive his will concerning you: *Behold, this is pleasing unto your Lord, and the angels rejoice over you; the alms of your prayers have come up into the ears of the Lord of Sabaoth, and are recorded in the book of the names of the sanctified, even them of the celestial world.* (D&C 88:1-2.)

Call a solemn assembly, even of those who are the first laborers in this last kingdom. (D&C 88:70.)

Call your solemn assembly, as I have commanded you. (D&C 88:117; similar scripture, D&C 109:6.)

They who are not chosen have sinned a very grievous sin, in that they are walking in darkness at noon-day. And for this cause I gave unto you a commandment that you should call your solemn assembly, *that your fastings and your mourning might come up into the ears of the Lord of Sabaoth, which is by interpretation, the creator of the first day, the beginning and the end.* (D&C 95:6-7.)

Call your solemn assemblies, and speak often one to another. (D&C 133:6.)

Mercy

(See also Forgiving Others.)

The Lord extends mercy to us by allowing us to repent of our sins. We thereby let his atonement meet the demands of justice in our behalf. Then, as we are given mercy, we are commanded to give it to others—"See that you are merciful"—by which we are once more blessed with mercy: "then shall ye receive your reward; yea, ye shall have mercy restored unto you again." (Alma 41:14.) In other words, "Blessed are the merciful: for they shall obtain mercy." (Matt. 5:7.)

James explains, "He shall have judgment without mercy, that hath shewed no mercy." (James 2:13.) But if we do show mercy, then the Lord's mediating gift of mercy becomes the key to eternal life.

Commandments and Promises

The righteous sheweth mercy, and giveth. (Ps. 37:21.)

The merciful man *doeth good to his own soul.* (Prov. 11:17.)

He that despiseth his neighbour *sinneth:* but he that hath mercy on the poor, *happy is he.* (Prov. 14:21.)

Turn thou to thy God: keep mercy and judgment, and wait on thy God continually. (Hosea 12:6.)

He hath shewed thee, O man, what is good; and what doth the Lord require of thee, but to do justly, and to love mercy, and to walk humbly with thy God? (Micah 6:8.)

Execute true judgment, and shew mercy and compassions every man to his brother. (Zech. 7:9.)

Blessed are the merciful: *for they shall obtain mercy.* (Matt. 5:7; similar scripture, 3 Ne. 12:7.)

Woe unto you, scribes and Pharisees, hypocrites! for ye pay tithe of mint and anise and cummin, and have omitted the weightier matters of the law, judgment, mercy, and faith: these ought ye to have done, and not to leave the other undone. (Matt. 23:23.)

Be ye therefore merciful, as your Father also is merciful. (Luke 6:36.)

He that sheweth mercy, [let him do it] with cheerfulness. (Rom. 12:8.)

Put on therefore, as the elect of God, holy and beloved, bowels of mercies, kindness, humbleness of mind, meekness, longsuffering; forbearing one another, and forgiving one another, if any man have a quarrel against any: even as Christ forgave you, so also do ye. (Col. 3:12-13.)

He shall have judgment without mercy, that hath shewed no mercy; and mercy rejoiceth against judgment. (James 2:13.)

[Alma to Corianton] See that you are merciful unto your brethren; deal justly, judge righteously, and do good continually; and if ye do all these things *then shall ye receive your reward; yea, ye shall have mercy restored unto you again.* (Alma 41:14.)

Mercy hath compassion on mercy *and claimeth her own.* (D&C 88:40.)

Mourning

(See also Adversity, Reacting to; Loving Others; Repentance.)

Some people are afraid to love because they are afraid to lose that love. They withhold their caring so that they will not suffer. The Lord tells us this is not his way. Those who mourn are indeed blessed, he says. They have chosen to love others; they have accepted the risks of charity. Those who mourn for their own shortcomings have chosen a similar path of caring.

For those who accept this initial risk and possible burden, the Lord gives an ultimate promise: "They shall be comforted." (Matt. 5:4.) To the sorrowful who seek him in supplication, he promises joy.

Commandments and Promises

It is better to go to the house of mourning, than to go to the house of feasting: for that is the end of all men; and the living will lay it to his heart. Sorrow is better than laughter: for by the sadness of the countenance *the heart is made better*. The heart of the wise is in the house of mourning; but the heart of fools is in the house of mirth. (Eccl. 7:2-4.)

Turn ye even to me with all your heart, and with fasting, and with weeping, and with mourning. (Joel 2:12.)

Blessed are they that mourn: *for they shall be comforted.* (Matt. 5:4; similar scripture, 3 Ne. 12:4.)

Blessed are ye that weep now: *for ye shall laugh.* (Luke 6:21.)

Be afflicted, and mourn, and weep: let your laughter be turned to mourning, and your joy to heaviness. (James 4:9.)

Thou shalt live together in love, insomuch that thou shalt weep for the loss of them that die, and more especially for those that have not hope of a glorious resurrection. (D&C 42:45.)

All they who have mourned *shall be comforted.* (D&C 101:14.)

If thou art sorrowful, call on the Lord thy God with supplication, *that your souls may be joyful.* (D&C 136:29.)

Murder and Violence

(See also Peace.)

The scriptures condemn murder and violence, and God sternly punishes those who willfully deprive others of life: "He that kills shall not have forgiveness in this world, nor in the world to come; . . . he that killeth shall die." (D&C 42:18-19.) The Lord, however, does not say he is speaking of those who kill others in battle, though he does not justify war except in certain cases. (See Alma 43:46-47 and 48:14-16.) Nor does he say he is speaking of accidental or negligent death, where the result is far more serious than the intent. Otherwise, murderers will not inherit the kingdom of God and will have their part in the second death. (See Gal. 5:19-20 and Rev. 21:8.)

Commandments and Promises

The earth also was corrupt before God, and the earth was filled with violence. . . . And God said unto Noah, *The end of all flesh is come before me;* for the earth is filled with violence through them; and, behold, *I will destroy them with the earth.* (Gen. 6:11-13; similar scripture, Moses 8:28-30.)

Whoso sheddeth man's blood, *by man shall his blood be shed: for in the image of God made he man.* And you, be ye fruitful, and multiply; bring forth abundantly in the earth, and multiply therein. (Gen. 9:6-7.)

Cursed be their anger, for it was fierce; and their wrath, for it was cruel: *I will divide them in Jacob, and scatter them in Israel.* (Gen. 49:7.)

Thou shalt not kill. (Ex. 20:13; similar scriptures, Deut. 5:17, Mosiah 13:21, D&C 59:6.)

Cursed be he that smiteth his neighbour secretly. And all the people shall say, Amen. *Cursed* be he that taketh reward to slay an innocent person. And all the people shall say, Amen. *Cursed* be he that confirmeth not all the words of this law to do them. And all the people shall say, Amen. (Deut. 27:24-26.)

The Lord trieth the righteous: but the wicked and him that loveth violence *his soul hateth.* (Ps. 11:5.)

Trust not in oppression. (Ps. 62:10.)

Envy thou not the oppressor, and choose none of his ways. For the froward *is abomination to the Lord: but his secret* is with the righteous. (Prov. 3:31-32.)

He that is cruel *troubleth his own flesh.* (Prov. 11:17.)

A man that doeth violence to the blood of any person *shall flee to the pit;* let no man stay him. (Prov. 28:17.)

Woe to thee that spoilest, and thou wast not spoiled; and dealest treacherously, and they dealt not treacherously with thee! when thou shalt cease to spoil, *thou shalt be spoiled;* and when thou make an end to deal treacherously, *they shall deal treacherously with thee.* (Isa. 33:1.)

Do no wrong, do no violence to the stranger, the fatherless, nor the widow, neither shed innocent blood in this place. (Jer. 22:3.)

Woe to the bloody city, to the pot whose scum is therein, and whose scum is not gone out of it! *bring it out piece by piece; let no lot fall upon it.... Woe to the bloody city! I will even make the pile for fire great ... that the scum of it may be consumed.* (Ezek. 24:6-11.)

Jesus said, Thou shalt do no murder. (Matt. 19:18.)

From within, out of the heart of men, proceed evil thoughts, . . . murders, thefts, . . . blasphemy, . . . all these evil things come from within, and *defile the man.* (Mark 7:21-23.)

The soldiers likewise demanded of him, saying, And what shall we do? And he said unto them, Do violence to no man. (Luke 3:14.)

The works of the flesh are manifest, which are these; . . . hatred, variance, emulations, wrath, strife, seditions, heresies, envyings, murders, . . . and such like: of the which I tell you before, as I have also told you in time past, that they which do such things *shall not inherit the kingdom of God.* (Gal. 5:19-21.)

A bishop must be blameless, . . . not soon angry, . . . no striker. (Titus 1:7.)

He that said, Do not commit adultery, said also, Do not kill. Now if thou commit no adultery, yet if thou kill, *thou art become a transgressor of the law.* (James 2:11.)

Let none of you suffer as a murderer. (1 Pet. 4:15.)

Murderers . . . *shall have their part in the lake which burneth with fire and brimstone: which is the second death.* (Rev. 21:8.)

Wo unto the murderer who deliberately killeth, *for he shall die.* (2 Ne. 9:35.)

I will punish the world for evil, and the wicked for their iniquity; *I will cause the arrogancy of the proud to cease, and will lay down the haughtiness of the terrible.* (2 Ne. 23:11.)

The Lord God hath commanded that men should not murder; . . . that they should not have malice; that they should not contend one with another, . . . for whoso doeth them *shall perish.* (2 Ne. 26:32.)

Whosoever murdereth against the light and knowledge of God, *it is not easy for him to obtain forgiveness.* (Alma 39:6.)

The Lord had said unto them [Nephites], and also unto their fathers, that: Inasmuch as ye are not guilty of the first offense, neither the second, ye shall not suffer yourselves to be slain by the hands of your enemies. And again, the Lord has said that: Ye shall defend your families even unto bloodshed. (Alma 43:46-47.)

The Nephites were taught to defend themselves against their enemies, even to the shedding of blood if it were necessary; yea, and they were also taught never to give an offense, yea, and never to raise the sword except it were against an enemy, except it were to preserve their lives. And this was their faith, that by so doing *God would prosper them in the land,* or in other words, if they were faithful in keeping the commandments of God *that he would prosper them in the land; yea, warn them to flee, or to prepare for war, according to their danger; and also, that God would make it known unto them whither they should go to defend themselves against their enemies, and by so doing, the Lord would deliver them.* (Alma 48:14-16.)

[Moroni to Ammoron] I would tell you concerning *that awful hell that awaits to receive* such murderers as thou and thy brother have been, except ye repent and withdraw your murderous purposes. (Alma 54:7.)

Even at this time ye [Nephites] are ripening, because of your murders and your fornication and wickedness, *for everlasting destruction;* yea, and except ye repent *it will come unto you soon.* (Hel. 8:26.)

Turn, all ye Gentiles, from your wicked ways; and repent of your evil doings, . . . of your murders, . . . and your strifes, . . . and come unto me, and be baptized in my name, *that ye may receive a remission of your sins, and be filled with the Holy Ghost, that ye may be numbered with my people who are of the house of Israel.* (3 Ne. 30:2.)

I command thee that thou shalt not . . . seek thy neighbor's life. (D&C 19:25.)

Whosoever shall lay their hands upon you by violence, ye shall command to be smitten in my name; and, behold, *I will smite them according to your words, in mine own due time.* (D&C 24:16.)

I speak unto the church. Thou shalt not kill; and he that kills *shall not have forgiveness in this world, nor in the world to come.* And again, I say, thou shalt not kill; but he that killeth *shall die.* (D&C 42:18-19.)

If any persons among you shall kill *they shall be delivered up and dealt with according to the laws of the land; for remember that he hath no forgiveness.* (D&C 42:79.)

Wo be unto man that sheddeth blood of animals or that wasteth flesh and hath no need. (D&C 49:21; see also JST Gen. 9:11.)

Wo unto all those that discomfort my people, and drive, and murder, and testify against them, saith the Lord of Hosts; *a generation of vipers shall not escape the damnation of hell.* (D&C 121:23.)

If a man marry a wife according to my word, and they are sealed by the Holy Spirit of promise, according to mine appointment, and he or she shall commit any sin or transgression of the new and everlasting covenant whatever, and all manner of blasphemies, and if they commit no murder wherein they shed innocent blood, *yet they shall come forth in the first resurrection, and enter into their exaltation; but they shall be destroyed in the flesh, and shall be delivered unto the buffetings of Satan unto the day of redemption, saith the Lord God.* (D&C 132:26.)

Murmuring and Complaining
(See also Blasphemy and Evil Communication.)

Petty complaining is not worthy of God's sons and daughters. Even when we apparently have cause to complain, we are commanded not to complain, especially about God. We should consider what happened to the men that Moses sent to search the land, who "made all the congregation to murmur against him, by bringing up a slander upon the land." (Num. 14:36.) "Neither murmur ye, as some of them also murmured," Paul counseled, "and were destroyed of the destroyer." (1 Cor. 10:10.)

Our times are no less wicked and perverse, our leaders no less accessible to slander. We could complain as did Moses' men, but we are commanded not to. Murmuring and complaining wound our souls, damaging the protection of righteousness and allowing evil influences to take hold in us.

Commandments and Promises

The Lord spake unto Moses and Aaron, saying, How long shall I bear with this evil congregation, which murmur against me? I have heard the murmurings of the children of Israel, which they murmur against me. Say unto them, As truly as I live, saith the Lord, as ye have spoken in mine ears, *so will I do to you: your carcases shall fall in this wilderness; and all that were numbered of you, according to your whole number, from twenty years old and upward,* which have murmured against me, *doubtless ye shall not come into the land.* (Num. 14:26-30.)

Say not thou, What is the cause that the former days were better than these? for thou dost not enquire wisely concerning this. (Eccl. 7:10.)

The soldiers likewise demanded of him, saying, And what shall we do? And he said unto them, Do violence to no man, neither accuse any falsely; and be content with your wages. (Luke 3:14.)

Jesus therefore answered and said unto them, Murmur not among yourselves. (John 6:43.)

Neither murmur ye, as some of them also murmured, *and were destroyed of the destroyer.* (1 Cor. 10:10.)

Do all things without murmurings and disputings: *that ye be blameless and harmless, the sons of God, without rebuke, in the midst of a crooked and perverse nation, among whom ye shine as lights in the world; holding forth the word of life; that I [Paul] may rejoice in the day of Christ, that I have not run in vain, neither laboured in vain.* (Philip. 2:14-16.)

Let your conversation be without covetousness; and be content with such things as ye have: for *he hath said, I will never leave thee, nor forsake thee.* (Heb. 13:5.)

Thou shalt be favored of the Lord, because thou hast not murmured. (1 Ne. 3:6.)

I, Nephi, said unto them that they should murmur no more against their father. (1 Ne. 17:49.)

I command you, my servant Joseph, that you shall say unto him [Martin Harris], that he shall do no more, nor trouble me any more concerning this matter [of the Book of Mormon manuscript]. (D&C 5:29.)

Do not murmur, my son, for it is wisdom in me that I have dealt with you after this manner. (D&C 9:6.)

Murmur not because of the things which thou hast not seen, for they are withheld from thee and from the world, which is wisdom in me in a time to come. (D&C 25:4.)

Name of Jesus Christ, Bearing the

(See also Blasphemy and Evil Communication; Prayer; Purity and Singleness of Heart.)

At baptism we take upon ourselves the name of Jesus Christ. Each time we renew our baptismal covenant through partaking of the sacrament, we witness that we are "willing to take upon [us]" his name. The Lord, in return, promises that his Spirit will always be with us. (See Moro. 4:3.) Then, once we take upon ourselves the name of Christ, we are responsible for the way we use his name. If we use the Savior's name in vain, we are under condemnation. (D&C 63:61-63.)

We can use the Lord's name righteously: we pray in his name, give blessings in his name, speak and teach in his name. The Lord said to Joseph Smith and Sidney Rigdon in the early days of the Restoration, "Declare whatsoever thing ye declare in my name, in solemnity of heart, in the spirit of meekness." (D&C 100:7.) He instructed Thomas B. Marsh, president of the Quorum of the Twelve, thusly, "Admonish [the Twelve] for my name's sake, . . . and be ye faithful before me unto my name." (D&C 112:12.)

However, being careful how we use the Savior's name and how we represent him to the world is not enough. A greater task is required: we must do *all* that we do in the name of Christ. The Lord commands us directly several times throughout scripture, "Whatsoever ye do in word or deed, do all in the name of the Lord Jesus." (Col. 3:17.) Such complete consecration does, indeed, help us achieve salvation.

Commandments and Promises

They shall put my name upon the children of Israel; *and I will bless them.* (Num. 6:27.)

Thou shalt fear the Lord thy God, and serve him, and shalt swear by his name. (Deut. 6:13; similar scripture, Deut. 10:20.)

All people of the earth shall see that thou [Israel] art called by the name of the Lord; *and they shall be afraid of thee.* (Deut. 28:10.)

Blessed be he that cometh in the name of the Lord: *we have blessed you out of the house of the Lord.* (Ps. 118:26.)

Fear not: for I am with thee: *I will bring thy seed from the east, and gather thee from the west; I will say to the north, Give up; and to the south, Keep not back: bring my sons from far, and my daughters from the ends of the earth;* even every one that is called by my name: for I have created him for my glory, I have formed him; yea, I have made him. (Isa. 43:5-7.)

Every one that hath forsaken houses, or brethren, or sisters, or father, or mother, or wife, or children, or lands, for my name's sake, *shall receive an hundredfold, and shall inherit everlasting life.* (Matt. 19:29.)

Whatsoever ye do in word or deed, do all in the name of the Lord Jesus, giving thanks to God and the Father by him. (Col. 3:17.)

If ye be reproached for the name of Christ, *happy are ye; for the spirit of glory and of God resteth upon you:* on their part he is evil spoken of, but on your part he is glorified. (1 Pet. 4:14.)

I know that if ye shall follow the Son, with full purpose of heart, acting no hypocrisy and no deception before God, but with real intent, repenting of your sins, witnessing unto the Father that ye are willing to take upon you the name of Christ, by baptism—yea, by following your Lord and your Savior down into the water, according to his word, behold, *then shall ye receive the Holy Ghost; yea, then cometh the baptism of fire and of the Holy Ghost; and then can ye speak with the tongue of angels, and shout praises unto the Holy One of Israel.* (2 Ne. 31:13.)

[The Lord] had said unto me: Whatsoever thing ye shall ask in faith, believing that ye shall receive in the name of Christ, *ye shall receive it.* (Enos 1:15.)

There is no other head whereby ye can be made free. There is no other name whereby salvation cometh; therefore, I would that ye should take upon you the name of Christ, all you that have entered into the covenant with God that ye should be obedient unto the end of your lives. *And it shall come to pass that* whosoever doeth this *shall be found at the right hand of God, for he shall know the name by which he is called; for he shall be called by the name of Christ. And now it shall come to pass, that* whosoever shall not take upon him the name of Christ *must be called by some other name; therefore, he findeth himself on the left hand of God.* (Mosiah 5:8-10.)

I would that ye should remember also, that this is the name that I said I should give unto you that never should be blotted out, except it be through transgression; therefore, take heed that ye do not trans-gress, *that the name be not blotted out of your hearts.* I say unto you, I would that ye should remember to retain the name written always in your hearts, *that ye are not found on the left hand of God, but that ye hear and know the voice by which ye shall be called, and also, the name by which he shall call you.* (Mosiah 5:11-12.)

Take upon you the name of Christ. (Alma 34:38.)

Whatsoever ye shall do, ye shall do it in my name; therefore ye shall call the church in my name; and ye shall call upon the Father in my name that he will bless the church for my sake. And how be it my church save it be called in my name? . . . If it be called in my name then it is my church, if it so be that they are built upon my gospel. Verily I say unto you, that ye are built upon my gospel; therefore ye shall call whatsoever things ye do call, in my name; therefore if ye call upon the Father, for the church, if it be in my name *the Father will hear you.* (3 Ne. 27:7-9.)

See that ye are not baptized unworthily; see that ye partake not of the sacrament of Christ unworthily; but see that ye do all things in worthiness, and do it in the name of Jesus Christ, the Son of the living God; and if ye do this, and endure to the end, *ye will in nowise be cast out.* (Morm. 9:29.)

[sacrament prayer] O God, the Eternal Father, we ask thee in the name of thy Son, Jesus Christ, to bless and sanctify this bread to the souls of all those who partake of it; that they may eat in remembrance of the body of thy Son, and witness unto thee, O God, the Eternal Father, that they are willing to take upon them the name of thy Son, and always remember him, and keep his commandments which he hath given them, *that they may always have his Spirit to be with them.* Amen. (Moro. 4:3; similar scripture, D&C 20:77.)

None were received unto baptism save they took upon them the name of Christ, having a determination to serve him to the end. (Moro. 6:3.)

Where two or three are gathered together in my name, as touching one thing, *behold, there will I be in the midst of them—even so am I in the midst of you.* (D&C 6:32.)

Take upon you the name of Christ, and speak the truth in soberness. (D&C 18:21.)

Jesus Christ is the name which is given of the Father, and there is none other name given whereby man can be saved; wherefore, all men must take upon them the name which is given of the Father, for in that name shall they be called at the last day; wherefore, if they know not the name by which they are called, *they cannot have place in the kingdom of my Father.* (D&C 18:23-25.)

If they desire to take upon them my name with full purpose of heart, they are called to go into all the world to preach my gospel unto every creature. And they are they who are ordained of me to baptize in my name, according to that which is written. (D&C 18:28-29.)

Every member of the church of Christ having children is to bring them unto the elders before the church, who are to lay their hands upon them in the name of Jesus Christ, and bless them in his name. (D&C 20:70.)

All things must be done in the name of Christ, whatsoever you do in the Spirit. (D&C 46:31.)

Let all men beware how they take my name in their lips—for behold, verily I say, that many there be who are under this condemnation, who use the name of the Lord, and use it in vain, having not authority. (D&C 63:61-62.)

Organize yourselves; prepare every needful thing; and establish a house, even a house of prayer, a house of fasting, a house of faith, a house of learning, a house of glory, a house of order, a house of God; *that your incomings may be in the name of the Lord; that your outgoings may be in the name of the Lord; that all your salutations may be in the name of the Lord, with uplifted hands unto the Most High.* (D&C 88:119-120; similar scripture, D&C 109:8.)

Declare whatsoever thing ye declare in my name, in solemnity of heart, in the spirit of meekness, in all things. *And I give unto you this promise, that* inasmuch as ye do this *the Holy Ghost shall be shed forth in bearing record unto all things whatsoever ye shall say.* (D&C 100:7-8.)

[to Thomas B. Marsh] Pray for thy brethren of the Twelve. Admonish them sharply for my name's sake, and let them be admonished for all their sins, and be ye faithful before me unto my name. (D&C 112:12.)

If a man be called of my Father, as was Aaron, by mine own voice, and by the voice of him that sent me, and I have endowed him with the keys of the power of this priesthood, if he do anything in my name, according to my law and by my word, *he will not commit sin, and I will justify him.* (D&C 132:59.)

Thou shalt do all that thou doest in the name of the Son, and thou shalt repent and call upon God in the name of the Son forevermore. (Moses 5:8.)

Obedience

(See also Faith; Following God and His Servants; Knowing God and His Ways; Loving God.)

The Syrian nobleman Naaman approached the prophet Elisha to be healed of leprosy. Without seeing Naaman in person, Elisha had a messenger tell him, "Wash in the Jordan seven times, and thy flesh shall come again to thee, and thou shalt be clean. But Naaman was wroth." He was angered that Elisha had not healed him in person. "He turned and went away in a rage." Naaman's servants reasoned with him that if the prophet had commanded "some great thing," he surely would have done it. "How much rather then, when he saith to thee, Wash, and be clean?" So Naaman did as the servants suggested, as Elisha had commanded, and was healed. (2 Kgs. 5:9-14.)

The principle of obedience is taught throughout scripture, from Adam onward. An angel came to Adam and asked, "Why dost thou offer sacrifices unto the Lord?" Adam replied, "I know not, save the Lord commanded me." Then, having proved himself through obedience, Adam was instructed in the meaning of his sacrifice. Wisdom and understanding came after compliance.

One purpose of obedience in man's mortality is explained by Abraham's account of the events preceding the creation: "And we will make an earth whereon these may dwell; and we will prove them herewith, to see if they will do all things whatsoever the Lord their God shall command them." (Abr. 3:24-25.) The Lord, however, does not expect or want us to live our entire lives in blind compliance; by so doing we would never learn the ways of God. Sometimes, though, the reasons behind a commandment are not immediately clear. At those times, we would do well to say with Nephi, "I will go and do the things which the Lord hath commanded, for I know that the Lord giveth no commandments unto the children of men, save he shall prepare a way for them that they may accomplish the thing which he commandeth them." (1 Ne. 3:7.) Often then, in the doing, we can see God's reasoning and come to know and love him more.

Commandments and Promises

[the Lord to Abraham] By myself have I sworn, saith the Lord, for because thou hast done this thing, and hast not withheld thy son, thine only son: *that in blessing I will bless thee, and in multiplying I will multiply thy seed as the stars of the heaven, and as the sand which is upon the sea shore; and thy seed shall possess the gate of his enemies; and in thy seed shall all the nations of the earth be blessed;* because thou hast obeyed my voice. (Gen. 22:16-18.)

The Lord appeared unto him [Isaac], and said, Go not down into Egypt; dwell in the land which I shall tell thee of; sojourn in this land, and *I will be with thee, and will bless thee; for unto thee, and unto thy seed, I will give all these countries, and I will perform the oath which I sware unto Abraham thy father; and I will make thy seed to multiply as the stars of heaven, and will give unto thy seed all these countries; and in thy seed shall all the nations of the earth be blessed;* because that Abraham obeyed my voice, and kept my charge, my commandments, my statutes, and my laws. (Gen. 26:2-5.)

[the Lord to Moses] If thou wilt diligently hearken to the voice of the Lord thy God, and wilt do that which is right in his sight, and wilt give ear to his commandments, and keep all his statutes, *I will put none of these diseases upon thee, which I have brought upon the Egyptians: for I am the Lord that healeth thee.* (Ex. 15:26.)

[the Lord to Israel] If ye will obey my voice indeed, and keep my covenant, *then ye shall be a peculiar treasure unto me above all people: for all the earth is mine: and ye shall be unto me a kingdom of priests, and an holy nation.* (Ex. 19:5-6.)

I the Lord thy God am a jealous God, . . . *shewing mercy* unto thousands of them that love me, and keep my commandments. (Ex. 20:5-6; similar scriptures, Deut. 5:9-10, Mosiah 13:13-14.)

The Lord said unto Moses, Whosoever hath sinned against me, *him will I blot out of my book.* (Ex. 32:33.)

Ye shall therefore keep my statutes and my judgments, and shall not commit any of these abominations: neither any of your own nation, nor any stranger that sojourneth among you. (Lev. 18:26.)

Therefore shall ye keep mine ordinance, that ye commit not any one of these abominable customs, which were committed before you, and that ye defile not yourselves therein: I am the Lord your God. (Lev. 18:30.)

Ye shall keep my statutes. (Lev. 19:19.)

Therefore shall ye observe all my statutes, and all my judgments, and do them: I am the Lord. (Lev. 19:37.)

Ye shall keep my statutes, and do them: I am the Lord *which sanctify you.* (Lev. 20:8.)

Ye shall therefore keep all my statutes, and all my judgments, and do them: *that the land, whither I bring you to dwell therein, spue you not out.* (Lev. 20:22.)

Therefore shall ye keep my commandments, and do them: I am the Lord. (Lev. 22:31.)

If ye walk in my statutes, and keep my commandments, and do them; *then I will give you rain in due season, and the land shall yield her increase, and the trees of the field shall yield their fruit. And your threshing shall reach unto the vintage, and the vintage shall reach unto the sowing time: and ye shall eat your bread to the full, and dwell in your land safely. And I will give peace in the land, and ye shall lie down, and none shall make you afraid: and I will rid evil beasts out of the land, neither shall the sword go through your land. And ye shall chase your enemies, and they shall fall before you by the sword. And five of you shall chase an hundred, and an hundred of you shall put ten thousand to flight: and your enemies shall fall before you by the sword. For I will have respect unto you, and make you fruitful, and multiply you, and establish my covenant with you. And ye shall eat old store, and bring forth the old because of the new. And I will set my tabernacle among you: and my soul shall not abhor you. And I will walk among you, and will be your God, and ye shall be my people.* (Lev. 26:3-12.)

If ye walk contrary unto me, and will not hearken unto me; *I will bring seven times more plagues upon you* according to your sins. *I will also send wild beasts among you, which shall rob you of your chil-*

dren, and destroy your cattle, and make you few in number; and your high ways shall be desolate. And if ye will not be reformed by me by these things, but will walk contrary unto me; *then will I also walk contrary unto you, and will punish you yet seven times* for your sins. *And I will bring a sword upon you, that shall avenge the quarrel of my covenant: and when ye are gathered together within your cities, I will send the pestilence among you; and ye shall be delivered into the hand of the enemy. And when I have broken the staff of your bread, ten women shall bake your bread in one oven, and they shall deliver you your bread again by weight: and ye shall eat, and not be satisfied.* And if ye will not for all this hearken unto me, but walk contrary unto me; *then I will walk contrary unto you also in fury; and I, even I, will chastise you seven times* for your sins. *And ye shall eat the flesh of your sons, and the flesh of your daughters shall ye eat. And I will destroy your high places, and cut down your images, and cast your carcases upon the carcases of your idols, and my soul shall abhor you. And I will make your cities waste, and bring your sanctuaries unto desolation, and I will not smell the savour of your sweet odours. . . . Your enemies which dwell therein shall be astonished at it. And I will scatter you among the heathen, and will draw out the sword after you. . . . Then shall the land enjoy her sabbaths, as long as it lieth desolate, and ye be in your enemies' land. . . . Upon them that are left alive of you I will send a faintness into their hearts in the lands of their enemies; and the sound of a shaken leaf shall chase them; and they shall flee, as fleeing from a sword; and they shall fall when none pursueth. . . . Ye shall have no power to stand before your enemies. And ye shall perish among the heathen, and the land of your enemies shall eat you up. And they that are left of you shall pine away in their iniquity in your enemies' lands.* (Lev. 26:21-39.)

Hearken, O Israel, unto the statutes and unto the judgments, which I teach you, for to do them, *that ye may live, and go in and possess the land which the Lord God of your fathers giveth you.* Ye shall not add unto the word which I command you, neither shall ye diminish ought from it, *that ye may keep the commandments of the Lord your God which I command you.* (Deut. 4:1-2.)

When thou art in tribulation, and all these things are come upon thee, even in the latter days, if thou turn to the Lord thy God, and shalt be obedient unto his voice; (for the Lord thy God is a merciful God;) *he will not forsake thee, neither destroy thee, nor forget the covenant of thy fathers which he sware unto them.* (Deut. 4:30-31.)

Thou shalt keep therefore his statutes, and his commandments, which I command thee this day, *that it may go well with thee, and with thy children after thee, and that thou mayest prolong thy days upon the earth, which the Lord thy God giveth thee, for ever.* (Deut. 4:40.)

Ye shall observe to do therefore as the Lord your God hath commanded you: ye shall not turn aside to the right hand or to the left. Ye shall walk in all the ways which the Lord your God hath commanded you, *that ye may live, and that it may be well with you, and that ye may prolong your days in the land which ye shall possess.* (Deut. 5: 32-33.)

Ye shall diligently keep the commandments of the Lord your God, and his testimonies, and his statutes, which he hath commanded thee. (Deut. 6:17.)

The Lord commanded us to do all these statutes, to fear the Lord our God, for our good always, *that he might preserve us alive, as it is at this day. And it shall be our righteousness,* if we observe to do all these commandments before the Lord our God, as he hath commanded us. (Deut. 6:24-25.)

Know therefore that the Lord thy God, he is God, the faithful God, *which keepeth covenant and mercy with them* that love him and keep his commandments *to a thousand generations; and repayeth them* that hate him *to their face, to destroy them: he will not be slack to him* that hateth him, *he will repay him to his face.* Thou shalt therefore keep the commandments, and the statutes, and the judgments, which I command thee this day, to do them. Wherefore it shall come to pass, if ye hearken to these judgments, and keep, and do them, *that the Lord thy God shall keep unto thee the covenant and the mercy which he sware unto thy fathers: and he will love thee, and bless thee, and multiply thee: he will also bless the fruit of thy womb, and the fruit of thy land, thy corn, and thy wine, and thine oil, the increase of thy kine, and the flocks of thy sheep, in the land which he sware unto thy fathers to give thee. Thou shalt be blessed above all people: there shall not be male or female barren among you, or among your cattle. And the Lord will take away from thee all sickness, and will put none of the evil diseases of Egypt, which thou knowest, upon thee; but will lay them upon all them that hate thee. And thou shalt consume all the people which the Lord thy God shall deliver thee;* thine eye shall have no pity upon them: neither shalt thou serve their gods; *for that will be a snare unto thee.* (Deut. 7:9-16.)

Thou shalt keep the commandments of the Lord thy God, to walk in his ways, and to fear him. (Deut. 8:6.)

Now, Israel, what doth the Lord thy God require of thee, but to fear the Lord thy God, to walk in all his ways, and to love him, and to serve the Lord thy God will all thy heart and with all thy soul, to keep the commandments of the Lord, and his statutes, which I command thee this day for thy good? (Deut. 10:12-13.)

Thou shalt love the Lord thy God, and keep his charge, and his statutes, and his judgments, and his commandments, alway. (Deut. 11:1.)

Therefore shall ye keep all the commandments which I command you this day, *that ye may be strong, and go in and possess the land, whither ye go to possess it.* (Deut. 11:8.)

It shall come to pass, if ye shall hearken diligently unto my commandments which I command you this day, to love the Lord your God, and to serve him with all your heart and with all your soul, *that I will give you the rain of your land in his due season, the first rain and the latter rain, that thou mayest gather in thy corn, and thy wine, and thine oil. And I will send grass in thy fields for thy cattle, that thou mayest eat and be full.* (Deut. 11:13-15.)

If ye shall diligently keep all these commandments which I command you, to do them, to love the Lord your God, to walk in all his ways, and to cleave unto him; *then will the Lord drive out all these nations from before you, and ye shall possess greater nations and mightier than yourselves. Every place whereon the soles of your feet shall tread shall be yours: from the wilderness and Lebanon, from the river, the river Euphrates, even unto the uttermost sea shall your coast be. There shall no man be able to stand before you: for the Lord your God shall lay the fear of you and the dread of you upon all the land that ye shall tread upon, as he hath said unto you.* (Deut. 11:22-25.)

I set before you this day a blessing and a curse; a blessing, if ye obey the commandments of the Lord your God, which I command you this day: *and a curse,* if ye will not obey the commandments of the Lord your God, but turn aside out of the way which I command you this day, to go after other gods, which ye have not known. (Deut. 11:26-28.)

Ye shall observe to do all the statutes and judgments which I set before you this day. (Deut. 11:32.)

What thing soever I command you, observe to do it: thou shalt not add thereto, nor diminish from it. (Deut. 12:32.)

Ye shall walk after the Lord your God, and fear him, and keep his commandments, and obey his voice, and ye shall serve him, and cleave unto him. (Deut. 13:4.)

Take heed, and hearken, O Israel; this day thou art become the people of the Lord thy God. Thou shalt therefore obey the voice of the Lord thy God, and do his commandments and his statutes, which I command thee this day. (Deut. 27:9-10.)

Let your heart therefore be perfect with the Lord our God, to walk in his statutes, and to keep his commandments, as at this day. (1 Kgs. 8:61.)

Thus saith God, Why transgress ye the commandments of the Lord, *that ye cannot prosper?* because ye have forsaken the Lord, *he hath also forsaken you.* (2 Chr. 24:20.)

Remember, I beseech thee, the word that thou commandest thy servant Moses, saying, If ye transgress, *I will scatter you abroad among the nations.* (Neh. 1:8.)

Blessed is the man that walketh not in the counsel of the ungodly, nor standeth in the way of sinners, nor sitteth in the seat of the scornful.

But his delight is in the law of the Lord; and in his law doth he meditate day and night. *And he shall be like a tree planted by the river of water, that bringeth forth his fruit in his season; his leaf also shall not wither; and whatsoever he doeth shall prosper.* (Ps. 1:1-3.)

The fear of the Lord is the beginning of wisdom: *a good understanding have all they* that do his commandments: his praise endureth for ever. (Ps. 111:10.)

Blessed is the man that feareth the Lord, that delighteth greatly in his commandments. *His seed shall be mighty upon earth: the generation of the upright shall be blessed. Wealth and riches shall be in his house: and his righteousness endureth for ever.* (Ps. 112:1-3.)

Blessed is every one that feareth the Lord; that walketh in his ways. (Ps. 128:1.)

The eyes of the Lord preserve knowledge, and he overthroweth the words of the transgressor. (Prov. 22:12.)

Whoso keepeth the commandment *shall feel no evil thing.* (Eccl. 8:5.)

Fear God, and keep his commandments: for this is the whole duty of man. For God shall bring every work into judgment, with every secret thing, whether it be good, or whether it be evil. (Eccl. 12:13-14.)

If ye be willing and obedient, *ye shall eat the good of the land.* (Isa. 1:19.)

The *destruction* of the transgressors and of the sinners shall be together, and they that forsake the Lord *shall be consumed. For they shall be ashamed of the oaks which ye have desired, and ye shall be confounded for the gardens that ye have chosen.* (Isa. 1:28-29.)

As the fire devoureth the stubble, and the flame consumeth the chaff, so their root shall be as rottenness, and their blossom shall go up as dust: because they have cast away the law of the Lord of hosts, and despised the word of the Holy One of Israel. (Isa. 5:24.)

O that thou hadst hearkened to my commandments! *then had thy peace been as a river, and thy righteousness as the waves of the sea: thy seed also had been as the sand, and the offspring of thy bowels like the gravel thereof; his name should not have been cut off nor destroyed from before me.* (Isa. 48:18-19; similar scripture, 1 Ne. 20:18-19.)

I will bring evil upon this people, even the fruit of their thoughts, because they have not hearkened unto my words, nor to my law, but rejected it. (Jer. 6:19.)

This thing commanded I them, saying, Obey my voice, *and I will be your God, and ye shall be my people:* and walk ye in all the ways that I have commanded you, *that it may be well unto you.* (Jer. 7:23.)

Because they have forsaken my law which I set before them, and have not obeyed my voice, neither walked therein; but have walked after the imagination of their own heart, and after Baalim, which their fathers taught them: *therefore thus saith the Lord of hosts, the God of Israel; Behold, I will feed them, even this people, with wormwood, and give them water of gall to drink. I will scatter them also among the heathen, whom neither they nor their fathers have known: and I will send a sword after them, till I have consumed them.* (Jer. 9:13-16.)

Cursed be the man that obeyeth not the words of this covenant, which I commanded your fathers in the day that I brought them forth out of the land of Egypt, from the iron furnace, saying, Obey my voice, and do them, according to all which I command you: *so shall ye be my people, and I will be your God; that I may perform the oath which I have sworn unto your fathers, to give them a land flowing with milk and honey, as it is this day.* (Jer. 11:3-5.)

I shall speak concerning a nation, and concerning a kingdom, *to build and to plant it;* if it do evil in my sight, that it obey not my voice, *then I will repent of the good, wherewith I said I would benefit them.* (Jer. 18:9-10.)

If so be they will hearken, and turn every man from his evil way, *that I may repent me of the evil, which I purpose to do unto them* because of the evil of their doings. And thou shalt say unto them, Thus saith the Lord; If ye will not hearken to me, to walk in my law, which I have set before you, to hearken to the words of my servants the prophets, whom I sent unto you, both rising up early, and sending them, but ye have not hearkened; *then will I make this house like Shiloh, and will make this city a curse to all the nations of the earth.* (Jer. 26:3-6.)

Obey, I beseech thee, the voice of the Lord, which I speak unto thee: *so it shall be well unto thee, and thy soul shall live.* (Jer. 38:20.)

I have this day declared it to you; but ye have not obeyed the voice of the Lord your God, nor any thing for the which he hath sent me unto you. *Now therefore know certainly that ye shall die by the sword, by the famine, and by the pestilence, in the place whither ye desire to go and to sojourn.* (Jer. 42:21-22.)

They are not humbled even unto this day, neither have they feared, nor walked in my law, nor in my statutes, that I set before you and before your fathers. Therefore thus saith the Lord of hosts, the God of Israel; *Behold, I will set my face against you for evil, and to cut off all Judah. And I will take the remnant of Judah, that have set their faces to go into the land of Egypt to sojourn there, and they shall all be consumed, and fall in the land of Egypt; they shall even be consumed by the sword and by the famine: they shall die, from the least even unto the greatest, by the sword and by the famine: and they shall be an execration, and an astonishment, and a curse, and a reproach. For I will punish them that dwell in the land of Egypt, as I have punished Jerusalem by the sword, by the famine, and by the pestilence: so that none of the remnant of Judah, which are gone into the land of Egypt to sojourn there, shall escape or remain, that they should return into the land of Judah, to the which they have a desire to return to dwell there: for none shall return but such as shall escape.* (Jer. 44:10-14.)

Because ye have burned incense, and because ye have sinned against the Lord, and have not obeyed the voice of the Lord, nor walked in his law, nor in his statutes, nor in his testimonies; *therefore this evil is happened unto you, as at this day.* (Jer. 44:23.)

If a man be just, and do that which is lawful and right, . . . hath walked in my statutes, and hath kept my judgments, to deal truly; *he is just, he shall surely live, saith the Lord God.* (Ezek. 18:5-9.)

[Daniel] prayed . . . , *O Lord, the great and dreadful God, keeping the covenant and mercy* to them that love him, and to them that keep his commandments. (Dan. 9:4.)

They that are far off shall come and build in the temple of the Lord, and ye shall know that the Lord of hosts hath sent me unto you. And this shall come to pass, if ye will diligently obey the voice of the Lord your God. (Zech. 6:15.)

When the tempter came to him, he said, If thou be the Son of God, command that these stones be made bread. But he answered and said, It is written, Man shall not live by bread alone, but by every word that proceedeth out of the mouth of God. (Matt. 4:3-4; similar scripture, Luke 4:3-4.)

Whosoever therefore shall break one of these least commandments, and shall teach men so, *he shall be called the least in the kingdom of heaven:* but whosoever shall do and teach them, *the same shall be called great in the kingdom of heaven.* (Matt. 5:19; see also JST Matt. 5:21.)

Not every one that saith unto me, Lord, Lord, *shall enter into the kingdom of heaven;* but he that doeth the will of my Father which is in heaven. (Matt. 7:21; similar scripture, 3 Ne. 14:21; see also JST Matt. 7:31.)

Whosoever heareth these sayings of mine, and doeth them, I will liken him unto a wise man, which built his house upon a rock: *and the rain descended, and the floods came, and the winds blew, and beat upon that house; and it fell not:* for it was founded upon a rock. And every one that heareth these sayings of mine, and doeth them not, shall be likened unto a foolish man, which built his house upon the sand: *and the rain descended, and the floods came, and the winds blew, and beat upon that house; and it fell: and great was the fall of it.* (Matt. 7:24-27; similar scriptures, Luke 6:47-49; 3 Ne. 14:24-27.)

Whosoever shall do the will of my Father which is in heaven, *the same is my brother, and sister, and mother.* (Matt. 12:50; similar scriptures, Mark 3:35; Luke 8:21.)

If thou wilt enter into life, keep the commandments. (Matt. 19:17.)

Blessed are they that hear the word of God, and keep it. (Luke 11:28.)

If any man will do his will, *he shall know of the doctrine, whether it be of God, or whether I speak of myself.* (John 7:17.)

Then said Jesus to those Jews which believed on him, If ye continue in my word, *then are ye my disciples indeed; and ye shall know the truth, and the truth shall make you free.* (John 8:31-32.)

If a man keep my saying, *he shall never see death.* (John 8:51.)

If ye love me, keep my commandments. *And I will pray the Father, and he shall give you another Comforter, that he may abide with you for ever; even the Spirit of truth; whom the world cannot receive, because it seeth him not, neither knoweth him: but ye know him; for he dwelleth with you, and shall be in you.* (John 14:15-17.)

He that hath my commandments, and keepeth them, he it is that loveth me: and he that loveth me *shall be loved of my Father, and I will love him, and will manifest myself to him.* (John 14:21.)

If ye keep my commandments, *ye shall abide in my love; even as I have kept my Father's commandments, and abide in his love.* (John 15:10.)

We ought to obey God rather than man. (Acts 5:29.)

We are his witnesses of these things; and so is also *the Holy Ghost, whom God hath given* to them that obey him. (Acts 5:32.)

As many as have sinned in the law *shall be judged by the law; (for not the hearers of the law are just before God,* but the doers of the law *shall be justified. . . .)* (Rom. 2:12-13.)

Know ye not, that to whom ye yield yourselves servants to obey, *his servants ye are to whom ye obey;* whether of sin *unto death,* or of obedience *unto righteousness?* (Rom. 6:16.)

Let every soul be subject unto the higher powers. For there is no power but of God: the powers that be are ordained of God. Whosoever therefore resisteth the power, resisteth the ordinance of God: and they that resist *shall receive to themselves damnation. . . .* Wherefore ye must needs be subject, not only for wrath, but also for conscience sake. (Rom. 13:1-5; see also JST Rom. 13:1.)

Servants, be obedient to them that are your masters according to the flesh, with fear and trembling, in singleness of your heart, as unto

Christ; not with eyeservice, as menpleasers; but as the servants of Christ, doing the will of God from the heart; with good will doing service, as to the Lord, and not to men: knowing that whatsoever good thing any man doeth, *the same shall he receive of the Lord, whether he be bond or free.* (Eph. 6:5-8.)

To you who are troubled rest with us, when *the Lord Jesus shall be revealed from heaven with his mighty angels, in flaming fire taking vengeance* on them that know not God, and that obey not the gospel of our Lord Jesus Christ: *who shall be punished with everlasting destruction from the presence of the Lord, and from the glory of his power.* (2 Thes. 1:7-9.)

I charge thee before God, and the Lord Jesus Christ, and the elect angels, that thou observe these things without preferring one before another, doing nothing by partiality. (1 Tim. 5:21.)

If we sin wilfully after that we have received the knowledge of the truth, *there remaineth no more sacrifice for sins.* (Heb. 10:26.)

Obey them that have the rule over you, and submit yourselves: for they watch for your souls, as they that must give account, that they may do it with joy, and not with grief: *for that is unprofitable for you.* (Heb. 13:17.)

Submit yourselves therefore to God. Resist the devil, *and he will flee from you.* (James 4:7.)

Gird up the loins of your mind, be sober, and hope to the end *for the grace that is to be brought unto you at the revelation of Jesus Christ;* as obedient children, not fashioning yourselves according to the former lusts in your ignorance: but as he which hath called you is holy, so be ye holy in all manner of conversation; because it is written, Be ye holy; for I am holy. (1 Pet. 1:13-16.)

Seeing *ye have purified your souls* in obeying the truth through the Spirit unto unfeigned love of the brethren, see that ye love one another with a pure heart fervently. (1 Pet. 1:22.)

Unto you therefore which believe he is precious: but unto them which be disobedient, *the stone which the builders disallowed, the same is made the head of the corner, and a stone of stumbling, and a rock of offence, even to them which stumble at the word,* being disobedient: whereunto also they were appointed. (1 Pet. 2:7-8.)

Hereby we do know that we know him, if we keep his commandments. He that saith, I know him, and keepeth not his commandments, *is a liar, and the truth is not in him.* But whoso keepeth his word, *in him verily is the love of God perfected: hereby know we that we are in him.* (1 Jn. 2:3-5.)

The world passeth away, and the lust thereof: but he that doeth the will of God *abideth for ever.* (1 Jn. 2:17.)

He that keepeth his commandments *dwelleth in him, and he in him. And hereby we know that he abideth in us, by the Spirit which he hath given us.* (1 Jn. 3:24.)

This is love, that we walk after his commandments. This is the commandment, That, as ye have heard from the beginning, ye should walk in it. (2 Jn. 1:6.)

Whosoever transgresseth, and abideth not in the doctrine of Christ, *hath not God.* He that abideth in the doctrine of Christ, *he hath both the Father and the Son.* (2 Jn. 1:9.)

Blessed is he that readeth, and they that hear the words of this prophecy, and keep those things which are written therein: for the time is at hand. (Rev. 1:3.)

Blessed are they that do his commandments, *that they may have right to the tree of life, and may enter in through the gates into the city.* (Rev. 22:14.)

[to Nephi] Inasmuch as thou shalt keep my commandments, *thou shalt be made a ruler and a teacher over thy brethren.* (1 Ne. 2:22.)

[to Nephi] Inasmuch as thy seed shall keep my commandments, *they shall prosper in the land of promise.* (1 Ne. 4:14.)

If it so be that the children of men keep the commandments of God *he doth nourish them, and strengthen them, and provide means whereby they can accomplish the thing which he has commanded them.* (1 Ne. 17:3.)

I will prepare the way before you, if it so be that ye shall keep my commandments; wherefore, inasmuch as ye shall keep my commandments *ye shall be led towards the promised land; and ye shall know that it is by me that ye are led.* (1 Ne. 17:13.)

If ye shall be obedient to the commandments, and endure to the end, *ye shall be saved at the last day.* (1 Ne. 22:31.)

I, Lehi, have obtained a promise, that inasmuch as those whom the Lord God shall bring out of the land of Jerusalem shall keep his commandments, *they shall prosper upon the face of this land; and they shall be kept from all other nations, that they may possess this land unto themselves.* And if it so be that they shall keep his commandments *they shall be blessed upon the face of this land, and there shall be none to molest them, nor to take away the land of their inheritance; and they shall dwell safely forever.* (2 Ne. 1:9.)

[Lehi to his sons] Inasmuch as ye shall keep my commandments *ye shall prosper in the land;* but inasmuch as ye will not keep my commandments *ye shall be cut off from my presence.* (2 Ne. 1:20; similar scripture, 2 Ne. 4:4.)

[Lehi to Zoram] If ye shall keep the commandments of the Lord, *the Lord hath consecrated this land for the security of thy seed with the seed of my son.* (2 Ne. 1:32.)

[Lehi to Joseph] *May the Lord consecrate also unto thee this land, which is a most precious land, for thine inheritance and the inheritance of thy seed with thy brethren, for thy security forever,* if it so be that ye shall keep the commandments of the Holy One of Israel. (2 Ne. 3:2.)

Wo unto him that has the law given, yea, that has all the commandments of God, like unto us, and that transgresseth them, and that wasteth the days of his probation, *for awful is his state!* (2 Ne. 9:27.)

Inasmuch as it shall be expedient, ye [Nephites] must keep the performances and ordinances of God until the law be fulfilled which was given to Moses. (2 Ne. 25:30.)

[Nephi to his people] After Christ shall have risen from the dead he shall show himself unto you, my children, and my beloved brethren; and the words which he shall speak unto you shall be the law which ye shall do. (2 Ne. 26:1.)

I, Nephi, would not suffer that ye should suppose that ye are more righteous than the Gentiles shall be. For behold, except ye shall keep the commandments of God *ye shall all likewise perish.* (2 Ne. 30:1.)

This people shall keep my commandments, saith the Lord of Hosts, *or cursed be the land for their sakes.* (Jacob 2:29.)

Blessed art thou; for because ye have been diligent in laboring with me in my vineyard, and have kept my commandments, and have brought unto me again the natural fruit, that my vineyard is no more corrupted, and the bad is cast away, *behold ye shall have joy with me* because of the fruit of my vineyard. (Jacob 5:75.)

The Lord would not suffer, after he had led them out of the land of Jerusalem and kept and preserved them from falling into the hands of their enemies, yea, he would not suffer that the words should not be verified, which he spake unto our fathers, saying that: Inasmuch as ye will not keep my commandments *ye shall not prosper in the land.* (Omni 1:6; similar scripture, Jarom 1:9.)

[King Benjamin to his sons] I would that ye should keep the commandments of God, *that ye may prosper in the land according to the promises which the Lord made unto our fathers.* (Mosiah 1:7.)

All that he requires of you is to keep his commandments; and he has promised you that if ye would keep his commandments *ye should prosper in the land; and he never doth vary from that which he hath said;* therefore, if ye do keep his commandments *he doth bless you and prosper you.* (Mosiah 2:22.)

After ye have known and have been taught all these things, if ye should transgress and go contrary to that which has been spoken, that ye do withdraw yourselves from the Spirit of the Lord, that it may have no place in you to guide you in wisdom's paths that ye may be blessed, prospered, and preserved—I say unto you, that the man that doeth this, *the same cometh out in open rebellion against God; therefore he listeth to obey the evil spirit, and becometh an enemy to all righteousness; therefore, the Lord has no place in him, for he dwelleth not in unholy temples.* (Mosiah 2:36-37.)

Consider on *the blessed and happy state* of those that keep the commandments of God. *For behold, they are blessed in all things, both temporal and spiritual;* and if they hold out faithful to the end *they are received into heaven, that thereby they may dwell with God in a state of never-ending happiness.* (Mosiah 2:41.)

I [King Benjamin] would that ye should remember also, that this is the name that I said I should give unto you that never should be blotted out, except it be through transgression; therefore, take heed that ye do not transgress, *that the name be not blotted out of your hearts.* (Mosiah 5:11.)

Abinadi said unto them: I know if ye keep the commandments of God *ye shall be saved.* (Mosiah 12:33.)

Come and fear not, and lay aside every sin, which easily doth beset you, *which doth bind you down to destruction,* yea, come and go forth, and show unto your God that ye are willing to repent of your sins and enter into a covenant with him to keep his commandments, and witness it unto him this day by going into the waters of baptism. And whosover doeth this, and keepeth the commandments of God from thenceforth, *the same will remember that I say unto him, yea, he will remember that I have said unto him, he shall have eternal life, according to the testimony of the Holy Spirit, which testifieth in me.* (Alma 7:15-16.)

[Be] diligent in keeping the commandments of God at all times. (Alma 7:23.)

Do ye not remember the words which he spake unto Lehi, saying that: Inasmuch as ye shall keep my commandments, *ye shall prosper in the land?* And again it is said that: Inasmuch as ye will not keep my commandments *ye shall be cut off from the presence of the Lord.* (Alma 9:13.)

[Alma to Helaman] Inasmuch as ye shall keep the commandments of God *ye shall prosper in the land;* and ye ought to know also, that inasmuch as ye will not keep the commandments of God *ye shall be cut off from his presence.* (Alma 36:30; similar scripture, Alma 36:1.)

[Alma to Helaman] I tell you by the spirit of prophecy, that if ye transgress the commandments of God, *behold, these things which are sacred shall be taken away from you by the power of God, and ye shall be delivered up unto Satan, that he may sift you as chaff before the wind.* (Alma 37:15.)

I command you, my son Helaman, that ye be diligent in fulfilling all my words, and that ye be diligent in keeping the commandments of God as they are written. (Alma 37:20.)

O, remember, my son, and learn wisdom in thy youth; yea, learn in thy youth to keep the commandments of God. (Alma 37:35.)

This was their [the Nephites'] faith, that . . . if they were faithful in keeping the commandments of God that he *would prosper them in the land; yea, warn them to flee, or to prepare for war, according to their danger; and also, that God would make it known unto them whither they should go to defend themselves against their enemies, and by so doing, the Lord would deliver them;* and this was the faith of Moroni, and his heart did glory in it; not in the shedding of blood but in doing good, in preserving his people, yea, in keeping the commandments of God, yea, and resisting iniquity. Yea, verily, verily I say unto you, if all men had been, and were, and ever would be, like unto Moroni, *behold, the very powers of hell would have been shaken forever; yea, the devil would never have power over the hearts of the children of men.* (Alma 48:15-17.)

Blessed art thou [Lehi] and thy children; and *they shall be blessed,* inasmuch as they shall keep my commandments *they shall prosper in the land.* But remember, inasmuch as they will not keep my commandments *they shall be cut off from the presence of the Lord. And we see that these promises have been verified to the people of Nephi;* for it has been their quarrelings and their contentions, yea, their murderings, and their plunderings, their idolatry, their whoredoms, and their abominations, which were among themselves, *which brought upon them their wars and their destructions.* And those who were faithful in keeping the commandments of the Lord *were delivered at all times,* whilst thousands of their wicked brethren *have been consigned to bondage, or to perish by the sword, or to dwindle in unbelief, and mingle with the Lamanites.* (Alma 50:20-22.)

Insomuch as the children of Lehi have kept his commandments *he hath blessed them and prospered them according to his word.* (3 Ne. 5:22.)

Whoso remembereth these sayings of mine and doeth them, *him will I raise up at the last day.* (3 Ne. 15:1.)

I have given unto you the commandments; therefore keep my commandments. And this is the law and the prophets, for they truly testified of me. (3 Ne. 15:10.)

They . . . did drink of it [sacramental wine] and were filled; and they gave unto the multitude, and they did drink, and they were filled. And when the disciples had done this, Jesus said unto them: *Blessed are ye* for this thing which ye have done, for this is fulfilling my commandments, and this doth witness unto the Father that ye are willing to do that which I have commanded you. (3 Ne. 18:9-10.)

Blessed are ye if ye shall keep my commandments, which the Father hath commanded me that I should give unto you. (3 Ne. 18:14.)

Keep these sayings which I have commanded you *that ye come not under condemnation; for wo unto him whom the Father condemneth.* (3 Ne. 18:33.)

The reason why *he ceaseth to do miracles among the children of men* is because that they dwindle in unbelief, and depart from the right way, and know not the God in whom they should trust. (Morm. 9:20.)

[sacramental prayer] O God, the Eternal Father, we ask thee in the name of thy Son, Jesus Christ, to bless and sanctify this bread to the souls of all those who partake of it; that they may eat in remembrance of the body of thy Son, and witness unto thee, O God, the Eternal Father, that they are willing to take upon them the name of thy

Son, and always remember him, and keep his commandments' which he hath given them, *that they may always have his Spirit to be with them.* Amen. (Moro. 4:3 similar scripture, D&C 20:77.)

[to Joseph Smith] Be firm in keeping the commandments wherewith I have commanded you; and if you do this, *behold I grant unto you eternal life, even if you should be slain.* (D&C 5:22.)

[to Joseph Smith] There are many that lie in wait to destroy thee from off the face of the earth; and for this cause, *that thy days may be prolonged,* I have given unto thee these commandments. Yea, for this cause I have said: Stop, and stand still until I command thee, *and I will provide means whereby thou mayest accomplish the thing* which I have commanded thee. And if thou art faithful in keeping my commandments, *thou shalt be lifted up at the last day.* (D&C 5:33-35.)

Keep my commandments. (D&C 6:6; similar scriptures, D&C 8:5; 11:6, 9, 18; 12:6; 14:6.)

Keep my commandments, and assist to bring forth my work, according to my commandments, *and you shall be blessed.* (D&C 6:9.)

Be faithful and diligent in keeping the commandments of God, *and I will encircle thee in the arms of my love.* (D&C 6:20.)

Be faithful, keep my commandments, *and ye shall inherit the kingdom of heaven.* (D&C 6:37.)

Do this thing which I have commanded you [Oliver Cowdery], *and you shall prosper.* Be faithful, and yield to no temptation. (D&C 9:13.)

This is your work, to keep my commandments, yea, with all your might, mind and strength. (D&C 11:20.)

Keep my commandments in all things. (D&C 14:6.)

If you keep my commandments and endure to the end *you shall have eternal life, which gift is the greatest of all the gifts of God.* (D&C 14:7.)

If he [Joseph] shall be diligent in keeping my commandments he shall be blessed unto eternal life. (D&C 18:8.)

You have that which is written before you; wherefore, you must perform it according to the words which are written. (D&C 18:30.)

[to Oliver Cowdery and David Whitmer] After that you have received this [Doctrine and Covenants 18], you must keep my commandments in all things; *and by your hands I will work a marvelous work among the children of men, unto the convincing of many of their sins, that they may come unto repentance, and that they may come unto the kingdom of my Father. Wherefore, the blessings which I give unto you are above all things.* And after that you have received this, if you keep not my commandments *you cannot be saved in the kingdom of my Father.* (D&C 18:46.)

Misery thou [Martin Harris] shalt receive if thou wilt slight these counsels, yea, *even the destruction of thyself and property.* (D&C 19:33.)

Wherefore, meaning the church, thou shalt give heed unto all his [Joseph Smith's] words and commandments which he shall give unto you as he receiveth them, walking in all holiness before me. (D&C 21:4.)

Keep my commandments continually, *and a crown of righteousness thou shalt receive.* And except thou do this, *where I am you cannot come.* (D&C 25:15.)

Thou shalt be obedient unto the things which I shall give unto him [Joseph Smith], even as Aaron, to declare faithfully the commandments and the revelations, with power and authority unto the church. (D&C 28:3.)

Be diligent in keeping my commandments, *and you shall be blessed unto eternal life.* (D&C 30:8.)

[to Thomas B. Marsh] Go your way whithersoever I will, *and it shall be given you by the Comforter what you shall do and whither you shall go.* (D&C 31:11.)

Ye shall remember the church articles and covenants to keep them. (D&C 33:14.)

Keep all the commandments and covenants by which ye are bound; *and I will cause the heavens to shake for your good, and Satan shall tremble and Zion shall rejoice upon the hills and flourish.* (D&C 35:24.)

He that receiveth my law and doeth it, *the same is my disciple;* and he that saith he receiveth it and doeth it not, *the same is not my disciple, and shall be cast out from among you.* (D&C 41:5.)

Hearken and hear and obey the law which I shall give unto you. (D&C 42:2.)

[The elders, priests, and teachers] shall observe the covenants and church articles to do them, and these shall be their teachings, as they shall be directed by the Spirit. (D&C 42:13.)

If thou lovest me thou shalt serve me and keep all my commandments. (D&C 42:29.)

They who have not faith to do these things, but believe in me, *have power to become my sons;* and inasmuch as they break not my laws *thou* [the Church] *shalt bear their infirmities.* (D&C 42:52.)

He that doeth according to these things *shall be saved,* and he that doeth them not *shall be damned* if he so continue. (D&C 42:60.)

Ye shall observe the laws which ye have received and be faithful. (D&C 42:66.)

Every person who belongeth to this church of Christ, shall observe to keep all the commandments and covenants of the church. (D&C 42:78.)

Keep all my commandments. (D&C 43:35.)

Go forth as I have commanded you. (D&C 49:26.)

He that prayeth, whose spirit is contrite, *the same is accepted of me* if he obey mine ordinances. (D&C 52:15.)

He that will not take up his cross and follow me, and keep my commandments, *the same shall not be saved.* Behold, I, the Lord, command; and he that will not obey *shall be cut off in mine own due time,* after I have commanded and the commandment is broken. (D&C 56:2-3.)

Blessed is he that keepeth my commandments, whether in life or in death; and he that is faithful in tribulation, *the reward of the same is greater in the kingdom of heaven.* (D&C 58:2.)

My law shall be kept on this land. Let no man think he is ruler; but let God rule him that judgeth, according to the counsel of his own will, or, in other words, him that counseleth or sitteth upon the judgment seat. Let no man break the laws of the land, for he that keepeth the laws of God hath no need to break the laws of the land. Wherefore, be subject to the powers that be, until he reigns whose right it is to reign. (D&C 58:19-22.)

It is not meet that I should command in all things; for he that is compelled in all things, the same is a slothful and not a wise servant; *wherefore he receiveth no reward.* Verily I say, men should be anxiously engaged in a good cause, and do many things of their own free will, and bring to pass much righteousness; for the power is in them, wherein they are agents unto themselves. And inasmuch as men do good *they shall in nowise lose their reward.* But he that doeth not anything until he is commanded, and receiveth a commandment with doubtful heart, and keepeth it with slothfulness, *the same is damned.* (D&C 58:26-29.)

Let the wicked take heed, and let the rebellious fear and tremble; and let the unbelieving hold their lips, *for the day of wrath shall come upon them as a whirlwind, and all flesh shall know that I am God.* (D&C 63:6.)

He that endureth in faith and doeth my will, *the same shall overcome, and shall receive an inheritance upon the earth when the day of transfiguration shall come.* (D&C 63:20.)

Unto him that keepeth my commandments *I will give the mysteries of my kingdom, and the same shall be in him a well of living water, springing up unto everlasting life.* (D&C 63:23.)

Keep these sayings, for they are true and faithful. (D&C 66:11; similar scripture, D&C 71:11.)

These sayings are true and faithful; wherefore, transgress them not, neither take therefrom. (D&C 68:34.)

If you will that *I give unto you a place in the celestial world*, you must prepare yourselves by doing the things which I have commanded you and required of you. (D&C 78:7.)

Do the things which I have commanded you. (D&C 78:20.)

Inasmuch as ye keep not my sayings, which I give unto you, *ye become transgressors; and justice and judgment are the penalty which is affixed unto my law.* (D&C 82:4.)

I give unto you directions how you may act before me, *that it may turn to you for your salvation. I, the Lord, am bound* when ye do what I say; but when ye do not what I say, *ye have no promise.* (D&C 82:9-10.)

All saints who remember to keep and do these sayings [Word of Wisdom], walking in obedience to the commandments, *shall receive health in their navel and marrow to their bones; and shall find wisdom and great treasures of knowledge, even hidden treasures; and shall run and not be weary, and shall walk and not faint. And I, the Lord, give them a promise, that the destroying angel shall pass by them, as the children of Israel, and not slay them.* (D&C 89:18-21.)

Every soul who forsaketh his sins and cometh unto me, and calleth on my name, and obeyeth my voice, and keepeth my commandments, *shall see my face and know that I am.* (D&C 93:1.)

If you keep my commandments *you shall receive of his fulness, and be glorified in me as I am in the Father; therefore, I say unto you, you shall receive grace for grace.* (D&C 93:20.)

No man receiveth a fulness unless he keepeth his commandments. He that keepeth his commandments *receiveth truth and light, until he is glorified in truth and knoweth all things.* (D&C 93:27-28.)

Inasmuch as you keep my sayings *you shall not be confounded in this world, nor in the world to come.* (D&C 93:52.)

It is my will that you should build a house [of the Lord]. If you keep my commandments *you shall have power to build it.* If you keep not my commandments, *the love of the Father shall not continue with you, therefore you shall walk in darkness.* (D&C 95:11-12.)

Zion shall escape if she observe to do all things whatsoever I have commanded her. But if she observe not to do whatsoever I have commanded her, *I will visit her according to all her works, with sore affliction, with pestilence, with plague, with sword, with vengeance, with devouring fire.* (D&C 97:25-26.)

Forsake all evil and cleave unto all good, *that ye shall live by every word which proceedeth forth out of the mouth of God.* (D&C 98:11.)

If ye observe to do whatsoever I command you, *I, the Lord, will turn away all wrath and indignation from you, and the gates of hell shall not prevail against you.* (D&C 98:22.)

All that call upon the name of the Lord, and keep his commandments, *shall be saved.* (D&C 100:17.)

I, the Lord, have suffered the affliction to come upon them, wherewith they have been afflicted, in consequence of their transgressions. (D&C 101:2.)

Those who call themselves after my name might be chastened for a little season with a sore and grievous chastisement, because they did not hearken altogether unto the precepts and commandments which I gave unto them. (D&C 103:4.)

Inasmuch as they keep not my commandments, and hearken not to observe all my words, *the kingdoms of the world shall prevail against them.* (D&C 103:8.)

Inasmuch as some of my servants have not kept the commandment, but have broken the covenant through covetousness, and with feigned words, *I have cursed them with a very sore and grievous curse.* (D&C 104:4.)

Thus saith the Lord unto you, my servant Lyman: *Your sins are forgiven you,* because you have obeyed my voice in coming up hither this morning to receive counsel of him whom I have appointed. (D&C 108:1.)

I will appear unto my servants, and speak unto them with mine own voice, if my people will keep my commandments, and do not pollute this holy house. (D&C 110:8.)

Whosoever ye shall send in my name, by the voice of your brethren, the Twelve, duly recommended and authorized by you, shall have power to open the door of my kingdom unto any nation whithersoever ye shall send them—inasmuch as they shall humble themselves before me, and abide in my word, and hearken to the voice of my Spirit. (D&C 112:21-22.)

If ye love me, keep my commandments; *and the sickness of the land shall redound to your glory.* (D&C 124:87.)

If a person *gains more knowledge and intelligence in this life* through his diligence and obedience than another, *he will have so much the advantage in the world to come.* (D&C 130:19.)

There is a law, irrevocably decreed in heaven before the foundations of this world, *upon which all blessings are predicated—and when we obtain any blessing from God,* it is by obedience to that law *upon which it is predicated.* (D&C 130:20-21.)

All who will have a blessing at my hands shall abide the law which was appointed *for that blessing,* and the conditions thereof, as were instituted from before the foundations of the world. (D&C 132:5.)

Except ye abide my law *ye cannot attain to this glory.* (D&C 132:21; see also 132:19-20.)

There are none to deliver you; for ye obeyed not my voice when I called to you out of the heavens; ye believed not my servants, and when they were sent unto you ye received them not. *Wherefore, they sealed up the testimony and bound up the law, and ye were delivered over unto darkness.* (D&C 133:71-72.)

Go thy way and do as I have told you, and fear not thine enemies; for they shall not have power to stop my work. (D&C 136:17.)

Be diligent in keeping all my commandments, *lest judgments come upon you, and your faith fail you, and your enemies triumph over you.* (D&C 136:42.)

We will prove them herewith, to see if they will do all things whatsoever the Lord their God shall command them; and they who keep their first estate *shall be added upon;* and they who keep not their first estate *shall not have glory in the same kingdom with those who keep their first estate;* and they who keep their second estate *shall have glory added upon their heads for ever and ever.* (Abr. 3:25-26.)

Offenses

Violence is not necessarily physical; it can be mental or emotional. It is this intangible damage that one can do to another which the Lord condemns in passages about offenses, just as he condemns physical violence. He commands us not to be offensive to one another, "neither to the Jews, nor the Gentiles, nor to the church of God." (1 Cor. 10:32.) And while he commands us to not offend others, he also says he will "cut off" those who "make a man an offender for a word." (Isa. 29:20-21.) Perhaps most importantly, we are to work with offenders to reclaim them and to maintain peace in the Church, or to avoid them when they refuse help.

Commandments and Promises

A brother offended *is harder to be won than a strong city:* and their contentions *are like the bars of a castle.* (Prov. 18:19.)

All that watch for iniquity *are cut off:* that make a man an offender for a word, and lay a snare for him that reproveth in the gate. (Isa. 29:20-21; similar scripture, 2 Ne. 27:31-32.)

Whoso shall offend one of these little ones which believe in me, *it were better for him that a millstone were hanged about his neck, and that he were drowned in the depth of the sea. Woe* unto the world because of offences: for it must needs be that offences come; *but woe to that man by whom the offence cometh!* (Matt. 18:6-7; similar scriptures, Mark 9:42, Luke 17:1-2.)

Mark them which cause divisions and offences contrary to the doctrine which ye have learned; and avoid them. (Rom. 16:17.)

Give none offence, neither to the Jews, nor to the Gentiles, nor to the church of God. (1 Cor. 10:32.)

Giving no offence in any thing, that the ministry be not blamed: but in all things approving ourselves as the ministers of God, in much patience, in afflictions, in necessities, in distresses. (2 Cor. 6:3-4.)

In many things we offend all. If any man offend not in word, *the same is a perfect man, and able also to bridle the whole body.* (James 3:2.)

If thy brother or sister offend thee, thou shalt take him or her between him or her and thee alone; and if he or she confess *thou shalt be reconciled.* And if he or she confess not thou shalt deliver him or her up unto the church, not to the members, but to the elders. And it shall be done in a meeting, and that not before the world. And if thy brother or sister offend many, he or she shall be chastened before many. And if any one offend openly, he or she shall be rebuked openly, *that he or she may be ashamed.* And if he or she confess not, *he or she shall be delivered up unto* the law of God. If any shall offend in secret, he or she shall be rebuked in secret, *that he or she may have opportunity to confess in secret to him or her* whom he or she has offended, *and to God, that the church may not speak reproachfully of him or her.* (D&C 42:88-92.)

Wo to him by whom this offense cometh, *for it had been better for him that he had been drowned in the depth of the sea.* (D&C 54:5.)

Opposing God and His Servants

Life has only two sides: God's and Satan's. God commands us to be on his side. He tells us that if we are not with God, we are against him.

Our complex human natures may result in our being evil in some ways and righteous in others. This means that we must watch for and eliminate those traits and attitudes which pull us from God.

In what ways do we oppose God? Scripture lists such things as tempting him, forsaking him, rebelling against him, rejecting his word, contending with him, persecuting his people, fighting his people, being angry because of his truths, speaking against his works, perverting his ways, and denying him.

Those who oppose and fight God or his servants suffer serious consequences. They are cursed, cast down, and damned. Those who contend with God's servants will find that God will contend with them. Those who resist being subject to God will be damned, "for there is no power but of God: the powers that be are ordained of God. Whosoever therefore resisteth the power, resisteth the ordinance of God: and they that resist shall receive to themselves damnation." (Rom. 13:1-2.) Little hope remains to those who resist God unless they repent.

Commandments and Promises

If ye forsake the Lord, and serve strange gods, *then he will turn and do you hurt, and consume you, after that he hath done you good.* (Josh. 24:20.)

If ye will fear the Lord, and serve him, and obey his voice, and not rebel against the commandment of the Lord, *then shall both ye and also the king that reigneth over you continue following the Lord your God:* but if ye will not obey the voice of the Lord, but rebel against the commandment of the Lord, *then shall the hand of the Lord be against you, as it was against your fathers.* (1 Sam. 12:14-15.)

[Saul rebuked by Samuel] Rebellion is as the sin of witchcraft, and stubbornness is as iniquity and idolatry. Because thou hast rejected the word of the Lord, *he hath also rejected thee from being king.* (1 Sam. 15:23.)

Thine hand shall find out all thine enemies: *thy right hand shall find out* those that hate thee. *Thou shalt make them as a fiery oven in the time of thine anger: the Lord shall swallow them up in his wrath, and the fire shall devour them. Their fruit shalt thou destroy from the earth, and their seed from among the children of men.* (Ps. 21:8-10.)

Envy thou not the oppressor, and choose none of his ways. For the froward *is abomination to the Lord: but his secret is* with the righteous. (Prov. 3:31-32.)

Woe unto him that striveth with his Maker! Let the potsherd strive with the potsherds of the earth. Shall the clay say to him that fashioneth it, What makest thou? or thy work, He hath no hands? (Isa. 45:9.)

Thus saith the Lord, *Even the captives of the mighty shall be taken away, and the prey of the terrible shall be delivered: for I will contend with him* that contendeth with thee, *and I will save thy children. And I will feed them* that oppress thee *with their own flesh; and they shall be drunken with their own blood, as with sweet wine: and all flesh shall know that I the Lord am thy Saviour and thy Redeemer, the mighty One of Jacob.* (Isa. 49:25-26; similar scripture, 2 Ne. 6:17-18.)

Israel was holiness unto the Lord, and the firstfruits of his increase: all that devour him *shall offend; evil shall come upon them, saith the Lord.* (Jer. 2:3.)

It is written again, Thou shalt not tempt the Lord thy God. (Matt. 4:7; similar scripture, Luke 4:12.)

Whosoever shall deny me before men, *him will I also deny before my Father which is in heaven.* (Matt. 10:33.)

He that is not with me *is against me;* and he that gathereth not with me *scattereth abroad.* (Matt. 12:30.)

Let every soul be subject unto the higher powers. For there is no power but of God: the powers that be are ordained of God. Whosoever therefore resisteth the power, *resisteth the ordinance of God:* and they that resist *shall receive to themselves damnation.* (Rom. 13:1-2; see also JST Rom. 13:1.)

Neither let us tempt Christ, as some of them also tempted, *and were destroyed of serpents.* (1 Cor. 10:9.)

If we sin wilfully after that we have received the knowledge of the truth, *there remaineth no more sacrifice for sins.* (Heb. 10:26.)

[to Nephi] Inasmuch as thy brethren shall rebel against thee, *they shall be cut off from the presence of the Lord.* And inasmuch as thou shalt keep my commandments, *thou shalt be made a ruler and a teacher over thy brethren.* For behold, in that day that they shall rebel against me, *I will curse them even with a sore curse, and they shall have no power over thy seed except* they shall rebel against me also. And if it so be that they rebel against me, *they shall be a scourge unto thy seed, to stir them up in the ways of remembrance.* (1 Ne. 2:21-24.)

The Spirit of the Lord ceaseth soon to strive with them; for behold, they have rejected the prophets, and Jeremiah have they cast into prison. And they have sought to take away the life of my father, insomuch that they have driven him out of the land. (1 Ne. 7:14.)

Every nation which shall war against thee, O house of Israel, *shall be turned one against another, and they shall fall into the pit which they digged to ensnare the people of the Lord.* And all that fight against Zion *shall be destroyed,* and that great whore, who hath perverted the right ways of the Lord, yea, that great and abominable church, *shall tumble to the dust and great shall be the fall of it.* (1 Ne. 22:14.)

When the time cometh that they shall dwindle in unbelief, after they have received so great blessings from the hand of the Lord—having a knowledge of the creation of the earth, and all men, knowing the great and marvelous works of the Lord from the creation of the world; having power given them to do all things by faith; having all the commandments from the beginning, and having been brought by his infinite goodness into this precious land of promise—behold, I say, if the day shall come that they will reject the Holy One of Israel, the true Messiah, their Redeemer and their God, behold, *the judgments of him that is just shall rest upon them. Yea, he will bring other nations unto them, and he will give unto them power, and he will take away from them the lands of their possessions, and he will cause them to be scattered and smitten. Yea, as one generation passeth to another there shall be bloodsheds, and great visitations among them.* (2 Ne. 1:10-12.)

[to the sons of Lehi, excepting Nephi] Rebel no more against your brother, whose views have been glorious. (2 Ne. 1:24.)

Thus prophesied Joseph, saying: Behold, that seer will the Lord bless; and they that seek to destroy him *shall be confounded; for this promise, which I have obtained of the Lord, of the fruit of my loins, shall be fulfilled.* (2 Ne. 3:14.)

They that fight against Zion and the covenant people of the Lord *shall lick up the dust of their feet;* and the people of the Lord *shall not be ashamed.* (2 Ne. 6:13.)

He that fighteth against Zion, both Jew and Gentile, both bond and free, both male and female, *shall perish;* for they are they who are the whore of all the earth; for they who are not for me are against me, saith our God. (2 Ne. 10:16; similar scripture, 2 Ne. 10:13.)

Wo unto them that fight against God and the people of his church. (2 Ne. 25:14.)

After the Messiah shall come there shall be signs given unto my people of his birth, and also of his death and resurrection; *and great and terrible shall that day be unto the wicked, for they shall perish; and they perish* because they cast out the prophets, and the saints, and stone them, and slay them; wherefore the cry of the blood of the saints shall ascend up to God from the ground against them. (2 Ne. 26:3.)

They that kill the prophets, and the saints, *the depths of the earth shall swallow them up, saith the Lord of Hosts; and mountains shall cover them, and whirlwinds shall carry them away, and buildings shall fall upon them and crush them to pieces and grind them to powder. And they shall be visited with thunderings, and lightnings, and earthquakes, and all manner of destructions, for the fire of the anger of the Lord shall be kindled against them, and they shall be as stubble, and the day that cometh shall consume them, saith the Lord of Hosts.* (2 Ne. 26:5-6.)

All the nations that fight against Zion, and that distress her, *shall be as a dream of a night vision; yea, it shall be unto them, even as unto a hungry man which dreameth, and behold he eateth but he awaketh and his soul is empty; or like unto a thirsty man which dreameth, and behold he drinketh but he awaketh and behold he is faint, and his soul hath appetite; yea, even so shall the multitude of all the nations be* that fight against Mount Zion. (2 Ne. 27:3; similar scripture, Isa. 29:7-8.)

Wo unto all those who tremble, and are angry because of the truth of God! For behold, he that is built upon the rock *receiveth it with gladness;* and he that is built upon a sandy foundation *trembleth lest he shall fall.* (2 Ne. 28:28.)

I will show unto them that fight against my word and against my people, who are of the house of Israel, *that I am God, and that I covenanted with Abraham that I would remember his seed forever.* (2 Ne. 29:14.)

The hand of providence hath smiled upon you most pleasingly, that you have obtained many riches; and because some of you have obtained more abundantly than that of your brethren ye are lifted up in the pride of your hearts, and wear stiff necks and high heads because of the costliness of your apparel, and persecute your brethren because ye suppose that ye are better than they. And now, my brethren, do ye suppose that God justifieth you in this thing? Behold, I say unto you, Nay. *But he condemneth you, and* if ye persist in these things *his judgments must speedily come unto you.* (Jacob 2:13-14.)

After ye have known and have been taught all these things, if ye should transgress and go contrary to that which has been spoken, that ye do withdraw yourselves from the Spirit of the Lord, that it may have no place in you to guide you in wisdom's paths *that ye may be blessed, prospered, and preserved*—I say unto you, that the man that doeth this, the same cometh out in open rebellion against God; therefore he listeth to obey the evil spirit, and becometh an enemy to all righteousness; *therefore, the Lord has no place in him, for he dwelleth not in unholy temples.* Therefore if that man repenteth not, and remaineth and dieth an enemy to God, *the demands of divine justice do awaken his immortal soul to a lively sense of his own guilt, which doth cause him to shrink from the presence of the Lord, and doth fill his breast with guilt, and pain, and anguish, which is like an unquenchable fire, whose flame ascendeth up forever and ever. And now I say unto you, that mercy hath no claim on that man; therefore his final doom is to endure a never-ending torment.* (Mosiah 2:36-39.)

Wo, wo unto him who knoweth that he rebelleth against God! *For salvation cometh to none such except it be through repentance and faith on the Lord Jesus Christ.* (Mosiah 3:12.)

The Lord redeemeth none such that rebel against him and die in their sins; yea, even all those that have perished in their sins ever since the world began, that have wilfully rebelled against God, that have known the commandments of God, and would not keep them; *these are they that have no part in the first resurrection.* (Mosiah 15:26.)

Remember that he that persists in his own carnal nature, and goes on in the ways of sin and rebellion against God, *remaineth in his fallen state and the devil hath all power over him. Therefore he is as though there was no redemption made,* being an enemy to God; and also is the devil an enemy to God. (Mosiah 16:5.)

The Amlicites knew not that they were fulfilling the words of God when they began to mark themselves in their foreheads; nevertheless they had come out in open rebellion against God; *therefore it was expedient that the curse should fall upon them.* (Alma 3:18.)

Is there one among you that doth make a mock of his brother, or that heapeth upon him persecutions? *Wo* unto such an one, for he is not prepared, and the time is at hand that he must repent or *he cannot be saved!* (Alma 5:30-31.)

Has not the Lord expressly promised and firmly decreed, that if ye will rebel against him that *ye shall utterly be destroyed from off the face of the earth?* (Alma 9:24.)

No more deny the coming of Christ. (Alma 34:37.)

Contend no more against the Holy Ghost, but . . . receive it, and take upon you the name of Christ. (Alma 34:38.)

Wo unto this people, because of this time which has arrived, that ye do cast out the prophets, and do mock them, and cast stones at them, and do slay them, and do all manner of iniquity unto them, even as they did of old time. (Hel. 13:24.)

Wo unto him that spurneth at the doings of the Lord; yea, wo unto him that shall deny the Christ and his works! Yea, *wo* unto him that shall deny the revelations of the Lord, and that shall say the Lord no longer worketh by revelation, or by prophecy, or by gifts, or by tongues, or by healings, or by the power of the Holy Ghost! Yea, and *wo* unto him that shall say at that day, to get gain, that there can be no miracle wrought by Jesus Christ; *for he that doeth this shall become like unto the son of perdition, for whom there was no mercy, according to the word of Christ!* (3 Ne. 29:5-7.)

He that shall breathe out wrath and strifes against the work of the Lord, and against the covenant people of the Lord who are the house of Israel, and shall say: We will destroy the work of the Lord, and the Lord will not remember his covenant which he hath made unto the house of Israel—*the same is in danger to be hewn down and cast into the fire.* (Morm. 8:21.)

Who can stand against the works of the Lord? Who can deny his sayings? Who will rise up against the almighty power of the Lord? Who will despise the works of the Lord? Who will despise the children of Christ? Behold, all ye who are despisers of the works of the Lord, *for ye shall wonder and perish.* O then despise not, and wonder not, but hearken unto the words of the Lord. (Morm. 9:26-27.)

He that will contend against the word of the Lord, *let him be accursed;* and he that shall deny these things, *let him be accursed; for unto them will I show no greater things, saith Jesus Christ; for I am he who speaketh.* (Esther 4:8.)

Wo be unto them that shall pervert the ways of the Lord after this manner, *for they shall perish* except they repent. (Moro. 8:16.)

Deny not the gifts of God, for they are many; and they come from the same God. (Moro. 10:8.)

If ye by the grace of God are perfect in Christ, and deny not his power, *then are ye sanctified in Christ by the grace of God, through the shedding of the blood of Christ, which is in the covenant of the Father unto the remission of your sins, that ye become holy, without spot.* (Moro. 10:33.)

The rebellious *shall be pierced with much sorrow; for their iniquities shall be spoken upon the housetops, and their secret acts shall be revealed.* (D&C 1:3.)

If they reject my words, and this part of my gospel and ministry, blessed are ye, for they can do no more unto you than unto me. And even if they do unto you even as they have done unto me, *blessed are ye, for you shall dwell with me in glory.* But if they reject not my words, which shall be established by the testimony which shall be given, *blessed are they, and then shall ye have joy in the fruit of your labors.* (D&C 6:29-31.)

Seek not to counsel your God. (D&C 22:4.)

It shall come to pass that whosoever shall lay their hands upon you by violence, *ye shall command to be smitten in my name; and, behold, I will smite them according to your words, in mine own due time.* (D&C 24:16.)

Mine anger is kindled against the rebellious, *and they shall know mine arm and mine indignation, in the day of visitation and of wrath upon the nations.* (D&C 56:1.)

Let the wicked take heed, and let the rebellious fear and tremble; and let the unbelieving hold their lips, *for the day of wrath shall come upon them as a whirlwind, and all flesh shall know that I am God.* (D&C 63:6.)

The rebellious *shall be cut off out of the land of Zion, and shall be sent away, and shall not inherit the land.* For, verily I say that the rebellious are not of the blood of Ephraim, *wherefore they shall be plucked out.* (D&C 64:35-36.)

Wo unto that house, or that village or city that rejecteth you [priesthood holders], or your words, or your testimony concerning me. *Wo,* I say again, unto that house, or that village or city that rejecteth you, or your words, or your testimony of me; for I, the Almighty, have laid my hands upon the nations, *to scourge them for their wickedness.* (D&C 84:94-96.)

Whoso rejecteth you *shall be rejected of my Father and his house.* (D&C 99:4.)

The destroyer I have sent forth to destroy and lay waste mine enemies; *and not many years hence they shall not be left to pollute mine heritage, and to blaspheme my name upon the lands which I have consecrated for the gathering together of my saints.* (D&C 105:15.)

Call ye, therefore, upon them with loud proclamation, and with your testimony, fearing them not, for they are as grass, and all their glory as the flower thereof which soon falleth, *that they may be left also without excuse—and that I may visit them in the day of visitation, when I shall unveil the face of my covering, to appoint the portion* of the oppressor among hypocrites, *where there is gnashing of teeth,* if they reject my servants and my testimony which I have revealed unto them. (D&C 124:7-8.)

Let all the saints rejoice, therefore, and be exceedingly glad; for Israel's God is their God, and *he will mete out a just recompense of reward upon the heads* of all their oppressors. (D&C 127:3.)

Order

God's universe is orderly; his creations function according to an established pattern. Man, too, is a creation of order. He grows and learns in order, and he is commanded to choose orderliness rather than confusion as he exercises agency in patterning his life.

Our lives and spirits can be put in order even if, through disobedience, we have disordered them. Just as we are told to have our homes in order, we can put our lives in order so that we follow the pattern the Savior established for us. In this manner, we can become worthy of being one of God's creations, and we can learn and grow as the Lord would have us do.

Commandments and Promises

Let all things be done decently and in order. (1 Cor. 14:40.)

We hear that there are some which walk among you disorderly, working not at all, but are busybodies. Now them that are such we command and exhort by our Lord Jesus Christ, that with quietness they work, and eat their own bread. (2 Thes. 3:11-12.)

See that all these things are done in wisdom and order; for it is not requisite that a man should run faster than he has strength. And again, it is expedient that he should be diligent, *that thereby he might win the prize*; therefore, all things must be done in order. (Mosiah 4:27.)

All things must be done in order, and by common consent in the church, by the prayer of faith. (D&C 28:13.)

Let the work of the gathering be not in haste, nor by flight; but let it be done as it shall be counseled by the elders of the church at the conferences, according to the knowledge which they receive from time to time. (D&C 58:56.)

This is the will of the Lord your God concerning his saints, that they should assemble themselves together unto the land of Zion, not in haste, *lest there should be confusion, which bringeth pestilence.* (D&C 63:24.)

Assemble yourselves together, and organize yourselves, and prepare yourselves, and sanctify yourselves; yea, purify your hearts, and cleanse your hands and your feet before me, *that I may make you clean; that I may testify unto your Father, and your God, and my God, that you are clean from the blood of this wicked generation; that I may fulfil this promise, this great and last promise, which I have made unto you, when I will.* (D&C 88:74-75.)

Organize yourselves; prepare every needful thing; and establish a house, even a house of prayer, a house of fasting, a house of faith, a house of learning, a house of glory, a house of order, a house of God. (D&C 88:119; similar scripture, D&C 109:8.)

Set in order your houses; keep slothfulness and uncleanness far from you. (D&C 90:18.)

If you will be delivered you shall set in order your own house. (D&C 93:43.)

First set in order thy house. (D&C 93:44.)

Let not your gathering be in haste, nor by flight; but let all things be prepared before you. (D&C 101:68.)

Patience

(See also Adversity, Reacting to; Enduring to the End; Waiting on God.)

Patience is necessary for faith, for self-mastery, for perfection. It is one of the ways to nourish the "tree springing up unto everlasting life." (Alma 32:41.) It is prerequisite to being fruitful in the knowledge of God and having spiritual vision. (2 Pet. 1:5-9.) It is essential if we are to become instruments in God's hands. (Alma 26:27.)

The Lord emphasizes particularly that we must be patient in affliction—"For our light affliction, which is but for a moment, worketh for us a far more exceeding and eternal weight of glory." (2 Cor. 4:17.) As the Lord instructed Joseph Smith and Sidney Rigdon, "These things remain to overcome through patience," with the promise "that such may receive a more exceeding and eternal weight of glory." (D&C 63:66.) It is the principle by which we can endure and overcome, and turn experience into learning or adversity into blessings.

Commandments and Promises

Rest in the Lord, and wait patiently for him: fret not thyself because of him who prospereth in his way, because of the man who bringeth wicked devices to pass. (Ps. 37:7.)

[Be] rejoicing in hope; patient in tribulation; continuing instant in prayer. (Rom. 12:12.)

In all things approving ourselves as the ministers of God, in much patience, in afflictions, in necessities, in distresses, in stripes, in imprisonments, in tumults, in labours, in watchings, in fastings. (2 Cor. 6:4-5.)

I therefore, the prisoner of the Lord, beseech you that ye walk worthy of the vocation wherewith ye are called, with all lowliness and meekness, with longsuffering, forbearing one another in love. (Eph. 4:1-2.)

Put on therefore, as the elect of God, holy and beloved, bowels of mercies, kindness, humbleness of mind, meekness, longsuffering; forbearing one another, and forgiving one another, if any man have a quarrel against any: even as Christ forgave you, so also do ye. (Col. 3:12-13.)

Now we exhort you, brethren, warn them that are unruly, comfort the feebleminded, support the weak, be patient toward all men. (1 Thes. 5:14.)

Follow after . . . love, patience, meekness. (1 Tim. 6:11.)

The servant of the Lord must not strive; but be gentle unto all men, apt to teach, patient, in meekness instructing those that oppose themselves; *if God peradventure will give them repentance to the acknowledging of the truth; and that they may recover themselves out of the snare of the devil, who are taken captive by him at his will.* (2 Tim. 2:24-26.)

Speak thou the things which become sound doctrine: that the aged men be . . . sound in . . . patience. (Titus 2:1-2.)

Ye have need of patience, that, after ye have done the will of God, *ye might receive the promise.* (Heb. 10:36.)

Seeing we also are compassed about with so great a cloud of witnesses, let us lay aside every weight, and the sin which doth so easily beset us, and let us run with patience the race that is set before us. (Heb. 12:1.)

Count it all joy when ye fall into divers temptations; knowing this, that the trying of your faith worketh patience. But let patience have her perfect work, *that ye may be perfect and entire, wanting nothing.* (James 1:2-4; see also JST James 1:2.)

Be patient therefore, brethren, *unto the coming of the Lord.* Behold, the husbandman waiteth *for the precious fruit of the earth,* and hath long patience for it, *until he receive the early and latter rain.* Be ye also patient; stablish your hearts: for the coming of the Lord draweth nigh. (James 5:7-8.)

Take, my brethren, the prophets, who have spoken in the name of the Lord, for an example of suffering affliction, and of patience. (James 5:10.)

What glory is it, if, when ye be buffeted for your faults, ye shall take it patiently? but if, when ye do well, and suffer for it, ye take it patiently, *this is acceptable with God.* For even hereunto were ye called: because Christ also suffered for us, leaving us an example, that ye should follow his steps: who did no sin, neither was guile found in his mouth: who, when he was reviled, reviled not again; when he suffered, he threatened not; but committed himself to him that judgeth righteously. (1 Pet. 2:20-23.)

Beside this, giving all diligence, add to your faith virtue; and to virtue knowledge; and to knowledge temperance; and to temperance patience; and to patience godliness; and to godliness brotherly kindness; and to brotherly kindness charity. For if these things be in you, and abound, *they make you that ye shall neither be barren nor unfruitful in the knowledge of our Lord Jesus Christ.* But he that lacketh these things *is blind, and cannot see afar off, and hath forgotten that he was purged from his old sins.* (2 Pet. 1:5-9.)

I would that ye should be humble, and be submissive and gentle; easy to be entreated; full of patience and long-suffering. (Alma 7:23.)

[Become] humble, meek, submissive, patient, full of love and all long-suffering. (Alma 13:28.)

The Lord said unto them [Alma and the sons of Mosiah] also: Go forth among the Lamanites, thy brethren, and establish my word; yet ye shall be patient in long-suffering and afflictions, *that ye may show forth good examples unto them in me, and I will make an instrument of thee in my hands unto the salvation of many souls.* (Alma 17:11.)

The Lord comforted us [sons of Mosiah] and said: Go amongst thy brethren, the Lamanites, and bear with patience thine afflictions, *and I will give unto you success.* (Alma 26:27.)

If ye will nourish the word, yea, nourish the tree as it beginneth to grow, by your faith with great diligence, and with patience, looking forward to the fruit thereof, *it shall take root; and behold it shall be a tree springing up unto everlasting life.* And because of your diligence and your faith and your patience with the word in nourishing it, that it may take root in you, behold, *by and by ye shall pluck the fruit thereof, which is most precious, which is sweet above all that is sweet, and which is white above all that is white, yea, and pure above all that is pure; and ye shall feast upon this fruit even until ye are filled, that ye hunger not, neither shall ye thirst.* Then, *my brethren, ye shall reap the rewards* of your faith, and your diligence, and patience, and long-suffering, waiting for the tree *to bring forth fruit unto you.* (Alma 32:41-43.)

Have patience, and that ye bear with all manner of afflictions; that ye do not revile against those who do cast you out because of your exceeding poverty, *lest ye become sinners like unto them;* but that ye have patience, and bear with those afflictions, with a firm hope that ye shall one day rest from all your afflictions. (Alma 34:40-41.)

Remember . . . temperance, patience, . . . diligence. (D&C 4:6.)

Be patient; be sober; be temperate; have patience, faith, hope and charity. (D&C 6:19.)

[to Oliver Cowdery] Be patient, my son, for it is wisdom in me, and it is not expedient that you should translate at this present time. (D&C 9:3.)

Marvel not that I said unto you [Joseph Smith]: Here is wisdom, show it [initial translation of Book of Mormon] not unto the world— for I said, show it not unto the world, *that you may be preserved.* Behold, I do not say that you shall not show it unto the righteous; but as you cannot always judge the righteous, or as you cannot always tell the wicked from the righteous, therefore I say unto you, hold your peace until I shall see fit to make all things known unto the world concerning the matter. (D&C 10:35-37.)

[to Hyrum Smith] Keep my commandments; hold your peace; appeal unto my Spirit; yea, cleave unto me with all your heart, *that you may assist in bringing to light those things of which has been spoken—yea, the translation of my work;* be patient until you shall accomplish it. (D&C 11:18-19.)

His [Joseph Smith's] word ye shall receive, as if from mine own mouth, in all patience and faith. For by doing these things *the gates of hell shall not prevail against you; yea, and the Lord God will disperse the powers of darkness from before you, and cause the heavens to shake for your good, and his name's glory.* (D&C 21:5-6.)

Be patient in afflictions, for thou shalt have many. (D&C 24:8; similar scriptures, D&C 31:9, 66:9.)

Be patient in tribulation until I come. (D&C 54:10.)

These things remain to overcome through patience, *that such may receive a more exceeding and eternal weight of glory, otherwise, a greater condemnation.* (D&C 63:66.)

Ye are not able to abide the presence of God now, neither the ministering of angels; wherefore, continue in patience *until ye are perfected.* (D&C 67:13.)

[Wait] patiently on the Lord, for your prayers have entered into the ears of the Lord of Sabaoth, and are recorded with this seal and testament—*that the Lord hath sworn and decreed that they shall be granted. Therefore, he giveth this promise unto you, with an immutable covenant that they shall be fulfilled; and all things wherewith you have been afflicted shall work together for your good, and to my name's glory, saith the Lord.* (D&C 98:2-3.)

I speak unto you concerning your families—if men will smite you, or your families, once, and ye bear it patiently and revile not against them, neither seek revenge, *ye shall be rewarded;* but if ye bear it not patiently, *it shall be accounted unto you as being meted out as a just measure unto you.* (D&C 98:23-24.)

Seek the face of the Lord always, that in patience *ye may possess your souls, and ye shall have eternal life.* (D&C 101:38.)

The decisions of these quorums, or either of them, are to be made in all righteousness, in holiness, and lowliness of heart, meekness and long suffering, and in faith, and virtue, and knowledge, temperance, patience, godliness, brotherly kindness and charity; *because the promise is,* if these things abound in them *they shall not be unfruitful in the knowledge of the Lord.* (D&C 107:30-31.)

Wait patiently until the solemn assembly shall be called of my servants, *then you shall be remembered with the first of mine elders, and receive right by ordination with the rest of mine elders whom I have chosen. Behold, this is the promise of the Father unto you* if you continue faithful. (D&C 108:4-5.)

No power or influence can or ought to be maintained by virtue of the priesthood, only by persuasion, by long-suffering, by gentleness and meekness, and by love unfeigned; by kindness, and pure knowledge, *which shall greatly enlarge the soul without hypocrisy, and without guile.* (D&C 121:41-42.)

Let your diligence, and your perseverance, and patience, and your works be redoubled, *and you shall in nowise lose your reward, saith the Lord of Hosts.* (D&C 127:4.)

Peace

(See also Example, Being an; Murmuring and Complaining; Murder and Violence.)

While some wars are prophesied, war is not God's way. God continually commands his people to seek and to love peace, and to fight only as he commands. For the latter days, the Lord enjoins his people to "sue for peace, not only to the people that have smitten you, but also to all people; and lift up an ensign of peace, and make a proclamation of peace." In addition, Paul writes, "If it be possible, as much as lieth in you, live peaceably with all men." (Rom. 12:18.)

Sometimes, of course, that is not possible. And so we have this commandment: "Ye must lay down your weapons of war, and delight no more in the shedding of blood, and take them not again, save it be that God shall command you." (Morm. 7:4.) As he did with the Nephites, the Lord commands us when to fight. Section 98 of the Doctrine and Covenants carefully defines conditions for warfare. First, God must command it. Second, if war is proclaimed by the opposition, God's people are to raise a standard of peace to them, not once, but three times. Then if peace is not accepted, the people of God are to bring the testimony to the Lord, who will "give unto them a commandment, and justify them in going out to battle." When war is approached in this manner, the Lord promises that he will "fight their battles, and their children's battles, and their children's children's, until they [have] avenged themselves on all their enemies." (D&C 98:34-37.)

Commandments and Promises

When thou comest nigh unto a city to fight against it, then proclaim peace unto it. (Deut. 20:10.)

Depart from evil, and do good; seek peace, pursue it. (Ps. 34:14.)

Pray for the peace of Jerusalem. (Ps. 122:6.)

Say not thou, I will recompense evil; but wait on the Lord, *and he shall save thee.* (Prov. 20:22.)

These are the things that ye shall do; Speak ye every man the truth to his neighbour; execute the judgment of truth and peace in your gates: and let none of you imagine evil in your hearts against his neighbour; and love no false oath: *for all these are things that I hate, saith the Lord.* (Zech. 8:16-17.)

Love the truth and peace. (Zech. 8:19.)

Blessed are the peacemakers: *for they shall be called the children of God.* (Matt. 5:9; similar scripture, 3 Ne. 12:9.)

If it be possible, as much as lieth in you, live peaceably with all men. (Rom. 12:18.)

Let us therefore follow after the things which make for peace, and things wherewith one may edify another. (Rom. 14:19.)

Be perfect, be of good comfort, be of one mind, live in peace; *and the God of love and peace shall be with you.* (2 Cor. 13:11.)

I therefore, the prisoner of the Lord, beseech you that ye walk worthy of the vocation wherewith ye are called, with all lowliness and meekness, with longsuffering, forbearing one another in love; endeavouring to keep the unity of the Spirit in the bond of peace. (Eph. 4:1-3.)

Let the peace of God rule in your hearts, to the which also ye are called in one body; and be ye thankful. (Col. 3:15.)

I exhort therefore, that, first of all, supplications, prayers, intercessions, and giving of thanks, be made for all men; for kings, and for all that are in authority; *that we may lead a quiet and peaceable life in all godliness and honesty.* (1 Tim. 2:1-2.)

Flee also youthful lusts: but follow righteousness, faith, charity, peace, with them that call on the Lord out of a pure heart. (2 Tim. 2:22.)

Follow peace with all men, and holiness, *without which no man shall see the Lord:* looking diligently lest any man fail of the grace of God; *lest any root of bitterness springing up trouble you, and thereby many be defiled.* (Heb. 12:14-15.)

The fruit of righteousness is sown in peace of them that make peace. (James 3:18.)

He that will love life, and see good days, let them refrain his tongue from evil, and his lips that they speak no guile: let him eschew evil, and do good; let him seek peace, and ensue it. *For the eyes of the Lord are* over the righteous, *and his ears are open unto their prayers: but the face of the Lord is against them* that do evil. (1 Pet. 3:10-12.)

Ye will not have a mind to injure one another, but to live peaceably, and to render to every man according to that which is his due. (Mosiah 4:13.)

Do that which will make for the peace of this people. (Mosiah 29:10.)

Inasmuch as ye are not guilty of the first offense, neither the second, ye shall not suffer yourselves to be slain by the hands of your enemies. (Alma 43:46.)

Know ye that ye must lay down your weapons of war, and delight no more in the shedding of blood, and take them not again, save it be that God shall command you. (Morm. 7:4.)

Renounce war and proclaim peace. (D&C 98:16.)

I speak unto you concerning your families—if men will smite you or your families, once, and ye bear it patiently and revile not against them, neither seek revenge, *ye shall be rewarded;* but if ye bear it not patiently, *it shall be accounted unto you as being meted out as a just measure unto you.* And again, if your enemy shall smite you the second time, and you revile not against your enemy, and bear it patiently, *your reward shall be an hundredfold.* And again, if he shall smite you the third time, and ye bear it patiently, *your reward shall be doubled unto you four-fold; and these three testimonies shall stand against your enemy* if he repent not, *and shall not be blotted out.* (D&C 98:23-27.)

This is the law that I gave unto mine ancients, that they should not go out unto battle against any nation, kindred, tongue, or people, save I, the Lord, commanded them. And if any nation, tongue, or people should proclaim war against them, they should first lift a standard of peace unto that people, nation, or tongue; and if that people did not accept the offering of peace, neither the second nor the third time, they should bring these testimonies before the Lord; then I, the Lord, would give unto them a commandment, and justify them in going out to battle against that nation, tongue, or people. *And I, the Lord, would fight their battles, and their children's battles, and their children's children's, until they had avenged themselves on all their enemies, to the third and fourth generation.* (D&C 98:33-37.)

If after thine enemy has come upon thee the first time, he repent and come unto thee praying thy forgiveness, thou shalt forgive him, and shalt hold it no more as a testimony against thine enemy—and so on unto the second and third time; and as oft as thine enemy repenteth of the trespass wherewith he has trespassed against thee, thou shalt forgive him, until seventy times seven. And if he trespass against thee and repent not the first time, nevertheless thou shalt forgive him. And if he trespass against thee the second time, and repent not, nevertheless thou shalt forgive him. And if he trespass against thee the third time, and repent not, thou shalt also forgive him. But if he trespass against thee the fourth time thou shalt not forgive him, but shalt bring these testimonies before the Lord; *and they shall not be blotted out until he repent and reward thee four-fold in all things* wherewith he has trespassed against thee. And if he do this, thou shalt forgive him with all thine heart; and if he do not this, *I, the Lord, will avenge thee of thine enemy an hundred-fold; and upon his children, and upon his children's children of all them that hate me, unto the third and fourth generation.* But if the children shall repent, or the children's children, and turn to the Lord their God, with all their hearts and with all their might, mind, and strength, and restore four-fold for all their trespasses wherewith they have trespassed, or wherewith their fathers have trespassed, or their fathers' fathers, *then thine indignation shall be turned away; and vengeance shall no more come upon them, saith the Lord thy God, and their trespasses shall never be brought any more as a testimony before the Lord against them.* (D&C 98:39-48.)

Sue for peace, not only to the people that have smitten you, but also to all people; and lift up an ensign of peace, and make a proclamation of peace unto the ends of the earth; and make proposals for peace unto those who have smitten you, according to the voice of the Spirit which is in you, *and all things shall work together for your good.* (D&C 105:38-40.)

Perfection

The Lord commands us to be perfect as he is perfect. For struggling mortals, this may sound like an impossible goal. However, the Lord tells us several ways to achieve this perfection.

We are commanded, "Be ye therefore perfect, even as your Father which is in heaven is perfect." (Matt. 5:48.) An additional translation of the word *perfect* from the Greek is "complete, finished, fully developed." In other words, when we have completed our growth, we should be as our Father in heaven is.

It is also possible to become perfect in one area, and then in another, and another. We can grow as Jesus did, grace by grace. We can serve and follow the Lord daily, task by task. We can do his will, act by act. We can allow time to perfect us through our patience. We can identify and forsake those things that matter to us more than God matters. In this way we become perfect, as God is perfect.

Commandments and Promises

The Lord appeared to Abram, and said unto him, I am the Almighty God; walk before me, and be thou perfect. *And I will make my covenant between me and thee, and will multiply thee exceedingly.* (Gen. 17:1-2.)

Thou shalt be perfect with the Lord thy God. (Deut. 18:13.)

Mark the perfect man, and behold the upright: *for the end of that man is peace.* (Ps. 37:37.)

The righteousness of the perfect *shall direct his way:* but the wicked *shall fall by his own wickedness.* (Prov. 11:5.)

Be ye therefore perfect, even as your Father which is in heaven is perfect. (Matt. 5:48; see also 3 Ne. 12:48.)

Jesus said unto him, If thou wilt be perfect, go and sell that thou hast, and give to the poor, *and thou shalt have treasure in heaven:* and come and follow me. (Matt. 19:21.)

The disciple is not above his master: but every one that is perfect *shall be as his master.* (Luke 6:40.)

Be perfect, be of good comfort, be of one mind, live in peace; *and the God of love and peace shall be with you.* (2 Cor. 13:11.)

Above all these things put on charity, which is the bond of perfectness. (Col. 3:14.)

Make you perfect in every good work to do his will, working in you that which is wellpleasing in his sight, through Jesus Christ. (Heb. 13:21.)

Count it all joy when ye fall into divers temptations; knowing this, that the trying of your faith *worketh patience.* But let patience have her perfect work, *that ye may be perfect and entire, wanting nothing.* (James 1:2-4; see also JST James 1:2.)

Whosoever shall keep the whole law, and yet offend in one point, he is guilty of all. (James 2:10.)

I would that ye should be perfect even as I, or your Father who is in heaven is perfect. (3 Ne. 12:48; see also Matt. 5:48.)

What manner of men ought ye to be? Verily I say unto you, even as I am. (3 Ne. 27:27.)

If ye by the grace of God are perfect in Christ, and deny not his power, *then are ye sanctified in Christ by the grace of God, through the shedding of the blood of Christ, which is in the covenant of the Father unto the remission of your sins, that ye become holy, without spot.* (Moro. 10:33.)

Ye are not able to abide the presence of God now, neither the ministering of angels; wherefore, continue in patience until ye are perfected. (D&C 67:13.)

Above all things, clothe yourselves with a bond of charity, as with a mantle, which is the bond of perfectness and peace. (D&C 88:125.)

Prayer

"After this manner therefore pray ye," Jesus instructs us. In the following prayer, he gives us an example for our own prayers to our Father in heaven. (See Matt. 6:9-13.)

"Our Father which art in heaven," he begins. We should realize to whom we speak when we pray: the God of all creation, God our eternal Father, a real father who loves us, who wants us to be happy and successful, who wants us to speak to him. *"Hallowed by thy name."* We should reverence and worship the being to whom we pray. This means that not only will we use his name with care, but we will also consider carefully all that we do in his name. *"Thy kingdom come."* As we pray, we should commit ourselves to helping build the kingdom of God on earth. We can confer with God about the ways we can help build his kingdom, however small they may be. *"Thy will be done in earth, as it is in heaven."* We need to commit ourselves to do his will. Praying is pointless if we want someone else to do the building or the obeying. This commitment is difficult to say and mean, yet once we promise the Lord to help with his work and do his will, we find that our will begins to match his.

"Give us this day our daily bread." All that we have comes from God, even if we work long hours to "earn" some of it. As we ask the Lord to supply our necessities, we acknowledge that they come from him, and commit ourselves to be worthy of them. *"And forgive us our debts, as we forgive our debtors."* We must forgive others if we are to be forgiven. Our sins, weaknesses, and deficiencies remain to impede us as long as we are unforgiving. *"And lead us not into temptation, but deliver us from evil."* We must ask God to always lead us, especially into sure and safe paths, and to deliver us from the evils that so easily beset us. If we do not ask, we may not be able to discern and to refuse all the carnal paths of the devil. *"For thine is the kingdom, and the power, and the glory, for ever."* Christ gives us a goal for life: the Lord's kingdom. We must recognize that the only genuine and eternal power and glory are the Father's. We must commit our-

selves to bring glory to God. The words *for ever* remind us that we speak of eternal things with eternal consequences. *"Amen."* With this word, we speak our "so be it" to our prayers. This is our seal to and ratification of our words.

Not every prayer will have all these elements. In a tense or dangerous situation, we may speak only a few pleading words. In like manner, we might offer a brief prayer of gratitude and joy that fills our hearts. Even so, the attitudes Jesus exemplifies in his prayer can be part of our attitudes and ultimately our character. As we pray like Jesus, we can become like him.

Commandments and Promises

As truly as I live, saith the Lord, as ye have spoken in mine ears, *so will I do to you.* (Num. 14:28.)

It may be the Lord thy God will hear all the words of Rab-shakeh, whom the king of Assyria his master hath sent to reproach the living God; and will reprove the words which the Lord thy God hath heard: wherefore lift up thy prayer for the remnant that are left. (2 Kgs. 19:4.)

Give thanks unto the Lord, call upon his name, make known his deeds among the people. (1 Chr. 16:8.)

Say ye, Save us, O God of our salvation, and gather us together, and deliver us from the heathen, *that we may give thanks to thy holy name, and glory in thy praise.* (1 Chr. 16:35.)

If I shut up heaven that there be no rain, or if I command the locusts to devour the land, or if I send pestilence among my people; if my people, which are called by my name, shall humble themselves, and pray, and seek my face, and turn from their wicked ways; *then will I hear from heaven, and will forgive their sin, and will heal their land.* (2 Chr. 7:13-14.)

Because thine heart was tender, and thou didst humble thyself before God, when thou heardest his words against this place, and against the inhabitants thereof, and humbledst thyself before me, and didst rend thy clothes, and weep before me; *I have even heard thee also, saith the Lord.* (2 Chr. 34:27.)

The eyes of the Lord are upon the righteous, *and his ears are open unto their cry.* . . . The righteous cry, *and the Lord heareth, and delivereth them out of all their troubles.* (Ps. 34:15, 17.)

Cast thy burden upon the Lord, and he shall sustain thee: *he shall never suffer the righteous to be moved.* (Ps. 55:22.)

Trust in him at all times; ye people, pour out your heart before him: *God is a refuge for us.* (Ps. 62:8.)

He shall deliver the needy when he crieth; the poor also, and him that hath no helper. (Ps. 72:12.)

He will regard the prayer of the destitute, and not despise their prayer. (Ps. 102:17.)

O give thanks unto the Lord; call upon his name: make known his deeds among the people. (Ps. 105:1.)

Seek ye the Lord while he may be found, call ye upon him while he is near. (Isa. 55:6.)

Pray not for this people for their good [because of their iniquity]. When they fast, *I will not hear their cry;* and when they offer burnt offering and an oblation, *I will not accept them: but I will consume them by the sword, and by the famine, and by the pestilence.* (Jer. 14:11-12.)

Then shall ye call upon me, and ye shall go and pray unto me, *and I will hearken unto you.* And ye shall seek me, *and find me,* when ye shall search for me with all your heart. (Jer. 29:12-13.)

Thus saith the Lord the maker thereof, the Lord that formed it, to establish it; the Lord is his name; call unto me, *and I will answer thee, and shew thee great and mighty things, which thou knowest not.* (Jer. 33:2-3.)

Whosoever shall call on the name of the Lord *shall be delivered: for in mount Zion and in Jerusalem shall be deliverance, as the Lord hath said, and in the remnant whom the Lord shall call.* (Joel 2:32.)

Ask ye of the Lord rain in the time of the latter rain; *so the Lord shall make bright clouds, and give them showers of rain, to every one grass in the field.* (Zech. 10:1.)

Beseech God that he will be gracious unto us. (Mal. 1:9.)

Ye have heard that it hath been said, Thou shalt love thy neighbour, and hate thine enemy. But I say unto you, Love your enemies, bless them that curse you, do good to them that hate you, and pray for them which despitefully use you, and persecute you: *that ye may be the children of your Father which is in heaven:* for he maketh his sun to rise on the evil and on the good, and sendeth rain on the just and on the unjust. (Matt. 5:43-45; similar scripture, 3 Ne. 12:43-45.)

When thou prayest, thou shalt not be as the hypocrites are: for they love to pray standing in the synagogues and in the corners of the streets, that they may be seen of men. *Verily I say unto you, They have their reward.* But thou, when thou prayest, enter into thy closet, and when thou hast shut thy door, pray to thy Father which is in secret; *and thy Father which seeth in secret shall reward thee openly.* (Matt. 6:5-6; similar scripture, 3 Ne. 13:5-6.)

When ye pray, use not vain repetitions, as the heathen do: for they think that they shall be heard for their much speaking. Be not ye therefore like unto them: for your Father knoweth what things ye have need of, before ye ask him. (Matt. 6:7-8; similar scripture, 3 Ne. 13:7-8.)

After this manner therefore pray ye: Our Father which art in heaven, Hallowed be thy name. Thy kingdom come. Thy will be done in earth, as it is in heaven. Give us this day our daily bread. And forgive us our debts, as we forgive our debtors. And lead us not into temptation, but deliver us from evil: For thine is the kingdom, and the power, and the glory, for ever. Amen. (Matt. 6:9-13; similar scriptures, Luke 11:1-4, 3 Ne. 13:9-13; see also JST Matt. 6:14 and Luke 11:4.)

Ask, *and it shall be given you;* seek *and ye shall find;* knock, *and it shall be opened unto you:* for every one that asketh *receiveth;* and he that seeketh *findeth;* and to him that knocketh *it shall be opened.* (Matt. 7:7-8; similar scriptures, Luke 11:9-10, 3 Ne. 14:7-8, 27:29; D&C 4:7, 6:5, 11:5, 12:5, 14:5, 49:26, 66:9, 103:35; see also JST Matt. 7:12-17; see also 2 Ne. 9:42; D&C 8:11, 88:62-63, 103:31.)

Pray ye therefore the Lord of the harvest, that he will send forth labourers into his harvest. (Matt. 9:38.)

All things, whatsoever ye shall ask in prayer, believing, *ye shall receive.* (Matt. 21:22.)

Watch and pray, *that ye enter not into temptation:* the spirit indeed is willing, but the flesh is weak. (Matt. 26:41; similar scripture, Mark 14:38.)

What things soever ye desire, when ye pray, believe that ye receive them, *and ye shall have them.* And when ye stand praying, forgive, if ye have ought against any: *that your Father also which is in heaven may forgive you your trespasses.* (Mark 11:24-25.)

He spake a parable unto them to this end, that man ought always to pray, and not to faint. (Luke 18:1.)

Watch ye therefore, and pray always, *that ye may be accounted worthy to escape all these things that shall come to pass, and to stand before the Son of man.* (Luke 21:36; see also JST Luke 21:36.)

Pray that ye enter not into temptation. (Luke 22:40.)

When he rose up from prayer, and was come to his disciples, he found them sleeping for sorrow, and said unto them, Why sleep ye? rise and pray, *lest ye enter into temptation.* (Luke 22:45-46.)

Whatsoever ye shall ask in my name, *that will I do, that the Father may be glorified in the Son.* If ye shall ask any thing in my name, *I will do it.* (John 14:13-14.)

If ye abide in me, and my words abide in you, ye shall ask what ye will, *and it shall be done unto you.* (John 15:7.)

It shall come to pass, that whosoever shall call on the name of the Lord *shall be saved.* (Acts 2:21.)

The Spirit also helpeth our infirmities: for we know not what we should pray for as we ought: *but the Spirit itself maketh intercession for us with groanings which cannot be uttered.* (Rom. 8:26.)

There is no difference between the Jew and the Greek: for *the same Lord over all is rich* unto all that call upon him. For whosoever shall call upon the name of the Lord *shall be saved.* (Rom. 10:12-13.)

Take the helmet of salvation, and the sword of the Spirit, which is the word of God: praying always with all prayer and supplication in the Spirit, and watching thereunto with all perseverance and supplication for all saints. (Eph. 6:17-18.)

Be careful for nothing; but in every thing by prayer and supplication with thanksgiving let your requests be made known unto God. *And the peace of God, which passeth all understanding, shall keep your hearts and minds through Christ Jesus.* (Philip. 4:6-7.)

Continue in prayer, and watch in the same with thanksgiving. (Col. 4:2.)

Pray without ceasing. In every thing give thanks: for this is the will of God in Christ Jesus concerning you. (1 Thes. 5:17-18.)

Brethren, pray for us. (1 Thes. 5:25.)

Pray for us, *that the word of the Lord may have free course, and be glorified, even as it is with you.* (2 Thes. 3:1.)

I exhort therefore, that, first of all, supplications, prayers, intercessions, and giving of thanks, be made for all men; for kings, and for all that are in authority; *that we may lead a quiet and peaceable life in all godliness and honesty.* For this is good and acceptable in the sight of God our Saviour. (1 Tim. 2:1-3.)

I will therefore that men pray every where, lifting up holy hands, without wrath and doubting. (1 Tim. 2:8.)

Pray for us: for we trust we have a good conscience, in all things willing to live honestly. (Heb. 13:18.)

If any of you lack wisdom, let him ask of God, that giveth to all men liberally, and upbraideth not; *and it shall be given him.* But let him ask in faith, nothing wavering. For he that wavereth *is like a wave of the sea driven with the wind and tossed. For let not that man think that he shall receive any thing of the Lord.* (James 1:5-7; see also D&C 42:68.)

Ye ask, *and receive not,* because ye ask amiss, that ye may consume it upon your lusts. (James 4:3.)

Is any among you afflicted? let him pray. Is any merry? let him sing psalms. Is any sick among you? let him call for the elders of the church; and let them pray over him, anointing him with oil in the name of the Lord: *and the prayer of faith shall save the sick, and the Lord shall raise him up; and if he have committed sins, they shall be forgiven him.* Confess your faults one to another, and pray one for another, *that ye may be healed.* The effectual fervent prayer of a righteous man *availeth much.* (James 5:13-16.)

If ye call on the Father, who without respect of persons judgeth according to every man's work, pass the time of your sojourning here in fear. (1 Pet. 1:17.)

The end of all things is at hand: be ye therefore sober, and watch unto prayer. (1 Pet. 4:7.)

Whatsoever we ask, *we receive of him,* because we keep his commandments, and do those things that are pleasing in his sight. (1 Jn. 3:22.)

This is the confidence that we have in him, that, if we ask any thing according to his will, *he heareth us:* and if we know that he hear us, whatsoever we ask, *we know that we have the petitions that we desired of him.* (1 Jn. 5:14-15.)

If ye will not harden your hearts, and ask me in faith, believing that ye shall receive, with diligence in keeping my commandments, *surely these things shall be made known unto you.* (1 Ne. 15:11.)

I know that *God will give liberally* to him that asketh. *Yea, my God will give me,* if I ask not amiss; therefore I will lift up my voice unto thee; yea, I will cry unto thee, my God, the rock of my righteousness. Behold, my voice shall forever ascend up unto thee, my rock and mine everlasting God. (2 Ne. 4:35.)

Whoso knocketh, *to him will he open;* and the wise, and the learned, and they that are rich, who are puffed up because of their learning, and their wisdom, and their riches—yea, they are they *whom he despiseth;* and save they shall cast these things away, and consider themselves fools before God, and come down in the depths of humility, *he will not open unto them. But the things of the wise and the prudent shall be hid from them forever—yea, that happiness which is prepared for the saints.* (2 Ne. 9:42-43.)

Pray unto him continually by day, and give thanks unto his holy name by night. (2 Ne. 9:52.)

After I have spoken these words, *if ye cannot understand them* it will be because ye ask not, neither do ye knock; *wherefore, ye are not brought into the light, but must perish in the dark.* (2 Ne. 32:4.)

I say unto you that ye must pray always, and not faint; that ye must not perform any thing unto the Lord save in the first place ye shall pray unto the Father in the name of Christ, *that he will consecrate thy performance unto thee, that thy performance may be for the welfare of thy soul.* (2 Ne. 32:9.)

Look unto God with firmness of mind, and pray unto him with exceeding faith, *and he will console you in your afflictions, and he will plead your cause, and send down justice upon those who seek your destruction.* (Jacob 3:1.)

Continue in fasting and praying, and endure to the end; *and as the Lord liveth ye will be saved.* (Omni 1:26.)

I would that ye should remember, and always retain in remembrance, the greatness of God, and your own nothingness, and his goodness and long-suffering towards you, unworthy creatures, and humble yourselves even in the depths of humility, calling on the name of the Lord daily, and standing steadfastly in the faith of that which is to come, which was spoken by the mouth of the angel. And behold, I say unto you that if ye do this *ye shall always rejoice, and be filled with the love of God, and always retain a remission of your sins; and ye shall grow in the knowledge of the glory of him that created you, or in the knowledge of that which is just and true.* (Mosiah 4: 11-12.)

If God, who has created you, on whom you are dependent for your lives and for all that ye have and are, *doth grant unto you whatsoever ye ask that is right,* in faith, believing that ye shall receive, O then, how ye ought to impart of the substance that ye have one to another. (Mosiah 4:21.)

He did deliver them because they did humble themselves before him; and because they cried mightily unto him *he did deliver them out of bondage;* and thus doth the Lord work with his power in all cases among the children of men, extending the arm of mercy towards them that put their trust in him. (Mosiah 29:20.)

The children of God were commanded that they should gather themselves together oft, and join in fasting and mighty prayer in behalf of the welfare of the souls of those who knew not God. (Alma 6:6.)

[Ask] for whatsoever things ye stand in need, both spiritual and temporal; always returning thanks unto God for whatsoever things ye do receive. (Alma 7:23.)

The Lord will be merciful unto all who call on his name. (Alma 9:17.)

Humble yourselves before the Lord, and call on his holy name, and watch and pray continually, *that ye may not be tempted above that which ye can bear, and thus be led by the Holy Spirit, becoming humble, meek, submissive, patient, full of love and all long-suffering.* (Alma 13:28.)

They had given themselves to much prayer, and fasting; *therefore they had the spirit of prophecy, and the spirit of revelation, and when they taught, they taught with power and authority of God.* (Alma 17:3.)

If thou wilt bow down before God, yea, if thou wilt repent of all thy sins, and will bow down before God, and call on his name in faith, believing that ye shall receive, *then shalt thou receive the hope which thou desirest.* (Alma 22:16.)

Cry unto him for mercy; for he is mighty to save. Yea, humble yourselves, and continue in prayer unto him. Cry unto him when ye are in
your fields, yea, over all your flocks. Cry unto him in your houses, yea,
over all your household, both morning, mid-day, and evening. Yea,
cry unto him against the power of your enemies. Yea, cry unto him
against the devil, who is an enemy to all righteousness. Cry unto him
over the crops of your fields, *that ye may prosper in them.* Cry over the
flocks of your fields, *that they may increase.* But this is not all; ye must
pour out your souls in your closets, and your secret places, and in
your wilderness. Yea, and when you do not cry unto the Lord, let your
hearts be full, drawn out in prayer unto him continually for your welfare, and also for the welfare of those who are around you. (Alma
34:18-27.)

Be watchful unto prayer continually, *that ye may not be led away by
the temptations of the devil, that he may not overpower you, that ye
may not become his subjects at the last day; for behold, he rewardeth
you no good thing.* (Alma 34:39.)

Cry unto God for all thy support; yea, let all thy doings be unto the
Lord, and whithersoever thou goest let it be in the Lord; yea, let all
thy thoughts be directed unto the Lord; yea, let the affections of thy
heart be placed upon the Lord forever. Counsel with the Lord in all
thy doings, *and he will direct thee for good;* yea, when thou liest down
at night lie down unto the Lord, *that he may watch over you in your
sleep;* and when thou risest in the morning let thy heart be full of
thanks unto God; and if ye do these things, *ye shall be lifted up at the
last day.* (Alma 37:36-37.)

Do not pray as the Zoramites do, for ye have seen that they pray to be
heard of men, and to be praised for their wisdom. (Alma 38:13.)

The Lord is merciful unto all who will, in the sincerity of their hearts,
call upon his holy name. (Hel. 3:27.)

[Aminadab to Nephites] Ye must repent, and cry unto the voice, even
until ye shall have faith in Christ, who was taught unto you by Alma,
and Amulek, and Zeezrom; and when ye shall do this, *the cloud of
darkness shall be removed from overshadowing you.* (Hel. 5:41.)

[Jesus to Nephites] Go ye unto your homes, and ponder upon the
things which I have said, and ask of the Father, in my name, that ye

may understand, and prepare your minds for the morrow, and I come unto you again. (3 Ne. 17:3.)

Ye must watch and pray always, *lest ye be tempted by the devil, and ye be led away captive by him.* And as I have prayed among you even so shall ye pray in my church, among my people who do repent and are baptized in my name. Behold I am the light; I have set an example for you. (3 Ne. 18:15-16.)

Ye must watch and pray always *lest ye enter into temptation; for Satan desireth to have you, that he may sift you as wheat.* Therefore ye must always pray unto the Father in my name. And whatsoever ye shall ask the Father in my name, which is right, believing that ye shall receive, *behold it shall be given unto you.* Pray in your families unto the Father, always in my name, *that your wives and your children may be blessed.* And behold, ye shall meet together oft; and ye shall not forbid any man from coming unto you when ye shall meet together, but suffer them that they may come unto you and forbid them not; but ye shall pray for them, and shall not cast them out; and if it so be that they come unto you oft ye shall pray for them unto the Father, in my name. (3 Ne. 18:18-23.)

Jesus said unto them: Pray on; nevertheless they did not cease to pray. (3 Ne. 19:26.)

He commanded [the multitude] that they should not cease to pray in their hearts. (3 Ne. 20:1.)

Whatsoever ye shall do, ye shall do it in my name; therefore ye shall call the church in my name; and ye shall call upon the Father in my name *that he will bless the church for my sake.* (3 Ne. 27:7.)

Whatsoever things ye shall ask the Father in my name *shall be given unto you.* (3 Ne. 27:28.)

Ask the Father in the name of Jesus for what things soever ye shall stand in need. Doubt not, but be believing, and begin as in times of old, and come unto the Lord with all your heart, and work out your own salvation with fear and trembling before him. . . . Ask not, that ye may consume it on your lusts, but ask with a firmness unshaken, that ye will yield to no temptation, but that ye will serve the true and living God. (Morm. 9:27-28.)

O Lord, thou hast given us a commandment that we must call upon thee, *that from thee we may receive according to our desires.* (Ether 3:2.)

When ye shall call upon the Father in my name, with a broken heart and a contrite spirit, *then shall ye know that the Father hath remembered the covenant which he made unto your fathers, O house of Israel.* (Ether 4:15.)

Whatsoever thing ye shall ask the Father in my name, which is good, in faith believing that ye shall receive, *behold, it shall be done unto you.* (Moro. 7:26.)

Pray unto the Father with all the energy of heart, *that ye may be filled with this love, which he hath bestowed upon all who are true followers of his Son, Jesus Christ; that ye may become the sons of God; that when he shall appear we shall be like him, for we shall see him as he is; that we may have this hope; that we may be purified even as he is pure.* (Moro. 7:48.)

Pray for them [the Nephites], my son, that repentance may come unto them. (Moro. 8:28.)

When ye shall receive these things, I would exhort you that ye would ask God, the Eternal Father, in the name of Christ, if these things are not true; and if ye shall ask with a sincere heart, with real intent, having faith in Christ, *he will manifest the truth of it unto you, by the power of the Holy Ghost. And by the power of the Holy Ghost ye may know the truth of all things.* (Moro. 10:4-5.)

Blessed art thou [Oliver Cowdery] for what thou hast done; for thou hast inquired of me, and behold, as often as thou hast inquired *thou hast received instruction of my Spirit. If it had not been so, thou wouldst not have come to the place where thou art at this time.* (D&C 6:14.)

[to Oliver Cowdery] Remember that without faith you can do nothing; therefore ask in faith. Trifle not with these things; do not ask for that which you ought not. Ask that you may know the mysteries of God, and that you may translate and receive knowledge from all those ancient records which have been hid up, that are sacred; and according to your faith *shall it be done unto you.* (D&C 8:10-11.)

You have not understood; you have supposed that I would give it unto you, when you took no thought save it was to ask me. But, behold, I say unto you, that you must study it out in your mind; then you must ask me if it be right, *and if it is right I will cause that your bosom shall burn within you; therefore, you shall feel that it is right. But if it be not right you shall have no such feelings, but you shall have a stupor of thought that shall cause you to forget the thing which is wrong.* (D&C 9:7-9.)

Pray always, *that you may come off conqueror; yea, that you may conquer Satan, and that you may escape the hands of the servants of Satan that do uphold his work.* (D&C 10:5.)

Appeal unto my Spirit. (D&C 11:18.)

It shall come to pass, that if you shall ask the Father in my name, in faith believing, *you shall receive the Holy Ghost, which giveth utterance, that you may stand as a witness of the things of which you shall both hear and see, and also that you may declare repentance unto this generation.* (D&C 14:8.)

Ask the Father in my name, in faith believing that you shall receive, *and you shall have the Holy Ghost, which manifesteth all things which are expedient unto the children of men.* (D&C 18:18.)

I command thee that thou shalt pray vocally as well as in thy heart; yea, before the world as well as in secret, in public as well as in private. (D&C 19:28.)

Pray always, *and I will pour out my Spirit upon you, and great shall be your blessing—yea, even more than if you should obtain treasures of earth and corruptibleness to the extent thereof.* (D&C 19:38.)

Let the church take heed and pray always, *lest they fall into temptation;* yea, and even let those who are sanctified take heed also. (D&C 20:33-34.)

You must take up your cross, in the which you must pray vocally before the world as well as in secret, and in your family, and among your friends, and in all places. (D&C 23:6.)

[to Joseph Smith] Thou shalt continue in calling upon God in my name, and writing the things which shall be given thee by the Comforter, and expounding all scriptures unto the church. (D&C 24:5.)

My soul delighteth in the song of the heart; yea, the song of the righteous is a prayer unto me, *and it shall be answered with a blessing upon their heads.* (D&C 25:12.)

Take the helmet of salvation, and the sword of my Spirit, which I will pour out upon you, and my word which I reveal unto you, and be agreed as touching all things whatsoever ye ask of me, and be faithful until I come, *and ye shall be caught up, that where I am ye shall be also.* (D&C 27:18.)

All things must be done in order, and by common consent in the church, by the prayer of faith. (D&C 28:13.)

Whatsoever ye shall ask in faith, being united in prayer according to my command, *ye shall receive.* (D&C 29:6.)

It is given unto you that ye may understand, because ye have asked it of me and are agreed. (D&C 29:33.)

Be you [Peter Whitmer] afflicted in all his [Oliver Cowdery's] afflictions, ever lifting up your heart unto me in prayer and faith, for his and your deliverance. (D&C 30:6.)

Pray always, *lest you enter into temptation and lose your reward.* (D&C 31:12.)

They shall pray always *that I may unfold the same [that which is written] to their understanding.* (D&C 32:4.)

Be faithful, praying always, having your lamps trimmed and burning, and oil with you, *that you may be ready at the coming of the Bridegroom.* (D&C 33:17.)

Whoso shall ask it in my name in faith, *they shall cast out devils; they shall heal the sick; they shall cause the blind to receive their sight, and the deaf to hear, and the dumb to speak, and the lame to walk.* (D&C 35:9.)

Arise and be baptized, and wash away your sins, calling on my name, *and you shall receive my Spirit, and a blessing so great as you never have known.* (D&C 39:10.)

By the prayer of your faith *ye shall receive my law, that ye may know how to govern my church and have all things right before me.* (D&C 41:3.)

As ye have assembled yourselves together according to the commandment wherewith I commanded you, and are agreed as touching this one thing, and have asked the Father in my name, *even so ye shall receive.* (D&C 42:3.)

The Spirit shall be given unto you by the prayer of faith; and if ye receive not the Spirit ye shall not teach. (D&C 42:14.)

If thou shalt ask, *thou shalt receive revelation upon revelation, knowledge upon knowledge, that thou mayest know the mysteries and peaceable things—that which bringeth joy, that which bringeth life eternal.* (D&C 42:61.)

He that lacketh wisdom, let him ask of me, *and I will give him liberally and upbraid him not.* (D&C 42:68; see also James 1:5-7.)

Ye are commanded in all things to ask of God, who giveth liberally; and that which the Spirit testifies unto you even so I would that ye should do in all holiness of heart, walking uprightly before me, considering the end of your salvation, doing all things with prayer and thanksgiving, *that ye may not be seduced by evil spirits, or doctrines of devils, or the commandments of men; for some are of men, and others of devils.* (D&C 46:7.)

He that asketh in Spirit *shall receive in Spirit.* (D&C 46:28.)

He that asketh in the Spirit asketh according to the will of God; *wherefore it is done even as he asketh.* (D&C 46:30.)

If ye are purified and cleansed from all sin, ye shall ask whatsoever you will in the name of Jesus and *it shall be done*. But know this, *it shall be given you what you shall ask; and as ye are appointed to the head, the spirits shall be subject unto you.* (D&C 50:29-30.)

He that prayeth, whose spirit is contrite, *the same is accepted of me* if he obey mine ordinances. (D&C 52:15.)

Pray always *that you enter not into temptation, that you may abide the day of his coming, whether in life or in death.* (D&C 61:39.)

Ye receive the Spirit through prayer. (D&C 63:64.)

Pray unto the Lord, call upon his holy name, make known his wonderful works among the people. Call upon the Lord *that his kingdom may go forth upon the earth, that the inhabitants thereof may receive it, and be prepared for the days to come, in the which the Son of Man shall come down in heaven, clothed in the brightness of his glory, to meet the kingdom of God which is set up on the earth.* (D&C 65:4-5.)

They shall also teach their children to pray, and to walk uprightly before the Lord. (D&C 68:28.)

A commandment I give unto them—that he that observeth not his prayers before the Lord in the season thereof, *let him be had in remembrance before the judge of my people.* (D&C 68:33.)

[to missionaries] Proclaim the things which I have commanded them—calling on the name of the Lord for the Comforter, *which shall teach them all things that are expedient for them*— praying always that they faint not; and inasmuch as they do this, *I will be with them even unto the end.* (D&C 75:9-11.)

Let them ask *and they shall receive,* knock *and it shall be opened unto them, and be made known from on high, even by the Comforter, whither they shall go.* (D&C 75:27.)

I will forgive you of your sins with this commandment—that you remain steadfast in your minds in solemnity and the spirit of prayer, in bearing testimony to all the world of those things which are communicated unto you. (D&C 84:61.)

Ye shall call upon me while I am near—draw near unto me *and I will draw near unto you;* seek me diligently *and ye shall find me;* ask; *and ye shall receive;* knock, *and it shall be opened unto you.* Whatsoever ye ask the Father in my name *it shall be given unto you, that is expedient for you;* and if ye ask anything that is not expedient for you, *it shall turn unto your condemnation.* (D&C 88:62-65.)

Let those whom they have warned in their traveling call on the Lord, and ponder the warning in their hearts which they have received, for a little season. (D&C 88:71.)

I give unto you a commandment that ye shall continue in prayer and fasting from this time forth. (D&C 88:76.)

Establish a house, even a house of prayer. (D&C 88:119; similar scripture, D&C 109:8.)

Pray always, *that ye may not faint, until I come.* (D&C 88:126.)

Search diligently, pray always, and be believing, *and all things shall work together for your good,* if ye walk uprightly and remember the covenant wherewith ye have covenanted one with another. (D&C 90:24.)

It shall come to pass that every soul who forsaketh his sins and cometh unto me, and calleth on my name, and obeyeth my voice, and keepeth my commandments, *shall see my face and know that I am.* (D&C 93:1.)

Pray always *lest that wicked one have power in you, and remove you out of your place.* (D&C 93:49.)

Fear not, let your hearts be comforted; yea, rejoice evermore, and in everything give thanks; waiting patiently on the Lord, for your prayers have entered into the ears of the Lord of Sabaoth, and are recorded with this seal and testament—*the Lord hath sworn and decreed that they shall be granted. Therefore, he giveth this promise unto you, with an immutable covenant that they shall be fulfilled; and all things wherewith you have been afflicted shall work together for your good, and to my name's glory, saith the Lord.* (D&C 98:1-3.)

All that call upon the name of the Lord, and keep his commandments, *shall be saved.* (D&C 100:17.)

In that day [the Millennium] whatsoever any man shall ask, *it shall be given unto him.* (D&C 101:27.)

Men ought always to pray and not to faint. (D&C 101:81.)

Pray ye, therefore, that their ears may be opened unto your cries, that I may be merciful unto them, that these things may not come upon them. (D&C 101:92.)

Behold this is my will; ask *and ye shall receive;* but men do not always do my will. (D&C 103:31.)

All victory and glory is brought to pass unto you through your diligence, faithfulness, and prayers of faith. (D&C 103:36.)

It is my will that you shall humble yourselves before me, and *obtain this blessing* [paying of debts] by your diligence and humility and the prayer of faith. And inasmuch as you are diligent and humble, and exercise the prayer of faith, *behold, I will soften the hearts of those to whom you are in debt, until I shall send means unto you for your deliverance.* (D&C 104:79-80.)

Inasmuch as ye are humble and faithful and call upon my name, behold, *I will give you the victory.* (D&C 104:82.)

Let all my people who dwell in the regions round about be very faithful, and prayerful, and humble before me, and reveal not the things which I have revealed unto them, until it is wisdom in me that they should be revealed. (D&C 105:23.)

Strengthen your brethren in all your conversation, in all your prayers, in all your exhortations, and in all your doings. (D&C 108:7.)

Be thou humble; *and the Lord thy God shall lead thee by the hand, and give thee answer to thy prayers.* (D&C 112:10.)

[to Thomas B. Marsh] Pray for thy brethren of the Twelve. (D&C 112:12.)

Let every man call upon the name of the Lord. (D&C 133:6.)

If thou art sorrowful, call on the Lord thy God with supplication, *that your souls may be joyful.* (D&C 136:29.)

Thou shalt do all that thou doest in the name of the Son, and thou shalt repent and call upon God in the name of the Son forevermore. (Moses 5:8.)

Preparedness

The Lord tells us in scripture and through living prophets what events are to come. He admonishes us to be prepared for them. He also tells us how to prepare: by seeking truth, righteousness, peace, faith, salvation, the Spirit; and with prayer, watchfulness, and supplication. (Eph. 6:13-18.)

The ten virgins spoken of in parable by Christ were all righteous, yet only five were prepared when the bridegroom came. (See Matt. 25:1-13.) As they were warned, so have we been warned. Our knowledge of the future need not give us fear. Instead, it can give us confidence—if we prepare.

Commandments and Promises

Draw thee waters for the siege, fortify thy strong holds. (Nahum 3:14.)

Watch therefore, for ye know neither the day nor the hour wherein the Son of man cometh. (Matt. 25:13.)

Let your loins be girded about, and your lights burning. (Luke 12:35.)

Be ye therefore ready also: for the Son of man cometh at an hour when ye think not. (Luke 12:40.)

Take heed to yourselves, *lest at any time your hearts be overcharged with surfeiting, and drunkenness, and cares of this life, and so that day come upon you unawares.* (Luke 21:34.)

Wherefore take unto you the whole armour of God, *that ye may be able to withstand in the evil day, and having done all, to stand.* Stand therefore, having your loins girt about with truth, and having on the breastplate of righteousness; and your feet shod with the preparation of the gospel of peace; above all, taking the shield of faith, *wherewith ye shall be able to quench all the fiery darts of the wicked.* And take the helmet of salvation, and the sword of the Spirit, which is the word of

God: praying always with all prayer and supplication in the Spirit, and watching thereunto with all perseverance and supplication for all saints. (Eph. 6:13-18; see also D&C 27:15-18.)

Gird up the loins of your mind, be sober. (1 Pet. 1:13.)

Prepare your souls for that glorious day when justice shall be administered unto the righteous, even the day of judgment, *that ye may not shrink with awful fear; that ye may not remember your awful guilt in perfectness.* (2 Ne. 9:46.)

Are ye stripped of pride? I say unto you, if ye are not ye are not prepared to meet God. Behold ye must prepare quickly; for the kingdom of heaven is soon at hand, *and such an one hath not eternal life.* Behold, I say, is there one among you who is not stripped of envy? I say unto you that such an one is not prepared; and I would that he should prepare quickly, for the hour is close at hand, and he knoweth not when the time shall come; *for such an one is not found guiltless.* (Alma 5:28-29.)

This life is the time for men to prepare to meet God; yea, behold the day of this life is the day for men to perform their labors. (Alma 34:32.)

Prepare ye, prepare ye for that which is to come, for the Lord is nigh. (D&C 1:12.)

Lift up your hearts and rejoice, and gird up your loins, and take upon you my whole armor, *that ye may be able to withstand the evil day, having done all, that ye may be able to stand.* Stand, therefore, having your loins girt about with truth, having on the breastplate of righteousness, and your feet shod with the preparation of the gospel of peace, which I have sent mine angels to commit unto you; taking the shield of faith *wherewith ye shall be able to quench all the fiery darts of the wicked;* and take the helmet of salvation, and the sword of my Spirit, which I will pour out upon you, and my word which I reveal unto you, and be agreed as touching all things whatsoever ye ask of me, and be faithful until I come, *and ye shall be caught up, that where I am ye shall be also.* (D&C 27:15-18; see also Eph. 6:13-18.)

The decree hath gone forth from the Father that they shall be gathered in unto one place upon the face of this land, to prepare their hearts and be prepared in all things against the day when tribulation and desolation are sent forth upon the wicked. (D&C 29:8.)

Be faithful, praying always, having your lamps trimmed and burning, and oil with you, *that you may be ready at the coming of the Bridegroom.* (D&C 33:17.)

Gird up your loins *and I will suddenly come to my temple.* (D&C 36:8.)

Gird up your loins and be prepared. *Behold, the kingdom is yours, and the enemy shall not overcome.* (D&C 38:9.)

If ye are prepared *ye shall not fear.* (D&C 38:30.)

Gird up your loins *lest ye be found among the wicked.* Lift up your voices and spare not. Call upon the nations to repent, both old and young, both bond and free, saying: Prepare yourselves for the great day of the Lord. (D&C 43:19-20.)

Be prepared for the days to come, in the which the Son of Man shall come down in heaven, clothed in the brightness of his glory, to meet the kingdom of God which is set up on the earth. (D&C 65:5.)

Gird up your loins and be sober. (D&C 73:6.)

Gird up your loins and be faithful, *and ye shall overcome all things, and be lifted up at the last day.* (D&C 75:22.)

A commandment I give unto you, to prepare and organize yourselves by a bond of everlasting covenant that cannot be broken. (D&C 78:11.)

With the sword and by bloodshed the inhabitants of the earth shall mourn; and with famine, and plague, and earthquake, and the thunder of heaven, and the fierce and vivid lightning also, shall the inhabitants of the earth be made to feel the wrath, and indignation, and chastening hand of an Almighty God, until the consumption decreed hath made a full end of all nations; that the cry of the saints, and of the blood of the saints, shall cease to come up into the ears of the Lord of Sabaoth, from the earth, to be avenged of their enemies. Wherefore, stand ye in holy places, and be not moved, until the day of the Lord come; for behold, it cometh quickly, saith the Lord. (D&C 87:6-8.)

Assemble yourselves together, and organize yourselves, and prepare yourselves, and sanctify yourselves; yea, purify your hearts, and cleanse your hands and your feet before me, *that I may make you clean; that I may testify unto your Father, and your God, and my God, that you are clean from the blood of this wicked generation; that I may fulfil this promise, this great and last promise, which I have made unto you, when I will.* (D&C 88:74-75.)

Tarry ye, and labor diligently, that ye may be perfected in your ministry to go forth among the Gentiles for the last time, as many as the mouth of the Lord shall name, to bind up the law and seal up the testimony, and to prepare the saints for the hour of judgment which is to come; *that their souls may escape the wrath of God, the desolation of abomination which awaits the wicked, both in this world and in the world to come.* (D&C 88: 84-85.)

Organize yourselves; prepare every needful thing. (D&C 88:119; similar scripture, D&C 109:8.)

It is my will, that all they who call on my name, and worship me according to mine everlasting gospel, should gather together, and stand in holy places; and prepare for the revelation which is to come, when the veil of the covering of my temple, in my tabernacle, which hideth the earth, shall be taken off, and all flesh shall see me together. (D&C 101:22-23.)

The coming of the Lord draweth nigh, and it overtaketh the world as a thief in the night—therefore, gird up your loins, *that you may be the children of light, and that day shall not overtake you as a thief.* (D&C 106:4-5.)

Gird up thy loins for the work. Let thy feet be shod also, for thou art chosen, and thy path lieth among the mountains, and among many nations. (D&C 112:7.)

Arise and gird up your loins, take up your cross, follow me, and feed my sheep. (D&C 112:14.)

Prepare thy heart to receive and obey the instructions which I am about to give unto you; for all those who have this law revealed unto them must obey the same. (D&C 132:3.)

Prepare ye, prepare ye, O my people; sanctify yourselves. (D&C 133:4.)

Yea, let the cry go forth among all people: Awake and arise and go forth to meet the Bridegroom; behold and lo, the Bridegroom cometh; go ye out to meet him. Prepare yourselves for the great day of the Lord. Watch, therefore, for ye know neither the day nor the hour. (D&C 133:10-11.)

Let not your flight be in haste, but let all things be prepared before you; and he that goeth, let him not look back *lest sudden destruction shall come upon him.* (D&C 133:15.)

Know this, if the good man of the house had known in what watch the thief would come, he would have watched, and would not have suffered his house to have been broken up, but would have been ready. Therefore be ye also ready, for in such an hour as ye think not, the Son of Man cometh. Who, then, is a faithful and wise servant, whom his lord hath made ruler over his household, to give them meat in due season? Blessed is that servant whom his lord, when he cometh, shall find so doing; and verily I say unto you, *he shall make him ruler over all his goods.* But if that evil servant shall say in his heart: My lord delayeth his coming, and shall begin to smite his fellow-servants, and to eat and drink with the drunken, *the lord of that servant shall come in a day when he looketh not for him, and in an hour that he is not aware of, and shall cut him asunder, and shall appoint him his portion with the hypocrites; there shall be weeping and gnashing of teeth.* (JS-M 1:47-54; similar scripture, Matt. 24:43-51.)

Purity

(See also Holiness; Purity and Singleness of Heart; Repentance; and Sanctification.)

Purity refers not only to a lack of obvious sins, but also to an absence of impure elements throughout. If we are pure, we are free of the pollutants of sin; we have not mixed into our souls the contaminants of wickedness.

The Lord instructs us to flee evil, to "touch no unclean thing" (Isa. 52:11), to strive for holiness, to repent, to be obedient and righteous, to seek sanctification—all reinforcing the symbol of purity. "Let us cleanse ourselves from all filthiness of the flesh and spirit," Paul wrote. (2 Cor. 7:1.) This purity covers the entirety of our behavior. If we are pure, we will be whole, undivided, and clean. We will do nothing to defile the body or spirit, because our spiritual well-being, our blessings, and our integrity depend on that purity.

Commandments and Promises

The righteous also shall hold on his way, and he that hath clean hands *shall be stronger and stronger.* (Job 17:9.)

Wherewithal shall a young man cleanse his way? by taking heed thereto according to thy word. (Ps. 119:9.)

Let thy garments be always white; and let thy head lack no ointment. (Eccl. 9:8.)

Wash you, make you clean; put away the evil of your doings from before mine eyes; cease to do evil. (Isa. 1:16.)

An highway shall be there, and a way, and it shall be called The way of holiness; the unclean *shall not pass over it;* but it shall be for those: *the wayfaring men, though fools, shall not err therein.* (Isa. 35:8.)

Depart ye, depart ye, go ye out from thence, touch no unclean thing; go ye out of the midst of her; be ye clean, that bear the vessels of the Lord. (Isa. 52:11; similar scripture, 3 Ne. 20:41; see also D&C 38:42.)

Thou blind Pharisee, cleanse first that which is within the cup and platter, *that the outside of them may be clean also.* (Matt. 23:26; similar scripture, Luke 11:39; see also Alma 60:23.)

In all things approving ourselves as the ministers of God . . . by pureness. (2 Cor. 6:4-6.)

Having therefore these promises, dearly beloved, let us cleanse ourselves from all filthiness of the flesh and spirit, perfecting holiness in the fear of God. (2 Cor. 7:1.)

Fornication, and all uncleanness, or covetousness, let it not be once named among you, as becometh saints; neither filthiness, nor foolish talking, nor jesting, which are not convenient: but rather giving of thanks. For this ye know, that no whoremonger, nor unclean person, nor covetous man, who is an idolater, *hath any inheritance in the kingdom of Christ and of God.* (Eph. 5:3-5.)

Whatsoever things are pure, . . . think on these things. (Philip. 4:8.)

Rebuke not an elder, but intreat him as a father; and the younger men as brethren; the elder women as mothers; the younger as sisters, with all purity. (1 Tim. 5:1-2.)

Neither be partaker of other men's sins: keep thyself pure. (1 Tim. 5:22.)

If a man therefore purge himself from these, *he shall be a vessel unto honour, sanctified, and meet for the master's use, and prepared unto every good work.* (2 Tim. 2:21.)

Unto the pure *all things are pure:* but unto them that are defiled and unbelieving *is nothing pure; but even their mind and conscience is defiled.* (Titus 1:15; see JST Titus 1:15.)

Now are we the sons of God, and it doth not yet appear what we shall be: but we know that, when he shall appear, we shall be like him; for we shall see him as he is. And every man that hath this hope in him *purifieth himself, even as he is pure.* (1 Jn. 3:2-3.)

Because thou sayest, I am rich, and increased with goods, and have need of nothing; and knowest not that thou art wretched, and miserable, and poor, and blind, and naked: I counsel thee to buy of me gold tried in the fire, *that thou mayest be rich;* and white raiment, *that thou mayest be clothed, and that the shame of thy nakedness do not appear;* and anoint thine eyes with eyesalve, *that thou mayest see.* (Rev. 3:17-18.)

The kingdom of God is not filthy, and *there cannot any unclean thing enter into the kingdom of God;* wherefore there must needs be a place of filthiness prepared for that which is filthy. (1 Ne. 15:34.)

There can no man be saved except his garments are washed white; yea, his garments must be purified until they are cleansed from all stain, through the blood of him of whom it has been spoken by our fathers, who should come to redeem his people from their sins. (Alma 5:21.)

An awful death cometh upon the wicked; *for they die as to things pertaining to things of righteousness;* for they are unclean, *and no unclean thing can inherit the kingdom of God; but they are cast out, and consigned to partake of the fruits of their labors or their works,* which have been evil; *and they drink the dregs of a bitter cup.* (Alma 40:26.)

God has said that the inward vessel shall be cleansed first, *and then shall the outer vessel be cleaned also.* (Alma 60:23; see also Matt. 23:26.)

There was not any man who could do a miracle in the name of Jesus save he were cleansed every whit from his iniquity. (3 Ne. 8:1.)

No unclean thing *can enter into his kingdom; therefore nothing entereth into his rest* save it be those who have washed their garments in my blood, because of their faith, and the repentance of all their sins, and their faithfulness unto the end. (3 Ne. 27:19.)

Be wise in the days of your probation; strip yourselves of all uncleanness. (Morm. 9:28.)

The Lord said unto me: *They shall not go forth unto the Gentiles* until the day that they shall repent of their iniquity, and become clean before the Lord. (Ether 4:6.)

Again I would exhort you that ye would come unto Christ, and lay hold upon every good gift, and touch not the evil gift, nor the unclean thing. (Moro. 10:30.)

He that is not purified *shall not abide the day.* (D&C 38:8.)

Go ye out from among the wicked. Save yourselves. Be ye clean that bear the vessels of the Lord. (D&C 38:42; see also Isa. 52:11.)

Let all things be done in cleanliness before me. (D&C 42:41.)

Purge ye out the iniquity which is among you. (D&C 43:11.)

No man is possessor of all things except he be purified and cleansed from all sin. And if ye are purified and cleansed from all sin, *ye shall ask whatsoever you will in the name of Jesus and it shall be done. But know this, it shall be given you what you shall ask; and as ye are appointed to the head, the spirits shall be subject unto you.* (D&C 50: 28-30.)

Great and marvelous are the works of the Lord, and the mysteries of his kingdom . . . for they are only to be seen and understood by the power of the Holy Spirit, which God bestows on those who love him, and purify themselves before him; *to whom he grants this privilege of seeing and knowing for themselves; that through the power and manifestation of the Spirit, while in the flesh, they may be able to bear his presence in the world of glory.* (D&C 76:114-118.)

Entangle not yourselves in sin, but let your hands be clean, until the Lord comes. (D&C 88:86.)

Cease to be unclean. (D&C 88:124.)

Set in order your houses; keep slothfulness and uncleanness far from you. (D&C 90:18.)

When our bodies are purified *we shall see that it [spirit] is all matter.* (D&C 131:8.)

No unclean thing *can dwell there, or dwell in his presence.* (Moses 6:57.)

Purity and Singleness of Heart

(See also Living God; Meditation and Purity of Thought; Purity.)

A spiritually pure heart is crucial to our salvation just as a physically beating heart is necessary to life. The Lord specifies that our hearts must be pure and our desires singly directed toward his standards: "Let your heart therefore be perfect with the Lord our God, to walk in his statutes, and to keep his commandments." (1 Kgs. 8:61.)

The Lord also explains the consequences of an impure heart: "Those things which proceed out of the mouth come forth from the heart; and they defile the man. For out of the heart proceed evil thoughts, murders, adulteries, fornications, thefts, false witness, blasphemies: these are the things which defile a man." (Matt. 15: 18-20.)

As Christ compares ritual impurities with impurity of heart, he indicates why purity and singleness of heart are so frequently commanded. To purify the heart is to strike at the roots of evil. To make the heart single to God's purposes and glory is to direct the soul's entire efforts toward the kingdom of heaven.

Commandments and Promises

Let your heart therefore be perfect with the Lord our God, to walk in his statutes, and to keep his commandments, as at this day. (1 Kgs. 8:61.)

Thou, Solomon my son, know thou the God of thy father, and serve him with a perfect heart and with a willing mind: for the Lord searcheth all hearts, and understandeth all the imaginations of the thoughts: if thou seek him, *he will be found of thee;* but if thou forsake him, *he will cast thee off for ever.* (1 Chr. 28:9.)

The eyes of the Lord run to and fro throughout the whole earth, *to shew himself strong in the behalf of them* whose heart is perfect toward him. (2 Chr. 16:9.)

He charged them, saying, Thus shall ye do in the fear of the Lord, faithfully, and with a perfect heart. (2 Chr. 19:9.)

412

Who shall ascend into the hill of the Lord? or who shall stand in his holy place? He that hath clean hands and a pure heart; . . . *He shall receive the blessing from the Lord, and righteousness from the God of his salvation.* (Ps. 24:3-5.)

Truly God is good to Israel, even to such as are of a clean heart. (Ps. 73:1.)

These . . . things doth the Lord hate: . . . a lying tongue, . . . an heart that deviseth wicked imaginations. (Prov. 6:16-18.)

Forasmuch as this people draw near me with their mouth, and with their lips do honour me, but have removed their heart far from me, and their fear toward me is taught by the precept of men: *therefore, behold, I will proceed to do a marvellous work among this people, even a marvellous work and a wonder: for the wisdom of their wise men shall perish, and the understanding of their prudent men shall be hid.* (Isa. 29:13-14; similar scripture, 2 Ne. 27:25-26.)

Therefore also now, saith the Lord, turn ye even to me with all your heart, and with fasting, and with weeping, and with mourning. (Joel 2:12.)

Blessed are the pure in heart: *for they shall see God.* (Matt. 5:8; similar scripture, 3 Ne. 12:8.)

Whosoever looketh on a woman to lust after her hath committed adultery with her already in his heart. (Matt. 5:28; similar scripture, 3 Ne. 12:28.)

The light of the body is the eye: if therefore thine eye be single, *thy whole body shall be full of light.* But if thine eye be evil, *thy whole body shall be full of darkness.* (Matt. 6:22-23; similar scriptures, Luke 11:34, 3 Ne. 13:22-23; see also JST Matt. 6:22.)

A good man out of the good treasure of the heart *bringeth forth good things:* and an evil man out of the evil treasure *bringeth forth evil things.* (Matt. 12:35; similar scripture, Luke 6:45.)

Those things which proceed out of the mouth come forth from the heart; *and they defile the man.* For out of the heart proceed evil thoughts, murders, adulteries, fornications, thefts, false witness, blasphemies: *these are the things which defile a man.* (Matt. 15: 18-19.)

God also gave them up to uncleanness through the lusts of their own hearts, to dishonour their own bodies between themselves. (Rom. 1:24.)

Whether therefore ye eat, or drink, or whatsoever ye do, do all to the glory of God. (1 Cor. 10:31.)

Servants, obey in all things your masters according to the flesh; not with eyeservice, as menpleasers; but in singleness of heart, fearing God: and whatsoever ye do, do it heartily, as to the Lord, and not unto men; *knowing that of the Lord ye shall receive the reward of the inheritance:* for ye serve the Lord Christ. (Col. 3:22-24.)

The end of the commandment is charity out of a pure heart, and of good conscience, and of faith unfeigned. (1 Tim. 1:5.)

Let us draw near with a true heart in full assurance of faith, having our hearts sprinkled from an evil conscience, and our bodies washed with pure water. (Heb. 10:22.)

Purify your hearts, ye double minded. (James 4:8.)

Seeing ye have purified your souls in obeying the truth through the Spirit unto unfeigned love of the brethren, see that ye love one another with a pure heart fervently: being born again, not of corruptible seed, but of incorruptible, by the word of God, which liveth and abideth for ever. (1 Pet. 1:22-23.)

Whose adorning let it not be that outward adorning of plaiting the hair, and of wearing of gold, or of putting on apparel; but let it be the hidden man of the heart, in that which is not corruptible, even the ornament of a meek and quiet spirit, *which is in the sight of God of great price.* For after this manner in the old time the holy women also, who trusted in God, adorned themselves, being in subjection unto their own husbands. (1 Pet. 3:3-5.)

Sanctify the Lord God in your hearts: and be ready always to give an answer to every man that asketh you a reason of the hope that is in you with meekness and fear. (1 Pet. 3:15.)

Wo unto the uncircumcised of heart, *for a knowledge of their iniquities shall smite them at the last day.* (2 Ne. 9:33.)

If ye shall follow the Son, with full purpose of heart, acting no hypocrisy and no deception before God, but with real intent, repenting of your sins, witnessing unto the Father that ye are willing to take upon you the name of Christ, by baptism—yea, by following your Lord and your Savior down into the water, according to his word, behold, *then shall ye receive the Holy Ghost; yea, then cometh the baptism of fire and of the Holy Ghost; and then can ye speak with the tongue of angels, and shout praises unto the Holy One of Israel.* (2 Ne. 31:13.)

[to Nephites] *Wo, wo,* unto you that are not pure in heart, that are filthy this day before God; for except ye repent *the land is cursed for your sakes; and the Lamanites,* which are not filthy like unto you, *nevertheless they are cursed with a sore cursing, shall scourge you even unto destruction.* (Jacob 3:3.)

I beseech of you in words of soberness that ye would repent, and come with full purpose of heart, and cleave unto God as he cleaveth unto you. (Jacob 6:5.)

[to Limhi's people] If ye will turn to the Lord with full purpose of heart, and put your trust in him, and serve him with all diligence of mind, if ye do this, *he will, according to his own will and pleasure, deliver you out of bondage.* (Mosiah 7:33.)

Let all thy doings be unto the Lord, and whithersoever thou goest let it be in the Lord. (Alma 37:36.)

[to Corianton] I command you, my son, in the fear of God, that ye refrain from your iniquities; that ye turn to the Lord with all your mind, might, and strength; that ye lead away the hearts of no more to do wickedly; but rather return unto them, and acknowledge your faults and that wrong which ye have done. (Alma 39:12-13.)

O ye house of Israel whom I have spared, *how oft will I gather you as a hen gathereth her chickens under her wings,* if ye will repent and return unto me with full purpose of heart. (3 Ne. 10:6.)

If ye shall come unto me, or shall desire to come unto me, and rememberest that thy brother hath aught against thee—go thy way unto thy brother, and first be reconciled to thy brother, and then come unto me with full purpose of heart, *and I will receive you.* (3 Ne. 12:23-24.)

I give unto you a commandment, that ye suffer none of these things to enter into your heart; for it is better that ye should deny yourselves of these things, wherein ye will take up your cross, *than that ye should be cast into hell.* (3 Ne. 12:29-30.)

Doubt not, but be believing, and begin as in times of old, and come unto the Lord with all your heart. (Morm. 9:27.)

O ye that embark in the service of God, see that ye serve him with all your heart, might, mind and strength, *that ye may stand blameless before God at the last day.* (D&C 4:2.)

Look unto me in every thought. (D&C 6:36.)

This is your work, to keep my commandments, yea, with all your might, mind and strength. (D&C 11:20.)

If they desire to take upon them my name with full purpose of heart, *they are called to go into all the world to preach my gospel unto every creature.* (D&C 18:28.)

It mattereth not what ye shall eat or what ye shall drink when ye partake of the sacrament, if it so be that ye do it with an eye single to my glory—remembering unto the Father my body which was laid down for you, and my blood which was shed for the remission of your sins. (D&C 27:2.)

This commandment shall be given unto the elders of my church, that every man which will embrace it with singleness of heart *may be ordained and sent forth, even as I have spoken.* (D&C 36:7.)

Thus saith the Lord unto you, my servant William [W. Phelps], yea, even the Lord of the whole earth, thou art called and chosen; and after thou hast been baptized by water, which if you do with an eye single to my glory, *you shall have a remission of your sins and a reception of the Holy Spirit by the laying on of hands.* (D&C 55:1.)

If he [Edward Partridge] repent not of his sins, which are unbelief and blindness of heart, let him take heed *lest he fall.* (D&C 58:15.)

They sought evil in their hearts, *and I, the Lord, withheld my Spirit.* (D&C 64:16.)

I, the Lord, require the hearts of the children of men. (D&C 64:22.)

The Lord requireth the heart and a willing mind; and the willing and obedient *shall eat the good of the land of Zion in these last days.* (D&C 64:34.)

If your eye be single to my glory, *your whole bodies shall be filled with light, and there shall be no darkness in you; and that body which is filled with light comprehendeth all things.* Therefore, sanctify yourselves that your minds become single to God, *and the days will come that you shall see him; for he will unveil his face unto you, and it shall be in his own time, and in his own way, and according to his own will.* (D&C 88:67-68.)

Assemble yourselves together, and organize yourselves, and prepare yourselves, and sanctify yourselves; yea, purify your hearts, and cleanse your hands and your feet before me, *that I may make you clean; that I may testify unto your Father, and your God, and my God, that you are clean from the blood of this wicked generation; that I may fulfil this promise, this great and last promise, which I have made unto you, when I will.* (D&C 88:74-75.)

Thus saith the Lord, let Zion rejoice, for this is Zion— THE PURE IN HEART; therefore, let Zion rejoice, *while all the wicked shall mourn.* (D&C 97:21.)

They that remain, and the pure in heart, *shall return, and come to their inheritances, they and their children, with songs of everlasting joy, to build up the waste places of Zion.* (D&C 101:18.)

Purify your hearts before me; and then go ye into all the world, and preach my gospel unto every creature who has not received it. (D&C 112:28.)

Cleanse your hearts and your garments, *lest the blood of this generation be required at your hands.* (D&C 112:33.)

If ye do this [1847 migration west] with a pure heart, in all faithfulness, *ye shall be blessed; you shall be blessed in your flocks, and in your herds, and in your fields, and in your houses, and in your families.* (D&C 136:11.)

Receiving and Following the Holy Ghost

(See also False Teachers and Teachings; Following God and His Servants; Spiritual Gifts.)

The Savior, before he died, taught his disciples of the Comforter who would follow him. Those who have been baptized and had the gift of the Holy Ghost conferred on them can have the companionship of this Comforter, or the Spirit, the rest of their lives. They lose that opportunity if they "grieve . . . the holy Spirit" through their unrighteousness. (Eph. 4:30.) They can also lose the Spirit simply through not following when it speaks.

The purpose of the Spirit is twofold: receiving and following the Holy Ghost enables us to perfect our lives and to build the kingdom. The Holy Ghost testifies of truth to all people. It helps us individually by telling us what we should say, and by guiding our actions and directions. It fills us with peace and joy. It teaches us all things and brings us closer to God and Jesus Christ. (See John 14:16-31 and 15:26–16:15.)

The Spirit also leads us in performing God's works. Nephi writes that when we speak by the power of the Holy Ghost, the Holy Ghost carries the message into the hearts of men. (2 Ne. 33:1.) The Lord declares that if those sent to teach the gospel in the latter days "humble themselves before me, and abide in my word, and hearken to the voice of my Spirit," they "shall have power to open the door of my kingdom unto any nation whithersoever [the First Presidency and the Twelve] shall send them." (D&C 112:21-22.) Few commandments have a greater or more widespread promise.

Commandments and Promises

Ye shall be brought before governors and kings for my sake, for a testimony against them and the Gentiles. But when they deliver you up, take no thought how or what ye shall speak: *for it shall be given you in that same hour what ye shall speak.* For it is not ye that speak, but the Spirit of your Father which speaketh in you. (Matt. 10:18-20.)

All manner of sin and blasphemy shall be forgiven unto men: but the blasphemy against the Holy Ghost *shall not be forgiven unto men.* (Matt. 12:31; see also JST Matt. 12:26.)

He that shall blaspheme against the Holy Ghost *hath never forgiveness, but is in danger of eternal damnation.* (Mark 3:29.)

When they shall lead you, and deliver you up, take no thought beforehand what ye shall speak, neither do ye premeditate: but *whatsoever shall be given you in that hour,* that speak ye: for it is not ye that speak, *but the Holy Ghost.* (Mark 13:11.)

Whosoever shall speak a word against the Son of man, *it shall be forgiven him:* but unto him that blasphemeth against the Holy Ghost *it shall not be forgiven.* And when they bring you unto the synagogues, and unto magistrates, and powers, take ye no thought how or what thing ye shall answer, or what ye shall say: *for the Holy Ghost shall teach you in the same hour what ye ought to say.* (Luke 12:10-12.)

[Christ] breathed on them, and saith unto them, Receive ye the Holy Ghost. (John 20:22.)

Now we are delivered from the law, that being dead wherein we were held; that we should serve in newness of spirit, and not in the oldness of the letter. (Rom. 7:6.)

They that are after the flesh *do mind the things of the flesh;* but they that are after the Spirit *the things of the Spirit.* For to be carnally minded *is death;* but to be spiritually minded *is life and peace.* (Rom. 8:5-6.)

Ye are not in the flesh, but in the Spirit, if so be that the Spirit of God dwell in you. Now if any man have not the Spirit of Christ, *he is none of his.* And if Christ be in you, the body *is dead* because of sin; but the Spirit *is life* because of righteousness. (Rom. 8:9-10; see also JST Rom. 8:10.)

Walk in the Spirit, *and ye shall not fulfil the lust of the flesh.* For the flesh lusteth against the Spirit, and the Spirit against the flesh: and these are contrary the one to the other: *so that ye cannot do the things that ye would.* But if ye be led of the Spirit, *ye are not under the law.* (Gal. 5:16-18.)

The fruit of the Spirit is love, joy, peace, longsuffering, gentleness, goodness, faith, meekness, temperance: against such there is no law. And *they that are Christ's* have crucified the flesh with the affections and lusts. If we live in the Spirit, let us also walk in the Spirit. (Gal. 5:22-25.)

He that soweth to his flesh *shall of the flesh reap corruption;* but he that soweth to the Spirit *shall of the Spirit reap life everlasting.* (Gal. 6:8.)

Grieve not the holy Spirit of God, *whereby ye are sealed unto the day of redemption.* (Eph. 4:30.)

It is impossible for those who were once enlightened, and have tasted of the heavenly gift, and were made partakers of the Holy Ghost, and have tasted the good word of God, and the powers of the world to come, if they shall fall away, *to renew them again unto repentance;* seeing they crucify to themselves the Son of God afresh, and put him to an open shame. (Heb. 6:4-6.)

If we sin wilfully after that we have received the knowledge of the truth, *there remaineth no more sacrifice for sins, but a certain fearful looking for of judgment and fiery indignation, which shall devour the adversaries.* (Heb. 10:26-27.)

To him that knoweth to do good, and doeth it not, *to him it is sin.* (James 4:17.)

If after they have escaped the pollutions of the world through the knowledge of the Lord and Saviour Jesus Christ, they are again entangled therein, and overcome, *the latter end is worse with them than the beginning. For it had been better for them* not to have known the way of righteousness, than, after they have known it, to turn from the holy commandment delivered unto them. *But it is happened unto them according to the true proverb, The dog is turned to his own vomit again; and the sow that was washed to her wallowing in the mire.* (2 Pet. 2:20-22.)

[Lehi] I would that ye should . . . choose eternal life, according to the will of his Holy Spirit; and not choose eternal death, according to the will of the flesh and the evil which is therein, *which giveth the spirit of the devil power to captivate, to bring you down to hell, that he may reign over you in his own kingdom.* (2 Ne. 2:28-29.)

After ye have repented of your sins, and witnessed unto the Father that ye are willing to keep my commandments, by baptism of water, and have received the baptism of fire and of the Holy Ghost, and can speak with a new tongue, yea, even with the tongue of angels, and after this should deny me, *it would have been better for you that ye had not known me.* (2 Ne. 31:14.)

If ye will enter in by the way, and receive the Holy Ghost, *it will show unto you all things what ye should do.* (2 Ne. 32:5.)

When a man speaketh by the power of the Holy Ghost *the power of the Holy Ghost carrieth it unto the hearts of the children of men.* But behold, there are many that harden their hearts against the Holy Spirit, that it hath no place in them; *wherefore, they cast many things away which are written and esteem them as things of naught.* (2 Ne. 33:1-2.)

Will ye reject these words? Will ye reject the words of the prophets; and will ye reject all the words which have been spoken concerning Christ, after so many have spoken concerning him; and deny the good word of Christ, and the power of God, and the gift of the Holy Ghost, and quench the Holy Spirit, and make a mock of the great plan of redemption, which hath been laid for you? Know ye not that if ye will do these things, *that the power of the redemption and the resurrection, which is in Christ, will bring you to stand with shame and awful guilt before the bar of God?* (Jacob 6:8-9.)

[Sherem] I fear lest I have committed the unpardonable sin, for I have lied unto God; for I denied the Christ, and said that I believed the scriptures; and they truly testify of him. And because I have thus lied unto God I greatly fear lest my case shall be awful; and I confess unto God. (Jacob 7:19.)

There is a wo pronounced upon him who listeth to obey that [evil] spirit; for if he listeth to obey him, and remaineth and dieth in his sins, *the same drinketh damnation to his own soul; for he receiveth for his wages an everlasting punishment,* having transgressed the law of God contrary to his own knowledge. (Mosiah 2:33.)

After ye have known and been taught all these things, if ye should transgress and go contrary to that which has been spoken, that ye do withdraw yourselves from the Spirit of the Lord, *that it may have no place in you to guide you in wisdom's paths that ye may be blessed, prospered, and preserved*—I say unto you, that the man that doeth this, *the same cometh out in open rebellion against God; therefore he listeth to obey the evil spirit, and becometh an enemy to all righteousness; therefore, the Lord has no place in him, for he dwelleth not in unholy temples.* (Mosiah 2:36-37.)

They, after being sanctified by the Holy Ghost, *having their garments made white, being pure and spotless before God, could not look upon sin save it were with abhorrence;* and there were many, exceedingly great many, who were made pure and entered into the rest of the Lord their God. (Alma 13:12.)

After a people have been once enlightened by the Spirit of God, and have had great knowledge of things pertaining to righteousness, and then have fallen away into sin and transgression, *they become more hardened, and thus their state becomes worse than though they had never known these things.* (Alma 24:30.)

He that knoweth good and evil, *to him it is given according to his desires, whether he desireth good or evil, life or death, joy or remorse of conscience.* (Alma 29:5.)

How much more cursed is he that knoweth the will of God and doeth it not, *than he* that only believeth, or only hath cause to believe, and falleth into transgression? (Alma 32:19.)

If ye give place, that a seed may be planted in your heart, behold, if it be a true seed, or a good seed, if ye do not cast it out by your unbelief, that ye will resist the Spirit of the Lord, behold, *it will begin to swell within your breasts;* and when you feel these swelling motions, ye will begin to say within yourselves—It must needs be that this is a good seed, or that the word is good, *for it beginneth to enlarge my soul; yea, it beginneth to enlighten my understanding, yea, it beginneth to be delicious to me.* (Alma 32:28.)

I desire that ye shall plant this word in the hearts, and as it beginneth to swell even so nourish it by your faith. *And behold, it will become a tree, springing up in you unto everlasting life. And then may God grant unto you that your burdens may be light, through the joy of his Son. And even all this can ye do* if ye will. (Alma 33:23.)

Contend no more against the Holy Ghost, but . . . receive it. (Alma 34:38.)

If ye deny the Holy Ghost when it once has had place in you, and ye know that ye deny it, behold, *this is a sin which is unpardonable;* yea, and whosoever murdereth against the light and knowledge of God, *it is not easy for him to obtain forgiveness.* (Alma 39:6.)

They [the Lamanites] have not sinned against that great knowledge which ye have received; *therefore the Lord will be merciful unto them; yea, he will lengthen out their days and increase their seed, even when thou shalt be utterly destroyed* except thou shalt repent. (Hel. 7:24.)

Repent, all ye ends of the earth, and come unto me and be baptized in my name, *that ye may be sanctified* by the reception of the Holy Ghost, *that ye may stand spotless before me at the last day.* (3 Ne. 27:20.)

They are denying the Holy Ghost. And after rejecting so great a knowledge, my son, *they must perish soon, unto the fulfilling of the prophecies which were spoken by the prophets, as well as the words of our Savior himself.* (Moro. 8:28-29.)

Put your trust in that Spirit which leadeth to do good—yea, to do justly, to walk humbly, to judge righteously; and this is my Spirit.

Verily, verily, I say unto you, I will impart unto you of my Spirit, which shall enlighten your mind, which shall fill your soul with joy. (D&C 11:12-13.)

Deny not the spirit of revelation, nor the spirit of prophecy, for *wo unto him* that denieth these things. (D&C 11:25.)

Learn of me, and listen to my words; walk in the meekness of my Spirit, *and you shall have peace in me.* (D&C 19:23.)

The elders are to conduct the meetings as they are led by the Holy Ghost, according to the commandments and revelations of God. (D&C 20:45.)

[to Oliver Cowdery] If thou art led at any time by the Comforter to speak or teach, or at all times by the way of commandment unto the church, thou mayest do it. But thou shalt not write by way of commandment, but by wisdom. (D&C 28:4-5.)

Go your way whithersoever I will, *and it shall be given you by the Comforter what you shall do and whither you shall go.* (D&C 31:11.)

I give unto thee a commandment, that thou shalt baptize by water, *and they shall receive the Holy Ghost by the laying on of the hands, even as the apostles of old.* (D&C 35:6.)

They shall observe the covenants and church articles to do them, and these shall be their teachings, as they shall be directed by the Spirit. *And the Spirit shall be given unto you by the prayer of faith;* and if ye receive not the Spirit ye shall not teach. (D&C 42:13-14.)

As ye shall lift up your voices by the Comforter, *ye shall speak and prophesy as seemeth me good.* (D&C 42:16.)

They that are wise and have received the truth, and have taken the Holy Spirit for their guide, and have not been deceived—*verily I say unto you, they shall not be hewn down and cast into the fire, but shall abide the day.* (D&C 45:57.)

It always has been given to the elders of my church from the beginning, and ever shall be, to conduct all meetings as they are directed and guided by the Holy Spirit. (D&C 46:2.)

That which the Spirit testifies unto you even so I would that ye should do in all holiness of heart, walking uprightly before me, considering the end of your salvation, doing all things with prayer and thanksgiving, *that ye may not be seduced by evil spirits, or doctrines of devils, or the commandments of men; for some are of men, and others of devils.* (D&C 46:7.)

This is an ensample unto all those who were ordained unto this priesthood, whose mission is appointed unto them to go forth—and this is the ensample unto them, that they shall speak as they are moved upon by the Holy Ghost. *And whatsoever they shall speak when moved upon by the Holy Ghost shall be scripture, shall be the will of the Lord, shall be the mind of the Lord, shall be the word of the Lord, shall be the voice of the Lord, and the power of God unto salvation. Behold, this is the promise of the Lord unto you, O ye my servants.* (D&C 68:2-5.)

Their children shall be baptized for the remission of their sins when eight years old, and receive the laying on of the hands. (D&C 68:27.)

All those who know my power, and have been made partakers thereof, and suffered themselves through the power of the devil to be overcome, and to deny the truth and defy my power—they are they who are the sons of perdition, of whom I say that *it had been better for them never to have been born; for they are vessels of wrath, doomed to suffer the wrath of God, with the devil and his angels in eternity; concerning whom I have said there is no forgiveness in this world nor in the world to come*—having denied the Holy Spirit after having received it, and having denied the Only Begotten Son of the Father, having crucified him unto themselves and put him to an open shame. *These are they who shall go away into the lake of fire and brimstone, with the devil and his angels—and the only ones on whom the second death shall have any power; yea, verily, the only ones who shall not be redeemed in the due time of the Lord, after the sufferings of his wrath.* (D&C 76:31-38.)

Of him unto whom much is given much is required; and he who sins against the greater light *shall receive the greater condemnation.* (D&C 82:3.)

Neither take ye thought beforehand what ye shall say; but treasure up in your minds continually the words of life, *and it shall be given you in the very hour that portion that shall be meted unto every man.* (D&C 84:85.)

Lift up your voices unto this people; speak the thoughts that I shall put into your hearts, *and you shall not be confounded before men; for it shall be given you in the very hour, yea, in the very moment, what ye shall say.* (D&C 100:5-6.)

Whosoever ye shall send in my name, by the voice of your brethren, the Twelve, duly recommended and authorized by you, shall have power to open the door of my kingdom unto any nation whithersoever ye shall send them—inasmuch as they shall humble themselves before me, and abide in my word, and hearken to the voice of my Spirit. (D&C 112:21-22.)

The blasphemy against the Holy Ghost, *which shall not be forgiven in the world nor out of the world,* is in that ye commit murder wherein ye shed innocent blood, and assent unto my death, after ye have received my new and everlasting covenant, saith the Lord God; and he that abideth not this law *can in nowise enter into my glory, but shall be damned, saith the Lord.* (D&C 132:27.)

[to Adam] If thou wilt turn unto me, and hearken unto my voice, and believe, and repent of all thy transgressions, and be baptized, even in water, in the name of mine Only Begotten Son, . . . *ye shall receive the gift of the Holy Ghost, asking all things in his name, and whatsoever ye shall ask, it shall be given you.* (Moses 6:52.)

Inasmuch as ye were born into the world by water, and blood, and the spirit, which I have made, and so became of dust a living soul, even so ye must be born again into the kingdom of heaven, of water, and of the Spirit, and be cleansed by blood, even the blood of mine Only Begotten; *that ye might be sanctified from all sin, and enjoy the words of eternal life in this world, and eternal life in the world to come, even immortal glory;* for by the water *ye keep the commandment;* by the Spirit *ye are justified,* and by the blood *ye are sanctified.* (Moses 6:59-60.)

Receiving God, His Teachings, and His Servants

(See also Coming to God; Listening to God and His Servants; Opposing God and His Servants.)

God's words, spoken by himself or by his servants, do us no good if we do not listen to them. And even listening to his words is worth nothing if we do not apply them. Furthermore, receiving God and his teachings also implies that what we have accepted must remain with us, with this promise: "If that which ye have heard from the beginning shall remain in you, ye also shall continue in the Son, and in the Father." (1 Jn. 2:24.)

As the Church was organized in 1830, the Lord commanded the members to receive Joseph Smith's words "as if from mine own mouth, in all patience and faith." By so doing, he promised the Saints, "The gates of hell shall not prevail against you; yea, and the Lord God will disperse the powers of darkness from before you, and cause the heavens to shake for your good, and his name's glory." (D&C 21:5-6.) By receiving God, we receive his protection, his wisdom, his love, his power, and his gift of eternal life.

Commandments and Promises

Hear, O my son, and receive my sayings; *and the years of thy life shall be many.* (Prov. 4:10.)

Hear instruction, and be wise, and refuse it not. (Prov. 8:33.)

Hear counsel, and receive instruction, *that thou mayest be wise in thy latter end.* (Prov. 19:20.)

Thou shalt speak all these words unto them; but they will not hearken to thee: thou shalt also call unto them; but they will not answer thee. But thou shalt say unto them, This is a nation that obeyeth not the voice of the Lord their God, nor receiveth correction: *truth is perished, and is cut off from their mouth.* (Jer. 7:27-28.)

Because thou hast rejected knowledge, *I will also reject thee, that thou shalt be no priest to me:* seeing thou hast forgotten the law of thy God, *I will also forget thy children.* (Hosea 4:6.)

He that receiveth you receiveth me, and he that receiveth me receiveth him that sent me. He that receiveth a prophet in the name of a prophet *shall receive a prophet's reward;* and he that receiveth a righteous man in the name of a righteous man *shall receive a righteous man's reward.* And whosoever shall give to drink unto one of these little ones a cup of cold water only in the name of a disciple, verily I say unto you, *he shall in no wise lose his reward.* (Matt. 10:40-42.)

Blessed are your eyes, for they see: *and your ears,* for they hear. For verily I say unto you, That many prophets and righteous men have desired to see those things which ye see, and have not seen them; and to hear those things which ye hear, and have not heard them. Hear ye therefore the parable of the sower. When any one heareth the word of the kingdom, and understandeth it not, *then cometh the wicked one, and catcheth away that which was sown in his heart.* This is he which received seed by the way side. But he that received the seed into stony places, the same is he that heareth the word, and anon with joy receiveth it; yet hath he not root in himself, but dureth for a while: for when tribulation or persecution ariseth because of the word, *by and by he is offended.* He also that received seed among the thorns is he that heareth the word; and the care of this world, and the deceitfulness of riches, choke the word, *and he becometh unfruitful.* But he that received seed into the good ground is he that heareth the word, and understandeth it; *which also beareth fruit, and bringeth forth, some an hundredfold, some sixty, some thirty.* (Matt. 13:16-23; see also JST Matt. 13:21.)

As many as received him, *to them gave he power to become the sons of God, even to them that believe on his name: which were born, not of blood, nor of the will of the flesh, nor of the will of man, but of God.* (John 1:12-13.)

Whosoever drinketh of the water that I shall give him *shall never thirst; but the water that I shall give him shall be in him a well of water springing up into everlasting life.* (John 4:14.)

I am the living bread which came down from heaven: if any man eat of this bread, *he shall live for ever:* and the bread that I will give is my flesh, *which I will give for the life of the world.* The Jews therefore strove among themselves, saying, How can this man give us his flesh to eat? Then Jesus said unto them, Verily, verily, I say unto you, Except ye eat the flesh of the Son of man, and drink his blood, *ye have no life in you.* Whoso eateth my flesh, and drinketh my blood, *hath eternal life; and I will raise him up at the last day.* For my flesh is meat indeed, and my blood is drink indeed. He that eateth my flesh, and drinketh my blood, *dwelleth in me, and I in him.* As the living Father hath sent me, and I live by the Father: so he that eateth me, *even he shall live by me.* This is that bread which came down from heaven: not as your fathers did eat manna, and are dead: he that eateth of this bread *shall live for ever.* (John 6:51-58; see also JST John 6:54.)

Jesus stood and cried, saying, If any man thirst, let him come unto me, and drink. (John 7:37.)

Receive ye one another, as Christ also received us to the glory of God. (Rom. 15:7.)

If any man think himself to be a prophet, or spiritual, let him acknowledge that the things that I write unto you are the commandments of the Lord. But if any man be ignorant, let him be ignorant. (1 Cor. 14:37-38.)

Let the peace of God rule in your hearts, to the which also ye are called in one body; and be ye thankful. Let the word of Christ dwell in you richly in all wisdom; teaching and admonishing one another in psalms and hymns and spiritual songs, singing with grace in your hearts to the Lord. (Col. 3:15-16.)

Despise not prophesyings. (1 Thes. 5:20.)

Then shall that Wicked be revealed, . . . whose coming is after the working of Satan with all power and signs and lying wonders, and with *all deceivableness of unrighteousness in them that perish;* because they received not the love of the truth, *that they might be saved.* (2 Thes. 2:8-10.)

Ye have forgotten the exhortation which speaketh unto you as unto children, My son, despise not thou the chastening of the Lord, nor faint when thou art rebuked of him: for whom the Lord loveth he chasteneth, and scourgeth every son whom he receiveth. If ye endure chastening, *God dealeth with you as with sons; for what son is he whom the father chasteneth not?* (Heb. 12:5-7.)

See that ye refuse not him that speaketh. For if they escaped not who refused him that spake on earth, *much more shall not we escape,* if we turn away from him that speaketh from heaven. (Heb. 12:25.)

Wherefore lay apart all filthiness and superfluity of naughtiness, and receive with meekness the engrafted word, *which is able to save your souls.* (James 1:21.)

Let that therefore abide in you, which ye have heard from the beginning. If that which ye have heard from the beginning shall remain in you, *ye also shall continue in the Son, and in the Father.* (1 Jn. 2:24.)

Wo be unto him that rejecteth the word of God! (2 Ne. 27:14.)

Wo be unto him that saith: We have received, and we need no more! (2 Ne. 28:27.)

I will give unto the children of men line upon line, precept upon precept, here a little and there a little; and *blessed* are those who hearken unto my precepts, and lend an ear unto my counsel, *for they shall learn wisdom;* for unto him that receiveth *I will give more;* and from them that shall say, We have enough, *from them shall be taken away even that which they have.* (2 Ne. 28:30.)

O all ye that are pure in heart, lift up your heads and receive the pleasing word of God, and feast upon his love; *for ye may,* if your minds are firm, *forever.* (Jacob 3:2.)

No man knoweth of his ways save it be revealed unto him; wherefore, brethren, despise not the revelations of God. (Jacob 4:8.)

Will ye reject the words of the prophets; and will ye reject all the words which have been spoken concerning Christ, after so many have spoken concerning him; and deny the good word of Christ, and the power of God, and the gift of the Holy Ghost, and quench the Holy Spirit, and make a mock of the great plan of redemption, which hath been laid for you? Know ye not that if ye will do these things, that *the power of the redemption and the resurrection, which is in Christ, will bring you to stand with shame and awful guilt before the bar of God? And according to the power of justice, for justice cannot be denied, ye must go away into that lake of fire and brimstone, whose flames are unquenchable, and whose smoke ascendeth up forever and ever, which lake of fire and brimstone is endless torment.* (Jacob 6:8-10.)

I desire that ye shall plant this word in your hearts, and as it beginneth to swell even so nourish it by your faith. *And behold, it will become a tree, springing up in you unto everlasting life. And then may God grant unto you that your burdens may be light, through the joy of his Son. And even all this can ye do* if ye will. (Alma 33:23.)

As many as have received me, *to them have I given to become the sons of God; and even so will I to as many* as shall believe on my name, *for behold, by me redemption cometh, and in me is the law of Moses fulfilled.* (3 Ne. 9:17.)

At that day when the Gentiles shall sin against my gospel, and shall reject the fulness of my gospel, and shall be lifted up in the pride of their hearts above all nations, and above all the people of the whole earth, and shall be filled with all manner of lyings, and of deceits, and of mischiefs, and all manner of hypocrisy, and murders, and priestcrafts, and whoredoms, and of secret abominations; and if they shall do all those things, and shall reject the fulness of my gospel, *behold, saith the Father, I will bring the fulness of my gospel from among them.* (3 Ne. 16:10.)

Whoso receiveth not the words of Jesus and the words of those whom he hath sent receiveth not him; *and therefore he will not receive them at the last day.* (3 Ne. 28:34.)

Whoso receiveth this record, and shall not condemn it because of the imperfections which are in it, *the same shall know of greater things than these.* (Morm. 8:12.)

If they reject not my words, which shall be established by the testimony which shall be given, *blessed are they, and then shall ye have joy in the fruit of your labors.* (D&C 6:31.)

As many as receive me, *to them will I give power to become the sons of God, even to them* that believe on my name. (D&C 11:30.)

Those who receive it [Jesus Christ's church] in faith, and work righteousness, *shall receive a crown of eternal life;* but those who harden their hearts in unbelief, and reject it, *it shall turn to their own condemnation.* (D&C 20:14-15.)

His word ye shall receive, as if from mine own mouth, in all patience and faith. For by doing these things *the gates of hell shall not prevail against you; yea, and the Lord God will disperse the powers of darkness from before you, and cause the heavens to shake for your good, and his name's glory.* (D&C 21:5-6.)

As many as received me, *gave I power to become my sons; and even so will I give unto as many* as will receive me, *power to become my sons.* (D&C 39:4.)

He that receiveth these things receiveth me; *and they shall be gathered unto me in time and in eternity.* (D&C 39:22.)

By the prayer of your faith ye shall receive my law, *that ye may know how to govern my church and have all things right before me.* (D&C 41:3.)

He that receiveth my law and doeth it, *the same is my disciple;* and he that saith he receiveth it and doeth it not, *the same is not my disciple, and shall be cast out from among you.* (D&C 41:5.)

I came unto mine own, and mine own received me not; but unto as many as received me *gave I power to do many miracles, and to become the sons of God; and even unto them that believed on my name gave I power to obtain eternal life.* (D&C 45:8.)

He that receiveth him [Jesus Christ] *shall be saved,* and he that receiveth him not *shall be damned.* (D&C 49:5.)

Inasmuch as ye have received me, *ye are in me and I in you.* (D&C 50:43.)

He that doeth not anything until he is commanded, and receiveth a commandment with doubtful heart, and keepeth it with slothfulness, *the same is damned.* (D&C 58:29.)

Blessed are you for receiving mine everlasting covenant, even the fulness of my gospel, sent forth unto the children of men, *that they might have life and be made partakers of the glories which are to be revealed in the last days*, as it was written by the prophets and apostles in days of old. (D&C 66:2.)

All they who receive this priesthood receive me, saith the Lord; for he that receiveth my servants receiveth me; and he that receiveth me receiveth my Father; and he that receiveth my Father receiveth my Father's kingdom; *therefore all that my Father hath shall be given him.* (D&C 84:35-38.)

Blessed are ye inasmuch as you receive these things. (D&C 84:60.)

Whoso receiveth you, *there I will be also, for I will go before your face. I will be on your right hand and on your left, and my Spirit shall be in your hearts, and mine angels round about you, to bear you up.* Whoso receiveth you receiveth me; *and the same will feed you, and clothe you, and give you money.* And he who feeds you, or clothes you, or gives you money, *shall in nowise lose his reward.* And he that doeth not these things *is not my disciple;* by this you may know my disciples. (D&C 84:88-91.)

Every man whose spirit receiveth not the light *is under condemnation.* (D&C 93:32.)

Who receiveth you receiveth me; *and you shall have power to declare my word in the demonstration of my Holy Spirit.* And who receiveth you as a little child, *receiveth my kingdom; and blessed are they, for they shall obtain mercy.* And whoso rejecteth you *shall be rejected of my Father and his house; and you shall cleanse your feet in the secret places by the way for a testimony against them.* (D&C 99:2-4.)

Strait is the gate, and narrow the way that leadeth unto the exaltation and continuation of the lives, and few there be that find it, because ye receive me not in the world neither do ye know me. But if ye receive me in the world, *then shall ye know me, and shall receive your exaltation; that where I am ye shall be also. This is eternal lives—to know the only wise and true God, and Jesus Christ, whom he hath sent. I am he.* Receive ye, therefore, my law. *Broad is the gate, and wide the way that leadeth to the deaths; and many there are that go in thereat,* because they receive me not, neither do they abide in my law. (D&C 132:22-25.)

Reconciliation

(See also Anger; Forgiving Others; Loving Others; Reproving Others.)

The Lord teaches that we must be reconciled to all men and to God, and to be reconciled to God, we must first be reconciled to others: "If ye shall come unto me, or shall desire to come unto me, and rememberest that thy brother hath aught against thee—go thy way unto thy brother, and first be reconciled to thy brother, and then come unto me with full purpose of heart." The Lord then gives this promise: "And I will receive you." (3 Ne. 12:23-24.) Reconciliation to God comes through aligning our will with his and repenting of our sins. "Reconcile yourselves to the will of God, and not to the will of the devil and the flesh," we are commanded. (2 Ne. 10:24.) "Be reconciled unto him through the atonement of Christ." (Jacob 4:11.)

Commandments and Promises

If thou meet thine enemy's ox or his ass going astray, thou shalt surely bring it back to him again. If thou see the ass of him that hateth thee lying under his burden, and wouldest forbear to help him, thou shalt surely help with him. (Ex. 23:4-5.)

If thou bring thy gift to the altar, and there rememberest that thy brother hath ought against thee; leave there thy gift before the altar, and go thy way; first be reconciled to thy brother, and then come and offer thy gift. Agree with thine adversary quickly, whiles thou art in the way with him; *lest at any time the adversary deliver thee to the judge, and the judge deliver thee to the officer, and thou be cast into prision. Verily I say unto thee, Thou shalt by no means come out thence, till thou hast paid the uttermost farthing.* (Matt. 5:23-26; similar scripture, 3 Ne. 12:25-26; see also 3 Ne. 12:23-24.)

If thy brother shall trespass against thee, go and tell him his fault between thee and him alone: *if he shall hear thee, thou hast gained thy brother.* But if he will not hear thee, then take with thee one or two more, that in the mouth of two or three witnesses every word may be established. And if he shall neglect to hear them, tell it unto the church: but if he neglect to hear the church, let him be unto thee as an heathen man and a publican. (Matt. 18:15-17.)

We are ambassadors for Christ, as though God did beseech you by us: we pray you in Christ's stead, be ye reconciled to God. (2 Cor. 5:20.)

Reconcile yourselves to the will of God, and not to the will of the devil and the flesh; and remember, after ye are reconciled unto God, that it is only in and through the grace of God that ye are saved. (2 Ne. 10:24.)

Be reconciled unto him through the atonement of Christ, his Only Begotten Son, *and ye may obtain a resurrection, according to the power of the resurrection which is in Christ, and be presented as the first-fruits of Christ unto God, having faith, and obtained a good hope of glory in him before he manifesteth himself in the flesh.* (Jacob 4:11.)

If ye shall come unto me, or shall desire to come unto me, and rememberest that thy brother hath aught against thee—go thy way unto thy brother, and first be reconciled to thy brother, and then come unto me with full purpose of heart, *and I will receive you.* (3 Ne. 12:23-24; see also Matt. 5:23-24.)

If thy brother or sister offend thee, thou shalt take him or her between him or her and thee alone; and if he or she confess thou shalt be reconciled. (D&C 42:88.)

Ye are also commanded not to cast any one who belongeth to the church out of your sacrament meetings; nevertheless, if any have trespassed, let him not partake until he makes reconciliation. (D&C 46:4.)

Rejoicing

(See also Cheerfulness; Worship.)

The ability to rejoice amid life's daily tasks is a gift from God, a gift we are commanded to seek. God does not want us to be light-minded, or to indulge in an excess of laughter, but he does want us to rejoice in him and in life. Yet how can God command us on one hand to mourn, and on the other hand to rejoice? The answer is in Solomon's words: "To every thing there is a season, a time to every purpose under the heaven: . . . a time to weep, and a time to laugh; a time to mourn, and a time to dance." (Eccl. 3:1, 4.) Thus rejoicing is, at times, appropriate, as the following causes indicate:

—"Break forth into joy, . . . for the Lord hath comforted his people, he hath redeemed Jerusalem." (Isa. 52:9.)

—"Sing and rejoice, . . . for, lo, I come, and I will dwell in the midst of thee." (Zech. 2:10.)

—"When men shall revile you, and persecute you, . . . Rejoice, . . . for great is your reward in heaven." (Matt. 5:11-12.)

—"Lift up your hearts and be glad, for I am in your midst, and am your advocate with the Father." (D&C 29:5.)

—"Rejoice, because your names are written in heaven." (Luke 10:20.)

—"Lift up your hearts and be glad, your redemption draweth nigh." (D&C 35:26.)

To rejoice correctly, we must be attuned to things eternal, for all of the commandments to rejoice reflect eternal rewards and God's eternal love.

Commandments and Promises

Glory ye in his holy name: let the heart of them rejoice that seek the Lord. (1 Chr. 16:10.)

Rejoice in the Lord, ye righteous; and give thanks at the remembrance of his holiness. (Ps. 97:12.)

438

Rejoice not when thine enemy falleth, and let not thine heart be glad when he stumbleth: *lest the Lord see it, and it displease him, and he turn away his wrath from him.* (Prov. 24:17-18.)

Break forth into joy, sing together, ye waste places of Jerusalem: for the Lord hath comforted his people, he hath redeemed Jerusalem. (Isa. 52:9; similar scriptures, Mosiah 15:30, 3 Ne. 16:19.)

Ye shall go out with joy, and be led forth with peace: the mountains and the hills shall break forth before you into singing, and all the trees of the field shall clap their hands. (Isa. 55:12.)

Rejoice ye with Jerusalem, and be glad with her, all ye that love her: rejoice for joy with her, all ye that mourn for her. (Isa. 66:10.)

Sing and rejoice, O daughter of Zion: for, lo, I come, and I will dwell in the midst of thee, saith the Lord. (Zech. 2:10.)

Rejoice greatly, O daughter of Zion; shout, O daughter of Jerusalem: behold, thy King cometh unto thee: he is just, and having salvation. (Zech. 9:9.)

Blessed are ye, when men shall revile you, and persecute you, and shall say all manner of evil against you falsely, for my sake. Rejoice, and be exceeding glad: *for great is your reward in heaven:* for so persecuted they the prophets which were before you. (Matt. 5:11-12; similar scripture, Luke 6:22-23.)

In this rejoice not, that the spirits are subject unto you; but rather rejoice, because your names are written in heaven. (Luke 10:20.)

Ye have heard how I said unto you, I go away, and come again unto you. If ye loved me, ye would rejoice, because I said, I go unto the Father: for my Father is greater than I. (John 14:28.)

[Be] rejoicing in hope. (Rom. 12:12.)

In all things approving ourselves as the ministers of God, in much patience, in afflictions, in necessities, in distresses. . . ; as sorrowful, yet alway rejoicing; as poor, yet making many rich; as having nothing, and yet possessing all things. (2 Cor. 6:4, 10.)

Rejoice in the Lord. (Philip. 3:1.)

Rejoice in the Lord alway: and again I say, Rejoice. (Philip. 4:4.)

Rejoice evermore. (1 Thes. 5:16.)

Is any merry? let him sing psalms. (James 5:13.)

Think it not strange concerning the fiery trial which is to try you, as though some strange thing happened unto you: but rejoice, inasmuch as ye are partakers of Christ's sufferings; *that, when his glory shall be revealed, ye may be glad also with exceeding joy.* (1 Pet. 4: 12-13.)

Let your hearts rejoice. (2 Ne. 9:52.)

Lift up your heads, and rejoice, and put your trust in God. (Mosiah 7:19.)

Blessed art thou, Alma; therefore, lift up thy head and rejoice, for thou hast great cause to rejoice; for thou hast been faithful in keeping the commandments of God from the time which thou receivedst thy first message from him. Behold, I am he that delivered it unto you. (Alma 8:15.)

Lift up thy heart and rejoice. (D&C 25:13; similar scripture, D&C 27:15.)

Lift up your hearts and be glad, for I am in your midst, and am your advocate with the Father; *and it is his good will to give you the kingdom.* (D&C 29:5.)

Lift up your heart and rejoice, for the hour of your mission is come; *and your tongue shall be loosed, and you shall declare glad tidings of great joy unto this generation.* (D&C 31:3.)

Lift up your hearts and be glad, your redemption draweth nigh. (D&C 35:26.)

Lift up your hearts and rejoice, for unto you the kingdom, or in other words, the keys of the church have been given. (D&C 42:69.)

On this day [the Sabbath] thou shalt do none other thing, only let thy food be prepared with singleness of heart *that thy fasting may be perfect, or, in other words, that thy joy may be full.* Verily, this is fasting and prayer, or in other words, rejoicing and prayer. And inasmuch as ye do these things with thanksgiving, with cheerful hearts and countenances, not with much laughter, for this is sin, but with a glad heart and a cheerful countenance—verily I say, that inasmuch as ye do this, *the fulness of the earth is yours, the beasts of the field and the fowls of the air, and that which climbeth upon the trees and walketh upon the earth; yea, and the herb, and the good things which come of the earth, whether for food or for raiment, or for houses, or for barns, or for orchards, or for gardens, or for vineyards; yea, all things which come of the earth, in the season thereof, are made for the benefit and the use of man, both to please the eye and to gladden the heart; yea, for food and for raiment, for taste and for smell, to strengthen the body and to enliven the soul.* (D&C 59:13-19.)

Hold a meeting and rejoice together, and offer a sacrament unto the Most High. (D&C 62:4.)

Hear, O ye heavens, and give ear, O earth, and rejoice ye inhabitants thereof, for the Lord is God, and beside him there is no Savior. (D&C 76:1.)

Verily, thus saith the Lord, let Zion rejoice, for this is Zion—THE PURE IN HEART; therefore, let Zion rejoice, while all the wicked shall mourn. (D&C 97:21.)

Fear not, let your hearts be comforted; yea, rejoice evermore, and in everything give thanks. (D&C 98:1.)

Let your hearts rejoice; for behold, and lo, I am with you even unto the end. (D&C 100:12.)

Let the hearts of your brethren rejoice, and let the hearts of all my people rejoice, who have, with their might, built this house [Kirtland Temple] to my name. (D&C 110:6.)

Remembering God and His Teachings

(See also Knowing God and His Ways; Meditation and Purity of Thought; Sacrament.)

The commandment to remember God is given often in scripture. It is so critical that it is mentioned twice in each sacrament prayer. We eat the bread and drink the water in remembrance of the body and blood of Christ, and we covenant to "always remember him." (Moro. 4:3; see also Moro. 5:2.) Ordinances and rituals such as the blessing and partaking of the sacrament help us keep God in remembrance. "This do in remembrance of me," Jesus said as he passed the first sacramental emblems to his apostles. (Luke 22:19.) "And if ye do always remember me," he told the Nephites, "ye shall have my Spirit to be with you." (3 Ne. 18:5-7.)

Commandments and Promises

Take heed unto yourselves, *lest ye forget the covenant of the Lord your God, which he made with you, and make you a graven image, or the likeness of any thing, which the Lord thy God hath forbidden thee.* (Deut. 4:23.)

Beware *lest thou forget the Lord*, which brought thee forth out of the land of Egypt, from the house of bondage. (Deut. 6:12.)

Beware that thou forget not the Lord thy God, in not keeping his commandments, and his judgments, and his statutes, which I command thee this day: *lest when thou hast eaten and art full, and hast built goodly houses, and dwelt therein; and when thy herds and thy flocks multiply, and thy silver and thy gold is multiplied, and all that thou hast is multiplied; then thine heart be lifted up, and thou forget the Lord thy God*, which brought thee forth out of the land of Egypt, from the house of bondage; who led thee through that great and terrible wilderness, wherein were fiery serpents, and scorpions, and drought, where there was no water; who brought thee forth water out of the rock of flint; who fed thee in the wilderness with manna, which thy fathers knew not, that he might humble thee, and that he might prove thee, to do thee good at thy latter end; *and thou say in thine heart, My power and the might of mine hand hath gotten me this wealth.* But thou shalt remember the Lord thy God: for it is he that giveth thee power to get wealth, that he may establish his covenant which he sware unto thy fathers, as it is this day. (Deut. 8:11-18.)

Therefore shall ye lay up these my words in your heart and in your soul, and bind them for a sign upon your hand, *that they may be as frontlets between your eyes.* (Deut. 11:18.)

Remember his marvellous works that he hath done, his wonders, and the judgments of his mouth. (1 Chr. 16:12; similar scripture, Ps. 105:5.)

Be ye mindful always of his covenant; the word which he commanded to a thousand generations; even of the covenant which he made with Abraham, and of his oath unto Isaac; and hath confirmed the same to Jacob for a law, and to Israel for an everlasting covenant, saying, Unto thee will I give the land of Canaan, the lot of your inheritance. (1 Chr. 16:15-18.)

Remember now thy Creator in the days of thy youth, while the evil days come not, nor the years draw nigh, when thou shalt say, I have no pleasure in them. (Eccl. 12:1.)

Because thou hast forgotten the God of thy salvation, and hast not been mindful of the rock of thy strength, *therefore shalt thou plant pleasant plants, and shalt set it with strange slips: in the day shalt thou make thy plant to grow, and in the morning shalt thou make thy seed to flourish: but the harvest shall be a heap in the day of grief and of desperate sorrow.* (Isa. 17:10-11.)

Put me in remembrance: let us plead together: declare thou, that thou mayest be justified. (Isa. 43:26.)

Remember these, O Jacob and Israel; for thou art my servant: I have formed thee; thou art my servant: *O Israel, thou shalt not be forgotten of me.* (Isa. 44:21.)

Remember this, and shew yourselves men: bring it again to mind, O ye transgressors. Remember the former things of old: for I am God, and there is none else; I am God, and there is none like me, declaring the end from the beginning, and from ancient times the things that are not yet done, saying, My counsel shall stand, and I will do all my pleasure: calling a ravenous bird from the east, the man that executeth my counsel from a far country: yea, I have spoken it, I will also bring it to pass; I have purposed it, I will also do it. (Isa. 46:8-11.)

Therefore will I scatter them as the stubble that passeth away by the wind of the wilderness. This is thy lot, the portion of thy measures from me, saith the Lord; because thou hast forgotten me, and trusted in falsehood. *Therefore will I discover thy skirts upon thy face, that thy shame may appear.* (Jer. 13:24-26.)

Seeing thou hast forgotten the law of thy God, *I will also forget thy children.* (Hosea 4:6.)

He took bread, and gave thanks, and brake it, and gave unto them, saying, This is my body which is given for you: this do in remembrance of me. (Luke 22:19.)

When he had given thanks, he brake it, and said, Take, eat: this is my body, which is broken for you: this do in remembrance of me. After the same manner also he took the cup, when he had supped, saying, This cup is the new testament in my blood: this do ye, as oft as ye drink it, in remembrance of me. (1 Cor. 11:24-25.)

I declare unto you the gospel which I preached unto you, which also ye have received, and wherein ye stand; *by which also ye are saved,* if ye keep in memory what I preached unto you, unless ye have believed in vain. (1 Cor. 15:1-2.)

When I call to remembrance the unfeigned faith that is in thee [Timothy], which dwelt first in thy grandmother Lois, and thy mother Eunice; and I am persuaded that in thee also. Wherefore I put thee in remembrance that thou stir up the gift of God, which is in thee by the putting on of my hands. (2 Tim. 1:5-6.)

Remember that Jesus Christ of the seed of David was raised from the dead according to my gospel. (2 Tim. 2:8.)

Remember ye the words which were spoken before of the apostles of our Lord Jesus Christ; how that they told you there should be mockers in the last time, who should walk after their own ungodly lusts. These be they who separate themselves, sensual, having not the Spirit. (Jude 1:17-19.)

Remember therefore how thou hast received and heard, and hold fast, and repent. (Rev. 3:3.)

Hearken diligently unto me, and remember the words which I have spoken. (2 Ne. 9:51.)

Seeing that our merciful God has given us so great knowledge concerning these things, let us remember him, and lay aside our sins, and not hang down our heads, for we are not cast off. (2 Ne. 10:20.)

Cheer up your hearts, and remember that ye are free to act for yourselves—to choose the way of everlasting death or the way of eternal life. (2 Ne. 10:23.)

I would that ye should remember, and always retain in remembrance, the greatness of God, and your own nothingness, and his goodness and long-suffering towards you, unworthy creatures, and humble yourselves even in the depths of humility, calling on the name of the Lord daily, and standing steadfastly in the faith of that which is to come, which was spoken by the mouth of the angel. And behold, I say unto you that if ye do this *ye shall always rejoice, and be filled with the love of God, and always retain a remission of your sins; and ye shall grow in the knowledge of the glory of him that created you, or in the knowledge of that which is just and true.* (Mosiah 4:11-12.)

He did exhort the people of Limhi and his brethren, all those that had been delivered out of bondage, that they should remember that it was the Lord that did deliver them. (Mosiah 25:16.)

I would that ye should do as I have done, in remembering the captivity of our fathers; for they were in bondage, and none could deliver them except it was the God of Abraham, and the God of Isaac, and the God of Jacob; and he surely did deliver them in their afflictions. (Alma 36:2.)

Remember that there is no other way nor means whereby man can be saved, only through the atoning blood of Jesus Christ, who shall come; yea, remember that he cometh to redeem the world. And remember also . . . that the Lord surely should come to redeem his people, but that he should not come to redeem them in their sins, but to redeem them from their sins. (Hel. 5:9-10.)

Remember the words which I have spoken. For behold, ye are they whom I have chosen to minister unto this people. (3 Ne. 13:25.)

Ye have heard the things which I taught before I ascended to my Father; therefore, whoso remembereth these sayings of mine and doeth them, *him will I raise up at the last day.* (3 Ne. 15:1.)

There shall one be ordained among you, and to him will I give power that he shall break bread and bless it and give it unto the people of my church, unto all those who shall believe and be baptized in my name. And this shall ye always observe to do, even as I have done, even as I have broken bread and blessed it and given it unto you. And this shall ye do in remembrance of my body, which I have shown unto you. And it shall be a testimony unto the Father that ye do always remember me. And if ye do always remember me *ye shall have my Spirit to be with you.* (3 Ne. 18:5-7.)

This [sacrament] shall ye alway do to those who repent and are baptized in my name; and ye shall do it in remembrance of my blood, which I have shed for you, that ye may witness unto the Father that ye do always remember me. And if ye do always remember me *ye shall have my Spirit to be with you.* And I give unto you a commandment that ye shall do these things. And if ye shall always do these things *blessed are ye, for ye are built upon my rock.* (3 Ne. 18:11-12.)

[sacrament prayer] O God, the Eternal Father, we ask thee in the name of thy Son, Jesus Christ, to bless and sanctify this bread to the souls of all those who partake of it; that they may eat in remembrance of the body of thy Son, and witness unto thee, O God, the Eternal Father, that they are willing to take upon them the name of thy son, and always remember him, and keep his commandments which he hath given them, *that they may always have his Spirit to be with them.* Amen. (Moro. 4:3; similar scripture, D&C 20:77.)

[sacrament prayer] O God, the Eternal Father, we ask thee, in the name of thy Son, Jesus Christ, to bless and sanctify this wine to the souls of all those who drink of it, that they may do it in remembrance of the blood of thy Son, which was shed for them; that they may witness unto thee, O God, the Eternal Father, that they do always remember him, *that they may have his Spirit to be with them.* Amen. (Moro. 5:2; similar scripture, D&C 20:79.)

I would exhort you that when ye shall read these things, if it be wisdom in God that ye should read them, that ye would remember how merciful the Lord hath been unto the children of men, from the creation of Adam even down until the time that ye shall receive these things, and ponder it in your hearts. (Moro. 10:3.)

Remember that he is the same yesterday, today, and forever, and that all these gifts of which I have spoken, which are spiritual, never will be done away, even as long as the world shall stand, only according to the unbelief of the children of men. (Moro. 10:19.)

I exhort you to remember these things [in the book of Moroni]; for the time speedily cometh that ye shall know that I lie not, for ye shall see me at the bar of God. (Moro. 10:27.)

Treasure up these words [to Oliver Cowdery] in thy heart. (D&C 6:20.)

Oh, remember these words [to Oliver Cowdery], and keep my commandments. (D&C 8:5.)

Remember the words of him who is the life and light of the world, your Redeemer, your Lord and your God. (D&C 10:70.)

Treasure these things [in Doctrine and Covenants 43] up in your hearts. (D&C 43:34.)

Always retain in your minds what those gifts are, that are given unto the church. (D&C 46:10.)

They shall remain under this condemnation until they repent and remember the new covenant, even the Book of Mormon and the former commandments which I have given them, not only to say, but to do according to that which I have written—*that they may bring forth fruit meet for their Father's kingdom; otherwise there remaineth a scourge and judgment to be poured out upon the children of Zion.* (D&C 84:57-58.)

Remember the great and last promise which I have made unto you [*that we shall see Christ*]. (D&C 88:69.)

Search diligently, pray always, and be believing, *and all things shall work together for your good*, if ye walk uprightly and remember the covenant wherewith ye have covenanted one with another. (D&C 90:24.)

Repentance

(See also Fleeing Evil; Forgiving Others.)

Much of Jesus' ministry was devoted to calling people to repentance, and a major part of his sacrifice was to cleanse from sin those who repent and are baptized. Furthermore, as he told Alma, "As often as my people repent will I forgive them their trespasses against me." (Mosiah 26:30.)

Jesus and his servants also specified what must be done to repent, although they did not specify what order the steps of repentance should follow. The repenter must consider his ways, cease his evil works, confess his sins, humbly and sincerely ask God for forgiveness, do God's will, and replace evil works with good works.

Through repentance, we are no longer bound by our past sins. We are renewed in spirit and made worthy of the blessings God reserves for the righteous, including his greatest blessing, exaltation. And even though repentance is a repeated thing, we have the Lord's assurance that we can, with his help, turn our weaknesses into strengths. "If they humble themselves before me, and have faith in me, then will I make weak things become strong unto them." (Ether 12:27.)

The reality of these changes and of the atonement are two of the Savior's greatest gifts. Jacob thus encourages us, "Seeing that our merciful God has given us so great knowledge concerning these things, let us remember him, and lay aside our sins, and not hang down our heads, for we are not cast off." (2 Ne. 10:20.).

Commandments and Promises

When thou art in tribulation, and all these things are come upon thee, even in the latter days, if thou turn to the Lord thy God, and shalt be obedient unto his voice; (for the Lord thy God is a merciful God;) *he will not forsake thee, neither destroy thee, nor forget the covenant of thy fathers which he sware unto them.* (Deut. 4:30-31.)

So shalt thou put away the guilt of innocent blood from among you, when thou shalt do that which is right in the sight of the Lord. (Deut. 21:9.)

If I shut up heaven that there be no rain, or if I command the locusts to devour the land, or if I send pestilence among my people; if my people, which are called by my name, shall humble themselves, and pray, and seek my face, and turn from their wicked ways; *then will I hear from heaven, and will forgive their sin, and will heal their land.* (2 Chr. 7:13-14.)

Depart from evil, and do good; seek peace, and pursue it. (Ps. 34:14.)

Be not wise in thine own eyes: fear the Lord, and depart from evil. (Prov. 3:7.)

He that covereth his sins *shall not prosper:* but whoso confesseth and forsaketh them *shall have mercy.* (Prov. 28:13.)

Remove sorrow from thy heart, and put away evil from thy flesh: for childhood and youth are vanity. (Eccl. 11:10.)

Wash you, make you clean; put away the evil of your doings from before mine eyes; cease to do evil; learn to do well; seek judgment, relieve the oppressed, judge the fatherless, plead for the widow. Come now, and let us reason together, saith the Lord: *though your sins be as scarlet, they shall be as white as snow; though they be red like crimson, they shall be as wool.* (Isa. 1:16-18.)

Turn ye unto him from whom the children of Israel have deeply revolted. (Isa. 31:6.)

Let the wicked forsake his way, and the unrighteous man his thoughts: and let him return unto the Lord, *and he will have mercy upon him;* and to our God, *for he will abundantly pardon.* (Isa. 55:7.)

Return, ye backsliding children, *and I will heal your backslidings.* (Jer. 3:22.)

If that nation, against whom I have pronounced, turn from their evil, *I will repent of the evil that I thought to do unto them.* (Jer. 18:8.)

Amend your ways and your doings, and obey the voice of the Lord your God; *and the Lord will repent him of the evil that he hath pronounced against you.* (Jer. 26:13; see also JST Jer. 26:13.)

Let us search and try our ways, and turn again to the Lord. (Lam. 3:40.)

If the wicked will turn from all his sins that he hath committed, and keep all my statutes, and do that which is lawful and right, *he shall surely live, he shall not die. All his transgressions that he hath committed, they shall not be mentioned unto him:* in his righteousness that he hath done *he shall live.* (Ezek. 18:21-22.)

Cast away from you all your transgressions, whereby ye have transgressed; and make you a new heart and a new spirit: *for why will ye die, O house of Israel? For I have no pleasure in the death of him that dieth,* saith the Lord God: wherefore turn yourselves, *and live ye.* (Ezek. 18:31-32.)

Whosoever heareth the sound of the trumpet, and taketh not warning; if the sword come, and take him away, *his blood shall be upon his own head.* (Ezek. 33:4.)

When I say unto the wicked, Thou shalt surely die; if he turn from his sin, and do that which is lawful and right; if the wicked restore the pledge, give again that he had robbed, walk in the statutes of life, without committing iniquity; *he shall surely live, he shall not die. None of his sins that he hath committed shall be mentioned unto him:* he hath done that which is lawful and right; *he shall surely live.* (Ezek. 33:14-16.)

When the righteous turneth from his righteousness, and committeth iniquity, *he shall even die thereby.* But if the wicked turn from his wickedness, and do that which is lawful and right, *he shall live thereby.* (Ezek. 33:18-19.)

Then said [the Lord] unto [Daniel], Fear not, Daniel: for from the first day that thou didst set thine heart to understand, and to chasten thyself before thy God, *thy words were heard, and I am come for thy words.* (Dan. 10:12.)

Come, and let us return unto the Lord: for he hath torn, *and he will heal us;* he hath smitten, *and he will bind us up.* (Hosea 6:1.)

Turn thou to thy God: keep mercy and judgment, and wait on thy God continually. (Hosea 12:6.)

Thus saith the Lord of hosts; Consider your ways. Ye have sown much, *and bring in little;* ye eat, *but ye have not enough;* ye drink, *but ye are not filled with drink;* ye clothe you, *but there is none warm;* and he that earneth wages *earneth wages to put it into a bag with holes.* Thus saith the Lord of hosts; Consider your ways. (Hag. 1:5-7.)

Bring forth therefore fruits meet for repentance. (Matt. 3:8.)

From that time Jesus began to preach, and to say, Repent: for the kingdom of heaven is at hand. (Matt. 4:17; similar scripture, Matt. 3:1-2, Alma 10:20.)

If thy right eye offend thee, pluck it out, and cast it from thee: *for it is profitable for thee that one of thy members should perish, and not that thy whole body should be cast into hell.* And if thy right hand offend thee, cut it off, and cast it from thee: *for it is profitable for thee that one of thy members should perish, and not that thy whole body should be cast into hell.* (Matt. 5:29-30; see also Matt. 18:8-9, JST Matt. 5:34.)

Why beholdest thou the mote that is in thy brother's eye, but considerest not the beam that is in thine own eye? Or how wilt thou say to thy brother, Let me pull out the mote of thine eye; and, behold, a beam is in thine own eye? Thou hypocrite, first cast out the beam out of thine own eye; *and then shalt thou see clearly to cast out the mote out of thy brother's eye.* (Matt. 7:3-5; similar scripture, Luke 6:41-42; see also JST Matt. 7:4-8.)

If thy hand or thy foot offend thee, cut them off, and cast them from thee: *it is better for thee to enter into life halt or maimed, rather than having two hands or two feet to be cast into everlasting fire.* And if thine eye offend thee, pluck it out, and cast it from thee: *it is better for thee to enter into life with one eye, rather than having two eyes to be cast into hell fire.* (Matt. 18:8-9; similar scripture, Mark 9:47; see also Matt. 5:29-30, JST Matt. 18:9.)

Woe unto you, scribes and Pharisees, hypocrites! for ye make clean the outside of the cup and of the platter, but within they are full of extortion and excess. Thou blind Pharisee, cleanse first that which is within the cup and platter, *that the outside of them may be clean also.* (Matt. 23:25-26.)

The time is fulfilled, and the kingdom of God is at hand: repent ye, and believe the gospel. (Mark 1:15.)

Bring forth therefore fruits worthy of repentance, and begin not to say within yourselves, We have Abraham to our father: for I say unto you, That God is able of these stones to raise up children unto Abraham. (Luke 3:8; see also JST Luke 3:13.)

Except ye repent, *ye shall all likewise perish.* (Luke 13:3.)

Peter said unto them, Repent, and be baptized every one of you in the name of Jesus Christ for the remission of sins, *and ye shall receive the gift of the Holy Ghost.* (Acts 2:38.)

Repent ye therefore, and be converted, *that your sins may be blotted out, when the times of refreshing shall come from the presence of the Lord.* (Acts 3:19.)

The times of this ignorance God winked at; but now commandeth all men every where to repent. (Acts 17:30.)

Being then made free from sin, *ye became the servants of righteousness.* (Rom. 6:18.)

The night is far spent, the day is at hand: let us therefore cast off the works of darkness, and let us put on the armour of light. Let us walk honestly, as in the day; not in rioting and drunkenness, not in chambering and wantonness, not in strife and envying. But put ye on the Lord Jesus Christ, and make not provision for the flesh, to fulfil the lusts thereof. (Rom. 13:12-14.)

Purge out therefore the old leaven, *that ye may be a new lump,* as ye are unleavened. For even Christ our passover is sacrificed for us: therefore let us keep the feast, not with old leaven, neither with the leaven of malice and wickedness; but with the unleavened bread of sincerity and truth. (1 Cor. 5:7-8.)

Put off concerning the former conversation the old man, which is corrupt according to the deceitful lusts; and be renewed in the spirit of your mind; and that ye put on the new man, which after God is created in righteousness and true holiness. (Eph. 4:22-24.)

Mortify therefore your members which are upon the earth; fornication, uncleanness, inordinate affection, evil concupiscence, and covetousness, which is idolatry: for which things' sake *the wrath of God cometh on the children of disobedience.* (Col. 3:5-6.)

The Lord knoweth them that are his. And, Let every one that nameth the name of Christ depart from iniquity. (2 Tim. 2:19.)

If a man therefore purge himself from these, *he shall be a vessel unto honour, sanctified, and meet for the master's use, and prepared unto every good work.* (2 Tim. 2:21.)

Seeing we also are compassed about with so great a cloud of witnesses, let us lay aside every weight, and the sin which doth so easily beset us, and let us run with patience the race that is set before us, looking unto Jesus the author and finisher of our faith; who *for the joy that was set before him* endured the cross, despising the shame, *and is set down at the right hand of the throne of God.* (Heb. 12:1-2.)

Lift up the hands which hang down, and the feeble knees; and make straight paths for your feet, *lest that which is lame be turned out of the way; but let it rather be healed.* (Heb. 12:12-13.)

Lay apart all filthiness and superfluity of naughtiness, and receive with meekness the engrafted word, which is able to save your souls. (James 1:21.)

Cleanse your hands, ye sinners; and purify your hearts, ye double minded. (James 4:8.)

Confess your faults one to another, and pray one for another, *that ye may be healed.* (James 5:16.)

If we confess our sins, *he is faithful and just to forgive us our sins, and to cleanse us from all unrighteousness.* (1 Jn. 1:9.)

Repent; *or else I will come unto thee quickly, and will fight against them with the sword of my mouth.* (Rev. 2:16.)

Remember therefore how thou hast received and heard, and hold fast, and repent. (Rev. 3:3.)

As many as I love, I rebuke and chasten: be zealous therefore, and repent. (Rev. 3:19.)

All nations, kindreds, tongues, and people shall dwell safely in the Holy One of Israel if it so be that they will repent. (1 Ne. 22:28.)

[Lehi to sons] Awake, my sons; put on the armor of righteousness. Shake off the chains with which ye are bound, and come forth out of obscurity, and arise from the dust. (2 Ne. 1:23.)

[God] gave commandment that all men must repent. (2 Ne. 2:21.)

Blessed are the Gentiles, they of whom the prophet has written; for behold, if it so be that they shall repent and fight not against Zion, and do not unite themselves to that great and abominable church, *they shall be saved.* (2 Ne. 6:12.)

Shake thyself from the dust; arise, sit down, O Jerusalem; loose thyself from the bands of thy neck, O captive daughter of Zion. (2 Ne. 8:25.)

Turn away from your sins; shake off the chains of him that would bind you fast; come unto that God who is the rock of your salvation. (2 Ne. 9:45.)

Seeing that our merciful God has given us so great knowledge concerning these things, let us remember him, and lay aside our sins, and not hang down our heads, for we are not cast off. (2 Ne. 10:20.)

If the inhabitants of the earth shall repent of their wickedness and abominations *they shall not be destroyed, saith the Lord of Hosts.* (2 Ne. 28:17.)

I will be merciful unto them [the Gentiles], saith the Lord God, if they will repent and come unto me; for mine arm is lengthened out all the day long, saith the Lord God of Hosts. (2 Ne. 28:32.)

As many of the Gentiles as will repent *are the covenant people of the Lord;* and as many of the Jews as will not repent *shall be cast off; for the Lord covenanteth with none save it be with them* that repent and believe in his Son, who is the Holy One of Israel. (2 Ne. 30:2.)

Wo, wo, unto you that are not pure in heart, that are filthy this day before God; for except ye repent *the land is cursed for your sakes; and the Lamanites, which are not filthy like unto you, nevertheless they are cursed with a sore cursing, shall scourge you even unto destruction. And the time speedily cometh, that* except ye repent *they shall possess the land of your inheritance, and the Lord God will lead away the righteous out from among you.* (Jacob 3:3-4.)

Hearken unto my words; arouse the faculties of your souls; shake yourselves that ye may awake from the slumber of death; and loose yourselves from the pains of hell *that ye may not become angels to the devil, to be cast into that lake of fire and brimstone which is the second death.* (Jacob 3:11.)

I beseech of you in words of soberness that ye would repent, and come with full purpose of heart, and cleave unto God as he cleaveth unto you. And while his arm of mercy is extended towards you in the light of the day, harden not your hearts. (Jacob 6:5.)

Repent ye, and enter in at the strait gate, and continue in the way which is narrow, *until ye shall obtain eternal life.* (Jacob 6:11.)

Wo, wo unto him who knoweth that he rebelleth against God! For *salvation cometh to none such* except it be through repentance and faith on the Lord Jesus Christ. (Mosiah 3:12.)

When that time cometh, none shall be found blameless before God, except it be little children, only through repentance and faith on the name of the Lord God Omnipotent. (Mosiah 3:21.)

Believe that ye must repent of your sins and forsake them, and humble yourselves before God; and ask in sincerity of heart that he would forgive you; and now, if you believe all these things see that ye do them. (Mosiah 4:10.)

Except they [people of King Noah] repent *I will visit them in mine anger.* And except they repent and turn to the Lord their God, behold, *I will deliver them into the hands of their enemies; yea, and they shall be brought into bondage; and they shall be afflicted by the hand of their enemies.* . . . Except this people repent and turn unto the Lord their God, *they shall be brought into bondage; and none shall deliver them, except it be the Lord the Almighty God. Yea, and it shall come to pass that when they shall cry unto me I will be slow to hear their cries; yea, and I will suffer them that they be smitten by their enemies.* And except they repent in sackcloth and ashes, and cry mightily to the Lord their God, *I will not hear their prayers, neither will I deliver them out of their afflictions.* (Mosiah 11:20-25; see also Mosiah 12:1.)

Except they [people of King Noah] repent *I will utterly destroy them from off the face of the earth; yet they shall leave a record behind them, and I will preserve them for other nations . . . that I may discover the abominations of this people to other nations.* (Mosiah 12:8.)

If he confess his sins before thee and me, and repenteth in the sincerity of his heart, *him shall ye forgive, and I will forgive him also.* Yea, and as often as my people repent *will I forgive them their trespasses against me.* (Mosiah 26:29-30.)

Whosoever repented of their sins and did confess them, *them he [Alma] did number among the people of the church;* and those that would not confess their sins and repent of their iniquity, *the same were not numbered among the people of the church, and their names were blotted out.* (Mosiah 26:35-36.)

Repent, *and I will receive you.* (Alma 5:33.)

Repent, for except ye repent *ye can in nowise inherit the kingdom of heaven.* (Alma 5:51.)

Whosoever did not belong to the church who repented of their sins *were baptized unto repentance, and were received into the church.* And it also came to pass that whosoever did belong to the church that did not repent of their wickedness and humble themselves before God—I mean those who were lifted up in the pride of their hearts— *the same were rejected, and their names were blotted out, that their names were not numbered among those of the righteous.* (Alma 6:2-3.)

Repent ye, and prepare the way of the Lord, and walk in his paths, which are straight; for behold, the kingdom of heaven is at hand, and the Son of God cometh upon the face of the earth. (Alma 7:9.)

He commandeth you [people of Ammonihah] to repent; and except ye repent, *ye can in nowise inherit the kingdom of God.* But behold, this is not all—he has commanded you to repent, *or he will utterly destroy you from off the face of the earth; yea, he will visit you in his anger, and in his fierce anger he will not turn away.* (Alma 9:12.)

[to people of Ammonihah] Ye ought to bring forth works which are meet for repentance, seeing that your hearts have been grossly hardened against the word of God, and seeing that ye are a lost and a fallen people. (Alma 9:30.)

Concerning the holy order, or this high priesthood, *there were many who were ordained and became high priests of God;* and it was on account of their exceeding faith and repentance, and their righteousness before God, they choosing to repent, and work righteousness rather than to perish; *therefore they were called after this holy order, and were sanctified, and their garments were washed white through the blood of the Lamb.* (Alma 13:10-11.)

I would that ye should humble yourselves before God, and bring forth fruit meet for repentance, *that ye may also enter into that rest.* (Alma 13:13.)

I wish from the inmost part of my heart, yea, with great anxiety even unto pain, that ye would hearken unto my words, and cast off your sins, and not procrastinate the day of your repentance. (Alma 13:27.)

May the Lord grant unto you repentance, *that ye may not bring down his wrath upon you, that ye may not be bound down by the chains of hell, that ye may not suffer the second death.* (Alma 13:30.)

His arm is extended to all people who will repent and believe on his name. (Alma 19:36.)

If thou wilt bow down before God, yea, if thou wilt repent of all thy sins, and will bow down before God, and call on his name in faith, believing that ye shall receive, *then shalt thou receive the hope which thou desirest.* (Alma 22:16.)

Whosoever repenteth *shall find mercy; and he that findeth mercy and endureth to the end the same shall be saved.* (Alma 32:13.)

He that truly humbleth himself, and repenteth of his sins, and endureth to the end, *the same shall be blessed—yea, much more blessed than they who are compelled to be humble because of their exceeding poverty.* (Alma 32:15.)

I would that, after ye have received so many witnesses, seeing that the holy scriptures testify of these things, ye come forth and bring fruit unto repentance. Yea, I would that ye would come forth and harden not your hearts any longer; for behold, now is the time and the day of your salvation; and therefore, if ye will repent and harden not your hearts, *immediately shall the great plan of redemption be brought about unto you.* (Alma 34:30-31.)

Do not procrastinate the day of your repentance until the end; for after this day of life, which is given us to prepare for eternity, behold, if we do not improve our time while in this life, *then cometh the night of darkness wherein there can be no labor performed.* (Alma 34:33.)

If ye have procrastinated the day of your repentance even until death, behold, *ye have become subjected to the spirit of the devil, and he doth seal you his; therefore, the Spirit of the Lord hath withdrawn from you, and hath no place in you, and the devil hath all power over you; and this is the final state of the wicked.* (Alma 34:35.)

The Lord saw that his people [the Jaredites] began to work in darkness, yea, work secret murders and abominations; therefore the Lord said if they did not repent *they should be destroyed from off the face of the earth.* (Alma 37:22.)

Cursed be the land forever and ever unto those workers of darkness and secret combinations, even unto destruction, except they repent before they are fully ripe. (Alma 37:31.)

[to Corianton] Ye cannot hide your crimes from God; and except ye repent *they will stand as a testimony against you at the last day.* Now my son, I would that ye should repent and forsake your sins, and go no more after the lusts of your eyes, but cross yourself in all these things; for except ye do this *ye can in nowise inherit the kingdom of God.* (Alma 39:8-9.)

[to Corianton] Turn to the Lord with all your mind, might, and strength; . . . lead away the hearts of no more to do wickedly; but rather return unto them, and acknowledge your faults and that wrong which ye have done. (Alma 39:13.)

If he hath repented of his sins, and desired righteousness until the end of his days, *even so he shall be rewarded unto righteousness. These are they that are redeemed of the Lord; yea, these are they that are taken out, that are delivered from that endless night of darkness; and thus they stand or fall;* for behold, they are their own judges, whether to do good or do evil. (Alma 41:6-7.)

If he has desired to do evil, and has not repented in his days, behold, *evil shall be done unto him, according to the restoration of God.* (Alma 42:28.)

[Alma to Corianton] My son, I desire that ye should let these things trouble you no more, and only let your sins trouble you, with that trouble which shall bring you down unto repentance. (Alma 42:29.)

Inasmuch as they did repent *they did begin to prosper.* (Hel. 4:15.)

There came a voice as if it were above the cloud of darkness, saying: Repent ye, repent ye, and seek no more to destroy my servants whom I have sent unto you to declare good tidings. (Hel. 5:29; similar scripture, Hel. 5:32.)

[Aminadab to Lamanites caught in cloud of darkness] You must repent, and cry unto the voice, even until ye shall have faith in Christ, who was taught unto you by Alma, and Amulek, and Zeezrom; and when ye shall do this, *the cloud of darkness shall be removed from overshadowing you.* (Hel. 5:41.)

O repent ye, repent ye! *Why will ye die?* Turn ye, turn ye unto the Lord your God. *Why has he forsaken you?* It is because you have hardened your hearts; yea, ye will not hearken unto the voice of the good shepherd; yea, *ye have provoked him to anger against you.* And behold, instead of gathering you, except ye will repent, behold, *he shall scatter you forth that ye shall become meat for dogs and wild beasts.* O, how could you have forgotten your God in the very day that he has delivered you? But behold, it is to get gain, to be praised of men, yea, and that ye might get gold and silver. And ye have set your hearts upon the riches and the vain things of this world, for the which ye do murder, and plunder, and steal, and bear false witness against your neighbor, and do all manner of iniquity. And for this cause *wo shall come unto you* except ye shall repent. For if ye will not repent, behold, *this great city, and also all those great cities which are round about, which are in the land of our possession, shall be taken away that ye shall have no place in them; for behold, the Lord will not grant unto you strength, as he has hitherto done, to withstand against your enemies. For behold, thus saith the Lord: I will not show unto the wicked of my strength, to one more than the other,* save it be unto those who repent of their sins, and hearken unto my words. Now therefore, I would that ye should behold, my brethren, that *it shall be better for the Lamanites than for you* except ye shall repent. (Hel. 7:17-23.)

Except ye repent *ye shall perish; yea, even your lands shall be taken from you, and ye shall be destroyed from off the face of the earth.* (Hel. 7:28.)

Even at this time ye are ripening, because of your murders and your fornication and wickedness, for everlasting destruction; yea, and except ye repent *it will come upon you soon.* (Hel. 8:26.)

For this cause, *that men might be saved,* hath repentance been declared. Therefore, *blessed* are they who will repent and hearken unto the voice of the Lord their God; *for these are they that shall be saved.* (Hel. 12:22-23.)

*Heavy destruction awaiteth this people, and it surely cometh unto this
people, and nothing can save this people* save it be repentance and
faith on the Lord Jesus Christ, who surely shall come into the world,
and shall suffer many things and shall be slain for his people. And
behold, an angel of the Lord hath declared it unto me [Samuel the
Lamanite], and he did bring glad tidings to my soul. And behold, I
was sent unto you to declare it unto you also, that ye might have glad
tidings; but behold ye would not receive me. Therefore, thus saith the
Lord: Because of the hardness of the hearts of the people of the
Nephites, except they repent *I will take away my word from them,
and I will withdraw my Spirit from them, and I will suffer them no
longer, and I will turn the hearts of their brethren against them.* (Hel.
13:6-8.)

If ye will repent and return unto the Lord your God *I will turn away
mine anger, saith the Lord; yea, thus saith the Lord, blessed are they*
who will repent and turn unto me, *but wo unto him* that repenteth
not. (Hel. 13:11.)

The resurrection of Christ redeemeth mankind, yea, even all mankind, and bringeth them back into the presence of the Lord. Yea, and
it bringeth to pass the condition of repentance, that whosoever repenteth *the same is not hewn down and cast into the fire;* but
whosoever repenteth not *is hewn down and cast into the fire; and
there cometh upon them again a spiritual death, yea, a second death,
for they are cut off again as to things pertaining to righteousness.*
Therefore repent ye, repent ye, lest by knowing these things and not
doing them ye shall suffer yourselves to come under condemnation,
and ye are brought down unto this second death. (Hel. 14:17-19.)

Except ye shall repent *your houses shall be left unto you desolate.* Yea,
except ye repent, *your women shall have great cause to mourn in the
day that they shall give suck; for ye shall attempt to flee and there
shall be no place for refuge; yea, and wo unto them which are with
child, for they shall be heavy and cannot flee; therefore, they shall be
trodden down and shall be left to perish.* (Hel. 15:1-2.)

Concerning the people of the Nephites: If they will not repent, and
observe to do my will, *I will utterly destroy them, saith the Lord,* because of their unbelief notwithstanding the many mighty works

which I have done among them; *and as surely as the Lord liveth shall these things be, saith the Lord.* (Hel. 15:17.)

Whoso repenteth and cometh unto me as a little child, *him will I receive, for of such is the kingdom of God. Behold, for such I have laid down my life, and have taken it up again;* therefore repent, and come unto me ye ends of the earth, and *be saved.* (3 Ne. 9:22.)

O ye house of Israel whom I have spared, *how oft will I gather you as a hen gathereth her chickens under her wings,* if ye will repent and return unto me with full purpose of heart. (3 Ne. 10:6.)

This is my doctrine, and it is the doctrine which the Father hath given unto me; and I bear record of the Father, and the Father beareth record of me, and the Holy Ghost beareth record of the Father and me; and I bear record that the Father commandeth all men, everywhere, to repent and believe in me. (3 Ne. 11:32.)

I have given you the law and the commandments of my Father, that ye shall believe in me, and that ye shall repent of your sins, and come unto me with a broken heart and a contrite spirit. Behold, ye have the commandments before you, and the law is fulfilled. Therefore come unto me *and be ye saved.* (3 Ne. 12:19-20.)

If the Gentiles will repent and return unto me, saith the Father, behold *they shall be numbered among my people,* O house of Israel. (3 Ne. 16:13.)

If the Gentiles do not repent after the blessing which they shall receive, after they have scattered my people—then shall ye, who are a remnant of the house of Jacob, go forth among them; and ye shall be in the midst of them who shall be many; and *ye shall be among them as a lion among the beasts of the forest, and as a young lion among the flocks of sheep, who, if he goeth through both treadeth down and teareth in pieces, and none can deliver.* (3 Ne. 20:15-16.)

At that day whosoever will not repent and come unto my Beloved Son, *them will I cut off from among my people, O house of Israel; and I will execute vengeance and fury upon them, even as upon the heathen, such as they have not heard.* But if they will repent and hearken unto my words, and harden not their hearts, *I will establish my church among them, and they shall come in unto the covenant and be numbered among this the remnant of Jacob, unto whom I have given this land for their inheritance.* (3 Ne. 21:20-22.)

Repent ye, and humble yourselves before him, *lest he shall come out in justice against you—lest a remnant of the seed of Jacob shall go forth among you as a lion, and tear you in pieces, and there is none to deliver.* (Morm. 5:24.)

Know ye that ye must come unto repentance, *or ye cannot be saved.* (Morm. 7:3.)

Know ye that ye must come to the knowledge of your fathers, and repent of all your sins and iniquities, and believe in Jesus Christ. (Morm. 7:5.)

If it so be that they repent and come unto the Father in the name of Jesus, *they shall be received into the kingdom of God.* (Ether 5:5.)

There was great calamity in all the land, for they [Jaredite prophets] had testified that *a great curse should come upon the land, and also upon the people, and that there should be a great destruction among them, such an one as never had been upon the face of the earth, and their bones should become as heaps of earth upon the face of the land* except they should repent of their wickedness. (Ether 11:6.)

In the days of Coriantor there also came many prophets, and prophesied of great and marvelous things, and cried repentance unto the people, and except they should repent *the Lord God would execute judgment against them to their utter destruction; and that the Lord God would send or bring forth another people to possess the land, by his power, after the manner by which he brought their fathers.* (Ether 11:20-21.)

He [Ether] did cry from the morning, even until the going down of the sun, exhorting the people to believe in God unto repentance *lest they should be destroyed.* (Ether 12:3.)

Neither did they *receive any unto baptism* save they came forth with a broken heart and a contrite spirit, and witnessed unto the church that they truly repented of all their sins. (Moro. 6:2.)

Whoso was found to commit iniquity, and three witnesses of the church did condemn them before the elders, and if they repented not, and confessed not, *their names were blotted out, and they were not numbered among the people of Christ.* But as oft as they repented and sought forgiveness, with real intent, *they were forgiven.* (Moro. 6:7-8.)

Come unto Christ, and be perfected in him, and deny yourselves of all ungodliness; and if ye shall deny yourselves of all ungodliness, and love God with all your might, mind and strength, *then is his grace sufficient for you, that by his grace ye may be perfect in Christ; and if by the grace of God ye are perfect in Christ, ye can in nowise deny the power of God.* (Moro. 10:32.)

He that repents and does the commandments of the Lord *shall be forgiven;* and he that repents not, *from him shall be taken even the light which he has received; for my Spirit shall not always strive with man, saith the Lord of Hosts.* (D&C 1:32-33.)

[to Joseph Smith] Remember, God is merciful; therefore, repent of that which thou hast done which is contrary to the commandment which I gave you, *and thou art still chosen, and art again called to the work;* except thou do this, *thou shalt be delivered up and become as other men, and have no more gift.* (D&C 3:10-11.)

A desolating scourge shall go forth among the inhabitants of the earth, and shall continue to be poured out from time to time, if they repent not, *until the earth is empty, and the inhabitants thereof are consumed away and utterly destroyed by the brightness of my coming.* (D&C 5:19.)

I command you, my servant Joseph, to repent and walk more uprightly before me, and to yield to the persuasions of men no more; and that you be firm in keeping the commandments wherewith I have commanded you. (D&C 5:21-22.)

Go your ways and sin no more. (D&C 6:35.)

I command all men everywhere to repent. (D&C 18:9.)

Surely every man must repent *or suffer,* for I, God, am endless. (D&C 19:4.)

I command you to repent, and keep the commandments which you have received by the hand of my servant Joseph Smith, Jun., in my name. (D&C 19:13.)

I command you to repent—repent *lest I smite you by the rod of my mouth, and by my wrath, and by my anger, and your sufferings be sore—how sore you know not, how exquisite you know not, yea, how hard to bear you know not. For behold, I, God have suffered these things for all, that they might not suffer* if they would repent; but if they would not repent *they must suffer even as I.* (D&C 19:15-17.)

[to Martin Harris] I command you again to repent, *lest I humble you with my almighty power;* and that you confess your sins, *lest you suffer these punishments of which I have spoken, of which in the smallest, yea, even in the least degree you have tasted at the time I withdrew my Spirit.* (D&C 19:20.)

We know that all men must repent and believe on the name of Jesus Christ, and worship the Father in his name, and endure in faith on his name to the end, *or they cannot be saved in the kingdom of God.* (D&C 20:29.)

All those who humble themselves before God, and desire to be baptized, and come forth with broken hearts and contrite spirits, and witness before the church that they have truly repented of all their sins, and are willing to take upon them the name of Jesus Christ, having a determination to serve him to the end, and truly manifest by their works that they have received of the Spirit of Christ unto the remission of their sins, *shall be received by baptism into his church.* (D&C 20:37.)

Go thy way and sin no more. (D&C 24:2.)

Repent and be baptized, every one of you, for a remission of your sins; yea, be baptized even by water, *and then cometh the baptism of fire and of the Holy Ghost.* (D&C 33:11.)

He that has committed adultery and repents with all his heart, and forsaketh it, and doeth it no more, *thou shalt forgive;* but if he doeth it again, *he shall not be forgiven, but shall be cast out.* (D&C 42: 25-26.)

He that sinneth and repenteth not *shall be cast out.* (D&C 42:28.)

I will that all men shall repent, for all are under sin, except those which I have reserved unto myself, holy men that ye know not of. (D&C 49:8.)

Believe on the name of the Lord Jesus, who was on the earth, and is to come, the beginning and the end; repent and be baptized in the name of Jesus Christ, according to the holy commandment, for the remission of sins; and whoso doeth this *shall receive the gift of the Holy Ghost, by the laying on of the hands of the elders of the church.* (D&C 49:12-14.)

Go forth as I have commanded you; repent of all your sins; ask and ye shall receive; knock and it shall be opened unto you. *Behold, I will go before you and be your rearward; and I will be in your midst, and you shall not be confounded.* (D&C 49:26-27.)

If your brethren desire to escape their enemies, let them repent of all their sins and become truly humble before me and contrite. (D&C 54:3.)

You have many things to do and to repent of; for behold, *your sins have come up unto me, and are not pardoned,* because you seek to counsel in your own ways. And your hearts are not satisfied. And ye obey not the truth, but have pleasure in unrighteousness. (D&C 56:14-15.)

If he repent not of his sins, which are unbelief and blindness of heart, let him take heed *lest he fall.* (D&C 58:15.)

He who has repented of his sins, *the same is forgiven, and I, the Lord, remember them no more.* (D&C 58:42.)

Remember that on this, the Lord's day, thou shalt offer thine oblations and thy sacraments unto the Most High, confessing thy sins unto thy brethren, and before the Lord. (D&C 59:12.)

Let the church repent of their sins, *and I, the Lord, will own them; otherwise they shall be cut off.* (D&C 63:63.)

I, the Lord, forgive sins unto those who confess their sins before me and ask forgiveness, who have not sinned unto death. (D&C 64:7.)

Him that repenteth not of his sins, and confesseth them not, *ye shall bring before the church, and do with him as the scripture saith unto you, either by commandment or by revelation.* (D&C 64:12.)

[to William McLellin] You are clean, but not all; repent, therefore, of those things which are not pleasing in my sight, saith the Lord, for the Lord will show them unto you. (D&C 66:3.)

Seek not to be cumbered. Forsake all unrighteousness. (D&C 66:10.)

I, the Lord, will not lay any sin to your charge; go your ways and sin no more; but unto that soul who sinneth *shall the former sins return, saith the Lord your God.* (D&C 82:7.)

They shall remain under this condemnation until they repent and re-member the new covenant, even the Book of Mormon and the former commandments which I have given them, not only to say, but to do according to that which I have written. (D&C 84:57.)

Every soul who forsaketh his sins and cometh unto me, and calleth on my name, and obeyeth my voice, and keepeth my command-ments, *shall see my face and know that I am.* (D&C 93:1.)

I give unto you a commandment, that ye shall forsake all evil and cleave unto all good, that ye shall live by every word which pro-ceedeth forth out of the mouth of God. (D&C 98:11.)

When we undertake to cover our sins, or to gratify our pride, our vain ambition, or to exercise control or dominion or compulsion upon the souls of the children of men, in any degree of unrighteousness, be-hold, *the heavens withdraw themselves; the Spirit of the Lord is grieved; and when it is withdrawn, Amen to the priesthood or the au-thority of that man. Behold, ere he is aware, he is left unto himself, to kick against the pricks, to persecute the saints, and to fight against God.* (D&C 121:37-38.)

The Lord . . . commandeth all men everywhere to repent. (D&C 133:16.)

Thou shalt do all that thou doest in the name of the Son, and thou shalt repent and call upon God in the name of the Son forevermore. (Moses 5:8.)

As many as believed in the Son, and repented of their sins, *should be saved;* and as many as believed not and repented not, *should be damned;* and the words went forth out of the mouth of God in a firm decree; *wherefore they must be fulfilled.* (Moses 5:15.)

Enoch, my son, prophesy unto this people, and say unto them— Repent, for thus saith the Lord: *I am angry with this people, and my fierce anger is kindled against them,* for their hearts have waxed hard, and their ears are dull of hearing, and their eyes cannot see afar off. (Moses 6:27.)

A hell I have prepared for them, if they repent not. (Moses 6:29.)

And the Lord said unto Noah: My Spirit shall not always strive with man, . . . and if men do not repent, *I will send in the floods upon them.* (Moses 8:17.)

[Noah speaking to the wicked] Believe and repent of your sins and be baptized in the name of Jesus Christ, the Son of God, even as our fathers, *and ye shall receive the Holy Ghost, that ye may have all things made manifest;* and if ye do not this, *the floods will come in upon you;* nevertheless they hearkened not. (Moses 8:24.)

Reproving Others

Reproving another can be appropriate and wise. Yet if done incorrectly, reproving can do more damage than the behavior which makes reproof necessary. Our loving Father, who reproves us himself, tells us when and how to reprove others.

Among the clearest of these instructions is a passage in the Doctrine and Covenants. After explaining that the power and influence of the priesthood can be maintained only "by persuasion, by long-suffering, by gentleness and meekness, and by love unfeigned; by kindness, and pure knowledge," the Lord explains how those qualities apply to reproof: "Reproving betimes [i.e., immediately] with sharpness, when moved upon by the Holy Ghost; and then showing forth afterwards an increase of love toward him whom thou hast reproved, lest he esteem thee to be his enemy; that he may know that thy faithfulness is stronger than the cords of death." (D&C 121: 41-44.)

Reproving must carry the qualities and attitudes listed in the first two verses—persuasion, long-suffering, gentleness, meekness, love, kindness—and reproof must be based on pure knowledge, not on rumor or speculation. Initiated only at the direction of the Holy Ghost, it should come soon after the offense and must be followed by a demonstration of increased love. In this way, a correct reproof will foster perfection and increase love and unity.

Commandments and Promises

Thou shalt not hate thy brother in thine heart: thou shalt in any wise rebuke thy neighbour, and not suffer sin upon him. (Lev. 19:17.)

Lord, who shall abide in thy tabernacle? who shall dwell in thy holy hill? . . . He that backbiteth not with his tongue, nor doeth evil to his neighbour, nor taketh up a reproach against his neighbour. . . . He that doeth these things *shall never be moved.* (Ps. 15:1-5; see JST Ps. 15:1.)

470

Reprove not a scorner, *lest he hate thee:* rebuke a wise man, and *he will love thee.* (Prov. 9:8.)

Chasten thy son while there is hope, and let not thy soul spare for his crying. (Prov. 19:18.)

Withhold not correction from the child. (Prov. 23:13.)

Let no man strive, nor reprove another: for thy people are as they that strive with the priest. (Hosea 4:4.)

Take heed to yourselves: If thy brother trespass against thee, rebuke him; and if he repent, forgive him. (Luke 17:3.)

If a man be overtaken in a fault, ye which are spiritual, restore such an one in the spirit of meekness; considering thyself, *lest thou also be tempted.* (Gal. 6:1.)

Have no fellowship with the unfruitful works of darkness, but rather reprove them. (Eph. 5:11.)

If any man obey not our word by this epistle, note that man, and have no company with him, *that he may be ashamed.* Yet count him not as an enemy, but admonish him as a brother. (2 Thes. 3:14-15.)

Rebuke not an elder, but intreat him as a father; and the younger men as brethren; the elder women as mothers; the younger as sisters, with all purity. (1 Tim. 5:1-2.)

Reprove, rebuke, exhort with all longsuffering and doctrine. (2 Tim. 4:2; see also JST 2 Tim. 4:2.)

Denying ungodliness and worldly lusts, we should live soberly, righteously, and godly, in this present world; looking for that blessed hope, and the glorious appearing of the great God and our Saviour Jesus Christ; who gave himself for us, that he might redeem us from all iniquity, and purify unto himself a peculiar people, zealous of good works. These things speak, and exhort, and rebuke with all authority. (Titus 2:12-15.)

A commandment I give unto you, which is the word of God, that ye revile no more against them [the Lamanites], because of the darkness of their skins; neither shall ye revile against them because of their filthiness; but ye shall remember your own filthiness, and remember that their filthiness came because of their fathers. (Jacob 3:9.)

[to Oliver Cowdery] Be diligent; stand by my servant Joseph, faithfully, in whatsoever difficult circumstances he may be for the word's sake. Admonish him in his faults, and also receive admonition of him. (D&C 6:18-19.)

Thou shalt take thy brother, Hiram Page, between him and thee alone, and tell him that those things which he hath written from that stone are not of me and that Satan deceiveth him. (D&C 28:11.)

[to Thomas B. Marsh, president of the Twelve] Pray for thy brethren of the Twelve. Admonish them sharply for my name's sake, and let them be admonished for all their sins. (D&C 112:12.)

[Reprove] betimes with sharpness, when moved upon by the Holy Ghost; and then showing forth afterwards an increase of love toward him whom thou hast reproved, *lest he esteem thee to be his enemy.* (D&C 121:43.)

Retaliation

(See also Forgiving Others; Peace; Reproving Others.)

Christ teaches us that, no matter what is done to us, we are not to "render evil for evil" (1 Thes. 5:15), but instead we should "have patience, and bear with those afflictions, with a firm hope that [we] shall one day rest from all [our] afflictions." (Alma 34:41.) We are neither to contend with contenders, nor revile with revilers. Otherwise, we would "become sinners like unto them." (Alma 34:40.) Instead, Jesus says, "Love your enemies, . . . do good to them that hate you, and pray for them which despitefully use you, and persecute you." (Matt. 5:43-45.) "If thine enemy hunger, feed him; if he thirst, give him drink." (Rom. 12:20.) Refraining from the natural impulse toward retaliation may be difficult, but the promise for such self-control is rich: "Ye may be the children of your Father which is in heaven." (Matt. 5:45.)

Commandments and Promises

Thou shalt not avenge, nor bear any grudge against the children of thy people, but thou shalt love thy neighbour as thyself: I am the Lord. (Lev. 19:18.)

Say not thou, I will recompense evil; but wait on the Lord, *and he shall save thee.* (Prov. 20:22.)

Say not, I will do so to him as he hath done to me: I will render to the man according to his work. (Prov. 24:29.)

Ye have heard that it hath been said, Thou shalt love thy neighbour, and hate thine enemy. But I say unto you, Love your enemies, bless them that curse you, do good to them that hate you, and pray for them which despitefully use you, and persecute you; *that ye may be the children of your Father which is in heaven:* for he maketh his sun to rise on the evil and on the good, and sendeth rain on the just and on the unjust. (Matt. 5:43-45; similar scriptures, Luke 6:27-28, 3 Ne. 12:43-45.)

Unto him that smiteth thee on the one cheek offer also the other; and him that taketh away thy cloke forbid not to take thy coat also. (Luke 6:29; see also JST Luke 6:29-30.)

Bless them which persecute you: bless, and curse not. (Rom. 12:14.)

Recompense to no man evil for evil. Provide things honest in the sight of all men. (Rom. 12:17.)

Avenge not yourselves, but rather give place unto wrath: for it is written, Vengeance is mine; *I will repay, saith the Lord.* Therefore if thine enemy hunger, feed him; if he thirst, give him drink: for in so doing *thou shalt heap coals of fire on his head.* (Rom. 12:19-20.)

Being reviled, we bless; being persecuted, we suffer it; being defamed, we intreat. (1 Cor. 4:12-13.)

See that none render evil for evil unto any man; but ever follow that which is good, both among yourselves, and to all men. (1 Thes. 5:15.)

Be ye all of one mind, having compassion one of another, love as brethren, be pitiful, be courteous: not rendering evil for evil, or railing for railing: but contrariwise blessing; knowing that ye are thereunto called, *that ye should inherit a blessing.* (1 Pet. 3:8-9.)

I would exhort you to have patience, and that ye bear with all manner of afflictions; that ye do not revile against those who do cast you out because of your exceeding poverty, *lest ye become sinners like unto them;* but that ye have patience, and bear with those afflictions, with a firm hope that ye shall one day rest from all your afflictions. (Alma 34:40-41.)

Man shall not smite, neither shall he judge; for judgment is mine, saith the Lord, and vengeance is mine also, *and I will repay.* (Morm. 8:20.)

Thou shalt do it [publish glad tidings] with all humility, trusting in me, reviling not against revilers. (D&C 19:30.)

Revile not against those that revile. (D&C 31:9.)

If men will smite you, or your families, once, and ye bear it patiently and revile not against them, neither seek revenge, *ye shall be rewarded;* but if ye bear it not patiently, *it shall be accounted unto you as being meted out as a just measure unto you.* And again, if your enemy shall smite you the second time, and you revile not against your enemy, and bear it patiently, *your reward shall be an hundredfold.* And again, if he shall smite you the third time, and ye bear it patiently, *your reward shall be doubled unto you four-fold; and these three testimonies shall stand against your enemy if he repent not, and shall not be blotted out.* (D&C 98:23-27.)

Revelation

(See also Following God and His Servants; Listening to God and His
Servants; Looking to God; Prayer; Receiving and Following the
Holy Ghost; Spiritual Awareness.)

God speaks to us through many means. When Joseph Smith, as a
young man, asked for guidance, his answer was a visitation of the
Father and the Son. His direction came from the mouth of Jesus
Christ. When Oliver Cowdery requested a further witness, the Lord
told him in a revelation given through Joseph Smith, "Did I not speak
peace to your mind concerning the matter? What greater witness can
you have than from God?" (D&C 6:23.) The Savior has visited men,
spoken aloud to them, spoken to them through others, and prompted them through the Holy Ghost. Joseph Smith wrote in a revelation
of "the still small voice, which whispereth through and pierceth all
things, and often times it maketh my bones to quake while it maketh
manifest." (D&C 85:6.)

God commands us to seek divine communication, but to ask God
for a specific type or intensity of revelation would be as presumptuous as asking for a specific answer. Instead, we must seek God's
counsel in faith, having studied the matter ourselves, knowing that
when we ask God, God answers.

Commandments and Promises

Ask, *and it shall be given you*; seek, *and ye shall find*; knock, and it
shall be opened unto you: for every one that asketh *receiveth*; and he
that seeketh *findeth*; and to him that knocketh *it shall be opened*.
(Matt. 7:7-8; similar scriptures, Luke 11:9-10; 3 Ne. 14:7-8, 27:29;
D&C 4:7, 6:5, 11:5, 12:5, 14:5, 49:26, 66:9; see also 2 Ne. 9:42, D&C
75:27, JST Matt. 7:12-17.)

He hath filled the hungry *with good things;* and the rich *he hath sent
empty away.* (Luke 1:53.)

Blessed are ye that hunger now: *for ye shall be filled.* (Luke 6:21; see
also 3 Ne. 12:6.)

Be ye not unwise, but understanding what the will of the Lord is. (Eph. 5:17.)

Quench not the Spirit. (1 Thes. 5:19.)

If any of you lack wisdom, let him ask of God, that giveth to all men liberally, and upbraideth not; *and it shall be given him.* But let him ask in faith, nothing wavering. For he that wavereth is like a wave of the sea driven with the wind and tossed. *For let not that man think that he shall receive any thing of the Lord.* (James 1:5-7; see also D&C 42:68.)

Laying aside all malice, and all guile, and hypocrisies, and envies, and all evil speakings, as newborn babes, desire the sincere milk of the word, *that ye may grow thereby: if so be ye have tasted that the Lord is gracious.* (1 Pet. 2:1-3.)

He that diligently seeketh *shall find; and the mysteries of God shall be unfolded unto them, by the power of the Holy Ghost, as well in these times as in times of old, and as well in times of old as in times to come; wherefore, the course of the Lord is one eternal round.* (1 Ne. 10:19.)

After I have spoken these words, *if ye cannot understand them* it will be because ye ask not, neither do ye knock; *wherefore, ye are not brought into the light, but must perish in the dark.* (2 Ne. 32:4.)

Blessed are all they who do hunger and thirst after righteousness, *for they shall be filled with the Holy Ghost.* (3 Ne. 12:6; similar scripture, Matt. 5:6; see also Luke 6:21.)

I beseech of you, brethren, that ye should search diligently in the light of Christ *that ye may know good from evil;* and if ye will lay hold upon every good thing, and condemn it not, *ye certainly will be a child of Christ.* (Moro. 7:19.)

When ye shall receive these things, I would exhort you that ye would ask God, the Eternal Father, in the name of Christ, if these things are not true; and if ye shall ask with a sincere heart, with real intent, having faith in Christ, *he will manifest the truth of it unto you, by the power of the Holy Ghost. And by the power of the Holy Ghost ye may know the truth of all things.* (Moro. 10:4-5.)

Blessed art thou [Oliver Cowdery] for what thou hast done; for thou hast inquired of me, and behold, as often as thou hast inquired *thou hast received instruction of my Spirit.* If it had not been so, *thou wouldst not have come to the place where thou art at this time.* (D&C 6:14.)

If you [Oliver Cowdery] desire a further witness, cast your mind upon the night that you cried unto me in your heart, that you might know concerning the truth of these things. *Did I not speak peace to your mind concerning the matter? What greater witness can you have than from God?* (D&C 6:22-23.)

Oliver Cowdery, verily, verily, I say unto you, that *assuredly as the Lord liveth, who is your God and your Redeemer, even so surely shall you receive a knowledge of whatsoever things* you shall ask in faith, with an honest heart, believing that you shall receive a knowledge. . . . *Yea, behold, I will tell you in your mind and in your heart, by the Holy Ghost, which shall come upon you and which shall dwell in your heart. Now, behold, this is the spirit of revelation; behold, this is the spirit by which Moses brought the children of Israel through the Red Sea on dry ground. Therefore this is thy gift;* apply unto it, and *blessed art thou, for it shall deliver you out of the hands of your enemies, when, if it were not so, they would slay you and bring your soul to destruction.* (D&C 8:1-4.)

[to Oliver Cowdery] Ask that you may know the mysteries of God, and that you may translate and receive knowledge from all those ancient records which have been hid up, that are sacred; and according to your faith *shall it be done unto you.* (D&C 8:11.)

[to Oliver Cowdery] You must study it out in your mind; then you must ask me if it be right, *and if it is right I will cause that your bosom shall burn within you; therefore, you shall feel that it is right. But if it be not right you shall have no such feelings, but you shall have a stupor of thought that shall cause you to forget the thing which is wrong.* (D&C 9:8-9.)

I will impart unto you of my Spirit, which shall enlighten your mind, which shall fill your soul with joy; and then shall ye know, or by this shall you know, all things whatsoever you desire of me, which are per-

taining unto things of righteousness, in faith believing in me that you shall receive. (D&C 11:13-14.)

[to Hyrum Smith] Seek not to declare my word, but first seek to obtain my word, *and then shall your tongue be loosed; then,* if you desire, *you shall have my Spirit and my word, yea, the power of God unto the convincing of men.* (D&C 11:21.)

Ask the Father in my name, in faith believing that you shall receive, *and you shall have the Holy Ghost, which manifesteth all things which are expedient unto the children of men.* (D&C 18:18.)

He that lacketh wisdom, let him ask of me, *and I will give him liberally and upbraid him not.* (D&C 42:68; see also James 1:5.)

Let them ask *and they shall receive,* knock *and it shall be opened unto them, and be made known from on high, even by the Comforter, whither they shall go.* (D&C 75:27; see also Matt. 7:7-8.)

Search diligently, pray always, and be believing, *and all things shall work together for your good,* if ye walk uprightly and remember the covenant wherewith ye have covenanted one with another. (D&C 90:24.)

If any man shall seek to build up himself, and seeketh not my counsel, *he shall have no power, and his folly shall be made manifest.* Seek ye; and keep all your pledges one with another; and covet not that which is thy brother's. (D&C 136:19-20.)

Righteousness

(See also Fleeing Evil; Obedience.)

The power of righteousness is evident in the Book of Mormon account of Moroni. After describing Moroni's righteousness, the account reads: "If all men had been, and were, and ever would be, like unto Moroni, behold, the very powers of hell would have been shaken forever; yea, the devil would never have power over the hearts of the children of men." (Alma 48:17.)

Righteousness gives us power. Choosing God's ways instead of the adversary's diversions protects us from evil influences and binds Satan's powers over us.

The scriptures also symbolize righteousness as protection. Paul writes of "the armour of righteousness" and "the breastplate of righteousness." (2 Cor 6:7 and Eph. 6:14.) The Lord uses the same image in a similar statement in the Doctrine and Covenants. (See D&C 27:16.)

Paul explains that all who wrestle with unrighteousness learn this: "For we wrestle not against flesh and blood, but against principalities, against powers, against the rulers of the darkness of this world, against spiritual wickedness in high places. Wherefore take unto you the whole armour of God, that ye may be able to withstand in the evil day, and having done all, to stand." (Eph. 6:12-13.).

Commandments and Promises

Thou shalt do that which is right and good in the sight of the Lord: *that it may be well with thee, and that thou mayest go in and possess the good land which the Lord sware unto thy fathers, to cast out all thine enemies from before thee, as the Lord hath spoken.* (Deut. 6: 18-19.)

The Lord rewarded me according to my righteousness: according to the cleanness of my hands *hath he recompensed me.* (2 Sam. 22:21.)

Blessed is the man that walketh not in the counsel of the ungodly, nor standeth in the way of sinners, nor sitteth in the seat of the scornful. But his delight is in the law of the Lord; and in his law doth he meditate day and night. *And he shall be like a tree planted by the rivers of water, that bringeth forth his fruit in his season; his leaf also shall not wither; and whatsoever he doeth shall prosper.* The ungodly *are not so: but are like the chaff which the wind driveth away.* Therefore the ungodly *shall not stand in the judgment,* nor sinners *in the congregation of the righteous. For the Lord knoweth the way* of the righteous: *but the way* of the ungodly *shall perish.* (Ps. 1:1-6.)

Stand in awe, and sin not: commune with your own heart upon your bed, and be still. (Ps. 4:4.)

Thou art not a God that hath pleasure in wickedness: *neither shall evil dwell with thee.* (Ps. 5:4.)

Thou, Lord, wilt bless the righteous; *with favour wilt thou compass him as with a shield.* (Ps. 5:12.)

The Lord trieth the righteous: but the wicked and him that loveth violence *his soul hateth.* (Ps. 11:5.)

Lord, who shall abide in thy tabernacle? who shall dwell in thy holy hill? He that walketh uprightly, and worketh righteousness, and speaketh the truth in his heart. (Ps. 15:1-2; see also Ps. 15:1.)

Many sorrows shall be to the wicked: but he that trusteth in the Lord, *mercy shall compass him about.* (Ps. 32:10.)

The face of the Lord is against them that do evil, *to cut off the remembrance of them from the earth.* The righteous cry, *and the Lord heareth, and delivereth them out of all their troubles.* (Ps. 34:16-17.)

Evil shall slay the wicked: and they that hate the righteous *shall be desolate.* (Ps. 34:21.)

Evildoers *shall be cut off:* but those that wait upon the Lord, *they shall inherit the earth. For yet a little while, and* the wicked *shall not be: yea, thou shalt diligently consider his place, and it shall not be.* (Ps. 37:9-10.)

The wicked plotteth against the just, and gnasheth upon him with his teeth. *The Lord shall laugh at him: for he seeth that his day is coming.* The wicked have drawn out the sword, and have bent their bow, to cast down the poor and needy, and to slay such as be of upright conversation. *Their sword shall enter into their own heart, and their bows shall be broken.* A little that a righteous man hath is better than the riches of many wicked. *For the arms* of the wicked *shall be broken: but the Lord upholdeth* the righteous. *The Lord knoweth the days* of the upright: *and their inheritance shall be for ever. They shall not be ashamed in the evil time: and in the days of famine they shall be satisfied.* But the wicked *shall perish,* and the enemies of the Lord *shall be as the fat of lambs: they shall consume; into smoke shall they consume away.* (Ps. 37:12-20.)

The steps of a good man *are ordered by the Lord: and he delighteth in his way. Though he fall, he shall not be utterly cast down: for the Lord upholdeth him with his hand. I have been young, and now am old; yet have I not seen* the righteous *forsaken, nor his seed begging bread.* He is ever merciful, and lendeth; *and his seed is blessed.* Depart from evil, and do good; *and dwell for evermore. For the Lord loveth judgment, and forsaketh not his saints; they are preserved for ever: but the seed* of the wicked *shall be cut off.* The righteous *shall inherit the land, and dwell therein for ever.* The mouth of the righteous speaketh wisdom, and his tongue talketh of judgment. The law of God is in his heart; none of his steps shall slide. The wicked watcheth the righteous, and seeketh to slay him. *The Lord will not leave him in his hand, nor condemn him when he is judged.* (Ps. 37:23-33.)

All the horns of the wicked also *will I cut off;* but the horns of the righteous *shall be exalted.* (Ps. 75:10.)

The righteous *shall flourish like the palm tree: he shall grow like a cedar in Lebanon.* (Ps. 92:12.)

Ye that love the Lord, hate evil: *he preserveth the souls of his saints; he delivereth them out of the hand of the wicked. Light is sown* for the righteous, *and gladness* for the upright in heart. (Ps. 97:10-11.)

Blessed are they that keep judgment, and he that doeth righteousness at all times. (Ps. 106:3.)

Unto the upright *there ariseth light in the darkness:* he is gracious, and full of compassion, and righteous. (Ps. 112:4.)

Surely the righteous shall give thanks unto thy name: the upright *shall dwell in thy presence.* (Ps. 140:13.)

The Lord preserveth all them that love him: but all the wicked *will he destroy.* (Ps. 145:20.)

He layeth up sound wisdom for the righteous: *he is a buckler* to them that walk uprightly. (Prov. 2:7.)

Envy thou not the oppressor, and choose none of his ways. For the froward *is abomination to the Lord: but his secret is* with the righteous. *The curse of the Lord is in the house* of the wicked: *but he blesseth the habitation* of the just. (Prov. 3:31-33.)

Enter not into the path of the wicked, and go not in the way of evil men. Avoid it, pass not by it, turn from it, and pass away. (Prov. 4: 14-15.)

The fear of the Lord is to hate evil: pride, and arrogancy, and the evil way, and the froward mouth, *do I hate.* (Prov. 8:13.)

The Lord will not suffer the soul of the righteous *to famish: but he casteth away the substance of the wicked.* (Prov. 10:3.)

Blessings are upon the head of the just: *but violence covereth the mouth* of the wicked. *The memory* of the just *is blessed: but the name* of the wicked *shall rot.* (Prov. 10:6-7.)

The mouth of a righteous man *is a well of life: but violence covereth the mouth* of the wicked. (Prov. 10:11.)

The fear of the wicked, *it shall come upon him: but the desire* of the righteous *shall be granted. As the whirlwind passeth, so is* the wicked *no more:* but the righteous *is an everlasting foundation.* (Prov. 10: 24-25.)

The years of the wicked *shall be shortened. The hope* of the righteous *shall be gladness: but the expectation* of the wicked *shall perish.* (Prov. 10:27-28.)

The righteousness of the perfect *shall direct his way:* but the wicked *shall fall by his own wickedness.* The righteousness of the upright *shall deliver them:* but transgressors *shall be taken in their own naughtiness.* When a wicked man dieth, *his expectation shall perish: and the hope* of the unjust men *perisheth.* The righteous *is delivered out of trouble,* and the wicked *cometh in his stead.* (Prov. 11:5-8.)

The wicked worketh a deceitful work: but to him that soweth righteousness *shall be a sure reward.* As righteousness *tendeth to life:* so he that pursueth evil *pursueth it to his own death.* (Prov. 11:18-19.)

He that diligently seeketh good *procureth favour:* but he that seeketh mischief, *it shall come unto him.* (Prov. 11:27.)

The fruit of the righteous *is a tree of life;* and he that winneth souls *is wise.* Behold, the righteous *shall be recompensed in the earth: much more* the wicked and the sinner. (Prov. 11:30-31.)

Righteousness keepeth him that is upright *in the way:* but wickedness *overthroweth the sinner.* (Prov. 13:6.)

The light of the righteous *rejoiceth: but the lamp* of the wicked *shall be put out.* (Prov. 13:9.)

The house of the wicked *shall be overthrown: but the tabernacle* of the upright *shall flourish.* (Prov. 14:11.)

The sacrifice of the wicked *is an abomination to the Lord:* but the prayer of the upright *is his delight. The way* of the wicked is *an abomination unto the Lord: but he loveth* him that followeth after righteousness. (Prov. 15:8-9.)

It is joy to the just to do judgment: *but destruction shall be* to the workers of iniquity. (Prov. 21:15.)

Better is the poor that walketh in his uprightness, than he that is perverse in his ways, though he be rich. (Prov. 28:6.)

Whoso walketh uprightly *shall be saved:* but he that is perverse in his ways *shall fall at once.* (Prov. 28:18.)

Be not over much wicked, neither be thou foolish: *why shouldest thou die before thy time?* (Eccl. 7:17.)

Be not hasty to go out of his [God's] sight: stand not in an evil thing. (Eccl. 8:3.)

It shall not be well with the wicked, *neither shall he prolong his days, which are as a shadow;* because he feareth not before God. (Eccl. 8:13.)

Say ye to the righteous, *that it shall be well with him: for they shall eat the fruit of their doings. Woe* unto the wicked! *it shall be ill with him: for the reward of his hands shall be given him.* (Isa. 3:10-11; see also 2 Ne. 13:10-11.)

The Lord shall have no joy in their young men, neither shall have mercy on their fatherless and widows: for every one is an hypocrite and an evildoer, and every mouth speaketh folly. For all this *his anger is not turned away, but his hand is stretched out still.* For wickedness *burneth as the fire: it shall devour the briers and thorns, and shall kindle in the thickets of the forest, and they shall mount up like the lifting up of smoke. Through the wrath of the Lord of hosts is the land darkened, and the people shall be as the fuel of the fire: no man shall spare his brother.* (Isa. 9:17-19; similar scripture, 2 Ne. 19:17-19.)

I will punish the world for their evil, and the wicked for their iniquity. (Isa. 13:11; similar scripture, 2 Ne. 23:11.)

The terrible one *is brought to nought,* and the scorner *is consumed,* and all that watch for iniquity *are cut off.* (Isa. 29:20; similar scripture, 2 Ne. 27:31.)

There is no peace, saith the Lord, unto the wicked. (Isa. 48:22; similar scriptures, Isa. 57:21, 1 Ne. 20:22.)

Keep ye judgment, and do justice: for my salvation is near to come, and my righteousness to be revealed. *Blessed* is the man that doeth this, and the son of man that layeth hold on it; that keepeth the sabbath from polluting it, and keepeth his hand from doing any evil. (Isa. 56:1-2.)

The wicked *are like the troubled sea, when it cannot rest, whose waters cast up mire and dirt.* (Isa. 57:20.)

The Lord's hand is not shortened, that it cannot save; neither his ear heavy, that it cannot hear: but your iniquities *have separated between you and your God,* and your sins *have hid his face from you, that he will not hear.* (Isa. 59:1-2.)

Therefore is judgment far from us, neither doth justice overtake us: we wait for light, but behold obscurity; for brightness, but we walk in darkness. We grope for the wall like the blind, and we grope as if we had no eyes: we stumble at noonday as in the night; we are in desolate places as dead men. We roar all like bears, and mourn sore like doves: we look for judgment, but there is none; for salvation, but it is far off from us. For our transgressions are multiplied before thee, and our sins testify against us: for our transgressions are with us; and as for our iniquities, we know them; in transgressing and lying against the Lord, and departing away from our God, speaking oppression and revolt, conceiving and uttering from the heart words of falsehood. *And judgment is turned away backward, and justice standeth afar off:* for truth is fallen in the street, and equity cannot enter. Yea, truth faileth; and he that departeth from evil *maketh himself a prey:* and the Lord saw it, *and it displeased him* that there was no judgment. (Isa. 59:9-15.)

I also will choose their delusions, and will bring their fears upon them; because when I called, none did answer; when I spake, they did not hear: but they did evil before mine eyes, and chose that *in which I delighteth not.* (Isa. 66:4.)

Stand ye in the ways, and see, and ask for the old paths, where is the good way, and walk therein, *and ye shall find rest for your souls.* (Jer. 6:16.)

The Lord our God hath put us to silence, and given us water of gall to drink, because we have sinned against the Lord. (Jer. 8:14.)

The Lord ... will give them that are wicked *to the sword,* saith the Lord. Thus saith the Lord of hosts, Behold, evil shall go forth from nation to nation, *and a great whirlwind shall be raised up from the coasts of the earth. And the slain of the Lord shall be at that day from one end of the earth even unto the other end of the earth: they shall not be lamented, neither gathered, nor buried; they shall be dung upon the ground.* (Jer. 25:31-33.)

Son of man, I have made thee a watchman unto the house of Israel: therefore hear the word at my mouth, and give them warning from me. When I say unto the wicked, *Thou shalt surely die;* and thou givest him not warning, nor speakest to warn the wicked from his wicked way to save his life; the same wicked man *shall die in his iniquity; but his blood will I require at thine hand.* Yet if thou warn the wicked, and he turn not from his wickedness, nor from his wicked way, *he shall die in his iniquity; but thou hast delivered thy soul.* Again, When a righteous man doth turn from his righteousness, and commit iniquity, and I lay a stumblingblock before him, *he shall die:* because thou hast not given him warning, *he shall die in his sin, and his righteousness which he hath done shall not be remembered; but his blood will I require at thine hand.* Nevertheless if thou warn the righteous man, that the righteous sin not, and he doth not sin, *he shall surely live,* because he is warned; *also thou hast delivered thy soul.* (Ezek. 3:17-21.)

The soul that sinneth, *it shall die.* The son shall not bear the iniquity of the father, neither shall the father bear the iniquity of the son: the righteousness of the righteous shall be upon him, and the wickedness of the wicked shall be upon him. But if the wicked will turn from all his sins that he hath committed, and keep all my statutes, and do that which is lawful and right, *he shall surely live, he shall not die.* All his transgressions that he hath committed, *they shall not be mentioned unto him:* in his righteousness that he hath done *he shall live.* (Ezek. 18:20-22.)

When the righteous turneth away from his righteousness, and committeth iniquity, and doeth according to all the abominations that the wicked man doeth, *shall he live? All his righteousness that he hath done shall not be mentioned:* in his trespass that he hath trespassed, and in his sin that he hath sinned, *in them shall he die.* (Ezek. 18:24.)

When a righteous man turneth away from his righteousness, and committeth iniquity, and dieth in them; for his iniquity that he hath done *shall he die*. Again, when the wicked man turneth away from his wickedness that he hath committed, and doeth that which is lawful and right, *he shall save his soul alive*. Because he considereth, and turneth away from all his transgressions that he hath committed, *he shall surely live, he shall not die*. (Ezek. 18:26-28.)

I will judge you, O house of Israel, every one according to his ways, saith the Lord God. Repent, and turn yourselves from all your transgressions; *so iniquity shall not be your ruin*. Cast away from you all your transgressions, whereby ye have transgressed; and make you a new heart and a new spirit: *for why will ye die, O house of Israel?* (Ezek. 18:30-31.)

When I shall say to the righteous, *that he shall surely live;* if he trust to his own righteousness, and commit iniquity, *all his righteousness shall not be remembered;* but for his iniquity that he hath committed, *he shall die for it.* (Ezek. 33:13.)

When the righteous turneth from his righteousness, and committeth iniquity, *he shall even die thereby.* (Ezek. 33:18.)

The wicked shall do wickedly: and *none* of the wicked *shall understand; but* the wise *shall understand.* (Dan. 12:10.)

Seek good, and not evil, *that ye may live: and so the Lord, the God of hosts, shall be with you, as ye have spoken.* (Amos 5:14.)

The day cometh, that shall burn as an oven; and all the proud, yea, and all that do wickedly, *shall be stubble: and the day that cometh shall burn them up, saith the Lord of hosts, that it shall leave them neither root nor branch.* (Mal. 4:1; similar scriptures, 1 Ne. 22:15, 2 Ne. 26:4, 3 Ne. 25:1, D&C 29:9, 64:24, 133:64.)

Blessed are they which do hunger and thirst after righteousness, *for they shall be filled.* (Matt. 5:6; see also 3 Ne. 12:6.)

Except your righteousness shall exceed the righteousness of the scribes and Pharisees, *ye shall in no case enter into the kingdom of heaven.* (Matt. 5:20.)

If thine eye be evil, *thy whole body shall be full of darkness.* If therefore the light that is in thee be darkness, *how great is that darkness!*
(Matt. 6:23; similar scripture, 3 Ne. 13:23.)

*Not every one that saith unto me, Lord, Lord, shall enter into the king-
dom of heaven;* but he that doeth the will of my Father which is in
heaven. Many will say to me in that day, Lord, Lord, have we not
prophesied in thy name? and in thy name have cast out devils? and in
thy name done many wonderful works? And then will I profess unto
them, *I never knew you: depart from me,* ye that work iniquity. (Matt.
7:21-23; see also JST Matt. 7:31.)

Then shall the righteous *shine forth as the sun in the kingdom of their
father.* (Matt. 13:43; similar scripture, Alma 40:25.)

[God] will render to every man according to his deeds: to them who by
patient continuance in well doing seek for glory and honour and immortality, *eternal life:* but unto them that are contentious, and do not
obey the truth, but obey unrighteousness, *indignation and wrath,
tribulation and anguish,* upon every soul of man that doeth evil, of
the Jew first, and also of the Gentile; *but glory, honour, and peace,* to
every man that worketh good, to the Jew first, and also to the Gentile.
(Rom. 2:6-10.)

Let not sin therefore reign in your mortal body, *that ye should obey it
in the lusts thereof.* Neither yield ye your members as instruments of
unrighteousness unto sin: but yield yourselves unto God, as those
that are alive from the dead, and your members as instruments of
righteousness unto God. (Rom. 6:12-13.)

I speak after the manner of men because of the infirmity of your
flesh: for as ye have yielded your members servants to uncleanness
and to iniquity *unto iniquity;* even so now yield your members servants to righteousness *unto holiness.* (Rom. 6:19.)

Now being made free from sin, and become servants to God, *ye have
your fruit unto holiness, and the end everlasting life.* For the wages of
sin *is death.* (Rom. 6:22-23.)

If thou do that which is evil, be afraid; *for he beareth not the sword in vain: for he is the minister of God, a revenger to execute wrath* upon him that doeth evil. (Rom. 13:4.)

Awake to righteousness, and sin not; for some have not the knowledge of God. (1 Cor. 15:34.)

In all things approving ourselves as the ministers of God, in much patience, in afflictions, in necessities, in distresses, in stripes, in imprisonments, in tumults, in labours, in watchings, in fastings; by pureness, by knowledge, by longsuffering, by kindness, by the Holy Ghost, by love unfeigned, by the word of truth, by the power of God, by the armour of righteousness on the right hand and on the left. (2 Cor. 6:4-7.)

The works of the flesh are manifest, which are these; Adultery, fornication, uncleanness, lasciviousness, idolatry, witchcraft, hatred, variance, emulations, wrath, strife, seditions, heresies, envyings, murders, drunkenness, revellings, and such like: of the which I tell you before, as I have also told you in time past, that they which do such things *shall not inherit the kingdom of God.* (Gal. 5:19-21.)

Take unto you the whole armour of God, *that ye may be able to withstand in the evil day, and having done all, to stand.* Stand therefore, having your loins girt about with truth, and having on the breastplate of righteousness; and your feet shod with the preparation of the gospel of peace; above all, taking the shield of faith, *wherewith ye shall be able to quench all the fiery darts of the wicked.* And take the helmet of salvation, and the sword of the Spirit, which is the word of God: praying always with all prayer and supplication in the Spirit, and watching thereunto with all perseverance and supplication for all saints. (Eph. 6:13-18; similar scripture, D&C 27:15-18.)

For this cause God shall send them strong delusion, that they should believe a lie: that they all might be damned who believed not the truth, but had pleasure in unrighteousness. (2 Thes. 2:11-12.)

Study to shew thyself approved unto God, a workman that needeth not to be ashamed, rightly dividing the word of truth. (2 Tim. 2:15.)

When lust hath conceived, *it bringeth forth sin:* and sin, when it is finished, *bringeth forth death.* (James 1:15.)

The eyes of the Lord are over the righteous, *and his ears are open unto their prayers: but the face of the Lord is against* them that do evil. (1 Pet. 3:12.)

Let none of you suffer as a murderer, or as a thief, or an an evildoer, or as a busybody in other men's matters. (1 Pet. 4:15.)

Giving all diligence, add to your faith virtue; and to virtue knowledge; and to knowledge temperance; and to temperance patience; and to patience godliness; and to godliness brotherly kindness; and to brotherly kindness charity. For if these things be in you, and abound, *they make you that ye shall neither be barren nor unfruitful in the knowledge of our Lord Jesus Christ.* But he that lacketh these things *is blind, and cannot see afar off, and hath forgotten that he was purged from his old sins.* (2 Pet. 1:5-9.)

He that doeth righteousness *is righteous, even as he is righteous.* He that committeth sin *is of the devil; for the devil sinneth from the beginning.* (1 Jn. 3:7-8; see also JST 1 Jn. 3:8.)

In this the children of God are manifest, and the children of the devil: whoever doeth not righteousness *is not of God,* neither he that loveth not his brother. (1 Jn. 3:10.)

The fearful, and unbelieving, and the abominable, and murderers, and whoremongers, and sorcerers, and idolaters, and all liars, *shall have their part in the lake which burneth with fire and brimstone: which is the second death.* (Rev. 21:8; similar scripture, D&C 63:17.)

Remember, O man, *for all thy doings thou shalt be brought into judgment.* Wherefore, if ye have sought to do wickedly in the days of your probation, *then ye are found unclean before the judgment-seat of God; and no unclean thing can dwell with God; wherefore, ye must be cast off forever.* (1 Ne. 10:20-21.)

He raiseth up a righteous nation, *and destroyeth* the nations of the wicked. (1 Ne. 17:37.)

The righteous *need not fear, for they are those who shall not be con-founded.* But it is the kingdom of the devil, which shall be built up among the children of men, which kingdom is established among them which are in the flesh—for the time speedily shall come that all churches which are built up to get gain, and all those who are built up to get power over the flesh, and those who are built up to become popular in the eyes of the world, and those who seek the lusts of the flesh and the things of the world, and to do all manner of iniquity; yea, in fine, all those who belong to the kingdom of the devil *are they who need fear, and tremble, and quake; they are those who must be brought low in the dust; they are those who must be consumed as stubble; and this is according to the words of the prophet.* And the time cometh speedily that the righteous *must be led up as calves of the stall, and the Holy One of Israel must reign in dominion, and might, and power, and great glory.* . . . And because of the righ-teousness of his people, *Satan has no power; wherefore, he cannot be loosed for the space of many years; for he hath no power over the hearts of the people, for they dwell in righteousness, and the Holy One of Israel reigneth.* (1 Ne. 22:22-26.)

[to Zoram, the servant of Laban] Because thou hast been faithful *thy seed shall be blessed with his seed, that they dwell in prosperity long upon the face of this land; and nothing,* save it shall be iniquity among them, *shall harm or disturb their prosperity upon the face of this land forever.* (2 Ne. 1:31.)

They who are righteous *shall be righteous still,* and they who are filthy *shall be filthy still;* wherefore, they who are filthy *are the devil and his angels; and they shall go away into everlasting fire, prepared for them; and their torment is as a lake of fire and brimstone, whose flame ascendeth up forever and ever and has no end.* (2 Ne. 9:16.)

Because of their [the Jews'] iniquities, *destructions, famines, pesti-lences, and bloodshed shall come upon them; and they who shall not be destroyed shall be scattered among all nations.* (2 Ne. 10:6.)

Say unto the righteous that *it is well with them; for they shall eat the fruit of their doings. Wo unto the wicked, for they shall perish; for the reward of their hands shall be upon them!* (2 Ne. 13:10-11; see also Isa. 3:10-11.)

The day shall come that the Lord God will speedily visit the inhabitants of the earth; and in that day that they are fully ripe in iniquity *they shall perish.* (2 Ne. 28:16.)

The Lord did visit them in great judgment; nevertheless, he did spare the righteous *that they should not perish, but did deliver them out of the hands of their enemies.* (Omni 1:7.)

[King Benjamin to people of Zarahemla] I say unto you, that if this highly favored people of the Lord should fall into transgression, and become a wicked and an adulterous people, that *the Lord will deliver them up, that thereby they become weak like unto their brethren; and he will no more preserve them by his matchless and marvelous power, as he has hitherto preserved our fathers.* (Mosiah 1:13.)

They shall be judged, every man according to his works, whether they be good, or whether they be evil. And if they be evil *they are consigned to an awful view of their own guilt and abominations, which doth cause them to shrink from the presence of the Lord into a state of misery and endless torment, from whence they can no more return; therefore they have drunk damnation to their own souls.* (Mosiah 3:25.)

If ye do not watch yourselves, and your thoughts, and your words, and your deeds, and observe the commandments of God, and continue in the faith of what ye have heard concerning the coming of our Lord, even unto the end of your lives, *ye must perish.* And now, O man, remember, *and perish not.* (Mosiah 4:30.)

This generation [people of King Noah], because of their iniquities, *shall be brought into bondage, and shall be smitten on the cheek; yea, and shall be driven by men, and shall be slain; and the vultures of the air, and the dogs, yea, and the wild beasts, shall devour their flesh. . . . I will smite this my people with sore afflictions, yea, with famine and with pestilence; and I will cause that they shall howl all the day long. Yea, and I will cause that they shall have burdens lashed upon their backs; and they shall be driven before like a dumb ass. And it shall come to pass that I will send forth hail among them, and it shall smite them; and they shall also be smitten with the east wind; and insects shall pester their land also, and devour their grain. And they shall be smitten with a great pestilence—and all this will I do* because of their iniquities and abominations. (Mosiah 12:2-7.)

The names of the righteous *shall be written in the book of life, and unto them will I grant an inheritance at my right hand.* (Alma 5:58.)

[Alma to people of Ammonihah] I say unto you, that if ye persist in your wickedness that *your days shall not be prolonged in the land, for the Lamanites shall be sent upon you;* and if ye repent not *they shall come in a time when you know not, and ye shall be visited with utter destruction; and it shall be according to the fierce anger of the Lord.* (Alma 9:18.)

The Lord hath said he dwelleth not in unholy temples, but in the hearts of the righteous *doth he dwell;* yea, and he has also said that the righteous *shall sit down in his kingdom, to go no more out; but their garments should be made white through the blood of the Lamb.* (Alma 34:36.)

There is a curse upon all this land [the Americas], that destruction shall come upon all those workers of darkness, *according to the power of God,* when they are fully ripe. (Alma 37:28.)

The spirits of those who are righteous *are received into a state of happiness, which is called paradise, a state of rest, a state of peace, where they shall rest from all their troubles and from all care, and sorrow. And then shall it come to pass,* that the spirits of the wicked, yea, who are evil—for behold, they chose evil works rather than good; therefore the spirit of the devil did enter into them, and take possession of their house—*and these shall be cast out into outer darkness; there shall be weeping, and wailing, and gnashing of teeth, and this because of their own iniquity, being led captive by the will of the devil. Now this is the state of the souls of the wicked, yea, in darkness, and a state of awful, fearful looking for the fiery indignation of the wrath of God upon them; thus they remain in this state, as well as the righteous in paradise, until the time of their resurrection.* (Alma 40:12-14.)

If their works are evil *they shall be restored unto them for evil. Therefore, all things shall be restored to their proper order, every thing to*

*its natural frame—mortality raised to immortality, corruption to in-
corruption—raised to endless happiness to inherit the kingdom of
God, or to endless misery to inherit the kingdom of the devil, the one on
the one hand, the other on the other—the one raised to happiness according to his desires of happiness, or good according to his desires of
good; and the other to evil according to his desires of evil;* for as he has
desired to do evil all the day long *even so shall he have his reward of
evil when the night cometh. And so it is on the other hand.* If he hath
repented of his sins, and desired righteousness until the end of his
days, *even so he shall be rewarded unto righteousness. These are they
that are redeemed of the Lord; yea, these are they that are taken out,
that are delivered from that endless night of darkness; and thus they
stand or fall; for behold, they are their own judges, whether to do good
or do evil.* (Alma 41:4-7.)

All men that are in a state of nature, or I would say, in a carnal state,
*are in the gall of bitterness and in the bonds of iniquity; they are with-
out God in the world,* and they have gone contrary to the nature of
God; therefore, *they are in a state contrary to the nature of happiness.*
(Alma 41:11.)

Wo be unto you because of that great abomination which has come
among you; and ye have united yourselves unto it, yea, to that secret
band which was established by Gadianton! (Hel. 7:25.)

Ye were separated from among them [the other sheep] because of their
iniquity *that they know not of you.* (3 Ne. 15:19.)

At that day when the Gentiles shall sin against my gospel, and shall
reject the fulness of my gospel, and shall be lifted up in the pride of
their hearts above all nations, and above all the people of the whole
earth, and shall be filled with all manner of lyings, and of deceits,
and of mischiefs, and all manner of hypocrisy, and murders, and
priestcrafts, and whoredoms, and of secret abominations; and if
they shall do all those things, and shall reject the fulness of my gospel, behold, saith the Father, *I will bring the fulness of my gospel from
among them.* (3 Ne. 16:10.)

Wickedness did prevail upon the face of the whole land [of the
Nephites and Lamanites], insomuch that *the Lord did take away his*

beloved disciples, and the work of miracles and of healing did cease because of the iniquity of the people. *And there were no gifts from the Lord and the Holy Ghost did not come upon any,* because of their wickedness and unbelief. (Morm. 1:13-14.)

The Lord will remember the prayers of the righteous, *which have been put up unto him for them.* (Morm. 5:21.)

See that ye do all things in worthiness, and do it in the name of Jesus Christ, the Son of the living God; and if ye do this, and endure to the end, *ye will in nowise be cast out.* (Morm. 9:29.)

I will forgive thee [brother of Jared] and thy brethren of their sins; but thou shalt not sin any more, for ye shall remember that my Spirit will not always strive with man; wherefore, if ye will sin until ye are fully ripe *ye shall be cut off from the presence of the Lord.* (Ether 2:15.)

Come unto Christ, and lay hold upon every good gift, and touch not the evil gift, nor the unclean thing. (Moro. 10:30.)

You must walk uprightly before me and sin not. (D&C 18:31.)

I revoke not the judgments which I shall pass, but *woes shall go forth, weeping, wailing and gnashing of teeth,* yea, to those who are found on my left hand. (D&C 19:5.)

If thou art faithful and walk in the paths of virtue before me, *I will preserve thy life, and thou shalt receive an inheritance in Zion.* (D&C 25:2.)

[Joseph Smith to six elders] At this time your sins are forgiven you, therefore ye receive these things; but remember to sin no more, *lest perils shall come upon you.* (D&C 29:3.)

Let every man esteem his brother as himself, and practise virtue and holiness before me. (D&C 38:24.)

[in the Millennium] He that liveth in righteousness *shall be changed in the twinkling of an eye,* and the earth shall pass away so as by fire. And the wicked *shall go away into unquenchable fire, and their end no man knoweth on earth, nor ever shall know, until they come before me in judgment.* (D&C 43:32-33.)

Ye must practise virtue and holiness before me continually. (D&C 46:33.)

Let every man beware *lest he do that which is not in truth and righteousness before me.* (D&C 50:9.)

Let the wicked take heed, and let the rebellious fear and tremble; and let the unbelieving hold their lips, for the day of wrath shall come upon them as a whirlwind, and all flesh shall know that I am God. (D&C 63:6.)

Every man should take righteousness in his hands and faithfulness upon his loins, and lift a warning voice unto the inhabitants of the earth; and declare both by word and by flight that *desolation shall come* upon the wicked. (D&C 63:37.)

Abide ye in the liberty wherewith ye are made free; entangle not yourselves in sin, but let your hands be clean, until the Lord comes. (D&C 88:86.)

Cease from all your light speeches, from all laughter, from all your lustful desires, from all your pride and light-mindedness, and from all your wicked doings. (D&C 88:121.)

Set in order your houses; keep slothfulness and uncleanness far from you. (D&C 90:18.)

Search diligently, pray always, and be believing, and *all things shall work together for your good,* if ye walk uprightly and remember the covenant wherewith ye have covenanted one with another. (D&C 90:24.)

Vengeance cometh speedily upon the ungodly as the whirlwind; and who shall escape it? The Lord's scourge shall pass over by night and by day, and the report thereof shall vex all people; yea, it shall not be stayed until the Lord come; for the indignation of the Lord is kindled against their abominations and all their wicked works. (D&C 97: 22-24.)

Mine indignation is soon to be poured out without measure upon all nations; and this will I do when the cup of their iniquity is full. (D&C 101:11.)

The decisions of these quorums, or either of them, are to be made in all righteousness, in holiness, and lowliness of heart, meekness and long suffering, and in faith, and virtue, and knowledge, temperance, patience, godliness, brotherly kindness and charity; *because the promise is,* if these things abound in them *they shall not be unfruitful in the knowledge of the Lord.* (D&C 107:30-31.)

Be ye as wise as serpents and yet without sin; *and I will order all things for your good, as fast as ye are able to receive them.* (D&C 111:11.)

Let thy bowels also be full of charity towards all men, and to the household of faith, and let virtue garnish thy thoughts unceasingly; *then shall thy confidence wax strong in the presence of God; and the doctrine of the priesthood shall distil upon thy soul as the dews from heaven. The Holy Ghost shall be thy constant companion, and thy scepter an unchanging scepter of righteousness and truth; and thy dominion shall be an everlasting dominion, and without compulsory means it shall flow unto thee forever and ever.* (D&C 121:45-46.)

We believe in being honest, true, chaste, benevolent, virtuous, and in doing good to all men; indeed, we may say that we follow the admonition of Paul—We believe all things, we hope all things, we have endured many things, and hope to be able to endure all things. If there is anything virtuous, lovely, or of good report or praiseworthy, we seek after these things. (A of F 13.)

Sabbath Observance

(See also Sacrament; Worship.)

From the times of the ancients, the Lord has commanded that man keep the Sabbath holy and unpolluted. It is the Lord's day, but, paradoxically, it is also for man. Although the Israelites were given specific, strict commandments for Sabbath observance, the early members of the restored Church were not. When Joseph Smith asked the Lord about the Sabbath, which the early Saints found difficult to observe on the Missouri frontier, the Lord replied with generalities: the people should offer sacraments, rest from their labors, confess their sins, prepare their food with singleness of heart, and observe the day with thanksgiving and glad hearts. (D&C 59:12-15.)

The Lord's intent in ordaining a Sabbath, however, is the same in all dispensations: "Wherefore the Sabbath was given unto man for a day of rest; and also that man should glorify God." (JST Mark 2:26.) By choosing one day in seven for rest, for worship, for doing good, for offering sacraments, and for comparing his life with God's ways; man can focus on and draw closer to God and things of eternal significance.

Commandments and Promises

In the first day there shall be an holy convocation, and in the seventh day there shall be an holy convocation to you; no manner of work shall be done in them, save that which every man must eat, that only may be done of you. (Ex. 12:16.)

Remember the sabbath day, to keep it holy. Six days shalt thou labour, and do all thy work: but the seventh day is the sabbath of the Lord thy God: in it thou shalt not do any work, thou, nor thy son, nor thy daughter, thy manservant, nor thy maidservant, nor thy cattle, nor thy stranger that is within thy gates: for in six days the Lord made heaven and earth, the sea, and all that in them is, and rested the seventh day: *wherefore the Lord blessed the sabbath day, and hallowed it.* (Ex. 20:8-11; similar scriptures, Deut. 5:12-14, Mosiah 13:16-19.)

Six days thou shalt do thy work, and on the seventh day thou shalt rest: *that thine ox and thine ass may rest, and the son of thy hand-maid, and the stranger, may be refreshed.* (Ex. 23:12.)

Six days may work be done; but in the seventh is the sabbath of rest, holy to the Lord. . . . Wherefore the children of Israel shall keep the sabbath, to observe the sabbath throughout their generations, for a perpetual covenant. It is a sign between me and the children of Israel for ever. (Ex. 31:15-17.)

Six days thou shalt work, but on the seventh day thou shalt rest: in earing time and in harvest thou shalt rest. (Ex. 34:21.)

Ye shall fear every man his mother, and his father, and keep my sab-baths: I am the Lord your God. (Lev. 19:3.)

Ye shall keep my sabbaths, and reverence my sanctuary: I am the Lord. (Lev. 19:30.)

Six days shall work be done: but the seventh day is the sabbath of rest, an holy convocation; ye shall do no work therein: it is the sabbath of the Lord in all your dwellings. (Lev. 23:3.)

Remember that thou wast a servant in the land of Egypt, and that the Lord thy God brought thee out thence through a mighty hand and by a stretched out arm: therefore the Lord thy God commanded thee to keep the sabbath day. (Deut. 5:15.)

Blessed is the man that doeth this, and the son of man that layeth hold on it; that keepeth the sabbath from polluting it, and keepeth his hand from doing any evil. (Isa. 56:2.)

If thou turn away thy foot from the sabbath, from doing thy pleasure on my holy day; and call the sabbath a delight, the holy of the Lord, honourable; and shalt honour him, not doing thine own ways, nor finding thine own pleasure, nor speaking thine own words: *then shalt thou delight thyself in the Lord; and I will cause thee to ride upon the high places of the earth, and feed thee with the heritage of Jacob thy father: for the mouth of the Lord hath spoken it.* (Isa. 58:13-14.)

Take heed to yourselves, and bear no burden on the sabbath day, nor bring it in by the gates of Jerusalem; neither carry forth a burden out of your houses on the sabbath day, neither do ye any work, but hallow ye the sabbath day, as I commanded your fathers. (Jer. 17: 21-22.)

I gave them my sabbaths, to be a sign between me and them, *that they might know that I am the Lord that sanctify them.* (Ezek. 20:12.)

Hallow my sabbaths; *and they shall be a sign between me and you, that ye may know that I am the Lord your God.* (Ezek. 20:20.)

What man shall there be among you, that shall have one sheep, and if it fall into a pit on the sabbath day, will he not lay hold on it, and lift it out? How much then is a man better than a sheep? Wherefore it is lawful to do well on the sabbath days. (Matt. 12:11-12.)

He commanded them that they should observe the sabbath day, and keep it holy, and also every day they should give thanks to the Lord their God. (Mosiah 18:23.)

That thou mayest more fully keep thyself unspotted from the world, thou shalt go to the house of prayer and offer up thy sacraments upon my holy day; for verily this is a day appointed unto you to rest from your labors, and to pay thy devotions unto the Most High. (D&C 59: 9-10.)

Remember that on this, the Lord's day, thou shalt offer thine oblations and thy sacraments unto the Most High, confessing thy sins unto thy brethren, and before the Lord. (D&C 59:12.)

On this day [the sabbath] thou shalt do none other thing, only let thy food be prepared with singleness of heart *that thy fasting may be perfect, or, in other words, that thy joy may be full. Verily, this is fasting and prayer, or in other words, rejoicing and prayer. . . . Verily I say, that inasmuch as ye do this, the fulness of the earth is yours, the beasts of the field and the fowls of the air, and that which climbeth upon the trees and walketh upon the earth; yea, and the herb, and the good things which come of the earth, whether for food or for raiment, or for houses, or for barns, or for orchards, or for gardens, or for vineyards.* (D&C 59:13-17.)

The inhabitants of Zion shall also observe the Sabbath day to keep it holy. (D&C 68:29.)

Sacrament

(See also Baptism and Spiritual Rebirth; Name of Christ, Bearing the; Obedience; Remembering God and His Teachings.)

At the Last Supper the Lord had his apostles eat and drink in remembrance of him. When we partake of the sacrament, we follow that example. By partaking of the sacrament regularly, we can then find strength and silently renew our resolve to be righteous.

Through the sacrament we renew baptismal covenants: to take upon us the name of Jesus Christ, to keep his commandments, and to remember him. In return, we have the promise that we will always have his Spirit to be with us.

The sacrament can be a time of repentance and cleansing. It can be a moment when we promise that we will keep our covenants with God, even if we have broken those covenants in the past. However, if we partake of the sacrament unworthily, if we are breaking covenants and are not genuinely seeking forgiveness and repentance, we eat and drink damnation to our souls. (See 3 Ne. 18:29.)

Since we all sin, how can we ever partake of the sacrament worthily? Worthiness hinges on repentance, on the willingness to retrench and to seek perfection. When time, actions and attitudes mirror true repentance, we may partake worthily, and when we do, we have this promise: "He that eateth this bread eateth of my body to his soul; and he that drinketh of this wine drinketh of my blood to his soul; and his soul shall never hunger nor thirst, but shall be filled." (3 Ne. 20:8.)

Commandments and Promises

As they were eating, Jesus took bread, and blessed it, and brake it, and gave it to the disciples, and said, Take, eat; this is my body. And he took the cup, and gave thanks, and gave it to them, saying, Drink ye all of it; for this is my blood of the new testament, which is shed for many for the remission of sins. (Matt. 26:26-28; similar scripture, Mark 14:22-24; see also JST Matt. 26:22-25 and Mark 14:20-25.)

He took bread, and gave thanks, and brake it, and gave unto them, saying, This is my body which is given for you: this do in remembrance of me. Likewise also the cup after supper, saying, This cup is the new testament in my blood, which is shed for you. (Luke 22: 19-20.)

Whosoever shall eat this bread, and drink this cup of the Lord, unworthily, *shall be guilty of the body and blood of the Lord.* But let a man examine himself, and so let him eat of that bread, and drink of that cup. For he that eateth and drinketh unworthily, *eateth and drinketh damnation to himself, not discerning the Lord's body. For this cause many are weak and sickly among you, and many sleep.* (1 Cor. 11:27-30.)

There shall one be ordained among you, and to him will I give power that he shall break bread and bless it and give it unto the people of my church, unto all those who shall believe and be baptized in my name. And this shall ye always observe to do, even as I have done, even as I have broken bread and blessed it and given it unto you. And this shall ye do in remembrance of my body, which I have shown unto you. And it shall be a testimony unto the Father that ye do always remember me. And if ye do always remember me *ye shall have my Spirit to be with you.* (3 Ne. 18:5-7.)

This shall ye always do to those who repent and are baptized in my name; and ye shall do it in remembrance of my blood, which I have shed for you, that ye may witness unto the Father that ye do always remember me. And if ye do always remember me *ye shall have my Spirit to be with you.* (3 Ne. 18:11.)

This is the commandment which I give unto you, that ye shall not suffer any one knowingly to partake of my flesh and blood unworthily, when ye shall minister it; for whoso eateth and drinketh my flesh and blood unworthily *eateth and drinketh damnation to his soul;* therefore if ye know that a man is unworthy to eat and drink of my flesh and blood ye shall forbid him. Nevertheless, ye shall not cast him out from among you, but ye shall minister unto him and shall pray for him unto the Father, in my name; and if it so be that he repenteth and is baptized in my name, then shall ye receive him, and shall minister unto him of my flesh and blood. (3 Ne. 18:28-30.)

He that eateth this bread eateth of my body to his soul; and he that drinketh of this wine drinketh of my blood to his soul; *and his soul shall never hunger nor thirst, but shall be filled.* (3 Ne. 20:8.)

See that ye partake not of the sacrament of Christ unworthily. (Morm. 9:29.)

[sacrament prayer] O God, the Eternal Father, we ask thee in the name of thy Son, Jesus Christ, to bless and sanctify this bread to the souls of all those who partake of it; that they may eat in remembrance of the body of thy Son, and witness unto thee, O God, the Eternal Father, that they are willing to take upon them the name of thy Son, and always remember him, and keep his commandments which he hath given them, *that they may always have his Spirit to be with them.* Amen. (Moro. 4:3; similar scripture, D&C 20:77.)

[sacrament prayer] O God, the Eternal Father, we ask thee, in the name of thy Son, Jesus Christ, to bless and sanctify this wine to the souls of all those who drink of it, that they may do it in remembrance of the blood of thy Son, which was shed for them; that they may witness unto thee, O God, the Eternal Father, that they do always remember him, *that they may have his Spirit to be with them.* Amen. (Moro. 5:2; similar scripture, D&C 20:79.)

It mattereth not what ye shall eat or what ye shall drink when ye partake of the sacrament, if it so be that ye do it with an eye single to my glory—remembering unto the Father my body which was laid down for you, and my blood which was shed for the remission of your sins. (D&C 27:2.)

That thou mayest more fully keep thyself unspotted from the world, thou shalt go to the house of prayer and offer up thy sacraments upon my holy day. (D&C 59:9.)

Assemble yourselves upon the land of Zion; and hold a meeting and rejoice together, and offer a sacrament unto the Most High. (D&C 62:4.)

Sacredness

(See also Holiness.)

To remain holy, sacred things must be treated with reverence and respect. If they are desecrated, their holiness is defiled. The Lord commands us to keep sacred those things he has made sacred. The sacredness of an experience, a vow, or a doctrine can be polluted if treated too lightly; and through failure to maintain sacredness, we are cut off from God's enlightenment: "Your minds in times past have been darkened because of unbelief, and because you have treated lightly the things you have received." (D&C 84:54.)

Sacredness is similarly inherent in God's words, his name, and his house. In a vision to Joseph Smith in the Kirtland Temple, the Lord said: "I have accepted this house, and my name shall be here; and I will manifest myself to my people in mercy in this house. Yea, I will appear unto my servants, and speak unto them with mine own voice, if my people will keep my commandments, and do not pollute this holy house." (D&C 110:7-8.)

The Kirtland Temple was eventually desecrated after the Saints left Kirtland; but other such houses of the Lord have been built to God's name and glory. And those who honor both the promises made there and the sanctity of the Lord's house have the Lord's enlightenment and blessings.

Commandments and Promises

Ye shall keep my sabbaths, and reverence my sanctuary: I am the Lord. (Lev. 19:30.)

Give not that which is holy unto the dogs, neither cast ye your pearls before swine, *lest they trample them under their feet, and turn again and rend you.* (Matt. 7:6; similar scripture, 3 Ne. 14:6; see also JST Matt. 7:9-11.)

[Christ] said unto them that sold doves [in the temple], Take these things hence; make not my Father's house an house of merchandise. (John 2:16.)

[Alma to his son Helaman] I also command you that ye keep a record of this people, according as I have done, upon the plates of Nephi, and keep all these things sacred which I have kept, even as I have kept them; for it is for a wise purpose that they are kept. (Alma 37:2.)

My son [Helaman], see that ye take care of these sacred things. (Alma 37:47.)

It was because of . . . making a mock of that which was sacred, . . . *they were left in their own strength; therefore they did not prosper, but were afflicted and smitten, and driven before the Lamanites, until they had lost possession of almost all their lands.* (Hel. 4:12-13.)

[to Joseph Smith] Make not thy gift known unto any save it be those who are of thy faith. Trifle not with sacred things. (D&C 6:12.)

It is not meet that the things which belong to the children of the kingdom should be given to them that are not worthy, or to dogs, or the pearls to be cast before swine. (D&C 41:6.)

These words are given unto you, and they are pure before me; wherefore, beware how you hold them, *for they are to be answered upon your souls in the day of judgment.* (D&C 41:12.)

Remember that that which cometh from above is sacred, and must be spoken with care, and by constraint of the Spirit; *and in this there is no condemnation, and ye receive the Spirit through prayer; wherefore, without this there remaineth condemnation.* (D&C 63:64.)

Your minds in times past have been darkened because of unbelief, and because you have treated lightly the things you have received. (D&C 84:54.)

A commandment I give unto them [that believe], that they shall not boast themselves of these things [signs], neither speak them before the world; for these things are given unto you for your profit and for salvation. (D&C 84:73.)

All they who receive the oracles of God, let them beware how they hold them *lest they are accounted as a light thing, and are brought under condemnation thereby, and stumble and fall when the storms descend, and the winds blow, and the rains descend, and beat upon their house.* (D&C 90:5.)

Ye shall not suffer any unclean thing to come in unto it [the Kirtland Temple]; *and my glory shall be there, and my presence shall be there. But if there shall come into it any unclean thing, my glory shall not be there; and my presence shall not come into it.* (D&C 94:8-9.)

Inasmuch as my people build a house unto me in the name of the Lord, and do not suffer any unclean thing to come into it, that it be not defiled, *my glory shall rest upon it; yea, and my presence shall be there, for I will come into it, and all the pure in heart that shall come into it shall see God. But if it be defiled I will not come into it, and my glory shall not be there; for I will not come into unholy temples.* (D&C 97:15-17.)

Let not that which I have appointed be polluted by mine enemies, by the consent of those who call themselves after my name. (D&C 101:97.)

Let all my people who dwell in the regions round about be very faithful, and prayerful, and humble before me, and reveal not the things which I have revealed unto them, until it is wisdom in me that they should be revealed. (D&C 105:23.)

I will appear unto my servants, and speak unto them with mine own voice, if my people will keep my commandments, and do not pollute this holy house. (D&C 110:8.)

Sacrifice

(See also Contrite Heart and Spirit; Obedience; Tithes and Offerings.)

The principle of sacrifice dates from Adam, who was required to sacrifice and was later told it was done in similitude of the sacrifice to be made by Christ. (Moses 5:5-7.) Later, God commanded Abraham to sacrifice his son Isaac, although a ram was provided instead at the last moment. Both were blessed for their willingness to comply with the commandment to sacrifice.

Jesus, however, ended blood offerings, as he explained to the Nephites: "Ye shall offer up unto me no more the shedding of blood; yea, your sacrifices and your burnt offerings shall be done away, for I will accept none of your sacrifices and your burnt offerings." He then explained what was acceptable and expected: "Ye shall offer for a sacrifice unto me a broken heart and a contrite spirit." (3 Ne. 9:20.)

The commandment to have a broken heart and contrite spirit might not be easy when life requires more than we would choose to endure or offer. When we are disappointed, we cannot become bitter; when we feel persecuted, we cannot indulge in hatred; when we succeed, we cannot become proud; when we sin, we must repent. We might not be asked to sacrifice the firstlings of our flock, as was Adam, or our only son, as was Abraham, but we are commanded to sacrifice our sins, our pride, our hardheartedness, our bitterness, and resentment. We may be asked especially to give up those things we love more than we love God.

Sacrifices have changed since the times of Adam and Abraham, but the Lord still blesses those who give the required offering: "Him will I baptize with fire and with the Holy Ghost." (3 Ne. 9:19-20.)

Commandments and Promises

Offer the sacrifices of righteousness, and put your trust in the Lord. (Ps. 4:5.)

Keep thy foot when thou goest to the house of God, and be more ready to hear, than to give the sacrifice of fools: for they consider not that they do evil. (Eccl. 5:1.)

He that findeth his life *shall lose it:* and he that loseth his life for my sake *shall find it.* (Matt. 10:39; see also JST Matt. 10:34.)

Whosoever will save his life *shall lose it:* and whosoever will lose his life for my sake *shall find it.* (Matt. 16:25; see also JST Matt. 16: 27-29.)

Every one that hath forsaken houses, or brethren, or sisters, or father, or mother, or wife, or children, or lands, for my name's sake, *shall receive an hundredfold, and shall inherit everlasting life.* (Matt. 19:29.)

Whosoever will come after me, let him deny himself, and take up his cross, and follow me. For whosoever will save his life *shall lose it;* but whosoever shall lose his life for my sake and the gospel's, *the same shall save it.* (Mark 8:34-35; see also JST Mark 8:37-38.)

Every one shall be salted with fire, and every sacrifice *shall be salted with salt.* Salt is good: but if the salt have lost his saltness, wherewith will ye season it? Have salt in yourselves, and have peace one with another. (Mark 9:49-50.)

Peter began to say unto him, Lo, we have left all, and have followed thee. And Jesus answered and said, Verily I say unto you, There is no man that hath left house, or brethren, or sisters, or father, or mother, or wife, or children, or lands, for my sake, and the gospel's, *but he shall receive an hundredfold now in this time, houses, and brethren, and sisters, and mothers, and children, and lands, with persecutions; and in the world to come eternal life.* (Mark 10:28-30.)

Whosoever will save his life *shall lose it:* but whosoever will lose his life for my sake, *the same shall save it. For what is a man advantaged, if he gain the whole world, and lose himself, or be cast away?* (Luke 9:24-25; see also JST Luke 9:24-25.)

If any man come to me, and hate not his father, and mother, and wife, and children, and brethren, and sisters, yea, and his own life also, *he cannot be my disciple.* And whosoever doth not bear his cross, and come after me, *cannot be my disciple.* (Luke 14:26-27; see also JST Luke 14:26.)

Whosoever he be of you that forsaketh not all that he hath, *he cannot be my disciple.* (Luke 14:33.)

Whosoever shall seek to save his life *shall lose it;* and whosoever shall lose his life *shall preserve it.* (Luke 17:33.)

He that loveth his life *shall lose it;* and he that hateth his life in this world *shall keep it unto life eternal.* (John 12:25.)

I beseech you therefore, brethren, by the mercies of God, that ye present your bodies a living sacrifice, holy, acceptable unto God, which is your reasonable service. (Rom. 12:1.)

I count all things but loss for the excellency of the knowledge of Christ Jesus my Lord: for whom I have suffered the loss of all things, and do count them but dung, *that I may win Christ, and be found in him, not having mine own righteousness, which is of the law, but that which is through the faith of Christ, the righteousness which is of God by faith: that I may know him, and the power of his resurrection, and the fellowship of his sufferings, being made conformable unto his death.* (Philip. 3:8-10.)

To do good and to communicate forget not: for with such sacrifices *God is well pleased.* (Heb. 13:16.)

Come unto him [Christ], and offer your whole souls as an offering unto him. (Omni 1:26.)

Ye shall offer up unto me no more the shedding of blood; yea, your sacrifices and your burnt offerings shall be done away, for I will accept none of your sacrifices and your burnt offerings. And ye shall offer for a sacrifice unto me a broken heart and a contrite spirit. And whoso cometh unto me with a broken heart and a contrite spirit, *him will I baptize with fire and with the Holy Ghost, even as the Lamanites, because of their faith in me at the time of their conversion, were baptized with fire and with the Holy Ghost, and they knew it not.* (3 Ne. 9:19-20.)

Thou shalt offer a sacrifice unto the Lord thy God in righteousness, even that of a broken heart and a contrite spirit. (D&C 59:8.)

It is a day of sacrifice, and a day for the tithing of my people; for he that is tithed *shall not be burned at his coming.* (D&C 64:23.)

The Lord requireth the heart and a willing mind; and the willing and obedient *shall eat the good of the land of Zion in these last days.* (D&C 64:34.)

All among them who know their hearts are honest, and are broken, and their spirits contrite, and are willing to observe their covenants by sacrifice—yea, every sacrifice which I, the Lord, shall command— *they are accepted of me.* (D&C 97:8.)

All they who have given their lives for my name *shall be crowned.* (D&C 101:15.)

Let no man be afraid to lay down his life for my sake; for whoso layeth down his life for my sake *shall find it again.* (D&C 103:27.)

Salvation, Working Out

(See also Seeking God.)

Through Christ's atonement, salvation is offered to all, though not all accept it. Salvation means we are saved from our sins through repentance, baptism, and righteousness.

"Work out your own salvation with fear and trembling," Paul wrote the Philippian believers. (Philip. 2:12.) Alma repeats, "Ye should work out your salvation with fear before God." (Alma 34:37.) Mormon counsels similarly. (See Morm. 9:27.) But why fear and tremble? Because, if we do not work out our salvation, we forgo partaking of the Savior's mediating atonement. We are left to our sins— to suffer for them ourselves, to die in them, to live their consequences in eternity.

Commandments and Promises

Seek good, and not evil, *that ye may live: and so the Lord, the God of hosts, shall be with you, as ye have spoken.* (Amos 5:14.)

Lay not up for yourselves treasures upon earth, *where moth and rust doth corrupt, and where thieves break through and steal:* but lay up for yourselves treasures in heaven, *where neither moth nor rust doth corrupt, and where thieves do not break through nor steal:* for where your treasure is, *there will your heart be also.* (Matt. 6:19-21.)

Seek ye first the kingdom of God, and his righteousness; *and all these things shall be added unto you.* (Matt. 6:33; similar scripture, 3 Ne. 13:33; see also JST Matt. 6:38.)

Strive to enter in at the strait gate: for many, I say unto you, will seek to enter in, and shall not be able. (Luke 13:24.)

Labour not for the meat which perisheth, but for that meat which endureth unto everlasting life, which the Son of man shall give unto you. (John 6:27.)

Take unto you the whole armour of God, *that ye may be able to withstand in the evil day, and having done all, to stand.* Stand therefore, having your loins girt about with truth, and having on the breastplate of righteousness; and your feet shod with the preparation of the gospel of peace; above all, taking the shield of faith, *wherewith ye shall be able to quench all the fiery darts of the wicked.* And take the helmet of salvation, and the sword of the Spirit, which is the word of God: praying always with all prayer and supplication in the Spirit, and watching thereunto with all perseverance and supplication for all saints; and for me, *that utterance may be given unto me.* (Eph. 6:13-19; similar scripture, D&C 27:15-18.)

This one thing I do, forgetting those things which are behind, and reaching forth unto those things which are before, I press toward the mark for the prize of the high calling of God in Christ Jesus. Let us therefore, as many as be perfect, be thus minded: and if in any thing ye be otherwise minded, *God shall reveal even this unto you.* (Philip. 3:13-15.)

If ye then be risen with Christ, seek those things which are above, where Christ sitteth on the right hand of God. Set your affection on things above, not on things on the earth. (Col. 3:1-2.)

God hath not appointed us to wrath, but to obtain salvation by our Lord Jesus Christ. (1 Thes. 5:9.)

Lay hold on eternal life, whereunto thou art also called. (1 Tim. 6:12.)

Choose eternal life, according to the will of his Holy Spirit. (2 Ne. 2:28.)

With joy shall ye draw water out of the wells of salvation. (2 Ne. 22:3.)

He doeth not anything save it be for the benefit of the world; for he loveth the world, even that he layeth down his own life *that he may draw all men unto him.* Wherefore, he commandeth none that they shall not partake of his salvation. (2 Ne. 26:24.)

Before ye seek for riches, seek ye for the kingdom of God. (Jacob 2:18.)

I desire that ye should remember these things, and that ye should work out your salvation with fear before God, and that ye should no more deny the coming of Christ. (Alma 34:37.)

Work out your salvation with fear and trembling before him [the Lord]. (Morm. 9:27; similar scripture, Philip. 2:12.)

Seek the kingdom of God, *and all things shall be added according to that which is just.* (D&C 11:23.)

Thou shalt lay aside the things of this world, and seek for the things of a better. (D&C 25:10.)

If ye seek the riches which it is the will of the Father to give unto you, *ye shall be the richest of all people, for ye shall have the riches of eternity;* and it must needs be that the riches of the earth are mine to give; but beware of pride, *lest ye become as the Nephites of old.* (D&C 38:39.)

Go ye out from among the wicked. Save yourselves. (D&C 38:42.)

That which the Spirit testifies unto you even so I would that ye should do in all holiness of heart, walking uprightly before me, considering the end of your salvation, doing all things with prayer and thanksgiving, *that ye may not be seduced by evil spirits, or doctrines of devils, or the commandments of men; for some are of men, and others of devils.* (D&C 46:7.)

Care not for the body, neither the life of the body; but care for the soul, and for the life of the soul. (D&C 101:37.)

Sanctification

(See also Holiness; Receiving and Following the Holy Ghost.)

Sanctification changes and makes us spotless from sin. (See 3 Ne. 27:20.) It opens us to revelations and manifestations. (See Ether 4:7.) It enables us to "bring forth works which are meet for repentance." (Alma 5:54.) It brings us gifts of the Spirit: "love, joy, peace, long-suffering, gentleness, goodness, faith, meekness, temperance." (Gal. 5:22.) Then once our garments are "made white, being pure and spotless before God," we cannot look upon sin with anything but abhorrence. (Alma 13:12.)

We cannot sanctify ourselves without help. Sanctification is a condition brought about by the Holy Ghost, given through the grace of Jesus Christ to those who seek it. Yet despite our inability to achieve it on our own, we are told repeatedly to sanctify ourselves. That it is possible is illustrated in the following examples:

—"They did fast and pray oft, and did wax stronger and stronger in their humility, and firmer and firmer in the faith of Christ, unto the filling their souls with joy and consolation, yea, even to the purifying and the sanctification of their hearts, which sanctification cometh because of their yielding their hearts unto God." (Hel. 3:35.)

—"Repent, all ye ends of the earth, and come unto me and be baptized in my name, that ye may be sanctified by the reception of the Holy Ghost." (3 Ne. 27:20.)

—"They shall exercise faith in me, saith the Lord, even as the brother of Jared did, that they may become sanctified in me." (Ether 4:7.)

—"Sanctification through the grace of our Lord and Savior Jesus Christ is just and true, to all those who love and serve God with all their mights, minds, and strength." (D&C 20:31.)

Fasting, prayer, humility, faith, yielding our hearts to God, repentance, coming to Christ, baptism, loving and serving God, all these will aid us in obtaining sanctification through the Holy Ghost. And, as with so many other commandments, the commandment ultimately becomes its own blessing.

Commandments and Promises

For I am the Lord your God: ye shall therefore sanctify yourselves, and ye shall be holy; for I am holy. (Lev. 11:44; similar scripture, Lev. 20:7.)

This is the will of God, even your sanctification, that ye should abstain from fornication: that every one of you should know how to possess his vessel in sanctification and honour; not in the lust of concupiscence, even as the Gentiles which know not God. (1 Thes. 4:3-5.)

God hath from the beginning chosen you to salvation through sanctification of the Spirit and belief of the truth. (2 Thes. 2:13.)

Let us draw near with a true heart in full assurance of faith, having our hearts sprinkled from an evil conscience, and our bodies washed with pure water. (Heb. 10:22.)

There were many who were ordained and became high priests of God; and it was on account of their exceeding faith and repentance, and their righteousness before God, they choosing to repent and work righteousness rather than to perish; *therefore they were called after this holy order, and were sanctified, and their garments were washed white through the blood of the Lamb. Now they, after being sanctified by the Holy Ghost, having their garments made white, being pure and spotless before God, could not look upon sin save it were with abhorrence.* (Alma 13:10-12.)

They did fast and pray oft, and did wax stronger and stronger in their humility, and firmer and firmer in the faith of Christ, unto the filling their souls with joy and consolation, yea, *even to the purifying and the sanctification of their hearts, which sanctification cometh* because of their yielding their hearts unto God. (Hel. 3:35.)

Now this is the commandment: Repent, all ye ends of the earth, and come unto me and be baptized in my name, *that ye may be sanctified by the reception of the Holy Ghost, that ye may stand spotless before me at the last day.* (3 Ne. 27:20.)

In that day that they shall exercise faith in me, saith the Lord, even as the brother of Jared did, *that they may become sanctified in me, then will I manifest unto them the things which the brother of Jared saw, even to the unfolding unto them all my revelations, saith Jesus Christ.* (Ether 4:7.)

Inasmuch as they do repent and receive the fulness of my gospel, and become sanctified, *I will stay mine hand in judgment.* (D&C 39:18.)

Ye shall become instructed in the law of my church, and be sanctified by that which ye have received, and ye shall bind yourselves to act in all holiness before me—that inasmuch as ye do this, *glory shall be added to the kingdom which ye have received.* Inasmuch as ye do it not, *it shall be taken, even that which ye have received.* (D&C 43: 9-10.)

Purge ye out the iniquity which is among you; sanctify yourselves before me. (D&C 43:11.)

Sanctify yourselves *and ye shall be endowed with power, that ye may give even as I have spoken.* (D&C 43:16.)

Sanctify yourselves that your minds become single to God, *and the days will come that you shall see him; for he will unveil his face unto you, and it shall be in his own time, and in his own way, and according to his own will.* (D&C 88:68.)

I give unto you, who are the first laborers in this last kingdom, a commandment that you assemble yourselves together, and organize yourselves, and prepare yourselves, and sanctify yourselves; yea, purify your hearts, and cleanse your hands and your feet before me, *that I may make you clean; that I testify unto your Father, and your God, that you are clean from the blood of this wicked generation; that I may fulfil this promise [seeing God], this great and last promise, which I have made unto you, when I will.* (D&C 88:74-75.)

First let my army become very great, and let it be sanctified before me, *that it may become fair as the sun, and clear as the moon, and that her banners may be terrible unto all nations; that the kingdoms of this world may be constrained to acknowledge that the kingdom of Zion is in very deed the kingdom of our God and his Christ;* therefore, let us become subject unto her laws. (D&C 105:31-32.)

Prepare ye, O my people; sanctify yourselves. (D&C 133:4.)

Unto him that repenteth and sanctifieth himself before the Lord *shall be given eternal life.* (D&C 133:62.)

Seeking God

(See also Coming to God; Glorifying God; Looking to God; Prayer.)

Since our mortality separates us from the presence of God, we are commanded to seek him. Even when we feel that sin has taken us far from God, God's love keeps him close to us, as Paul declares: "For I am persuaded, that neither death, nor life, nor angels, nor principalities, nor powers, nor things present, nor things to come, nor height, nor depth, nor any other creature, shall be able to separate us from the love of God, which is in Christ Jesus our Lord." (Rom. 8: 38-39.) Previously Paul had promised that "all nations of men . . . should seek the Lord, if they are willing to find him, for he is not far from every one of us." (JST Acts 17:26-27.) Perhaps we will not see him, but we can have the comfort and joy of his presence. And we know that only by seeking him will we find him.

Commandments and Promises

If from thence thou shalt seek the Lord thy God, *thou shalt find him,* if thou seek him with all thy heart and with all thy soul. (Deut. 4:29.)

Glory ye in his holy name: let the heart of them rejoice that seek the Lord. Seek the Lord and his strength, seek his face continually. (1 Chr. 16:10-11.)

If I shut up heaven that there be no rain, or if I command the locusts to devour the land, or if I send pestilence among my people; if my people, which are called by my name, shall humble themselves, and pray, and seek my face, and turn from their wicked ways; *then will I hear from heaven, and will forgive their sin, and will heal their land.* (2 Chr. 7:13-14.)

The Lord is with you, while ye be with him; and if ye seek him, *he will be found of you;* but if ye forsake him, *he will forsake you.* (2 Chr. 15:2.)

They that know thy name will put their trust in thee: for *thou, Lord, hast not forsaken them* that seek thee. (Ps. 9:10.)

Your heart shall live that seek God. (Ps. 69:32.)

Seek the Lord, and his strength: seek his face evermore. (Ps. 105:4.)

Seek ye the Lord while he may be found, call ye upon him while he is near. (Isa. 55:6.)

Ye shall seek me, *and find me,* when ye shall search for me with all your heart. (Jer. 29:13.)

The Lord is good unto them that wait for him, to the soul that seeketh him. (Lam. 3:25.)

It is time to seek the Lord, *till he come and rain righteousness upon you.* (Hosea 10:12.)

Seek the Lord, *and ye shall live.* (Amos 5:6; similar scripture, Amos 5:4.)

Seek him that maketh the seven stars and Orion, and turneth the shadow of death into the morning, and maketh the day dark with night: that calleth for the waters of the sea, and poureth them out upon the face of the earth: The Lord is his name. (Amos 5:8.)

Seek ye first the kingdom of God, and his righteousness; *and all these things shall be added unto you.*(Matt. 6:33; similar scripture, 3 Ne. 13:33; see also JST Matt. 6:38.)

[All nations of men] should seek the Lord, if haply they might feel after him, *and find him,* though he be not far from every one of us. (Acts 17:27; see also JST Acts 17:27.)

Blessed art thou, Nephi, because of thy faith, for thou hast sought me diligently with lowliness of heart. (1 Ne. 2:19.)

I would commend you to seek this Jesus of whom the prophets and apostles have written, *that the grace of God the Father, and also the Lord Jesus Christ, and the Holy Ghost, which beareth record of them, may be and abide in you forever.* (Ether 12:41.)

They who have sought me early *shall find rest to their souls.* (D&C 54:10.)

Seek me diligently *and ye shall find me.* (D&C 88:63.)

He that seeketh me early *shall find me, and shall not be forsaken.* (D&C 88:83.)

Seek the face of the Lord always, *that in patience ye may possess your souls, and ye shall have eternal life.* (D&C 101:38.)

If any man shall seek to build up himself, and seeketh not my counsel, *he shall have no power, and his folly shall be made manifest.* (D&C 136:19-20.)

Serving God

(See also Authority and Stewardship; False Gods; Loving God
and His Teachings; Obedience; Serving Others.)

The commandment to serve God and its promise were made
clear to those who emigrated to the Americas with Lehi: "This land is
consecrated unto him whom he shall bring. And if it so be that they
shall serve him according to the commandments which he hath
given, it shall be a land of liberty unto them; wherefore, they shall
never be brought down into captivity; if so, it shall be because of iniquity; for if iniquity shall abound cursed shall be the land for their
sakes, but unto the righteous it shall be blessed forever." (2 Ne. 1:7.)
The Lamanites and Nephites alternated between righteous service to
God and iniquity. Iniquity was their final choice, and their civiliza-
tions were destroyed and thrust into centuries of darkness.

All of us are commanded to serve God with all our heart, might,
mind and strength. (See D&C 4:2.) We are told to serve joyfully and
diligently while obeying his commandments and doing his works. In
addition, we know that when we serve our fellowmen, we are serving
him. Then, through service to God, we receive his help, protection,
and sanctification.

Commandments and Promises

Ye shall serve the Lord your God, *and he shall bless thy bread, and thy
water; and I will take sickness away from the midst of thee.* (Ex.
23:25.)

Thou shalt fear the Lord thy God, and serve him. (Deut. 6:13.)

Israel, what doth the Lord thy God require of thee, but to fear the
Lord thy God, to walk in all his ways, and to love him, and to serve the
Lord thy God with all thy heart and with all thy soul, to keep the commandments of the Lord, and his statutes, which I command thee this
day *for thy good?* (Deut. 10:12-13.)

Thou shalt fear the Lord thy God; him shalt thou serve. (Deut. 10:20.)

522

Ye shall walk after the Lord your God, and fear him, and keep his commandments, and obey his voice, and ye shall serve him, and cleave unto him. (Deut. 13:4.)

Because thou servedst not the Lord thy God with joyfulness, and with gladness of heart, for the abundance of all things; *therefore shalt thou serve thine enemies which the Lord shall send against thee, in hunger, and in thirst, and in nakedness, and in want of all things: and he shall put a yoke of iron upon thy neck, until he have destroyed thee.* (Deut. 28:47-48.)

Fear the Lord, and serve him in sincerity and in truth: and put away the gods which your fathers served on the other side of the flood, and in Egypt; and serve ye the Lord. And if it seem evil unto you to serve the Lord, choose you this day whom ye will serve; whether the gods which your fathers served that were on the other side of the flood, or the gods of the Amorites, in whose land ye dwell: but as for me and my house, we will serve the Lord. (Josh. 24:14-15.)

If ye will fear the Lord, and serve him, and obey his voice, and not rebel against the commandment of the Lord, *then shall both ye and also the king that reigneth over you continue following the Lord your God.* (1 Sam. 12:14.)

Fear not: ye have done all this wickedness: yet turn not aside from following the Lord, but serve the Lord with all your heart; and turn ye not aside: *for then should ye go after vain things, which cannot profit nor deliver; for they are vain.* (1 Sam. 12:20-21.)

Serve the Lord with gladness. (Ps. 100:2.)

Thou shalt worship the Lord thy God, and him only shalt thou serve. (Matt 4:10.)

Inasmuch as ye have done it unto one of the least of these my brethren, *ye have done it unto me.* (Matt. 25:40.)

If any man serve me, let him follow me; *and where I am, there shall also my servant be:* if any man serve me, *him will my Father honour.* (John 12:26.)

Now being made free from sin, and become servants to God, *ye have your fruit unto holiness, and the end everlasting life.* (Rom. 6:22.)

[Be] fervent in spirit; serving the Lord. (Rom. 12:11.)

Ye are bought with a price; be not ye the servants of men. (1 Cor. 7:23.)

Be ye stedfast, unmoveable, always abounding in the work of the Lord, forasmuch as ye know that your labour *is not in vain in the Lord.* (1 Cor. 15:58.)

We receiving a kingdom which cannot be moved, let us have grace, whereby we may serve God acceptably with reverence and godly fear. (Heb. 12:28.)

This land is consecrated unto him whom he shall bring. And if it so be that they shall serve him according to the commandments which he hath given, *it shall be a land of liberty unto them; wherefore, they shall never be brought down into captivity; if so,* it shall be because of iniquity; for if iniquity shall abound *cursed shall be the land for their sakes,* but unto the righteous *it shall be blessed forever.* (2 Ne. 1:7; see also Ether 2:9, 12.)

If ye [people of Limhi] will turn to the Lord with full purpose of heart, and put your trust in him, and serve him with all diligence of mind, if ye do this, *he will, according to his own will and pleasure, deliver you out of bondage.* (Mosiah 7:33.)

Thou [Alma] art my servant; *and I covenant with thee that thou shalt have eternal life;* and thou shalt serve me and go forth in my name, and shalt gather together my sheep. (Mosiah 26:20.)

No weapon that is formed against thee shall propser; and every tongue that shall revile against thee in judgment thou shalt condemn. This is the heritage of the servants of the Lord, and their righteousness *is of me, saith the Lord.* (3 Ne. 22:17.)

We can behold the decrees of God concerning this land, that it is a land of promise; and whatsoever nation shall possess it shall serve

God, *or they shall be swept off when the fulness of his wrath shall come upon them. And the fulness of his wrath cometh upon them* when they are ripened in iniquity. (Ether 2:9; see also 2 Ne. 1:7.)

This is a choice land, and whatsoever nation shall possess it shall be free from bondage, and from captivity, and from all other nations under heaven, if they will but serve the God of the land, who is Jesus Christ, who hath been manifested by the things which we have written. (Ether 2:12; see also 2 Ne. 1:7.)

O ye that embark in the service of God, see that ye serve him with all your heart, might, mind and strength, *that ye may stand blameless before God at the last day.* Therefore, if ye have desires to serve God *ye are called to the work.* (D&C 4:2-3.)

[God] gave unto them commandments that they should love and serve him, the only living and true God, and that he should be the only being whom they should worship. (D&C 20:19.)

We know also, that *sanctification through the grace of our Lord and Savior Jesus Christ is just and true,* to all those who love and serve God with all their mights, minds, and strength. (D&C 20:31.)

All those who humble themselves before God, and desire to be baptized, and come forth with broken hearts and contrite spirits, and witness before the church that they have truly repented of all their sins, and are willing to take upon them the name of Jesus Christ, having a determination to serve him to the end, and truly manifest by their works that they have received of the Spirit of Christ unto the remission of their sins, *shall be received by baptism into his church.* (D&C 20:37.)

I will bless all those who labor in my vineyard *with a mighty blessing, and they shall believe on his [Joseph Smith's] words, which are given him through me by the Comforter, which manifesteth that Jesus was crucified by sinful men for the sins of the world, yea, for the remission of sins unto the contrite heart.* (D&C 21:9.)

Thou shalt devote all thy service in Zion; *and in this thou shalt have strength.* (D&C 24:7.)

If thou lovest me thou shalt serve me and keep all my commandments. (D&C 42:29.)

Thou shalt love the Lord thy God with all thy heart, with all thy might, mind, and strength; and in the name of Jesus Christ thou shalt serve him. (D&C 59:5.)

Whoso is faithful unto the obtaining these two priesthoods of which I have spoken, and the magnifying their calling, *are sanctified by the Spirit unto the renewing of their bodies. They become the sons of Moses and of Aaron and the seed of Abraham, and the church and kingdom, and the elect of God.* (D&C 84:33-34.)

Serving Others

(See also Good Works; Serving God.)

Immediately after the feast of the passover, Jesus washed the feet of his apostles. Peter objected and Jesus then taught an important principle of discipleship: "If I then, your Lord and Master, have washed your feet; ye also ought to wash one another's feet. For I have given you an example, that ye should do as I have done to you. Verily, verily, I say unto you, The servant is not greater than his lord; neither he that is sent greater than he that sent him." (John 13:14-16.)

The Lord expects us to serve others, whether we are leaders or servants. In fact, service to others is essential to religion: "Pure religion and undefiled before God and the Father is this, To visit the fatherless and widows in their affliction, and to keep himself unspotted from the world." (James 1:27.) In the process of acting and caring for the benefit of others, we serve God: "When ye are in the service of your fellow beings ye are only in the service of your God." (Mosiah 2:17.) By serving others and God, we become more like Christ, developing the charity and qualities necessary for godhood.

Commandments and Promises

Ye shall not afflict any widow, or fatherless child. If thou afflict them in any wise, and they cry at all unto me, *I will surely hear their cry; and my wrath shall wax hot, and I will kill you with the sword; and your wives shall be widows, and your children fatherless.* (Ex. 22:22-24.)

When ye reap the harvest of your land, thou shalt not wholly reap the corners of thy field, neither shalt thou gather the gleanings of thy harvest. And thou shalt not glean thy vineyard, neither shalt thou gather every grape of thy vineyard; thou shalt leave them for the poor and stranger: I am the Lord your God. (Lev. 19:9-10; similar scripture, Lev. 23:22.)

Thou shalt not curse the deaf, nor put a stumblingblock before the blind, but shalt fear thy God: I am the Lord. (Lev. 19:14.)

If a stranger sojourn with thee in your land, ye shall not vex him. But the stranger that dwelleth with you shall be unto you as one born among you, and thou shalt love him as thyself; for ye were strangers in the land of Egypt: I am the Lord your God. (Lev. 19:33-34.)

Love ye therefore the stranger: for ye were strangers in the land of Egypt. (Deut. 10:19.)

If there be among you a poor man of one of thy brethren within any of thy gates in thy land which the Lord thy God giveth thee, thou shalt not harden thine heart, nor shut thine hand from thy poor brother: but thou shalt open thine hand wide unto him, and shalt surely lend him sufficient for his need, in that which he wanteth. (Deut. 15:7-8.)

Thou shalt surely give him [thy poor brother], and thine heart shall not be grieved when thou givest unto him: *because that for this thing the Lord thy God shall bless thee in all thy works, and in all that thou puttest thine hand unto.* For the poor shall never cease out of the land: therefore I command thee, saying, Thou shalt open thine hand wide unto thy brother, and thy poor, and to thy needy, in thy land. (Deut. 15:10-11.)

Thou shalt not see thy brother's ass or his ox fall down by the way, and hide thyself from them: thou shalt surely help him to lift them up again. (Deut. 22:4.)

Cursed be he that perverteth the judgment of the stranger, fatherless, and widow. (Deut. 27:19.)

Blessed is he that considereth the poor: *the Lord will deliver him in time of trouble.* (Ps. 41:1.)

Withhold not good from them to whom it is due, when it is in the power of thine hand to do it. Say not unto thy neighbour, Go, and come again, and to morrow I will give; when thou hast it by thee. (Prov. 3:27-28.)

He that hath pity upon the poor *lendeth unto the Lord*; and that which he hath given *will he pay him again.* (Prov. 19:17.)

Whoso stoppeth his ears at the cry of the poor, *he also shall cry himself, but shall not be heard.* (Prov. 21:13.)

Rob not the poor, because he is poor: neither oppress the afflicted in the gate: *for the Lord will plead their cause, and spoil the soul* of those that spoiled them. (Prov. 22:22-23.)

He that giveth unto the poor *shall not lack:* but he that hideth his eyes *shall have many a curse.* (Prov. 28:27.)

Open thy mouth for the dumb in the cause of all such as are appointed to destruction. Open thy mouth, judge righteously, and plead the cause of the poor and needy. (Prov. 31:8-9.)

Do no violence to the stranger, the fatherless, nor the widow. (Jer. 22:3.)

Execute true judgment, and shew mercy and compassions every man to his brother: and oppress not the widow, nor the fatherless, the stranger, nor the poor; and let none of you imagine evil against his brother in your heart. (Zech. 7:9-10.)

If any man will sue thee at the law, and take away thy coat, let him have thy cloke also. And whosoever shall compel thee to go a mile, go with him twain. Give to him that asketh thee, and from him that would borrow of thee turn not thou away. (Matt. 5:40-42.)

All things whatsoever ye would that men should do to you, do ye even so to them: for this is the law and the prophets. (Matt. 7:12; similar scriptures, Luke 6:31, 3 Ne. 14:12.)

Heal the sick, cleanse the lepers, raise the dead, cast out devils: freely ye have received, freely give. (Matt. 10:8.)

Whoso shall receive one such little child in my name *receiveth me.* But whoso shall offend one of these little ones which believe in me, *it were better for him that a millstone were hanged about his neck, and that he were drowned in the depth of the sea. Woe unto the world* because of offences! for it must needs be that offences come; *but woe to that man* by whom the offence cometh! (Matt. 18:5-7.)

Take heed that ye despise not one of these little ones; for I say unto you, That in heaven their angels do always behold the face of my Father which is in heaven. (Matt. 18:10.)

Then were there brought unto him little children, that he should put his hands on them, and pray: and the disciples rebuked them. But Jesus said, Suffer little children, and forbid them not, to come unto me: for of such is the kingdom of heaven. (Matt. 19:13-14; similar scriptures, Mark 10:13-14, Luke 18:15-16; see also JST Matt. 19:13.)

Jesus said unto him, *If thou wilt be perfect,* go and sell that thou hast, and give to the poor, *and thou shalt have treasure in heaven:* and come and follow me. (Matt. 19:21; see also Luke 18:22.)

Call no man your father upon the earth: for one is your Father, which is in heaven. Neither be ye called masters: for one is your Master, even Christ. But he that is greatest among you *shall be your servant.* (Matt. 23:9-11; see also JST Matt. 23:6-7.)

Whosoever shall receive one of such children in my name, *receiveth me: and whosoever shall receive me, receiveth not me, but him that sent me.* (Mark 9:37; see also JST Mark 9:34-35.)

He that hath two coats, let him impart to him that hath none; and he that hath meat, let him do likewise. (Luke 3:11.)

Whosoever shall receive this child in my name *receiveth me:* and whosoever shall receive me *receiveth him that sent me: for he that is least among you all, the same shall be great.* (Luke 9:48.)

When thou makest a dinner or a supper, call not thy friends, nor thy brethren, neither thy kinsmen, nor thy rich neighbours; *lest they also bid thee again, and a recompence be made thee.* But when thou makest a feast, call the poor, the maimed, the lame, the blind: *and thou shalt be blessed; for they cannot recompense thee: for thou shalt be recompensed at the resurrection of the just.* (Luke 14:12-14.)

[Jesus to a rich man] Yet lackest thou one thing: sell all that thou hast, and distribute unto the poor, *and thou shalt have treasure in heaven:* and come, follow me. (Luke 18:22; see also Matt. 19:21.)

If I then, your Lord and Master, have washed your feet; ye also ought to wash one another's feet. For I have given you an example, that ye should do as I have done to you. Verily, verily, I say unto you, The servant is not greater than his lord; neither he that is sent greater than he that sent him. (John 13:14-16.)

I have shewed you all things, how that so labouring ye ought to support the weak, and to remember the words of the Lord Jesus, how he said, *It is more blessed* to give than to receive. (Acts 20:35.)

Now we are delivered from the law, that being dead wherein we were held; that we should serve in newness of spirit, and not in the oldness of the letter. (Rom. 7:6.)

Rejoice with them that do rejoice, and weep with them that weep. (Rom. 12:15.)

We then that are strong ought to bear the infirmities of the weak, and not to please ourselves. (Rom. 15:1.)

Ye have been called unto liberty; only use not liberty for an occasion to the flesh, but by love serve one another. (Gal. 5:13.)

Bear ye one another's burdens, and so fulfil the law of Christ. (Gal. 6:2.)

Ye masters, do the same things unto them [servants], forbearing threatening: knowing that your Master also is in heaven; neither is there respect of persons with him. (Eph. 6:9.)

Servants, obey in all things your masters according to the flesh; not with eyeservice, as menpleasers; but in singleness of heart, fearing God: and whatsoever ye do, do it heartily, as to the Lord, and not unto men; *knowing that of the Lord ye shall receive the reward of the inheritance:* for ye serve the Lord Christ. (Col. 3:22-24.)

Wherefore comfort one another with these words. (1 Thes. 4:18.)

Let as many servants as are under the yoke count their own masters worthy of all honour, *that the name of God and his doctrine be not blasphemed.* And they that have believing masters, let them not despise them, because they are brethren; but rather do them service, because they are faithful and beloved, *partakers of the benefit.* These things teach and exhort. (1 Tim. 6:1-2.)

Exhort servants to be obedient unto their own masters, and to please them well in all things; not answering again; not purloining, but shewing all good fidelity; that they may adorn the doctrine of God our Saviour in all things. (Titus 2:9-10.)

Be not forgetful to entertain strangers: for thereby some have entertained angels unawares. Remember them that are in bonds, as bound with them; and them which suffer adversity, as being yourselves also in the body. (Heb. 13:2-3.)

Pure religion and undefiled before God and the Father is this, To visit the fatherless and widows in their affliction, and to keep himself unspotted from the world. (James 1:27.)

Be ye all of one mind, having compassion one of another, love as brethren, be pitiful, be courteous: not rendering evil for evil, or railing for railing: but contrariwise blessing; knowing that ye are thereunto called, *that ye should inherit a blessing.* (1 Pet. 3:8-9.)

Use hospitality one to another without grudging. (1 Pet. 4:9.)

Hereby perceive we the love of God, because he laid down his life for us: and we ought to lay down our lives for the brethren. But whoso hath this world's good, and seeth his brother have need, and shutteth up his bowels of compassion from him, *how dwelleth the love of God in him?* (1 Jn. 3:16-17.)

Thou doest faithfully whatsoever thou doest to the brethren, and to strangers. . . . We therefore ought to receive such, *that we might be fellowhelpers to the truth.* (3 Jn. 1:5-8.)

After ye have obtained a hope in Christ *ye shall obtain riches*, if ye seek them; and ye will seek them for the intent to do good—to clothe the naked, and to feed the hungry, and to liberate the captive, and administer relief to the sick and the afflicted. (Jacob. 2:19.)

When ye are in the service of your fellow beings *ye are only in the service of your God.* (Mosiah 2:17.)

Ye yourselves will succor those that stand in need of your succor; ye will administer of your substance unto him that standeth in need; and ye will not suffer that the beggar putteth up his petition to you in vain, and turn him out to perish. Perhaps thou shalt say: The man has brought upon himself his misery; therefore I will stay my hand, and will not give unto him of my food, nor impart unto him of my substance that he may not suffer, for his punishments are just—but I say unto you, O man, whosoever doeth this the same hath great cause to repent; and except he repenteth of that which he hath done *he perisheth forever, and hath no interest in the kingdom of God.* (Mosiah 4:16-18.)

If ye judge the man who putteth up his petition to you for your substance that he perish not, and condemn him, *how much more just will be your condemnation* for withholding your substance, which doth not belong to you but to God, to whom also your life belongeth; and yet ye put up no petition, nor repent of the thing which thou hast done. I say unto you, *wo be unto that man, for his substance shall perish with him;* and now, I say these things unto those who are rich as pertaining to the things of the world. (Mosiah 4:22-23.)

For the sake of these things which I have spoken unto you—that is, *for the sake of retaining a remission of your sins from day to day, that ye may walk guiltless before God*—I would that ye should impart of your substance to the poor, every man according to that which he hath, such as feeding the hungry, clothing the naked, visiting the sick and administering to their relief, both spiritually and temporally, according to their wants. (Mosiah 4:26.)

Alma commanded that the people of the church should impart of their substance, every one according to that which he had; if he have more abundantly he should impart more abundantly; and of him that had but little, but little should be required; and to him that had not should be given. And thus they should impart of their substance of their own free will and good desires towards God, and to those priests that stood in need, yea, and to every needy, naked soul. (Mosiah 18:27-28.)

This great loss of the Nephites, and the great slaughter which was among them, would not have happened had it not been for their wickedness and their abomination which was among them; yea, and it was among those also who professed to belong to the church of God. And it was because of the pride of their hearts, because of their exceeding riches, yea, it was because of their oppression to the poor, withholding their food from the hungry, withholding their clothing from the naked, and smiting their humble brethren upon the cheek, making a mock of that which was sacred, denying the spirit of prophecy and of revelation, murdering, plundering, lying, stealing, committing adultery, rising up in great contentions, and deserting alway into the land of Nephi, among the Lamanites—and because of this their great wickedness, and their boastings in their own strength, *they were left in their own strength; therefore they did not prosper, but were afflicted and smitten, and driven before the Lamanites, until they had lost possession of almost all their lands.* (Hel. 4:11-13.)

I give unto you the church in these parts a commandment, that certain men among them shall be appointed, and they shall be appointed by the voice of the church; and they shall look to the poor and the needy, and administer to their relief that they shall not suffer; and send them forth to the place which I have commanded them. (D&C 38:34-35.)

Thou shalt not speak evil of thy neighbor, nor do him any harm. (D&C 42:27.)

Thou wilt remember the poor, and consecrate of thy properties for their support that which thou hast to impart unto them, with a covenant and a deed which cannot be broken. (D&C 42:30.)

If thou obtainest more than that which would be for thy support, thou shalt give it into my storehouse, *that all things may be done according to that which I have said.* (D&C 42:55.)

Ye must visit the poor and the needy and administer to their relief, *that they may be kept until all things may be done* according to my law which ye have received. (D&C 44:6.)

Remember in all things the poor and the needy, the sick and the afflicted, for he that doeth not these things, *the same is not my disciple.* (D&C 52:40.)

[to missionaries] If any man shall give unto any of you a coat, or a suit, take the old and cast it unto the poor, and go on your way rejoicing. (D&C 84:105.)

If any man shall take of the abundance which I have made, and impart not his portion, according to the law of my gospel, unto the poor and the needy, *he shall, with the wicked, lift up his eyes in hell, being in torment.* (D&C 104:18.)

Let him [Vinson Knight] lift up his voice long and loud, in the midst of the people, to plead the cause of the poor and the needy; and let him not fail, neither let his heart faint; *and I will accept of his offerings, for they shall not be unto me as the offerings of Cain, for he shall be mine, saith the Lord.* Let his family rejoice and turn away their hearts from affliction; *for I have chosen him and anointed him, and he shall be honored in the midst of his house, for I will forgive all his sins, saith the Lord.* (D&C 124:75-76.)

Sexual Morality

(See also Marriage; Purity of Heart.)

While commandments forbidding unchastity emphasize the negative, chastity itself is a positive virtue. It is the basis for cleanliness, purity, and sanctification of body and soul, and therefore the foundation for all the blessings attendant to those qualities.

In scriptures relating to marriage, the Lord commands that husband cleave to wife. Thus, in marriage, a man and woman are capable not only of procreation, but of binding themselves spiritually and emotionally to each other. On the other hand, similar sexual behavior outside of marriage will alienate people from the Lord and his Spirit and can bind them through sin into obsessions that dominate and rule.

Sexual sins are among the most serious sins. The sin of adultery is second only to murder in seriousness. (See Alma 39:3-7.) Homosexuality is also condemned severely by the Lord. (See Rom. 1:24-28.) Whatever the level of seriousness, all sexual sins defile the godliness in men and women and pull them away from God and his Son. Sins of immorality are unworthy behavior for sons and daughters of deity and demonstrate that they "have not so learned Christ." (Eph. 4:20.)

Commandments and Promises

Thou shalt not commit adultery. (Ex. 20:14; similar scriptures, Deut. 5:18, Matt. 19:18, Mosiah 13:22, D&C 59:6.)

Thou shalt not lie with mankind, as with womankind: *it is abomination.* Neither shalt thou lie with any beast to defile thyself therewith: neither shall any woman stand before a beast to lie down thereto: *it is confusion.* (Lev. 18:22-23.)

The woman shall not wear that which pertaineth unto a man, neither shall a man put on a woman's garment: for all that do so *are abomination unto the Lord thy God.* (Deut. 22:5.)

Cursed be he that lieth with his father's wife; because he uncovereth his father's skirt. . . . *Cursed* be he that lieth with any manner of beast. . . . *Cursed* be he that lieth with his sister, the daughter of his father, or the daughter of his mother. . . . *Cursed* be he that lieth with his mother in law. (Deut. 27:20-23.)

Lust not after her beauty in thine heart; neither let her take thee with her eyelids. (Prov. 6:25.)

Whoso committeth adultery with a woman *lacketh understanding:* he that doeth it *destroyeth his own soul. A wound and dishonour shall he get; and his reproach shall not be wiped away.* (Prov. 6: 32-33.)

Ye have heard that it was said by them of old time, Thou shalt not commit adultery: but I say unto you, That whosoever looketh on a woman to lust after her hath committed adultery with her already in his heart. (Matt. 5:27-28; similar scripture, 3 Ne. 12:28.)

From within, out of the heart of men, proceed evil thoughts, adulteries, fornications, . . . lasciviousness, . . . foolishness: all these evil things come from within, and *defile the man.* (Mark 7:21-23.)

God also gave them up to uncleanness through the lusts of their own hearts, to dishonour their own bodies between themselves: who changed the truth of God into a lie, and worshipped and served the creature more than the Creator, who is blessed for ever. Amen. For this cause *God gave them up unto vile affections:* for even their women did change the natural use into that which is against nature: and likewise also the men, leaving the natural use of the woman, burned in their lust one toward another; men with men working that which is unseemly, *and receiving in themselves that recompence of their error which was meet.* And even as they did not like to retain God in their knowledge, *God gave them over to a reprobate mind, to do those things which are not convenient.* (Rom. 1:24-28.)

Let not sin therefore reign in your mortal body, that ye should obey it in the lusts thereof. Neither yield ye your members as instruments of unrighteousness unto sin: but yield yourselves unto God, as those that are alive from the dead, and your members as instruments of righteousness unto God. (Rom. 6:12-13.)

They that are after the flesh do mind the things of the flesh; but they that are after the Spirit the things of the Spirit. For to be carnally minded *is death;* but to be spiritually minded *is life and peace.* Because the carnal mind is enmity against God: for it is not subject to the law of God, neither indeed can be. So then they that are in the flesh *cannot please God.* (Rom. 8:5-8; see also JST Rom. 8:8.)

If ye live after the flesh, *ye shall die:* but if ye through the Spirit do mortify the deeds of the body, *ye shall live.* For as many as are led by the Spirit of God, *they are the sons of God.* (Rom. 8:13-14.)

Put ye on the Lord Jesus Christ, and make not provision for the flesh, to fulfil the lusts thereof. (Rom. 13:14.)

Know ye not that ye are the temple of God, and that the Spirit of God dwelleth in you? If any man defile the temple of God, *him shall God destroy;* for the temple of God is holy, which temple ye are. (1 Cor. 3:16-17; see also D&C 93:35.)

Know ye not that the unrighteous *shall not inherit the kingdom of God?* Be not deceived: neither fornicators, nor idolators, nor adulterers, nor effeminate, nor abusers of themselves with mankind. (1 Cor. 6:9.)

The body is not for fornication, but for the Lord; and the Lord for the body. (1 Cor. 6:13.)

Flee fornication. Every sin that a man doeth is without the body; but he that committeth fornication sinneth against his own body. (1 Cor. 6:18.)

These things [the deeds of ancient Israel] were our examples, to the intent we should not lust after evil things, as they also lusted. (1 Cor. 10:6.)

Neither let us commit fornication, as some of them [the Israelites] committed, *and fell in one day three and twenty thousand.* (1 Cor. 10:8.)

Ye have been called unto liberty; only use not liberty for an occasion to the flesh, but by love serve one another. (Gal. 5:13.)

Now the works of the flesh *are manifest,* which are these; Adultery, fornication, uncleanness, lasciviousness, . . . of the which I tell you before, as I have also told you in time past, that they which do such things *shall not inherit the kingdom of God.* (Gal. 5:19-21.)

This I say therefore, and testify in the Lord, that ye henceforth walk not as other Gentiles walk, in the vanity of their mind, *having the understanding darkened, being alienated from the life of God* through the ignorance that is in them, because of the blindness of their heart: who being past feeling have given themselves over unto lasciviousness, to work all uncleanness with greediness. But ye have not so learned Christ. (Eph. 4:17-20.)

Fornication, and all uncleanness, or covetousness, let it not be once named among you, as becometh saints; neither filthiness, nor foolish talking, nor jesting, which are not convenient: but rather giving of thanks. For this ye know, that no whoremonger, nor unclean person, nor covetous man, who is an idolater, *hath any inheritance in the kingdom of Christ and of God.* (Eph. 5:3-5.)

Mortify therefore your members which are upon the earth; fornication, uncleanness, inordinate affection, evil concupiscence, and covetousness, which is idolatry: for which things' sake *the wrath of God cometh on the children of disobedience.* (Col. 3:5-6.)

This is the will of God, even your sanctification, that ye should abstain from fornication: that every one of you should know how to possess his vessel in sanctification and honour; not in the lust of concupiscence, even as the Gentiles which know not God. (1 Thes. 4:3-5.)

Flee also youthful lusts: but follow righteousness, faith, charity, peace, with them that call on the Lord out of a pure heart. (2 Tim. 2:22.)

Marriage is honourable in all, and the bed undefiled: but whoremongers and adulterers *God will judge.* (Heb. 13:4.)

When lust hath conceived, *it bringeth forth sin:* and sin, when it is finished, *bringeth forth death.* (James 1:15.)

Gird up the loins of your mind, be sober, and hope to the end *for the grace that is to be brought unto you at the revelation of Jesus Christ;* as obedient children, not fashioning yourselves according to the former lusts in your ignorance. (1 Pet. 1:13-14.)

Abstain from fleshly lusts, *which war against the soul.* (1 Pet. 2:11.)

Whereby are given unto us exceeding great and precious promises: that by these ye might be partakers of the divine nature, having escaped the corruption that is in the world through lust. (2 Pet. 1:4.)

The Lord knoweth how to deliver the godly *out of temptations, and to reserve* the unjust *unto the day of judgment to be punished:* but chiefly them that walk after the flesh in the lust of uncleanness, and despise government. (2 Pet. 2:9-10.)

The abominable, . . . and whoremongers . . . *shall have their part in the lake which burneth with fire and brimstone: which is the second death.* (Rev. 21:8.)

Wo unto them who commit whoredoms, *for they shall be thrust down to hell.* (2 Ne. 9:36.)

The Lord God hath commanded that men . . . should not commit whoredoms; . . . for whoso doeth them *shall perish.* (2 Ne. 26:32.)

All those who commit whoredoms, and pervert the right way of the Lord, *wo, wo, wo be unto them, saith the Lord God Almighty, for they shall be thrust down to hell!* (2 Ne. 28:15.)

They [wicked husbands and men of the Lord's people] shall not lead away captive the daughters of my people because of their tenderness, *save I shall visit them with a sore curse, even unto destruction;* for they shall not commit whoredoms, like unto them of old, saith the Lord of Hosts. (Jacob 2:33.)

I, Jacob, spake many more things unto the people of Nephi, warning them against fornication and lasciviousness, and every kind of sin, *telling them the awful consequences.* (Jacob 3:12.)

My son [Corianton], I would that ye should repent and forsake your sins, and go no more after the lusts of your eyes, but cross yourself in all these things; for except ye do this *ye can in nowise inherit the king-dom of God.* Oh, remember, and take it upon you, and cross yourself in these things. (Alma 39:9.)

Suffer not yourself to be led away by any vain or foolish thing; suffer not the devil to lead away your heart again after those wicked harlots. (Alma 39:11.)

Because of their . . . committing adultery, they were left in their own strength; *therefore they did not prosper, but were afflicted and smitten, and driven before the Lamanites, until they had lost possession of almost all their lands.* (Hel. 4:12-13.)

At that day when the Gentiles shall sin against my gospel, . . . and shall be filled with all manner of . . . whoredoms, and secret abominations, . . . behold, saith the Father, *I will bring the fulness of my gospel from among them.* (3 Ne. 16:10.)

Thou shalt love thy wife with all thy heart, and shalt cleave unto her and none else. And he that looketh upon a woman to lust after her shall deny the faith, *and shall not have the Spirit;* and if he repents not *he shall be cast out.* Thou shalt not commit adultery; and he that committeth adultery, and repenteth not, *shall be cast out.* But he that has committed adultery and repents with all his heart, and forsaketh it, and doeth it no more, *thou shalt forgive;* but if he doeth it again, *he shall not be forgiven, but shall be cast out.* (D&C 42:22-26.)

Whatever persons among you, having put away their companions for the cause of fornication, or in other words, if they shall testify before you in all lowliness of heart that this is the case, *ye shall not cast them out from among you;* but if ye shall find that any persons have left their companions for the sake of adultery, and they themselves are the offenders, and their companions are living, *they shall be cast out from among you.* (D&C 42:74-75.)

There were among you adulterers and adulteresses; some of whom have turned away from you, and others remain with you that hereafter shall be revealed. Let such beware and repent speedily, *lest judgment shall come upon them as a snare, and their folly shall be made manifest, and their works shall follow them in the eyes of the people.* (D&C 63:14-15.)

He that looketh on a woman to lust after her, or if any shall commit adultery in their hearts, *they shall not have the Spirit, but shall deny the faith and shall fear. Wherefore, I, the Lord, have said that . . . the whoremonger . . . shall have their part in that lake which burneth with fire and brimstone, which is the second death.* (D&C 63:16-17.)

[to William McLellin] Commit not adultery—a temptation with which thou hast been troubled. (D&C 66:10.)

Cease from all your . . . lustful desires. (D&C 88:121.)

Man is the tabernacle of God, even temples; and whatsoever temple is defiled, *God shall destroy that temple.* (D&C 93:35; see also 1 Cor. 3:16-17.)

As ye have asked concerning adultery, verily, verily, I say unto you, if a man receiveth a wife in the new and everlasting covenant, and if she be with another man, and I have not appointed unto her by the holy anointing, she hath committed adultery *and shall be destroyed.* If she be not in the new and everlasting covenant, and she be with another man, she has committed adultery. And if her husband be with another woman, and he was under a vow, he hath broken his vow and hath committed adultery. And if she hath not committed adultery, but is innocent and hath not broken her vow, and she knoweth it, and I reveal it unto you, my servant Joseph, *then shall you have power, by the power of my Holy Priesthood, to take her and give her unto him that hath not committed adultery but hath been faithful; for he shall be made ruler over many.* (D&C 132:41-44.)

Signs and Miracles, Seeking

(See also Believing in God; Faith; Prayer; Spiritual Gifts.)

Signs and miracles are a function of belief. Many who demonstrate even fledgling faith are comforted, enlightened, or healed through signs and miracles performed with God's priesthood. Signs and miracles encourage God's followers and sometimes even spare their lives. However, God explains clearly that signs and miracles are not a shortcut to faith, that "faith cometh not by signs," but that "signs come by faith, not by the will of men, nor as they please, but by the will of God." (D&C 63:9-10.)

The Lord also says that he is not pleased with those who seek after signs and wonders for faith. This is not a condemnation of all who seek signs and miracles. Instead, the motivation behind sign-seeking should be for the good of men unto the Lord's glory. (See D&C 63:12.) The difference is not in the nature of the sign or request but in the reason why the sign is sought. Seeking them to build faith is fruitless and damaging; God's power should be invoked for selfless, not selfish, reasons.

Asking a miracle at God's hand is not always wrong, even a miracle benefiting the person asking for it. As Moroni counseled: "Ask the Father in the name of Jesus for what things soever ye shall stand in need. . . . Ask not, that ye may consume it on your lusts, but ask with a firmness unshaken, that ye will yield to no temptation, but that ye will serve the true and living God." (Morm. 9:27-28.)

Commandments and Promises

An evil and adulterous generation seeketh after a sign; and *there shall no sign be given to it, but the sign of the prophet Jonas.* (Matt. 12:39; similar scriptures, Matt. 16:4, Mark 8:12, Luke 11:29.)

Jesus saith unto him, Thomas, because thou hast seen me, thou hast believed: *blessed* are they that have not seen, and yet have believed. (John 20:29.)

[Alma to Korihor] Thou hast had signs enough; will ye tempt your God? Will ye say, Show unto me a sign, when ye have the testimony of all these thy brethren, and also all the holy prophets? (Alma 30:44.)

Ask the Father in the name of Jesus for what things soever ye shall stand in need. . . . Ask not, that ye may consume it on your lusts, but ask with a firmness unshaken, that ye will yield to no temptation, but that ye will serve the true and living God. (Morm. 9:27-28.)

Require not miracles, except I shall command you, except casting out devils, healing the sick, and against poisonous serpents, and against deadly poisons. (D&C 24:13.)

Beware lest ye are deceived; *and that ye may not be deceived* seek ye earnestly the best gifts, always remembering for what they are given; for verily I say unto you, *they are given for the benefit of those* who love me and keep all my commandments, and him that seeketh so to do; *that all may be benefited* that seek or that ask of me, that ask and not for a sign that they may consume it upon their lusts. (D&C 46:8-9.)

He that seeketh signs *shall see signs, but not unto salvation.* (D&C 63:7.)

Faith cometh not by signs, but *signs follow* those that believe. Yea, *signs come* by faith, not by the will of men, nor as they please, but by the will of God. Yea, *signs come* by faith, *unto mighty works,* for without faith *no man pleaseth God; and with whom God is angry he is not well pleased; wherefore, unto such he showeth no signs, only in wrath unto their condemnation. Wherefore, I, the Lord, am not pleased* with those among you who have sought after signs and wonders for faith, and not for the good of men unto my glory. (D&C 63:9-12.)

Soberness

(See also Foolishness.)

The Lord expects us to be sober about serious things. While we are commanded to be cheerful and to rejoice, we are cautioned against lightmindedness. Peter writes, "The end of all things is at hand: be ye therefore sober, and watch unto prayer." (1 Pet. 4:7.) The Lord says in latter-day revelation, "Let the solemnities of eternity rest upon your minds." (D&C 43:34.)

We can have a glad heart, be cheerful, and yet be sober. Sobriety indicates reflection about matters of consequence, and reflection about eternity can bring us to the realization that we can take life seriously and still find joy in it.

Commandments and Promises

They mocked the messengers of God, and despised his words, and misused his prophets, *until the wrath of the Lord arose against his people, till there was no remedy.* (2 Chr. 36:16.)

Be ye not mockers, *lest your bands be made strong: for I have heard from the Lord God of hosts a consumption, even determined upon the whole earth.* (Isa. 28:22.)

I say, through the grace given unto me, to every man that is among you, not to think of himself more highly than he ought to think; but to think soberly, according as God hath dealt to every man the measure of faith. (Rom. 12:3.)

Let it not be once named among you, as becometh saints; neither filthiness, nor foolish talking, nor jesting, which are not convenient. (Eph. 5:4.)

Let us not sleep, as do others; but let us watch and be sober. (1 Thes. 5:6.)

Let us, who are of the day, be sober, putting on the breastplate of faith and love; and for an helmet, the hope of salvation. (1 Thes. 5:8.)

A bishop must be . . . vigilant, sober, of good behaviour, . . . not a brawler . . . ; one that ruleth well his own house, having his children in subjection with all gravity. . . . Likewise must the deacons be grave, not doubletongued. (1 Tim. 3:2-4, 8.)

A bishop must be . . . sober, just, holy, temperate. (Titus 1:7-8.)

Speak thou the things which become sound doctrine: that the aged men be sober, grave, temperate. . . . The aged women likewise . . . ; that they teach the young women to be sober, . . . to be discreet. Young men likewise exhort to be sober minded. In all things shewing thyself a pattern of good works: in doctrine shewing uncorruptness, gravity, sincerity, sound speech, that cannot be condemned; *that he that is of the contrary part may be ashamed, having no evil thing to say of you.* (Titus 2:1-8.)

Denying ungodliness and worldly lusts, we should live soberly, righteously, and godly, in this present world. (Titus 2:12.)

Gird up the loins of your mind, be sober. (1 Pet. 1:13.)

The end of all things is at hand: be ye therefore sober, and watch unto prayer. (1 Pet. 4:7.)

Be sober, be vigilant; because your adversary the devil, as a roaring lion, walketh about, seeking whom he may devour. (1 Pet. 5:8.)

Will ye . . . make a mock of the great plan of redemption, which hath been laid for you? Know ye not that if ye will do these things, *that the power of the redemption and the resurrection, which is in Christ, will bring you to stand with shame and awful guilt before the bar of God?* (Jacob 6:8-9.)

Ye will teach them [your children] to walk in the ways of truth and soberness. (Mosiah 4:15.)

Go unto this people and declare the word, and be sober. (Alma 37:47.)

Teach the word unto this people. Be sober. (Alma 38:15.)

Go thy way, declare the word with truth and soberness, *that thou mayest bring souls unto repentance, that the great plan of mercy may have claim upon them.* (Alma 42:31.)

Because of . . . making a mock of that which was sacred, . . . *they were left in their own strength; therefore they did not prosper, but were afflicted and smitten before the Lamanites, until they had lost possession of almost all their lands.* (Hel. 4:12-13.)

Fools mock, *but they shall mourn.* (Ether 12:26.)

Be sober; be temperate. (D&C 6:19.)

Perform with soberness the work which I have commanded you. (D&C 6:35.)

Speak the truth in soberness. (D&C 18:21.)

Treasure these things up in your hearts, and let the solemnities of eternity rest upon your minds. Be sober. (D&C 43:34-35.)

Inasmuch as ye do these things [Sabbath observance, fasting, and prayer] with thanksgiving, with cheerful hearts and countenances, not with much laughter, for this is sin, but with a glad heart and a cheerful countenance—verily I say, that inasmuch as ye do this, *the fulness of the earth is yours, the beasts of the field and the fowls of the air, and that which climbeth upon the trees and walketh upon the earth.* (D&C 59:15-16.)

Gird up your loins and be watchful and be sober, looking forth for the coming of the Son of Man, for he cometh in an hour you think not. (D&C 61:38.)

Gird up your loins and be sober. (D&C 73:6.)

Your minds in times past have been darkened because of unbelief, and because you have treated lightly the things you have received. (D&C 84:53.)

I will forgive you of your sins with this commandment—that you remain steadfast in your minds in solemnity and the spirit of prayer, in bearing testimony to all the world of those things which are communicated unto you. (D&C 84:61.)

Cast away your idle thoughts and your excess laughter far from you. (D&C 88:69.)

Cease from all your light speeches, from all laughter, from all your lustful desires, from all your pride and light-mindedness, and from all your wicked doings. (D&C 88:121.)

Declare whatsoever thing ye declare in my name, in solemnity of heart, in the spirit of meekness, in all things. *And I give unto you this promise, that* inasmuch as ye do this *the Holy Ghost shall be shed forth in bearing record unto all things whatsoever ye shall say.* (D&C 100:7-8.)

Spiritual Awareness

(See also Honest in Heart; Listening to God and His Servants; Receiving and Following the Holy Ghost; Revelation.)

To receive inspiration and revelation, we must be aware of spiritual things. We must learn to recognize the voice of God when he speaks quietly. We must train our spiritual senses to be receptive and discerning.

Much of our spiritual awareness depends on our overcoming "the natural man" in us. "You shall see me and know that I am—not with the carnal neither natural mind, but with the spiritual," the Lord declares. (D&C 67:10.) "The natural man receiveth not the things of the Spirit of God: for they are foolishness unto him: neither can he know them, because they are spiritually discerned." (1 Cor. 2:14.) This spiritual discernment Paul speaks of is not impossible to achieve. It can come as we become true saints: "The natural man is an enemy to God . . . unless he yields to the enticings of the Holy Spirit, and putteth off the natural man and becometh a saint through the atonement of Christ the Lord, and becometh as a child, submissive, meek, humble, patient, full of love, willing to submit to all things which the Lord seeth fit to inflict upon him, even as a child doth submit to his father." (Mosiah 3:19.) This process of yielding to the Holy Spirit, of bringing the Spirit into our lives step by step, is the key to becoming spiritually aware.

Commandments and Promises

Woe unto them that call evil good, and good evil; that put darkness for light, and light for darkness; that put bitter for sweet, and sweet for bitter! (Isa. 5:20; similar scripture, 2 Ne. 15:20.)

Though the Lord give you the bread of adversity, and the water of affliction, *yet shall not thy teachers be removed into a corner any more, but thine eyes shall see thy teachers: and thine ears shall hear a word behind thee, saying, This is the way, walk ye in it, when ye turn to the right hand, and when ye turn to the left.* (Isa. 30:20-21.)

549

Hear, ye deaf; and look, ye blind, *that ye may see.* (Isa. 42:18.)

The Lord's hand is not shortened, that it cannot save; neither his ear heavy, that it cannot hear: but your iniquities *have separated between you and your God,* and your sins *have hid his face from you, that he will not hear.* (Isa. 59:1-2.)

Therefore is judgment far from us, neither doth justice overtake us: we wait for light, but behold obscurity; for brightness, but we walk in darkness. We grope for the wall like the blind, and we grope as if we had no eyes; we stumble at noonday as in the night; we are in desolate places as dead men. We roar all like bears, and mourn sore like doves: we look for judgment, but there is none; for salvation, but it is far off from us. For our transgressions are multiplied before thee, and our sins testify against us: for our transgressions are with us; and as for our iniquities, we know them. (Isa. 59:9-12.)

Therefore speak I to them in parables; because they seeing see not; and hearing they hear not, neither do they understand. And in them is fulfilled the prophecy of Esaias, which saith, By hearing ye shall hear, and shall not understand; and seeing ye shall see, and shall not perceive: for this people's heart is waxed gross, and their ears are dull of hearing, and their eyes they have closed; lest at any time they should see with their eyes, and hear with their ears, and should understand with their heart, and should be converted, and I should heal them. But *blessed* are your eyes, for they see: and your ears, for they hear. (Matt. 13:13-16.)

Ye blind guides, which strain at a gnat, and swallow a camel. *Woe* unto you, scribes and Pharisees, hypocrites! for ye make clean the outside of the cup and of the platter, but within they are full of extortion and excess. Thou blind Pharisee, cleanse first that which is within the cup and platter, *that the outside of them may be clean also.* (Matt. 23:24-26; see also JST Matt. 23:21.)

No man knoweth who the Son is, but the Father; and who the Father is, but the Son, and he to whom the Son will reveal him. (Luke 10:22; see also JST Luke 10:23.)

They that are after the flesh do mind the things of the flesh; but they that are after the Spirit the things of the Spirit. For to be carnally minded *is death;* but to be spiritually minded *is life and peace.* Because the carnal mind *is enmity against God:* for it is not subject to the law of God, neither indeed can be. So then they that are in the flesh *cannot please God.* But ye are not in the flesh, but in the Spirit, if so be that the Spirit of God dwell in you. Now if any man have not the Spirit of Christ, *he is none of his.* And if Christ be in you, *the body is dead* because of sin; *but the Spirit is life* because of righteousness. But if the Spirit of him that raised up Jesus from the dead dwell in you, *he that raised up Christ from the dead shall also quicken your mortal bodies by his Spirit that dwelleth in you.* (Rom 8:5-11; see also JST Rom. 8:8-10.)

The natural man *receiveth not the things of the Spirit of God:* for they are foolishness unto him: *neither can he know them,* because they are spiritually discerned. But he that is spiritual *judgeth all things, yet he himself is judged of no man.* (1 Cor. 2:14-15.)

Because thou sayest, I am rich, and increased with goods, and have need of nothing; and knowest not that thou art wretched, and miserable, and poor, and blind, and naked: I counsel thee to buy of me gold tried in the fire, *that thou mayest be rich;* and white raiment, *that thou mayest be clothed, and that the shame of thy nakedness do not appear;* and anoint thine eyes with eyesalve, *that thou mayest see.* (Rev. 3:17-18.)

Remember, to be carnally-minded *is death,* and to be spiritually-minded *is life eternal.* (2 Ne. 9:39.)

The Jews were a stiffnecked people; and they despised the words of plainness, and killed the prophets, and sought for things that they could not understand. Wherefore, because of their blindness, which blindness came by looking beyond the mark, *they must needs fall; for God hath taken away his plainness from them, and delivered unto them many things which they cannot understand,* because they desired it. And because they desired it God hath done it, *that they may stumble.* (Jacob 4:14.)

When ye shall rend that veil of unbelief which doth cause you to remain in your awful state of wickedness, and hardness of heart, and blindness of mind, *then shall the great and marvelous things which have been hid up from the foundation of the world from you—yea,* when ye shall call upon the Father in my name, with a broken heart and a contrite spirit, *then shall ye know that the Father hath remembered the covenant which he made unto your fathers, O house of Israel.* (Ether 4:15.)

No man has seen God at any time in the flesh, except quickened by the Spirit of God. Neither can any natural man *abide the presence of God,* neither after the carnal mind. Ye are not able to abide the presence of God now, neither the ministering of angels; wherefore, continue in patience *until ye are perfected.* Let not your minds turn black; and when ye are worthy, in mine own due time, *ye shall see and know that which was conferred upon you by the hands of my servant Joseph Smith.* (D&C 67:11-14.)

If your eye be single to my glory, *your whole bodies shall be filled with light, and there shall be no darkness in you;* and that body which is filled with light *comprehendeth all things.* (D&C 88:67.)

Let thy bowels also be full of charity towards all men, and to the household of faith, and let virtue garnish thy thoughts unceasingly; *then shall thy confidence wax strong in the presence of God; and the doctrine of the priesthood shall distil upon thy soul as the dews from heaven. The Holy Ghost shall be thy constant companion, and thy scepter an unchanging scepter of righteousness and truth; and thy dominion shall be an everlasting dominion, and without compulsory means it shall flow unto thee forever and ever.* (D&C 121:45-46.)

Spiritual Gifts

(See also Signs and Miracles, Seeking.)

We are given different spiritual gifts. Some have the gift of healing, others the gift of being healed; some have the gift of tongues, others the gift of interpretation; some have the gift of believing; others the gift of faith; some have the gift of teaching, others the gift of understanding. (See 1 Cor. 12:31.) What gifts we have, however, is not as important as wisely using those we have: "Forasmuch as ye are zealous of spiritual gifts, seek that ye may excel to the edifying of the Church." (1 Cor. 4:12.)

As with signs and miracles, we are commanded to seek spiritual gifts not to "consume it upon [our] lusts," but "that all may be benefited that seek or that ask of me." (D&C 46:9.) The Lord cautions believers "that they shall not boast themselves of these things, neither speak them before the world; for these things are given unto you for your profit and for salvation." (D&C 84:73.) Treated as sacred and purposeful, spiritual gifts can bless us and witness to believers the authenticity of the power of God.

Commandments and Promises

The prophet that hath a dream, let him tell a dream; and he that hath my word, let him speak my word faithfully. (Jer. 23:28.)

Heal the sick, cleanse the lepers, raise the dead, cast out devils: freely ye have received, freely give. (Matt. 10:8.)

These signs shall follow them that believe; *In my name shall they cast out devils; they shall speak with new tongues; they shall take up serpents; and if they drink any deadly thing, it shall not hurt them: they shall lay hands on the sick, and they shall recover.* (Mark 16:17-18; similar scripture, Morm. 9:24; see also D&C 84:65-72.)

Having then gifts differing according to the grace that is given to us, whether prophecy, let us prophesy according to the proportion of faith; or ministry, let us wait on our ministering: or he that teacheth, on teaching; or he that exhorteth, on exhortation: he that giveth, let him do it with simplicity; he that ruleth, with diligence; he that sheweth mercy, with cheerfulness. (Rom. 12:6-8.)

Covet earnestly the best gifts. (1 Cor. 12:31.)

Follow after charity, and desire spiritual gifts, but rather that ye may prophesy. For he that speaketh in an unknown tongue speaketh not unto men, but unto God: for no man understandeth him; howbeit in the spirit he speaketh mysteries. He that prophesieth *speaketh unto men to edification, and exhortation, and comfort.* He that speaketh in an unknown tongue *edifieth himself;* but he that prophesieth *edifieth the church.* I would that ye all spake with tongues, but rather that ye prophesied: for *greater is he* that prophesieth than he that speaketh with tongues, except he interpret, *that the church may receive edifying.* (1 Cor. 14:1-5.)

Even so ye, forasmuch as ye are zealous of spiritual gifts, seek that ye may excel to the edifying of the church. (1 Cor. 14:12.)

If any man speak in an unknown tongue, let it be by two, or at the most by three, and that by course; and let one interpret. But if there be no interpreter, let him keep silence in the church; and let him speak to himself, and to God. Let the prophets speak two or three, and let the other judge. If any thing be revealed to another that sitteth by, let the first hold his peace. For ye may all prophesy one by one, *that all may learn, and all may be comforted.* And the spirits of the prophets are subject to the prophets. For God is not the author of confusion, but of peace, as in all churches of the saints. (1 Cor. 14:27-33.)

Covet to prophesy, and forbid not to speak with tongues. (1 Cor. 14:39.)

Neglect not the gift that is in thee, which was given thee by prophecy, with the laying on of the hands of the presbytery. (1 Tim. 4:14.)

As every man hath received the gift, even so minister the same one to another, as good stewards of the manifold grace of God. If any man speak, let him speak as the oracles of God; if any man minister, let him do it as of the ability which God giveth: *that God in all things may be glorified through Jesus Christ,* to whom be praise and dominion for ever and ever. (1 Pet. 4:10-11.)

He that prophesieth, let him prophesy to the understanding of men; for the Spirit speaketh the truth and lieth not. Wherefore, it speaketh of things as they really are, and of things as they really will be; wherefore, *these things are manifested unto us plainly, for the salvation of our souls.* (Jacob 4:13.)

Come unto God, the Holy One of Israel, and believe in prophesying, and in revelations, and in the ministering of angels, and in the gift of speaking with tongues, and in the gift of interpreting languages, and in all things which are good. (Omni 1:25.)

Remember that every good gift cometh of Christ. (Moro. 10:18.)

Remember that he is the same yesterday, today, and forever, and that *all these gifts of which I have spoken, which are spiritual, never will be done away, even as long as the world shall stand,* only according to the unbelief of the children of men. (Moro. 10:19.)

Now I speak unto all the ends of the earth—that *if the day cometh that the power and gifts of God shall be done away among you,* it shall be because of unbelief. *And wo be unto the children of men if this be the case;* for there shall be none that doeth good among you, no not one. For if there be one among you that doeth good, *he shall work by the power and gifts of God.* (Moro. 10:24-25.)

Come unto Christ, and lay hold upon every good gift, and touch not the evil gift, nor the unclean thing. (Moro. 10:30.)

I am God, and mine arm is not shortened; and *I will show miracles, signs, and wonders,* unto all those who believe on my name. And whoso shall ask it in my name in faith, *they shall cast out devils; they shall heal the sick; they shall cause the blind to receive their sight, and the deaf to hear, and the dumb to speak, and the lame to walk.* And *the time speedily cometh that great things are to be shown forth unto the children of men;* but without faith *shall not anything be shown forth except desolations upon Babylon.* (D&C 35:8-11.)

He that hath faith in me to be healed, and is not appointed unto death, *shall be healed.* He who hath faith to see *shall see.* He who hath faith to hear *shall hear.* The lame who hath faith to leap *shall leap.* And they who have not faith to do these things, but believe in me, *have power to become my sons;* and inasmuch as they break not my laws *thou shalt bear their infirmities.* (D&C 42:48-52.)

That ye may not be deceived seek ye earnestly the best gifts, always remembering for what they are given; for verily I say unto you, they are given *for the benefit of those* who love me and keep all my commandments, and him that seeketh so to do; *that all may be benefited* that seek or that ask of me, that ask and not for a sign that they may consume it upon their lusts. (D&C 46:8-9.)

Always remember, and always retain in your minds what those gifts are, that are given unto the church. (D&C 46:10.)

These signs shall follow them that believe—*In my name they shall do many wonderful works; in my name they shall cast out devils; in my name they shall heal the sick; in my name they shall open the eyes of the blind, and unstop the ears of the deaf; and the tongue of the dumb shall speak; and if any man shall administer poison unto them it shall not hurt them; and the poison of a serpent shall not have power to harm them.* But a commandment I give unto them, that they shall not boast themselves of these things, neither speak them before the world; for these things are given unto you for your profit and for salvation. (D&C 84:65-73.)

Steadfastness/Enduring to the End

(See also Faithfulness.)

Nephi once questioned those who had received baptism by water and by fire. In speaking of the marvels of that experience, he asked: "After ye have gotten into this strait and narrow path, I would ask if all is done?" He answered, "Nay," and then gave us the principle and blessing of steadfastness and enduring to the end: "Ye must press forward with a steadfastness in Christ, having a perfect brightness of hope, and a love of God and of all men. Wherefore, if ye shall press forward, feasting upon the word of Christ, and endure to the end, behold, thus saith the Father: Ye shall have eternal life." (2 Ne. 31: 19-20.)

What greater gift can we receive from God than eternal life? Because of this, though endurance and steadfastness often suggest joylessness, the perseverance the gospel requires is not so. It is filled with a brightness of hope, a love of God and man, and a feast on the words of Christ. Even in the terrible death of Stephen the martyr, "he, being full of the Holy Ghost, looked up stedfastly into heaven, and saw the glory of God, and Jesus." With this vision full in his heart, as he was being stoned, he called upon God and said, "Lord Jesus, receive my spirit." He kneeled down and, in words that echoed those of Jesus on the cross, cried out, "Lord, lay not this sin to their charge." (Acts 7:55-60.) Hardly the words of a grim, despairing, frustrated, or joyless man!

Stephen stood fast to the end despite persecution and imminent death. We are commanded to do as Stephen did: to stand fast in our faith, our loyalty, our purpose, our deeds; to endure to the end of this life and embark in the hereafter upon eternal life.

557

Commandments and Promises

Ye shall be hated of all men for my name's sake: but he that endureth to the end *shall be saved*. (Matt. 10:22; similar scripture, Mark 13:13.)

No man, having put his hand to the plough, and looking back, *is fit for the kingdom of God*. (Luke 9:62.)

If ye continue in my word, *then are ye my disciples indeed*. (John 8:31.)

[God] will render to every man according to his deeds: to them who by patient continuance in well doing seek for glory and honour and immortality, *eternal life*. (Rom. 2:6-7.)

Behold therefore the goodness and severity of God: on them which fell, *severity*; but toward thee, *goodness*, if thou continue in his goodness: *otherwise thou also shalt be cut off*. (Rom. 11:22.)

Know ye not that they which run in a race run all, but one receiveth the prize? So run, *that ye may obtain*. (1 Cor. 9:24.)

Be ye stedfast, unmoveable, always abounding in the work of the Lord, forasmuch as ye know that your labour *is not in vain in the Lord*. (1 Cor. 15:58.)

Watch ye, stand fast in the faith, quit you like men, be strong. (1 Cor. 16:13.)

Stand fast therefore in the liberty wherewith Christ hath made us free, and be not entangled again with the yoke of bondage. (Gal. 5:1.)

Let us not be weary in well doing: *for in due season we shall reap*, if we faint not. (Gal. 6:9.)

Take unto you the whole armour of God, *that ye may be able to withstand in the evil day, and having done all, to stand*. Stand therefore, having your loins girt about with truth, and having on the breastplate of righteousness; and your feet shod with the preparation of the gospel of peace; above all, taking the shield of faith, *wherewith ye shall be able to quench all the fiery darts of the wicked.* And take the helmet of salvation, and the sword of the Spirit, which is the word of God: praying always with all prayer and supplication in the Spirit, and watching thereunto with all perseverance and supplication for all saints. (Eph. 6:13-18.)

Stand fast in the Lord. (Philip. 4:1.)

You, *that were sometime alienated and enemies in your mind* by wicked works, *yet now hath he reconciled in the body of his flesh through death, to present you holy and unblameable and unreproveable in his sight:* if ye continue in the faith grounded and settled, and be not moved away from the hope of the gospel, which ye have heard, and which was preached to every creature which is under heaven. (Col. 1:21-23.)

As ye have therefore received Christ Jesus the Lord, so walk ye in him: rooted and built up in him, and stablished in the faith, as ye have been taught, abounding therein with thanksgiving. (Col. 2:6-7.)

Prove all things; hold fast that which is good. (1 Thes. 5:21.)

Stand fast, and hold the traditions which ye have been taught, whether by word, or our epistle. (2 Thes. 2:15.)

Hold fast the form of sound words, which thou hast heard of me, in faith and love which is in Christ Jesus. (2 Tim. 1:13.)

Thou therefore endure hardness, as a good soldier of Jesus Christ. (2 Tim. 2:3.)

Continue thou in the things which thou hast learned and hast been assured of, knowing of whom thou hast learned them; and that from a child thou hast known the holy scriptures, *which are able to make thee wise unto salvation through faith which is in Christ Jesus.* (2 Tim. 3:14-15.)

Moses verily was faithful in all his house, as a servant . . . ; but Christ as a son over his own house; *whose house are we,* if we hold fast the confidence and the rejoicing of the hope firm unto the end. (Heb. 3: 5-6.)

We are made partakers of Christ, if we hold the beginning of our confidence stedfast unto the end. (Heb. 3:14.)

Seeing then that we have a great high priest, that is passed into the heavens, Jesus the Son of God, let us hold fast our profession. (Heb. 4:14.)

Seeing we also are compassed about with so great a cloud of witnesses, let us lay aside every weight, and the sin which doth so easily beset us, and let us run with patience the race that is set before us, looking unto Jesus the author and finisher of our faith; who for the joy that was set before him endured the cross. (Heb. 12:1-2.)

If ye endure chastening, *God dealeth with you as with sons;* for what son is he whom the father chasteneth not? (Heb. 12:7.)

We count them happy which endure. (James 5:11.)

Resist [the adversary] stedfast in the faith, knowing that the same afflictions are accomplished in your brethren that are in the world. (1 Pet. 5:9.)

Seeing ye know these things before, beware *lest ye also*, being led away with the error of the wicked, *fall* from your own stedfastness. (2 Pet. 3:17; see also JST 2 Pet. 3:17.)

Fear none of those things which thou shalt suffer: . . . be thou faithful unto death, *and I will give thee a crown of life*. (Rev. 2:10.)

Remember therefore how thou hast received and heard, and hold fast, and repent. If therefore thou shalt not watch, *I will come on thee as a thief, and thou shalt not know what hour I will come upon thee.* (Rev. 3:3.)

I come quickly; hold that fast which thou hast, *that no man take thy crown.* (Rev. 3:11.)

If they endure unto the end *they shall be lifted up at the last day, and shall be saved in the everlasting kingdom of the Lamb.* (1 Ne. 13:37.)

If ye shall be obedient to the commandments, and endure to the end, *ye shall be saved at the last day.* (1 Ne. 22:31.)

They who have endured the crosses of the world, and despised the shame of it, *they shall inherit the kingdom of God, which was prepared for them from the foundation of the world, and their joy shall be full forever.* (2 Ne. 9:18.)

If they will not repent and believe in his name, and be baptized in his name, and endure to the end, *they must be damned.* (2 Ne. 9:24.)

The righteous that hearken unto the words of the prophets, and destroy them not, but look forward unto Christ with steadfastness for the signs which are given, notwithstanding all persecution—behold, *they are they which shall not perish. But the Son of righteousness shall appear unto them; and he shall heal them, and they shall have peace with him, until three generations shall have passed away, and many of the fourth generation shall have passed away in righteousness.* (2 Ne. 26:8-9.)

Unless a man shall endure to the end, in following the example of the Son of the living God, *he cannot be saved.* (2 Ne. 31:16.)

Ye must press forward with a steadfastness in Christ, having a perfect brightness of hope, and a love of God and of all men. Wherefore, if ye shall press forward, feasting upon the word of Christ, and endure to the end, behold, thus saith the Father: *Ye shall have eternal life.* (2 Ne. 31:20.)

O all ye that are pure in heart, lift up your heads and receive the pleasing word of God, and feast upon his love; *for ye may*, if your minds are firm, *forever.* (Jacob 3:2.)

Come unto him, and offer your whole souls as an offering unto him, and continue in fasting and praying, and endure to the end; and as the Lord liveth *ye will be saved.* (Omni 1:26.)

Consider on *the blessed and happy state* of those that keep the commandments of God. For behold, *they are blessed in all things, both temporal and spiritual*; and if they hold out faithful to the end *they are received into heaven, that thereby they may dwell with God in a state of neverending happiness.* (Mosiah 2:41.)

Humble yourselves even in the depths of humility, calling on the name of the Lord daily, and standing steadfastly in the faith of that which is to come. . . . If ye do this *ye shall always rejoice, and be filled with the love of God, and always retain a remission of your sins; and ye shall grow in the knowledge of the glory of him that created you, or in the knowledge of that which is just and true.* (Mosiah 4:11-12.)

If ye do not watch yourselves, and your thoughts, and your words, and your deeds, and observe the commandments of God, and continue in the faith of what ye have heard concerning the coming of our Lord, even unto the end of your lives, *ye must perish.* (Mosiah 4:30.)

I would that ye should be steadfast and immovable, always abounding in good works, *that Christ, the Lord God Omnipotent, may seal you his, that you may be brought to heaven, that ye may have everlasting salvation and eternal life.* (Mosiah 5:15.)

It is he that cometh *to take away the sins of the world, yea, the sins of every man* who steadfastly believeth on his name. (Alma 5:48.)

He that truly humbleth himself, and repenteth of his sins, and endureth to the end, *the same shall be blessed.* (Alma 32:15.)

Blessed is he that endureth to the end. (Alma 38:2.)

Look unto me, and endure to the end, *and ye shall live;* for unto him that endureth to the end *will I give eternal life.* (3 Ne. 15:9.)

Whoso taketh upon him my name, and endureth to the end, the same *shall be saved at the last day.* (3 Ne. 27:6.)

Whoso repenteth and is baptized in my name *shall be filled;* and if he endureth to the end, behold, *him will I hold guiltless before my Father at that day when I shall stand to judge the world.* And he that endureth not unto the end, *the same is he that is also hewn down and cast into the fire, from whence they can no more return.* (3 Ne. 27: 16-17.)

See that ye do all things in worthiness, and do it in the name of Jesus Christ, the Son of the living God; and if ye do this, and endure to the end, *ye will in nowise be cast out.* (Morm. 9:29.)

Blessed is he that is found faithful unto my name at the last day, *for he shall be lifted up to dwell in the kingdom prepared for him from the foundation of the world.* (Ether 4:19.)

If thou wilt do good, yea, and hold out faithful to the end, *thou shalt be saved in the kingdom of God, which is the greatest of all the gifts of God; for there is no gift greater than the gift of salvation.* (D&C 6:13.)

Stand fast in the work wherewith I have called you, *and a hair of your head shall not be lost, and you shall be lifted up at the last day.* (D&C 9:14.)

Whosoever is of my church, and endureth of my church to the end, *him will I establish upon my rock, and the gates of hell shall not prevail against them.* (D&C 10:69.)

If you keep my commandments and endure to the end *you shall have eternal life, which gift is the greatest of all the gifts of God.* (D&C 14:7.)

As many as repent and are baptized in my name, which is Jesus Christ, and endure to the end, *the same shall be saved.* (D&C 18:22.)

As many as would believe and be baptized in his holy name, and endure in faith to the end, *should be saved.* (D&C 20:25.)

All men must repent and believe on the name of Jesus Christ, and worship the Father in his name, and endure in faith to the end, *or they cannot be saved in the kingdom of God.* (D&C 20:29.)

Be steadfast. (D&C 31:9.)

Blessed are they who are faithful and endure, whether in life or in death, *for they shall inherit eternal life.* (D&C 50:5.)

He that endureth in faith and doeth my will, *the same shall overcome, and shall receive an inheritance upon the earth when the day of transfiguration shall come.* (D&C 63:20.)

He that is faithful and endureth *shall overcome the world.* (D&C 63:47.)

All things must come to pass in their time. Wherefore, be not weary in well-doing, for ye are laying the foundation of a great work. And out of small things *proceedeth that which is great.* (D&C 64:32-33.)

Continue in these things even unto the end, *and you shall have a crown of eternal life at the right hand of my Father.* (D&C 66:12.)

Be faithful; stand in the office which I have appointed unto you; succor the weak, lift up the hands which hang down, and strengthen the feeble knees. (D&C 81:5.)

I will forgive you of your sins with this commandment—that you remain steadfast in your minds in solemnity and the spirit of prayer, in bearing testimony to all the world of those things which are communicated unto you. (D&C 84:61.)

Blessed are ye if ye continue in my goodness, a light unto the Gentiles, and through this priesthood, a savior unto my people Israel. (D&C 86:11.)

Stand ye in holy places, and be not moved, until the day of the Lord come; for behold, it cometh quickly, saith the Lord. (D&C 87:8.)

All those who will not endure chastening, but deny me, *cannot be sanctified.* (D&C 101:5.)

Whosoever ye shall send in my name, by the voice of your brethren, the Twelve, duly recommended and authorized by you, *shall have power to open the door of my kingdom unto any nation whithersoever ye shall send them*—inasmuch as they shall humble themselves before me, and abide in my word, and hearken to the voice of my Spirit. (D&C 112:21-22.)

My son [Joseph Smith], *peace be unto thy soul; thine adversity and thine afflictions shall be but a small moment; and then,* if thou endure it well, *God shall exalt thee on high; thou shalt triumph over all thy foes.* (D&C 121:7-8.)

All thrones and dominions, principalities and powers, shall be revealed and set forth upon all who have endured valiantly for the gospel of Jesus Christ. (D&C 121:29.)

Hold on thy way, *and the priesthood shall remain with thee; for their bounds are set, they cannot pass. Thy days are known, and thy years shall not be numbered less;* therefore, fear not what man can do, *for God shall be with you forever and ever.* (D&C 122:9.)

Let your diligence, and your perseverance, and patience, and your works be redoubled, *and you shall in nowise lose your reward saith the Lord of Hosts.* (D&C 127:4.)

He that remaineth steadfast and is not overcome, *the same shall be saved.* (JS–M 1:11.)

Stealing

(See also Covetousness; Honesty.)

The Lord condemns false dealings, exaggerated charges, fraud, robbery, withholding wages, borrowing without returning, and plundering. "He that stealeth and will not repent shall be cast out." (D&C 42:20.) Stealing does more than just defile the thief and deprive another of what is rightfully his; it deprives those that the victim and the thief might otherwise have been able to help. Paul says of this that the thief should cease stealing: "Rather let him labour, . . . that he may have to give to him that needeth." (Eph. 4:28.) King Benjamin teaches that if we do not return what we borrow, we might cause our "neighbor to commit sin also." (Mosiah 4:28.)

Commandments and Promises

Thou shalt not steal. (Ex. 20:15; similar scriptures, Deut. 5:19, Matt. 19:18, Mark 10:19, Rom. 13:9, Mosiah 13:22, D&C 59:6.)

Ye shall not steal, neither deal falsely, neither lie one to another. (Lev. 19:11.)

Thou shalt not defraud thy neighbour, neither rob him: the wages of him that is hired shall not abide with thee all night until the morning. (Lev. 19:13.)

Lord, who shall abide in thy tabernacle? who shall dwell in thy holy hill? . . . He that putteth not out his money to usury, nor taketh reward against the innocent. He that doeth these things *shall never be moved.* (Ps. 15:1, 5; see also JST Ps. 15:1.)

Trust not in oppression, and become not vain in robbery: if riches increase, set not your heart upon them. (Ps. 62:10.)

Divers weights *are an abomination unto the Lord;* and a false balance *is not good.* (Prov. 20:23.)

The robbery of the wicked *shall destroy them.* (Prov. 21:7.)

Whoso robbeth his father or his mother, and saith, It is no transgression; *the same is the companion of a destroyer.* (Prov. 28:24.)

Woe unto him that buildeth his house by unrighteousness, and his chambers by wrong; that useth his neighbour's service without wages, and giveth him not for his work. (Jer. 22:13.)

Every one that stealeth *shall be cut off as on this side according to it.* (Zech. 5:3.)

From within, out of the heart of men, proceed evil thoughts, . . . thefts, covetousness, . . . all these evil things come from within, *and defile the man.* (Mark 7:21-23.)

Then came also publicans to be baptized, and said unto him, Master, what shall we do? And he said unto them, Exact no more than that which is appointed you. (Luke 3:12-13; see also JST Luke 3:19-20.)

Be not deceived: neither fornicators, . . . nor thieves, nor covetous, . . . nor extortioners, *shall inherit the kingdom of God.* (1 Cor. 6:9-10.)

Let him that stole steal no more: but rather let him labour, working with his hands the thing which is good, *that he may have to give to him that needeth.* (Eph. 4:28.)

This is the will of God, even your sanctification, . . . that no man go beyond and defraud his brother in any matter: *because that the Lord is the avenger of all such,* as we also have forewarned you and testified. (1 Thes. 4:3, 6.)

Exhort servants to be obedient unto their own masters, and to please them well in all things; not answering again; not purloining, but shewing all good fidelity; that they may adorn the doctrine of God our Saviour in all things. (Titus 2:9-10.)

Let none of you suffer as . . . a thief. (1 Pet. 4:15.)

The Lord God hath commanded that men . . . should not steal; . . . that they should not envy; . . . for *whoso doeth them shall perish.* (2 Ne. 26:32.)

Whosoever among you borroweth of his neighbor should return the thing that he borroweth, according as he doth agree, *or else thou shalt commit sin; and perhaps thou shalt cause thy neighbor to commit sin also.* (Mosiah 4:28.)

Those priests who did go forth among the people did preach against all [stealing, robbing, plundering, etc.], crying that these things ought not so to be. (Alma 16:18.)

They ought not . . . to plunder, nor to steal. (Alma 23:3.)

This great loss of the Nephites, and the great slaughter which was among them, would not have happened had it not been for their wickedness and their abomination which was among them; yea, and it was among those also who professed to belong to the church of God. And it was because of . . . their exceeding riches, yea, it was because of their oppression to the poor, withholding their food from the hungry, withholding their clothing from the naked, . . . plundering, . . . stealing. (Hel. 4:11-12.)

Thou shalt not steal; and he that stealeth and will not repent *shall be cast out.* (D&C 42:20.)

Thou shalt not take thy brother's garment; thou shalt pay for that which thou shalt receive of thy brother. (D&C 42:54.)

If he or she shall steal, *he or she shall be delivered up unto the law of the land.* (D&C 42:85.)

Strong, Being

Being strong is both a commandment and a blessing. In modern revelations the Lord explains some qualities that reap the blessing of strength:

—"He that trembleth under my power shall be made strong, and shall bring forth fruits of praise and wisdom." (D&C 52:17.)

—"He that is faithful shall be made strong in every place; and I, the Lord, will go with you." (D&C 66:8.)

—"Let thy bowels also be full of charity towards all men, and to the household of faith, and let virtue garnish thy thoughts unceasingly; then shall thy confidence wax strong in the presence of God." (D&C 121:45.)

On the other hand, we must guard against weakness. To increase our steadfastness and strength, we are commanded: "Take unto you the whole armour of God, . . . having your loins girt about with truth, and having on the breastplate of righteousness; and your feet shod with the preparation of the gospel of peace; above all, taking the shield of faith, wherewith ye shall be able to quench all the fiery darts of the wicked. And take the helmet of salvation, and the sword of the Spirit, which is the word of God: praying always with all prayer and supplication in the Spirit, and watching thereunto with all perseverance and supplication for all saints." (Eph. 6:13-18.)

Commandments and Promises

Be strong and of a good courage, fear not, nor be afraid of them: for the Lord thy God, he it is that doth go with thee; *he will not fail thee, nor forsake thee.* (Deut. 31:6.)

Have not I commanded thee? Be strong and of good courage; be not afraid, neither be thou dismayed: for the Lord thy God is with thee whithersoever thou goest. (Josh. 1:9.)

[to Gideon] Go in this thy might, and thou shalt save Israel from the hand of the Midianites: have not I sent thee? (Judg. 6:14.)

Give unto the Lord, ye kindreds of the people, give unto the Lord glory and strength. (1 Chr. 16:28.)

Be ye strong therefore, and let not your hands be weak: *for your work shall be rewarded.* (2 Chr. 15:7.)

Give unto the Lord, O ye mighty, give unto the Lord glory and strength. Give unto the Lord the glory due unto his name; worship the Lord in the beauty of holiness. (Ps. 29:1-2.)

Whatsoever thy hand findeth to do, do it with thy might. (Eccl. 9:10.)

Say to them that are of a fearful heart, Be strong, fear not: behold, *your God will come with vengeance, even God with a recompence; he will come and save you.* (Isa. 35:4.)

Awake, awake; put on thy strength, O Zion. (Isa. 52:1; similar scriptures, 2 Ne. 8:24, 3 Ne. 20:36.)

Be strong, all ye people of the land, saith the Lord, and work: for I am with you, saith the Lord of hosts. (Hag. 2:4.)

Let your hands be strong, ye that hear in these days these words by the mouth of the prophets, which were in the day that the foundation of the house of the Lord of hosts was laid, that the temple might be built. (Zech. 8:9.)

Watch ye, stand fast in the faith, quit you like men, be strong. (1 Cor. 16:13.)

Be strong in the Lord, and in the power of his might. Put on the whole armour of God, *that ye may be able to stand against the wiles of the devil.* (Eph. 6:10-11.)

Take unto you the whole armour of God, *that ye may be able to withstand in the evil day, and having done all, to stand.* Stand therefore, having your loins girt about with truth, and having on the breastplate of righteousness; and your feet shod with the preparation of the gospel of peace; above all, taking the shield of faith, *wherewith ye shall be able to quench all the fiery darts of the wicked.* And take the helmet of salvation, and the sword of the Spirit, which is the word of God. (Eph. 6:13-17; similar scripture, D&C 27:15-18.)

[Nephi to his brothers] Let us go up; let us be strong like unto Moses. (1 Ne. 4:2.)

They did fast and pray oft, and did wax stronger and stronger in their humility, and firmer and firmer in the faith of Christ, *unto the filling their souls with joy and consolation, yea, even to the purifying and the sanctification of their hearts, which sanctification cometh* because of their yielding their hearts unto God. (Hel. 3:35.)

Be ye strong from henceforth; fear not, for the kingdom is yours. (D&C 38:15.)

If any man among you be strong in the Spirit, let him take with him him that is weak, *that he may be edified in all meekness, that he may become strong also.* (D&C 84:106.)

Teaching the Gospel

The most frequently repeated specific commandment in the scriptures is the charge to take the gospel to those who do not have it. Those spreading the gospel should teach only basic doctrines, such as faith, repentance, and baptism. "Of tenets thou shalt not talk," the Lord told Martin Harris, "but thou shalt declare repentance and faith on the Savior, and remission of sins by baptism, and by fire, yea, even the Holy Ghost." (D&C 19:31.) That idea is repeated throughout scripture.

The Lord stresses that those who teach the gospel must be prepared. "Seek not to declare my word, but first seek to obtain my word," the Lord told Hyrum Smith. "Then shall your tongue be loosed; then, if you desire, you shall have my Spirit and my word, yea, the power of God unto the convincing of men." (D&C 11:21.) Those who prepare to assist in this work must also "be humble and full of love, having faith, hope, and charity, being temperate in all things." (D&C 12:8.) The Lord tells his followers that "faith, hope, charity and love, with an eye single to the glory of God, qualify [them] for the work." (D&C 4:5.)

Once called, missionaries are urged to serve God wholeheartedly, with all their heart, might, mind, and strength. (See D&C 4:2.) They should not be overly concerned with worldly things, such as coats, purse, or scrip. Those in the Lord's service who live by faith, knowing the Lord will provide, are promised that "all these things shall be added unto [them]." (Matt. 6:33.) And if they are successful in bringing just one soul to Jesus into the heavenly kingdom of his Father, they will be able to rejoice with him or her eternally. (See D&C 18: 14-16.)

Commandments and Promises

Take heed to thyself, and keep thy soul diligently, *lest thou forget the things which thine eyes have seen, and lest they depart from thy heart all the days of thy life:* but teach them thy sons, and thy sons' sons. (Deut. 4:9.)

The Lord commanded me [Moses] at that time to teach you [Israel] statutes and judgments, *that ye might do them in the land whither ye go over to possess it.* (Deut. 4:14.)

Hear, O Israel: The Lord our God is one Lord: and thou shalt love the Lord thy God with all thine heart, and with all thy soul, and with all thy might. And these words, which I command thee this day, shall be in thine heart: and thou shalt teach them diligently unto thy children, and shalt talk of them when thou sittest in thine house, and when thou walkest by the way, and when thou liest down, and when thou risest up. (Deut. 6:4-7.)

Give thanks unto the Lord, call upon his name, make known his deeds among the people. (1 Chr. 16:8.)

Declare his glory among the heathen; his marvellous works among all nations. (1 Chr. 16:24.)

Say among the heathen that the Lord reigneth: the world also shall be established that it shall not be moved: he shall judge the people righteously. (Ps. 96:10.)

Speak not in the ears of a fool: for he will despise the wisdom of thy words. (Prov. 23:9.)

In that day shall ye say, Praise the Lord, call upon his name, declare his doings among the people, make mention that his name is exalted. (Isa. 12:4; similar scripture, 2 Ne. 22:4.)

Prepare the table, watch in the watchtower, eat, drink: arise, ye princes, and anoint the shield. For thus hath the Lord said unto me, Go, set a watchman, let him declare what he seeth. (Isa. 21:5-6.)

Bring forth the blind people that have eyes, and the deaf that have ears. Let all the nations be gathered together, and let the people be assembled: who among them can declare this, and shew us former things? let them bring forth their witnesses, *that they may be justified:* or let them hear, *and say, It is truth.* (Isa. 43:8-9.)

Cry aloud, spare not, lift up thy voice like a trumpet, and shew my people their transgression, and the house of Jacob their sins. (Isa. 58:1.)

Ye that make mention of the Lord, keep not silence. (Isa. 62:6.)

Go and proclaim these words toward the north, and say, Return, thou backsliding Israel, saith the Lord; *and I will not cause mine anger to fall upon you: for I am merciful, saith the Lord, and I will not keep anger for ever.* (Jer. 3:12.)

The word that came to Jeremiah from the Lord, saying, Hear ye the words of this covenant, and speak unto the men of Judah, and to the inhabitants of Jerusalem; and say thou unto them, Thus saith the Lord God of Israel; *Cursed* be the man that obeyeth not the words of this covenant. (Jer. 11:1-3.)

The prophet that hath a dream, let him tell a dream; and he that hath my word, let him speak my word faithfully. (Jer. 23:28.)

Sing with gladness for Jacob, and shout among the chief of the nations: publish ye, praise ye, and say, O Lord save thy people, the remnant of Israel. (Jer. 31:7.)

Hear the word of the Lord, O ye nations, and declare it in the isles afar off, and say, He that scattered Israel will gather him, and keep him, as a shepherd doth his flock. (Jer. 31:10.)

The Lord hath brought forth our righteousness: come, and let us declare in Zion the work of the Lord our God. (Jer. 51:10.)

Son of man, I have made thee a watchman unto the house of Israel: therefore hear the word at my mouth, and give them warning from me. When I say unto the wicked, Thou shalt surely die; and thou givest him not warning, nor speakest to warn the wicked from his wicked way, to save his life; *the same wicked man shall die in his iniquity; but his blood will I require at thine hand.* Yet if thou warn the wicked, and he turn not from his wickedness, nor from his wicked way, *he shall die in his iniquity; but thou hast delivered thy soul.* Again, When a righteous man doth turn from his righteousness, and commit iniquity, and I lay a stumblingblock before him, *he shall die:* because thou hast not given him warning, *he shall die in his sin, and his righteousness which he hath done shall not be remembered; but his blood will I require at thine hand.* Nevertheless if thou warn the righteous man, that the righteous sin not, and he doth not sin, *he shall surely live,* because he is warned; *also thou hast delivered thy soul.* (Ezek. 3:17-21.)

Son of man, set thy face toward Jerusalem, and drop thy word toward the holy places, and prophesy against the land of Israel, and say to the land of Israel, Thus saith the Lord; Behold, I am against thee, and will draw forth my sword out of his sheath, and will cut off from thee the righteous and the wicked. (Ezek. 21:1-3.)

If thou warn the wicked of his way to turn from it; if he do not turn from his way, *he shall die in his iniquity; but thou hast delivered thy soul.* Therefore, O thou son of man, speak unto the house of Israel; Thus ye speak, saying, If our transgressions and our sins be upon us, and we pine away in them, how should we then live? Say unto them, *As I live, saith the Lord God, I have no pleasure in the death* of the wicked; but that the wicked turn from his way and live: turn ye, turn ye from your evil ways; *for why will ye die, O house of Israel?* Therefore, thou son of man, say unto the children of thy people, The righteousness of the righteous *shall not deliver him in the day of his transgression:* as for the wickedness of the wicked, *he shall not fall thereby in the day that he turneth* from his wickedness; *neither shall the righteous be able to live for his righteousness* in the day that he sinneth. (Ezek. 33:9-12.)

Thou son of man, prophesy unto the mountains of Israel, and say, Ye mountains of Israel, hear the word of the Lord. (Ezek. 36:1.)

Put ye in the sickle, for the harvest is ripe: come, get you down; for the press is full, the fats overflow; for their wickedness is great. (Joel 3:13.)

The word of the Lord came unto Jonah the son of Amittai, saying, Arise, go to Nineveh, that great city, and cry against it; for their wickedness is come up before me. (Jonah 1:1-2.)

The word of the Lord came unto Jonah the second time, saying, Arise, go unto Nineveh, that great city, and preach unto it the preaching that I bid thee. (Jonah 3:1-2.)

Whosoever therefore shall break one of these least commandments, and shall teach men so, *he shall be called the least in the kingdom of heaven:* but whosoever shall do and teach them, *the same shall be called great in the kingdom of heaven.* (Matt. 5:19; see also JST Matt. 5:21.)

Go ye into the world, and care not for the world; for the world will hate you, and will persecute you, and will turn you out of their synagogues. Nevertheless, ye shall go forth from house to house, teaching the people; *and I will go before you. And your heavenly Father will provide for you, whatsoever things ye need for food, what ye shall eat; and for raiment, what ye shall wear or put on.* Therefore I say unto you, Take no thought for your life, what ye shall eat, or what ye shall drink; nor yet for your body, what ye shall put on. Is not the life more than meat, and the body than raiment? Behold the fowls of the air: for they sow not, neither do they reap, nor gather into barns; yet your heavenly Father feedeth them. Are ye not much better than they? Which of you by taking thought can add one cubit unto his stature? And why take ye thought for raiment? Consider the lilies of the field, how they grow; they toil not, neither do they spin: and yet I say unto you, That even Solomon in all his glory was not arrayed like one of these. Wherefore, if God so clothe the grass of the field, which to day is, and to morrow is cast into the oven, *shall he not much more clothe you,* O ye of little faith? Therefore take no thought, saying, What shall we eat? or, What shall we drink? or Wherewithal shall we be clothed? (For after all these things do the Gentiles seek:) for your heavenly Father knoweth that ye have need of all these things. But seek ye first the kingdom of God, and his righteousness; *and all these things shall be added unto you.* Take therefore no thought for the morrow: for the morrow shall take thought for the things of itself. Sufficient unto the day is the evil thereof. (JST Matt. 6:25-27 and Matt. 6:25-34; similar scriptures, Luke 12:22-31, 3 Ne. 25-34, D&C 84:81-84; see also JST Matt. 6:34, 38, Luke 12:30, 34.)

Give not that which is holy unto the dogs, neither cast ye your pearls before swine, *lest they trample them under their feet, and turn again and rend you.* (Matt. 7:6; see also JST Matt. 7:9-11.)

The harvest truly is plenteous, but the labourers are few; pray ye therefore the Lord of the harvest, that he will send forth labourers into his harvest. (Matt. 9:37-38.)

As ye go, preach, saying, The kingdom of heaven is at hand. Heal the sick, cleanse the lepers, raise the dead, cast out devils: freely ye have received, freely give. Provide neither gold, nor silver, nor brass in your purses, nor scrip for your journey, neither two coats, neither shoes, nor yet staves: for the workman is worthy of his meat. And into whatsoever city or town ye shall enter, enquire who in it is worthy; and there abide till ye go thence. And when ye come into an house, salute it. And if the house be worthy, let your peace come upon it: but if it be not worthy, let your peace return to you. And whosoever shall not receive you, nor hear your words, when ye depart out of that house or city, shake off the dust of your feet. Verily I say unto you, *It shall be more tolerable for the land of Sodom and Gomorrha in the day of judgment, than for that city*. Behold, I send you forth as sheep in the midst of wolves: be ye therefore wise as serpents, and harmless as doves. (Matt. 10:7-16; see also Mark 6:7-11, Luke 9:2-5, 10:3-4, D&C 84:86.)

When they persecute you in this city, flee ye into another: for verily I say unto you, Ye shall not have gone over the cities of Israel, till the Son of man be come. (Matt. 10:23.)

What I tell you in darkness, that speak ye in light: and what ye hear in the ear, that preach ye upon the housetops. (Matt. 10:27.)

Whosoever therefore shall confess me before men, *him will I confess also before my Father which is in heaven*. But whosoever shall deny me before men, *him will I also deny before my Father which is in heaven*. (Matt. 10:32-33.)

Go ye therefore, and teach all nations, baptizing them in the name of the Father, and of the Son, and of the Holy Ghost: teaching them to observe all things whatsoever I have commanded you: *and, lo, I am with you alway, even unto the end of the world*. (Matt. 28:19-20.)

He called unto him the twelve, and began to send them forth by two and two; and gave them power over unclean spirits; and commanded them that they should take nothing for their journey, save a staff only; no scrip, no bread, no money in their purse. But be shod with sandals; and not put on two coats. (Mark 6:7-9; see also Matt. 10:9-10.)

The gospel must first be published among all nations. (Mark 13:10.)

Afterward he appeared unto the eleven as they sat at meat, and up-braided them with their unbelief and hardness of heart, because they believed not them which had seen him after he was risen. And he said unto them, Go ye into all the world, and preach the gospel to every creature. (Mark 16:14-15.)

He sent them to preach the kingdom of God, and to heal the sick. And he said unto them, Take nothing for your journey, neither staves, nor scrip, neither bread, neither money; neither have two coats apiece. (Luke 9:2-3; see also Matt. 10:9-10.)

He said unto another, Follow me. But he said, Lord, suffer me first to go and bury my father. Jesus said unto him, Let the dead bury their dead: but go thou and preach the kingdom of God. (Luke 9:59-60.)

Carry neither purse, nor scrip, nor shoes: and salute no man by the way. (Luke 10:4; see also Matt. 10:9-10.)

And in the same house remain, eating and drinking such things as they give: for the labourer is worthy of his hire. Go not from house to house. And into whatsoever city ye enter, and they receive you, eat such things as are set before you: and heal the sick that are therein, and say unto them, The kingdom of God is come nigh unto you. But into whatsoever city ye enter, and they receive you not, go your ways out into the streets of the same, and say, Even the very dust of your city, which cleaveth on us, we do wipe off against you: notwithstanding be ye sure of this, that the kingdom of God is come nigh unto you. But I say unto you, that *it shall be more tolerable in that day for Sodom, than for that city*. (Luke 10:7-12; see also Matt. 10:12-15.)

When thou art converted, strengthen thy brethren. (Luke 22:32.)

As my Father hath sent me, even so I send you. (John 20:21.)

Let all the house of Israel know assuredly, that God hath made that same Jesus, whom ye have crucified, both Lord and Christ. (Acts 2:36.)

He commanded us [the apostles] to preach unto the people, and to testify that it is he which was ordained of God to be the Judge of quick and dead. (Acts 10:42.)

Having then gifts differing according to the grace that is given to us, whether prophecy, let us prophesy according to the proportion of faith; or ministry, let us wait on our ministering: or he that teacheth, on teaching; or he that exhorteth, on exhortation. (Rom. 12:6-8.)

Even so hath the Lord ordained that they which preach the gospel should live of the gospel. (1 Cor. 9:14.)

In all things approving ourselves as the ministers of God, in much patience, in afflictions, in necessities, in distresses, in stripes, in imprisonments, in tumults, in labours, in watchings, in fastings; by pureness, by knowledge, by longsuffering, by kindness, by the Holy Ghost, by love unfeigned, by the word of truth, by the power of God, by the armour of righteousness on the right hand and on the left. (2 Cor. 6:4-7.)

Let no corrupt communication proceed out of your mouth, but that which is good to the use of edifying, *that it may minister grace unto the hearers.* (Eph. 4:29.)

Let the word of Christ dwell in you richly in all wisdom; teaching and admonishing one another in psalms and hymns and spiritual songs, singing with grace in your hearts to the Lord. (Col. 3:16.)

Take heed unto thyself, and unto the doctrine; continue in them: for in doing this *thou shalt both save thyself, and them that hear thee.* (1 Tim. 4:16.)

They that have believing masters, let them not despise them, because they are brethren; but rather do them service, because they are faithful and beloved, partakers of the benefit. These things teach and exhort. (1 Tim. 6:2.)

Charge them that are rich in this world, that they be not highminded, nor trust in uncertain riches, but in the living God, who giveth us richly all things to enjoy; that they do good, that they be rich in good works, ready to distribute, willing to communicate; *laying up in store for themselves a good foundation against the time to come, that they may lay hold on eternal life.* (1 Tim. 6:17-19.)

The things that thou hast heard of me among many witnesses, the same commit thou to faithful men, who shall be able to teach others also. (2 Tim. 2:2.)

The servant of the Lord must not strive; but be gentle unto all men, apt to teach, patient, in meekness instructing those that oppose themselves; if God peradventure will give them repentance to the acknowledging of the truth; and *that they may recover themselves out of the snare of the devil,* who are taken captive by him at his will. (2 Tim. 2:24-26.)

Preach the word; be instant in season, out of season; reprove, rebuke, exhort with all longsuffering and doctrine. (2 Tim. 4:2; see also JST 2 Tim. 4:2.)

Watch thou in all things, endure afflictions, do the work of an evangelist, make full proof of thy ministry. (2 Tim. 4:5.)

The grace of God that bringeth salvation hath appeared to all men, teaching us that, denying ungodliness and worldly lusts, we should live soberly, righteously, and godly, in this present world; looking for that blessed hope, and the glorious appearing of the great God and our Saviour Jesus Christ; who gave himself for us, that he might redeem us from all iniquity, and purify unto himself a peculiar people, zealous of good works. These things speak, and exhort, and rebuke with all authority. Let no man despise thee. (Titus 2:11-15.)

Exhort one another daily, while it is called To day; *lest any of you be hardened through the deceitfulness of sin.* (Heb. 3:13.)

Let us consider one another to provoke unto love and to good works: not forsaking the assembling of ourselves together, as the manner of some is; but exhorting one another: and so much the more, as ye see the day approaching. (Heb. 10:24-25.)

If any of you do err from the truth, and one convert him; let him know, that he which converteth the sinner from the error of his way *shall save a soul from death, and shall hide a multitide of sins.* (James 5:19-20.)

I beseech you as strangers and pilgrims, abstain from fleshly lusts, which war against the soul; having your conversation honest among the Gentiles: that, whereas they speak against you as evildoers, they may by your good works, which they shall behold, *glorify God in the day of visitation.* (1 Pet. 2:11-12.)

Sanctify the Lord God in your hearts: and be ready always to give an answer to every man that asketh you a reason of the hope that is in you with meekness and fear: having a good conscience; that, whereas they speak evil of you, as of evildoers, *they may be ashamed* that falsely accuse your good conversation in Christ. (1 Pet. 3:15-16; see also JST 1 Pet. 3:16.)

If any man speak, let him speak as the oracles of God; if any man minister, let him do it as of the ability which God giveth: *that God in all things may be glorified through Jesus Christ.* (1 Pet. 4:11.)

The elders which are among you I exhort, who am also an elder, and a witness of the sufferings of Christ, and also a partaker of the glory that shall be revealed: Feed the flock of God which is among you, taking the oversight thereof, not by constraint, but willingly; not for filthy lucre, but of a ready mind; neither as being lords over God's heritage, but being ensamples to the flock. *And when the chief Shepherd shall appear, ye shall receive a crown of glory that fadeth not away.* (1 Pet. 5:1-4.)

Building up yourselves on your most holy faith, praying in the Holy Ghost, keep yourselves in the love of God, looking for the mercy of our Lord Jesus Christ unto eternal life. And of some have compassion, making a difference: and others save with fear, pulling them out of the fire; hating even the garment spotted by the flesh. (Jude 1:20-23.)

Blessed are they who shall seek to bring forth my Zion at that day, *for they shall have the gift and the power of the Holy Ghost;* and if they endure unto the end *they shall be lifted up at the last day, and shall be saved in the everlasting kingdom of the Lamb;* and whoso shall publish peace, yea, tidings of great joy, *how beautiful upon the mountains shall they be.* (1 Ne. 13:37.)

He hath commanded his people that they should persuade all men to repentance. (2 Ne. 26:27.)

We did magnify our office unto the Lord, taking upon us the responsibility, *answering the sins of the people upon our own heads* if we did not teach them the word of God with all diligence; wherefore, by laboring with our might *their blood might not come upon our garments; otherwise their blood would come upon our garments, and we would not be found spotless at the last day.* (Jacob 1:19.)

He that prophesieth, let him prophesy to the understanding of men; for the Spirit speaketh the truth and lieth not. Wherefore, it speaketh of things as they really are, and of things as they really will be; wherefore, these things are manifested unto us plainly, *for the salvation of our souls.* (Jacob 4:13.)

Let us go to and labor with our might this last time, for behold the end draweth nigh, and this is for the last time that I shall prune my vineyard. Graft in the branches; begin at the last that they may be first, and that the first may be last, and dig about the trees, both old and young, the first and the last. (Jacob 5:62-63.)

If ye teach the law of Moses, also teach that it is a shadow of those things which are to come—teach them that redemption cometh through Christ the Lord, who is the very Eternal Father. (Mosiah 16:14-15.)

He commanded them that they should teach nothing save it were the things which he had taught, and which had been spoken by the mouth of the holy prophets. Yea, even he commanded them that they should preach nothing save it were repentance and faith on the Lord, who had redeemed his people. And he commanded them that there should be no contention one with another, but that they should look forward with one eye, having one faith and one baptism, having their hearts knit together in unity and in love one towards another. And thus he commanded them to preach. *And thus they became the children of God.* (Mosiah 18:19-22.)

[to Alma] Thou art my servant; *and I covenant with thee that thou shalt have eternal life;* and thou shalt serve me and go forth in my name, and shalt gather together my sheep. (Mosiah 26:20.)

It is given unto many to know the mysteries of God; nevertheless they are laid under a strict command that they shall not impart only according to the portion of his word which he doth grant unto the children of men, according to the heed and diligence which they give unto him. (Alma 12:9.)

Go forth among the Lamanites, thy brethren, and establish my word; yet ye [the sons of Mosiah] shall be patient in long-suffering and afflictions, *that ye may show forth good examples unto them in me, and I will make an instrument of thee in my hands unto the salvation of many souls.* (Alma 17:10-11.)

[Alma to Helaman] Ye shall keep these secret plans of their oaths and their covenants from this people, and only their wickedness and their murders and their abominations shall ye make known unto them; and ye shall teach them to abhor such wickedness and abominations and murders; and ye shall also teach them that these people [Jaredites] were destroyed on account of their wickedness and abominations and their murders. (Alma 37:29.)

[Alma to Helaman] Trust not those secret plans unto this people, but teach them an everlasting hatred against sin and iniquity. Preach unto them repentance, and faith on the Lord Jesus Christ; teach them to humble themselves and to be meek and lowly in heart; teach them to withstand every temptation of the devil, with their faith on the Lord Jesus Christ. Teach them to never be weary of good works, but to be meek and lowly in heart; for such shall find rest to their souls. (Alma 37:32-34.)

Go unto this people and declare the word, and be sober. (Alma 37:47.)

As ye have begun to teach the word even so I would that ye should continue to teach; and I would that ye would be diligent and temperate in all things. (Alma 38:10.)

Go, my son [Shiblon], and teach the word unto this people. Be sober. (Alma 38:15.)

Go thy way, declare the word with truth and soberness, *that thou mayest bring souls unto repentance, that the great plan of mercy may have claim upon them. And may God grant unto you even according to my words.* (Alma 42:31.)

Blessed art thou, Nephi, for those things which thou hast done; for I have beheld how thou hast with unwearyingness declared the word, which I have given unto thee, unto this people. And thou hast not feared them, and hast not sought thine own life, but hast sought my will, and to keep my commandments. And now, because thou hast done this with such unwearyingness, *behold, I will bless thee forever; and I will make thee mighty in word and in deed, in faith and in works; yea, even that all things shall be done unto thee according to thy word, for thou shalt not ask that which is contrary to my will.* (Hel. 10:4-5.)

Whoso shall declare more or less than this [repentance and baptism], and establish it for my doctrine, the same cometh of evil, and is not built upon my rock; but he buildeth upon a sandy foundation, *and the gates of hell stand open to receive such when the floods come and the winds beat upon them.* Therefore, go forth unto this people, and declare the words which I have spoken, unto the ends of the earth. (3 Ne. 11:40-41.)

When Jesus had expounded all the scriptures in one, which they had written, he commanded them that they should teach the things which he had expounded unto them. (3 Ne. 23:14.)

Thus said Jesus Christ, the Son of God, unto his disciples who should tarry, yea, and also to all his disciples, in the hearing of the multitude: Go ye into all the world, and preach the gospel to every creature. (Morm. 9:22.)

This thing shall ye teach—repentance and baptism unto those who are accountable and capable of committing sin; yea, teach parents that they must repent and be baptized, and humble themselves as their little children, and that they shall all be saved with their little children. (Moro. 8:10.)

Notwithstanding their hardness, let us labor diligently; for if we should cease to labor, *we should be brought under condemnation;* for we have a labor to perform whilst in this tabernacle of clay, *that we may conquer the enemy of all righteousness, and rest our souls in the kingdom of God.* (Moro. 9:6.)

The voice of warning shall be unto all people, by the mouths of my disciples, whom I have chosen in these last days. And they shall go forth *and none shall stay them*, for I the Lord have commanded them. (D&C 1:4-5.)

They who go forth, bearing these tidings unto the inhabitants of the earth, to them is power given to seal both on earth and in heaven, the unbelieving and rebellious; yea, verily, to seal them up unto the day *when the wrath of God shall be poured out* upon the wicked *without measure*—unto the day *when the Lord shall come to recompense unto every man* according to his work, *and measure to every man* according to the measure which he has measured to his fellow man. (D&C 1:8-10.)

[The Lord] also gave commandments to others, that they should proclaim these things unto the world; and all this *that it might be fulfilled, which was written by the prophets.* (D&C 1:18.)

Therefore, O ye that embark in the service of God, see that ye serve him with all your heart, might, mind and strength, *that ye may stand blameless before God at the last day.* Therefore, if ye have desires to serve God *ye are called to the work; for behold the field is white* already to harvest; and lo, he that thrusteth in his sickle with his might, *the same layeth up in store that he perisheth not, but bringeth salvation to his soul;* and faith, hope, charity, and love, with an eye single to the glory of God qualify him for the work. Remember faith, virtue, knowledge, temperance, patience, brotherly kindness, godliness, charity, humility, diligence. (D&C 4:2-6.)

Say nothing but repentance unto this generation. (D&C 6:9; similar scripture, D&C 11:9.)

[to Oliver Cowdery] If they reject my words, and this part of my gospel and ministry, *blessed are ye, for they can do no more unto you than unto me.* And even if they do unto you even as they have done unto me, *blessed are ye, for you shall dwell with me in glory.* But if they reject not my words, which shall be established by the testimony which shall be given, blessed are they, *and then shall ye have joy in the fruit of your labors.* (D&C 6:29-31.)

[to Hyrum Smith] I command you that you need not suppose that you are called to preach until you are called. Wait a little longer, until you shall have my word, my rock, my church, and my gospel, that you may know of a surety my doctrine. (D&C 11:15-16.)

[to Hyrum Smith] Seek not to declare my word, but first seek to obtain my word, and then shall your tongue be loosed; then, if you desire, *you shall have my Spirit and my word, yea, the power of God unto the convincing of men.* (D&C 11:21.)

Whosoever will thrust in his sickle and reap, the same is called of God. (D&C 12:4.)

No one can assist in this work except he shall be humble and full of love, having faith, hope, and charity, being temperate in all things, whatsoever shall be entrusted to his care. (D&C 12:8.)

If you shall ask the Father in my name, in faith believing, you shall receive the Holy Ghost, which giveth utterance, that you may stand as a witness of the things of which you shall both hear and see, and also that you may declare repentance unto this generation. (D&C 14:8.)

Thou art David [Whitmer], and thou art called to assist; which thing if ye do, and are faithful, *ye shall be blessed both spiritually and temporally, and great shall be your reward.* (D&C 14:11.)

Remember the worth of souls is great in the sight of God. (D&C 18:10.)

You are called to cry repentance unto this people. And if it so be that you should labor all your days in crying repentance unto this people, and bring, save it be one soul unto me, *how great shall be your joy with him in the kingdom of my Father!* And now, if your joy will be great with one soul that you have brought unto me into the kingdom of my Father, *how great will be your joy* if you should bring many souls unto me! (D&C 18:14-16.)

You must preach unto the world, saying: You must repent and be baptized, in the name of Jesus Christ. (D&C 18:41.)

I command you [Martin Harris] that you preach naught but repentance, and show not these things unto the world until it is wisdom in me. For they cannot bear meat now, but milk they must receive; wherefore, they must not know these things, *lest they perish.* (D&C 19:21-22.)

Thou shalt declare glad tidings, yea, publish it upon the mountains, and upon every high place, and among every people that thou shalt be permitted to see. (D&C 19:29.)

Of tenets thou [Martin Harris] shalt not talk, but thou shalt declare repentance and faith on the Savior, and remission of sins by baptism, and by fire, yea, even the Holy Ghost. (D&C 19:31.)

Speak freely to all; yea, preach, exhort, declare the truth, even with a loud voice, with a sound of rejoicing, crying—Hosanna, hosanna, blessed be the name of the Lord God! (D&C 19:37.)

The duty of the members after they are received by baptism.—The elders or priests are to have a sufficient time to expound all things concerning the church of Christ to their understanding, previous to their partaking of the sacrament and being confirmed by the laying on of the hands of the elders, so that all things may be done in order. (D&C 20:68.)

I will bless all those who labor in my vineyard *with a mighty blessing,* and they shall believe on his [Joseph Smith's] words, which are given him through me by the Comforter, which manifesteth that Jesus was crucified by sinful men for the sins of the world, yea, for the remission of sins unto the contrite heart. (D&C 21:9.)

Make known thy calling unto the church, and also before the world, *and thy heart shall be opened to preach the truth from henceforth and forever.* (D&C 23:2.)

At all times, and in all places, he [Oliver Cowdery] shall open his mouth and declare my gospel as with the voice of a trump, both day and night. *And I will give unto him strength such as is not known among men.* (D&C 24:12.)

[to Joseph Smith, Oliver Cowdery, and John Whitmer] You shall let your time be devoted to the studying of the scriptures, and to preaching, and to confirming the church at Colesville, and to performing your labors on the land, such as is required, until after you shall go to the west to hold the next conference; and then it shall be made known what you shall do. (D&C 26:1.)

[to Oliver Cowdery] Thou shalt be obedient unto the things which I shall give unto him [Joseph Smith], even as Aaron, to declare faithfully the commandments and the revelations, with power and authority unto the church. (D&C 28:3.)

[to Oliver Cowdery] You shall go unto the Lamanites and preach my gospel unto them. (D&C 28:8.)

[to Oliver Cowdery] Thou must open thy mouth at all times, declaring my gospel with the sound of rejoicing. (D&C 28:16.)

Ye are chosen out of the world to declare my gospel with the sound of rejoicing, as with the voice of a trump. (D&C 29:4.)

I say unto you, my servant John [Whitmer], that thou shalt commence from this time forth to proclaim my gospel, as with the voice of a trump. . . . Your whole labor shall be in Zion, with all your soul, from henceforth; yea, you shall ever open your mouth in my cause, not fearing what man can do, for I am with you. (D&C 30:9-11.)

Lift up your heart and rejoice, for the hour of your mission is come; and your tongue shall be loosed, and you shall declare glad tidings of great joy unto this generation. (D&C 31:3.)

[to Thomas B. Marsh] Thrust in your sickle with all your soul, *and your sins are forgiven you, and you shall be laden with sheaves upon your back, for the laborer is worthy of his hire. Wherefore, your family shall live.* (D&C 31:5.)

Concerning my servant Parley P. Pratt, behold, I say unto him that as I live I will that he shall declare my gospel and learn of me, and be meek and lowly of heart. And that which I have appointed unto him is that he shall go with my servants, Oliver Cowdery and Peter Whitmer, Jun., into the wilderness among the Lamanites. And Ziba Peterson also shall go with them; and *I myself will go with them and be in their midst; and I am their advocate with the Father, and nothing shall prevail against them.* (D&C 32:1-3.)

Ye are called to lift up your voices as with the sound of a trump, to declare my gospel unto a crooked and perverse generation. (D&C 33:2.)

[to Ezra Thayre and Northrup Sweet] The field is white already to harvest; wherefore, thrust in your sickles, and reap with all your might, mind, and strength. Open your mouths *and they shall be filled, and you shall become even as Nephi of old, who journeyed from Jerusalem in the wilderness.* Yea, open your mouths and spare not, *and you shall be laden with sheaves upon your backs, for lo, I am with you.* Yea, open your mouths *and they shall be filled,* saying: Repent, repent, and prepare ye the way of the Lord, and make his paths straight; for the kingdom of heaven is at hand; yea, repent and be baptized, every one of you, for a remission of your sins; yea, be baptized even by water, and then cometh the baptism of fire and of the Holy Ghost. (D&C 33:7-11.)

More blessed are you because you are called of me to preach my gospel. (D&C 34:5.)

Lift up your voice and spare not, for the Lord God hath spoken; therefore prophesy, *and it shall be given by the power of the Holy Ghost.* (D&C 34:10.)

I give unto thee a commandment, that thou shalt baptize by water, and they shall receive the Holy Ghost by the laying on of the hands, even as the apostles of old. (D&C 35:6.)

This calling and commandment give I unto you concerning all men—that as many as shall come before my servants Sidney Rigdon and Joseph Smith, Jun., embracing this calling and commandment, shall be ordained and sent forth to preach the everlasting gospel among the nations—crying repentance, saying: Save yourselves from this untoward generation, and come forth out of the fire, hating even the garments spotted with the flesh. And this commandment shall be given unto the elders of my church, that every man which will embrace it with singleness of heart may be ordained and sent forth, even as I have spoken. (D&C 36:4-7.)

Teach one another according to the office wherewith I have appointed you. (D&C 38:23.)

I give unto you a commandment, that every man, both elder, priest, teacher, and also member, go to with his might, with the labor of his hands, to prepare and accomplish the things which I have commanded. And let your preaching be the warning voice, every man to his neighbor, in mildness and in meekness. (D&C 38:40-41.)

[to James Covill] Arise and be baptized, and wash away your sins, calling on my name, and you shall receive my Spirit, and a blessing so great as you never have known. And if thou do this, I have prepared thee for a greater work. Thou shalt preach the fulness of my gospel, which I have sent forth in these last days, the covenant which I have sent forth to recover my people, which are of the house of Israel. *And it shall come to pass that power shall rest upon thee; thou shalt have great faith, and I will be with thee and go before thy face.* (D&C 39: 10-12.)

Lay to with your might and call faithful laborers into my vineyard, that it may be pruned for the last time. (D&C 39:17.)

Go forth, crying with a loud voice, saying: The kingdom of heaven is at hand; crying: Hosanna! blessed be the name of the Most High God. Go forth baptizing with water, preparing the way before my face for the time of my coming. (D&C 39:19-20.)

Ye shall go forth in the power of my Spirit, preaching my gospel, two by two, in my name, lifting up your voices as with the sound of a trump, declaring my word like unto angels of God. And ye shall go forth baptizing with water, saying: Repent ye, repent ye, for the kingdom of heaven is at hand. And from this place ye shall go forth into the regions westward; and inasmuch as ye shall find them that will receive you ye shall build up my church in every region. (D&C 42:6-8.)

It shall not be given to any one to go forth to preach my gospel, or to build up my church, except he be ordained by some one who has authority, and it is known to the church that he has authority and has been regularly ordained by the heads of the church. And again, the elders, priests and teachers of this church shall teach the principles of my gospel, which are in the Bible and the Book of Mormon, in the which is the fulness of the gospel. And they shall observe the covenants and church articles to do them, and these shall be their teachings, as they shall be directed by the Spirit. And the Spirit shall be given unto you by the prayer of faith; and if ye receive not the Spirit ye shall not teach. And all this ye shall observe to do as I have commanded concerning your teaching, until the fulness of my scriptures is given. And as ye shall lift up your voices by the Comforter, *ye shall speak and prophesy as seemeth me good.* (D&C 42:11-16.)

It is expedient that thou shouldst hold thy peace concerning them [scriptures], and not teach them until ye have received them in full. And I give unto you a commandment that then ye shall teach them unto all men; for they shall be taught unto all nations, kindreds, tongues and people. (D&C 42:57-58.)

My servants shall be sent forth to the east and to the west, to the north and to the south. And even now, let him that goeth to the east teach them that shall be converted to flee to the west, and this in consequence of that which is coming on the earth, and of secret combinations. Behold, thou shalt observe all these things, *and great shall be thy reward; for unto you it is given to know the mysteries of the kingdom, but unto the world it is not given to know them.* (D&C 42: 63-65.)

I give unto you a commandment, that when ye are assembled together ye shall instruct and edify each other, *that ye may know how to act and direct my church, how to act upon the points of my law and commandments, which I have given.* (D&C 43:8.)

Hearken ye elders of my church, whom I have appointed: Ye are not sent forth to be taught, but to teach the children of men the things which I have put into your hands by the power of my Spirit; and ye are to be taught from on high. Sanctify yourselves *and ye shall be endowed with power, that ye may give even as I have spoken.* (D&C 43:15-16.)

Lift up your voices and spare not. Call upon the nations to repent, both old and young, both bond and free, saying: Prepare yourselves for the great day of the Lord. (D&C 43:20.)

Labor ye, labor ye in my vineyard for the last time—for the last time call upon the inhabitants of the earth. (D&C 43:28.)

I give unto you a commandment that you shall go and preach my gospel which ye have received, even as ye have received it. (D&C 49:1.)

My servant Leman [Copley] shall be ordained unto this work, that he may reason with them, not according to that which he has received of them, but according to that which shall be taught him by you my servants; *and by so doing I will bless him, otherwise he shall not prosper.* (D&C 49:4.)

I give unto you a commandment that ye go among this people, and say unto them, like unto mine apostle of old, whose name was Peter: Believe on the name of the Lord Jesus, who was on the earth, and is to come, the beginning and the end; repent and be baptized in the name of Jesus Christ, according to the holy commandment, for the remission of sins; and whoso doeth this shall receive the gift of the Holy Ghost, by the laying on of the hands of the elders of the church. (D&C 49:11-14.)

I the Lord ask you this question—unto what were ye ordained? To preach my gospel by the Spirit, even the Comforter which was sent forth to teach the truth. (D&C 50:13-14.)

He that preacheth and he that receiveth, understand one another, *and both are edified and rejoice together.* (D&C 50:22.)

He that is ordained of God and sent forth, *the same is appointed to be the greatest, notwithstanding he is the least and the servant of all. Wherefore, he is possessor of all things; for all things are subject unto him, both in heaven and on the earth, the life and the light, the Spirit and the power, sent forth by the will of the Father through Jesus Christ, his Son.* (D&C 50:26-27.)

Let them journey thence preaching the word by the way, saying none other things than that which the prophets and apostles have written, and that which is taught them by the Comforter through the prayer of faith. Let them go two by two, and thus let them preach by the way in every congregation, baptizing by water, and the laying on of the hands by the water's side. (D&C 52:9-10.)

He that speaketh, whose spirit is contrite, whose language is meek and edifieth, *the same is of God* if he obey mine ordinances. (D&C 52:16.)

Let them labor with their families, declaring none other things than the prophets and apostles, that which they have seen and heard and most assuredly believe, *that the prophecies may be fulfilled.* (D&C 52:36.)

Let the residue of the elders watch over the churches, and declare the word in the regions round about them; and let them labor with their own hands that there be no idolatry nor wickedness practised. (D&C 52:39.)

Take upon you mine ordination, even that of an elder, to preach faith and repentance and remission of sins, according to my word, and the reception of the Holy Spirit by the laying on of hands. (D&C 53:3.)

Assemble yourselves together; and they who are not appointed to stay in this land, let them preach the gospel in the regions round about; and after that let them return to their homes. Let them preach by the way, and bear testimony of the truth in all places, and call upon the rich, the high and the low, and the poor to repent. And let them build up churches, inasmuch as the inhabitants of the earth will repent. (D&C 58:46-48.)

The sound must go forth from this place into all the world, and unto the uttermost parts of the earth—the gospel must be preached unto every creature, with signs following them that believe. (D&C 58:64.)

Let them lift up their voice and declare my word with loud voices, without wrath or doubting, lifting up holy hands upon them. For I am able to make you holy, *and your sins are forgiven you.* And let the residue take their journey from St. Louis, two by two, and preach the word, not in haste, among the congregations of the wicked, until they return to the churches from whence they came. And *all this for the good of the churches*; for this intent have I sent them. (D&C 60:7-9.)

They have been sent to preach my gospel among the congregations of the wicked; wherefore, I give unto them a commandment, thus: Thou shalt not idle away thy time, neither shalt thou bury thy talent *that it may not be known.* (D&C 60:13.)

[Proclaim] my word among the congregations of the wicked, not in haste, neither in wrath nor with strife. And shake off the dust of thy feet against those who receive thee not, not in their presence, lest thou provoke them, but in secret; and wash thy feet, as a testimony against them in the day of judgment. (D&C 60:14-15.)

Let them journey and declare the word among the congregations of the wicked, inasmuch as it is given: And inasmuch as they do this *they shall rid their garments, and they shall be spotless before me.* (D&C 61:33-34.)

Be faithful, and declare glad tidings unto the inhabitants of the earth, or among the congregations of the wicked. (D&C 62:5.)

Every man should take righteousness in his hands and faithfulness upon his loins, and lift a warning voice unto the inhabitants of the earth; and declare both by word and by flight that desolation shall come upon the wicked. (D&C 63:37.)

Those who desire in their hearts, in meekness, to warn sinners to repentance, let them be ordained unto this power. (D&C 63:57.)

Make known his wonderful works among the people. (D&C 65:4.)

It is my will that you should proclaim my gospel from land to land, and from city to city, yea, in those regions round about where it has not been proclaimed. (D&C 66:5.)

This is an ensample unto all those who were ordained unto this priesthood, whose mission is appointed unto them to go forth—and this is the ensample unto them, that they shall speak as they are moved upon by the Holy Ghost. *And whatsoever they shall speak when moved upon by the Holy Ghost shall be scripture, shall be the will of the Lord, shall be the mind of the Lord, shall be the word of the Lord, shall be the voice of the Lord, and the power of God unto salvation. Behold, this is the promise of the Lord unto you, O ye my servants.* (D&C 68:2-5.)

Go ye into all the world, preach the gospel to every creature, acting in the authority which I have given you, baptizing in the name of the Father, and of the Son, and of the Holy Ghost. (D&C 68:8.)

Proclaim unto the world in the regions round about, and in the church also, for the space of a season, even until it shall be made known unto you. (D&C 71:2.)

It is my will that you should go forth and not tarry, neither be idle but labor with your might—lifting up your voices as with the sound of a trump, proclaiming the truth according to the revelations and commandments which I have given you. (D&C 75:3-4.)

In whatsoever house ye enter, and they receive you not, ye shall depart speedily from that house, and shake off the dust of your feet as a testimony against them. *And you shall be filled with joy and gladness; and know this, that in the day of judgment you shall be judges of that house, and condemn them; and it shall be more tolerable for the heathen in the day of judgment, than for that house.* (D&C 75:20-22.)

Let all such as can obtain places for their families, and support of the church for them, not fail to go into the world, whether to the east or to the west, or to the north, or to the south. (D&C 75:26.)

[to Frederick G. Williams] I acknowledge him [Joseph Smith] and will bless him, and also thee, inasmuch as thou art faithful in counsel, in the office which I have appointed unto you, in prayer always, vocally and in thy heart, in public and in private, also in thy ministry in proclaiming the gospel in the land of the living, and among thy brethren. (D&C 81:3.)

I will forgive you of your sins with this commandment—that you remain steadfast in your minds in solemnity and the spirit of prayer, in bearing testimony to all the world of those things which are communicated unto you. Therefore, go ye into all the world; and unto whatsoever place ye cannot go ye shall send, *that the testimony may go from you into all the world unto every creature.* (D&C 84:61-62.)

I say unto all those to whom the kingdom has been given—from you it must be preached unto them, that they shall repent of their former evil works; for they are to be upbraided for their evil hearts of unbelief, and your brethren in Zion for their rebellion against you at the time I sent you. And again I say unto you, my friends, for from henceforth I shall call you friends, it is expedient that I give unto you this commandment, that ye become even as my friends in days when I was with them, traveling to preach the gospel in my power. (D&C 84:76-77.)

Any man that shall go and preach this gospel of the kingdom, and fail not to continue faithful in all things, *shall not be weary in mind, neither darkened, neither in body, limb, nor joint; and a hair of his head shall not fall to the ground unnoticed. And they shall not go hungry, neither athirst.* (D&C 84:80.)

Neither take ye thought beforehand what ye shall say; but treasure up in your minds continually the words of life, *and it shall be given you in the very hour that portion that shall be meted unto every man.* Therefore, let no man among you, for this commandment is unto all the faithful who are called of God in the church unto the ministry, from this hour take purse or scrip, that goeth forth to proclaim this gospel of the kingdom. Behold, I send you out to reprove the world of all their unrighteous deeds, and to teach them of a judgment which is to come. *And whoso receiveth you, there I will be also, for I will go before your face. I will be on your right hand and on your left, and my Spirit shall be in your hearts, and mine angels round about you, to bear you up.* (D&C 84:85-88.)

He that receiveth you not, go away from him alone by yourselves, and cleanse your feet even with water, pure water, whether in heat or in cold, and bear testimony of it unto your Father which is in heaven, and return not again unto that man. (D&C 84:92.)

Search diligently and spare not. (D&C 84:94.)

Take with you those who are ordained unto the lesser priesthood, and send them before you to make appointments, and to prepare the way, and to fill appointments that you yourselves are not able to fill. (D&C 84:107.)

Go ye forth as your circumstances shall permit, in your several callings, unto the great and notable cities and villages, reproving the world in righteousness of all their unrighteous and ungodly deeds, setting forth clearly and understandingly the desolation of abomination in the last days. (D&C 84:117.)

Blessed are ye if ye continue in my goodness, a light unto the Gentiles, and through this priesthood, a savior unto my people Israel. (D&C 86:11.)

Teach one another the doctrine of my kingdom. Teach ye diligently *and my grace shall attend you, that you may be instructed more perfectly in theory, in principle, in doctrine, in the law of the gospel, in all things that pertain unto the kingdom of God, that are expedient for you to understand; of things both in heaven and in the earth, and under the earth; things which have been, things which are, things which must shortly come to pass; things which are at home, things which are abroad; the wars and the perplexities of the nations, and the judgments which are on the land; and a knowledge also of countries and of kingdoms—that ye may be prepared in all things* when I shall send you again to magnify the calling whereunto I have called you, and the mission with which I have commissioned you. Behold, I sent you out to testify and warn the people, and it becometh every man who hath been warned to warn his neighbor. (D&C 88:77-81.)

Tarry ye, and labor diligently, *that you may be perfected in your ministry* to go forth among the Gentiles for the last time, as many as the mouth of the Lord shall name, to bind up the law and seal up the testimony, and to prepare the saints for the hour of judgment which is to come; *that their souls may escape the wrath of God, the desolation of abomination which awaits the wicked, both in this world and in the world to come.* (D&C 88:84-85.)

As all have not faith, seek ye diligently and teach one another words of wisdom; yea, seek ye out of the best books words of wisdom; seek learning, even by study and also by faith. (D&C 88:118; similar scripture, D&C 109:7.)

Appoint among yourselves a teacher, and let not all be spokesmen at once; but let one speak at a time and let all listen unto his sayings, that when all have spoken *that all may be edified of all, and that every man may have an equal privilege.* (D&C 88:122.)

Renounce war and proclaim peace, and seek diligently to turn the hearts of the children to their fathers, and the hearts of the fathers to the children; and again, the hearts of the Jews unto the prophets, and the prophets unto the Jews; *lest I come and smite the whole earth with a curse, and all flesh be consumed before me.* (D&C 98:16-17.)

Lift up your voices unto this people; speak the thoughts that I shall put into your hearts, *and you shall not be confounded before men; for it shall be given you in the very hour, yea, in the very moment, what ye shall say.* But a commandment I give unto you, that ye shall declare whatsoever thing ye declare in my name, in solemnity of heart, in the spirit of meekness, in all things. *And I give unto you this promise, that inasmuch as ye do this the Holy Ghost shall be shed forth in bearing record unto all things whatsoever ye shall say.* (D&C 100:5-8.)

Strengthen your brethren in all your conversation, in all your prayers, in all your exhortations, and in all your doings. (D&C 108:7.)

[to Thomas B. Marsh] Let thy heart be of good cheer before my face; and thou shalt bear record of my name, not only unto the Gentiles, but also unto the Jews; and thou shalt send forth my word unto the ends of the earth. Contend thou, therefore, morning by morning; and day after day let thy warning voice go forth; and when the night cometh let not the inhabitants of the earth slumber, because of thy speech. (D&C 112:4-5.)

Arise and gird up your loins, take up your cross, follow me, and feed my sheep. (D&C 112:14.)

[to Thomas B. Marsh] Whithersoever they shall send you, go ye, *and I will be with you;* and in whatsoever place ye shall proclaim my name *an effectual door shall be opened unto you, that they may receive my word.* (D&C 112:19.)

Purify your hearts before me; and then go ye into all the world, and preach my gospel unto every creature who has not received it. (D&C 112:28.)

Let the residue continue to preach from that hour, and if they will do this in all lowliness of heart, in meekness and humility, and long-suffering, *I, the Lord, give unto them a promise that I will provide for their families; and an effectual door shall be opened for them, from henceforth.* (D&C 118:3.)

Call ye, therefore, upon them [the leaders of the world] with loud proclamation, and with your testimony, fearing them not, for they are as grass, and all their glory as the flower thereof which soon falleth, that they may be left also without excuse. (D&C 124:7.)

It is my will that my servant Lyman Wight should continue in preaching for Zion, in the spirit of meekness, confessing me before the world; *and I will bear him up as on eagles' wings; and he shall beget glory and honor to himself and unto my name.* (D&C 124:18.)

Let him [Vinson Knight] lift up his voice long and loud, in the midst of the people, to plead the cause of the poor and the needy; and let him not fail, neither let his heart faint; *and I will accept of his offerings.* (D&C 124:75.)

[to Brigham Young] I therefore command you to send my word abroad, and take especial care of your family from this time, henceforth and forever. (D&C 126:3.)

Send forth the elders of my church unto the nations which are afar off; unto the islands of the sea; send forth unto foreign lands; call upon all nations, first upon the Gentiles, and then upon the Jews. (D&C 133:8.)

The Lord said unto Enoch: Go forth and do as I have commanded thee, *and no man shall pierce thee.* Open thy mouth, *and it shall be filled, and I will give thee utterance, for all flesh is in my hands, and I will do as seemeth me good.* Say unto this people: Choose ye this day, to serve the Lord God who made you. *Behold my Spirit is upon you, wherefore all thy words will I justify; and the mountains shall flee before you, and the rivers shall turn from their course; and thou shalt abide in me, and I in you;* therefore walk with me. (Moses 6:32-34.)

Teach it unto your children, that all men, everywhere, must repent, or *they can in nowise inherit the kingdom of God,* for no unclean thing can dwell there. . . . Therefore I give unto you a commandment, to teach these things freely unto your children. (Moses 6:57-58.)

The Lord ordained Noah after his own order, and commanded him that he should go forth and declare his Gospel unto the children of men, even as it was given unto Enoch. (Moses 8:19.)

Temperance

The self-restraint or moderation we are commanded to seek is an avoidance of the extreme. Extremist beliefs or practices damage our perspective and hinder our ability to follow the Spirit of God. On the other hand, there is strength in temperance. The Lord commands, "See that ye bridle all your passions, that ye may be filled with love." (Alma 38:12.) A bridle does not lessen the strength of an animal; it channels and directs that strength for useful means. Likewise, our energies must be bridled and controlled to be of use to the Lord. We are told, "No one can assist in this work except he . . . [be] temperate in all things, whatsoever shall be entrusted to his care." (D&C 12:8.)

Commandments and Promises

The drunkard and the glutton *shall come to poverty.* (Prov. 23:21.)

The night is far spent, the day is at hand; let us therefore cast off the works of darkness, and let us put on the armour of light. Let us walk honestly, as in the day; not in rioting and drunkenness, not in chambering and wantonness, not in strife and envying. (Rom. 13:12-14.)

Glorify God in your body, and in your spirit, which are God's. (1 Cor. 6:20.)

Let your moderation be known unto all men. (Philip. 4:5.)

Study to be quiet. (1 Thes. 4:11.)

Speak thou the things which become sound doctrine: That the aged men be sober, grave, temperate. (Titus 2:1-2.)

The grace of God that bringeth salvation hath appeared to all men, teaching us that, denying ungodliness and worldly lusts, we should live soberly, righteously, and godly, in this present world. (Titus 2:11-12.)

Giving all diligence, add to your faith virtue; and to virtue knowledge; and to knowledge temperance; and to temperance patience;

and to patience godliness; and to godliness brotherly kindness; and to brotherly kindness charity. For if these things be in you, and abound, *they make you that ye shall neither be barren nor unfruitful in the knowledge of our Lord Jesus Christ.* (2 Pet. 1:5-8.)

I would that ye should be humble, and be submissive and gentle; easy to be entreated; full of patience and long-suffering; being temperate in all things. (Alma 7:23..)

I would that ye would be diligent and temperate in all things. (Alma 38:10.)

Use boldness, but not overbearance; and also see that ye bridle all your passions, *that ye may be filled with love.* (Alma 38:12.)

Remember . . . temperance, patience, brotherly kindness, . . . humility. (D&C 4:6.)

Be patient; be sober; be temperate. (D&C 6:19.)

No one can assist in this work except he shall be humble and full of love, having faith, hope, and charity, being temperate in all things, whatsoever shall be entrusted to his care. (D&C 12:8.)

It pleaseth God that he hath given all these things unto man; for unto this end were they made to be used, with judgment, not to excess, neither by extortion. (D&C 59:20.)

The decisions of these quorums, or either of them, are to be made in all righteousness, in holiness, and lowliness of heart, meekness and long suffering, and in faith, and virtue, and knowledge, temperance, patience, godliness, brotherly kindness and charity; *because the promise is, if these things abound in them they shall not be unfruitful in the knowledge of the Lord.* (D&C 107:30-31.)

Testifying

(See also Example, Being an; Opposing God and His Servants; Teaching the Gospel.)

As believers in Jesus Christ, we are commanded to bear witness of his reality and divinity, his ministry and message. We are to be steadfast "in bearing testimony to all the world of those things which are communicated" to us from God. (D&C 84:61.) The Lord also tells us it is appropriate to bear witness of the Lord's good works, his compassion, his words, his divine Sonship, his mortality, his resurrection, and his second coming. However, our testimonies must come from more than our mouths or hearts. They must show in our lives, for our lives bear witness of the depth of our testimonies.

Commandments and Promises

When thy son asketh thee in time to come, saying, What mean the testimonies, and the statutes, and the judgments, which the Lord our God hath commanded you? Then thou shalt say unto thy son, We were Pharaoh's bondmen in Egypt; and the Lord brought us out of Egypt with a mighty hand: and the Lord shewed signs and wonders, great and sore, upon Egypt, upon Pharaoh, and upon all his household, before our eyes: and he brought us out from thence, that he might bring us in, *to give us the land which he sware unto our fathers.* And the Lord commanded us to do all these statutes, to fear the Lord our God, *for our good always, that he might preserve us alive, as it is at this day. And it shall be our righteousness,* if we observe to do all these commandments before the Lord our God, as he hath commanded us. (Deut. 6:20-25.)

Ye are my witnesses, saith the Lord, and my servant whom I have chosen: *that ye may know and believe me, and understand that I am he: before me there was no God formed, neither shall there be after me.* (Isa. 43:10.)

Jesus saith unto him, See thou tell no man; but go thy way, shew thyself to the priest, and offer the gift that Moses commanded, for a testimony unto them. (Matt. 8:4.)

Whosoever therefore shall confess me before men, *him will I confess also before my Father which is in heaven.* But whosoever shall deny me before men, *him will I also deny before my Father which is in heaven.* (Matt. 10:32-33.)

When he was come into the ship, he that had been possessed with the devil prayed him that he might be with him. Howbeit Jesus suffered him not, but saith unto him, Go home to thy friends, and tell them how great things the Lord hath done for thee, and hath had compassion on thee. (Mark 5:18-19.)

Whosoever shall confess me before men, *him shall the Son of man also confess before the angels of God.* But he that denieth me before men *shall be denied before the angels of God.* (Luke 12:8.)

If thou shalt confess with thy mouth the Lord Jesus, and shalt believe in thine heart that God hath raised him from the dead, *thou shalt be saved.* For with the heart man believeth *unto righteousness;* and with the mouth confession is made *unto salvation.* (Rom. 10:9-10.)

Be not thou therefore ashamed of the testimony of our Lord, nor of me his prisoner: but be thou partaker of the afflictions of the gospel according to the power of God. (2 Tim. 1:8.)

If we deny him, *he also will deny us.* (2 Tim. 2:12.)

Let us hold fast the profession of our faith without wavering. (Heb. 10:23.)

Who is a liar but he that denieth that Jesus is the Christ? He is antichrist, that denieth the Father and the Son. Whosoever denieth the Son, *the same hath not the Father:* [but] he that acknowledgeth the Son *hath the Father also.* (1 Jn. 2:22-23.)

The right way is to believe in Christ, and deny him not; and Christ is the Holy One of Israel; wherefore ye must bow down before him, and worship him with all your might, mind, and strength, and your whole soul; and if ye do this *ye shall in nowise be cast out.* (2 Ne. 25:29.)

This great loss of the Nephites, and the great slaughter which was among them, would not have happened had it not been for their wickedness and their abomination which was among them; yea, and it was among those also who professed to belong to the church of God. And it was because of the pride of their hearts, because of their exceeding riches, yea, it was because of their oppression to the poor, withholding their food from the hungry, withholding their clothing from the naked, and smiting their humble brethren upon the cheek, making a mock of that which was sacred, denying the spirit of prophecy and of revelation. (Hel. 4:11-12.)

[sacrament prayer] O God, the Eternal Father, we ask thee in the name of thy Son, Jesus Christ, to bless and sanctify this bread to the souls of all those who partake of it; that they may eat in remembrance of the body of thy Son, and witness unto thee, O God, the Eternal Father, that they are willing to take upon them the name of thy Son, and always remember him, and keep his commandments which he hath given them, *that they may always have his Spirit to be with them.* (Moro. 4:3; similar scriptures, Moro. 5:2, D&C 20:77, 79.)

I, the Lord, am God, and have given these things unto you, my servant Joseph Smith, Jun., and have commanded you that you should stand as a witness of these things. (D&C 5:2.)

In the mouth of two or three witnesses shall every word be established. (D&C 6:28; similar scripture, D&C 128:3.)

If you shall ask the Father in my name, in faith believing, *you shall receive the Holy Ghost, which giveth utterance, that you may stand as a witness of the things of which you shall both hear and see, and also that you may declare repentance unto this generation.* (D&C 14:8.)

These words are not of men nor of man, but of me; wherefore, you shall testify they are of me and not of man; for it is my voice which speaketh them unto you; for they are given by my Spirit unto you, and by my power you can read them one to another; and save it were by my power you could not have them; *wherefore, you can testify that you have heard my voice, and know my words.* (D&C 18:34-36.)

The members shall manifest before the church, and also before the elders, by a godly walk and conversation, that they are worthy of it, that there may be works and faith agreeable to the holy scriptures—walking in holiness before the Lord. (D&C 20:69.)

Ye are blessed, for the testimony which ye have borne *is recorded in heaven for the angels to look upon; and they rejoice over you, and your sins are forgiven you.* (D&C 62:3.)

Ye shall bear record of me, even Jesus Christ, that I am the Son of the living God, that I was, that I am, and that I am to come. (D&C 68:6.)

They are bodies terrestrial, and not bodies celestial, and differ in glory as the moon differs from the sun. These are they who are not valiant in the testimony of Jesus; *wherefore, they obtain not the crown over the kingdom of our God.* (D&C 76:78-79.)

I will forgive you of your sins with this commandment—that you remain steadfast in your minds in solemnity and the spirit of prayer, in bearing testimony to all the world of those things which are communicated unto you. (D&C 84:61.)

All those who will not endure chastening, but deny me, *cannot be sanctified.* (D&C 101:5.)

It is my will that my servant Lyman Wight should continue in preaching for Zion, in the spirit of meekness, confessing me before the world; *and I will bear him up as on eagles' wings; and he shall beget glory and honor to himself and unto my name.* (D&C 124:18.)

When any of you are baptized for your dead, let there be a recorder, and let him be eye-witness of your baptisms; let him hear with his ears, *that he may testify of a truth,* saith the Lord. (D&C 127:6.)

Thankfulness

Thankfulness should be a quality every person possesses, for we have received much, including our lives, this earth, and the restored gospel. Moreover, the Lord expects us to give abundantly to bless others: "Freely ye have received, freely give." (Matt. 10:8.) Through thankfulness, we can also maintain a proper perspective of eternal things and not be overwhelmed by the petty cares of this world.

The Lord furthermore asks that we acknowledge him through gratitude. Those who, without thankfulness, claim not to see God's influence are spiritually blinded. They not only offend God, but they deny themselves a knowledge of God and his ways and deprive themselves of the blessings the Lord bestows on the faithful.

Commandments and Promises

When thou hast eaten and art full, then thou shalt bless the Lord thy God for the good land which he hath given thee. (Deut. 8:10.)

O give thanks unto the Lord; for he is good; for his mercy endureth for ever. (1 Chr. 16:34; similar scripture, Ps. 136:1.)

Enter into his gates with thanksgiving, and into his courts with praise: be thankful unto him, and bless his name. (Ps. 100:4.)

Fornication, and all uncleanness, or covetousness, let it not be once named among you, as becometh saints; neither filthiness, nor foolish talking, nor jesting, which are not convenient: but rather giving of thanks. (Eph. 5:3-4.)

[Give] thanks always for all things unto God and the Father in the name of our Lord Jesus Christ. (Eph. 5:20.)

As ye have therefore received Christ Jesus the Lord, so walk ye in him: rooted and built up in him, and stablished in the faith, as ye have been taught, abounding therein with thanksgiving. (Col. 2:6-7.)

Let the peace of God rule in your hearts, to the which also ye are called in one body; and be ye thankful. (Col. 3:15.)

Whatsoever ye do in word or deed, do all in the name of the Lord Jesus, giving thanks to God and the Father by him. (Col. 3:17.)

Continue in prayer, and watch in the same with thanksgiving. (Col. 4:2.)

In every thing give thanks: for this is the will of God in Christ Jesus concerning you. (1 Thes. 5:18.)

I exhort therefore, that first of all, supplications, prayers, intercessions, and giving of thanks, be made for all men; for kings, and for all that are in authority; *that we may lead a quiet and peaceable life in all godliness and honesty.* For this is good and acceptable in the sight of God our Saviour. (1 Tim. 2:1-3.)

Every creature of God is good, and nothing to be refused, if it be received with thanksgiving: for it is sanctified by the word of God and prayer. (1 Tim. 4:4-5.)

Men shall be lovers of their own selves, covetous, . . . unthankful . . . : from such turn away. . . . *But they shall proceed no further: for their folly shall be manifest unto all men.* (2 Tim. 3:2-5, 9.)

By him therefore let us offer the sacrifice of praise to God continually, that is, the fruit of our lips giving thanks to his name. (Heb. 13:15.)

Pray unto him continually by day, and give thanks unto his holy name by night. (2 Ne. 9:52.)

[Alma] commanded them that they should observe the sabbath day, and keep it holy, and also every day they should give thanks to the Lord their God. (Mosiah 18:23.)

I would that ye should be humble, . . . always returning thanks unto God for whatsoever things ye do receive. (Alma 7:23.)

Blessed be the name of our God; let us sing to his praise, yea, let us give thanks to his holy name, for he doth work righteousness forever. (Alma 26:8.)

Live in thanksgiving daily, for the many mercies and blessings which he doth bestow upon you. (Alma 34:38.)

Counsel with the Lord in all thy doings, and he will direct thee for good; yea, when thou liest down at night lie down unto the Lord, *that he may watch over you in your sleep;* and when thou risest in the morning let thy heart be full of thanks unto God; and if ye do these things, *ye shall be lifted up at the last day.* (Alma 37:37.)

Ye do not remember the Lord your God in the things with which he hath blessed you, but ye do always remember your riches, not to thank the Lord your God for them; yea, your hearts are not drawn out unto the Lord, but they do swell with great pride, unto boasting, and unto great swelling, envyings, strifes, malice, persecutions, and murders, and all manner of iniquities. For this cause *hath the Lord God caused that a curse should come upon the land, and also upon your riches, and this because of your iniquities.* (Hel. 13:22-23.)

Condemn me [Moroni] not because of mine imperfection, neither my father, because of his imperfection, neither them who have written before him; but rather give thanks unto God that he hath made manifest unto you our imperfections, *that ye may learn to be more wise than we have been.* (Morm. 9:31.)

That which the Spirit testifies unto you even so I would that ye should do in all holiness of heart, walking uprightly before me, considering the end of your salvation, doing all things with prayer and thanksgiving, *that ye may not be seduced by evil spirits, or doctrines of devils, or the commandments of men;* for some are of men, and others of devils. (D&C 46:7.)

Ye must give thanks unto God in the Spirit for whatsoever blessing ye are blessed with. (D&C 46:32.)

Thou shalt thank the Lord thy God in all things. (D&C 59:7.)

Inasmuch as ye do these things [fasting and prayer] with thanksgiving, with cheerful hearts and countenances, not with much laughter, for this is sin, but with a glad heart and a cheerful countenance— verily I say, that inasmuch as ye do this, *the fulness of the earth is yours, the beasts of the field and the fowls of the air, and that which climbeth upon the trees and walketh upon the earth; yea, and the herb, and the good things which come of the earth, whether for food or for raiment, or for houses, or for barns, or for orchards, or for gardens, or for vineyards.* (D&C 59:15-17.)

He who receiveth all things with thankfulness *shall be made glorious; and the things of this earth shall be added unto him, even an hundred fold, yea, more.* (D&C 78:19.)

Rejoice evermore, and in everything give thanks. (D&C 98:1.)

Now the year of my redeemed is come; *and they shall mention the loving kindness of their Lord, and all that he has bestowed upon them according to his goodness, and according to his loving kindness, forever and ever.* (D&C 133:52.)

If thou art merry, praise the Lord with singing, with music, with dancing, and with a prayer of praise and thanksgiving. (D&C 136:28.)

Tithes and Offerings

(See also Generosity; Sacrifice.)

The Prophet Joseph Smith asked the Lord in 1838, "O Lord, show unto thy servants how much thou requirest of the properties of thy people for a tithing." The Lord's response included this commandment: "Those who have thus been tithed shall pay one-tenth of all their interest annually; and this shall be a standing law unto them forever, for my holy priesthood, saith the Lord." (D&C 119, headnote and v. 4.)

The commandment to pay a tithe was not new in Joseph Smith's time. The Old Testament prophet Malachi explains tithing in words repeated by the Lord when he visited the Nephites after his death. Malachi explains that paying tithing brings both spiritual and temporal rewards: the Lord will open the windows of heaven, rebuke Satan, and bless our labors with fruitfulness. (See Mal. 3:10-12.)

The Lord also commands us to give generously through other offerings, such as fast offerings, which benefit the needy. And while it is not required that we pay tithing and offerings before we pay other obligations, the scriptures specify giving "the firstlings of your herds" and "the first fruits of all thine increase." (Deut. 12:6 and Prov. 3:9.) Whenever we pay tithing, it is clear that we should not do it as an afterthought, or only if there happens to be enough left over. We should pay it wholeheartedly and willingly, grateful for the chance to contribute to God's work.

Commandments and Promises

Thither ye shall bring your burnt offerings, and your sacrifices, and your tithes, and heave offerings of your hand, and your vows, and your freewill offerings, and the firstlings of your herds and of your flocks. (Deut. 12:6.)

Thou shalt truly tithe all the increase of thy seed, that the field bringeth forth year by year. (Deut. 14:22.)

Honour the Lord with thy substance, and with the firstfruits of all thine increase. (Prov. 3:9.)

Will a man rob God? Yet ye have robbed me. But ye say, Wherein have we robbed thee? In tithes and offerings. *Ye are cursed with a curse:* for ye have robbed me, even this whole nation. Bring ye all the tithes into the storehouse, *that there may be meat in mine house,* and prove me now herewith, saith the Lord of hosts, *if I will not open you the windows of heaven, and pour you out a blessing, that there shall not be room enough to receive it. And I will rebuke the devourer for your sakes, and he shall not destroy the fruits of your ground; neither shall your vine cast her fruit before the time in the field; saith the Lord of hosts. And all nations shall call you blessed: for ye shall be a delightsome land, saith the Lord of hosts.* (Mal. 3:8-12; similar scripture, 3 Ne. 24:8-12.)

Render therefore unto Caesar the things which are Caesar's; and unto God the things that are God's. (Matt. 22:21; similar scripture, Mark 12:17.)

Woe unto you, scribes and Pharisees, hypocrites! for ye pay tithe of mint and anise and cummin, and have omitted the weightier matters of the law, judgment, mercy, and faith: these ought ye to have done, and not to leave the other undone. (Matt. 23:23; similar scripture, Luke 11:42.)

Give alms of such things as ye have; *and, behold, all things are clean unto you.* (Luke 11:41; see also JST Luke 11:42.)

For this cause pay ye tribute also: for they are God's ministers, attending continually upon this very thing. (Rom. 13:6; see also JST Rom. 13:6-7.)

I would that ye should do alms unto the poor; but take heed that ye do not your alms before men to be seen of them; *otherwise ye have no reward of your Father who is in heaven.* Therefore, when ye shall do your alms do not sound a trumpet before you, as will hypocrites do in the synagogues and in the streets, *that they may have glory of men. Verily I say unto you, they have their reward.* But when thou doest alms let not thy left hand know what thy right hand doeth; that thine alms may be in secret; *and thy Father who seeth in secret, himself shall reward thee openly.* (3 Ne. 13:1-4; similar scripture, Matt. 6:1-4.)

Thou wilt remember the poor, and consecrate of thy properties for their support that which thou hast to impart unto them, with a covenant and a deed which cannot be broken. (D&C 42:30.)

Now it is called today until the coming of the Son of Man, and verily it is a day of sacrifice, and a day for the tithing of my people; for he that is tithed *shall not be burned at his coming.* (D&C 64:23.)

It is contrary to the will and commandment of God that those who receive not their inheritance by consecration, agreeable to his law, which he has given, that he may tithe his people, *to prepare them against the day of vengeance and burning*, should have their names enrolled with the people of God. (D&C 85:3.)

Let it [temple] be built speedily, by the tithing of my people. (D&C 97:11.)

If any man shall take of the abundance which I have made, and impart not his portion, according to the law of my gospel, unto the poor and the needy, *he shall, with the wicked, lift up his eyes in hell, being in torment.* (D&C 104:18.)

Those who have thus been tithed shall pay one-tenth of all their interest annually; and this shall be a standing law unto them forever, for my holy priesthood, saith the Lord. (D&C 119:4.)

Trusting in God
(See also Waiting on God.)

The Lord commands that our ultimate trust be in him: "Commit thy way unto the Lord," the Psalmist says. (Ps. 37:5.) We can trust in God by learning and obeying his words. We trust by following the Psalmist's admonition and promise, "Cast thy burden upon the Lord, and he shall sustain thee." (Ps. 55:22.) We show trust for God by approaching him in faithful prayer.

We can learn to trust in the same way that we recognize and trust the godliness in those we know. Trust grows as each demonstration of trust is met with honor and integrity. In the same way, we can develop trust for God by trusting him increasingly. Perhaps our first sign of trust may be a simple prayer. As our feelings of trust in God grow, we will find that we turn to him continually, and we will know that he is the God in whom we should trust.

Commandments and Promises

The sons of Reuben, and the Gadites, and half the tribe of Manasseh . . . made war with the Hagarites, with Jetur, and Nephish, and Nodab. *And they were helped against them, and the Hagarites were delivered into their hand, and all that were with them:* for they cried to God in the battle, and he was intreated of them; because they put their trust in him. (1 Chr. 5:18-20.)

The children of Israel were brought under at that time, and the children of Judah prevailed, because they relied upon the Lord God of their fathers. (2 Chr. 13:18.)

Blessed are all they that put their trust in him. (Ps. 2:12.)

Offer the sacrifices of righteousness, and put your trust in the Lord. (Ps. 4:5.)

Let all those that put their trust in thee rejoice: let them ever shout for joy, *because thou defendest them:* let them also that love thy name be joyful in thee. (Ps. 5:11.)

They that know thy name will put their trust in thee: *for thou, Lord, hast not forsaken them that seek thee.* (Ps. 9:10.)

He is a buckler to all those that trust in him. (Ps. 18:30.)

Oh how great is thy goodness, which thou hast laid up for them that fear thee; which thou hast wrought for them that trust in thee before the sons of men! (Ps. 31:19.)

He that trusteth in the Lord, *mercy shall compass him about.* (Ps. 32:10.)

Blessed is the man that trusteth in him. (Ps. 34:8.)

None of them that trust in him *shall be desolate.* (Ps. 34:22.)

Trust in the Lord, and do good; *so shalt thou dwell in the land, and verily thou shalt be fed.* (Ps. 37:3.)

Commit thy way unto the Lord; trust also in him; *and he shall bring it to pass. And he shall bring forth thy righteousness as the light, and thy judgment as the noonday.* Rest in the Lord, and wait patiently for him: fret not thyself because of him who prospereth in his way, because of the man who bringeth wicked devices to pass. (Ps. 37:5-7.)

The Lord shall help them, and deliver them: he shall deliver them from the wicked, and save them, because they trust in him. (Ps. 37:40.)

Blessed is that man that maketh the Lord his trust. (Ps. 40:4.)

Cast thy burden upon the Lord, *and he shall sustain thee.* (Ps. 55:22.)

Trust in him at all times; ye people, pour out your heart before him: God is a refuge for us. (Ps. 62:8.)

The righteous *shall be glad in the Lord, and shall trust in him; and all* the upright in heart *shall glory.* (Ps. 64:10.)

O Lord of hosts, *blessed* is the man that trusteth in thee. (Ps. 84:12.)

O Israel, trust thou in the Lord: he is their help and their shield. O house of Aaron, trust in the Lord: he is their help and their shield. Ye that fear the Lord, trust in the Lord: he is their help and their shield. (Ps. 115:9-11.)

It is better to trust in the Lord than to put confidence in princes. (Ps. 118:9.)

They that trust in the Lord *shall be as mount Zion, which cannot be removed, but abideth for ever.* (Ps. 125:1.)

Put not your trust in princes, nor in the son of man [mortals], in whom there is no help. (Ps. 146:3.)

Trust in the Lord with all thine heart; and lean not unto thine own understanding. (Prov. 3:5.)

He that trusteth in his riches *shall fall.* (Prov. 11:28.)

Whoso trusteth in the Lord, *happy is he.* (Prov. 16:20.)

He that putteth his trust in the Lord *shall be made fat.* He that trusteth in his own heart *is a fool.* (Prov. 28:25-26.)

Whoso putteth his trust in the Lord *shall be safe.* (Prov. 29:25.)

He is a shield unto them that put their trust in him. (Prov. 30:5.)

He that putteth his trust in me *shall possess the land, and shall inherit my holy mountain; and shall say, Cast ye up, cast ye up, prepare the way, take up the stumblingblock out of the way of my people.* (Isa. 57:13-14.)

Therefore will I scatter them as the stubble that passeth away by the wind of the wilderness. This is thy lot, the portion of thy measures from me, saith the Lord; because thou hast forgotten me, and trusted in falsehood. *Therefore will I discover thy skirts upon thy face, that thy shame may appear.* (Jer. 13:24-26.)

Thus saith the Lord; Cursed be the man that trusteth in man, and maketh flesh his arm, and whose heart departeth from the Lord. *For he shall be like the heath in the desert, and shall not see when good cometh; but shall inhabit the parched places in the wilderness, in a salt land and not inhabited. Blessed is the man* that trusteth in the Lord, and whose hope the Lord is. *For he shall be as a tree planted by the waters, and that spreadeth out her roots by the river, and shall not see when heat cometh, but her leaf shall be green; and shall not be careful in the year of drought, neither shall cease from yielding fruit.* (Jer. 17:5-8.)

I will surely deliver thee, and thou shalt not fall by the sword, but thy life shall be for a prey unto thee: because thou hast put thy trust in me, saith the Lord. (Jer. 39:18.)

Ye have plowed wickedness, ye have reaped iniquity; ye have eaten the fruit of lies: because thou didst trust in thy way, in the multitude of thy mighty men. *Therefore shall a tumult arise among thy people, and all thy fortresses shall be spoiled.* (Hosea 10:13-14.)

The Lord is good, a strong hold in the day of trouble; and *he knoweth them* that trust in him. (Nahum 1:7.)

Take no thought for your life, what ye shall eat, or what ye shall drink; nor yet for your body, what ye shall put on. Is not the life more than meat, and the body than raiment? (Matt. 6:25; similar scripture, Luke 12:22-23; see also JST Matt. 6:25-27.)

Why take ye thought for raiment? Consider the lilies of the field, how they grow; they toil not, neither do they spin: and yet I say unto you, That even Solomon in all his glory was not arrayed like one of these. Wherefore, if God so clothe the grass of the field, which to day is, and to morrow is cast into the oven, *shall he not much more clothe you,* O ye of little faith? Therefore take no thought, saying, What shall we eat? or, What shall we drink? or, Wherewithal shall we be clothed? (For after all these things do the Gentiles seek:) for your heavenly Father knoweth that ye have need of all these things. (Matt. 6:28-32; similar scripture, D&C 84:81-84; see also JST Matt. 6:34.)

Take therefore no thought for the morrow: for the morrow shall take thought for the things of itself. Sufficient unto the day is the evil thereof. (Matt. 6:34; similar scripture, D&C 84:84.)

Beware of men: for they will deliver you up to the councils, and they will scourge you in their synagogues; and ye shall be brought before governors and kings for my sake, for a testimony against them and the Gentiles. But when they deliver you up, take no thought how or what ye shall speak: *for it shall be given you in that same hour what ye shall speak. For it is not ye that speak, but the Spirit of your Father which speaketh in you.* (Matt. 10:17-20.)

Therefore we both labour and suffer reproach, because we trust in the living God, who is the Saviour of all men, specially of those that believe. (1 Tim. 4:10.)

Charge them that are rich in this world, that they be not high-minded, nor trust in uncertain riches, but in the living God, *who giveth us richly all things to enjoy;* that they do good, that they be rich in good works, ready to distribute, willing to communicate; laying up in store for themselves *a good foundation against the time to come, that they may lay hold on eternal life.* (1 Tim. 6:17-19.)

Cast not away therefore your confidence, *which hath great recompence of reward.* (Heb. 10:35.)

Let them that suffer according to the will of God commit the keeping of their souls to him in well doing, as unto a faithful Creator. (1 Pet. 4:19.)

Humble yourselves therefore under the mighty hand of God, that he may exalt you in due time: casting all your care upon him; for he careth for you. (1 Pet. 5:6-7.)

All mankind were in a lost and in a fallen state, and ever would be save they should rely on this Redeemer. (1 Ne. 10:6.)

O Lord, I have trusted in thee, and I will trust in thee forever. I will not put my trust in the arm of flesh; for I know that *cursed is he* that putteth his trust in the arm of flesh. Yea, *cursed is he* that putteth his trust in man or maketh flesh his arm. (2 Ne. 4:34.)

Lift up your heads, and rejoice, and put your trust in God, in that God who was the God of Abraham, and Isaac, and Jacob; and also, that

God who brought the children of Israel out of the land of Egypt, and caused that they should walk through the Red Sea on dry ground, and fed them with manna that they might not perish in the wilderness; and many more things did he do for them. (Mosiah 7:19.)

[to people of Limhi] If ye will turn to the Lord with full purpose of heart, and put your trust in him, and serve him with all diligence of mind, if ye do this, *he will, according to his own will and pleasure, deliver you out of bondage.* (Mosiah 7:33.)

Whosoever putteth his trust in him *the same shall be lifted up at the last day.* (Mosiah 23:22.)

He did deliver them because they did humble themselves before him; and because they cried mightily unto him *he did deliver them out of bondage; and thus doth the Lord work with his power in all cases among the children of men, extending the arm of mercy towards them* that put their trust in him. (Mosiah 29:20.)

I [Alma] have been supported under trials and troubles of every kind, yea, and in all manner of afflictions; yea, *God has delivered me from prison, and from bonds, and from death;* yea, and I do put my trust in him, *and he will still deliver me.* (Alma 36:27.)

He doth not command us that we shall subject ourselves to our enemies, but that we should put our trust in him, *and he will deliver us.* (Alma 61:13.)

The Lord in his great infinite goodness doth bless and prosper those who put their trust in him. (Hel. 12:1.)

The reason why he ceaseth to do miracles among the children of men is because that they dwindle in unbelief, and depart from the right way, and know not the God in whom they should trust. (Morm. 9:20.)

The weak things of the world shall come forth and break down the mighty and strong ones, that man should not counsel his fellow man, neither trust in the arm of flesh. (D&C 1:19.)

Put your trust in that Spirit which leadeth to do good—yea, to do justly, to walk humbly, to judge righteously; and this is my Spirit. *Verily, verily, I say unto you, I will impart unto you of my Spirit, which shall enlighten your mind, which shall fill your soul with joy; and then shall ye know, or by this shall you know, all things whatsoever you desire of me, which are pertaining unto things of righteousness,* in faith believing in me that you shall receive. (D&C 11:12-14.)

[to the Three Witnesses] You must rely upon my word, which if you do with full purpose of heart, *you shall have a view of the plates, and also of the breastplate, the sword of Laban, the Urim and Thummim, which were given to the brother of Jared upon the mount, when he talked with the Lord face to face, and the miraculous directors which were given to Lehi while in the wilderness, on the borders of the Red Sea.* (D&C 17:1.)

If you know that they are true, behold, I give unto you a commandment, that you rely upon the things which are written. (D&C 18:3.)

Thou shalt do it [publish glad tidings] with all humility, trusting in me, reviling not against revilers. (D&C 19:30.)

Let him [Newel K. Whitney] trust in me *and he shall not be confounded; and a hair of his head shall not fall to the ground unnoticed.* (D&C 84:116.)

Fear not, let your hearts be comforted; yea, rejoice evermore, and in everything give thanks. (D&C 98:1.)

Let not your hearts be troubled; for in my Father's house are many mansions, *and I have prepared a place for you; and where my Father and I am, there ye shall be also.* (D&C 98:18.)

Let your hearts be comforted; for *all things shall work together for good* to them that walk uprightly, *and to the sanctification of the church.* (D&C 100:15.)

Let your hearts be comforted concerning Zion; for all flesh is in mine hands; be still and know that I am God. (D&C 101:16.)

Concern not yourselves [Joseph Smith and other Church leaders] about your debts, for I will give you power to pay them. Concern not yourselves about Zion, for I will deal mercifully with her. Tarry in this place, and in the regions round about; *and the place where it is my will that you should tarry, for the main, shall be signalized unto you by the peace and power of my Spirit, that shall flow unto you.* (D&C 111:5-8.)

Understanding

(See also Knowing God and His Ways; Wisdom.)

If we do not understand God's teachings and ways, we have only ourselves to blame. "If ye cannot understand [the words of Christ] it will be because ye ask not, neither do ye knock; wherefore, ye are not brought into the light, but must perish in the dark." (2 Ne. 32:4.) We are commanded to seek understanding, with the insight that "knowledge of the holy is understanding." (Prov. 9:10.)

When we have sought and gained understanding, the Lord can speak to a greater level of understanding. Nephi writes, "My soul delighteth in plainness; for after this manner doth the Lord God work among the children of men. For the Lord giveth light unto the understanding; for he speaketh unto men according to their language, unto their understanding." (2 Ne. 31:3.) With that realization, we ought to take seriously the repeated statement, "Whoso readeth, let him understand." (Matt. 24:15.)

Commandments and Promises

God said unto him [Solomon], Because thou hast asked this thing, and hast not asked for thyself long life; neither hast asked riches for thyself, nor hast asked the life of thine enemies; but hast asked for thyself understanding to discern judgment; *behold, I have done according to thy words: lo, I have given thee a wise and an understanding heart; so that there was none like thee before thee, neither after thee shall any arise like unto thee.* (1 Kgs. 3:11-12.)

To depart from evil *is understanding.* (Job 28:28.)

Get wisdom, get understanding: forget it not; neither decline from the words of my mouth. Forsake her not, *and she shall preserve thee:* love her, *and she shall keep thee.* Wisdom is the principal thing; therefore get wisdom: and with all thy getting get understanding. (Prov. 4:5-7.)

O ye simple, understand wisdom: and, ye fools, be ye of an understanding heart. (Prov. 8:5.)

Forsake the foolish, *and live;* and go in the way of understanding. (Prov. 9:6.)

The knowledge of the holy *is understanding.* (Prov. 9:10.)

The man that wandereth out of the way of understanding *shall remain in the congregation of the dead.* (Prov. 21:16.)

Buy the truth, and sell it not; also wisdom, and instruction, and understanding. (Prov. 23:23.)

Fear not, Daniel: for from the first day that thou didst set thine heart to understand, and to chasten thyself before thy God, *thy words were heard, and I am come for thy words.* (Dan. 10:12.)

When any one heareth the word of the kingdom, and understandeth it not, *then cometh the wicked one, and catcheth away that which was sown in his heart.* This is he which received seed by the way side. (Matt. 13:19.)

He called the multitude, and said unto them, Hear, and understand. (Matt. 15:10.)

Whoso readeth, let him understand. (Matt. 24:15; similar scriptures, Mark 13:14, 3 Ne. 10:14, D&C 57:9, JS–M 1:12.)

Be not children in understanding: howbeit in malice be ye children, but in understanding be men. (1 Cor. 14:20.)

Be ye not unwise, but understanding what the will of the Lord is. (Eph. 5:17.)

[Nephi to his brothers] Now after I have spoken these words, if ye cannot understand them it will be because ye ask not, neither do ye knock; *wherefore, ye are not brought into the light, but must perish in the dark.* (2 Ne. 32:4.)

[Jesus during his visit to the Americas] Ponder upon the things which I have said, and ask of the Father, in my name, that ye may understand, and prepare your minds for the morrow, and I come unto you again. (3 Ne. 17:3.)

Whoso readeth, let him understand and receive also; for unto him that receiveth *it shall be given more abundantly, even power.* (D&C 71:5-6.)

Whoso readeth it, let him understand, for the Spirit manifesteth truth. (D&C 91:4.)

Unity
(See also Church Organization and Government; Contention; Edifying and Strengthening Others; Forgiving Others; Marriage; Prayer.)

God's church must be unified to have his sanction. "Be one; and if ye are not one ye are not mine." (D&C 38:27.) The Saints must be united not only through fellowship and love, but through teachings and ordinances.

In a prayer for the apostles and saints, the Savior speaks of his unity with his Father: "That they all may be one; as thou, Father, art in me, and I in thee, that they also may be one in us: that the world may believe that thou hast sent me. And the glory which thou gavest me I have given them; that they may be one, even as we are one: I in them, and thou in me, that they may be made perfect in one; and that the world may know that thou hast sent me, and hast loved them, as thou hast loved me." (John 17:21-23.)

Alma's example of Church leadership illustrates this kind of unity: "Alma, having authority from God, ordained priests; . . . and he commanded them that they should teach nothing save it were the things which he had taught, and which had been spoken by the mouth of the holy prophets. . . . And he commanded them that there should be no contention one with another, but that they should look forward with one eye, having one faith and one baptism, having their hearts knit together in unity and in love one towards another. And thus he commanded them to preach. And thus they became the children of God." (Mosiah 18:18-22.)

Commandments and Promises

How good and how pleasant it is for brethren to dwell together in unity! (Ps. 133:1.)

Every kingdom divided against itself *is brought to desolation;* and every city or house divided against itself *shall not stand.* (Matt. 12:25; similar scriptures, Mark 3:24-25, Luke 11:17.)

Rejoice with them that do rejoice, and weep with them that weep. Be of the same mind one toward another. Mind not high things, but condescend to men of low estate. Be not wise in your own conceits. (Rom. 12:15-16.)

Now I beseech you, brethren, by the name of our Lord Jesus Christ, that ye all speak the same thing, and that there be no divisions among you; but that ye be perfectly joined together in the same mind and in the same judgment. (1 Cor. 1:10.)

Be perfect, be of good comfort, be of one mind, live in peace; *and the God of love and peace shall be with you.* (2 Cor. 13:11.)

I therefore, the prisoner of the Lord, beseech you that ye walk worthy of the vocation wherewith ye are called, with all lowliness and meekness, with longsuffering, forbearing one another in love; endeavouring to keep the unity of the Spirit in the bond of peace. (Eph. 4:1-3.)

Only let your conversation be as it becometh the gospel of Christ: that whether I come and see you, or else be absent, I may hear of your affairs, that ye stand fast in one spirit, with one mind striving together for the faith of the gospel. (Philip. 1:27.)

If there be therefore any consolation in Christ, if any comfort of love, if any fellowship of the Spirit, if any bowels and mercies, fulfil ye my joy, that ye be likeminded, having the same love, being of one accord, of one mind. (Philip. 2:1-2.)

Be ye all of one mind, having compassion one of another, love as brethren, be pitiful, be courteous. (1 Pet. 3:8.)

Arise from the dust, my sons, and be men, and be determined in one mind and in one heart, united in all things, *that ye may not come down into captivity; that ye may not be cursed with a sore cursing; and also, that ye may not incur the displeasure of a just God upon you, unto the destruction, yea, the eternal destruction of both soul and body.* (2 Ne. 1:21-22.)

He commanded them that there should be no contention one with another, but that they should look forward with one eye, having one faith and one baptism, having their hearts knit together in unity and in love one towards another. And thus he commanded them to preach. *And thus they became the children of God.* (Mosiah 18:21-22.)

According as I have commanded you thus shall ye baptize. And there shall be no disputations among you, as there have hitherto been; neither shall there be disputations among you concerning the points of my doctrine, as there have hitherto been. (3 Ne. 11:28.)

All things shall be done by common consent in the church, by much prayer and faith, for all things you shall receive by faith. (D&C 26:2.)

Be agreed as touching all things whatsoever ye ask of me, and be faithful until I come, *and ye shall be caught up, that where I am ye shall be also.* (D&C 27:18.)

All things must be done in order, and by common consent in the church, by the prayer of faith. (D&C 28:13.)

As it is written—Whatsoever ye shall ask in faith, being united in prayer according to my command, *ye shall recieve.* (D&C 29:6.)

It is given unto you that ye may understand, because ye have asked it of me and are agreed. (D&C 29:33.)

Be you [Peter Whitmer] afflicted in all his [Oliver Cowdery's] afflictions, ever lifting up your heart unto me in prayer and faith, for his and your deliverance. (D&C 30:6.)

Be one; and if ye are not one *ye are not mine.* (D&C 38:27.)

Hearken, O ye elders of my church whom I have called, behold I give unto you a commandment, that ye shall assemble yourselves together to agree upon my word. (D&C 41:2.)

As ye have assembled yourselves together according to the commandment wherewith I commanded you, and are agreed as touching this one thing, and have asked the Father in my name, *even so ye shall receive.* (D&C 42:3.)

With one heart and with one mind, gather up your riches that ye may purchase an inheritance which shall hereafter be appointed unto you. (D&C 45:65.)

Let every man deal honestly, and be alike among this people, and receive alike, *that ye may be one, even as I have commanded you.* (D&C 51:9.)

Let every man stand in his own office, and labor in his own calling; and let not the head say unto the feet it hath no need of the feet; for without the feet how shall the body be able to stand? Also the body hath need of every member, that all may be edified together, that the system may be kept perfect. (D&C 84:109-110; see also 1 Cor. 12: 12-27.)

Every decision made by either of these quorums must be by the unanimous voice of the same; that is, every member in each quorum must be agreed to its decisions, in order to make their decisions of the same power or validity one with the other. (D&C 107:27.)

Waiting on God
(See also Patience; Trusting in God; Watchfulness.)

What we want or what is prophesied may not come to pass as soon as we would have it happen. Until then, or even until the Lord himself comes again, we are commanded to wait. Even if evil men prosper or wickedness occurs, we are to continue waiting—continuing our own righteous efforts, with faith that God will keep his word. Those who wait patiently for the Lord's blessings or deliverance then have his promise that he shall strengthen their hearts, and they have the assurance that the Lord will save and bless them.

Commandments and Promises

Wait on the Lord: be of good courage, *and he shall strengthen thine heart:* wait, I say, on the Lord. (Ps. 27:14.)

Rest in the Lord, and wait patiently for him: fret not thyself because of him who prospereth in his way, because of the man who bringeth wicked devices to pass. (Ps. 37:7.)

Those that wait upon the Lord, *they shall inherit the earth.* (Ps. 37:9.)

My soul, wait thou only upon God; for my expectation is from him. (Ps. 62:5.)

Say not thou, I will recompense evil; but wait on the Lord, *and he shall save thee.* (Prov. 20:22.)

They that wait upon the Lord *shall renew their strength; they shall mount up with wings as eagles; they shall run, and not be weary; and they shall walk, and not faint.* (Isa. 40:31.)

I will lift up mine hand to the Gentiles, and set up my standard to the people: and they shall bring thy sons in their arms, and thy daughters shall be carried upon their shoulders. And kings shall be thy nursing fathers, and their queens thy nursing mothers: they shall bow down to thee with their face toward the earth, and lick up the dust of thy feet;

and thou shalt know that I am the Lord: for they shall not be ashamed that wait for me. (Isa. 49:22-23; similar scripture, 1 Ne. 21:22-23.)

My righteousness is near; my salvation is gone forth, and mine arms shall judge the people; the isles shall wait upon me, and on mine arm shall they trust. (Isa. 51:5; similar scripture, 2 Ne. 8:5.)

The Lord is good unto them that wait for him, to the soul that seeketh him. *It is good* that a man should both hope and quietly wait for the salvation of the Lord. (Lam. 3:25-26.)

Turn thou to thy God: keep mercy and judgment, and wait on thy God continually. (Hosea 12:6.)

Wait ye upon me, saith the Lord, until the day that I rise up to the prey. (Zeph. 3:8.)

Ye yourselves [be] like unto men that wait for their Lord, when he will return from the wedding; *that when he cometh and knocketh, they may open unto him immediately.* (Luke 12:36.)

[Wait] patiently on the Lord, for your prayers have entered into the ears of the Lord of Sabaoth, and are recorded with this seal and testament—the Lord hath sworn and decreed that they shall be granted. *Therefore, he giveth this promise unto you, with an immutable covenant that they shall be fulfilled; and all things wherewith you have been afflicted shall work together for your good, and to my name's glory, saith the Lord.* (D&C 98:2-3.)

O God, . . . how great things thou hast prepared for him that waiteth for thee. (D&C 133:45.)

Watchfulness

(See also Preparedness; Waiting on God.)

We are commanded to be watchful, both for the coming of Christ and for our own souls, lest the adversary overtake us in our weaknesses. Since we do not know when the Lord will come, we are told, "Watch, therefore, that ye may be ready." (D&C 50:46.) We are told to be "looking forth for the great day of the Lord to come, even for the signs of the coming of the Son of Man." (D&C 45:39.) We are also commanded to "watch and pray continually," with the promise that, if we do so, we will not be tempted beyond what we can bear, and we will be led by the Spirit in love, faith, and hope, into salvation. (Alma 13:27-29.)

Commandments and Promises

Prepare the table, watch in the watchtower, eat, drink: arise, ye princes, and anoint the shield. For thus hath the Lord said unto me, Go, set a watchman, let him declare what he seeth. (Isa. 21:5-6.)

He that dasheth in pieces is come up before thy face: keep the munition, watch the way, make thy loins strong, fortify thy power mightily. (Nahum 2:1.)

Watch therefore, for ye know neither the day nor the hour wherein the Son of man cometh. (Matt. 25:13; see also JS–M 1:46.)

Watch and pray, *that ye enter not into temptation:* the spirit indeed is willing, but the flesh is weak. (Matt. 26:41; similar scripture, Mark 14:38.)

Take ye heed: behold, I have foretold you all things. (Mark 13:23.)

Take ye heed, watch and pray: for ye know not when the time is. For the Son of man is as a man taking a far journey, who left his house, and gave authority to his servants, and to every man his work, and commanded the porter to watch. Watch ye therefore: for ye know not when the master of the house cometh, at even, or at midnight, or at the cockcrowing, or in the morning: *lest coming suddenly he find you sleeping*. And what I say unto you I say unto all, Watch. (Mark 13: 33-37.)

Watch ye therefore, and pray always, *that ye may be accounted worthy to escape all these things that shall come to pass, and to stand before the Son of man*. (Luke 21:36; see also JST Luke 21:36.)

Take heed therefore unto yourselves, and to all the flock, over the which the Holy Ghost hath made you overseers, to feed the church of God, which he hath purchased with his own blood. (Acts 20:28.)

Wherefore let him that thinketh he standeth take heed *lest he fall*. (1 Cor. 10:12.)

Watch ye, stand fast in the faith, quit you like men, be strong. (1 Cor. 16:13.)

If a man be overtaken in a fault, ye which are spiritual, restore such an one in the spirit of meekness; considering thyself, *lest thou also be tempted*. (Gal. 6:1.)

Beware of dogs, beware of evil workers, beware of the concision. (Philip. 3:2.)

Let us not sleep, as do others; but let us watch and be sober. For they that sleep sleep in the night; and they that be drunken are drunken in the night. But let us, who are of the day, be sober, putting on the breastplate of faith and love; and for an helmet, the hope of salvation. (1 Thes. 5:6-8.)

Take heed unto thyself, and unto the doctrine; continue in them: for in doing this *thou shalt both save thyself, and them that hear thee*. (1 Tim. 4:16.)

Watch thou in all things, endure afflictions, do the work of an evangelist, make full proof of thy ministry. (2 Tim. 4:5.)

Take heed, brethren, lest there be in any of you an evil heart of unbelief, in departing from the living God. (Heb. 3:12.)

Unto them that look for him *shall he appear the second time without sin unto salvation.* (Heb. 9:28.)

The end of all things is at hand: be ye therefore sober, and watch unto prayer. (1 Pet. 4:7.)

Be sober, be vigilant; because your adversary the devil, as a roaring lion, walketh about, seeking whom he may devour. (1 Pet. 5:8.)

Look to yourselves, *that we lose not those things which we have wrought, but that we receive a full reward.* (2 Jn. 1:8.)

Be watchful, and strengthen the things which remain, that are ready to die: for I have not found thy works perfect before God. . . . If therefore thou shalt not watch, *I will come on thee as a thief, and thou shalt not know what hour I will come upon thee.* (Rev. 3:2-3.)

If ye do not watch yourselves, and your thoughts, and your words, and your deeds, and observe the commandments of God, and continue in the faith of what ye have heard concerning the coming of our Lord, even unto the end of your lives, *ye must perish.* And now, O man, remember, *and perish not.* (Mosiah 4:30.)

I wish from the inmost part of my heart, yea, with great anxiety even unto pain, that ye would hearken unto my words, and cast off your sins, and not procrastinate the day of your repentance; but that ye would humble yourselves before the Lord, and call on his holy name, and watch and pray continually, *that ye may not be tempted above that which ye can bear, and thus be led by the Holy Spirit, becoming humble, meek, submissive, patient, full of love and all long-suffering; having faith on the Lord; having a hope that ye shall receive eternal life; having the love of God always in your hearts, that ye may be lifted up at the last day and enter into his rest.* (Alma 13:27-29.)

I also exhort you, my brethren, that ye be watchful unto prayer continually, *that ye may not be led away by the temptations of the devil, that he may not overpower you, that ye may not become his subjects at the last day; for behold, he rewardeth you no good thing.* (Alma 34:39.)

Ye must watch and pray always, *lest ye be tempted by the devil, and ye be led away captive by him.* (3 Ne. 18:15.)

Ye must watch and pray always *lest ye enter into temptation; for Satan desireth to have you, that he may sift you as wheat.* (3 Ne. 18:18.)

Then shall my revelations which I have caused to be written by my servant John be unfolded in the eyes of all the people. Remember, when ye see these things, ye shall know that the time is at hand that they shall be made manifest in very deed. (Ether 4:16.)

Let the church take heed and pray always, *lest they fall into temptation;* yea, and even let those who are sanctified take heed also. (D&C 20:33-34.)

Then they shall look for me, *and, behold, I will come; and they shall see me in the clouds of heaven, clothed with power and great glory; with all the holy angels;* and he that watches not for me *shall be cut off.* (D&C 45:44.)

Beware lest ye are deceived; *and that ye may not be deceived* seek ye earnestly the best gifts, always remembering for what they are given. (D&C 46:8.)

Let every man beware *lest he do that which is not in truth and righteousness before me.* (D&C 50:9.)

Watch, therefore, *that ye may be ready.* (D&C 50:46.)

Gird up your loins and be watchful and be sober, looking forth for the coming of the Son of Man, for he cometh in an hour you think not. (D&C 61:38.)

Let the wicked take heed, and let the rebellious fear and tremble; and let the unbelieving hold their lips, for the day of wrath shall come upon them as a whirlwind, and all flesh shall know that I am God. (D&C 63:6.)

Beware from henceforth, and refrain from sin, *lest sore judgments fall upon your heads.* (D&C 82:2.)

Watch, for the adversary spreadeth his dominions, and darkness reigneth. (D&C 82:5.)

I now give unto you a commandment to beware concerning yourselves, to give diligent heed to the words of eternal life. For you shall live by every word that proceedeth forth from the mouth of God. (D&C 84:43-44.)

Watch, therefore, for ye know neither the day nor the hour. (D&C 133:11.)

So likewise, mine elect, when they shall see all these things, they shall know that he is near, even at the doors. (JS–M 1:39; similar scripture, Matt. 24:33.)

What I say unto one, I say unto all men; watch, therefore, for you know not at what hour the Lord doth come. (JS–M 1:46; similar scripture, Matt. 24:42.)

Willingness

(See also Initiative; Obedience.)

The Lord expects not only obedience, but willing obedience—we must serve "with a perfect heart and with a willing mind." (1 Chr. 28:9.) All good and righteous things should be done willingly. When we submit to God's will, we should submit willingly; when we assume the baptismal responsibilities of mourning with those that mourn, comforting those in need of comfort, witnessing of Christ, we should do it willingly. We should especially be willing to bear the name of Jesus Christ, for "blessed is this people who are willing to bear my name; for in my name shall they be called; and they are mine." (Mosiah 26:18.)

Commandments and Promises

Thou, Solomon my son, know thou the God of thy father, and serve him with a perfect heart and with a willing mind: for the Lord searcheth all hearts, and understandeth all the imaginations of the thoughts: if thou seek him, *he will be found of thee;* but if thou forsake him, *he will cast thee off for ever.* (1 Chr. 28:9.)

If ye be willing and obedient, *ye shall eat the good of the land.* (Isa. 1:19.)

If I do this thing willingly, *I have a reward:* but if against my will, *a dispensation of the gospel is committed unto me.* (1 Cor. 9:17.)

Charge them that are rich in this world, that they be not high-minded, nor trust in uncertain riches, but in the living God, who giveth us richly all things to enjoy; that they do good, that they be rich in good works, ready to distribute, willing to communicate; *laying up in store for themselves a good foundation against the time to come, that they may lay hold on eternal life.* (1 Tim. 6:17-19.)

Put them in mind to be subject to principalities and powers, to obey magistrates, to be ready to every good work. (Titus 3:1.)

The elders which are among you I exhort, who am also an elder, and a witness of the sufferings of Christ, and also a partaker of the glory that shall be revealed: Feed the flock of God which is among you, taking the oversight thereof, not by constraint, but willingly; not for filthy lucre, but of a ready mind; neither as being lords over God's heritage, but being ensamples to the flock. *And when the chief Shepherd shall appear, ye shall receive a crown of glory that fadeth not away.* (1 Pet. 5:1-4.)

The natural man is an enemy to God, and has been from the fall of Adam, and will be, forever and ever, unless he yields to the enticings of the Holy Spirit, and putteth off the natural man and becometh a saint through the atonement of Christ the Lord, and becometh as a child, submissive, meek, humble, patient, full of love, willing to submit to all things which the Lord seeth fit to inflict upon him, even as a child doth submit to his father. (Mosiah 3:19.)

[Alma at the waters of Mormon] As ye are desirous to come into the fold of God, and to be called his people, and are willing to bear one another's burdens, that they may be light; yea, and are willing to mourn with those that mourn; yea, and comfort those that stand in need of comfort, and to stand as witnesses of God at all times and in all things, and in all places that ye may be in, even until death, *that ye may be redeemed of God, and be numbered with those of the first resurrection, that ye may have eternal life.* (Mosiah 18:8-9.)

Blessed is this people who are willing to bear my name; *for in my name shall they be called; and they are mine.* (Mosiah 26:18.)

Come and fear not, and lay aside every sin, which easily doth beset you, which doth bind you down to destruction, yea, come and go forth, and show unto your God that ye are willing to repent of your sins and enter into a covenant with him to keep his commandments, and witness it unto him this day by going into the waters of baptism. And whosoever doeth this, and keepeth the commandments of God from thenceforth, *the same will remember that I say unto him, yea, he will remember that I have said unto him, he shall have eternal life, according to the testimony of the Holy Spirit, which testifieth in me.* (Alma 7:15-16.)

Now I would that ye should be . . . easy to be entreated. (Alma 7:23.)

[sacrament prayer] O God, the Eternal Father, we ask thee in the name of thy Son, Jesus Christ, to bless and sanctify this bread to the souls of all those who partake of it; that they may eat in remembrance of the body of thy Son, and witness unto thee, O God, the Eternal Father, that they are willing to take upon them the name of thy Son, and always remember him, and keep his commandments which he hath given them, that they may always have his Spirit to be with them. (Moro. 4:3; similar scripture, D&C 20:77.)

The Lord requireth the heart and a willing mind; and the willing and the obedient *shall eat the good of the land of Zion in these last days.* (D&C 64:34.)

Wisdom

(See also Knowing God and His Ways; Knowledge;
Understanding.)

As the Savior sent forth his twelve apostles to preach, he instructed them, "I send you forth as sheep in the midst of wolves: be ye therefore wise as serpents, and harmless as doves." (Matt. 10:16.) This injunction is equally important today; while we should be aware of both godly and evil ways, we should ourselves remain guileless. "Be ye as wise as serpents and yet without sin," the Lord declares in latter days, "and I will order all things for your good, as fast as ye are able to receive them." (D&C 111:11.)

The Lord also tells us how to gain wisdom: "Seek ye diligently and teach one another words of wisdom: yea, seek ye out of the best books words of wisdom; seek learning, even by study and also by faith." (D&C 88:118.) And he promises that if we will ask him in faith, without wavering, he will give us wisdom: "If any of you lack wisdom, let him ask of God, that giveth to all men liberally, and upbraideth not; and it shall be given him. But let him ask in faith, nothing wavering." (James 1:5-6.) By thus increasing in wisdom, we become more like our maker, who is himself the embodiment of all wisdom.

Commandments and Promises

The fear of the Lord, that is wisdom. (Job 28:28.)

Whoso is wise, and will observe these things, *even they shall understand the lovingkindness of the Lord.* (Ps. 107:43.)

Keep sound wisdom and discretion: *so shall they be life unto thy soul, and grace to thy neck. Then shalt thou walk in thy way safely, and thy foot shall not stumble. When thou liest down, thou shalt not be afraid: yea, thou shalt lie down, and thy sleep shall be sweet.* (Prov. 3:21-24.)

The wise *shall inherit glory.* (Prov. 3:35.)

Get wisdom, get understanding: forget it not; neither decline from the words of my mouth. Forsake her not, *and she shall preserve thee: love her, and she shall keep thee.* Wisdom is the principal thing; therefore get wisdom: and with all thy getting get understanding. Exalt her, *and she shall promote thee: she shall bring thee to honour,* when thou dost embrace her. *She shall give to thine hand an ornament of grace: a crown of glory shall she deliver to thee.* (Prov. 4:5-9.)

Attend unto wisdom, and bow thine ear to my understanding: *that thou mayest regard discretion, and that thy lips may keep knowledge.* (Prov. 5:1-2.)

Hear instruction, and be wise, and refuse it not. (Prov. 8:33.)

The wise in heart will receive commandments. (Prov. 10:8.)

He that handleth a matter wisely *shall find good:* and whoso trusteth in the Lord, *happy is he.* The wise in heart *shall be called prudent.* (Prov. 16:20-21.)

Hear thou, my son, and be wise, and guide thine heart in the way. (Prov. 23:19.)

Buy the truth, and sell it not; also wisdom, and instruction, and understanding. (Prov. 23:23.)

Eat thou honey, because it is good; and the honeycomb, which is sweet to thy taste: *so shall the knowledge of wisdom be unto thy soul:* when thou hast found it, *then there shall be a reward, and thy expectation shall not be cut off.* (Prov. 24:13-14.)

Whoso walketh wisely, *he shall be delivered.* (Prov. 28:26.)

Whoso loveth wisdom *rejoiceth his father.* (Prov. 29:3.)

None of the wicked *shall understand;* but the wise *shall understand.* (Dan. 12:10.)

I send you forth as sheep in the midst of wolves: be ye therefore as wise as serpents, and harmless as doves. (Matt. 10:16.)

I would have you wise unto that which is good, and simple concerning evil. (Rom. 16:19.)

See then that ye walk circumspectly, not as fools, but as wise, redeeming the time, because the days are evil. Wherefore be ye not unwise, but understanding what the will of the Lord is. (Eph. 5:15-17.)

Let the word of Christ dwell in you richly in all wisdom; teaching and admonishing one another in psalms and hymns and spiritual songs, singing with grace in your hearts to the Lord. (Col. 3:16.)

Walk in wisdom toward them that are without, redeeming the time. (Col. 4:5.)

If any of you lack wisdom, let him ask of God, that giveth to all men liberally, and upbraideth not; *and it shall be given him.* But let him ask in faith, nothing wavering. For he that wavereth is like a wave of the sea driven with the wind and tossed. For let not that man think that he shall receive any thing of the Lord. (James 1:5-7; see also D&C 42:68.)

O be wise; what can I say more? (Jacob 6:12.)

See that all these things are done in wisdom and order; for it is not requisite that a man should run faster than he has strength. And again, it is expedient that he should be diligent, *that thereby he might win the prize;* therefore, all things must be done in order. (Mosiah 4:27.)

O, remember, my son, and learn wisdom in thy youth; yea, learn in thy youth to keep the commandments of God. (Alma 37:35.)

Be wise in the days of your probation. (Morm. 9:28.)

Inasmuch as they sought wisdom *they might be instructed.* (D&C 1:26.)

Seek not for riches but for wisdom, *and behold, the mysteries of God shall be unfolded unto you, and then shall you be made rich. Behold, he that hath eternal life is rich.* (D&C 6:7; similar scripture, D&C 11:7.)

Treasure up wisdom in your bosoms, *lest the wickedness of men reveal these things unto you by their wickedness, in a manner which shall speak in your ears with a voice louder than that which shall shake the earth.* (D&C 38:30.)

He that lacketh wisdom, let him ask of me, *and I will give him liberally and upbraid him not.* (D&C 42:68; see also James 1:5.)

They that are wise and have received the truth, and have taken the Holy Spirit for their guide, and have not been deceived—*verily I say unto you, they shall not be hewn down and cast into the fire, but shall abide the day.* (D&C 45:57.)

Whoso is found a faithful, a just, and a wise steward *shall enter into the joy of his Lord, and shall inherit eternal life.* (D&C 51:19.)

He who is faithful and wise in time *is accounted worthy to inherit the mansions prepared for him of my Father.* (D&C 72:4.)

As all have not faith, seek ye diligently and teach one another words of wisdom; yea, seek ye out of the best books words of wisdom; seek learning, even by study and also by faith. (D&C 88:118; similar scripture, D&C 109:7.)

Be ye as wise as serpents and yet without sin; *and I will order all things for your good, as fast as ye are able to receive them.* (D&C 111:11.)

Let him that is ignorant learn wisdom by humbling himself and calling upon the Lord his God, *that his eyes may be opened that he may see, and his ears opened that he may hear.* (D&C 136:32.)

Word of God, Studying the

(See also Following God and His Servants; Knowing God and His Ways; Listening to God and His Servants; Obedience; Remembering God and His Teachings; Revelation.)

Record-keeping has been commanded of all those who receive the words of the Lord: "I command all men, both in the east and in the west, and in the north, and in the south, and in the islands of the sea, that they shall write the words which I speak unto them." These words will then be used to judge us: "For out of the books which shall be written I will judge the world, every man according to their works, according to that which is written." (2 Ne. 29:11.) No wonder the Lord commands us to study his and God's words—we must know by what standards we are to be judged.

Through study of the scriptures we will learn what we must know and do to live this life well and prepare adequately for the next: "All scripture is given by inspiration of God, and is profitable for doctrine, for reproof, for correction, for instruction in righteousness: that the man of God may be perfect, throughly furnished unto all good works." (2 Tim. 3:16-17.) In the words of God we may find comfort as well as counsel, enlightenment as well as commandment, and inspiration as well as exhortation. So rich are the words of God that Nephi tells us, "Feast upon the words of Christ; for behold, the words of Christ will tell you all things what ye should do." (2 Ne. 32:3.)

Commandments and Promises

[instructions to kings] It shall be, when he sitteth upon the throne of his kingdom, that he shall write him a copy of this law in a book out of that which is before the priests the Levites: and it shall be with him, and he shall read therein all the days of his life: *that he may learn to fear the Lord his God, to keep all the words of this law and these statutes, to do them.* (Deut. 17:18-19.)

[to Moses] When all Israel is come to appear before the Lord thy God in the place which he shall choose, thou shalt read this law before all Israel in their hearing. Gather the people together, men, and women, and children, and thy stranger that is within thy gates, *that they may hear, and that they may learn, and fear the Lord your God, and observe to do all the words of this law: and that their children, which have not known anything, may hear, and learn to fear the Lord your God.* (Deut. 31:11-13.)

[to Joshua] This book of the law shall not depart out of thy mouth; but thou shalt meditate therein day and night, *that thou mayest observe to do according to all that is written therein: for then thou shalt make thy way prosperous, and then thou shalt have good success.* (Josh. 1:8.)

Seek ye out of the book of the Lord, and read: no one of these shall fail, none shall want her mate: for my mouth it hath commanded. (Isa. 34:16.)

Man shall not live by bread alone, but by every word that proceedeth out of the mouth of God. (Matt. 4:4; similar scripture, Luke 4:4; see also Deut. 8:3, D&C 84:44, 98:11.)

Ye do err, not knowing the scriptures, nor the power of God. (Matt. 22:29.)

Search the scriptures; for in them ye think ye have eternal life: and they are they which testify of me. (John 5:39.)

Whatsoever things were written aforetime were written for our learning, *that we* through patience and comfort of the scriptures *might have hope.* (Rom. 15:4.)

Till I come, give attendance to reading, to exhortation, to doctrine. (1 Tim. 4:13.)

From a child thou hast known the holy scriptures, *which are able to make thee wise unto salvation through faith which is in Christ Jesus. All scripture is given by inspiration of God, and is profitable for doctrine, for reproof, for instruction in righteousness: that the man of God may be perfect, throughly furnished unto all good works.* (2 Tim. 3:15-17)

Blessed is he that readeth, and they that hear the words of this prophecy, and keep those things which are written therein. (Rev. 1:3.)

Hear ye the words of the prophet, ye who are a remnant of the house of Israel, a branch who have been broken off; hear ye the words of the prophet, which were written unto all the house of Israel, and liken them unto yourselves, *that ye may have hope as well as your brethren from whom ye have been broken off.* (1 Ne. 19:24.)

If ye shall press forward, feasting upon the word of Christ, and endure to the end, *behold, thus saith the Father: Ye shall have eternal life.* (2 Ne. 31:20.)

Feast upon the words of Christ; *for behold, the words of Christ will tell you all things what ye should do.* (2 Ne. 32:3.)

You that will not partake of the goodness of God, and respect the words of the Jews, and also my words, and the words which shall proceed forth out of the mouth of the Lamb of God, behold, I bid you an everlasting farewell, for *these words shall condemn you at the last day.* (2 Ne. 33:14.)

[King Benjamin to his sons] I would that ye should remember to search them [the plates of Nephi] diligently, *that ye may profit thereby.* (Mosiah 1:7.)

The scriptures are before you; if ye will wrest them *it shall be to your own destruction.* (Alma 13:20.)

Just as surely as this director did bring our fathers, by following its course, to the promised land, shall the words of Christ, if we follow their course, *carry us beyond this vale of sorrow into a far better land of promise.* (Alma 37:45.)

Whosoever will may lay hold upon the word of God, *which is quick and powerful, which shall divide asunder all the cunning and the snares and the wiles of the devil, and lead the man of Christ in a strait and narrow course across that everlasting gulf of misery which is pre-*

pared to engulf the wicked—and land their souls, yea, their immortal souls, at the right hand of God in the kingdom of heaven, to sit down with Abraham, and Isaac, and with Jacob, and with all our holy fathers, to go no more out. (Hel. 3:29-30.)

Whoso readeth, let him understand; he that hath the scriptures, let him search them, and see and behold if all these deaths and destructions by fire, and by smoke, and by tempests, and by whirlwinds, and by the opening of the earth to receive them, and all these things are not unto the fulfilling of the prophecies of many of the holy prophets. (3 Ne. 10:14.)

Ye remember that I spake unto you, and said that when the words of Isaiah should be fulfilled—behold they are written, ye have them before you, therefore search them. (3 Ne. 20:11.)

Ye ought to search these things. Yea, a commandment I give unto you that ye search these things diligently; for great are the words of Isaiah. (3 Ne. 23:1.)

Search the prophets, for many there be that testify of these things. (3 Ne. 23:5.)

Repent, and be baptized in the name of Jesus, and lay hold upon the gospel of Christ, which shall be set before you, not only in this record but also in the record which shall come unto the Gentiles from the Jews, which record shall come from the Gentiles unto you. (Morm. 7:8.)

Search the prophecies of Isaiah. (Morm. 8:23.)

Look ye unto the revelations of God; for behold, the time cometh at that day when all these things must be fulfilled. (Morm. 8:33.)

I would exhort you that when ye shall read these things, if it be wisdom in God that ye should read them, that ye would remember how merciful the Lord hath been unto the children of men, from the creation of Adam even down until the time that ye shall receive these things, and ponder it in your hearts. And when ye shall receive these things, I would exhort you that ye would ask God, the Eternal Father, in the name of Christ, if these things are not true; and if ye shall ask with a sincere heart, with real intent, having faith in Christ, *he will manifest the truth of it unto you, by the power of the Holy Ghost. And by the power of the Holy Ghost ye may know the truth of all things.* (Moro. 10:3-5.)

Search these commandments, for they are true and faithful, and the prophecies and promises which are in them shall all be fulfilled. (D&C 1:37.)

Seek not to declare my word, but first seek to obtain my word, *and then shall your tongue be loosed.* (D&C 11:21.)

Study my word which hath gone forth among the children of men, and also study my word which shall come forth among the children of men, or that which is now translating. (D&C 11:22.)

I give unto you a commandment, that you rely upon the things which are written; for in them are all things written concerning the foundation of my church, my gospel, and my rock. (D&C 18:3-4.)

[to Joseph Smith, Oliver Cowdery, and John Whitmer] You shall let your time be devoted to the studying of the scriptures. (D&C 26:1.)

I give unto you a commandment that then ye shall teach them [the scriptures] unto all men; for they shall be taught unto all nations, kindreds, tongues and people. (D&C 42:58.)

I now give unto you a commandment to beware concerning yourselves, to give diligent heed to the words of eternal life. For you shall live by every word that proceedeth forth from the mouth of God. (D&C 84:43-44; similar scripture, D&C 98:11; see also Deut. 8:3; Matt. 4:4, Luke 4:4.)

Neither take ye thought beforehand what ye shall say; but treasure up in your minds continually the words of life, *and it shall be given you in the very hour that portion that shall be meted unto every man.* (D&C 84:85.)

Search diligently, pray always, and be believing, *and all things shall work together for your good,* if ye walk uprightly and remember the covenant wherewith ye have covenanted one with another. (D&C 90:24.)

Work

(See also Diligence; Initiative; Worldliness.)

The commandment to work has existed since the time of Adam, and since his time men have been able to turn their time and energy into sustenance, goods, property, and security. To work for "filthy lucre," however, or to sell portions of our lives to satiate worldly desires or greed is sinful. But to use honest gain for righteous purposes, such as husbands supporting their families or potential missionaries working for their mission funds, is blessed. By working diligently and honestly within our strength and means, we can eliminate individual poverty, both of the world and of the soul.

Commandments and Promises

[to Adam] Because thou hast hearkened unto the voice of thy wife, and hast eaten of the tree, of which I commanded thee, saying, Thou shalt not eat of it: *cursed is the ground for thy sake; in sorrow shalt thou eat of it all the days of thy life; thorns also and thistles shall it bring forth to thee; and thou shalt eat the herb of the field; in the sweat of thy face shalt thou eat bread, till thou return unto the ground;* for out of it wast thou taken: for dust thou art, and unto dust shalt thou return. (Gen. 3:17-19; similar scripture, Moses 4:23-25.)

Go to the ant, thou sluggard; consider her ways, and be wise: which having no guide, overseer, or ruler, provideth her meat in the summer, and gathereth her food in the harvest. (Prov. 6:6-8.)

The soul of the sluggard *desireth, and hath nothing:* but the soul of the diligent *shall be made fat.* (Prov. 13:4.)

Slothfulness *casteth into a deep sleep;* and an idle soul *shall suffer hunger.* (Prov. 19:15.)

He that tilleth his land *shall have plenty of bread:* but he that followeth after vain persons *shall have poverty enough.* (Prov. 28:19.)

Be strong, all ye people of the land, saith the Lord, and work: for I am with you, saith the Lord of hosts. (Hag. 2:4.)

If a man think himself to be something, when he is nothing, he deceiveth himself. But let every man prove his own work, *and then shall he have rejoicing in himself alone, and not in another.* For every man shall bear his own burden. (Gal. 6:3-5.)

Let him that stole steal no more: but rather let him labour, working with his hands the thing which is good, that he may have to give to him that needeth. (Eph. 4:28.)

Study to be quiet, and to do your own business, and to work with your own hands, as we commanded you. (1 Thes. 4:11.)

Even when we were with you, this we commanded you, that if any would not work, neither should he eat. For we hear that there are some which walk among you disorderly, working not at all, but are busybodies. Now them that are such we command and exhort by our Lord Jesus Christ, that with quietness they work, and eat their own bread. (2 Thes. 3:10-12.)

If any provide not for his own, and specially for those of his own house, *he hath denied the faith, and is worse than an infidel.* (1 Tim. 5:8.)

Do not spend money for that which is of no worth, nor your labor for that which cannot satisfy. (2 Ne. 9:51.)

He also commanded them that the priests whom he had ordained should labor with their own hands for their support. (Mosiah 18:24.)

All their priests and teachers should labor with their own hands for their support, in all cases save it were in sickness, or in much want; and doing these things, *they did abound in the grace of God.* (Mosiah 27:5.)

[to Joseph Smith] Do not run faster or labor more than you have strength and means provided to enable you to translate; but be diligent unto the end. (D&C 10:4.)

Let all thy garments be plain, and their beauty the beauty of the work of thine own hands. (D&C 42:40.)

Thou shalt not be idle; for he that is idle *shall not eat the bread nor wear the garments of the laborer*. (D&C 42:42.)

Let the residue of the elders watch over the churches, and declare the word in the regions round about them; and let them labor with their own hands that there be no idolatry nor wickedness practised. (D&C 52:39.)

Wo unto you poor men, whose hearts are not broken, whose spirits are not contrite, and whose bellies are not satisfied, and whose hands are not stayed from laying hold upon other men's goods, whose eyes are full of greediness, and who will not labor with your own hands! (D&C 56:17.)

They have been sent to preach my gospel among the congregations of the wicked; wherefore, I give unto them a commandment, thus: Thou shalt not idle away thy time, neither shalt thou bury thy talent that it may not be known. (D&C 60:13.)

The inhabitants of Zion also shall remember their labors, inasmuch as they are appointed to labor, in all faithfulness; for the idler *shall be had in remembrance before the Lord*. (D&C 68:30.)

It is my will that you should go forth and not tarry, neither be idle but labor with your might. (D&C 75:3.)

Every man who is obliged to provide for his own family, let him provide, *and he shall in nowise lose his crown*; and let him labor in the church. Let every man be diligent in all things. And the idler *shall not have place in the church*, except he repent and mend his ways. (D&C 75:28-29.)

Cease to be idle. (D&C 88:124.)

Set in order your houses; keep slothfulness and uncleanness far from you. (D&C 90:18.)

He that is slothful *shall not be counted worthy to stand*, and he that learns not his duty and shows himself not approved *shall not be counted worthy to stand*. (D&C 107:100.)

Let your diligence, and your perseverance, and patience, and your works be redoubled, *and you shall in nowise lose your reward, saith the Lord of Hosts.* (D&C 127:4.)

Worldliness

The first commandment God gave man was, "Be fruitful, and multiply, and replenish the earth, and subdue it: and have dominion over the fish of the sea, and over the fowl of the air, and over every living thing that moveth upon the earth." (Gen. 1:28.) If man did not subdue the world, the world would subdue and overcome him. If we choose, the world can become our classroom for the learning of mortality. As the Lord told Joseph Smith, "all these things shall give thee experience, and shall be for thy good." (D&C 122:7.)

But if we are not cautious and strong, the world will overcome and bury us in its influences. We are commanded: "Love not the world, neither the things that are in the world. If any man love the world, the love of the Father is not in him. For all that is in the world, the lust of the flesh, and the lust of the eyes, and the pride of life, is not of the Father, but is of the world. And the world passeth away, and the lust thereof: but he that doeth the will of God abideth for ever." (1 Jn. 2:15-17.)

The power is available for us to overcome the world, to resist the evil in our lives. "For whatsoever is born of God overcometh the world: and this is the victory that overcometh the world, even our faith. Who is he that overcometh the world, but he that believeth that Jesus is the Son of God?" (1 Jn. 5:4-5.) Through faith and through the diligent obedience that faith inspires we can overcome the world.

Commandments and Promises

If riches increase, set not your heart upon them. (Ps. 62:10.)

Labour not to be rich: cease from thine own wisdom. (Prov. 23:4.)

He that maketh haste to be rich *shall not be innocent.* (Prov. 28:20.)

Lay not up for yourselves treasures upon earth, where moth and rust doth corrupt, and where thieves break through and steal: but lay up for yourselves treasures in heaven, where neither moth nor rust doth corrupt, and where thieves do not break through nor steal: *for where your treasure is, there will your heart be also.* (Matt. 6:19-21; similar scripture, 3 Ne. 13:19-21.)

How hardly shall they that have riches *enter into the kingdom of God!* And the disciples were astonished at his words. But Jesus answereth again, and saith unto them, Children, *how hard it is for them* that trust in riches *to enter into the kingdom of God!* (Mark 10:23-24.)

Woe unto you that are rich! *for ye have received your consolation.* (Luke 6:24.)

Sell that ye have, and give alms; provide yourselves bags which wax not old, a treasure in the heavens that faileth not, where no thief approacheth, neither moth corrupteth. For where your treasure is, *there will your heart be also.* (Luke 12:33-34.)

Labour not for the meat which perisheth, but for that meat which endureth *unto everlasting life, which the Son of man shall give unto you:* for him hath God the Father sealed. (John 6:27.)

If ye live after the flesh, *ye shall die:* but if ye through the Spirit do mortify the deeds of the body, *ye shall live. For as many as are led by the Spirit of God, they are the sons of God.* (Rom. 8:13-14.)

Be not conformed to this world: but be ye transformed by the renewing of your mind, that ye may prove what is that good, and acceptable, and perfect, will of God. (Rom. 12:2.)

Be not overcome of evil, but overcome evil with good. (Rom. 12:21.)

The night is far spent, the day is at hand: let us therefore cast off the works of darkness, and let us put on the armour of light. Let us walk honestly, as in the day; not in rioting and drunkenness, not in chambering and wantonness, not in strife and envying. But put ye on the Lord Jesus Christ, and make not provision for the flesh, to fulfil the lusts thereof. (Rom. 13:12-14.)

Let no man deceive himself. If any man among you seemeth to be wise in this world, let him become a fool, *that he may be wise.* For the wisdom of this world *is foolishness with God. For it is written, He taketh the wise in their own craftiness.* (1 Cor. 3:18-19.)

Neither give place to the devil. (Eph. 4:27.)

If ye then be risen with Christ, seek those things which are above, where Christ sitteth on the right hand of God. Set your affection on things above, not on things on the earth. (Col. 3:1-2.)

In like manner also, that women adorn themselves in modest apparel, with shamefacedness and sobriety; not with broided hair, or gold, or pearls, or costly array; but (which becometh women professing godliness) with good works. (1 Tim. 2:9-10.)

Having food and raiment let us be therewith content. But they that will be rich *fall into temptation and a snare, and into many foolish and hurtful lusts, which drown men in destruction and perdition.* For the love of money *is the root of all evil:* which while some coveted after, *they have erred from the faith, and pierced themselves through with many sorrows.* But thou, O man of God, flee these things; and follow after righteousness, godliness, faith, love, patience, meekness. (1 Tim. 6:8-11.)

The grace of God that bringeth salvation hath appeared to all men, teaching us that, denying ungodliness and worldly lusts, we should live soberly, righteously, and godly, in this present world; looking for that blessed hope, and the glorious appearing of the great God and our Savior Jesus Christ; who gave himself for us, that he might redeem us from all iniquity, and purify unto himself a peculiar people, zealous of good works. These things speak, and exhort, and rebuke with all authority. (Titus 2:11-15.)

Pure religion and undefiled before God and the Father is this, To visit the fatherless and widows in their affliction, and to keep himself unspotted from the world. (James 1:27; see also JST James 1:27.)

Submit yourselves therefore to God. Resist the devil, *and he will flee from you.* (James 4:7.)

Go to now, ye rich men, weep and howl *for your miseries that shall come upon you.* Your riches are corrupted, and your garments are motheaten. Your gold and silver is cankered; and *the rust of them shall be a witness against you, and shall eat your flesh as it were fire.* Ye have heaped treasure together for the last days. Behold, the hire of the labourers who have reaped down your fields, which is of you kept back by fraud, crieth: and *the cries of them which have reaped are entered into the ears of the Lord of sabaoth.* Ye have lived in pleasure on the earth, and been wanton; ye have nourished your hearts, as in a day of slaughter. (James 5:1-5.)

Whose [wives'] adorning let it not be that outward adorning of plaiting the hair, and of wearing of gold, or of putting on of apparel; but let it be the hidden man of the heart, in that which is not corruptible, even the ornament of a meek and quiet spirit, *which is in the sight of God of great price.* (1 Pet. 3:3-4.)

Love not the world, neither the things that are in the world. If any man love the world, *the love of the Father is not in him.* For all that is in the world, the lust of the flesh, and the lust of the eyes, and the pride of life, *is not of the Father,* but is of the world. (1 Jn. 2:15-16.)

Ye are of God, little children, and have overcome them: because greater is he that is in you, than he that is in the world. They are of the world: *therefore speak they of the world, and the world heareth them.* We are of God: he that knoweth God *heareth us;* he that is not of God *heareth not us.* Hereby know we the spirit of truth, and the spirit of error. (1 Jn. 4:4-6.)

He that overcometh *shall not be hurt of the second death.* (Rev. 2:11.)

To him that overcometh *will I give to eat of the hidden manna, and will give him a white stone, and in the stone a new name written, which no man knoweth saving he that receiveth it.* (Rev. 2:17.)

He that overcometh, and keepeth my works unto the end, *to him will I give power over the nations: and he shall rule them with a rod of iron; as the vessels of a potter shall they be broken to shivers: even as I received of my Father. And I will give him the morning star.* (Rev. 2: 26-28; see also JST Rev. 2:26-27.)

He that overcometh, *the same shall be clothed in white raiment; and I will not blot out his name out of the book of life, but I will confess his name before my Father, and before his angels.* (Rev. 3:5.)

Him that overcometh *will I make a pillar in the temple of my God, and he shall go no more out: and I will write upon him the name of my God, and the name of the city of my God, which is new Jerusalem, which cometh down out of heaven from my God: and I will write upon him my new name.* (Rev. 3:12.)

Because thou sayest, I am rich, and increased with goods, and have need of nothing; and knowest not that thou art wretched, and miserable, and poor, and blind, and naked: I counsel thee to buy of me gold tried in the fire, *that thou mayest be rich*; and white raiment, *that thou mayest be clothed, and that the shame of thy nakedness do not appear*; and anoint thine eyes with eyesalve, *that thou mayest see.* (Rev. 3:17-18.)

He that overcometh *shall inherit all things; and I will be his God, and he shall be my son.* (Rev. 21:7.)

Wo unto the rich, who are rich as to the things of the world. For because they are rich they despise the poor, and they persecute the meek, and their hearts are upon their treasures; *wherefore, their treasure is their god. And behold, their treasure shall perish with them also.* (2 Ne. 9:30.)

Do not spend money for that which is of no worth, nor your labor for that which cannot satisfy. (2 Ne. 9:51.)

The hand of providence hath smiled upon you most pleasingly, that you have obtained many riches; and because some of you have obtained more abundantly than that of your brethren *ye are lifted up in the pride of your hearts, and wear stiff necks and high heads* because of the costliness of your apparel, *and persecute your brethren because ye suppose that ye are better than they.* And now, my brethren, do ye suppose that God justifieth you in this thing? Behold, I say unto you, *Nay. But he condemneth you*, and if ye persist in these things *his judgments must speedily come unto you.* (Jacob 2:13-14.)

After ye have obtained a hope in Christ ye shall obtain riches, if ye seek them; and ye will seek them for the intent to do good—to clothe the naked, and to feed the hungry, and to liberate the captive, and administer relief to the sick and the afflicted. (Jacob 2:19.)

Seek not after riches nor the vain things of this world; for behold, you cannot carry them with you. (Alma 39:14.)

Whoso shall hide up treasures in the earth *shall find them again no more,* because of the great curse of the land, save he be a righteous man and shall hide it up unto the Lord. For I will, saith the Lord, that they shall hide up their treasures unto me; and *cursed be they* who hide not up their treasures unto me; for none hideth up their treasures unto me save it be the righteous; and he that hideth not up his treasures unto me, *cursed is he, and also the treasure, and none shall redeem it because of the curse of the land. And the day shall come that they shall hide up their treasures,* because they have set their hearts upon riches; and because they have set their hearts upon their riches, and I will hide up their treasures when they shall flee before their enemies; because they will not hide them up unto me, *cursed be they and also their treasures; and in that day shall they be smitten; saith the Lord. . . . Ye are cursed* because of your riches, *and also are your riches cursed* because ye have set your hearts upon them, and have not hearkened unto the words of him who gave them unto you. Ye do not remember the Lord your God in the things with which he hath blessed you, but ye do always remember your riches, not to thank the Lord your God for them; yea, your hearts are not drawn out unto the Lord, but they do swell with great pride, unto boasting, and unto great swelling, envyings, strifes, malice, persecutions, and murders, and all manner of iniquities. For this cause hath the Lord God caused that *a curse should come upon the land, and also upon your riches,* and this because of your iniquities. (Hel. 13:18-23.)

Seek not for riches but for wisdom; *and, behold, the mysteries of God shall be unfolded unto you, and then shall you be made rich. Behold, he that hath eternal life is rich.* (D&C 11:7; similar scripture, D&C 6:7.)

Thou shalt lay aside the things of this world, and seek for the things of a better. (D&C 25:10.)

I, the Lord, who was crucified for the sins of the world, give unto you a commandment that you shall forsake the world. (D&C 53:2.)

Wo unto you rich men, that will not give your substance to the poor, *for your riches will canker your souls; and this shall be your lamentation in the day of visitation, and of judgment, and of indignation: The harvest is past, the summer is ended, and my soul is not saved!* (D&C 56:16.)

I will that ye should overcome the world; *wherefore I will have compassion upon you.* (D&C 64:2.)

Worship

(See also False Gods; Thankfulness.)

Worship turns our thoughts to eternal things and makes us more aware of God's influence in our lives. It attunes us to the Holy Ghost and gives us the humility to accept direction: "In all thy ways acknowledge him, and he shall direct thy paths." (Prov. 3:6.) This channeling purifies our intents, and our desires become one with the Lord. Then he can give us the desires of our hearts. (See Ps. 37:4.) The Lord explains the intricate relationship between worship and its blessings in this scripture: "I give unto you these sayings that you may understand and know how to worship, and know what you worship, that you may come unto the Father in my name, and in due time receive of his fulness. For if you keep my commandments you shall receive of his fulness, and be glorified in me as I am in the Father; therefore, I say unto you, you shall receive grace for grace." (D&C 93:19-20.)

Commandments and Promises

Give thanks unto the Lord, call upon his name, make known his deeds among the people. Sing unto him, sing psalms unto him, talk ye of all his wondrous works. (1 Chr. 16:8-9.)

Sing unto the Lord, all the earth; shew forth from day to day his salvation. (1 Chr. 16:23.)

Great is the Lord, and greatly to be praised: he also is to be feared above all gods. (1 Chr. 16:25.)

Give unto the Lord, ye kindreds of the people, give unto the Lord glory and strength. Give unto the Lord the glory due unto his name: bring an offering, and come before him: worship the Lord in the beauty of holiness. Fear before him, all the earth: the world also shall be stable, that it be not moved. Let the heavens be glad, and let the earth rejoice: and let men say among the nations, The Lord reigneth. Let the sea roar, and the fulness thereof: let the fields rejoice, and all that is therein. (1 Chr. 16:28-32.)

659

Ye that fear the Lord, praise him; all ye the seed of Jacob, glorify him; and fear him, all ye the seed of Israel. (Ps. 22:23.)

Give unto the Lord, O ye mighty, give unto the Lord glory and strength. Give unto the Lord the glory due unto his name; worship the Lord in the beauty of holiness. (Ps. 29:1-2.)

Be glad in the Lord, and rejoice, ye righteous: and shout for joy, all ye that are upright in heart. (Ps. 32:11.)

Rejoice in the Lord, O ye righteous: for praise is comely for the upright. (Ps. 33:1.)

Delight thyself also in the Lord; *and he shall give thee the desires of thine heart.* (Ps. 37:4.)

O clap your hands, all ye people; shout unto God with the voice of triumph. (Ps. 47:1.)

Make a joyful noise unto God, all ye lands: sing forth the honour of his name: make his praise glorious. Say unto God, How terrible art thou in thy works! through the greatness of thy power shall thine enemies submit themselves unto thee. (Ps. 66:1-3.)

O bless our God, ye people, and make the voice of his praise to be heard. (Ps. 66:8.)

Bless ye God in the congregations, even the Lord, from the fountain of Israel. (Ps. 68:26.)

Sing unto God, ye kingdoms of the earth; O sing praises unto the Lord. (Ps. 68:32.)

Ascribe ye strength unto God: his excellency is over Israel, and his strength is in the clouds. (Ps. 68:34.)

Let the heaven and earth praise him, the seas, and every thing that moveth therein. (Ps. 69:34.)

Sing aloud unto God our strength: make a joyful noise unto the God of Jacob. (Ps. 81:1.)

O come, let us worship and bow down: let us kneel before the Lord our maker. (Ps. 95:6.)

O sing unto the Lord a new song: sing unto the Lord, all the earth. Sing unto the Lord, bless his name; shew forth his salvation from day to day. (Ps. 96:1-2.)

Give unto the Lord, O ye kindreds of the people, give unto the Lord glory and strength. Give unto the Lord the glory due unto his name: bring an offering, and come into his courts. O worship the Lord in the beauty of holiness: fear before him, all the earth. (Ps. 96:7-9.)

Let the heavens rejoice, and let the earth be glad; let the sea roar, and the fulness thereof. (Ps. 96:11.)

O sing unto the Lord a new song; for he hath done marvellous things: his right hand, and his holy arm, hath gotten him the victory. (Ps. 98:1.)

Exalt ye the Lord our God, and worship at his footstool; for he is holy. (Ps. 99:5.)

Make a joyful noise unto the Lord, all ye lands. Serve the Lord with gladness; come before his presence with singing. (Ps. 100:1-2.)

Enter into his gates with thanksgiving, and into his courts with praise: be thankful unto him, and bless his name. (Ps. 100:4.)

O give thanks unto the Lord; call upon his name: make known his deeds among the people. Sing unto him, sing psalms unto him: talk ye of all his wondrous works. Glory ye in his holy name: let the heart of them rejoice that seek the Lord. (Ps. 105:1-3.)

Praise ye the Lord. (Ps. 105:45; similar scriptures, Ps. 112:1, 113:9, 149:9.)

Praise ye the Lord. O give thanks unto the Lord; for he is good: for his mercy endureth for ever. (Ps. 106:1.)

O give thanks unto the Lord, for he is good: for his mercy endureth for ever. (Ps. 107:1; similar scriptures, Ps. 118:1, 136:1-3, 26.)

Praise ye the Lord. Praise, O ye servants of the Lord, praise the name of the Lord. (Ps. 113:1.)

O praise the Lord all ye nations: praise him, all ye people. For his merciful kindness is great toward us: and the truth of the Lord endureth for ever. Praise ye the Lord. (Ps. 117:1-2.)

Bless ye the Lord, all ye servants of the Lord, which by night stand in the house of the Lord. Lift up your hands in the sanctuary, and bless the Lord. (Ps. 134:1-2.)

Praise ye the Lord. Praise ye the name of the Lord; praise him, O ye servants of the Lord. Ye that stand in the house of the Lord, in the courts of the house of our God, praise the Lord; for the Lord is good: sing praises unto his name; for it is pleasant. (Ps. 135:1-3.)

Bless the Lord, O house of Israel: bless the Lord, O house of Aaron: bless the Lord, O house of Levi: ye that fear the Lord, bless the Lord. (Ps. 135:19-20.)

Praise ye the Lord. Praise the Lord, O my soul. (Ps. 146:1.)

Praise ye the Lord: for it is good to sing praises unto our God; for it is pleasant; and praise is comely. (Ps. 147:1.)

Sing unto the Lord with thanksgiving; sing praise upon the harp unto our God. (Ps. 147:7.)

Praise the Lord, O Jerusalem; praise thy God, O Zion. (Ps. 147:12.)

Praise ye the Lord. Praise ye the Lord from the heavens: praise him in the heights. (Ps. 148:1.)

Praise ye the Lord. Sing unto the Lord a new song, and his praise in the congregation of saints. (Ps. 149:1.)

Praise ye the Lord. Praise God in his sanctuary: praise him in the firmament of his power. Praise him for his mighty acts: praise him according to his excellent greatness. Praise him with the sound of the trumpet: praise him with the psaltery and harp. Praise him with the timbrel and dance: praise him with stringed instruments and organs. Praise him upon the loud cymbals: praise him upon the high sounding cymbals. Let every thing that hath breath praise the Lord. Praise ye the Lord. (Ps. 150:1-6.)

In all thy ways acknowledge him, *and he shall direct thy paths.* (Prov. 3:6.)

In that day shall he say, Praise the Lord, call upon his name, declare his doings among the people, make mention that his name is exalted. Sing unto the Lord; for he hath done excellent things: this is known in all the earth. Cry out and shout, thou inhabitant of Zion: for great is the Holy One of Israel in the midst of thee. (Isa. 12:4-6; similar scripture, 2 Ne. 22:4-6.)

Glorify ye the Lord in the fires, even the name of the Lord God of Israel in the isles of the sea. (Isa. 24:15.)

Hear, ye that are far off, what I have done; and, ye that are near, acknowledge my might. (Isa. 33:13.)

Sing unto the Lord a new song, and his praise from the end of the earth, ye that go down to the sea, and all that is therein; the isles, and the inhabitants thereof. Let the wilderness and the cities thereof lift up their voice, the villages that Kedar doth inhabit: let the inhabitants of the rock sing, let them shout from the top of the mountains. Let them give glory unto the Lord, and declare his praise in the islands. (Isa. 42:10-12.)

Give glory to the Lord your God, *before he cause darkness, and before your feet stumble upon the dark mountains, and, while ye look for light, he turn it into the shadow of death, and make it gross darkness.* (Jer. 13:16.)

Sing unto the Lord, praise ye the Lord: for he hath delivered the soul of the poor from the hand of evildoers. (Jer. 20:13.)

Let us lift up our heart with our hands unto God in the heavens. (Lam. 3:41.)

The Lord is in his holy temple: let all the earth keep silence before him. (Hab. 2:20.)

Be silent, O all flesh, before the Lord: for he is raised up out of his holy habitation. (Zech. 2:13.)

Whoso will not come up of all the families of the earth unto Jerusalem to worship the King, the Lord of hosts, *even upon them shall be no rain.* (Zech. 14:17.)

Thou shalt worship the Lord thy God, and him only shalt thou serve. (Matt. 4:10; similar scripture, Luke 4:8.)

He that glorieth, let him glory in the Lord. (1 Cor. 1:31; similar scripture, 2 Cor. 10:17.)

Ye are bought with a price: therefore glorify God in your body, and in your spirit, which are God's. (1 Cor. 6:20.)

Be not drunk with wine, wherein is excess; but be filled with the Spirit; speaking to yourselves in psalms and hymns and spiritual songs, singing and making melody in your heart to the Lord; giving thanks always for all things unto God and the Father in the name of our Lord Jesus Christ; submitting yourselves one to another in the fear of God. (Eph. 5:18-21.)

Let the word of Christ dwell in you richly in all wisdom; teaching and admonishing one another in psalms and hymns and spiritual songs, singing with grace in your hearts to the Lord. (Col. 3:16.)

By him [Christ] therefore let us offer the sacrifice of praise to God continually, that is, the fruit of our lips giving thanks to his name. (Heb. 13:15.)

Is any among you afflicted? let him pray. Is any merry? let him sing psalms. (James 5:13.)

Sanctify the Lord God in your hearts. (1 Pet. 3:15.)

If any man speak, let him speak as the oracles of God; if any man minister, let him do it as of the ability which God giveth: *that God in all things may be glorified through Jesus Christ,* to whom be praise and dominion for ever and ever. (1 Pet. 4:11.)

If any man suffer as a Christian, let him not be ashamed; but let him glorify God on this behalf. (1 Pet. 4:16.)

[Nephi about his brothers] Now, they said: We know of a surety that the Lord is with thee, for we know that it is the power of the Lord that has shaken us. And they fell down before me, and were about to worship me, but I would not suffer them, saying: I am thy brother, yea, even thy younger brother; wherefore, worship the Lord thy God, and honor thy father and thy mother, *that thy days may be long in the land which the Lord thy God shall give thee.* (1 Ne. 17:55.)

The right way is to believe in Christ, and deny him not; and Christ is the Holy One of Israel; wherefore ye must bow down before him, and worship him with all your might, mind, and strength, and your whole soul; and if ye do this *ye shall in nowise be cast out.* (2 Ne. 25:29.)

Worship God, in whatsoever place ye may be in, in spirit and in truth. (Alma 34:38.)

You shall fall down and worship the Father in my name. (D&C 18:40.)

[God] gave unto them commandments that they should love and serve him, the only living and true God, and that he should be the only being whom they should worship. (D&C 20:19.)

All men must repent and believe on the name of Jesus Christ, and worship the Father in his name, and endure in faith on his name to the end, *or they cannot be saved in the kingdom of God.* (D&C 20:29.)

Thy vows shall be offered up in righteousness on all days and at all times. (D&C 59:11.)

Let no man glory in man, but rather let him glory in God, who shall subdue all enemies under his feet. (D&C 76:61.)

I give unto you these sayings *that you may understand and know how to worship, and know what you worship, that you may come unto the Father in my name, and in due time receive of his fulness.* (D&C 93:19.)

If thou art merry, praise the Lord with singing, with music, with dancing, and with a prayer of praise and thanksgiving. (D&C 136:28.)

Worship God, for him only shalt thou serve. (Moses 1:15.)

Zeal

(See also Agency, Use of; Diligence; Obedience.)

The Lord wants us to be firmly and clearly on the side of righteousness. "Because thou art lukewarm, and neither cold nor hot, I will spue thee out of my mouth." (Rev. 3:16.) The Lord does not ask just for our zeal; he asks for zealous righteousness, wisely and knowledgeably applied, as with the people of Ammon. That zeal was directed to good works, to honesty, to faith, to abhorrence toward violence, and "thus they were a zealous and beloved people, a highly favored people of the Lord." (Alma 27:30.) When our repentance, good works, and service are zealous, we please the Lord.

Commandments and Promises

I give unto him [Phineas] my covenant of peace: and he shall have it, and his seed after him, even the covenant of an everlasting priesthood; because he was zealous for his God. (Num. 25:12-13.)

[Be] fervent in spirit; serving the Lord. (Rom. 12:11.)

It is good to be zealously affected always in a good thing, and not only when I am present with you. (Gal. 4:18.)

Whatsoever ye do, do it heartily, as to the Lord, and not unto men; knowing that of the Lord *ye shall receive the reward of the inheritance:* for ye serve the Lord Christ. (Col. 3:23-24.)

I know thy works, that thou art neither cold nor hot: I would thou wert cold or hot. So then because thou art lukewarm, and neither cold nor hot, *I will spue thee out of my mouth.* (Rev. 3:15-16.)

As many as I love, I rebuke and chasten: be zealous therefore, and repent. (Rev. 3:19.)

Men should be anxiously engaged in a good cause, and do many things of their own free will, and bring to pass much righteousness. (D&C 58:27.)